MAMMALS OF THE SEA
Biology and Medicine

This book is dedicated to

TUFFY

the singularly unique *Tursiops truncatus*
from whom we learned so much—truly
the most purposeful porpoise.

MAMMALS OF THE SEA
Biology and Medicine

Edited by

SAM H. RIDGWAY

Research Veterinarian
Ocean Sciences Department
Naval Undersea Research and Development Center
San Diego, California

CHARLES C THOMAS • PUBLISHER
Springfield • Illinois • U.S.A.

Published and Distributed Throughout the World by

CHARLES C THOMAS • PUBLISHER

Bᴀɴɴᴇʀsᴛᴏɴᴇ Hᴏᴜsᴇ

301–327 East Lawrence Avenue, Springfield, Illinois, U.S.A.

Nᴀᴛᴄʜᴇᴢ Pʟᴀɴᴛᴀᴛɪᴏɴ Hᴏᴜsᴇ

735 North Atlantic Boulevard, Fort Lauderdale, Florida, U.S.A.

With THOMAS BOOKS *careful attention is given to all details of manufacturing and design. It is the Publisher's desire to present books that are satisfactory as to their physical qualities and artistic possibilities and appropriate for their particular use.* THOMAS BOOKS *will be true to those laws of quality that assure a good name and good will.*

CONTRIBUTORS

ROBERT L. BROWNELL, JR.

Los Angeles County Museum of Natural History
Los Angeles, California
and
Department of Pathology
The Johns Hopkins University
Baltimore, Maryland

DAVID K. CALDWELL

Communication Sciences Laboratory
Florida State Museum
University of Florida
Gainesville, Florida

MELBA C. CALDWELL

Communication Sciences Laboratory
University of Florida
Gainesville, Florida

MURRAY D. DAILEY

Department of Biology
California State College
Long Beach, California

NORBERT J. FLANIGAN

Chairman, Department of Biology
St. Norbert's College
West De Pere, Wisconsin

MURRAY B. GARDNER

Department of Pathology
School of Medicine
University of Southern California
County–USC Medical Center
Los Angeles, California

ROBERT F. GREEN

Biologist-Anatomist, Life Sciences Division
Ventura College
Ventura, California

KARL W. KENYON

Biologist, Bureau of Sport Fisheries and Wildlife
United States Department of the Interior
Sand Point Naval Air Station
Seattle, Washington

DEBORAH DUFFIELD KULU

Department of Genetics
University of Hawaii
Honolulu, Hawaii

MASAHARU NISHIWAKI

Ocean Research Institute
University of Tokyo
Nakano, Tokyo, Japan

SAM H. RIDGWAY

Research Veterinarian
Ocean Sciences Department
Naval Undersea Research and Development Center
San Diego, California

JOHN G. SIMPSON

Research Veterinarian
Head, Clinical Pathology Branch
Marine Bioscience Facility
Naval Undersea Research and Development Center
Point Mugu, California
Department of Pathology
School of Medicine
University of Southern California
County–USC Medical Center
Los Angeles, California

Special Thanks

to

DR. WM. B. McLEAN

DR. CARL O. HOLMQUIST

DR. SIDNEY R. GALLER

These men are scientists and managers who in the late 1950's and early 1960's stimulated the United States Navy to undertake research with dolphins and other marine mammals. This research directly or indirectly made most of this book possible.

PREFACE

The first International Symposium on Cetacean Research was held in Washington, D.C., in 1963. During the session on practical problems, both Dr. Kenneth S. Norris, who chaired the meeting, and F. G. Wood, who chaired that particular session, suggested that I try to establish an information exchange regarding medical care and husbandry among persons working with marine mammals. An effort was made to start such a data clearinghouse, but it failed quite miscrably.

In the years since the first symposium, biomedical information has developed fairly rapidly; thus, when Mr. Payne Thomas contacted me about the need for a monograph in this field, I was eager to see if a useful text could be developed to fill the practical need for information and at the same time serve as a valuable reference for scientists, teachers, and students.

Therefore, we set out to cover the basic biological and medical sciences as they relate to marine mammals rather than to develop an advanced treatise on current research in the field. The contributors were chosen because of their capability and willingness to cover a specific area.

I felt that the text should contain a brief introduction to each species of marine mammal, giving certain basic information about that species. I asked Dr. Masaharu Nishiwaki to cover the cetaceans, pinnipeds, and sirenians, and his introduction to these three orders appears as Chapter 1. At Dr. Nishiwaki's insistence, I asked Dr. Karl Kenyon, the world's foremost authority on the sea otter, to introduce that species in Chapter 2. In those chapters, we have included illustrations of all those species for which specimens or photographs have been available. We hope that these illustrations will be helpful in species identification, though age, sex, and individual variation must be taken into account when comparing them with the actual animal. We also hope that our scientific colleagues around the world will apprise us of any variations that they find between these illustrations and the animals that they observe in the field. The taxonomy of some groups of marine mammals continues to be a matter of controversy, and we have not tried to still that controversy in this work. Dr. Nishiwaki has classified the Pinnipedia, Cetacea, and Sirenia according to the best evidence available today, but he is careful to point out that certain groups may have to be reclassified and others combined when more studies have been conducted with larger numbers of specimens.

Chapters 3, 4, and 5 deal primarily with anatomy and are designed to convey basic information about the structure of marine mammals, with special emphasis on structural detail required for identification of pathology. Chapters 6 and 7 deal with behavior, senses, and communication, with emphasis on those factors important in maintaining a colony of marine mammals. In Chapter 8, some new techniques for the evolutionary comparison of marine mammals are discussed, and current theories as to the origin of modern-day cetaceans and pinnipeds are reviewed.

Parasites appear to be the most important disease problem in wild populations of marine mammals and are therefore one of the first problems that must be dealt with in a captive group. Chapter 9 represents the first complete check list available on these parasites as well as a tabulation on host locality and a discussion of some of the more important genera. Chapter 10 is a discussion of the marine mammal and his aquatic environment. Here we provide information on our current state of knowledge concerning physiology, medicine, and husbandry and indulge in some speculation about the future.

Throughout this text we have been purposefully reckless in our use of the common terms porpoise and dolphin and we have employed them interchangeably in most cases. Following W. E. Schevill, we recognize no clear distinction between modern day Herringhoggidae and the dolphins of early Greek literature!

I am greatly indebted to many people who were helpful in this effort. Mr. Steve Leatherwood assisted in virtually every phase of the manuscript preparation. My wife, Jeanette, assisted with all the correspondence and manuscript preparation. Maria Ridge, Pam Hayslett, and Victoria Vargas typed the final manuscript, and Margaretta Fuller and Ruth Jackson helped with earlier drafts. I also want to thank many others for their assistance and valuable support. These include Mr. Bill Gilmartin, Mr. B. L. Scronce, Mr. M. F. Wintermantel, Mr. B. A. Powell, Mr. M. E. Conboy, Mr. F. G. Wood, Dr. C. Scott Johnson, Mr. George Anderson, Dr. Don Wilson, Capt. Charles B. Bishop, Mr. John Ropek, Mr. Stanley Marcus, Dr. Sam Rothman, Dr. Jack Collins, and Mr. H. B. Stone.

S.H.R.

CONTENTS

Contents   xiii

MAMMALS OF THE SEA
Biology and Medicine

Chapter 1

GENERAL BIOLOGY

Masaharu Nishiwaki

This chapter is intended to serve as an introduction and guide to the various species comprising the group of aquatic animals known collectively as the marine mammals. The following are the three basic taxonomic categories (orders) of marine mammals: Cetacea, which includes the porpoises (or dolphins), and whales; Pinnipedia, which includes seals, sea lions, and walruses; and Sirenia or sea cows. Another marine mammal, the sea otter, *Enhydra lutris*, a member of the order Carnivora, will be discussed separately (Chapter 2).

The morphological descriptions are included primarily to distinguish each species from others in the same genus. The more fundamental characteristics, those common to the genus, are included in the description of genus, family, or suborder. Illustrations are provided for all the species for which a specimen has been available. The scientific names are printed in italics, and when they appear for the first time are followed by the christener and the year of naming.

Relative body measurements are important for species identification, but since specific, detailed data is required only by specialists, little is included in this text. Mentions of body size usually refer to the size of the average adult, though there is occasional reference to maximum length. Where only a limited number of animals of a species have been accurately measured, the reported sizes represent an estimate based on the specimens available.

MEASUREMENTS

The measurements used by the author are as follows:

Total length: Measurement in a line parallel to the body axis from the front tip of the rostrum to the notch at the posterior edge of the tail flukes.

Head and Body: Total length minus length of posterior appendages (not used for cetaceans).

MAXIMUM WIDTH OF SKULL: Generally, zygomatic breadth of pinnipeds, mastoid breadth of other species.

MAXIMUM WIDTH OF BRAINCASE: Cranial measurement above the zyomatic region.

UPPER CHEEK TEETH: Distance between anterior edge of upper cuspidate tooth and posterior end of last molar, measured either at the crown or alveolus of the tooth (method of measurement must be mentioned).

UPPER TOOTH ROW: Total length of the upper tooth row is generally measured from the anterior end of the first incisor to the posterior end of the last molar tooth. Cetacea are always measured at the alveolus. Because some species lack teeth on the upper jaw, the lower tooth row should also be measured and recorded.

LENGTH OF SKULL: Although the length of the skull is measured at three positions, the condylobasal length is most commonly used.

1. *Maximum condylobasal length.* The linear distance from the posterior surface of the occipital condyles to the anterior end of the maxillary (not including teeth). The condylobasal length in Cetacea is equivalent to the total length of the skull.

2. *Total length of the skull.* A linear measurement from the anterior to the posterior end of the skull, parallel to the body axis (teeth excluded).

3. *Basilar length.* A linear measurement from the front end of the foramen magnum to the posterior end of the central incisor tooth socket, parallel to the body axis (not applicable to cetaceans).

BODY MEASUREMENTS: These are all linear measurements and are taken parallel to the body axis.

1. Total length, from the tip of snout (upper jaw) to the notch in the tail flukes.
2. From tip of snout to center of blowhole.
3. From tip of snout to center of eye.
4. From tip of snout to gape (corner of mouth).
5. From tip of snout to anterior insertion of flipper.
6. From tip of snout to tip of flipper.
7. From ear opening to center of eye.
8. From notch of flukes to tip of dorsal fin.
9. From notch of flukes to center of anus.
10. From notch of flukes to center of the genital opening.
11. From notch of flukes to center of navel.
12. From notch of flukes to posterior end of ventral grooves.

FLIPPER:

1. From anterior insertion to tip of flipper.

2. From axilla to tip.
3. Maximum width.
4. From anterior insertion to tip around the curve.

DORSAL FIN:
  1. Length of base (not necessarily parallel to the body axis).
  2. Height.
  3. From anterior insertion to tip around the curve.
  4. Posterior insertion to tip around the curve.

TAIL FLUKE:
  1. Total width (or spread) of flukes (straight line measurement).
  2. From notch to tip of fluke (both sides).
  3. From notch to nearest point on anterior border.
  4. From notch to anterior insertion.

CLASSIFICATION OF VETEBRAL BONES: Derivation of the vertebral formula is based upon this classification.
  1. *Cervical vertebrae* (C). The first seven vertebrae posterior to the skull. These are lacking rib attachment. The cervical vertebrae are fused in some species, completely free in others. When they are fused, the vertebra can be detected and counted by observing the number of nerve bundles arising from the spinal cord. Occasionally, the cervical vertebrae are found to have attached, but incomplete, bones. These are termed cervical ribs and are not considered to be true ribs.
  2. *Thoracic vertebrae* (T). The vertebrae to which true ribs are attached. The first one to several ribs are generally joined to the sternum. The last rib is often a "floating rib" with no direct attachment to a vertebrae. For this reason it is easily overlooked. The number of thoracic vertebrae is equivalent to the number of rib pairs.
  3. *Lumbar vertebrae* (L). The vertebrae to which neither ribs nor chevron bones attach. They are easily identified by their transverse processes.
  4. *Caudal vertebrae* (Ca). The vertebrae to which the chevron bones attach. The chevrons serve as attachments for caudal muscles. Although the anterior chevrons are distinct and easily recognized, those associated with the most posterior vetebrae are difficult to distinguish. Further, many of those vertebrae lack attachment to ossified chevrons. For this reason, the number of caudal vertebrae is not equivalent to the number of chevron bones.

PHALANGEAL FORMULA: I and II refer to the first and second fingers respectively. Because it is difficult to separate the metacarpals, (generally one per finger) and phalanges, the number of bones indicated includes both type.

DENTAL FORMULA: There are a variety of ways to indicate dental formula. For example, odontocetes usually have a large number of uniform teeth and the author indicates the number of teeth by a formula such as, $\frac{22\text{-}27}{23\text{-}28}$. The numbers above the line refer to the teeth of the upper jaw, those below the line the teeth of the lower jaw. The range of individual variation is indicated for both upper and lower jaws.

CETACEA

There are three suborders of Cetacea: Archaeoceti, Mystacoceti, and Odontoceti. The first, represented from the Eocene (a specimen known as Zeuglodontia), Oligocene, and Miocene epochs, includes only extinct species and is not discussed in this chapter. The remaining two are distinguishable from each other primarily by their types of dentition and the structure of their skulls.

All species of Cetacea have teeth, at least in the gums, during the fetal period. In the Mystacoceti, however, those teeth never emerge from the gums, even after birth, but are replaced instead by baleen plates which emerge from the palatine ridges and serve as food collectors. Odontoceti, on the other hand, have no baleen and retain their teeth after birth. There are some species in which those teeth remain inside the gums throughout life and others in which the tooth shape and position differ between the sexes, the females having smaller teeth which sometimes do not emerge at all. Though some fossil Odontoceti have polyform teeth, most living species have uniform teeth. Unlike most other mammals, Odontoceti have permanent dentition and no milk teeth.

The living animals included in the order Cetacea range in size from 1 to 30 m and have the basic mammalian characteristics but unlike other mammals, including members of the order Pinnipedia and Sirenia, spend their entire lives in the water. In adapting to that completely aquatic life, their bodies have become generally spindle shaped and streamlined. Some have a dorsal fin, others do not. The forelimbs are transformed into fin-shaped flippers, and though a trace of rear limbs appears as a projection on the early developing fetus, the rear limbs have degenerated and cannot be observed externally after birth. The skin at the end of the tail has developed into a horizontally positioned swimming organ known as a fluke. Just under the epidermis there is a relatively thick blubber layer, formed of fat and dermis, which aids in maintaining body temperature and in reducing specific gravity. The nostrils have migrated to the top of the head, permitting the animals to breathe while swimming at full speed (examination of the skeleton shows that the nares actually open about the middle of the face and that the forward elongation of the jaws causes the "overhead" appearance of the blowhole).

Fetuses of all cetacean species have hair on their snouts, like the rough or tactile hairs around the mouth of a dog or cat. Though most Odontoceti loose their external hairs soon after birth, Mystacoceti retain them as sensory organs throughout their lives.

Cetaceans have an extraordinarily well-developed skull, flexible back-bones, and ten to twenty ribs. Odontoceti have a well-developed sternum, but Mystacoceti have a small sternum which is joined to only one or two pairs of ribs. (Considering this rather weak thoracic structure, it is not surprising that stranded baleen whales may suffocate under their own weight.) Whales lack clavicles. Except for the joint with the scapula, there is no moveable joint in the forelegs. There are always traces of pelvic bones, but those bones are not joined to vertebrae. Traces of femur and fibula are attached to the pelvic bone of some species of Balaenidae. At the anterior portion of the coccyx, the V-shaped chevrons are very dis-tinctive. The vertebrae lie along the midline, but neither they nor any other bones extend into the tail flukes.

The gestation period of Mystacoceti is most frequently eleven months or slightly more; that of Odontoceti is generally a year or slightly more (sperm whales remain pregnant sixteen months). One pair of nipples is located at either side of the genital slit. There is one calf per pregnancy, and lactation continues for six to eighteen months.

Suborder Mystacoceti

The distinguishing characteristics of the suborder Mystacoceti are as follows:

1a.
1. Outer opening of nostril bipartite.
2. Teeth absent throughout life after birth.
3. Baleen plates present.
4. Convex profile of upper surface of skull (mainly maxillae and pre-maxillae).
5. Comparatively small sternum and poor skeletal construction of thorax.

Members of even the smallest species of this suborder reach a length of 6 m as adults. Although the fetus has teeth on both the upper and lower jaws, they are degenerated and absorbed by the time of birth and are re-placed by from 150 to 400 baleen plates on the palatine ridges of an adult. The shape, color, and number of baleen plates vary according to species.

The skull is extraordinarily large, comprising one-third of the total body length in some species. The cervical vetebrae are fused in some species but separated in others. Only one or two pairs of ribs join the sternum. Although the bones of the rear legs are usually absent, some species of Balaenidae retain traces of femur and fibula. Even in those species, however, such bones never form any external legs except during fetal life. Generally, a cecum exists in members of this suborder. Baleen whales feed mainly on krill (small crustaceans), but some species also eat small pelagic fishes.

The three living families are Balaenidae, Eschrichtiidae, and Balaenopteridae.

Family Balaenidae

Some characteristics of Balaenidae are the following:
2a.

1. No ventral grooves or creases in skin of throat.
2. Head length more than one-fourth of total body length.
3. Maxillae, premaxillae, and vomer construct a long narrow arch.
4. Long and narrow baleen plates; more than two hundred plates on a side.
5. Seven cervicals all fused.

This family is characterized by very narrow, curved maxillary and premaxillary bones. There are baleens along the lower side of the maxillary. The condylobasal length of the skull relative to the total length increases as individuals grow, sometimes attaining over one-fourth of the total length. There are neither grooves on the abdomen nor throat creases. The three living genera are Balaena, Eubalaena, and Caperea, each represented by a single species. Some scientists unite genus *Balaena* and genus *Eubalaena* and form a separate independent family with genus *Caperea*.

Balaena

Some characteristics of *Balaena* are the following:
3a.

1. Size large, more than 15 m in body length.
2. No dorsal fin, flippers fairly large.
3. Baleen plates long and narrow (2.5 m and 30 cm respectively); more than three hundred plates on each side.
4. Five fingers in flippers.
5. Body color blueish gray with pale spots.
6. No bonnets (wart-like projections on skin).

Balaena mysticetus

Figure 1–1. *Balaena mysticetus*, known as the Greenland right whale, named by Linnaeus in 1758.

OTHER COMMON NAMES: Bowhead, great polar whale, arctic right whale.

MORPHOLOGY: Greenland right whales are believed to reach a maximum body length of 20 m. Measurements of 30.3 to 30.6 m were once recorded, but later measurement of condylobasal length (which is approximately one-third of total length) of these two specimens confirmed that the reports were in error. These errors were probably caused by exaggeration or by measurement along the curve of the body. The valid measure of body length is the straight line from the tip of the maxillary to the notch in the tail flukes.

The body of these whales is generally blueish gray. Scoresby (1874) reported seeing a specimen in which the white portion (light coloring on underside) extended to the anterior part of the upper jaw. He also reported that some specimens are covered with white spots, that white or gray coloring predominates with old individuals, that the newborn are blue-black in color, and that the nursing young are pale blue to grayish blue. Many individuals have pale spots all over the body.

The flukes are about 6 to 8 m in width (total spread). The blowholes are located about 5 m behind the tip of upper jaw, near the highest point on the body. There are approximately 360 yellowish-white baleen plates, 35 cm wide and 3 m long, on each side.

The skull is very large (see Chapter 4). The maxillary and mandible are long and narrow but widen near the eyes. The mandibles extend forward along the lower edge of the lower jaw and are rather flat horizontally. The vertebral formula is $C7 + T13 + L10–13 + Ca22–24 = 53–55$. The phalangeal formula is I: 1, II: 3–4, III: 4–5, IV: 3–4, and V: 2–3. There is a trace of hind-leg bones.

DISTRIBUTION AND MIGRATION: This species is limited to the northern hemisphere. During the summer it is found in the Arctic Sea, but when the sea begins to ice over it moves southward in what is presumably not an extensive migration.

ABUNDANCE: This was the most important species in sixteenth and seventeenth century whaling and was abundant at that time. However, over-whaling has severely reduced the population, and at present, it is believed that only a few small groups exist near Greenland.

FOOD: The primary food is small plankton, mostly of the genus *Calanus* or *Copepoda*. The primary feeding ground appears to be near the icefields of the Arctic.

REPRODUCTION: Copulations occur in late summer, and adults accompanying young are frequently observed in spring. There is generally one fetus per pregnancy, but Scoresby (1874) reported seeing what appeared to be twins nursing and illustrated his observation.

Eubalaena

Some characteristics of *Eubalaena* are the following:
3b.
1. Size large, more than 15 m in body length.
2. No dorsal fin, flippers fairly large.
3. Baleen plates long and narrow (2.0 m and 30 cm respectively); less than 250 plates on each side.
4. Five fingers in flippers.
5. Body color blueish black with no pale spots.
6. Bonnets present.

Eubalaena glacialis

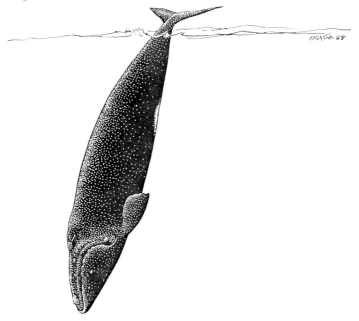

Figure 1–2. *Eubalaena glacialis*, known as the right whale, named by Borowski in 1781.

OTHER COMMON NAME: Black right whale.

MORPHOLOGY: This species is easily identifiable by its round and fat body and by the bonnets (large wart-like areas formed on the external skin) which are its most characteristic feature. The largest bonnet is located at the anterior of the upper jaw, and the next largest are found on both sides of the anterior portion of the lower jaw behind the blowhole. On the outside of the lower jaw, there is a series of several small, raised areas, each one of which is the base of an apparently tactile hair. The upper ridge of the lower lip is quite bumpy. The head comprises about one-fourth of the total length and the total spread of the tail flukes equals about 35 percent of the body length. Both maxillary and premaxillary are projected forward with a curve, forming an arch. The bristles of the olive black baleen plates are much rougher than those of *Balaena mysticetus*.

The maximum body lengths recorded to date are 16.5 m in the Atlantic and 17.8 m in the Pacific. The newborn are about 5 to 6 m long. The grayish blue body color of the young darkens with growth to the blueish black to black color of adults. White spots of irregular shape are often found on the abdomen near the navel. The tongue is thick, blueish gray in color and relatively smaller than that of other species of Mystacoceti. The mammillae are located at the inguinal region, and the mammary glands are very thick (as much as 10 cm even in immature females).

The testis, which may be only 1 to 2 kg in juveniles, may grow as large as 1,000 kg in weight in a fully matured breeding male. The blubber is very thick (as thick as 40 cm at the breast and heavy portion of back) and contains fat of good quality. The vertebral formula is C7 + T14–15 + L11–10 + Ca25 = 56–57. There are fourteen to fifteen pairs of ribs. The phalangeal formula is I: 3, II: 5, III: 6, IV: 4 (+1), and V: 4. The number of finger bones is subject to some individual variation.

DISTRIBUTION: In the southern hemisphere, *Eubalaena* are found south of 20°S and north of 50°S and in the northern hemisphere they are found between 20°N and 70°N in both the Pacific and Atlantic Oceans. Some inhabit the Arctic Sea. Since the distribution and migrations of this species in the Atlantic Ocean are often confused with those of the Greenland right whale, the northern limit of its distribution has not yet been determined.

ABUNDANCE: The abundance of *Eubalaena* in the southern hemisphere is unknown, but since reports of sightings of this species are very rare, they are considered very scarce. At present, slaughter of black right whales is prohibited by the International Whaling Convention. Sightings in the Pacific are more frequent than in the Atlantic. In the North Pacific, some animals are found north of the Bering Strait, in the Arctic Sea. The total world population is estimated to be from a few hundred to one thousand animals.

FOOD: This species is rather selective, feeding mostly on small copepods (*Calanus, Microcalanus, Pseudocalanus, Oithona,* and *Metridia*).

REPRODUCTION: Copulations have been observed from February to April, but the breeding season probably lasts about half a year. The gestation period is twelve months, and there is one fetus per pregnancy.

BEHAVIOR: Black right whales are slow swimmers. During their migrations they generally swim 2 or 3 knots (3.7 to 5.6 km/hr) and even when startled they swim no faster than 5 knots (9.3 km/hr). While swimming, they will blow two or three times per minute for several minutes and then make a longer and probably deeper dive for ten to twenty minutes. With each breath, two blows, one from each nostril, are visible to a height of 4 to 8 m above the animal. Although they may make deep dives, *Eubalaena* are not believed to dive as deeply as other species of Mystacoceti.

PARASITES: It was formerly believed that this species had a variety of external parasites. In recent studies, however, though two species of a parasitic whale lice were found all over the body, there were no acorn barnacles or ship barnacles. Black right whales simply do not migrate into warm water where the larvae of these barnacles are abundant.

MISCELLANEOUS: The length-weight relationship is as follows:[*]

* Based on data collected by the Japan Whale Research Institute since 1956.

Sex	Length	Body Weight (Excluding Blood and Feces)
F	11.7M	22,866kg
M	12.4	22,247
F	14.1	46,866
M	14.7	51,826
M	15.1	55,254
M	16.1	65,690
M	17.0	65,756
M	17.1	67,197

Caperea

Some characteristics of *Caperea* are the following:

3c.

1. Size small, less than 6 m in body length (smallest of the Mystaco-ceti).
2. Dorsal fin present, flippers small.
3. Four fingers in flippers.
4. Body color entirely black.
5. No bonnets.

Caperea marginata

Figure 1–3. *Caperea marginata*, known as the pygmy right whale, named by Gray in 1846.

MORPHOLOGY: This species is placed in the family Balaenidae because of the following characteristics: the seven cervical vertebrae are all fused together, there are no throat grooves, the maxillary and premaxillary are projected in an arch shape, and the baleen is long in relation to its width.

This is the smallest of the Mystacoceti, reaching a maximum length of 6 m. In those specimens of which the body color has been described, the body is black with a pale abdomen. The baleen plates, numbering 230 on a side, are pale yellowish white with a brown fringe along the exterior edge. Therefore, when the row is observed outside, the baleen plates appear brown in color. The eyes appear black. The condylobasal length is about one-fourth of the total body length (123 to 496 cm in one specimen). Although a sternum is believed to exist, none has yet been described. The dorsal fin is about 15 cm high. The vertebrae are presumably $C7 + T17 + L2 + Ca14–15 = 40–41$. Seventeen pairs of ribs are attached to seventeen dorsal (or thoracic) vertebrae.

Although the internal organs of this species have not yet been studied extensively, the skelton indicates a relatively large mass of internal organs. In a 3.3 m specimen, the small intestine was 40 m long, twelve times the body length. The same specimen had a 1.7 m large intestine and unlike most cetaceans, a 20 cm cecum.

DISTRIBUTION: This species is limited to the southern hemisphere. Specimens have been reported washed onto beaches in Australia, New Zealand, South Africa, and South America.

FAMILY ESCHRICHTIIDAE

Some characteristics of Eschrichtiidae are the following:
2b.
1. No ventral grooves, but 2 to 4 furrows of skin are visible on the throat.
2. Head length comprises one-fourth to one-fifth of total body length.
3. Maxillae, premaxillae, and vomer slightly curved forward.
4. Baleen plates, yellowish white, thick and short; 140 to 180 plates on a side.
5. No dorsal fin, but several humps situated on dorsal surface of the tail stock.
6. Four fingers in flipper.
7. Seven cervical vertebrae all separated.

This family has only one genus, and that genus consists of but one species, *Eschrichtius gibbosus,* found at present only in the North Pacific.

Eschrichtius

Eschrichtius gibbosus

Figure 1–4. *Eschrichtius gibbosus,* known as the California gray whale, named by Erxleben in 1777.

MORPHOLOGY: In appearance, the genus Eschrichtius is midway between the Balaenidae and Balaenopteridae. The largest female ever recorded was 15.0 m, but the average is 12.7 m. The largest male recorded was 15.3 m, but the average is 12.2 m. In both male and female, the girth is largest around the base of the flippers and decreases towards the tail. The body is gray, dark gray or blueish gray.

The proportion of head to body length is relatively small. The skull of this species is wider than Balaenidae but narrower than Balaenopteridae. The maxillary projects forward with less of a downward curve than that of Balaenidae. Although there is no dorsal fin, there is a chain of seven to fifteen small bumps on the dorsum of the last one-third of the body. This chain of bumps starts around the intersection of the anus and continues to the base of the tail flukes. The tail flukes are of intermediate size, the tip-to-tip distance reaching one-fourth of the body length.

Most commonly two but sometimes four, grooves about 1.5 m long run along the throat parallel to the body axis. The half of the body posterior to the flippers is quite rough and is usually covered with injuries and scars from the animal's rubbing against sand, rock, and other objects. Those scars and the baleen plates are often covered with barnacles. Whale lice are also abundant.

The upper jaw has 140 to 180 baleen plates on each side. The baleen is light yellowish white, 40 to 50 cm long and has very rough, thick bristles. This species has many tactile hairs (more than any other species of whale) located at the upper and lower jaws and on the forehead near the blowhole. There are no bumps at the base of these hairs. The eyes are located just posterior to the angle of gape and are oval in shape. The upper eyelids are only slightly longer than the lower lids. Wrinkles above each eyelid form a circle around the eye. This may be due to the shape of the skull. The auditory openings are located about midway between the eyes and the anterior insertion of the flippers. The opening is large enough that one can put a pencil into it. The blowholes are located slightly behind the highest portion of the rostrum. The two holes form somewhat of a V shape with the apex in the anterior and the open portion at the posterior end. The tongue is narrow, thick, and salmon-pink with a gray tip. The blubber is generally 15 to 20 cm thick but may reach 35 cm in thickness over certain areas of the body. It is usually very light yellow but sometimes appears light pink.

The flipper has four fingers, often identifiable from outside by a difference in color between the skin over the finger bones and the skin between. That difference in skin color is natural in some individuals, but is often caused by abrasion of the finger parts. The first finger does not exist. The phalangeal formula is II: 3, III: 3, IV: 4 and V: 1. The vertebral formula

is $C7 + T14 + L12 + Ca23 = 56$. The seven cervical vertebrae are all
separated. The first, second, and eighth to fourteenth pairs of ribs are uni-
cuspid (single headed) and the third to seventh pairs are bicuspid. The
pelvic bones are relatively large.

DISTRIBUTION: There are two groups of Eschrichtiidae in the North Pacific:
one which migrates along the Pacific coast of North America and a smaller
population which makes seasonal migrations in the western North Pacific.

MIGRATION: According to past observations made in Korea, the group in
the western North Pacific migrates southward along the coast of Korea
from late November through late January. They appear in the waters off
Ulsan every year after November 20, increase rapidly to a peak in December, and then begin to move out, completely disappearing by late January.

The southward migrants can be divided into three groups. The earliest
group appears in late November through mid-January and consists mainly
of pregnant females. The second group, coming in pods of several non-
pregnant females in the company of twenty to thirty males, increases to a
maximum in late December and then disappears in mid-January. The
third group, the immature males, usually less than 11.5 m in length, appears
in the waters of Ulsan in early November through late January. These
immature males are not a large percentage of the population and presumably migrate simply to avoid the cold waters of the North. Although
the migrations of this population are not well known further south than
Ulsan, it is believed that they may breed in the waters north of the Goto
Islands, south of Kyushu, or west to the Cheju-do Island. They may not
migrate as far south as Ryukyu.

The northward migration takes place between March and May. During
this time, pods composed of only several whales begin to follow paths
further off shore than the paths of the southern migration in search of
the abundant food of the northern North Pacific. Individuals enter the
Okhotsk Sea in June and then migrate further into the Aleutian waters.
In the past, this species passed through the waters off the east coast of
Japan, and catches were recorded along the east coasts of Kyushu and
Shikoku, in the area of Wakayama. In recent years, however, there has
been no record of capture or observation of this species off the east coast
of Japan.

The eastern Pacific population migrates along the coast of North America
in late December and January, arriving in abundance along the California
peninsula (Baja California) and the Gulf of California in January through
March. During the southward migration, the same three distinctive seg-
regations which exist in the waters off Korea may be observed in this
population. This indicates that the southward migration is a breeding

migration. The animals parturate and nurse the juveniles in the lagoons and calm coastal seas. Some animals are left on the beach (in shallow lagoons and bays) during the ebb tide and return to the sea during high tide.

The northward migration takes place in late February to early April. The animals move along the coast as far north as Vancouver Island and then cross the Gulf of Alaska towards the Aleutian chain. The passage of this species through the eastern Aleutian Islands is not recorded. It is assumed that they move westward south of the chain as far west as 180° and then enter the Bering Sea, where they feed. Some appear to go on further through the Bering Strait into the Arctic Sea and spend late June through September there.

ABUNDANCE: This species was once very abundant in coastal waters. They were the first whales to be sought by the American whaling ships and were exploited extensively by the coastal natives both because of their proximity to shore during migration and because they are probably the easiest species to catch. The abundance of gray whales was reduced first in the eastern Pacific.

Extensive whaling of the gray whales began off the east coast of Korea around 1900, and in twenty years, the western population was also nearly destroyed. The International Whaling Convention prohibited the slaughter of this species. (Recently the United States Government granted permission for the capture of a hundred gray whales each year to determine whether further protection is necessary.) American scientists currently estimate the stocks along the Pacific coast of America at 9,000.

FOOD: Gray whales reportedly take no food during their southward migration but feed constantly during the northward migration. As discussed earlier, gray whales pass through the waters off Ulsan going northward in late March to May, and off the eastern coasts of Siberia in late April to late May, spending some time in the waters off the west coast of Sakhalin and Hokkaido. In addition to copepods, these whales presumably feed on herring eggs and schooling fishes and some sea cucumbers have been recorded from stomach contents.

REPRODUCTION: During their southward migration, all the pregnant whales are close to delivery (fetuses are 3 to 4 m in length). On the other hand, during the northward migration, all the pregnant whales have fetuses of only 10 to 30 cm in length. This indicates that the parturition and impregnation are peaked in February, and that gestation is about twelve months.

BEHAVIOR: Gray whales blow three to five times in fairly rapid succession between shallow dives and then may make a longer, deeper dive (perhaps 100 m in depth and 1000 m in distance) of seventeen to eighteen minutes' duration. When they are making shallow dives, their flukes do not break the water, but when they are diving deep, their flukes come out high in the air. Gray whales' usual swimming speed is 3 to 4 knots but they may reach 7 to 8 knots when fleeing.

When the blow is observed from behind, the vapor column from the two blowholes is loosely separated, though not completely distinct as is the case with the right whale. When observed from the side, only one blow is distinguishable.

FAMILY BALAENOPTERIDAE

Some characteristics of Balaenopteridae are the following:
2c.
    1. Ventral grooves present.
    2. Head length less than one-fourth of body length.
    3. Maxillae broad and do not curve strongly with premaxillae and vomer.
    4. Baleen plates short compared to breadth; more than 200 baleen plates on each side.
    5. Dorsal fin present.
    6. Four fingers in flipper.
    7. Seven cervical vertebrae all separated.

This family includes the most abundant of the baleen whales. Although balaenopterids are found in all oceans, the northern populations do not intermingle with southern populations because of the half-year lag in seasons between the northern and southern hemispheres.

The body color varies among species and individuals. Balaenopteridae have a large number of short, wide baleen plates. The skull has a flat, wide snout, and the mandibles are widely separated, forming a large mouth. The parietal bone extends as far forward as the suture behind the nasal bone. The frontal bone does not extend as far back as the top of the cranium. The occipital bone extends forward beyond the orbital fossa as far as the squamosal bone. The cavity on the surface of the squamosal bone is deep. The ribs form an arch as they join the transverse process of the vertebrae. Two genera are included in this family: Balaenoptera and Megaptera.

Balaenoptera

Some characteristics of *Balaenoptera* are the following:
4a.
    1. Ventral grooves more than forty (count between flippers).
    2. Flipper length less than one-seventh of body length.

Balaenoptera musculus

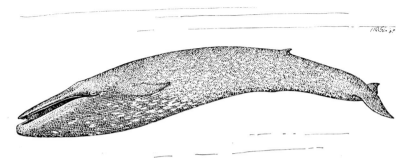

Figure 1–5. *Balaenoptera musculus,* known as the blue whale, named by Linnaeus in 1758.

Balaenoptera musculus also have these characteristics:
5a.
  1. Ventral grooves reach navel.
6a.
  2. More than 300 baleen plates.
7a.
  3. Baleen plates all black.

OTHER COMMON NAMES: Sibbald's rorqual, great whale.

MORPHOLOGY: The blue whale is the largest animal that has ever existed on earth. According to the International Whaling statistics, the largest ever recorded was a 31 m female taken from the Antarctic Ocean. The largest male, also taken from the Antarctic, was 30 m long. It has been impossible to weigh such a large body; therefore, the total weights have been estimated by weighing individually the parts of the body, separated on the deck of a whaling factory ship, and later totaling them. Since such a totaling does not include some of the blood and body fluid lost during sectioning, that sum is increased by 10 to 13 per cent to estimate the total weight. A specimen 24.4 m weighed 81,000 kg by this method. The relation between weight and length is represented by the equation $Y = aX^b$, where Y is body weight, X is body length, a is a constant (specific to each species), and b is a coefficient (variable according to body shape). In the case of this species the length-weight relation is represented by the following

$$Y(t) = 0.00151X \, (\text{feet})^{2.49}$$

The body is saxe blue with some splashed patterns formed by pale spots on the dorsal skin. Some animals have white flecks on the ventral grooves from the rear margin toward the thorax. Some also have white stripes, called white patches, across the axis near the anus, around the genital opening, or around the flippers. The undersurfaces of the flippers and flukes are also saxe blue, and there is a radiant pattern of pale color, called striation, on the lower surface of the tail flukes. The color of this pattern varies with individuals and with stocks and is considered genotypic. Although these patterns tend to fade out as the animal ages, striations may be used to identify different stocks of whales.

The flippers are relatively small, reaching only one-eighth to one-seventh of the body length. The dorsal fin is shorter than that of the fin whale or sei whale. The baleen plates, including the filaments, are all black and are as much as 90 to 110 cm long and 50 to 60 cm wide. The mammary glands lie along the ventral axis on either side of the genital slit. During lactation, each gland may be 2 m long, 60 cm wide, and 30 cm thick.

A wide maxillary (even at the tip) is characteristic of the skull. This wide upper jaw is quite apparent when swimming blue whales are observed from above. Generally, there is no vestige of the femur on the pelvic bone. The sternum is small but strong, and the blade of scapula is large. The vertebral formula is $C7 + T15 + L15 + Ca26\text{--}27 = 63\text{--}64$. The flippers have four fingers, and the phalangeal formula is I: 4 (4–5), II: 7 (5–8, IV: 6 (5–7), and V: 4 (3–4).

DISTRIBUTION AND MIGRATION: Blue whales are found in the North Pacific, North Atlantic, Antarctic Ocean, etc. Those in the northern hemisphere are shorter than those in the Antarctic Sea (by approximately 1.5 m at the same age). However, there is no apparent racial difference among them. There is no exchange of populations between the northern and southern hemispheres. The population in the southern hemisphere extends from the warm waters near the equator, where the animals migrate in the fall for breeding, to the vicinity of the packed ice around Antarctic, where they move during the summer.

The population in the northern hemisphere is found in both the Atlantic and Pacific, the Atlantic population venturing as far north as the drifting ice and the Pacific population extending as far north as the Aleutian chain, though not into the Bering Sea.

ABUNDANCE: Since the beginning of Norwegian whaling, blue whales have been extensively exploited. As a result of years of overkilling, the stocks of this species in the Antarctic Ocean have decreased greatly to the present population of only 20,000 to 30,000 animals. The stock size in the North Pacific is estimated as 1,000 to 1,500. The population in the Atlantic is very small, probably no more than 500.

FOOD: Blue whales seem to be very selective feeders, preferring small euphausiids. Their distribution is limited to the waters where euphausiids are abundant. Small fish that are sometimes found in the stomach contents are probably swallowed incidentally during feeding.

REPRODUCTION: In the southern hemisphere, *Balaenoptera musculus* breed in temperate seas during July and August. After ten to eleven months of pregnancy, they return to these seas for parturition. The newborn are 7 to 8 m in length. Lactating mother whales with juveniles are often observed in December and January. The lactation period presumably lasts for six to eight more months and the mother can be impregnated for the next winter.

It was once believed, using cerumen (ear plug) counting as a basis for age determination, that blue whales reached sexual maturity in 8 to 10 years. Current evidence suggests 23 to 30 years is more accurate. Females reach maturity at approximately 23.4 m, males at 22.6 m.

BEHAVIOR: The blows reach as high as 10 to 15 m.

LONGEVITY: Studies on cerumen indicate that this species lives to about ninety years and rarely over one hundred years.

PARASITES: Most of the external parasites are crustacea, mainly whale lice and barnacles. These apparently may also propagate on the skin. A paint-brush-like crustacea called pennella is also a common skin parasite. Besides these, yellow layers of diatoms are often found over the skin of whales which have spent the winter in the northern North Pacific. Animals so affected are called sulphur bottoms. Nematodes and cestodes are sometimes found in the digestive system, and cysts of cestodes are found under the skin.

VARIATIONS: Ichihara (1966) proposed as a subspecies the pygmy blue whale, *Balaenoptera musculus brevicauda*.

Balaenoptera physalus

Figure 1–6. *Balaenoptera physalus*, known as the fin whale, named by Linnaeus in 1758.

7b.

Balaenoptera physalus have baleen plates which are mainly bluish gray with one third of the forepart on the right side being yellowish white.

OTHER COMMON NAMES: Finback, common rorqual.

MORPHOLOGY: According to the International Whale statistics, the largest male and female ever caught were both 26.8 m specimens taken in the Antarctic Ocean. Females average 19.7 m and males 19.5 m.

The dorsal surface is brownish black, fading gradually but irregularly into white on the abdomen. Some animals appear yellow to green because of the diatoms which may cling to the outer layer of skin. Two dark areas are clearly visible, passing from the vicinity of the flippers toward the grooves. Another black stripe runs from the middle of the tail to the anus. On the back, behind the blowholes, at a plane running through the intersection of the base of the flippers, a V-shaped pattern of lighter color expands backward. A stripe of pale to white color runs back and upwards from the external ear opening on each side. The upper jaw is symmetric in color (except on the baleen plates), but the lower jaw is black on the left side and white on the right. When observed from the outside, the left baleen plates are blueish-gray, while the front one-half to one-third of the right baleen plates is yellowish-white. All the bristles are brownish-gray. The largest plates are 70 to 90 cm long. The average number of baleen plates varies from 350 to 360. A pair of mammillae is located at the inguinal region but is generally hidden in the mammillary valeculae.

The skull is fairly flat, though not as flat as that of the blue whale, and the mouth is large. The flippers are short, reaching only one-eleventh of the total body length. The fluke is less than one-fourth of body length. The small but very distinctive dorsal fin is positioned on the dorsum at the level of the anus. The eyes, located above and behind the corner of the mouth, are small. Two blowholes are located on the axis of the dorsal surface a little in front of the plane of the eyes. There are from fifty to one hundred tactile hairs growing on both the upper and lower jaws, and there is a distinct clump of hairs at the tip of the lower jaws. Fifty to sixty ventral grooves run as far back as the navel.

The vertebral formula is $C7 + T15 + L14–16 + Ca25–27 = 60–63$. The maxillaries are nearly as wide as those of the blue whale. The blade of the scapula is well developed and the flipper has four fingers of I: 4, II: 7, IV: 7, and V: 4.

DISTRIBUTION: Fin whales inhabit all oceans but are not found in coastal waters. The largest population is in the Antarctic. In the North Pacific they may be seen in the Bering Sea and Arctic Ocean.

MIGRATION AND ABUNDANCE: The fin whales generally migrate to areas of colder water in the summer for feeding and to warmer seas in the winter for breeding. The present Antarctic population is estimated at 80,000. They are less abundant in the northern hemisphere, with approximately 15,000 living in the North Pacific and 5,000 in the North Atlantic.

FOOD: Fin whales, particularly in the Antarctic Ocean, are fond of such small crustaceans as euphausiids, *Calanus*, and *Mysis*. Fish found in the stomach contents may sometimes be swallowed accidentally, but in the

North Pacific, fin whales have been reported to feed on the small pelagic fishes such as herring, mackerel, saury, and tomcod, and even on squids.

REPRODUCTION: Fin whales are generally considered to be monogamous and much affectionate behavior has been observed. They migrate to polar waters for feeding in summer and then return to the lower latitude in winter for parturition. Pregnancy lasts eleven to twelve months, and the newborn are about 6.4 m in both northern and southern hemispheres. Juveniles attain sexual maturity in eight to ten years.

BEHAVIOR: When they are, making shallow dives, fin whales take a breath of about five seconds duration every two to three minutes. The blow may be visible as high as 6 to 10 m. After making several of these short dives, the whale will make a longer, deeper dive (probably no greater than 200 m) of about fifteen minutes which it will begin quietly without bringing its flukes out of the water.

This species is the fastest and most active of the Mystacoceti. For that reason, it was seldom caught before the development of the fast catcher boats of today. Even now, the catcher boats must follow the animal for over thirty minutes at a speed of 18 knots before the whale begins to tire and the boat can close within range. As it is chased by the whaler, the fin whale will not bring its flukes out of the water, but it may raise its head so far out of the water that the ventral grooves are visible to observers on the chase boats. Its maximum swimming speed is probably over 20 knots, and its cruising speed about 8 knots. No other species of whale can swim for such long periods of time at such high speeds.

LONGEVITY: Based on the study of cerumen, fin whales are assumed to live ninety to one hundred years.

PARASITES: The external parasites include whale lice, penella, acorn and ship barnacles, protozoa, and bacteria, all of which produce some surface injuries. The microorganisms often cause secondary infections on the lamprey marks. Here, as with blue whales, these infections often leave characteristic white scars. Internal parasites include nematodes and cestodes in the digestive system and cysts of parasites in the muscle or under the skin.

MISCELLANEOUS: The migration routes of this species are very well studied through the use of marking harpoons. The marking harpoon is a stainless steel tube with a cone-shaped head that is filled with lead. It is shot from an 18 mm rifle at the dorsal or waist part of the whale as the boat approaches the animal. The date, location, estimated body length, and species are recorded at the time of the marking and these data are provided to all the member countries of International Whaling Convention. The harpoons remain in the muscle or blubber and may later be recovered if the whale is killed.

VARIATIONS: As in the case of other species of Mystacoceti, fin whales in the northern hemisphere are smaller by approximately 1.5 m at the age of sexual and physical maturity than those in the southern hemisphere, though they are usually the same size at birth. On the east longitude whaling ground of the Antaractic Ocean, the average body size of fin whales increases from east to west while the vitamin A content of the liver oil and the number of ovulations decrease. Recent studies have related these occurrences to variations in the food supply. In the stocks which inhabit the South China Sea and Yellow Sea, males attain sexual maturity at a length of 15.6 m, females at 17.8 m. In other stocks in the northern hemisphere, males attain sexual maturity at 17.4 m, females at 18.6 m.

Balaenoptera edeni

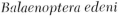
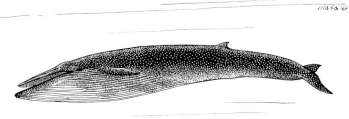

Figure 1–7. *Balaenoptera edeni*, known as Bryde's whale, named by Anderson in 1878.

7c.

Balaenoptera edeni can be distinguished by their baleen plates which are all slate gray with dark-colored bristles.

MORPHOLOGY: Both sexes of this species reach a maximum size of about 14.5 m, 1.5 m smaller than the sei whale. The mean lengths are 13 m for females and 12 m for males. Although the border between the dark dorsal and white ventral surfaces is even less noticeable in Bryde's whale than in the sei whale, the body colors of these two species are generally quite similar. The inner surface of the flippers and the undersurface of the tail flukes are gray. The dorsal fin is moderate in size and height, leans backwards, and resembles that of fin whales. There are about forty-five ventral grooves.

The baleen plates are approximately 50 cm in length and short, relative to width. There are approximately three hundred plates on each side. An interval between the left and right rows of baleen plates exposes a wide area of palatine. The maxillary and premaxillary do not curve downward but project forward rather straightly. The corners of the mandible extend backward beyond its joints. Its cross section is rounded laterally and appears to be thicker than that of the sei whale.

A main ridge runs along the axis from the tip of the jaw to the center of the blowholes. This main ridge is flanked on the outer surface of the upper jaw on each side by a subridge. The sei whale lacks these ridges. Several tactile hairs grow along the outside of those ridges. Other tactile hairs are found in the same location as in other Balaenopteridae.

The vertebral formula is $C7 + T13 + L13 + Ca21 = 54$. There are generally thirteen, but sometimes fourteen, pairs of ribs. The first ribs are bicuspid. The groove which separates the two heads of each rib is about 10 cm deep and the shape of the two heads is very distinctive and characteristic of this species. The neural spines of the dorsal and lumbar vertebrae have a pronounced posterior. The flipper have four fingers of I: 6, II: 5, IV: 5, and V: 3.

DISTRIBUTION: Bryde's whales' distribution is limited to the North Pacific, Central Pacific, South Atlantic, and Indian Oceans, between 40°N and 40°S and within areas where the water temperature is over 20°C. They are seldom found in the waters of higher latitude, except where there are warm water projections.

ABUNDANCE: Although the present level of population has not been estimated, no indication of declining population has been presented. However, the migration of this whale is not as extensive as those by some other species and is confined to a smaller overall area; thus, the world population size may not be large.

FOOD: Although this species may feed on small planktonic Crustacea, the main food items seem to be squid and such pelagic fishes as sardine, mackerel, and saury. They are also fond of sand lancers. Olsen (1913) reported on a specimen that had eaten a great number of sharks, and Fraser (1936) reported that a Bryde's whale fed on herring.

REPRODUCTION: Males attain sexual maturity at 12 m and females at 12.5 m.

BEHAVIOR: Blows are not high but give the impression of being very thick, like those of the fin whale. These whales generally breathe only two or three times between deeper more prolonged dives. They often form a very dense school, with tens of whales or sometimes over a hundred being observed at one sighting.

PARASITES: External parasites include acorn and ship barnacles, penella, whale lice, and *Balaenophilis unisetus* (on baleens). Many *Bolbosoma* (hooked cestodes) are found in the intestine, but none of the more frequent internal parasites found in other species of Balaenopteridae are commonly reported in this species.

Balaenoptera bonaerensis

Figure 1–8. *Balaenoptera bonaerensis,* known as the New Zealand piked whale, named by Burmeister in 1867.

Balaenoptera bonaerensis can be distinguished by the following characteristics:

6b.

1. Less than three hundred baleen plates.
2. Color of baleen plates all yellowish white with grayish brown outer margin.

OTHER COMMON NAME: Antarctic minke whale.

MORPHOLOGY: The animals of this species lack the white band on the flippers that is a characteristic of the little piked whale. The maximum body length is about 10 m for both sexes. The body is charcoal gray on the back and white on the abdomen. The dorsal fin is distinct and there are about sixty ventral grooves that reach the navel. The baleens are very characteristic. Both anterior and posterior portions are light yellow, but the posterior baleens are also fringed on the outer edges with grayish brown. That fringe is wide in front and narrow in back. There are 250 plates on each side which reach a maximum length of 3.0 cm.

Balaenoptera acutorostrata

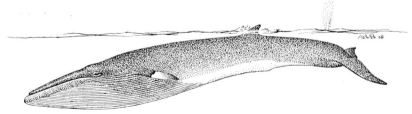

Figure 1–9. *Balaenoptera acutorostrata,* known as the little piked whale, named by Lacépède in 1804.

The distinguishing characteristics of *Balaenoptera acutorostrata* are as follows:

5b.

    1. Ventral grooves do not reach navel.

8a.

    2. White band on the flippers.

    3. Baleen plates yellowish white.

OTHER COMMON NAMES: Lesser rorqual, minke whale, and little finner.

MORPHOLOGY: This species is the smallest of the Balaenopteridae. The largest specimen reported was 10.2 m in length. In Japanese waters, specimens over 9.2 m are rarely found. The maximum weight is about 10,000 kg, and the average weight of animals 8 m in length is about 6,000 kg.

The body is slender and spindle shaped, and the rostrum is sharply pointed. The total spread of the tail flukes (along the axis) is almost one-fourth of the body length. The dorsal fin is high, slightly falcate, and located in the last one-third of the body. There are about sixty fine ventral grooves between the left and right flippers that do not reach as far back as the navel.

The dorsal surface of the body is black (often grayish) and the ventral surface is white. Unlike the irregular pattern of the sei whale or Bryde's whale, the boundary between the two colors of the piked whale is almost a straight line. The ventral side of the caudal penduncle is gray. The bottom surface of the tail flukes is light gray to sky gray, fringed with black extending from the upper surface of the flukes. The inside surface of the flippers is sky gray. A band of white color runs across the outer surface of each flipper. The boundary between this white band and the black portion of the back of the body is very distinct along the base of the flippers, while it turns gradually into dark gray near the end of the flipper. The baleen plates are yellowish white and sometimes fringed with dark brown. The white bristles of the approximately 280 to 300 baleens on each side are relatively fine. The piked whales of the Atlantic Ocean have more baleens, on the average, than those of the Pacific. The biggest baleen of individuals is 15 to 30 cm long and 5 to 12 cm wide.

The projection of the maxillary and mandible is not so marked as in other species of this family. The maxillary is even sharper at the end than that of the sei whale and is widened toward the inside (or toward premaxillary) at the base. This indicates that the nasal cavity is large and wide. The vertebral formula is $C7 + T11 + L12 + Ca\ 17–19 = 49$ (47–49). The sternum is relatively large and cross shaped. There are generally ten chevron bones.

MIGRATION AND ABUNDANCE: During the spring through summer months, the population near Japan migrates in coastal waters north into the Bering Sea and further through the Bering Strait into the Arctic Ocean. Though this species is not so coastal as the gray whale, individuals do frequent coastal waters and are often accidentally caught by Japanese coastal set nets. During the autumn and winter, the return migration southward follows a path further off shore. Groups are small and segregated into mature and immature individuals. Immature specimens, particularly immature males, do not migrate extensively into cold waters. Females tend to venture further into colder waters than do the males.

The migration of this species near Norway is very similar to that observed near Japan. There, piked whales migrate north along Norway coming close to the border of the U.S.S.R. The Norwegian whalers hunted them around Bear Island and Spitzbergen in the Arctic Ocean, butchering the whales aboard the boats.

Although distribution in the southern hemisphere has not been studied, information obtained in the North Pacific indicates that those found in the iced sea of the Antarctic Ocean are probably mature females. This species goes further into iced seas than any other species and has been observed extending the head vertically to breathe through holes or cracks in the ice.

Despite an annual catch of 3,000 to 3,500 animals by Norwegian whalers, the North Atlantic population has not decreased. The total population is estimated as 50,000 to 70,000 whales. The Pacific stock is much smaller, probably totalling only about 10,000 whales.

FOOD: English scientists reported that piked whales in the North Sea fed on the abundant herring. Jonsgard (1951) reported that individuals of this species distributed near the Norwegian coasts feed mostly on fish, while those found in the Arctic Ocean feed on euphausiids. Those found near Japan also have a wide selection of food including euphausiids, copepods, *Calanus*, sardines, sand lancers, cod, pollacks, atka mackerel, saury, mackerel, and squid.

REPRODUCTION: In the North Pacific, breeding occurs in February through April and parturitions occur in January through May after a pregnancy of ten to eleven months. The newborn are 2.8 to 3.0 m long, and lactation lasts about six months. A study of the growth curve of fetuses indicates that the peak of the breeding season is in early March. Males attain sexual maturity at 6.6 to 7.1 m, females at 7.3 m. In this respect, there is very little difference between Atlantic and Pacific groups.

Jonsgard (1951) reported that female piked whales in the Atlantic average one birth per year. Omura (1956) reported that those near Japan give one birth per 1 or 1½ years. This rate of reproduction is higher than that in most other species of Mystacoceti.

BEHAVIOR: Although blows reach only about 2 m in height, they appear large relative to body size. These whales stay on the surface for several seconds between shallow dives, each of which lasts for five to seven minutes. Their maximum swimming velocity is 10 to 15 knots (or to 24 km/hr) and their normal speed is 9 to 11 km/hr.

VARIATIONS: Some racial difference is assumed to exist between Atlantic and Pacific stocks. Although the body colors of the two stocks are nearly identical, the average size of the Atlantic animals is 0.2 to 0.6 m larger, and their maximum size 1.2 m longer, than those of the Pacific animals. On the other hand, in animals from the Pacific stock, the dorsal fin is higher and slightly more anterior, the tail flukes are wider, and the distance from the notch of the flukes to the center of the anus is shorter than in Atlantic animals. Although a few scientists have reported some differences in the skull, there appears to be too little variation between these two groups to warrant establishing a subspecies.

Balaenoptera borealis

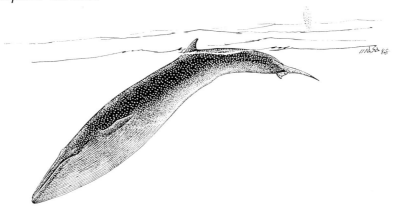

Figure 1–10. *Balaenoptera borealis,* known as the sei whale, named by Lesson in 1828.

Balaenoptera borealis can be distinguished by the following:
8b.
1. No white band on the flippers.
2. Baleen plates all black with fine white bristles.

OTHER COMMON NAMES: Rudolphi's rorqual, northern rorqual, pollack whale, Japan finner, and sardine whale.

MORPHOLOGY: The biggest sei whales recorded in the International Whale statistics are an 18.5 m male and a 20 m female. However, the largest caught recently are 15 to 16 m in length.

The dorsal side is dark-chocolate colored, but the dorsal coloration extends fairly well onto the abdominal side. The transitional part is gray which fades with a wavy boundary into the white of the ventral side. The inner surface of the flippers and undersurface of the tail flukes are gray.

The dorsal fin is relatively large, high, and triangular in shape and extends backward. The size of the flipper relative to the body is smaller than in other balaenopteriids.

The species has sixty to sixty-five ventral grooves with some individual variations. The longest baleen plate is about 65 cm in length and 25 cm wide. The number of baleens varies from 300 to 400, with an average of 320 to 340. The tactile hairs are much less abundant than in the other species of this family. Those present grow near the external nasal openings on the outer surface of the upper jaw and on both sides and the tip of the lower jaw. The vertebral formula is $C7 + T14 + L13 + Ca22-23 = 56-57$. The flippers have four fingers of I: 3–4, II: 5–7, IV: 4–6, and V: 2–3.

DISTRIBUTION AND MIGRATION: Sei whales are found in the North Pacific, North Atlantic, and Antarctic Ocean. Almost all of the sei whales that inhabit the southern hemisphere migrate to high latitudes but are rarely seen as far as the vicinity of packed ice. Whalers have begun to concentrate on sei whales since the decline in abundance of blue whales and fin whales. During migration, several whales form a herd, but herds as large as one hundred whales are sometimes observed in the South Pacific.

ABUNDANCE: In the North Pacific, near Japan, this species is the most abundant of the Mystacoeti. Though approximately 500 to 1,000 sei whales are caught every year, there appears to have been no measurable decrease in the population size. The catch in the North Atlantic is less substantial, and since the immature whales are very small and rarely caught, the population reduction in that area does not appear to be serious. No estimate of the Atlantic population is available.

FOODS: Sei whales prefer small crustacea like *Calanus* and euphausiids but also feed on sand lancers, herrings, cod, pollack, saury, sardines, etc. (As the Japanese common name indicates, Iwashi-Kujira means "sardine whale.") The food is widely varied, but does not include benthic animals.

REPRODUCTION: Like the other balaenopteriids, sei whales breed and parturate in the temperate seas. The breeding season appears to occur from January to March in the northern hemisphere and six months later in the southern hemisphere. Sexually mature males appear to mate with one female and live with her during one breeding season. The exact location of breeding grounds is still unknown. Young are 4.5 to 4.8 m at birth. Lactation lasts for about six months.

Both sexes appear to attain sexual maturity at about eight years of age when, in the northern hemisphere, the male is about 13.5 m in length and the females are about 14.4 m. Animals in the southern hemisphere are larger by 0.9 m at the time of sexual maturity.

BEHAVIOR: The blows are similar to, but neither as high nor as thick as, those of fin whales. This species swims very fast and may be able to attain a maximum swimming velocity of 30 knots (or 50 km/hr) for a short time. However, they tire very rapidly.

LONGEVITY: To date, no sei whales over seventy years old have been found. Thus the longevity of this species is shorter than that of blue or fin whales.

PARASITES: External parasites are quite similar to those on other species of Mystacoceti. *Balaenophilus unisetus* propagate on the baleen plates, and when those plates are removed from the whale, its development can be observed under the microscope.

Megaptera

The genus *Megaptera* was named by Gray in 1864. Its members can be distinguished by the following characteristics:
4b.
1. Ventral grooves less than 30 (count between flippers).
2. Flipper length more than one-fourth of body length.
3. Color of baleen plates all blackish brown with dark colored bristles.

Megaptera novaeangliae

Figure 1–11. *Megaptera novaeangliae,* known as the humpback whale, named by Borowski in 1781.

MORPHOLOGY: According to the International Whaling statistics, the largest animals taken were a 19.0 m female and 17.5 m male. However, at present, even fully grown females hardly reach 15 m and males are even smaller. There are 15 to 20 ventral grooves, each almost 15 cm in width, reaching to the navel. Therefore, this species can be identified simply by the ventral surface. The dorsal fin is relatively small and is located slightly behind the intersection of the anus.

There are two rows of several bumps, each supporting one tactile hair, on each side of the upper jaw. On each side of the mouth there are 350 to 370 baleen plates, the external edges of which are usually less than 80 cm long. The flippers are quite long, reaching about one-third of the total body length. On the anterior edge of the flippers, there are serrations which appear to be related with the joints and ends of finger bones. The posterior edge of tail flukes normally contains notches.

The dorsum is black and the abdomen is white. The distance the black color extends down the side of the body varies from individual to individual and is believed to be a genetic characteristic. Some of the northern whales have no white portion. The outer surfaces of the flippers are generally black, with this black color sometimes extending (in various degrees) to the white inner surface of the flippers.

One humpback whale caught off Kyuquot, on the west coast of Vancouver Island, Canada, in July, 1919, had rear legs of 1.2 m in length (in which was found a bone 0.8 m long). One of these legs was cut off by a worker, but the other has been preserved at the United States National Museum in Washington, D. C.

The vertebral formula is C7 + T14 + L10 + Ca21–22 = 52–53. The flippers have four fingers of I: 2, II: 7, IV: 6, and V: 3.

DISTRIBUTION: In the southern hemisphere, humpback whales are distributed south of the equatorial zone to the packed-ice line and in the northern hemisphere north of the equatorial zone to about 70°N.

MIGRATION AND ABUNDANCE: In July through September, they are found in Aleutian waters where food is abundant. Some may enter the Arctic Sea via the Bering Strait but most are distributed along the Aleutian Island chain. There seems to be some segregation according to maturity. In September and October, they start a southward migration and are commonly seen near Hawaii and the Midway Islands. Their distribution in October through December is unknown, but it appears that they breed in waters of 10° to 20°N. In early January, a part of the stock migrates near Okinawa and Ogasawara. This migration is led by immature males, followed by the main group of paired mature males and females, then by some immature females and a few immature males. The last group is the lactating females accompanying young. They avoid the Kuroshio current that runs off east of Taiwan, turns to the east at the west end of Okinawa, and goes along the east coast of Japan, because it is a clear-water current and a poor source of food. In those years when the Kuroshio current is strong, the whales migrate far offshore and are rarely caught near the coast of Japan. Similar patterns of migration are observed in the eastern Pacific.

In the southern hemisphere, migration occurs primarily in the south-north direction. Therefore, the population in each section of the Antarctic Ocean must be evaluated independently from the others. The total of all populations may be 10,000 to 15,000 whales.

BEHAVIOR: In days when American whaling was prominent, several characteristic swimming behaviors of this species were described as breaching, rolling, finning, lobtailing, and scooping. On submerging for a deep dive, humpbacks almost always throw the large flukes high into the air. The duration of the more prolonged dives is fifteen to twenty minutes. The blows are quite characteristic, being wide, relative to height. The large flippers provide this whale with better than average underwater maneu-verability.

FOOD: The main food items are planktonic Crustacea. Cod, but not pelagic fish such as sardine, saury, or mackerel have been reported as food. Also, Fraser (1937) reported that one specimen had eaten six sea birds, *Phalacro-crax capillatus*. The birds can probably be regarded as foreign ingestia.

REPRODUCTION: The rate of reproduction is comparatively high. Pregnancy appears to last for ten to eleven months, and the female is bred again almost immediately after parturition. The newborn are 4.5 to 5.0 m and at the time of weaning, which occurs at up to ten months of age, the young humpback is 8 to 9 m in length. Upon attaining sexual maturity the males are 11.1 to 11.4 m, and the females are 11.4 to 12.0 m.

Suborder Odontoceti

Odontoceti can be distinguished by the following:
1b.
1. Outer opening of nostril is single.
2. Teeth are present.
3. Baleen plates are absent.
4. Profile of upper surface of skull (mainly maxillae and premaxillae) is concave.
5. Sternum is comparatively large (usually segmented) and skeletal construction of thorax is complete.

Odontoceti have only one external nasal opening, the two nasal cavities joining together at the external end forming one nostril. Generally, the mouth is small and narrow and contains teeth throughout life. In some species, the teeth are developed only in males and do not protrude from the gum in females. One species has only one pair of teeth on the lower jaw while some species have over fifty-five teeth on each side of both upper and lower jaws. Tooth number and size are quite variable and are thus very useful in classification.

The skull is asymmetric. The degree of fusions of cervical vertebrae varies, some species having seven separate cervical vertebrae and other species having all seven bones fused together. In contrast to the Mysta-coceti, Odontoceti have large sternums. They lack a cecum.

The foreleg or flipper always has five fingers, but the number of bones in each finger varies by species. This characteristic might be used in classification but is not widely used at present because the finger bones are rather hard to examine and there is some intraspecific variation. Although the rear legs are not present, a trace of the femur has been observed in some species.

The larger species seem to have wider areas of distribution. Generally, they do not remain in one area but make extensive south-north feeding migrations following favorable water temperatures. There are a few rare species (such as those of Platanistidae) which only inhabit specific rivers.

The breeding season in the larger odontocetes is thought to extend from late winter throughout spring. Some smaller species have two breeding seasons, one in spring and one in fall. Some Odontoceti form harems. Most species are also gregarious and tens to thousands of animals often group together to form one big herd. Most species feed on small fishes and squids.

The following ten families are established: Physeteridae, Kogiidae, Ziphiidae, Monodontidae, Plantanistidae, Delphinidae, Orcaellidae, Phocoenidae, Grampidae, and Globicephalidae.

Family Physeteridae

Members of the *Physeteridae* family have the following general characteristics:

9a.

1. Tip of lower jaw ends an appreciable distance behind foremost part of head.
2. Lower teeth functional, but upper teeth rudimentary and usually found within the gum.

10a.

3. Head massive, one-fourth to one-third of body length.
4. Blowhole far forward.
5. Functional teeth large, eighteen to twenty pairs, confined to lower jaw.
6. Dorsal fin an ill-defined hump.
7. First cervical vertebra free, second to seventh cervical vertebrae fused.

This family consist of only one genus which includes but one species.

Physeter

The genus *Physeter* was named by Linnaeus in 1758.

Physeter catodon

Figure 1–12. *Physeter catodon,* known as the sperm whale, named by Linnaeus in 1758.

OTHER COMMON NAME: Cachalot.

MORPHOLOGY: The largest specimens recorded in the International Whaling statistics are a 19 m male and a 17 m female. However, at present the largest males reach 16.5 to 18.0 m, though 18 m is rare. The females are even smaller at present reaching 11.4 to 13.2 m. Unlike the different Mystacoceti, there is very little local variation in size among sperm whales.

The morphology of this species is unique from all others. The forehead of the skull forms a concavity from which the flat maxillary projects forward. These parts resemble a man's hand with its palm upward. On the top of the skull, a wall composed of maxillary, frontal, squamosal, and occipital bones is projected vertically from the exoccipital bone. In the big hollow formed by this crest, together with the maxillary, there is a case filled by a unique tissue called spermaceti. The right nasal cavity runs under the case, turns upward at the tip of the maxillary, and opens into the blowhole, located at the tip of head. The left nasal cavity runs to the left side of the case and joins the right cavity just before it reaches the blowhole. There is a broad blind sack behind the case and in front of the hollow of the skull. The functions of spermaceti are yet unknown, but it may be involved in the very deep diving of this species.

Side views of the adult male show a very large head that comprises about one-third of the total body length. In the female, the proportion of head to the total body length is not as great. The nasal opening is slightly S shaped and positioned toward the left side. The lower jaw is narrow. In a specimen 15 m long, it was about 20 cm wide at the front end and about 70 cm wide near the corner of the mouth.

The teeth are conical in shape, oval in cross section, and about 10 cm in diameter in adults. On the upper jaw, there are no exposed teeth. Instead, there are sockets into which the lower teeth fit. The upper teeth, ten to sixteen in number, are usually wholly within the gum throughout life though on occasion they are exposed at the sockets. Fetal sperm whales have many three-pointed teeth, a characteristic which may be reminiscent of Squalodon, generally considered the ancestor of Physeteridae.

The flippers are relatively short and round. When the animal is viewed laterally, a big notch is visible at the point where the anus is located. A keel begins just behind the anus and gradually narrows toward the tail flukes. The dorsal fin consists of a chain of small bumps along the dorsal ridge, the first of which is particularly distinct. The number of bumps varies with individuals.

The body of sperm whales is slate gray or dark blueish gray, generally paler on the abdomen. The skin around the mouth, especially near the corners of the mouth, is particularly pale in color and almost white. The anterior end of the body is somewhat flat with white spots distributed in a spiral pattern. Some animals have a white spot on the navel. The inner surface of the flippers and undersurface of the tail flukes are the same color as the body. Sperm whales are light in color when they are young, darken as they mature, and begin to fade as they grow old. Therefore, though Moby Dick, the great white whale of the famous novel, is fictional, seeing a large old sperm whale makes the source of the legend understandable. There are records of the capture of a pure white sperm whale near Japan, but even though the color of the eyes was not recorded, that animal is assumed to have been an albino.

The vertebral formula is C7 + T11 + L8 + Ca24 = 50. The first cervical vertebra is free but articulates with the mass formed by the fusion of the next six cervical vertebrae. The first eight of the eleven pairs of ribs are two headed. The last pair is very small, even though it is joined to the vertebrae. The lumbar vertebrae are quite thick and strong. There are nine to ten caudal vertebrae between the tail flukes. Usually, the basihyal and thyrohyal of the tongue are not fused. The sternum consists of two rows each of two or three parts. It is developed to a greater extent than in any other species of whale. This may be a factor in the great deep-diving capability of sperm whales. A vestigial femur is sometimes found. It may articulate with, or be fused to, the pelvic bone. The flipper has five fingers of I: 1, II: 5, III: 5, IV: 4, and V: 3.

The adults have no hair. In fact, at an early stage of development in which the fetuses of various porpoises still have hairs, sperm whale fetuses have already lost all traces of hair. The mammary glands of the female are thick (about 25 to 30 cm thick while lactating) but narrow (about 30 to

35 cm wide at the same period) and may reach a length of 1.5 m. There is a pair of mammary openings located in the inguinal region.

DISTRIBUTION: Physeteridae occur between 70° and 70°S.

MIGRATION AND ABUNDANCE: Because the body of a sperm whale floats on the sea surface when the whale dies, catches of this whale were recorded even hundreds of years ago. During the eighteenth and nineteenth centuries, when American whaling was very active, a great number of sperm whales were caught in various oceans of the world and records of these catches, showing the distribution in those years, have been well preserved.

The ranges of males and females are different. Females do not migrate into the cold waters but stay within 40° latitude in both hemispheres. Because the gestation period is sixteen months and the breeding season is quite long, there are always some pregnant females in a group. Some bachelor groups, consisting of old males which are no longer sexually active, young males not yet sexually mature, and often even males at the peak of reproduction potential, are usually isolated from the others and migrate into the cold waters.

In the North Pacific, males migrate beyond the Aleutian chain into the Bering Sea, and catches have been recorded as far as 60°N. Males migrating to the cold water form the majority of animals caught by whalers and the catch of such a large number of males might reduce the population size even though these whales practice polygamy and excess males are not able to participate in reproduction. Tomilin (1935) of the U.S.S.R. stated that sperm whales do not migrate beyond Cape Navarin. Arseniev of the U.S.S.R. (1939) reported that they do not go north of Oleutorskii Bay, and Japanese whaling boats have never taken sperm whales near the Bering Strait or in the Chukchik Sea. The distribution in the North Atlantic has not been adequately studied, but sperm whales may be distributed as far north as 70°N.

No sperm whale marked in the northern hemisphere has ever been recaptured in the southern hemisphere and vice versa. There is no estimate of the population size of the world. The North Pacific population is evaluated at 70,000 to 100,000.

FOOD: Sperm whales feed on squid but may also eat fish and an occasional octopus. The squids include both the smaller species and the giant squids. Squid bills found in the stomach of sperm whales are often as large as a chlid's head. Parts of giant squid estimated to be as large as 10 m in length have been recovered from stomach contents. Suckers of the giant squid may leave scar marks of 5 to 6 cm in diameter near the mouth or on the head of the whales. Although sperm whales seldom eat small pelagic fishes

such as herring, mackerel, and sardine, they frequently eat demersal fishes
such as cod or ocean perch. The capacity of the first stomach is 1½ drums
(300 l), and more than half of the whales caught have a full stomach.

In addition to these regular food items, sperm whales are known to
ingest some exotic objects. At least one out of every 1,000 whales caught
has its first stomach one-third filled with sand. Approximately the same
numbers of whales have swallowed coconuts. Stomach contents may also
include pieces of rock, wood, or worn, round stones. The whale may
swallow these items accidentally while it is feeding on benthic animals.
On one occasion, the discovery of a glove in a sperm whale's stomach gave
rise to rumors that the whale had eaten a man and the glove was all that
remained undigested. It is more likely, however, that the glove was floating
in the open sea and was swallowed by the whale.

There have been no records of this species attacking human beings
directly. On the contrary, a recent *Life* magazine photograph showed a
SCUBA diver touching the tail flukes of a sperm whale.

REPRODUCTION: Sperm whales are polygamous, and during the breeding
season each breeding male has a harem. These harems are apparently
formed during the off-whaling season, and for that reason, surveys of
breeding behavior are difficult to conduct.

Sperm whales do not make any extensive breeding migrations but breed
during January through July at latitudes lower than 40°. In the northern
hemisphere, the peak of the breeding season is in April, and parturition
occurs in July and August after a 16-month gestation period. The newborn
are 4.0 to 4.5 m long. Lactation lasts about 13 months. By the end of
lactation, the young may be as large as 6.7 m. At the time they attain
sexual maturity, females are about 8.9 m long and males about 9.5 m long.
Although males just reaching sexual maturity produce the same sperm as
older males, the younger animals do not usually participate in reproduction.
On the other hand, females breed soon after becoming sexually mature,
and pregnant females 8.7 to 9.0 m long are frequently found.

The age of Odontoceti can usually be estimated from sectioned teeth
(Nishiwaki and Yagi, 1954). Using this method, it has been determined
that both males and females are nine years old when they attain sexual
maturity. Both continue to grow, however, and do not attain physical
maturity until they are twenty-four to twenty-five years old and 11 m long
(females) or twenty-nine years old and 15.9 m long (males).

BEHAVIOR: When the are swimming near the surface, sperm whales breathe
every two or three minutes. After a series of three to five shallow dives,
they begin a deep and impressively long dive. In the case of the large
whales (15 m) of the Antarctic Ocean, this deep dive may last in excess

of an hour. Several whalers have reported that diving sperm whales have still not reappeared even after the whalers have waited for an hour at the surface. Those animals near Japan rarely dive for such long periods (thirty to forty minutes maximum). The diving time of the female is generally shorter than that of the male, rarely reaching, and never exceeding thirty minutes. The height of the blow of a sperm whale is from 3 to 5 m and because of the position of the blowhole, projects forward from the head at an angle.

Two examples of cooperative protective behavior in sperm whales, though rarely encountered, are of interest. Zebras reportedly protect themselves from attacking lions by forming a radiant circle with their heads towards the center and kicking out at the approaching lions. A similar behavior occurred when, on a quiet day, a harpoon was shot into a school of twenty to thirty sperm whales. The whales formed a radiant circle around the wounded, slapping the water with their tail flukes. This defensive behavior, however, was an advantage to the whaler who was able to systematically harpoon the whales one by one. Sometimes, when the sea is calm, sperm whales may be seen sleeping while floating near the surface with the blowhole out of the water. They may be in a horizontal or upright position. On these occasions, there are usually a few members of the group milling near them, apparently on guard for possible danger.

Unlike the baleen whales, which rarely attack boats, a harpooned sperm whale may charge even the largest catcher boat of today, ramming it with its head. If he hits the screw or rudder, he may disable the boat. In the early days of whaling, such attacks by sperm whales often proved destructive to the whaling boats and fatal to men. Drawings of whaling activity during the eighteenth and ninteenth centuries, when this species was the primary target of American whalers, often depicted sperm whales overturning boats and biting or crushing them with their tails. Many of those drawings were carved on sperm whale teeth, a form of art known as *scrimshaw.*

Sperm whales are known to be deep divers. A cable ship working off the coast of South America discovered a dead sperm whale entangled in a submarine cable which had been set at a depth of 1200 m. The whale probably became entangled while it was feeding near the bottom. A similar incident was reported on a cable between Lisbon and Malaga which had been set at a depth of 2200 m.

Sperm whales are often seen playing on the ocean surface. Although they very seldom jump completely out of the water, they often pull half of their body out of the water or throw the tail flukes high into the air. They also slap the water surface with the flukes (lobtailing) or play with floating objects such as logs or seaweed.

LONGEVITY: Sperm whales are believed to live a maximum of seventy years.

PARASITES: The most important external parasites are diatoms. Here, as with other whales, parasitic diatoms tend to drop off in warm waters. Whale lice are found in some groups but are not found at all in others. Penella often infect animals in warm waters but tend to drop off in cold water. Barnacles of different species than those parasitic on Mystococeti are also found. Large colonies of ship barnacles frequently occur on the skin and the tooth ridge. *Anisakis*, a nematode genus, is the most common internal parasite, occurring in the digestive system, particularly the stomach. There are practically no whales which are not infested with these nematodes. Parasitic cysts are very common in the skin or blubber, but cestodes are relatively rare.

MISCELLANEOUS: Abnormalities occur frequently. For example, nearly one out of every two thousand whales has a severely deformed, twisted lower jaw that must be almost functionless, and many whales lack the tip of the flukes or flippers. The attacks of sharks or killer whales are among the many possible causes for such mutilations. Injuries sustained during the fights between sperm whales are generally shallow and leave lightly marked scars on the skin.

Ambergris is a unique substance sometimes found near the end of the large intestine and beginning of the rectum of sperm whales. Analysis of ambergris indicates that it contains many squid bills and other residuals of food. There are two main schools of thought on the causes of ambergris formation. The first theorizes that a lump of ambergris is formed when the whale is constipated for some unknown reason. The second uses the following chain of logic: the whales, particularly the adult males who are engaged in fighting among themselves, feed very little during the breeding season. The result is that there is little feces and a residue may remain undischarged inside the intestine until the whales begin feeding again in the spring. In some individuals, that residue may not be passed even after feeding resumes and remains as ambergris.

Whatever the causes of ambergris, its use as a stabilizer in perfumes once made it the most valuable of all whale products. Advances in technology which resulted in synthetic stabilizers caused the value of whale ambergris to wane, but recent reaffirmation of its quality has caused a rise in its value. In 1962, ambergris sold at an average of $100 per kilogram. The largest lump ever reported was an egg shaped mass, 50 cm in diameter, which weighed 60 kg. Despite the widespread belief that all ambergris is alike, the quality actually varies a great deal. The value of a given find is determined by the analysis of a small portion of the lump.

FAMILY KOGIIDAE

Kogiidae have the following characteristics:
10b.
1. Head comprises one-sixth of total body length.
2. Functional teeth small, slender, and curved, nine to sixteen pairs confined to lower jaw.
3. Dorsal fin well developed.
4. All cervical vertebrae fused.

This family consists of a single genus, *Kogia* (Gray, 1846), with two species of pygmy sperm whales. In the past, these whales were generally regarded as either a subfamily or as one genus under Physeteridae. However, because of the many important differences between the sperm whale and the pygmy sperm whales, the latter are treated in this work as a separate family, Kogiidae.

Kogia

Some characteristics of the *Kogia* genus are the following:
11a.
1. Total body length of adult more than 2.5 m. (Weight is more than 300 kg.).
2. Dorsal fin low and located posterior to center of back.
3. Condylobasal length of skull more than 350 mm.
4. Twelve to sixteen (rarely ten or eleven) pairs of mandibular teeth.
5. Mandibular symphysis long (86 to 120 mm) and ventrally keeled.

Kogia breviceps

Figure 1–13. *Kogia breviceps*, known as the pygmy sperm whale, named by Blainville in 1838.

OTHER COMMON NAME: Lesser cachalot.

MORPHOLOGY: The rostrum of this species projects forward in a triangular shape, and the mouth resembles that of a shark. The blowhole is slightly further anterior than in any other small odontocetes. There are no teeth in the upper jaw.

Although there is some individual variation, the width of the skull relative to the length is nearly 1 to 1. (In most odontocetes, the skull is much longer than it is wide.) The condylobasal length of an adult is between 390 and 470 mm (approximately one-seventh of body length). The dorsal cranial fossae are not cupped posteriorly, and the left fossa is conspicuously longer and narrower than the right. The pterygoid-basioccipital wings are elongated, and the foramen magnum is near the midpoint of the skull height. Although both the maxillary and mandible are relatively short, the vomer at the middle of the skull is long, almost reaching to the tip of the mandible.

The falcate dorsal fin is located slightly posterior to the middle of the body and is quite low (approximatey 15 to 20 cm in height). The flippers are fairly large, reaching approximately one-sixth of the body length, and are sharply pointed at the end. The flukes, however, are moderate in size, reaching a total spread of one-fifth the body length.

The dorsal skin is charcoal to gray, and the skin of the abdomen is gray to white. The transition of color from the back to the abdomen varies to a great extent between individuals. From the external ear backward, there is a zigzag-shaped white portion which also varies in pattern among individuals. The flippers are slate gray, with the inside surface slightly paler than the outside surface. Both surfaces of the tail flukes are gray or slate gray. Some individuals have some cherry pink color on the abdomen and some have blueish color on the back.

The body girth is greatest midway between the flippers and the dorsal fin. The caudal portion of the body is compressed vertically. Just behind the anus, the body is twice as high as it is wide. The abdominal cavity is extraordinarily large, appearing to be about twice the size of dolphins of comparable size.

The vertebral formula is $C7 + T13 + L9 + Ca27 = 56$. The seven cervical vertebrae are all fused together. Eight out of the thirteen pairs of ribs are two headed. There are seventeen chevrons, and those in the posterior part are divided into two, one on each side. The sternum is in three pieces and is joined by cartilage to four pairs of ribs. There is a neural spine up to the thirteen caudal vertebrae and a transverse process up to the tenth caudal vertebrae. The flippers have five fingers of I: 1, II: 8, III: 8, 1V: 7, and V: 5, with much variation in the number of bones, particularly in the fourth and fifth digits. However, since few of the specimens in the past have been studied by x-ray, the bones might have been mixed up during collection.

DISTRIBUTION AND ABUNDANCE: This species is widely distributed and mixes freely with *Kogia simus*. In the North Pacific, it is found in temperate and tropical waters. In the southern hemisphere, catches have been reported off Australia and New Zealand. In addition, there are records of stranded specimens from beaches of India, IndoChina, the Atlantic coast of North America, France, Holland, and Hawaii. Because *Kogia breviceps* is rarely seen, the size of the world population is unknown.

FOOD: This species presumably prefers squid, but the stomach contents of a specimen found on a beach in France included coastal crab as well as squid beaks.

REPRODUCTION: Very little is known about reproduction in this species. A female about 3 m long beached in Holland during December of 1925 reportedly had a 20 cm fetus. An animal caught in December 1924 reportedly had a 22.5 cm fetus.

Kogia simus

Figure 1–14. *Kogia simus,* known as Owen's pygmy sperm whale, named by Owen in 1866.

Kogia simus have the following characteristics:
11b.
1. Total body length of adult less than 2.5 m. (Weight is less than 300 kg).
2. Dorsal fin high, near center of back.
3. Condylobasal length of skull less than 300 mm.
4. Eight to eleven (rarely thirteen) pairs of mandibular teeth.
5. Mandibular symphysis short (37 to 46 mm) and ventral keel lacking.

MORPHOLOGY: Except for the size and position of the dorsal fin and the total body length, the gross appearance of this species closely resembles that of *Kogia breviceps*. The dorsal fin is comparatively high and is situated near the center of the back. The total body length is approximately 2.1 to 2.7 m in adults, slightly less than in *Kogia breviceps*.

The skull is proportionally smaller than in *Kogia breviceps*. The condylobasal length of the adults is between 260 and 300 mm (approximately one-eighth of the total body length). The dorsal cranial fossae are cupped posteriorly and are subsymmetrical. The pterigoid-basioccipital wings are short, and the foramen magnum is well below the midpoint of the skull height. The width of the skull relative to length is nearly 1 to 1. There are usually three vestigial teeth in the upper jaw. The vertebral formula is $C7 + T13 + L9 + Ca27 = 56$. The seven cervical vertebrae are fused together and resemble three bones fused.

DISTRIBUTION: With the exception of body and skull characteristics, *Kogia breviceps* and *Kogia simus* have not been studied separately. Therefore, it can only be assumed that the distribution of *Kogia simus* is the same as that of *Kogia breviceps*.

FAMILY ZIPHIIDAE

General characteristics of Ziphiidae are as follows:
9b.
　1. Lower jaw extends at least to the tip of the snout.
　2. Blowhole is some distance from tip of snout.
12a.
　3. Two conspicuous grooves on the surface of the throat form a V shape.
　4. Dorsal fin present, considerably posterior to middle of body.
　5. Notch of tail flukes usually shallow or absent.
　6. Anterior three or four cervical vertebrae fused.

The family Ziphiidae is divided into five genera of "middle-sized" whales (5 to 12 m in length). Individuals are characteristically spindle shaped, have distinct rostrums, and display V-shaped grooves on the ventral surface in the throat region. The flippers are generally small and slender and may be three times as long as they are wide. The flukes are relatively large, measuring about one-fourth of the body length from tip to tip.

In Ziphiidae, the notch that is usually present at the center of the posterior margin of the flukes of odontocetes is absent, extremely shallow, or replaced by a slight projection. The tips of the flukes are pointed and curved inward. The girth of the body is greatest in the middle, and the dorsal fin is located considerably posteriorly.

Berardius

The genus *Berardius* was named by Duvernoy in 1851. Its members can be distinguished by the following characteristics:

13a.
   1. Two pairs of large teeth in the lower jaw.
14a.
   2. Adult body length more than 10.0 m.
   3. Second pair of teeth situated some distance from the first pair.
   4. No special protuberance on maxillae.
   5. One to four cervical vertebrae fused.

Berardius bairdi

Figure 1–15. *Berardius bairdi*, known as Baird's beaked whale, named by Stejneger in 1883.

Some additional characteristics of *Berardius bairdi* are the following:
15a.
   1. Inhabits only the northern hemisphere.
   2. Condylobasal length about one-eighth of body length.
   3. Total spread of tail flukes about one-fourth and length of flipper about one-eleventh of body length, respectively.

MORPHOLOGY: The average adult is between 10.3 and 11.1 m, though females reach a maximum length of 12.8 m and males attain 12.0 m. The body is slate gray, but the abdominal side is slightly lighter. Some individuals have a few white spots on the ventral thorax or the abdomen. The flippers and tail flukes are about the same color as the back.

The head portion and rostrum are relatively long. The distance from the tip of the snout to the corner of the mouth is about one-twelfth to one-thirteenth of the body length. The distance from the tip of the snout to the blowhole is about one-eighth of the body length. The rostrum reaches

about one-sixteenth of the body length. The flippers have a characteristic
shape and reach one-eighth to one-ninth of the body length. The width
of the fluke is about one-fourth of the body length. The dorsal fin is triangular, but the tip does not extend backward. On the surface of the
throat, there are grooves of about 60 cm in length, forming reverse V
shapes. Often there are small narrow grooves beside the major ones.

The teeth are triangular in shape when viewed from the side and are
slightly larger in males (90 mm) than in females (85 to 90 mm). The teeth
average about 70 to 75 mm in width in both males and females. The dentine is very thin, and the secondary pulp cavity is choked with osteodentine. The skull is almost symmetric. The crests of maxillary and frontal
bones may be seen behind the nostril but are not as high as in genus
Mesoplodon. The nostril is round but wide, and the preorbital fossa are
distinct. The vertebral formula is $C7 + T10–11 + L12 + Ca17–19 = 46–49$. The first to third cervical vertebrae are fused. The sternum is composed of five joints.

DISTRIBUTION: In the western North Pacific, this species ranges around
the Kuril Islands and goes into the southern part of the Sea of Okhotsk.
Individuals are also found around the Bering Islands and in the Bering
Sea, but are not found north of the Bering Strait. On the American side
of the Pacific they have been recorded from Alaska to California.

MIGRATION AND ABUNDANCE: This species is second only to the "little piked
whale" as the most important species for the Japanese coastal whaling
industry. Land-based whalers operating from various parts of Japan catch
about 150 to 200 whales annually. Each year, the first catches on the Japanese Pacific Coast occur off the Boso Peninsula. Herds of whales approach Japan from the southeast and turn to the north, staying very close
to the peninsula in May and June. Thereafter, the herds seem to continue
northward, gradually dispersing, and reach the waters off Kinkazan in June
and August. They migrate as far north as the waters off Hokkaido. Southern as well as northern migrants are observed simultaneously from scouting
airplanes in the area of Sanriku and Hokkaido during September and
October. Judging from the "size frequency data" of catches, the present
level of harvest does not adversely affect the population.

FOOD: This species feeds primarily on squids and bottom fishes. In addition, the stomachs of some specimens have contained such benthic animals
as ascidians, sea cucumbers, starfishes, and crabs.

REPRODUCTION: The growth rate is not yet well known, but males attain
sexual maturity at a length of about 9.3 to 9.6 m and females at 10.0 to
10.3 m.

Breeding apparently occurs between late November and early May, and the growth curve of the fetuses of those animals collected near the Pacific coasts of Japan indicates that the peak is in February. The largest fetus ever collected was 4.5 m long, and a young whale observed soon after birth was 4.7 m long.

BEHAVIOR: Although Baird's beaked whales are generally found in herds, lone individuals are sometimes seen. Near Japan, they appear in coastal waters in what may be harem groups of ten to thirty whales, led by one big male. Judging from the frequency of reports of observations of herds by fishing boats and scouting airplanes, this species is abundant.

Normally, the diving behavior of Baird's beaked whales is typical of larger whales. They will make several shallow dives followed by a deep prolonged dive of about twenty minutes. The blow is low and spread. When they are harrassed, they may dive for over an hour, and if a whaler misses one of these animals, he may have a long wait before he has another chance. When they are harpooned in shallow waters, such as in the Okhotsk Sea, the whales of this species dive almost at a right angle to the surface and frequently hit the bottom.

PARASITES: The external parasites of this species include ship barnacles, whale lice, penella, acorn barnacles, protozoans, and bacteria, the last two of which leave white scar marks. Internal parasites include nematodes and *Onchocerca*, which infest the throat or liver. Occasionally, cysts of parasites are found in the blubber or in the inguinal portion of the internal wall of the abdominal cavity.

Berardius arnouxi

Beradius arnouxi, known as the southern beaked whale, was classified by Duvernoy in 1851. Some of its characteristics are as follows:
15b.
1. Inhabits only the southern hemisphere.
2. Condylobasal length about one-seventh of body length.
3. Total spread of tail flukes and length of flippers relative to total body length are greater than in *Berardius bairdi*.

MORPHOLOGY: Although *Berardius arnouxi* is morphologically similar to *B. bairdi*, the northern species, there are some important differences. The southern whale is smaller, has proportionally wider tail flukes and larger flippers, and has a larger head relative to total body length (one-seventh of total in southern whales, one-eighth of total in northern whales). In addition, the southern whale is slightly different in color. It has dark blue dorsal skin, various blue-gray mottled patterns on the side of the body, and gray or light gray on the abdomen.

DISTRIBUTION: This species is distributed only in the southern hemisphere
and occurs primarily near Australia, New Zealand, the Falkland Islands,
and South Shetland Island.

BEHAVIOR: Little is known about the behavior of the southern beaked
whales except that they do not form large herds.

Hyperoodon

The genus *Hyperoodon* was named by Lacépède in 1804. The following
are the general characteristics of its members:
14b.

1. Adult body length less than 10 m.
2. Second pair of teeth situated just behind the first pair.
3. Special protuberance on the upper surface of maxillae.
4. All cervical vertebrae fused.

Hyperoodon ampullatus

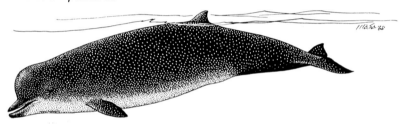

Figure 1–16. *Hyperoodon ampullatus*, known as the bottlenosed whale, named by For-
ster in 1770.

16a.

One characteristic of *Hyperoodan ampullatus* is that it only inhabits
the northern hemisphere.

MORPHOLOGY: This species is moderate in size. A 6.6 m specimen weighed
2200 kg. Adult males are 9.1 m, females 7.3 m. In both, the rostrum extends forward in characteristic fashion resembling the "bottlenose" that
prompted both the English and the Japanese common names. The forehead, which is round and high behind the rostrum, is particularly remarkable in males, increasing in size as the animal grows. This large forehead is probably used in fighting for the females. The size of the forehead
is apparently related mainly to the development of the maxillary bone.
In some individuals, the top of the forehead is flattened.

The relatively small eyes are situated behind and above the corner of
the mouth. The blowhole opens at the base of the heightened forehead
above the position of the eye. The small dorsal fin is located well behind
the midpoint of the body. It is curved backwards and the posterior edge
is sickle shaped. The flippers, too, are relatively small.

The dorsal surface is charcoal gray, while the ventral surface is very light gray. Both flippers and tail flukes are darker on both surfaces than the body. There is a pair of teeth at the anterior end of the lower jaw which may remain hidden inside the tooth ridge in many individuals even after they attain sexual maturity. The teeth are 4 to 5 cm in length and smaller than those of Cuvier's and Baird's beaked whales. In cross section, they are oval with a minimum diameter of 1.5 to 2.0 cm and a maximum diameter of 2.0 to 2.5 cm. In older whales, particularly males, these teeth gradually begin to fall out. Occasionally, vestigial teeth the size of toothpicks are found within the gums on either the upper or lower jaw. The vertebral formula is C7 + T9 + L9–11 + Ca18–20 = 43–46. The flipper has five fingers of I: 1, II: 5, III: 5, IV: 4, and V: 2.

DISTRIBUTION: In the Arctic Ocean, where the majority of bottlenosed whales occur, they are found both in the European and Asian sides but are not frequently seen off central Russia. Populations extend to waters off Newfoundland and Holland in the Atlantic Ocean. In the Pacific, they are found in the Bering Sea, Okhotsk Sea, and probably, but without certain confirmation, in the Japan Sea. They do not appear to be abundant in the eastern Pacific.

MIGRATION AND ABUNDANCE: Since many of these whales are found on the beaches of England, Holland, and France during autumn and winter, they may be migrating southward at this time of the year. In summer, they are assumed to remain in the North Sea and Arctic Ocean.

FOOD: Although bottlenosed whales, like the other members of this family, consume a wide variety of food, they seem to prefer squid.

REPRODUCTION: Very little is known about reproduction in the bottlenosed whale, but calves are about 3 m in length at the time of birth.

BEHAVIOR: This species generaly forms small herds of up to ten whales. Group strandings have been reported.

WHALING: In the late nineteenth century, after the diminishing of the Greenland right whales and before the beginning of the fin whale exploitation, this species was hunted extensively in the Arctic Ocean. In addition to the whale oil which was produced from the blubber, spermaceti was taken from the bulging forehead.

Hyperoodon planifrons

Figure 1–17. *Hyperoodon planifrons,* known as the southern bottlenosed whale, named by Flower in 1882.

16b.

Hyperoodon planifrons inhabits only the southern hemisphere.

MORPHOLOGY: This species is very similar in appearance to *Hyperoodon ampullatus.* The body is prussian blue on the dorsal surface and slightly brownish-gray on the ventral surface. The forehead is higher than the base of the rostrum. In fact, the most marked differences between this species and *Hyperoodon ampullatus* are that the forehead of the males projects to a greater extent in this species and the dorsal fin is larger in proportion to body length. The flukes are relatively large, and body length relative to fluke width is about 3.5 : 1. Males reach 9 m in length and females reach 7 m.

The vertebral formula is C7 + T9 + L10 + Ca20 = 46. In a specimen about 7 m long, the skull was about 1.4 m. The crest of the maxillary is quite high. The cartilage in the midde of the vomer ends at the base of the center of the nose and is not ossified. All the seven cervical vertebrae are fused, and, the first seven of the nine pairs of ribs are bicuspid. Although the sternum is four-jointed, the third and fourth pieces are often fused. The flipper has five fingers of I: 2, II: 6, III: 5, IV: 4–5, and V: 3. There are commonly ten chevrons. The pelvic bone is quite small in relation to the body length (about 10 cm long) and is positioned just under the last lumbar vertebra.

DISTRIBUTION: It is assumed that the whales inhabit the ocean encircling Antarctica, but they are seldom observed in the whaling ground along 60°S. A number of beached specimens have been collected from the beaches of Australia and New Zealand.

Ziphius

The genus *ziphius* was named by G. Cuvier in 1823. Some of its characteristics are the following:

17a.

    1. One pair of large conical teeth in the tip of the lower jaw.

18a.

    2. Only one pair of teeth in the tooth row; the other teeth always rudimentary.

Ziphius cavirostris

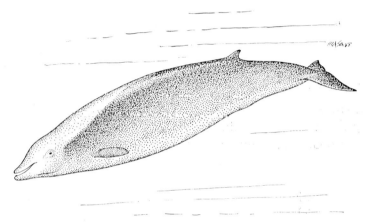

Figure 1–18. *Ziphius cavirostris*, known as Cuvier's beaked whale, named by G. Curvier in 1823.

OTHER COMMON NAME: Goose-beaked whale.

MORPHOLOGY: The males reach a length of about 6.4 m, and the females are slightly shorter. The color of goose-beaked whales varies from brown or gray to black and is very often pale in the face region. One young specimen caught near New Zealand was purplish dark blue on the back, brown on the side, white on the abdomen, and brown on the fluke. The mother whale, which was also caught on the same occasion, was ultra-marine on the back and white on the abdomen. The adult animal bore an abundance of oval white spots, particularly in the caudal region. These white spots (scars) are assumed to be the marks left by parasitic bacteria or protozoa.

The distance between the snout and the blowhole is short, reaching one-eighth to one-tenth of the body length. The entire skull is relatively wide. At the anterior joint of the orbital fossa, the width in proportion to the body length is largest among whales of this family. Occasionally, fifteen to forty vestigial teeth the size of toothpicks are found in the upper and lower jaws. The normal male tooth is about 7 cm in length and 4 cm in maximum diameter on its oval cross section. Females generally have teeth hidden inside the gum.

When viewed laterally, the lower jaw looks thicker than the upper jaw and the rostrum is short and broad. The trunk is relatively long, but the caudal portion behind the anus is short. The dorsal fin is triangular and curves backward with a convex posterior edge. The tail fluke has two very small notches at the center of its posterior edge. The vertebral formula is C7 + T9 + L11 + Ca20 = 47. The flippers are relatively small and have five fingers, the bones of which are I: 1, II: 3–6, III: 5–6, IV: 4, and V: 1–2.

DISTRIBUTION: *Ziphius cavirostris* is distributed in most of the oceans of the world. Though neither the northern nor southern limits have been determined, it is assumed that these whales do not migrate into the Bering Sea, the Arctic Ocean, or the Antarctic Ocean.

MIGRATION AND ABUNDANCE: Near Japan, *Ziphius cavirostris* migrates northward along the Izu Island chain toward the top of the Boso Peninsula and passes off Cape Choshi. They are known to go further north, passing to the southeast of Hakkaido, but their migration routes thereafter are not yet known.

Individuals of this species begin to appear regularly in Japanese waters in January and February. The frequency of sightings increases in May or June and reaches a peak in July to September. Thereafter, the abundance decreases, though some animals are seen throughout the year in one area or another.

FOOD: These whales feed on a wide variety of organisms, and though they prefer squid, they may also eat demersal fishes, sea cucumber, crabs, and even star fish.

REPRODUCTION: The capture of a swimming juvenile 3.1 m in length suggests that calves are probably less than 3.1 m at birth. Individuals are thought to attain sexual maturity at a length of 4.5 to 5.0 m. Adult males reach a maximum length of around 6.7 m. Females are an average of 30 cm larger. Near Japan, mature adult specimens of 5.4 to 6.5 m are most abundant.

BEHAVIOR: Very little is known about the behavior of this whale. The blows are neither very large nor conspicuous. When they are chased by catcher boats, they are seen to dive for as long as thirty minutes. When starting a deep dive, they show the flukes high in the air and dive almost at a right angle to the surface. Herds seem to be small, even during migration.

PARASITES: Most of the whales of this family are infested with *Onchocerca*, a parasite which forms a transparent cyst in the liver and larynx. Nematodes are frequently found in the stomach. Cysts, very similar to the ones found on the skin of sperm whales, are occasionally found in the skin, and nematodes are frequently found in the stomachs.

MISCELLANEOUS: This species is found beached more frequently than any other species of *Ziphiidae*. At least two to three beachings are reported annually on the Pacific Coasts of Japan, usually in Sagami Bay. Specimens have also been found ashore in Sweden, England, France, Spain, Corsica Island, east coast of the United States, west coast of the United States, South America, Cape of Good Hope in South Africa, India, Queensland (Australia), Tasmania, and New Zealand. It is not known whether beached whales are whales beaten during fights, old whales, or even sick whales.

Tasmacetus

18b.

The genus *Tasmacetus* was named by Oliver in 1937. Its principal characteristic is that its members have one pair of large teeth in the tip of the lower tooth row and some functional teeth in tooth rows.

Tasmacetus shepherdi

Figure 1–19. *Tasmacetus shepherdi*, known as the Tasman beaked whale, named by Oliver in 1937.

MORPHOLOGY: Because of the very small numbers of specimens that have been examined, a detailed description cannot be made. Generally, however, the body of these whales is about 6 m. The dorsal body surface is black, the ventral surface is white, and the side is covered with grayish-yellow stripes. The head is quite round and has a thick, short rostrum. The eyes are relatively large. The upper jaws contains nineteen functional teeth on each side, and the lower jaw has twenty-six relatively large teeth, as well as one pair of very large teeth at the front.

Members of the Family Ziphiidae usually have a small number of uniformly shaped teeth. The fact that this species has a dental formula of $\frac{19}{26}$ and a very well developed tooth structure may eventually result in its reclassification. For the time being, however, it is included as a new genus in this family, following Fraser (1948).

DISTRIBUTION: To date, the only three specimens reported were all from the Tasmanian Sea, near New Zealand. Their distribution in other areas is not known.

Mesoplodon
17b.

The genus *Mesoplodon* was named by Gervais in 1850. Its members can be distinguished by the fact that they have one pair of large flat teeth in the middle of the lower jaw. This genus consists of twelve species. However, the characteristics of some of them have not been clearly defined. More study is necessary.

Mesoplodon mirus

Figure 1–20. *Mesoplodon mirus,* known as True's beaked whale, named by True in 1913.

MORPHOLOGY: Although they resemble Cuvier's beaked whales, True's beaked whales have a longer rostrum, a smaller head (one-fifth of total body length), and a pair of teeth at the end of the slender lower jaw.

The dorsal surface is black, fading to slate gray on the side, and the abdominal skin is gray. There are frequently small yellow, purple, or pink spots on the body and occasionally a dark line in the center of the abdomen. In addition, there is a dark gray area on the ventral thorax. Some individuals have a pattern of brushed white around the navel and/or genitals. The flippers are quite dark and are attached low on the sides of the body, which reaches a maximum length of 4.8 to 5.2 m. The dorsal fin is located three-fourth of the distance posterior, and the tail fluke is wide with a small notch at the posterior edge.

The vertebral formula is C7 + T10 + L11 + Ca18 = 46. The phalangeal formula is I: 2, II: 4, III: 4, IV: 3, and V: 2. The first three cervical vertebrae are fused. The first seven pairs of ribs are two headed, and the first five of these are joined to the sternum by cartilage. The sternum consists of four sections.

DISTRIBUTION: True's beaked whales, like the other species of genus *Mesoplodon*, have very seldom been caught. Their presence is confirmed only in the North Atlantic. To date, none have been captured or even recorded in the North Pacific or in the southern hemisphere.

Mesoplodon pacificus

Mesoplodon pacificus known as Longman's beaked whale, was named by Longman in 1926. *Mesoplodon pacificus* was formerly considered a subspecies of *Mesoplodon mirus*, but Moore (1960) established it as a separate species. It is a relatively large whale, with a skull of over 1 m in length, and it has been found only in the South Pacific off southern Australia.

Mesoplodon hectori

Mesoplodon hectori, known as Hector's beaked whale, was named by Gray in 1871.

MORPHOLOGY: In this species, only certain features of the skull can be described. The premaxillary fossa is almost on the same plain as maxillary fossa, and there are no grooves along the maxillary. The distance from the premaxillary fossa to the occiput equals the maximum width of the skull. The pair of teeth in the lower jaw of *Mesoplodon hectori* is positioned within a portion of a suture of the mandible, somewhat away from the position where the pair of teeth is found in *Mesoplodon mirus*. Behind these teeth, there are several sockets where vestigial teeth are probably located in the young.

Mesoplodon gervaisi

Figure 1–21. *Mesoplodon gervaisi*, known as the Gulf Stream beaked whale, named by Deslongchamps in 1866.

MORPHOLOGY: The head of this species is relatively small. The slope from the forehead to the rostrum is very gentle. The premaxillary fossae are located in front of the maxillary fossae, and there are no side grooves on the maxillary. Here, as in *Mesoplodon hectori*, the teeth are present at the suture of the mandible. The body is higher than it is wide, and the dorsal fin is located in the posterior quarter of the body. The flippers reach only about one-twelfth of the body length. The flukes are also small and reach a total spread of about one-fifth of the body length. The dorsal body is grayish black, and the abdominal area is somewhat lighter.

The vertebral formula is C7 + T10 + L10 + Ca20 = 47. The first three cervical vertebrae are fused and the flipper has five fingers of I: 2, II: 6, III: 6, IV: 4, and V: 3, with some variations.

DISTRIBUTION: The holotype of this species was collected adrift in the English Channel. Most of the other specimens collected later came from the opposite side of the Atlantic: in Florida, New York, Long Island, the West Indies, Cuba, New Jersey, and Jamaica. None have been found in the Pacific or Indian Oceans.

Mesoplodon layardi

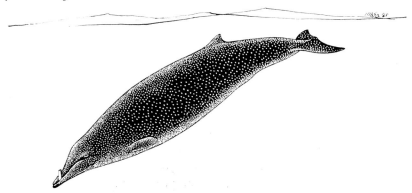

Figure 1–22. *Mesoplodon layardi,* known as the strap-toothed beaked whale, named by Gray in 1865.

MORPHOLOGY: Individuals of this species reach a maximum length of 5.0 to 5.8 m. The head is proportionally small, and the body, which is higher than it is wide, appears laterally compressed. The dorsal body and the flippers are charcoal gray and the ventral body is gray. The dorsal fin, located about two-thirds back on the body, is relatively small and curves slightly backward.

The teeth, which are flat, long, sharp, and covered with enamel, are located at the posterior end of the mandibular symphysis. Males have long, slender teeth which may migrate to the outside of the maxillary as the body grows. The common name of this whale derives from the fact that the teeth on the lower jaw may grow to encircle the upper jaw, giving the appearance that a string or strap is tied around the upper jaw.

DISTRIBUTION: Information on distribution is limited. To date, all reports of findings, have come from the southern hemisphere (New Zealand, Australia, South Africa, and the Falkland Islands).

Mesoplodon grayi

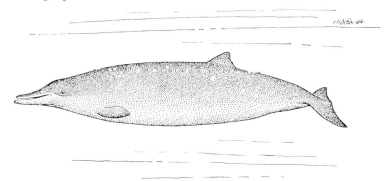

Figure 1–23. *Mesoplodon grayi,* known as the New Zealand scamperdown whale, named by Haast in 1876.

MORPHOLOGY: The body shape is typical for *Mesoplodon*. The rostrum is is sharply pointed, and the girth gently increases from the head to the body trunk and then gradually decreases from the dorsal fin towards the tail. Like *Mesoplodon layardi*, this species appears laterally compressed because it is higher than it is wide. The dorsal fin, which is positioned about one-third from the rear end, is high and triangular. Though the flippers are wider than in any other species of the genus, they are quite short (one-tenth to one eleventh of body length) and sharp at the end.

The dorsal body is olive drab, fading to brownish green on the abdomen, and except on the tail flukes and flippers, the ventral skin is quite pale. The V-shaped grooves on the throat are very distinct. The navel is located about the middle of the body. The blowhole is wide, opens anterior to the level of the eyes, and is positioned slightly to the left of the midline. The premaxillary fossa is positioned on or slightly behind the same cross section as the maxillary fossa. The side grooves of the maxillary are deep and very distinct.

The relatively small, triangular teeth are located at the posterior end of the mandibular symphysis. The teeth on the upper jaw are further posterior than those on the lower jaw. Ten or more vestigial teeth are often found at the base of the maxillary near the corners of the mouth. These may protrude from the gums, though they are usually buried inside the mucous membrane. The vertebral formula is $C7 + T10 + L11 + Ca20 = 48$. The first three cervical vertebrae are fused. The first five of ten pairs of ribs are bicuspid and there are ten chevrons. The flippers have five fingers of I: 1, II: 5, III: 5, IV: 4, and V: 3.

DISTRIBUTION: Although this species has been found only in the southern hemisphere, most frequently near New Zealand and Australia, it is also known to be distributed near Patagonia off South America. In 1874 an entire herd of twenty-eight whales beached itself on the Chatum Islands of New Zealand.

Mesoplodon bidens

Figure 1–24. *Mesoplodon bidens*, known as Sowerby's beaked whale, named by Sowerby in 1804.

MORPHOLOGY: This was the first species of *Mesoplodon* known. The body is typically spindle-shaped, is much higher than it is wide, and reaches a length of 5 m. The high triangular dorsal fin is located slightly posterior to the middle of the body and is curved backward at the tip. The flippers reach about one-eighth to one-ninth of the body length. The ends of the tail flukes are pointed backwards, and although there is no notch at the center of the posterior edge of the tail flukes, this area is rather concaved.

The entire body is charcoal gray, sometimes with a slightly blueish tint. Some individuals have a lighter-colored rostrum. Most specimens bear many scratches, wounds, and white scars all over the body.

When viewed laterally, the rostrum appears sharply pointed. The premaxillary fossa is positioned towards the rostrum from the maxillary fossa. There are no side grooves on the maxillary. The head comprises only one-sixth to one-seventh of the total body length. A pair of teeth is found on the lower jaw midway between the tip and the angle of gape. These relatively large teeth face upward while the tooth roots face forward. Frequently, small vestigial teeth, which commonly do not grow out of the tooth sockets, are found. The vertebral formula is C7 | T10 | L9 | Ca20 = 46. The five fingers of the flipper are I: 1, II: 6, III: 6, IV: 4, and V: 3.

DISTRIBUTION: This species is assumed to be distributed only in the Atlantic Ocean. Specimens have been reported from France, England, Holland, Belgium, Germany, Norway, Sweden, Italy, and the east coast of the United States. To date, none have been found in the Pacific or Indian Oceans.

REPRODUCTION: Concrete evidence on reproduction in this species is limited. A 1.55 m fetus was collected on December 18, 1892, and a 1.1 m fetus was collected on February 3, 1926. On April 18, 1957, a 5.15 m female washed ashore on the west coast of Norway, accompanied by a 3.15 m juvenile female (Jonsgård, 1957). The mother whale was not secreting milk.

Jonsgård (1957) assumed the following: that the breeding season is in February through April, that gestation is about twelve months, that the young are about 2.0 m in length at birth, that lactation lasts a year, and that the young may grow to 3.0 m by the end of lactation.

BEHAVIOR: In the *Book of Whales*, Beddard (1900) referred to an individual of this species which was kept alive out of water for two days after being collected in 1828. It ate bread and produced a low sound which resembled the mooing of a cow coming from inside a cave.

Mesoplodon ginkgodens

Figure 1–25. *Mesoplodon ginkgodens*, known as the Japanese beaked whale, named by Nishiwaki and Kamiya in 1958.

MORPHOLOGY: The body of this species is spindle-shaped and appears somewhat laterally compressed. The rostrum is long, and its tip appears sharp. On the lower jaw between the corner of the mouth and the teeth, there is a projection of skin which presses upward against the upper jaw. The dorsal fin is located toward the rear of the body. The flippers are rather small, reaching only one-ninth to one-tenth of the body length. There is almost no notch at the posterior edge of the tail flukes.

Although most of the body is midnight black, the abdominal skin is lighter in color, especially where white scars remain from parasitic protozoa and bacteria.

The premaxillary fossa is located considerably further anterior on the rostrum than the maxillary fossa. There are no side grooves along the maxillary. The teeth are quite flat and compressed. The width at the tooth crown is only about one-seventh of the depth. The location of a pair of the teeth found behind the mandibular symphysis varies somewhat according to sex. The vertebral formula is C7 + T10 + L10 + Ca21 = 48. Four of the seven cervical vertebrae are fused. The first seven of ten pairs of ribs are two-headed, and there are eleven chevrons. The flippers have five fingers, the bones of which are I: 1, II: 6, III: 5, IV: 4, and V: 3.

DISTRIBUTION: Japanese beaked whales are found in the southwest portion of the North Pacific.

Mesoplodon carlhubbsi

Figure 1–26. *Mesoplodon carlhubbsi*, known as Hubb's beaked whale, named by Moore in 1963.

MORPHOLOGY: The premaxillary fossa is on or slightly posterior to the cross section of the maxillary fossa. The side grooves along the maxillary are very shallow and indistinct. The preprocess of the maxillary projects high just inside the preorbital process at the base of the rostrum, giving the appearance of two preorbital processes on each side. The distance from the occipital condyles to the base of the rostrum is less than the maximum width of the skull. The flat large teeth on the lower jaw reach 9 cm in length, 16 to 17 cm or more in depth, and 1.4 cm in breadth. The navel is near the ventral midlength of the body. The flippers are small, reaching one-ninth of the body length. The dorsal fin is located on the same cross section as the anus, about one-third forward from the posterior end. The vertebral formula is C7 + T11 + L9 + Ca19 = 46. Only the first two cervical vertebrae are fused. The first seven out of eleven pairs of ribs are two-headed and the last two pairs of ribs are very short. There are eight to nine chevrons. The sternum has five sections. The phalangeal formula is I: 1, II: 5, III: 5, IV: 4, and V: 3.

DISTRIBUTION: This species has been found only in the North Pacific.

Mesoplodon stejnegeri

Figure 1–27. *Mesoplodon stejnegeri,* known as Stejneger's beaked whale.

OTHER COMMON NAME: Saber-toothed whale.

MORPHOLOGY: These whales are all black and may grow as large as 6 m. The maximum height of the body at the middle is greater than the width. The dorsal fin, which is triangular and curved at the tip, is positioned three-fifths to two-thirds of the distance posterior to the tip of the snout. There is a distinct keel on the tail sock from the anus posterior to the center of the flukes.

The holotype of this species is the skeleton of a juvenile which washed ashore in the Aleutian Islands. Although the poor development of the preorbital process of this specimen was originally attributed to its age, it was later confirmed in specimens from the west coast of the United States and from Japan that the preorbital fossa is poorly developed even in adults. The preorbital notch is also poorly developed and is almost as far from the occipital condyles as the skull is wide at its greatest width. The premaxillary fossa is located on or slightly posterior to the cross section of the maxillary fossa. The side groove along the maxillary is indistinct.

The width of the lower jaw increases rather suddenly just posterior to the teeth. The teeth, located on the lower jaw, are quite large (about 10 cm long, 16 to 17 cm deep, and 2.15 cm broad) and have a straight leading edge which faces forward and is frequently worn.

The vertebral formula is $C7 + T10 + L10 + Ca19 = 46$. The first to third cervical vertebrae are fused. The first seven out of ten pairs of ribs are bicuspid. There are nine to ten chevrons. The sternum is composed of five sections. The flipper has five fingers and the phalangeal formula is I: 1, II: 5, III: 4, IV: 4, and V: 3.

DISTRIBUTION: This species has been found only in the North Pacific.

Mesoplodon bowdoini

Mesoplodon bowdoini, known as Bowdoin's beaked whale, was named by Andrews in 1908.

MORPHOLOGY: In form, this species is very similar to *Mesoplodon stejnegeri.* The first specimens were collected in New Zealand, but many specimens collected and initially identified as *Mesoplodon bowdoini* were later corrected to some other species.

DISTRIBUTION: To date, this species has been found nowhere but in the South Pacific.

Mesoplodon densirostris

Figure 1–28. *Mesoplodon densirostris,* known as Blainville's beaked whale, named by Blainville in 1817.

MORPHOLOGY: The body reaches 4.5 m in length and is spindle shaped, the width being less than the height. The body height is greatest at the middle. The dorsal fin is located just behind the middle of the body and is triangular, high, sharp at the end, and curved backward. The flippers are rather small, reaching about one-tenth to one-eleventh of the body length, and are narrow and sharp at the tips. The notch in the middle of the posterior end of the tail flukes is negligible. The body is black with a very slightly lighter abdomen. The inside of the mouth is gray mixed with pink.

The premaxillary fossa is almost on or slightly posterior to the cross section of the maxillary fossa. The side grooves along the maxillary are very shallow and indistinct. The single pair of teeth is located on a large, wedge-shaped prominence behind the symphysis of the mandible, and the tip of the tooth faces backward. This prominence, which starts just in front of the eyes, is particularly marked in males. Although the tooth is fairly large, about 20 cm in depth, 9 cm in length, and 5 cm in breadth, only 1.0 to 1.5 cm is exposed. (The exposed portion looks like a bump on the prominence.) The remainder is buried in the gum.

The vertebral formula is $C7 + T11 + L9 + Ca20 = 47$. According to Raven (1942), the first seven of eleven pairs of ribs are two-headed and the first five pairs are joined to the sternum by cartilage. Cervical ribs, different from the ordinary ribs which form the thorax, are occasionally attached on the last cervical vertebra. The sternum is made of five segments, and though the flipper has five fingers, the phalangeal formula is not known.

DISTRIBUTION: Although reports have been limited, this species appears to be widely distributed. They have been reported from the Seychelles in the Indian Ocean, South Africa, Massachusetts, New Jersey, and Madeira. These reports indicate that these whales are distributed in the North Atlantic, South Atlantic, and Indian Oceans but not in the North Pacific. They further suggest that Blainville's beaked whale is a warm water species and may not venture poleward beyond 45° in either hemisphere.

FAMILY MONODONTIDAE

Monodontidae can be distinguished by the following:
12b.
   1. No grooves on throat.
   2. When present, dorsal fin at or near middle of body.
   3. Notch of tail flukes conspicuous.
19a.
   4. Seven cervical vertebrae all separate.
20a.
   5. Beak absent.
   6. Dorsal fin absent or rudimentary.
   7. Inhabit Arctic region.

This family consists of two genera each having a single species. Although the proportional measurements of the skulls of these two species are similar, the remarkable differences in the teeth have prompted some taxonomists to set up separate subfamilies for each of them. However, they are treated here as members of the same family.

Delphinapterus

The genus *Delphinapterus* was named by Lacépède in 1804. Its members have the following characteristics:

21a.
1. Eight to ten teeth in upper jaw.
2. Tooth length less than 5 cm.

Delphinapterus leucas

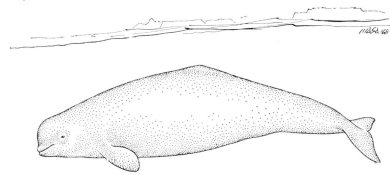

Figure 1–29. *Delphinapterus leucas,* known as the beluga, named by Pallas in 1776.

OTHER COMMON NAME: White whale.

MORPHOLOGY: The head is round and blunt and the mouth is large. Instead of a dorsal fin, there is a bump about 3 to 5 cm high and 10 cm long near the middle of the back. The flippers are round, wide and fan-shaped.

Adults are light ivory and seldom have scars or spots. However, the young (until ages 4 or 5) are marine blue gray, and younger individuals have dark, fine spots on the skin. These spots gradually become grayish-yellow as the whale matures, finally blending into white. Individuals may reach a length of 5.5 m, but the usual maximum length is from 3.7 to 4.3 m.

The premaxillary is flat and the portion in front of the nostril is slightly concaved. The skull is asymmetrical and the blowhole lies toward the left. The vertebral formula is C7 + T11–12 + L6–9 + Ca23–26 = 50–51. The flipper has five fingers of I: 1–2, II: 6–7, III: 4–5, IV: 2–4, and V: 2–4.

DISTRIBUTION: Belugas are found primarily in the Arctic Ocean but migrate as far south as 50°N. Sergeant and Brodie (1969 a,b) have recently summarized the migration and distribution of this species in northern Canadian waters.

MIGRATION AND ABUNDANCE: Canada conducts routine helicopter surveys around Hudson Bay in order to determine the abundance of belugas and regulate their catch. The white individuals are easy to spot against the background of blue water as they migrate along the east coast of North America from the Arctic. They occur in abundance in the Davis Strait, Hudson Bay, and the Gulf of St. Lawrence, and individuals frequently migrate up the St. Lawrence to Quebec. This species is also frequently observed along the Alaskan coasts, but an adequate survey of that population has not yet been made. Sightings of individuals have been recorded at Nulato, about 1120 km up the Yukon River. Belugas are also abundant along the northern coasts of Norway and Sweden. In cold winters, they migrate southward along these coast lines, sometimes going as far south as the Baltic Sea. In the U.S.S.R. belugas have been caught by beach seine. Current estimates of the entire world population range from 5,000 to 10,000 whales.

FOOD: White whales feed primarily on fairly large benthic fishes such as halibut and flounder but may also eat squid and crabs.

REPRODUCTION: Belugas breed in April and May and give birth in June and July, after fourteen months of pregnancy. At birth, the calf is about 1.5 m in length and dark in color.

BEHAVIOR: Normally, these whales form small family herds of five to ten individuals. During the southward migration, however, many families join to form a large herd of one hundred to two hundred whales. Belugas dive very well. When they are surfacing to breathe, their vocalizations can be heard even before they reach the surface.

LONGEVITY: This species is assumed to live thirty to fifty years, but studies on age determination are not yet adequate.

Monodon

The genus *Monodon* was named by Linnaeus in 1758. Its members have the following general characteristics:
21b.
1. One pair of teeth in upper jaw.
2. In the adult male, a tooth (usually only left side) is elongated more than 100 cm ahead of rostrum.

Monodon monoceros

Figure 1–30. *Monodon monoceros*, known as the narwhal, named by Linnaeus in 1758.

OTHER COMMON NAMES: Monodon, unicorn whale.

MORPHOLOGY: The maximum body length is about 4.0 to 4.5 m, excluding the length of the tooth. The larger measurements of early whaling days may have included the tooth. The head of this species is round but relatively small. A series of bumps about 5 cm high on the latter half of the back replaces the dorsal fin. The flippers are small, round, and blunt on the end.

In females, the teeth never erupt from the gum. After males attain sexual maturity, the tooth on their left upper jaw gradually grows forward in a counterclockwise spiral, often attaining a length of 2.5 m (two-thirds of the body length). On rare occasions, teeth develop on both sides.

The color of the skin varies with age. Young animals are dark blue gray, gradually changing to brownish gray as they mature. At the same time, many dark blue gray or steel gray spots become clear on the dorsal skin from the head to the tail flukes. There are seldom spots on the abdominal skin.

The maxillary and premaxillary are well developed. The root of the tooth extends into the skull 20 to 30 cm. The ratio of the condylobasal length to the maximum width of the skull is 2 to 1. The vertebral formula is C7 + T11–12 + L6–10 + Ca26–27 = 50–55. The flipper has five fingers with a phalangeal formula of 1: 1–2, II: 5–8, III: 4–6, IV: 2–4, and V· 2–3.

DISTRIBUTION AND ABUNDANCE: Narwhals are found in the Arctic Ocean, occuring in greater abundance near Russia than off American coasts. In spring, they migrate as far north as the packed ice fields. This species was once hunted with hand harpoons or spears for its strong teeth and for oil taken from its thick blubber (blubber thickness ranges from 5 to 10 cm with an average of 7 to 8 cm). When it is harpooned, the Narwhal dives diagonally into the sea as deep as 300 m but usually returns to the surface after only a few minutes and is easily caught. Since the population has declined and the demand for those materials has decreased, the hunting operations are much less active. The present population is estimated to be 1,000 to 3,000 animals.

FOOD: Narwhals feed mainly on squid but may also eat cod, rockfishes, flounders, shrimps, and crabs.

BEHAVIOR: Narwhals form small groups, generally consisting of ten or fewer individuals, which usually include males, females, and juveniles.

There are many theories on the function of the extraordinary long tooth. For example, one writer hypothesized that the tooth was developed for breaking breathing holes in packed ice. Another assumed that the tooth was used to dig the sea bottom in search of food. Still others speculated that the tooth is used like a whip to shepherd the school. To me, the most acceptable hypothesis is that the long tooth is a weapon employed by males in fights to win the females.

FAMILY PLATANISTIDAE

Platanistidae have the following characteristics:
20b.
1. Beak extremely long (one-sixth to one-seventh of body length).
2. Low dorsal fin present, base length long.
3. Inhabit fresh water in tropical or warmer regions.

The dolphins of this family inhabit only large freshwater rivers. Since they are believed to be morphologically similar to the ancestors of cetaceans, the study of skeletons of this family may provide important insight into the history of whales. Although the skulls of Platanistidae are very similar to those of Delphinidae, the ventricles are not nearly so compressed or well evolved. The cervical vertebrae are rather large, and there are generally eight pairs of two-headed ribs. The rostrum is very long and slender.

Platanista

The genus *Platanista* was named by Lesson in 1828. Its members have the following general characteristics:
22a.
1. Inhabit the Ganges.
2. Twenty-seven to thirty teeth in each row.

Platanista gangetica

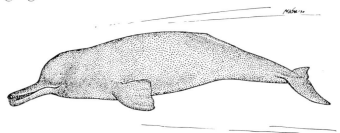

Figure 1–31. *Platanista gangetica,* known as the susu, named by Lebeck in 1801.

OTHER COMMON NAMES: Ganges River dolphin, gangetic dolphin, blind dolphin.

MORPHOLOGY: Adults reach a length of 2.3 m with a rostrum of about 30 cm in length. The blowhole opens in parallel to the body axis. The body is light tan to black. The eyes are extremely small and are believed to have no sight. The dorsal fin is located slightly posterior to the middle of the body. A keel runs from the dorsal fin to the center of the fluke. Another keel runs along the abdominal side from slightly posterior to the anus. The broad, large flippers are almost rectangular in shape. The fluke is wide and its posterior edge curves toward the center, where there is a notch.

The vertebral formula is $C7 + T10{-}11 + L7{-}8 + Ca24{-}25 = 49{-}51$. The finger bones are 1: 2, II: 4–5, III: 4–5, IV: 4–5, and V: 4–6. Five of the ten pairs of ribs are two headed. The cervical vertebrae are relatively large and long; thus, a definite neck portion is recognizable from the external appearance.

DISTRIBUTION: This species is limited to the Ganges, Brahmaputra and Indus River systems.

FOOD: Susu feed on demersal fish or shrimps. They appear to be blind and are believed to rake the mud with the rostrum, somewhat as ducks do, to find food.

BEHAVIOR: In order to breathe, this dolphin brings the tip of the rostrum, followed by about two-thirds of the body, out of the water and immediately dives again. This entire process takes only three seconds to complete and is repeated at thirty- to seventy-second intervals. Occasionally, the entire body leaves the water during breathing.

Inia

The genus *Inia* was named by D'Orbigny in 1834. Its members have the following general characteristics:

22b.

  1. Inhabit the Amazon.
  2. About thirty teeth in each row.

Inia geoffrensis

Figure 1–32. *Inia geoffrensis,* known as the Amazon dolphin, named by Blainville in 1817.

OTHER COMMON NAMES: Boutu, boto, bufeo, pink porpoise.

MORPHOLOGY: When fully grown, this species reaches a total length of 2.5 to 3.0 m. Both the upper and lower portions of the rostrum are sparsely covered with long, slender, heavy hairs. The forehead is rounded. The apex of the dorsal fin is located about two-thirds posterior to the snout. The flukes and flippers are relatively large and wide. The eyes are very small. The body is usually gray on the dorsal surface becoming paler on the sides.

DISTRIBUTION: This species is found in the upper Amazon River, as far as 2,500 km from the ocean. Individuals are most often reported from Iquitos, Peru, and Leticia, Columbia, but others are found in the Orinoco River of Venezuela.

BEHAVIOR: According to Bates, these dolphins usually swim in pairs. It is also reported that they have been observed copulating near the banks of the river while floating ventral side up at the surface of the water.

In February of 1965, the author observed a young 1.5 m male of this species at Steinhart Aquarium, San Francisco, California. The body was extremely soft and formed folds when the head was moved from its normal position. This dolphin sat with its flippers and tail flukes on the bottom of the tank, moving its head in all directions as if it were watching the outside with its very small eyes.

Pontoporia

The genus *Pontoporia* was named by Gray in 1846. Some of the characteristics of its members are as follows:

22c.
1. Inhabit the La Plata River.
2. More than fifty teeth in each row.

Pontoporia blainvillei

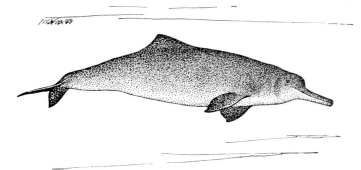

Figure 1–33. *Pontoporia blainvillei,* known as the La Plata river dolphin, named by Gervais in 1844.

OTHER COMMON NAME: Franciscana.

MORPHOLOGY: This species is much smaller than the Amazon dolphin, hardly reaching 1.5 m even when fully grown. The length of the rostrum relative to body length is the greatest of any species of dolphin. On each of the lower and upper jaws there are fifty to sixty very small sharp teeth. The head is round and the neck is prominent. The seven large cervical vertebrae are unfused, thus permitting the animal to make extensive movements with its head. There is a distinct dorsal fin near the middle of the back, the posterior portion of which continues as a keel toward the tail flukes. The flippers are large and triangular in shape. The first four pairs of ribs are two headed. The body is brownish or blueish but is generally pale. Some nearly white animals caught in the eastern part of the La Plata River are often called "White Ghost."

DISTRIBUTION: This species is found only in the La Plata River of South America and in coastal waters immediately adjacent to the river mouth.

Lipotes

The genus *Lipotes* was named by Miller in 1918. Some general characteristics are the following:

22d.
1. Inhabit the Tung Ting Lake.
2. Thirty-three to thirty-six teeth in each row.

Lipotes vexillifer

Figure 1–34. *Lipotes vexillifer,* known as the Chinese lake dolphin, named by Miller in 1918.

OTHER COMMON NAMES: Chinese River dolphin, white flag dolphin, pei c'hi.

MORPHOLOGY: When fully grown, this species reaches 2.2 m. The dorsal body is generally slate blue or gray and the ventral surface is white, though both those colors may be turned brown in mud. The narrow rostrum is about 30 cm long and has a very distinctive upturned tip. The blowhole is located just aft of the forehead and slightly to the left side. The triangular dorsal fin is located slightly past the center of the body. The anterior edge of the dorsal fin is slightly rounded or curled and the posterior edge is slightly falcate. The total spread of the tail flukes is about one-fourth of the body length. The flippers are white, round on the edge, and tapered at the tip. Like the Ganges dolphin, the Chinese Lake Dolphin's eyes are very small and thought to be functionless. The external ear openings are very prominent.

DISTRIBUTION: This species is found mainly in the Tung Ting Lake near the headwaters of the Yangtze River system of China.

FOOD: This species feeds primarily on fishes but also eats other animals in the mud. They relish freshwater shrimp that have a soft carapace. Miller (1918), who first scientifically reported this species, retrieved a bucketful of catfish from the stomach contents of the several specimens he collected.

REPRODUCTION: According to the natives around the Tung Ting Lake, when the water level of the lake increases in the spring, this species moves into the small, clear-water streams to breed.

BEHAVIOR: In the winter, when the level of the lake drops, these dolphins are easily seen. They generally travel in groups of three or four but sometimes form groups of ten or more individuals. They search the shallow muddy shore for bait fishes in much the same way ducks do.

Family Delphinidae

Delphinidae have the following general characteristics:
19b.
  1. Two or more cervical vertebrae are fused.
23a.
  2. Beak distinct.
  3. More than twenty teeth in each row of upper jaw.
  4. Less than 4 m in body length.

Delphinidae have a relatively large number of vertebrae, and only the first two cervical vertebrae are fused (in some old specimens, three or four are conjugated). All have a snout; and there are more than twenty teeth on each side of each of the upper and lower jaws. The tail flukes have a notch at the center of the posterior edge. The rostrum is more than twice as wide as it is long. The condylobasal length is more than 1.7 times the width. There are ten genera in this family: *Delphinus, Stenella, Lagenorhynchus, Cephalorhynchus, Tursiops, Sousa, Sotalia, Lagenodelphis, Lissodelphis, and Steno.*

Lissodelphis
24a.

The genus *Lissodelphis* was named by Golger in 1841. Its distinguishing characteristic is that it has no dorsal fin.

Lissodelphis borealis

Figure 1–35 *Lissodelphis borealis,* known as the Northern right whale dolphin, named by Peale in 1848.

Some characteristics of *Lissodelphis borealis* are the following:
25a.
  1. Slender body.
  2. Outer surface of flippers black.
  3. Inhabits northern hemisphere.

MORPHOLOGY: Adults of this species reach a length of approximately 2.3 m. The rostrum is extremely short and pointed at the tip. The body reaches a maximum girth about two-fifth of the body length from the tip of the snout. The flippers are relatively small, very narrow, sharply pointed, and reach a length comparable to about one-eighth of the total body length. The tail flukes are also small, reaching a total spread of one-seventh of the body length. The notch at the center of their posterior margin is deep.

Except for a white patch on the belly and a very small white spot at the end of the lower jaw, the body is all black. The ventral white patch is very narrow near the navel, widens again along the anus and the genital opening, and disappears on the keel of the tail stock.

The skull is very slender. The condylobasal length is 2.17 times the width of the skull. The rostrum is very slender but is only 2.18 times as long as it is wide. Although the end of the lower jaw is very narrow, the symphysis of the mandible is relatively short. The small teeth are all sharply pointed at the tip. Generally, the lower jaw has slightly more teeth than the upper jaw. The dental formula is $\frac{40\text{-}43}{42\text{-}46}$. The vertebral formula is C7 + T14–15 + L29–30 + Ca37–39 = 88–90. The first two cervical vertebrae are fused. The first five of the fourteen or fifteen pairs of ribs are two-headed, and the sternum has four sections. The flipper has five fingers, the bones of which are I: 1–2, II: 8, III: 9, IV: 3, and V: 2–3.

DISTRIBUTION AND ABUNDANCE: This species is restricted to the North Pacific Ocean, where it inhabits relatively warm waters. The population is estimated at more than 10,000.

FOOD: This species feeds mainly on squid and pelagic fish.

BEHAVIOR: *Lissodelphis borealis* generally form herds of two hundred or more individuals. Although the groups move very slowly, individuals can swim very fast, presumably as much as 35 km/hr.

VARIATIONS: Ogawa (1936) reported individuals caught off Kinkasan, Japan, which were slightly different from ordinary specimens. Although Ogawa considered the second group as *Lissodelphis peroni*, they will be treated in this work as *Lissodelphis borealis albiventris*, a subspecies of *Lissodelphis borealis*. The differences between the two subspecies are summarized as follows:

Lissodelphis borealis borealis

1. Dental formula: $\frac{40\text{-}43}{42\text{-}46}$.

2. On ventral surface, white color does not continue from tip of lower jaw to stalk of tail flukes. Dark color on throat. White area becomes narrow around navel.

3. Inner surface of flippers entirely black.

4. Undersurface of tail flukes dark.

Figure 1–36. Comparison of *L. b. borealis* and *L. b. albiventris.*

Lissodelphis borealis albiventris

1. Dental formula: $\frac{37\text{-}41}{40\text{-}43}$.
2. White color on ventral surface more extensive and continuing from tip of lower jaw to stalk of tail flukes.
3. Only lower half of inner surface of flippers black.
4. Undersurface of tail flukes white.

Lissodelphis peroni

Figure 1–37. *Lissodelphis peroni,* known as the southern right whale dolphin, named by Linnaeus in 1758.

Some distinguishing characteristics of *Lissodelphis peroni* are the following:

25b.

1. Body stouter.
2. Outer surface of flippers white.
3. Inhabit southern hemisphere.

MORPHOLOGY. In the Antarctic Ocean, the white abdominal portion of this species extends far up the side of the body, leaving very little black skin. The lower and upper jaws are black. The outer surface of the flippers

is white, and the outer surface of the tail flukes is black. Since there have
been no specimens collected in the Antarctic Ocean, no detailed description has been made.

DISTRIBUTION: This species occurs in the Antarctic Ocean.

BEHAVIOR: Lillie (1915) reported that both *Lissodelphis peroni* and *Lagenorhynchus obscurus* came close to his research boat, though the two
species never mixed.

Delphinus

The genus *Delphinus* was named by Linnaeus in 1758. Some of its
characteristics are the following:
24b.
   1. Distinct dorsal fin present.
26a.
   2. An angle (or a groove) present between beak and forehead, or fore-
      head makes a step from beak.
27a.
   3. Dorsal fin triangular, has light color near middle.
   4. Adults less than 2.15 m.
   5. Rostrum length more than 2.8 times its breadth.
   6. Greatest skull breadth less than one-half condylobasal length.
   7. Mandibular symphysis less than one-fifth of mandibular length.
   8. Maxillary groove present on palate.

Delphinus delphis

Figure 1–38. *Delphinus delphis,* known as the common dolphin, named by Linnaeus
in 1758.

MORPHOLOGY: Males are 10 to 20 cm larger than females, and individuals reach a length of 2.14 m. The keel is not pronounced on either the dorsal or ventral side. The medium-sized dorsal fin is triangular in shape, sharply pointed and curved slightly backward at the tip. The triangular flippers are also pointed at the tip. The total spread of the tail flukes is one-fifth to one-fourth of the body length.

The body color is distinctive and can be generally described, though there are individual variations. The dorsal surface is black, the ventral is white, and the sides are ochre and gray. Two arch-shaped boundaries overlap just beneath the dorsal fin and mark a triangular region of dark color. Below the arc line from the portion above the flipper toward the posterior end of the dorsal fin, the skin is gray. Above the line, the skin is midnight black. The portion of the body below the arc line drawn from just above and behind the anus toward the posterior edge of dorsal fin is gray. Two slate gray lines start from the eye, run backward and either join or run parallel to slate gray or yellow ochre (sometimes mustard yellow) portions which run from the anus forward. These lines are darker than those in the cape dolphin. Another black stripe runs towards the lower jaw from the base of flipper and eventually joins the black portion of the rostrum. In some specimens, this stripe extends forward along the lower edge of the lower jaw and then returns toward the posterior edge of the mouth forming a V shape which joins the dark portion on the upper edge of the lower jaw. In other specimens, it extends directly towards the posterior edge of the mouth. Several black bands inside the gray portion extend from the eyes toward the border of the rostrum. A gray, ivory, or white triangle commonly appears in the middle of the dorsal fin. Lighter stripes run from the blowhole towards the border of the forehead and rostrum.

The color changes after death. The triangle on the dorsal fin and the gray ochre stripes on the side of the body fade or disappear completely. The gray portion may turn to ochre, and the lower surface of the flippers may also fade into a paler color.

There are several hairs on each side of the upper jaw of the fetus, but these hairs are lost long before the animal attains maturity. The vertebral formula is $C7 + T14 + L21 + Ca31–32 = 73–74$. The first two of the seven cervical vertebrae are fused. Four to five of the fourteen pairs of ribs are double-headed. There are four sections in the sternum. The phalangeal formula is I: 2, II: 9, III: 6–7, IV: 3–4, and V: 1–2. Both the upper and lower jaws have forty to fifty relatively small (3 mm diameter) pointed teeth on each row.

DISTRIBUTION AND ABUNDANCE: As suggested by the English name, common dolphin, these animals occur frequently in the Atlantic Ocean and its adjacent seas, where the population is estimated at more than 30,000 individuals. They are also found in the Indian Ocean and in both the South and North Pacific but do not migrate into the cold waters. This species is not generally very abundant in Japanese waters. Small herds of one hundred to two hundred animals are found in the waters adjacent to Kyushu and Okinawa but rarely venture into coastal waters. The widely quoted statement that "the common dolphin is most frequently observed in the Japanese waters" probably resulted from confusion of this with other species and from confusion in common names.

Food: This species feeds chiefly on schools of migrating fish such as herring and sardines but may also eat squid.

Reproduction: Both males and females attain sexual maturity at a length of 1.7 to 1.8 m, at which time they are assumed to be three to four years old.

Longevity: Individuals are assumed to live twenty-five to thirty years.

Delphinus capensis

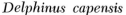

Figure 1–39. *Delphinus capensis*, known as the Cape dolphin, named by Gray in 1828.

Morphology: Although the body shape and the color patterns resemble those of the common dolphin, the rostrum in this species is much longer and the body colors are generally darker. Instead of the two dark stripes which run forward from the anus on the common dolphin, there is a single lighter stripe.

The length of the rostrum is about two-thirds of the condylobasal length and about 3.5 to 3.8 times the width of the rastrum. The dental formula of *Delphinus capensis* is $\frac{54-58}{51-55}$. The vertebral formula is C7 + T14 + L21 + Ca30 = 72. The first two cervical vertebrae are fused. The first five of the fourteen pairs of ribs are double headed.

DISTRIBUTION AND ABUNDANCE: Because many specimens have been captured or reported near the Cape of Good Hope in South Africa, it is assumed that this species is distributed in the Atlantic and Indian Oceans and prefers warmer waters to an even greater degree than the common dolphin. The cape dolphin has been reported near Japan but is assumed to inhabit only the warm waters near Kyushu. The population seems much smaller than that of the common dolphin.

Delphinus bairdi

Figure 1–40. *Delphinus bairdi,* known as the Pacific dolphin, named by Dall in 1873.

MORPHOLOGY: The body of this species is slightly heavier than that of the common dolphin and reaches a length of about 2.2 m. In addition, though they are generally quite similar, there are several significant differences between the Pacific dolphin and the common dolphin. First, the dark stripes which run from the eyes to the anus of the common dolphin are very light or absent and the yellow ochre stripes are absent in this species. The rostrum is slightly more slender than that of the common dolphin and reaches a length of more than 1.7 times the maximum width of the skull. The flippers have a wider base, and the stripe from the base of the flippers toward the lower jaw is lighter.

DISTRIBUTION: These animals are found in the North Pacific (from British Columbia, Canada, to Baja California, and Mexico) and often migrate near the coasts. They are not found in Japanese waters.

Stenella

The genus *Stenella* was named by Gray in 1866. Some of its characteristics are the following:

27b.
1. Dorsal fin leans backward, has no whitish color.
2. Adults less than 2.75 m long.
3. Rostrum length of skull more than 2.2 times its breadth.
4. Greatest breadth of skull less than one-half of condylobasal length.
5. Mandibular symphysis less than one-fifth of mandibular length.
6. No maxillary groove on palate.

Stenella caeruleoalba

Figure 1–41. *Stenella caeruleoalba*, known as the blue-white dolphin, named by Meyen in 1833.

MORPHOLOGY: The body is the typical spindle shape of dolphins and reaches a maximum length of 2.4 to 2.7 m. Males are usually 10 to 30 cm larger than females. The caudal portion of the body behind the anus is much thicker than that of the common dolphin. The relationship of length to weight in this species can be represented by the formula $W = 0.000006 \times L^{3.062}$, where W is body weight in kilograms and L is body length in centimeters. The triangular dorsal fin, located at the middle of the body, is not as high as that of the common dolphin. The flippers are triangular and curved inward slightly on their posterior edges. The total spread of the tail flukes is about one-fifth of the body length.

The dorsal body is dark prussian blue, and the abdomen, as far forward as the undersurface of the lower jaw, is white. The sides of both the upper and lower jaws are prussian blue, and the tip of the rostrum is particularly dark. Along the boundary, the dorsal blue and ventral white are gradated. A black stripe runs from the rostrum and frontal to the eye on each side, where it then divides into two stripes and continues from the eye to the anus. The eyes are completely encircled with blue. The flippers, dorsal fin, and tail flukes are black, but the undersurface of the flukes is somewhat lighter. A black stripe runs forward from the base of the flippers, finally joins the dark blue circle around the eye, and occasionally even extends as far as the angle of gape. That stripe does not run to the lower jaw. There are no small spots on any part of the body.

The vertebral formula is $C7 + T15 + L22 + Ca35 = 79$. The first two cervical vertebrae are fused together. Occasionally, the third or fourth cervical vertebrae are found conjugated, but such fusions are the result of old age. The first five pairs of ribs, all of which are joined to the sternum by sternal ribs, are two headed. The sternum has four sections. The skull is 2.3 times as long as it is wide. The rostrum comprises 56 percent of the skull length and is about 2.5 times as long as it is wide. The dental formula is $\frac{45\text{-}50}{43\text{-}49}$. The heavily enameled teeth are relatively small (about 14 to 15 mm long and 3 mm in diameter). The tips of the teeth are sharp and curved slightly inward.

The flippers have five fingers of I: 1, II: 9–10, III: 7, IV: 4, and V: 2.

DISTRIBUTION AND ABUNDANCE: This species is found in the Atlantic and Pacific Oceans and the Mediterranean Sea but has not been reported from the Indian Ocean. Since the collection of the first specimen in the estuary of the La Plata River, South America, individuals have been found in widely separated areas of the Atlantic Ocean (south of Greenland, near Jamaica, in the Mediterranean Sea and near South Africa) and in the Pacific. The size of the Atlantic population has not been determined, but the Pacific population appears to be between 150,000 and 200,000 animals. In fact, this appears to be the most abundant species in Japanese waters, and despite annual harvests of from 10,000 to 20,000 individuals, there is no indication that the population is declining. These animals are caught off the east coast of the Izu Peninsula during their southward migrations in September through December and off the west coast of the same peninsula during their return migrations northward in May through July. Their migrations north of the Sanriku coast of Kagoshima, Kyushu, have not been studied.

FOOD: The primary food of this species is squid, particularly *Loligo sp.* Many individuals bear numerous marks of squid sucker discs around the mouth.

REPRODUCTION: Studies of specimens caught at Kawana, Futo, and Inatori, on the east coast of the Izu Peninsula, revealed both large and small fetuses simultaneously in October through December. Specimens from Arari, on the west coast of the Izu Peninsula, similarly produced both large and small fetuses from May through July. This evidence suggests that this species has two distinct breeding seasons, one in spring and one in fall, that each season lasts for a long period of time, and that parturition may occur in spring or autumn. Lactation lasts from six to twelve months, and individuals attain sexual maturity at an age of 4 years and a length of 1.8 to 1.85 m.

BEHAVIOR: These dolphins are gregarious, forming large herds. Furthermore, several herds may group together to form a group of thousands of individuals. The largest I have observed included about three thousand animals, all of which were juveniles. Herds more often consist of five hundred to one thousand or fewer, individuals.

These animals are very cowardly, and large herds can be chased into a bay for harvesting. Several to more than ten boats participate in the drive in which the dolphins are scared in the proper direction by slapping the water surface, by throwing stones, or by beating a trumpet-shaped device designed to produce underwater noise.

LONGEVITY: This species is assumed to live twenty-five to 30 years.

Stenella styx

Figure 1–42. *Stenella styx*, known as Gray's porpoise, named by Gray in 1846.

MORPHOLOGY: Although these animals have frequently been considered *Stenella caeruleoalba*, there appears to be a distinct difference between the color patterns around the eyes of the two species. Two dark stripes run backward from the eye, one to the axilla and another toward the anus. A branch of the second stripe does not reach the anus. Another stripe runs from the anterior edge of the flipper to the corner of the mouth, fading in color after it passes under the eye. The eye is in the dark portion but is encircled with a white ring which resembles a pair of glasses.

The rostrum is greater than two-thirds of the condylobasal length. Both

jaws have forty-four to fifty teeth on each side. There are seventy-six vertebrae and fifteen pairs of ribs.

DISTRIBUTION: These animals are distributed from south of Greenland to
north of Jamaica (in the Atlantic Ocean). Since the holotype was collected
on the west coast of Africa, they must also be distributed in the southern
hemisphere. In the Pacific Ocean, they have been reported from the Bering
Sea as far south as Oregon. None have been reported from Japanese waters.

Stenella malayana

Stenella malayana, known as the Malayan Porpoise, was named by Lesson in 1826.

MORPHOLOGY: Fraser reported that this species attained a maximum size
of less than 1.8 m. However, Beddard (1900) indicated that individuals
may attain a length of 2.1 m. The body is all gray. There are thirty-nine
teeth in both the upper and lower jaws.

DISTRIBUTION: This species is distributed near the Indonesian Islands and
the Malay Peninsula.

Stenella longirostris

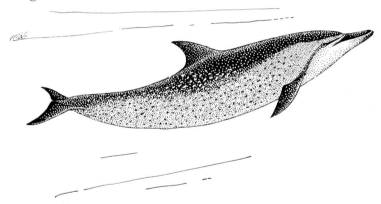

Figure 1–43. *Stenella longirostris,* known as the long-beaked porpoise, named by
Gray in 1871.

OTHER COMMON NAME: Long-snouted dolphin.

MORPHOLOGY: This species reaches a maximum length of about 2.1 m. The
dorsal body is charcoal-gray, while the ventral body is white or gray.
Numerous fine gray spots are scattered all over the body. The anterior half
of the body is darker than the posterior half. The boundary where the
dark dorsal and the light ventral surfaces fade together into gray runs in an
arch-like curve from behind the dorsal fin toward the head. The black
dorsal coloring narrows toward the front and reaches the border between

the frontal head and rostrum. The upper jaw of the beak and the tip and lip of the lower jaw are also black. A black stripe runs on each side from the eye to the border of the beak and frontal head. Another black line runs from the beak backward beyond the angle of gape. From the eye, a small, indistinct dark stripe runs backward to the base of the flippers. All the fins (flippers, dorsal fin, and fluke) are dark. There is no dark stripe from the eye to the anus. The dorsal fin, which is triangular and leans backwards, and the flippers are both small. There are forty-six to sixty-five (most commonly fifty-five) teeth on each side of both jaws. There are seventy-two to seventy-three vertebrae.

DISTRIBUTION: This species is abundant in the southern hemisphere. They are found near the Cape of Good Hope in the Indian Ocean and near Australia in the Pacific Ocean. In the northern hemisphere, some individuals are caught in Japanese waters west of Kyushu.

Stenella longirostris kunitomoi

Stenella longirostris kunitomoi, known as Ogawa's long-snouted dolphin, was named by Kuroda in 1952.

MORPHOLOGY: This subspecies was described from a skull specimen collected by Kunitomo in 1935 from a fishing boat operated south of the Goto Islands, Nagasaki Pref. The dental formula is $\frac{59-60}{50-61}$ and the rostrum is quite long. The skull is about 2.8 times as long as it is wide. The rostrum comprises about 63 percent of the skull length and is 3.4 times longer than it is wide. Ogawa stated that this subspecies differs from the holotype by lacking fine spots.

Five dolphins of *Stenella sp.* which this author observed at Sea Life Park in Hawaii in January, 1964, lacked any dots on the body, though they otherwise closely resembled *Stenella longirostris*. Although animals such as these, described by Ogawa, may constitute a new species, further study will be required.

Stenella microps

Stenella microps was named by Gray in 1871.

MORPHOLOGY: This species was described from a small-headed porpoise collected at Maria Madre Island in the Tres Marias Islands off Mexico. The species has a long rostrum which is narrow and sharp at the lip, broadest at the base of the preorbital process, and comprises over 60 percent of the total skull length. The skull is relatively small, reaching a maximum width of less than 15 cm. There are fifty-one teeth on each side of the lower jaw.

The flippers are rather small. There is a little bump immediately behind the anus in adult males. The skull and flippers of individuals of this species collected on the expeditions by the Erebus and the Terror of Great Britain are preserved at the British Museum.

BEHAVIOR: Information on behavior is limited. One distinctive behavior of *Stenella microps*, however, is that animals jump clear out of the water and spin themselves a few times in the air. The *Stenella* found near Hawaii also practice this maneuver.

Stenella attenuata

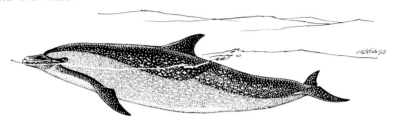

Figure 1–44. *Stenella attenuata*, known as the white-dotted dolphin, named by Gray in 1846.

OTHER COMMON NAME: Slender-beaked porpoise.

MORPHOLOGY: The triangular dorsal fin of this species is medium size but low, is located at the middle of the body, and leans backward. The flipper reaches a length of about two-fifteenths of the body length, is sharp, and curves backward. Males reach 2.0 to 2.1 m in length. The total spread of the tail flukes is about two-ninths of the body length. The caudal part is more slender than that of blue-white dolphin and resembles the common dolphin.

The body color of slender-beaked porpoises is very distinctive. Except on the dorsal skin, which is steel blue, and the rostrum, gray color dominates. When the animal is viewed laterally, the dark portion appears to begin at the middle of the frontal head and continue as far back as the posterior end of the dorsal fin. The boundary between the light and dark regions forms an arch which runs from the blow hole to the posterior edge of the dorsal fin. A charcoal-gray stripe runs from the base of the tail flukes to the anterior edge of the dorsal fin base. The rostrum is dark in color. Except for a white band along the axis on the abdomen, the rest of the body is gray.

In females, the skin around the mammilla is slightly lighter in color. The slate gray color of the lower jaw extends as far as the throat and in a dotted chain to the corner of the mouth. The lateral edge of the lower jaw is black, but the tips of both jaws are white. There are many small spots, gray in the dark portion of the body and white in the lighter portion.

There are no spots along the axis from the chest to the anus or along the axis of the dorsal side.

The flippers, dorsal fin, and tail flukes are all black but lack the spots. A black stripe which is less pronounced than that on the common or blue-white dolphins runs from the anterior edge of the flipper to the corner of the mouth. The eye is encircled with a black ring from which a black line stretches forward to join the black portion on the rostrum at a point above the corner of the mouth. When animals are alive, their dorsal skin reflects the light and appears purplish blue or very dark green while the abdominal skin, particularly that of pregnant or breeding individuals, shows pinkish color. A gray line runs to the boundary between the rostrum and forehead from each side of the blowhole.

The vertebral formula is $C7 + T15–16 + L18–19 + Ca37 = 78$. The first two pairs of ribs are two-headed, and five pairs are joined to the sternum. The rostrum is about 2.2 times as long as it is wide. Even though the rostrum is quite long, the large width between the preorbital joints keeps the ratio of rostrum length to width relatively small. The condylobasal length is slightly over twice the skull width. The rostrum length is about 55 percent of the condylobasal length. The flipper has five fingers, the bones of which are I: 2, II: 9, III: 7, IV: 3, and V: 1–2. The dental formula is $\frac{41-45}{40-43}$.

DISTRIBUTION: Besides the holotype, only a few specimens of this species have ever been collected. One was taken along the west coast of South Africa by the *Atlantide*, an exploratory boat of Denmark, and some were taken at the west coast of Izu Peninsula, Japan. In 1963, one was captured near Hawaii. Judging from such collections, this species may be present but not abundant in both the Atlantic and Pacific.

RELATED SPECIES: There are several groups which have color patterns which closely resemble those of this species. Each has some particular characteristic, but with further study some of those groups may be combined.

Stenella plagiodon

Figure 1–45. *Stenella plagiodon,* known as the spotted dolphin, named by Cope in 1866.

MORPHOLOGY: The maximum adult length is about 2.2 m. The body of the spotted dolphin resembles that of the white dotted dolphin in shape and color but the high forehead is more like that of the blue-white dolphin. The dorsal body is steel blue though slightly lighter than that of white dotted dolphin. There is no white color on the rostrum. The ventral skin is mostly light gray. There are many gray or steel blue dots scattered on the light skin and white or light gray dots on the dark skin. The dorsal fin is not large. The flippers, the dorsal fin, and the tail flukes all lack dots. The length of the rostrum is less than two-thirds of the condylobasal length. The dental formula is $\frac{34\text{-}37}{34\text{-}37}$. The total number of the vertebrae is sixty-eight to sixty-nine.

DISTRIBUTION: Spotted dolphins are not abundant and are found mainly in the Atlantic Ocean (along the United States and in the Gulf of Mexico). They are assumed to be distributed along the coasts of South America and Europe, as well.

Stenella graffmani

Figure 1–46. *Stenella graffmani,* known as Graffman's porpoise, named by Lönnberg in 1934.

MORPHOLOGY: This species reaches 2.4 m in length. The body is generally dark and contains numerous white or gray dots on the dorsal skin. Both the dorsal fin and flippers are relatively small. The length of the rostrum is less than two-thirds of the condylobasal length. Each of the jaws has forty-three to forty-seven teeth on each row. The relative proportion of head to total body length is smaller than in *Stenella plagiodon.*

DISTRIBUTION: Graffman's porpoises are distributed in the eastern tropical Pacific.

Stenella frontalis

Figure 1–47. *Stenella frontalis,* known as the bridled dolphin, named by G. Cuvier in 1829.

MOROPHOLOGY: This species reaches 1.8 to 1.9 m in length and resembles the blue-white dolphin in its shape. The rostrum is relatively short. The triangular dorsal fin is at the middle of the body and curves backward at the top. The flippers are relatively large, triangular, and sharp at the end. The total spread of the tail flukes is about one-fifth of the body length. The rostrum is about four-sevenths of the condylobasal length and about 2.4 times as long as it is wide. The eyes are encircled with black rings from which black stripes run forward, joining each other at the junction of the of the melon and the rostrum. A dark stripe runs from the anterior edge of the flipper to the angle of gape. Except at the head, the boundary between the gray side skin and the dark dorsal skin is indistinct. The gray on the side of the body gradually pales toward the abdomen, where it is almost white. The rostrum is black, the lower jaw is slightly paler, and the skin on the throat is gray. The dorsal fin and flukes are all black. The outer surfaces of the flippers are black, except near the tip, the inner surfaces are gray. The abdomen is covered with small black dots and the dorsal skin, particularly posterior to the dorsal fin, is covered with grayish white dots. The black anterior dorsal skin, the dorsal fin, and the tail flukes lack dots. The vertebral formula is $C7 + T15 + L19 + Ca36 = 77$. There are five to six pairs of two-headed ribs and twenty-eight chevrons. The flippers have five fingers of I: 2–3, II: 9, III: 7, IV: 3, and V: 2. The dental formula is $\frac{37\text{-}38}{37\text{-}38}$. However, Hall and Kelson (1959) reported thirty-five to forty-four teeth with the average of thirty-seven to thirty-eight and about seventy vertebrae in total.

DISTRIBUTION: This species is found in temperate zones of the Pacific, Atlantic, and Indian Oceans.

Lagenorhynchus

The genus *Lagenorhynchus* was named by Gray in 1846. Some of its principal characteristics are as follows:

27c.

1. Dorsal fin barely curves backward.
2. Adults less than 3 m long.
3. Rostrum length of skull about two times its breadth.
4. Greatest breadth of skull more than one-half of condylobasal length.
5. Mandibular symphysis less than one-fith of mandibular length.

Lagenorhynchus obliquidens

Figure 1–48. *Lagenorhynchus obliquidens,* known as the Pacific white-sided dolphin, named by Gill in 1865.

OTHER COMMON NAME: Pacific white-striped dolphin.

MORPHOLOGY: Although the rostrum of this species is not as distinct as it is in most species of *Lagenorhynchus*, it can nonetheless be distinguished from the frontal area (or melon). The body slims rapidly posterior to the anus and the keels of the tail stock are quite distinct from the ventral and dorsal sides, extending straight to the flukes. The falcate dorsal fin is very high. The flippers are medium sized, triangular, and broadest at the base. The tail flukes, also medium sized, reach a total spread of about one-sixth of the body length. The dorsal surface is black, fading gradually into gray on the side. A gray patch, resembling a brushed-on stripe, runs forward along the side from the back. The ventral body is white and where it overlays with the gray side patches, is distinctly marked with a black stripe which runs from the corner of the mouth along the base of the flippers to the anus. The dorsal fin is black and is marked on the posterior edge by a white, sickle-shaped area. The head, the upper jaw, and the lip of the lower jaw are black, but the lower jaw is white.

The white-sided dolphins caught near Japan are usually 2.1 to 2.2 m long and weigh 75 to 90 kg. This species does not reach 2.4 in length. Each of the upper and lower jaws has twenty-three to thirty-three small but sharp teeth, the round cross section of which has a diameter of about 3 to 4 mm. The vertebral formula is $C7 + T13–14 + L20–24 + Ca30–34 = 73–78$. The first six pairs of ribs are two-headed. The flipper has five fingers, the bones of which are I: 1–2, II: 6–8, III: 6, IV: 2–3, and V: 1–2.

DISTRIBUTION: This species is found in North Pacific waters north of the temperate zone and south of the Bering Sea. It is abundant in Japanese waters and along the coasts of North America from Baja California to Alaska and is particularly well known off the California coast, where large herds are frequently seen.

ABUNDANCE: The population size of this species near Japan alone is estimated as 30,000 to 50,000.

FOOD: Though *Lagenorhynchus obliquidens* appears to prefer squid, they may also feed on small pelagic fishes.

REPRODUCTION: Breeding and parturition both occur from spring to summer. At the base of the rostrum, the fetus sports several tactile hairs which are lost soon after birth. Newborn animals are about 1.2 m long, quite large when the adult size is considered.

BEHAVIOR: Although they often form small herds of twenty to one hundred individuals, observations in Japanese waters suggest that herds of hundreds or even a thousand dolphins are not unusual.

RELATED SPECIES: *Lagenorhynchus australis*, Peale's Porpoise.

Lagenorhynchus australis

Figure 1–49. *Lagenorhynchus australis*, known as Peale's porpoise, named by Peale in 1848.

MORPHOLOGY: Peale's porpoise reaches a length of 2.0 to 2.2 m. When viewed laterally, the outline of the animal slopes gradually from the top of the beak to the forehead, but the boundary between the rostrum and the forehead is clear. The falcate dorsal fin is medium in size and has a long base. The flippers are relatively small and curve backward. The medium-sized tail flukes have a very deep notch at the center of the posterior edge. The keels in front of the fluke on the dorsal, and ventral sides are very distinct. The dorsal body is charcoal-gray. The ventral body is white, and the breast region is gray. One black stripe runs to the corner of the mouth from the front base of the flippers and another from the posterior base of the flippers. The jaws, the area around the eyes, and the flippers are all black, though the flippers are surrounded by white. The black which encircles the eyes joins the black portion of the head. A white stripe, resembling a painted area, runs forward to the dorsal fin from each side of the caudal portion of the body. Both jaws have about thirty small teeth on each row.

DISTRIBUTION: This species is known only in the waters of southern South America.

Lagenorhynchus superciliosus

Lagenorhynchus superciliosus was named by Lesson and Gamot in 1826:

MORPHOLOGY: This species has been described only from a skeleton from the Cape of Good Hope. The vertebral formula is C7 + T13 + L20 + Ca33 = 73. The peterygoid is not fixed to the skull. The dental formula is $\frac{30\text{-}30}{30\text{-}30}$.

Lagenorhynchus thicolea

Lagenorhynchus thicolea, known as Gray's white-sided dolphin, was named by Gray in 1849.

MORPHOLOGY: Because this species was described from only one skull found on the west coast of North America, neither the size nor the color of the body are known. The skull has forty-five teeth on each row. The premaxillary is flat and narrow. The temporal fossae are small and round, and the rostrum is longer than one-half of the condylobasal length.

Lagenorhynchus acutus

Figure 1–50. *Lagenorhynchus acutus,* known as the Atlantic white-sided dolphin, named by Gray in 1828.

MORPHOLOGY: Adults reach a maximum length of about 2.7 m. The rostrum is short but distinct from the frontal area. The flippers are located forward on the body, and the high, falcate dorsal fin, which shows a separation in colors, is located slightly anterior to the midpoint of the body. The tail flukes reach about one-fifth to one-sixth of the total body length. The keels are very marked in the caudal region, and the dorsal keel continues to the dorsal fin. Although there are many individual variations in the distribution of colors on the body, the general patterns are as follows: The boundaries between the black dorsal and the white ventral surfaces are very distinct. A black line runs from the base of the all black flipper either to the corner of the mouth or to the eye. Another black line runs from the anus forward to the black dorsal portion. The lip of the lower jaw is either white or fringed with black.

The maxillary and premaxillary that form the rostrum are both flat in cross section. When measured along the body axis, the temporal fossa is long. The pterygoid is firmly fixed to the skull. On each row of the jaw, there are thirty to thirty-four relatively small, sharp teeth which have a cross-sectional diameter of about 5 mm. The vertebral formula is $C7 + T15 + L18–22 + Ca38–41 = 78–82$. Six of the fifteen pairs of ribs are two headed. The phalangeal formula is I: 1–2, II: 10, III: 6, IV: 2–3, and V: 2.

DISTRIBUTION: In the Atlantic Ocean, this species commonly occurs south of Greenland, off Norway (where it is the second most common small cetacean), near the Shetland and Orkney Islands in British waters, and off Cape Cod, Massachusetts. None have been found in tropical seas.

ABUNDANCE: Although an accurate evaluation of population size has not been made, population estimates range from 30,000 to 50,000 animals.

REPRODUCTION: The young are born in spring and summer after a ten-month gestation period. Parturition rarely takes place after midsummer (Guldberg and Nansen, 1894).

BEHAVIOR: *Lagenorhynchus acutus* form fairly large schools which often include more than a 1,000 individuals. Herds of thirty to forty animals have been reported beached in England.

Lagenorhynchus crusiger

Figure 1–51. *Lagenorhynchus crusiger*, known as Crusiger's white-sided dolphin, named by Quoy and Gaimard in 1824.

MORPHOLOGY: Although *Lagenorhynchus crusiger* and *Lagenorhynchus acutus* are morphologically similar, this animal is smaller in size, reaching only 1.6 to 1.8 m in length. The dorsal skin to the fluke, the rostrum, and lower jaw are all black. A black band, occassionally very broad under the dorsal fin, runs from the eye to the fluke on the side of the body. Each jaw has twenty-eight teeth on each side.

DISTRIBUTION: These animals are found in the South Pacific between 20°S and the drifting ice zone.

Lagenorhynchus wilsoni

Lagenorhynchus wilsoni, known as Wilson's hourglass dophin, was named by Lillie in 1915.

MORPHOLOGY: This species, though closely related to *Lagenorhynchus crusiger*, is slightly larger. It has a sharp rostrum, and the black bands which run along both sides of the body join on the ventral side below the flippers.

Lagenorhynchus fitzroyi

Figure 1–52. *Lagenorhynchus fitzroyi*, known as Fitzroy's dolphin, named by Waterhouse in 1836.

MORPHOLOGY: Although Beddard (1900) stated that this species might be the same as *Lagenorhynchus crusiger*, they will be treated in this work as two different species. The holotype was 1.62 m long, and Beddard gives the range as 1.4 to 1.9 m. The very tip of the beak is sharp. On side view, the beak is rounded, forming an arch-line that gradually shifts to the forehead. The dorsal black and the ventral white overlap on the sides of the body. The tip of the beak near the eyes, the lip on the lower jaw, and the tail flukes are all black. The flippers and dorsal fin are dark gray. A gray line, which is broader than that of *Lagenorhynchus acutus*, runs from the base of the flipper to the corner of the mouth. The dorsal black color projects in two stripes down and backwards in front of the dorsal fin. Another small black projection runs forward at the base of the tail flukes. There are twenty-eight teeth on each upper and twenty-four on each lower jaw. They are all curved but sharp at the tips. The pterygoid is fixed to the skull.

MISCELLANEOUS: The first specimen ever collected was speared in St. Joseph Bay during the expedition of the Beagle. This specimen was measured by Charles Darwin and illustrated by Captain Fitzroy, after whom it was named.

RELATED SPECIES: *Lagenorhynchus obscurus* (dusky dolphin).

Lagenorhynchus obscurus

Figure 1–53. *Lagenorhynchus obscurus*, known as the dusky dolphin, named by Gray in 1828.

MORPHOLOGY: There are thirty to thirty-two teeth on each side of both jaws. Adults reach a maximum of about 2.1 m. Although the body of this species resembles that of *Lagenorhynchus acutus* or *Lagenorhynchus obliquidens*, the rostrum is longer, and though the dorsal fin is relatively large, its posterior edge is straighter than that of *Lagenorhynchus acutus* or *Lagenorhynchus obliquidens*. The anterior edge of the fin is black while the posterior edge is white. There is a great deal of individual variation in body color. The following description is based on a specimen collected in South America: The dorsum, the flippers, and the tail flukes are all black. A thin black stripe runs from the base of the flippers to the eye and white brush-like stripes project in both directions from a point right behind the anus. The keels on the dorsal and the ventral bodies are black.

DISTRIBUTION: *Lagenorhynchus obscurus* is very common in New Zealand and is distributed in the water near the Falkland Islands off South America. Lillie (1915) reported that this species does not migrate south of 58°S.

FOOD: The primary stomach content of the specimens collected at the Falkland Islands was squid.

BEHAVIOR: After he observed this species from the *Terra Nova*, an exploratory ship, Lillie (1915) wrote, "When we approached the New Zealand coast, a large school came near the ship and laid around the bow, or followed the ship as if welcoming or seeing off the ship. They disappeared when we moved out of the warm waters."

Lagenorhynchus albirostris

Figure 1–54. *Lagenorhynchus albirostris,* known as the white-beaked dolphin, named by Gray in 1846.

MORPHOLOGY: Although the white portions are narrower than those of other members of the genus, the body of this species and the white coloration of the dorsal surface of the beak are typical of the genus. The tail flukes are moderate in size, and the body behind the anus is slender. The keels are quite marked. Individuals may reach a length of about 3 m but are generally somewhat smaller. The blubber is relatively thick. The rostrum is broad and reaches a length of about one-half of the condylobasal length. The premaxillary is flat but convexed slightly toward the rostrum. The ptyergoid is fixed to the skull, and the temporal fossa is oval.

There are twenty-six to twenty-seven teeth on each jaw, but there are sometimes more on the upper jaw than on the lower jaw. The teeth are an average of 6 mm in diameter, slightly larger than those of *Lagenorhynchus acutus.* The vertebral formula is C7 + T14–16 + L24–27 + Ca43–45 = 88–93. There are commonly ninety-three vertebrae. The first five pairs of ribs are two-headed. The flippers have five phalanges of I: 3, II: 7, III: 5, IV: 2, and V: 1.

DISTRIBUTION: The range of this species is shifted further north than that of *Lagenorhynchus acutus.* They are found only in the northern North Atlantic (the Davis Strait, northern Norway, the North Sea, and near Newfoundland).

FOOD: This species feeds on squid, octopus, cod, small cod, herring, capelin, and small crustacea. In addition, numerous hermit crabs were found in the stomach of one specimen and numerous snail shells in another.

REPRODUCTION: Parturition is assumed to take place in summer and many juveniles about 1.2 m in length have been reported beached in the later half of the year.

BEHAVIOR: Herds of more than 1,500 individuals are often formed.

Tursiops

The genus *Tursiops* was named by Gervais in 1855. Some characteristics of its members are as follows:

27d.
1. Dorsal fin triangular and bent slightly backward.
2. Adults more than 2.4 m, less than 4.0 m long.
3. Rostrum length of skull more than 2.2 times its breadth.
4. Greatest breadth of skull less than one-half of condylobasal length.
5. Mandibular symphysis less than one-fifth of mandibular length.

Tursiops truncatus

Figure 1–55. *Tursiops truncatus,* known as the bottlenosed dolphin, named by Montagu in 1821.

OTHER COMMON NAME: Bottlenosed porpoise.

MORPHOLOGY: This species reaches a length of 2.5 to 3 m. Males are 10 to 20 cm longer than females. The flippers are located forward on the body. The dorsal fin is located at the dorsal midlength, and the posterior end of its base is on the same cross section as the anus. The total spread of the tail flukes is about one-ninth of the body length. Because of the large melon, even though the rostrum of the skull is relatively long, the actual beak is rather short, comprising only one-twenty-first of the total body length. The dorsal surface is blueish steel gray or slate gray and makes a gradual transition to the pale ventral surface. A dark stripe runs from the blowhole to the base of the beak. In addition, there are often one or two dark lines running from the eye to the rostrum.

The vertebral formula is C7 + T13–14 + L15 + Ca29–30 = 65. Five of

the thirteen to fourteen pairs of ribs are two-headed. The sternum is in four
sections to which six pairs of ribs are joined. There are generally twenty-
two to twenty-four chevrons. The dental formula is $\frac{20 \cdot 23}{20 \cdot 23}$. The flipper has
five fingers, the bones of which are I: 2, II: 9, III: 7, IV: 4, and V: 2. The
teeth are relatively large (4 to 5 cm long, and 10 mm in diameter).

DISTRIBUTION: The bottlenosed dolphin is quite widely distributed. They
are the most common species along the Atlantic coast of America and are
frequently seen on the European Atlantic coasts. There was even a report
from New Zealand, though this author has not yet confirmed that report.

FOOD: Fish is the main food item but some squid may also be taken.

BEHAVIOR: Although these dolphins generally form small herds of two to
over ten individuals, groups as large as 100 to 500 have been seen. Their
actions are rather slow, they have very little fear of man, and they are
easily tamed. Some are caught by seine.

Tursiops gilli

Figure 1–56. *Tursiops gilli,* known as Gill's bottlenosed dolphin, named by Dall in
1873.

OTHER COMMON NAME: Cowfish.

MORPHOLOGY: Ogawa (1936) reported that this species generally reaches
2.65 m in length and does not grow longer than 3.0 m. Hall and Kelson
(1959) reported that they grow as large as 3.5 m in length. My own surveys
suggest that they may reach 3.7 m in length.

The body appears to be basically gray as a whole, with a slightly darker
dorsal suface. Although there is a black stripe from the eye forward, it is
very indistinct. The vertebral formula is $C7 + T14 + L15 + Ca29 = 65$
and the first five out of the fourteen pairs of ribs are two headed. (This
species has one or two more pairs of ribs than *Tursiops nuuanu*). The
phalangeal formula is I: 2, II: 9, III: 7, IV: 4, and V: 2. They have more
teeth than *Tursiops truncatus* or *Tursiops nuuanu*. The dental formula is
$\frac{20 \cdot 25}{20 \cdot 25}$.

DISTRIBUTION: This species is limited to the Pacific Ocean and is abundant
in the North Pacific. Most of the *Tursiops* which are caught near Japan

and kept in the aquaria and zoos there are assumed to be of this species (although they were once thought to be *Tursiops truncatus*).

FOOD: This species feeds primarily on fish but may also take some squid.

REPRODUCTION: There appear to be two breeding seasons, one in spring and one in fall. Most females breed and are impregnated in March to May, but those which are not successfully impregnated at this time may breed in autumn. The gestation period is eleven to twelve months long, and new-born calves are about 1.3 m. When females are kept in captivity, they tend to deliver premature calves about 1.2 m long which die within a month. When the calves are as large as 1.3 m in length at the time of birth, however, they generally survive. Mothers which have been in captivity for some time and are accustomed to the pool appear to be less likely to abort. In the first year after birth, juveniles grow to over 2 m in length. Females attain sexual maturity at an age of four to six years and a length of 2.7 to 2.9 m.

BEHAVIOR: This species is coastal, and groups sometimes appear to become residents of a particular area. Although herds generally consist of from a few to several tens of animals, herds of several hundreds are occasionally seen. They show little fear of humans and are easily tamed, though perhaps not as easily as *Tursiops truncatus*.

The swimming speed is not notably fast. Cruising herds move at about 7 knots (9 to 12 km/hr) and even escaping animals do not seem to exceed 20 knots (36 km/hr). They frequently follow ships cruising at 10 knots (18 km/hr) riding the bow waves. The breathing actions are gentle. These animals often jump completely out of the water, exposing the entire body.

LONGEVITY: *Tursiops gilli* probably live twenty-five to thirty years.

RELATED SPECIES: *Tursiops nuuanu* (Pacific bottlenosed dolphin).

Tursiops nuuanu

Figure 1–57. *Tursiops nuuanu,* known as the Pacific bottlenosed dolphin, named by Andrews in 1911.

MORPHOLOGY: Although the holotype of this species was less than 2.3 m long, the size of all other Pacific species of *Tursiops* would suggest that

that specimen was not an adult. The dorsal body is slate gray and the ventral body is white. The posterior end of the vomer is wide and the angles at the end are sharper than the right angle which is formed on the end of the vomer of *Tursiops gilli*. However, the differences between this characteristic of the two species is minor and cannot easily be used to distinguish them. The condylobasal length is at least 10 per cent less in *Tursiops nuuanu* than in *Tursiops gilli*. Ogawa (1936) described a wrinkle on the eyelid of *Tursiops nuuanu* that is absent in *Tursiops gilli*. The posterior end of the maxillary which forms the orbital fossa is almost straight, and the bone that constitutes the upper part of the orbital fossa is not thick. The mandibular condyle is relatively small, reaching less than one-half of the height of the mandible at the coronoid processes. The length of squamosal fossa along the body axis relative to the condylobasal length is less than that of other species. The dental formula is $\frac{18\text{-}20}{18\text{-}20}$.

DISTRIBUTION: *Tursiops nuuanu* are distributed in the Pacific Ocean, particularly in the tropical seas near Panama. It is not yet known whether they are found in the western Pacific. Ogawa (1936) stated, "*Tursiops gilli* found near Japan should be considered the same species as *Tursiops nuuanu*, since they closely resemble each other."

Tursiops aduncas

Figure 1–58. *Tursiops aduncas*, named by Ehrenbery in 1833.

MORPHOLOGY: The rostrum of this species is rather long and slender, but the condylobasal length is rather short. The vertebral formula is C7 + T13 + L15 + Ca27 = 62. The palatine has a sharp forward projection which extends beyond the line connecting the last tooth on each side.

DISTRIBUTION: This species has been collected from Australian waters, the Indian Ocean, and the South China Sea.

Tursiops parvimanus

   Tursiops parvimanus was named by Reinhardt in 1888.

MORPHOLOGY: Like *Tursiops aduncas*, this species has a vertebral formula of C7 + T13 + L15 + Ca27 = 62, but has a different phalangeal formula, I: 2, II: 6, II: 8, IV: 3, and V: 1. It has more bones in the third finger. One young specimen was collected from the Adriatic Sea. Lütken (1888) discussed the possibility that this species may be the same as *Tursiops aduncas*.

Tursiops gephyreus

Tursiops gephyreus was named by Lahille in 1908.

MORPHOLOGY: This species has fewer vertebrae and a slightly longer rostrum than *Tursiops truncatus*. It was collected from the vicinity of Argentina.

Tursiops abusalam

Tursiops abusalam was named by Ruppell in 1842.

MORPHOLOGY: Many scientists think that *Tursiops abusalam, Tursiops catalania* (Gray, 1862), and *Sotalia gadamu* (Owen, 1866) are the same species as *Tursiops aduncas*, but further studies on the taxonomy of the genus *Tursiops* are necessary. The vertebral formula is C7 + T12 + L16 + Ca26 = 61, and the dental formula is $\frac{26}{26}$.

DISTRIBUTION: *Tursiops abusalam* is found in the Red Sea.

Sousa

The distinguishing characteristics of members of the genus *Sousa* are the following:

27e.
1. Dorsal fin triangular and leans backward.
2. Adults less than 2.5 m long.
3. Rostrum length of skull more than 2.5 times its breadth.
4. Greatest breadth of skull less than one-half of condylobasal length.
5. Mandibular symphysis more than one-fifth of mandibular length.

Sousa plumbea

Figure 1–59. *Sousa plumbea,* known as the plumbeous dolphin, named by Cuvier in 1829.

OTHER COMMON NAME: Lead-colored dolphin.

MORPHOLOGY: This species resembles *Tursiops gilli* in appearance, but the body color is quite pale. The dorsal surface is lead color or light gray, and the abdominal skin is almost white. The maximum girth of the body is about the middle where the dorsal fin is located. The flippers are wide at the base and pointed at the tip.

The beak is long, and the distance from the tip of the snout to the eye is almost one-sixth of the body length, which may reach 2.4 m. The dental formula is $\frac{34-35}{34-35}$.

DISTRIBUTION: The plumbeous dolphin is found in the Indian Ocean, near Ceylon, Madras, the Malabar coast of India, and the Strait of Malacca. They are believed to be more pelagic than any other species of the genus *Sousa*.

RELATED SPECIES: *Sousa chinensis* (Chinese white dolphin).

Sousa chinensis

Sousa chinensis, known as the Chinese white dolphin, was named by Osbeck in 1765.

MORPHOLOGY: The body of this species is generally ivory, but the ventral skin is slightly pinkish. The dorsal fin, flippers, and tail flukes are brownish gray mingled with a little cherry pink. The eyes are black. On a specimen whose condylobasal length was 42 cm, the rostrum was 27 cm long and 7.5 cm wide at the base, and the skull measured 15 cm at the maximum width. The symphysis of the mandible is relatively long (about one-fifth of the length of the mandible). Although there are reportedly thirty-two teeth on each side of both jaws, one specimen examined was $\frac{37-37}{33-34}$. The vertebral formula is $C7 + T12 + L10 + Ca22 = 51$ and the phalangeal formula is I: 1, II: 7, III: 5, IV: 3, and V: 2.

DISTRIBUTION: The Chinese white dolphin is distributed in the South China Sea, mostly from the Amoy Bay to the Canton River.

Sousa borneensis

Sousa borneensis, known as the Bornean white dolphin, was named by Lydecker in 1901.

MORPHOLOGY: The dorsal fin is very low and is not concave on the posterior edge. The base of the dorsal fin extends toward the tail flukes and forms a keel. The entire body is a beautiful glossy white with many gray spots.

DISTRIBUTION: The Bornean white dolphin is distributed from the Gulf of Siam to the northwestern coast of Borneo.

Sousa lentiginosa

Sousa lentiginosa, known as the freckled (or speckled) dolphin, was named by Owen in 1866.

OTHER COMMON NAME: Bolla gadim.

MORPHOLOGY: The dorsal skin of this species is bluish steel gray, and the ventral skin is pale. Many spots of yellow ochre or lavender color are scattered over the body, and there are vertical stripes on the side. Adults reach a length of about 2.5 m and a weight of around 150 kg. The dorsal fin is relatively small, but its base is long and extends posterior to almost half the distance between the tip of the dorsal fin and the fluke. The flippers are round at the anterior edge and curve backwards at the end. There are about thirty teeth on each side of each jaw.

DISTRIBUTION: This species is known from the coast of south India and Ceylon.

Sousa teuszi

Sousa teuszi, known as the West African many-toothed dolphin, was named by Kükenthal in 1892.

MORPHOLOGY: This species reaches a length of 2.3 m and a weight of around 140 kg. The blubber is very thick. The blowhole sticks out in a tube-like form, making a small hump.

DISTRIBUTION: These dolphins are distributed off Senegal to the Cameroons of the west coast of Africa.

Steno

The genus *Steno* was named by Gray in 1846. Some of the characteristics of its members are as follows:
26b.
   1. Forehead rises from the beak in a gradual curve.
28a.
   2. Dorsal fin is triangular and bends backward slightly.
   3. Adults more than 1.8 but less than 2.5 m long.
   4. Rostrum length of skull more than three times its breadth.
   5. Greatest breadth of skull less than one-half of condylobasal length.
   6. Mandibular symphysis about one-fourth of mandibular length.

Steno bredanensis

Figure 1–60. *Steno bredanensis,* known as the rough-toothed dolphin, named by Lesson in 1828.

MORPHOLOGY: The maximum body length is 2.5 m. The relatively tall dorsal fin is located at the middle of the body and leans backward. The flippers are fairly long (about one-seventh of the body length) and the tail flukes are large, reaching a width equal to one-fourth of body length. Most of the body is charcoal gray or black, but there are irregular white patches on the underside. In addition, there are white, pale cherry pink, or ivory spots on various parts of the skin. These spots are presumably scars left by parasitic protozoa or bacteria.

The skull is very distinctive. The rostrum is almost two-thirds as long as the condylobasal length and over 3.1 times as long as it is wide. This high ratio results, at least in part, from the small size of the interval between the premaxillary processes. The mandibular symphysis is about one-quarter of the mandible's length. The pterygoid is fixed to the skull. In each jaw, there are twenty to twenty-seven fairly large teeth at the crown of which there are many vertical fine wrinkles. The vertebral formula is $C7 + T13 + L15–16 + Ca30–31 = 66$. Four or five pairs of ribs are two headed and five pairs of ribs are joined to the sternum. The flipper has five fingers, the bones of which are I: 3, II: 8–9, III: 6–7, IV: 6, and V: 2.

DISTRIBUTION: Rough-toothed dolphins are distributed in the temperate seas of the Atlantic, Indian, and North Pacific Oceans. Specimens have also been recorded near the Hawaiian Islands, Java, and the Bay of Biscay.

Cephalorhynchus

The genus *Cephalorhynchus* was named by Gray in 1846. Some of its characteristics are the following:

28b.
1. Dorsal fin small and neither pointed nor bent backward.
2. Adults less than 1.8 m.
3. Characteristic body color patterns.
4. Inhabit high latitudes of the southern hemisphere.

Cephalorhynchus commersoni

Figure 1–61. *Cephalorhynchus commersoni,* known as Commerson's dolphin, named by Lacépède in 1804.

OTHER COMMON NAMES: Piebald porpoise, Le Jacobite.

MORPHOLOGY: This species reaches a length of about 1.6 m. The rostrum is fairly sharply pointed at the tip, and its boundary with the forehead is indistinct. The dorsal fin is located slightly posterior to the middle of the body and is not pointed at the tip. The base of the fin is long. The flippers are round at the end and somewhat oval in overall shape. The notch at the posterior edge of the tail flukes is not so distinctive as in the other species of *Cephalorhynchus.*

The pattern of colors is very characteristic of this genus. The head and the region from the dorsal fin to the flukes are both black and the area between is white. On the underside, the skin is black in front of the flippers, and there is an oval patch in the throat region. Except for black patches around the anus and genital opening, the abdominal skin is all white. The lower surfaces of the tail flukes and the caudal peduncle are black. There are twenty-nine to thirty small, pointed teeth on each side of each jaw.

DISTRIBUTION: This species is found in the Strait of Magellan, Tierra del Fuego, and the Falkland Islands, off the southern tip of South America.

FOOD: Commerson's dolphin appears to feed on a wide variety of food items, including squids, euphausiids, and fishes. Judging from the appearance of the mouth and teeth, however, it is unlikely that they feed on large animals.

RELATED SPECIES: *Cephalorhynchus heavisidei* (*Heaviside's dolphin*).

Cephalorhynchus heavisidei

Figure 1–62. *Cephalorhynchus heavisidei*, known as Heaviside's dolphin, named by Gray in 1828.

MORPHOLOGY: Heaviside's dolphin reaches a length of 1.2 to 1.3 m. The dorsal body is black, and the ventral skin from the thorax to the anus is white. Except for the absence of white spots above the eyes, the black and white color patterns on the side of the body resemble those of the killer whale. When the animal is viewed laterally, the rostrum appears indistinct. The body reaches its maximum girth midway between the flippers and the dorsal fin. The triangular dorsal fin is located slightly posterior to the center of the body, is sharp at the end, and does not bend backward. The keels behind the dorsal fin and the anus are indistinct. The flippers are small, triangular, narrow, sharp at the end, and curve on the front edge. The tail flukes are small, narrow, and curve backward. Both jaws have twenty-five to thirty small sharp teeth on each side, and the lower jaw extends beyond the upper.

DISTRIBUTION: This species is known from cold seas in the southern hemisphere off the Cape of Good Hope of South Africa.

Cephalorhynchus hectori

Figure 1–63. *Cephalorhynchus hectori,* known as Hector's dolphin.

MORPHOLOGY: This species reaches a length of approximately 1.8 m. The beak is a little more prominent than that of *Cephalorhynchus heavisidei.* The small dorsal fin is located about the middle of the body and is low in profile. The dorsal keel is very low. The posterior and anterior edges of the flippers are almost parallel and the tips are rounded. The width of the relatively small tail flukes is less than one-fifth of the body length. The color pattern resembles that of *Cephalorhynchus heavisidei* except that in this species, the black portion near the flipper is wider and the white portion just above it extends to the lower jaw. There are thirty to thirty-two teeth on each side of each jaw.

DISTRIBUTION: Hector's dolphin is found only in the waters off New Zealand.

Cephalorhynchus albifrons

Figure 1–64. *Cephalorhynchus albifrons,* known as the white-headed dolphin.

MORPHOLOGY: The body of the white-headed dolphin is less than 1.3 m long and reaches its maximum girth about one-third back from the tip of the snout. The head is quite slender, and there are thirty-one to thirty-two teeth on each side of each jaw. The dorsal fin, which is located at the mid-point of the body length, is low and rounded on the end. The flippers are narrow and curve backward. The posterior edge of the tail flukes, which also curve backward, is considerably concave and marked by a deep notch. In front of the blowhole, the head is white. The white coloration extends behind the eyes. The skin around the blowhole, on the dorsal fin and tail flukes, and around the genital opening and anus are black, and the rest of the body is gray. There are two gray stripes on each side, one running from the base of the flipper forward towards the rostrum and another running forward from the caudal peduncle. Although this species is reportedly common in New Zealand waters, only a few specimens have been seen.

Cephalorhynchus eutropia

Cephalorhyncus eutropia, known as the white-bellied dolphin, was named by Gray in 1849.

MORPHOLOGY: The adult body length is about 1.4 m. The dorsal fin is rounded and the flippers are small. There is a marked curvature in the posterior edge on the tail flukes. The body is generally gray with white spots at the throat, behind the flippers, and on the abdomen.

DISTRIBUTION: The white-bellied dolphin is a very rare species which has been caught only off southern South America.

Sotalia

The genus *Sotalia* was named by Gray in 1866. Some of its principal characteristics are the following:
28c.
1. Dorsal fin triangular, curves backward only slightly.
2. Adults less than 1.85 m long.
3. Rostrum length of skull about 2.5 times its breadth.
4. Inhabit mainly large rivers in South America and their estuaries.

Sotalia fluviatilis

Figure 1–65. *Sotalia fluviatilis*, known as the Buffeo negro, named by Gervais and DeVille in 1853.

OTHER COMMON NAMES: Buffeo negro, pirayaguara, tucuxi, and Amazon dolphin.

MORPHOLOGY: This is the smallest of the cetaceans, averaging 1.1 m and reaching a maximum length of 1.2 m. The body is typically dolphin shaped. The dorsal body is brownish charcoal gray, while the ventral skin from the throat to the anus is cream yellow to ivory. The light ventral coloration projects from the anus toward the front of the dorsal fin in two bands. The dorsal fin and flippers are proportionately balanced to the small body. The tail flukes are not wide (tip to tip) but are quite broad. All the fins are the same color as the dorsal skin.

In one specimen whose condylobasal length was 38 cm, the rostrum comprised two-fifths of the skull length and was two-fifths as wide as it was long. There were thirty teeth on the upper jaw and thirty-one rather snaggled teeth in a disordered row on the lower jaw. The vertebral formula is C7 + T12 + L11 + Ca26 = 56. The first five pairs of ribs are two-headed and joined to the sternum. There are five fingers, the bones of which are I: 1, II: 8, III: 5, IV: 4, and V: 2.

DISTRIBUTION: This species is found 2,000 km and further upstream in the Amazon River and is often found with *Inia geoffrensis*.

Sotalia pallida

Sotalia pallida, known as buffeo blanco, was named by Gervais in 1855.

MORPHOLOGY: This species reportedly reaches a length of 1.7 m. They resemble buffeo negro in general appearance but have a thicker and shorter rostrum. The dorsal body is grayish ivory, and the ventral skin is somewhat lighter. The dorsal fin is relatively large. The dental formula is $\frac{30\text{-}31}{30\text{-}31}$.

DISTRIBUTION: This species has been recorded from Nauta, Peru, 2,560 km upstream of the Amazon River. Buffeo negro and buffeo blanco are spanish names which mean black dolphin and white dolphin, respectively. Some scientists believe that buffeo blanco is merely an adult buffeo negro and that both should be considered *Sotalia fluvitilis*.

Sotalia tucuxi

Sotalia tucuxi was named by Gray in 1856.

MOROPHOLOGY: This species is dull brownish gray all over. It has thirty teeth on each side of each jaw.

MISCELLANEOUS: Some scientists include this species, as well as *Sotalia pallida*, with *Sotalia fluviatilis*, and attribute the differences in body color to age variation.

Sotalia brasiliensis

Sotalia brasiliensis, known as the Brazilian dolphin, was named by Van Bénéden in 1875.

MORPHOLOGY: This species also resembles *Sotalia fluviatilis*. The dorsal skin is steel blue or dark-chocolate colored, and the ventral skin is white. The dental formula is $\frac{29\text{-}34}{29\text{-}34}$. There are fifty-four to fifty-five vertebrae, of which eleven to twelve are thoracic vertebrae.

DISTRIBUTION: This dolphin is reportedly so common in the Bay of Rio de Janeiro that one cannot cross the bay without seeing them playing near the ship.

Sotalia guianensis

Sotalia guianensis, known as the Guiana dolphin, was named by Van Bénéden in 1864.

MORPHOLOGY: This species resembles *Sotalia brasilensis* so closely that some scientists consider them the same species. The Guiana dolphin, however, has a dental formula of $\frac{32\text{-}35}{31\text{-}33}$, somewhat different from *Sotolia brasiliensis*, and a widely different distribution. Specimens 150 cm long weigh about 50 kg. Because of these differences, *Sotalia guianensis* is tentatively listed here as a different species.

DISTRIBUTION: These animals are found in the rivers of Guiana, in the northeast portion of South America.

Lagenodelphis

Lagenodelphis hosei

This genus and species were named by F. C. Fraser of the British Museum (Natural History), based on one skeletal specimen collected at the estuary of the Lutong River of the Sarawak Province of Borneo (northwest coast). Since the details of the outer characteristics are lacking, a description of this species cannot be made here.

FAMILY ORCAELIDAE

Some of the characteristics of Orcaelidae are as follows:
23b.
    1. Head blunt, without a distinct beak.
29a.
    2. Only two cervical vertebrae fused.
    3. Size small (less than 2.2 m).
    4. Less than twenty teeth in each row of upper jaw.

This new family is established by the author to include *Orcaella brevirostris* which was previously included in the Family Delphinidae.

Orcaella

The genus *Orcaella* was named by Gray in 1866.

Orcaella brevirostris

Figure 1–66. *Orcaella brevirostris,* known as the Irrawaddy dolphin, named by Owen in 1866.

MORPHOLOGY: The head of this dolphin is blunt, and though the rostrum is almost neligible, there is a lip-like swelling along the mouth. The well-developed eyes are located above the angle of the mouth. The external

auditory meatus opens behind the eyes. A neck is distinguishable from a
side view, particularly when the animal is poorly nourished. Fine tactile
hairs grow at 3 cm intervals along a line 2 cm above the mouth on each
side of the upper jaw of young animals. The first of those hairs is located
about 5 cm behind the tip of the snout. The blowhole is displaced to the
left of the body axis.

The dorsal fin, located slightly posterior to the midpoint of the body
length, is relatively short and curves backward at the top. There is a keel
running from the dorsal fin to the center of the tail fluke. The triangular,
tapered flippers are fairly large in size, reaching a length equal to one-
seventh of the body length. The anus is located about two-thirds back on
the ventral body surface. The dorsal body is dark blueish gray or black
and gradually becomes lighter toward the ventral side. Both surfaces of
the flippers, the dorsal fin, and the tail flukes are the same color as the
dorsal skin. The upper teeth are a little smaller in size than the lower teeth.
The dental formula is $\frac{15\text{-}17}{12\text{-}14}$, and there are more teeth on the upper jaw
than on the lower jaw. The skull is relatively short but broad, and the
rostrum is short and sharply pointed at the tip. The vertebral formula is
$C7 + T14 + L14 + Ca28 = 63$. Only the first and second cervical vertebrae are fused. The flipper has five fingers, the bones of which are I: 2, II:
8, III: 6, IV: 3, and V. 1. Occasionally the fifth finger is not ossified.

DISTRIBUTION: Irrawaddy dolphins are found primarily in coastal waters
of the Bay of Bengal, and in the Ganges, Brahmaputra, and Irrawaddy
Rivers. In addition, specimens have been caught at Port Vizagapatam,
off Madras, India, Singapore, Java, the Strait of Malacca, and the east coast
of the Malaya Peninsula, and others have been reported off northern
Australia.

FOOD: Food is apparently limited to fishes.

REPRODUCTION: According to Anderson (1871), a 2.1 m female captured
on June 1, 1871 had a full-term fetus 85 cm long (two-fifths the mother's
length).

BEHAVIOR: Although dolphins of this species are rarely seen swimming
alone, they generally form small herds of only a few individuals. According
to observations upstream in the Irrawaddy River, they swim by twisting
and rolling the body near the surface. They rarely expose the whole body
to the air and do not usually raise the tail flukes out of the water. These
dolphins generally inhabit waters of low salinity but apparently move out
to sea when the river is flooded.

MISCELLANEOUS: Anderson (1871) reported that the native fisherman on
the Irrawaddy River believe their dolphins have the power to entice fish

into the nets. They even name each dolphin and protect him. For that reason, it was reportedly difficult to obtain specimens.

RELATED SPECIES AND VARIATIONS: During his expedition to Yunnan, Anderson (1878) studied *Orcaella* and reported on *Orcaella fluminalis*, Anderson (1871). He compared it with *Orcaella brevirostris* as follows: (a) the dorsal fin is lower, smaller, and sharper near the top, (b) the melon is smaller and the rostrum is sharper, (c) the flippers are short and wide, (d) although the body colors are similar, this species has many scratches such as those on Risso's dolphin on the skin, (e) this species is not found at the estuary of the Irrawaddy River (where there is salt water) but about 1,280 km upstream in pure fresh water.

Ellerman and Morrison-Scott (1951) and Ellerman *et al.* (1953) divided Orcaellidae into two subspecies and assigned those from the Port of Vizagapatam, India to *Orcaella brevirostris* and those from the Irrawaddy River of Burma to *Orcaella brevirostris fluminalis*.

FAMILY PHOCOENIDAE

Phocoenidae have the following characteristics:

30a.

1. Light-colored anchor-shaped patches are absent on the ventral skin between the flippers.
2. More than five cervical vertebrae fused.
3. More than fifteen teeth in each row of upper jaw.
4. Body length less than 2.45 m.

The beak is not distinct. The head is gently curved from the tip of the snout to the blowhole. The lengths of upper and lower jaws are about equal. There are no grooves in the external skin of the throat. There is a notch at the center of the posterior edge of the fluke, and, usually, more than five cervical vertebrae are fused. This family includes three genera, *Neophocoena*, *Phocoenoides*, and *Phocoena*.

Neophocoena

31a.

The genus Neophocoena was named by Palmer in 1899. The most distinctive characteristic of its members is that they have no dorsal fins.

Neophocoena phocoenoides

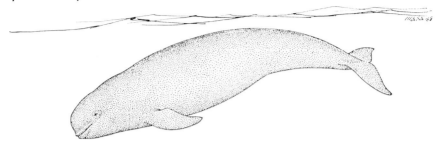

Figure 1–67. *Neophocoena phocoenoides,* known as the finless black porpoise, named by G. Cuvier in 1829.

OTHER COMMON NAME: Indian porpoise.

MORPHOLOGY: This species reaches a length of 1.9 m but is more commonly 1.5 m. The body gradually becomes thicker aft of the blowhole and reaches its maximum girth at the middle of the body. The flippers are about one-sixth of the body length. They are triangular and sharply pointed at the ends. The tail flukes are relatively large, reaching a total spread equal to about one-fourth of the body length. On the dorsal surface, where the dorsal fin should be located, there is a heightened section on which there is some round, scale-like tissue. The eyes are small and very indistinct. The body is generally blueish gray or slate gray (although there is much individual variation). Some individuals are paler on the ventral surface between the base of the flippers and the anus. The teeth are small, short, and compressed, and appear spade-shaped when viewed from the side. The upper and lower jaws have the same number of teeth. The dental formula is $\frac{15-19}{15-19}$. The skull is relatively flat and depressed. The length of the rostrum is about one-third of the condylobasal length. The breadth of the rostrum is almost equal to its length. The condylobasal length is about 1.5 times the greatest breadth of the skull. The vertebral formula is C7 + T13–14 + L11–14 + Ca28–31 = 60–63. The first five cervical vertebrae are fused. Usually there are fourteen pairs of ribs. Each flipper has five fingers, the bones of which are I: 2, II: 7, III: 6, IV: 4, and V: 2.

DISTRIBUTION: Finless black porpoises are widely distributed in coastal areas. They have been reported off the Cape of Good Hope toward the Indian Ocean, near Calcutta, Karachi, Singapore, Sumatra, Borneo, and Java, in the Strait of Malacca, in the East China Sea, and off the Japanese coast. Their northern limit is presently thought to be the Ojika Peninsula, Miyagi Prefecture in northern Japan. These animals venture into such protected inshore areas as Tokyo Bay, Ise Bay, and the Seto Inland Sea, and are seen occasionally in the Yangtze River as far upstream as the Tung Ting Lake.

FOOD: Although the main food item is small fish, this species also eats squid.

REPRODUCTION: Fraser (1937) reported that parturition occurs in October, and although the main season for parturition and breeding is the fall, both have also been observed in the spring.

Phocoenoides

The genus *Phocoenoides* was named by Andrews in 1911. Some of its principal characteristics are the following:
31b.
   1. Dorsal fin present.
32a.
   2. More than ninety vertebrae.
   3. White area of belly clearly separated from dorsal black.

Phocoenoides dalli dalli

Figure 1–68. *Phocoenoides dalli dalli,* known as the Dall porpoise, named by True in 1885.

MORPHOLOGY: Dall porpoises reach a length of 2.1 m and a weight of 145 kg. Males are larger than females. The body is thick and powerfully built. The head is rather small, comprising only about one-seventh of the total length. The lower jaw extends slightly beyond the tip of the upper jaw and the mouth opening slants slightly upward in a straight line. The dorsal body slopes gradually upward from the beak in a slight curve, levels off briefly around the blowhole and then continues upward rapidly toward the dorsal fin. The dorsal fin is located about two-fifths of the way from the snout to the flukes, is triangular, and curves slightly backward at the tip, and the body is thickest near its anterior insertion. At that point, the dorsoventral body is two-thirds as wide as it is high. Posterior to that point, the dorsal body gradually decreases in height. The caudal portion of the body comprises about one-fourth of the total length. The keels on both the dorsal and ventral sides of the caudal peduncle are quite distinct. The tail flukes are relatively small, reaching one-fifth the total body length. The small flippers are well forward in the body. Though the eyes are relatively small, they are very distinct. A distinct white portion which resembles a saddle on the undersurface of the animal begins just below the anterior insertion of the dorsal fin and ends at the anus.

The rostrum is relatively short, flat, and sharp on the end. Its length is 1.5 times its breadth and about three-fifths of the condylobasal length. The condylobasal length is 2.1 times the greatest length of the skull. The maxillary is rather short, and the mandible extends beyond the maxillary. The blowhole is large. The teeth are very small and in adults, rounded at the tips. The boundary between the crown and root is constricted. The dental formula is $\frac{23\text{-}28}{24\text{-}28}$, different from True's porpoise. There is an average of ninety-six vertebrae with a formula of C7 + T15–18 + L24–27 + Ca44–49 = 92–98. There are generally eighteen pairs of ribs, twelve of which are two-headed. All cervical vertebrae are fused, but the seventh can be separated by force. The flipper has five fingers of I: 2, II: 7, III: 5, IV: 3, and V: 1. There is always cartilage in the fifth finger, but the small ossified bone is often lost when specimens are prepared for presentation.

DISTRIBUTION: The Dall porpoise inhabits the cold waters of the North Pacific and migrates beyond the Aleutian chain into the Bering Sea. They are found along the coasts of Alaska and as far south as Baja California. Near Japan, they do not seem to migrate south of Choshi.

ABUNDANCE: Whaling fleets operating in Aleutian waters have reported a great many Dall porpoises. The population in the northwestern North Pacific may be as many as 30,000 to 50,000 animals.

FOOD: Dall porpoises feed on squid and schooling fishes.

BEHAVIOR: Kuroda (1953), Fraser (1937), and Hall and Kelson (1959), reported that Dall porpoises form small herds. The pelagic animals in Japanese waters do form herds of less than 100 individuals and groups approaching the coast tend to remain small. However, populations in the Aleutian waters and the Okhotsk Sea frequently form herds of 500 to 1,000 animals.

Dall porpoises are aggressive and relatively fast swimmers. When they race through the water, they slice through the surface to breathe, creating the characteristic spray by which this species can be identified.

MISCELLANEOUS: On February 18, 1963, a fisherman caught a completely black specimen 55 km off Kamaishi. There were several schools of five to ten True's and Dall porpoises in the area at that time. Two other black individuals were seen together. The specimen was a pregnant female 1.825 m long, weighing 102 kg. The fetus was a male, 32.5 cm in length.

Phocoenoides dalli truei

Figure 1–69. *Phocoenoides dalli truei,* known as True's porpoise, named by Andrews in 1911.

MORPHOLOGY: The body shape and color of this species closely resemble those of the Dall porpoise. Specimens reach a length of 2.1 m, though 2.0 m is more common, and a weight of 75 to 100 kg. The white coloration begins on the abdomen between the bases of the flippers and the anus and extends upward on the side of the body. In addition, a black anchor-shaped pattern on the abdomen extends forward from the anus. There are black spots on the nipple grooves. The edge of the dorsal fin and the posterior margin of the tail flukes are fringed with white. In both Dall and True's porpoises, there is considerable individual variation in the extension of these white fringes. Some specimens have white fringes at the flipper tips.

The skull is slender and the condylobasal length is 2.1 times the breadth of the skull. The rostrum is relatively small (three-sevenths of the condylobasal length) and is 1.5 times as long as it is wide. The dental formula is $\frac{19\text{-}23}{20\text{-}24}$. The vertebral formula is $C7 + T15\text{–}18 + L24\text{–}27 + Ca44\text{–}49 = 92\text{–}98$. All the cervical vertebrae are fused. The finger bones are I: 2, II: 7, III: 6, IV: 2 and V: 2. At the end of the metacarpus of the fifth finger, there is a cartilage which is sometimes ossified.

DISTRIBUTION: True's porpoise is limited to the northwestern part of the North Pacific, where it is found in warm waters more frequently than Dall porpoises. Although this species does not form very large herds, groups of 100 to 200 individuals have been observed. The aggressive swimming behavior and the spray characteristic of a Dall porpoise swimming at full speed is also characteristic of this species.

FOOD: True's porpoise is fond of squid but also feeds on schooling fish. Stomach content records of lantern fishes, which surface only during the night, indicate that these animals also feed at night.

REPRODUCTION: Since fetuses found in April and May were about 30 cm and others found in June were about 80 to 90 cm in length, the peak of parturition appears to be in summer.

MISCELLANEOUS: Although *Phocoenoides dalli dalli* and *Phocoenoides dalli truei* are similar in general appearance, they differ in proportional skull measurements, dental formulae, vertebral formulae, distribution, and adult size; these differences seem adequate to justify the establishment of a separate subspecies.

Phocoena

The genus *Phocoena* was named by G. Cuvier in 1817. Some of its characteristics are the following:

32b.

1. Less than seventy vertebrae.
2. White of underside gradually changes to black or gray of dorsum.

Phocoena phocoena

Figure 1–70. *Phocoena phocoena*, known as the common porpoise, named by Linnaeus in 1758.

Figure 1–71. Another view of *Phocoena phocoena*.

OTHER COMMON NAME: Harbor porpoise.

MORPHOLOGY: The common porpoise reaches a length of about 1.8 m and an average weight of 45 to 54 kg. The male is slightly larger than the female. The triangular dorsal fin is located slightly posterior to the midlength and leans forward. The dorsal surface is marine gray, while the ventral is white. The flippers and caudal peduncle are ultramarine, and the area at the base of the flippers is white. From the base of the flippers, a dark line runs forward to the angle of gape. Although there is a great deal of individual variation in the boundary between the dorsal gray and the ventral white, it is a zone of light gray. The first to sixth cervical vertebrae are all fused, but the seventh is free. The teeth are spade shaped, laterally compressed, and relatively small, reaching an average diameter of 2.5 mm at the crown. The dental formula is $\frac{23\text{-}28}{22\text{-}26}$.

DISTRIBUTION: Although this species is very common in the North Atlantic, it is also widely distributed in other parts of the world. In the Atlantic Ocean, the northern limit (Anderson, 1946) is Iceland, the White Sea, and the Davis Strait, and the southern limit is the Cape of Good Hope and the southern tip of South America. In the Pacific, they are found near the United States and Japan. Bobrinskoi (1944) reported that they also inhabit the Black Sea, the Sea of Azov, and the Mediterranean Sea. They are rarely seen in tropical waters.

MIGRATION AND ABUNDANCE: The common porpoise appears to be relatively abundant in the North Atlantic and in the eastern North Pacific, from Washington state northward, but somewhat scarce in the western North Pacific, where they only occasionally turn up in fish markets. The presence in the literature of the names *Phocoena phocoena* and *Phocoena vomerina* appears to result from confusion in nomenclature rather than from the actual existence of two different species.

FOOD: Though the main food items of this species are herring, small cods, and soles, they also eat squid and crustaceans. Occasionally, kelp or seaweed, sometimes with herring eggs attached, is found in their stomachs. When they chase herring, these porpoises are sometimes tangled and caught in gill nets set by fishermen.

BEHAVIOR: Common porpoises do not stay submerged for more than three or four minutes, They sometimes jump completely out of the water to breathe. When they are nursing, calves swim under the abdomen of the mother and both animals continue swimming. If the mother rolls or twists her body, the calf may bend her nipple at an angle to the axis of her body.

PARASITES: Cysts of many parasites are found in the blubber, parasitic flukes are reported in the liver, and some nematodes infest the throat.

VARIATIONS: Some scientists consider those *Phocoena* in the Black Sea a subspecies, *Phocoena phocoena relicta* (Abel, 1905).

Phocoena sinus

Figure 1–72. *Phocoena sinus,* known as the Gulf of California harbor porpoise, named by Norris and McFarland in 1958.

MORPHOLOGY: This is a new species was described by Norris from a skull found on the west coast of Mexico, inside the Gulf of California, in March of 1950. On the basis of the degree of ossification, the skull is assumed to be that of an adult, though it is smaller than that of any other species of this genus. Two other small adult skulls found subsequently support the possibility that members of this species are rather small or have a small head. When viewed laterally, the skull appears slightly curved. The rostrum extends further downwards than that of other *Phocoena* and the occipital condyles are somewhat lower on the skull. The general skull characteristics are intermediate between those of the common porpoise and those of the spectacled porpoise. The maxillary does not extend over the upper edge of the orbital fossa, and the premaxillary has a higher bump than the maxillary. The vomer is exposed at two locations of the palatal region, one in a diamond shape near the tip of the snout and the other in an oval shape at the front half of the palatine. The blowhole is relatively large and is located very much to the left at the top of the skull. The dental formula is $\frac{20\text{-}21}{18\text{-}18}$.

Phocoena dioptrica

Figure 1–73. *Phocoena dioptrica*, known as the spectacled porpoise, named by Lahille in 1912.

MORPHOLOGY: The average body length of this species is 1.8 m, but some individuals surpass 2.0 m. Unlike the case in the common porpoise, the maximum girth and the dorsal fin of the spectacled porpoise are both located at the midpoint of the body. The head is quite small and round. The flippers are triangular in shape, rounded at the tips, and located relatively close to the head. The anus is located rather close to the tail flukes, and the abdominal cavity is large. The body color is characteristic of this species. The entire abdomen is white, and the dorsal one-third is black. Hamilton (1941) observed that the white portion appears to expand as the animals age. A small but distinct boundary runs from the above the eye to the base of the tail flukes. The skin around the mouth is black. The eyes, which are located in the white portion of the body, are encircled with black. It is from this ring, which resembles a pair of spectacles and makes the eye appear larger than that of any other *Phocoena*, that this species derives its name.

The first five cervical vertebrae, one less than the common porpoise, are all fused. The vertebral formula is $C7 + T13 + L16 + Ca32 = 68$. Nine of the thirteen pairs of ribs are two headed. The last four pairs of ribs are single headed and when viewed laterally appear like the ribs of the pygmy right whale. The sternum is composed of four sections which seem to be fused together in a fairly early stage of development. There are eight pairs of sternal ribs and fifteen chevrons. The teeth are very small and appear spade-shaped when viewed from the side. The dental formula is $\frac{21-21}{17-17}$.

The anterior edges of the white flippers are gray, and a gray line runs from their base toward the corner of the mouth. The upper surface of the tail flukes is black, but the coloration is not continuous with the black of the dorsum. The undersurface of the tail flukes is white with gray lines radiating from the notch.

DISTRIBUTION: This is a rare species and the few specimens which have been collected to date were all found off South America from the La Plata River to South Georgia Island.

Phocoena spinipinnis

Figure 1–74. *Phocoena spinipinnis,* known as Burmeister's porpoise, named by Burmeister in 1865.

OTHER COMMON NAME: Black porpoise.

MORPHOLOGY: The body of this species is completely black and more closely resembles the shape of *Phocoenoides* than of *Phocoena*. The head is smaller and more slender than that of the common porpoise. The dorsal fin is located slightly posterior to the midpoint, and while its anterior edge is straight or slightly concave, the posterior edge is convex. Just anterior to the dorsal fin, there is a small spicular or scaly bump which is presumably vestigial. The keels on the caudal peduncle are distinct.

DISTRIBUTION: This species is found at the estuary of the La Plata River, off Cape Horn, and on the Pacific coast of South America as far north as Peru. It is considered very rare.

FAMILY GRAMPIDAE

The distinguishing characteristics of Grampidae are as follows:
30b.
  1. Anchor-shaped light-colored patch present on ventral skin between flippers.
  2. More than three cervical vertebrae fused.
  3. Usually less than fifteen teeth in each side of lower jaw.
  4. Adult body length more than 2.5 m.

33a.

5. Teeth absent in upper jaw.

Grampus griseus, Risso's dolphin is generally included in the family *Delphinidae*. However, it is established here as a new family for the following reasons: six cervical vertebrae are fused, there are no teeth in the upper jaw, and even fetal teeth seldom germinate in the upper jaw.

Grampus

The genus *Grampus* was named by Gray in 1828.

Grampus griseus

Figure 1–75. *Grampus griseus*, known as Risso's dolphin, named by G. Cuvier in 1812.

MORPHOLOGY: Adult Risso's dolphins are 4.0 to 4.3 m long. The anterior portion of the body is round and fat, but the posterior portion from the anus to the flukes is very slender. The keels on the dorsal and ventral surfaces are indistinct. The dorsal fin, located about the midpoint of the body length, is relatively long and narrow, sharply pointed on the end, and curved backward. The flippers resemble, but are somewhat shorter than, those of the family *Globicephalidae*. The tail flukes resemble those of beaked porpoises. When viewed laterally, the head resembles that of *Globicephalidae*, though the forehead is not as high. There is no beak. Along the body axis on the front of the head, there is a slight concave groove which is a unique characteristic of this species. The mouth opens fairly wide. There are no teeth in the upper jaw and only two to seven (average three or four) teeth on each lower jaw. Those teeth are relatively large (3.5 to 4.0 cm long and 1.5 cm in diameter) and are exposed from 2.5 to 3.0 cm.

The body is basically gray, but particularly in younger animals, the dorsal side is blueish and the ventral side is pale. In juveniles, the forehead and mouth are almost white. Though it is subject to some individual variation, there is an anchor-shaped portion on the abdomen between the flippers which may extend as far back as the anus. In some *Grampus*, the top of the dorsal fin and the anterior edges of the flukes and flippers are also pale. As these animals age, their color fades drastically. The dorsal body pales, and the abdomen and the forehead turn almost completely white. These changes, in combination with multiple body scars, make old animals appear almost completely white.

The rostrum of the skull is quite wide in front of the orbital fossa but, since teeth are lacking, narrows at the anterior end. The crest behind the nares is triangular and sharp at its summit. The premaxillary bone is wide at the rostrum and round on its external edge. The mandibular symphysis is short. The vertebral formula is $C7 + T12–13 + L18–19 + Ca30–31 = 68–69$. The first six cervical vertebrae are fused and form one big mass together with the seventh, a very thin vertebrae. The first six pairs of ribs are two headed. The flipper has five fingers of I: 2, II: 8–10, III: 5, IV: 3–5 and V: 1.

DISTRIBUTION: This species is widely distributed in the warm waters of the world. Though they generally prefer waters 10°C or warmer, one herd was reportedly discovered in water 5 to 6°C. They are found on both coasts of the Americas, near England, and between Cape Town and Singapore. Near Japan, they are found as far north as Hokkaido and the Kuril Islands area but seldom occur in the Okhotsk Sea. It has not been determined whether they inhabit the Japan Sea, but they are very frequently observed in the waters southward from the Sanriku Coasts (northeast of Japan).

FOOD: The most important food item is small squid, and when they are kept in captivity they are fed nothing else.

BEHAVIOR: They usually are found in relatively small herds of several to twenty individuals.

MISCELLANEOUS: Dr. Masayuki Nakajima reported that one individual, which died after three years and eight months in captivity at the Enoshima Marineland, Japan, had a pair of small teeth at the end of the upper jaw. The teeth were 3 cm long and 7 mm in maximum diameter, much smaller than the teeth of the lower jaw. There appeared to be four shallow sockets on each gum line, although only one had a tooth. Since Risso's dolphin generally lacks the upper teeth, this is rather an unusual example. An offspring of this animal has now been raised, and the growth of its teeth is of much interest.

FAMILY GLOBICEPHALIDAE

Even though this family was first established by Gray in 1866, it had not been commonly accepted and its members have usually been included in family *Delphinidae*. However, they are regarded as a separate family in this book for the following reasons: *Delphinidae* have a beak, a large number of teeth, a large number of vertebrae, and only two fused cervical vertebrae. In contrast, the *Globicephalidae* have no beak, fewer teeth, fewer vertebrae, in spite of relatively large body size, and more than three fused cervical vertebrae. The skull is generally broad but short. The rostrum is less than 1.5 times as long as it is wide. The condylobasal length is less than 1.6 times the greatest breadth of the skull. The volume of the ventricles of the brain relative to the skull is larger than in the dolphins. There are almost the same number of teeth on the upper and lower jaws, and there are not more than fifteen teeth on each row. *Delphinidae* have more than twenty teeth on each row.

Globicephala

The genus *Globicephala* was named by Lesson in 1828. Some of its principal characteristics are as follows:
33b.
1. Teeth present in upper jaw.
34a.
2. Dorsal fin situated on front half of body.
3. Height of dorsal fin shorter than length at base.

Globicephala scammoni

Figure 1–76. *Globicephala scammoni*, known as the blackfish, named by Cope in 1869.

OTHER COMMON NAMES: Pacific pilot whale.

MORPHOLOGY: The body of the blackfish is more dorsoventrally compressed than that of other pilot whales. The largest among *Globicephala* in the Pacific, they grow as long as 6.3 m. The entire body is black. Although the light, anchor-shaped patch which occurs on the underbelly of some pilot whales is generally absent in this species, some specimens, such as one being maintained at Marineland of the Pacific in California, do have such a marking.

The body is quite fat, and the maximum girth is at the middle, near the posterior of the dorsal fin. The dorsal fin is located about one-third from the anterior end (further forward than that of the other species of this genus). The anus is also located fairly forward, so the caudal portion of the body is relatively long. The keels on the tail stock are very distinct on both the dorsal and the ventral sides. The tail flukes reach a total spread of about one-fifth of the body length.

The flippers are narrow, pointed, and quite long (over one-fifth of the body length in some individuals). Though the last two-thirds of the flipper is curved backward, the curvature is not so extreme as it is in other pilot whales. Blackfish have a large mouth with eight to twelve teeth on each row. Most of the specimens collected near Japan, however, have only eight teeth on each side. The skull is short and wide, but the condylobasal length is greater than the greatest breadth of the skull. The rostrum is only slightly longer than it is wide. The premaxillary is extremely broad. The ventricles of the brain are relatively large. The vertebral formula is $C7 + T11 + L13 + Ca28 = 59$. The finger bones are I: 4, II: 10–14, III: 11, IV: 3, and V: 2.

DISTRIBUTION: This species is found only in the North Pacific. Near Japan, there are no records of their being captured south of the Izu Peninsula. Considerable numbers are taken annually off Sanriku, and some specimens are caught near Hokkaido, but few have been reported in the Okhotsk Sea (north of 44°N).

FOOD: In the wild, blackfish appear to have a strong preference for squid. In captivity, however, they may also eat such fish as mackerel.

BEHAVIOR: Herds of Pacific pilot whales may consist of as many as several hundred individuals and usually includes a few animals who lead the herd in migrating, escaping, and attacking. These pilot whales appear to be afraid of killer whales and may easily be chased into bays or inlets by killer-whale sound played in the water. Harassment by killer whales is believed to have caused entire herds of this, as well as other species of pilot whales, to beach themselves.

Globicephala macrorhyncha

Figure 1–77. *Globicephala macrorhyncha*, known as the shortfinned blackfish, named by Gray in 1846.

MORPHOLOGY: Males of this species reach a length of 6 m. The head is round and when viewed laterally, the mouth appears large. The front half of the body is quite chunky. The dorsal fin, located two-fifths from the anterior end, is relatively small and sharply curved backward. The body behind the anus is slender, and except in old males, the keels on the tail stock are indistinct. The total spread of the tail flukes is less than one-fifth of the body length. The length of the flippers is about one-sixth of the body length. The backward curving of the flippers is not pronounced, but the tip is sharply pointed. Most of the body is black, but the abdominal skin is lighter and there is a white cross or anchor-shaped patch between the flippers.

The skull is very large relative to the body size, and the rostrum is thick. The appearance of the premaxillary is one of the most important characteristics of the species. It is large and flat, becomes broader at the anterior, and when viewed from above, almost covers the maxillary. The blowhole is short but wide. These whales have fewer teeth than other members of the genus. The dental formula is $\frac{7\text{-}9}{7\text{-}9}$. The vertebral formula is C7 + T11 + L12 + Ca27 = 57. The phalangeal formula is I: 3, II: 9, III: 9, IV: 2, and V: 1.

DISTRIBUTION: They are found in the Pacific and Indian oceans and inhabit slightly warmer waters than *Globicephala scammoni*.

Globicephala melaena

Figure 1–78. *Globicephala melaena,* known as the pilot whale, named by Traill in 1809.

OTHER COMMON NAMES: Atlantic blackfish, caàing whale, calling whale.

MORPHOLOGY: When viewed laterally, *Globicephala melaena* have a round high forehead and no constriction between the head and body. Since the cervical vertebrae are very short, the flippers appear to be attached at the neck. The dorsal fin is located slightly anterior to the center of the body. Although the fin is high, it appears low because the base is relatively long. Although the body diameter declines from the midportion toward the tail flukes, the dorsal and ventral keels are very distinct. The flippers are about one-fifth of the body length and are pointed at the tips. A sharp backward curve begins just short of the flipper midlength.

The skin is generally charcoal gray, but the abdomen is a little lighter in color. The tips of dorsal fin and tail flukes are also slightly lighter in some individuals. A light-colored, melon-shaped patch runs toward the anus from a line between the bases of the flippers and the lower jaws.

The mouth is fairly large and there are eight to ten teeth on each row. Although the teeth are large, 5 cm in length and 1.5 cm in diameter, they are smaller than those of *Globicephala macrorhyncha.* The greatest breadth of the skull is shorter than the condylobasal length but considerably greater than the length of skull less the rostrum. Because of the broad premaxillary, the rostrum is flat. On typical specimens, the breadth and length of the rostrum are equal. The width of the premaxillary is greatest at the middle between the anterior end of the skull and external nasal opening, a characteristic which is quite unique for members of this genus. The nasal opening is broad. The thin wall of the vomer is high. The vertebral formula is $C7 + T11 + L12–13 + Ca28–29 = 58–60$. The phalanges are I: 3–4, II: 9–14, III: 9–11, IV: 2–3, V: 1–2.

DISTRIBUTION: This species has been reported as far north as Newfoundland, both on the American and European sides of the Atlantic Ocean.

FOOD: Although they feed mainly on squid, some reportedly eat schooling fishes as well.

MISCELLANEOUS: These animals are called pilot whales because European fisherman, who believed that there are always herring under these whales, use them to pilot their boats to herring.

Orcinus

The genus *Orcinus* was named by Fitzinder in 1860. Some of its principal characteristics are as follows:

34b.
1. Dorsal fin situated about middle of body.
2. Height of dorsal fin equal to or greater than the length of its base.

35a.
3. Adults more than 5 m long.

36a.
4. Four cervical vertebrae fused.
5. Cross sections of teeth are oval.

Orcinus orca

Figure 1–79. *Orcinus orca*, known as the killer whale, named by Linnaeus in 1758.

MORPHOLOGY: These whales are easily identified by their striking body colors and prominent dorsal fin. The dorsal body is black, and the ventral surface is white. The boundary between these two colors is quite distinct. A white oval spot, located above and slightly behind the eye, resembles a large eye from a distance. On the latter half of the body, the white ventral color projects well up the sides. Just behind the dorsal fin, there is generally a pale gray patch called the saddle which appears diamond shaped when viewed from above. The saddle is absent in some specimens. The lower jaw and, on some specimens, the lips of the upper jaw, are white. The lower surface of the flippers is black, but the underside of the tail flukes is commonly white fringed with black. When killer whales are born, the height of the dorsal fin related to body length is only slightly greater than that of the common dolphin. However, the proportion continues to increase as the animals age and is more than one-fourth the body length on a 9 m male. The dorsal fin is much larger in males than in females and may curve slightly forward at the tip in old bulls. More generally, however, the anterior edge of the fin curves slightly backward while the posterior edge is straight. The flippers are extremely large, round at the tips, and oval in shape. The tail flukes are thick and the total spread may be as much as one-fifth of the body length. Males reach a length of 9.6 m and females attain a length of 8.3 m (based on the measurements of specimens collected in Japanese coastal waters since 1948). However, a study of the body-length frequency distribution indicates that most of the adult males are 6.3 to 6.8 m long and most of the females are about 6.1 m.

Instead of a beak, killer whales have a slight demarcation which somewhat resembles an upper lip. The outline (or profile) of the body is very slightly constricted at the blowhole, but otherwise, the girth gradually increases from the head toward the cross section at the dorsal fin, where the maximum girth is attained. The caudal portion is slender. When viewed laterally, the mouth opening is as large as one-eleventh to one-twelfth of the body length. The eye is located above and behind the angle of gape, just under the white oval area, but since it is surrounded by black skin, it is not easily seen.

On both upper and lower jaws, there are ten to thirteen (most commonly twelve) conical teeth, oval in cross section, which are as long as 13 cm. These teeth are quite strong and the upper and lower teeth interlock when the jaws close. They are sharply pointed and curved inward and slightly backward at the tip. They are covered with enamel and the crown constitutes about one-third of the tooth. The rest is buried in the gum. The teeth of most odontocetes are used to seize prey, which is then swallowed whole. In addition, killer whales use their strong teeth to bite, tear off, and chew certain large food items.

The rostrum is very broad and long, and its length is commonly about 1.36 times its breadth. The condylobasal length is about 1.36 times the greatest breadth of the skull. The breadth of the thin premaxilla is very small in relation to that of the maxilla. The vertebral formula is C7 + T11–12 + L10 + Ca21–24 = 50–52 (most commonly total = 52). The first three to four cervical vertebrae are fused. The first six or seven out of twelve pairs of ribs are two headed. The flipper has five fingers, the bones of which are I: 2, II: 7, III: 5, IV: 4, and V: 3.

DISTRIBUTION: Killer whales are distributed widely in the oceans of the world.

MIGRATIONS AND ABUNDANCE: Although killer whales seem centered in the Atlantic and Pacific Oceans, they travel into most seas of the world. No other whales make such movements. Generally, other whale populations in the northern hemisphere are isolated from those in the southern hemisphere. In addition, there is usually not even intermingling between Atlantic and Pacific populations. For these reasons, there are usually species differences between whales of different areas. This general rule does not apply to killer whales however. There is a single species which travels extensively. They move through the Arctic and the Antarctic Seas, The North Pacific, the South Pacific, and further around South America to the North Atlantic. Such movements must take long periods of time.

FOOD: Killer whales appear to have a varied diet. About six hundred animals examined near Japan over a ten-year period indicated that fish were the main food items. The most abundant fishes in stomach contents were cod and flat fishes, but sardines, tuna, salmon, skipjack, and squid were also found. There were only rare reports of octopus, probably because octopus are nonschooling coastal dwellers. Next to fishes, dolphins and whales are the food items most frequently found. True's porpoises, Dall porpoises and white-sided dolphins were the cataceans most commonly retrieved from stomach contents. In addition, whaling vessels have frequently reported killer whales attacking sei whales, minke whales, Baird's whales, and pilot whales. Killer whales have also fed on large sharks, fur seals, and seals. The fact that of the six hundred specimens sampled, only thirty had empty stomachs, indicates that killer whales are excellent hunters. They also appear to be voracious eaters. Eschricht (1862) of Denmark reported finding thirteen dolphins and fourteen seals in the stomach of one 7 m killer whale. In addition to these twenty-seven animals, another seal was hung in the throat.

REPRODUCTION: Since fetuses of over 2.0 m have been recorded and a calf of 2.8 m in length was beached in 1927 in Britain, the calves may be around 2.5 m at the time of birth. Age determination by teeth indicates that females attain sexual maturity at an age of four years and a length of about 4.5 m.

BEHAVIOR: Killer whale herds are relatively small, ranging from only a few individuals to as many as forty or fifty whales. They are generally pelagic animals but occasionally enter into coastal waters (even into inland seas). They are rapid swimmers and are very thrilling to see in the ocean, with their large dorsal fins slicing the water at high speeds.

LONGEVITY: Killer whales presumably live over thirty-five years. At one time, the killer whale was classified as two species, *Orcinus orca*, the Atlantic killer whale, and *Orcinus rectipinna* (Cope, 1869), the Pacific killer whale. However, studies have indicated that there are not significant variations.

Pseudorca

The genus *Pseudorca* was named by Reinhardt in 1862. Its distinguishing skeletal characteristics are as follows:
36b.
  1. Cross sections of teeth circular.
  2. Six cervical vertebrae fused.

Pseudorca crassidens

Figure 1–80. *Pseudorca crassidens,* known as the false killer whale, named by Owen in 1846.

MORPHOLOGY: The head of this species is rounded, though not bulbous as in pilot whales, and is characterized by a large mouth opening. The flippers, located somewhat forward on the body, reach a length of about one-tenth of the body length, are sharply pointed at the tip, and curve backward on the anterior edge at the midlength. In most specimens, there are two prominences along the posterior edge of the flipper. The dorsal fin is relatively small and is located slightly anterior to the body midlength. The tip of the fin is pointed and the posterior edge is curved inward. The total spread of the tail flukes is about one-fifth of the body length. The keels on the caudal portion are not pronounced.

The body is all black and the color does not change with age. The anchor-shaped patterns, common on other species of the family, are scarcely seen on the underside. Male *Pseudorca crassidens* reach a length of 5.7 m, and females 5.0 m. There are eight to eleven large, strong teeth (about 8 cm long and 1.5 to 2.0 cm in diameter) on each side of each jaw. The vertebral formula is $C7 + T10 + L10 + Ca23 = 50$. Six of the ten pairs of ribs are two-headed. The phalangeal formula is I: 2, II: 8, III: 6, IV: 4, and V: 2.

DISTRIBUTION: This species may be found everywhere except in the colder seas.

FooD: The main food item is squid, but these whales also feed on fairly large fishes.

REPRODUCTION: The reports by Hall and Kelson (1959) and Fraser (1937) of fetuses of various sizes at the same time of the year indicates that breeding may occur throughout the year.

BEHAVIOR: Although large herds are believed to be rare, gatherings of several hundred to a thousand individuals are occasionally observed in warm waters in wintertime. These schools probably represent breeding migrations.

Feresa

The genus *Feresa* was named by Gray in 1871. Its principal chacteristics are the following:

35b.
1. Adults less than 3.1 m long.
2. Three cervical vertebrae fused.

37a.
3. Approximately seventy vertebrae.
4. Less than fifteen teeth in each row of upper jaw.

Feresa attenuata

Figure 1–81. *Feresa attenuata*, known as the slender blackfish, named by Gray in 1871.

OTHER COMMON NAMES: Slender pilot whale, pygmy killer whale.

MORPHOLOGY: Males reach 2.5 m in length and females 2.4 m. The body shape resembles that of the false killer whale. Although the body is generally black, there are several irregular white patches around the mouth, an oval white patch slightly posterior to the navel, and in some specimens, a distinctive light pattern on the side of the body. This pattern disappears after the animal dies, particularly when the skin has dried. As in pilot whales and Risso's dolphins, there is a light-colored, anchor-shaped patch between the flippers.

The flippers are about one-eighth of the body length, inserted well forward on the body, and do not curve backward as sharply on the anterior edge as those of *Globicephala* and *Pseudorca*. The triangular dorsal fin is sharply pointed at the end and is located near the middle of the back. Its posterior edge curves slightly inward. The tail flukes are typically dolphin shaped. When viewed laterally, the head is intermediate in appearance between *Globicephala* and *Pseudorca*. When viewed from above, it appears to be laterally compressed, narrowing toward the tip of the snout. The rostrum of the skull is about one-half as long as the condylobasal length, and three-fifths of its breadth. When viewed from above, the skull has a marked asymmetry to the left. The dental formula is $\frac{10\text{-}11}{11\text{-}13}$ but many specimens have one fewer teeth on the right side than on the left side. The vertebral formula is $C7 + T12 + L16\text{-}17 + Ca32\text{-}34 = 68\text{-}71$. The first three cervical vertebrae are fused. Five pairs of ribs are two headed.

DISTRIBUTION: Though found in the North Pacific, they have been sighted most frequently in Japanese waters. *Feresa attenuata* are also thought to inhabit the warm waters of the Atlantic Ocean.

MISCELLANEOUS: Gray (1871) described two species, *Feresa intermedia* and *Feresa attenuata*, based on the two skulls donated to the British Museum of Natural History. Since there were no records of *Feresa intermedia* from 1871 to 1952, it was assumed to be rare. In 1952, Munesato Yamado introduced the first whole skeleton, caught at Taiji, Wakayama Prefecture, Japan. Another specimen was later collected in the equatorial waters off West Africa. In January, 1963, fourteen specimens were captured alive at Sagami Bay and kept at the Ito Aquarium. Thirteen of the animals would take no food and died within ten days. The fourteenth was maintained for a month on sardines but died of acute pneumonia.

Peponocephala

The genus *Peponocephala* was named by Nishiwaki and Norris in 1966. Its distinguishing characteristics are as follows:
37b.
1. Approximately eighty vertebrae.
2. More than fifteen teeth in each row of upper jaw.

Peponocephala electra

Figure 1–82. *Peponocephala electra,* known as the many-toothed blackfish, named by Gray in 1846.

MORPHOLOGY: The males grow as large as 2.8 m in body length, and females are slightly shorter. Although the body shape is similar to that of the false killer whale and the slender blackfish, this animal has a much larger number of teeth. The body is mostly a dark gray which lightens slightly toward the underside. The skin of both lips and the area around the anus and the genital aperture are unpigmented. Other unpigmented patches are scattered just anterior to the navel (these are not usually scars left by parasites or bites). An anchor-shaped patch of light color is observed between the flippers.

These animals have no beak, but the head gradually expands from the tip of the snout. When observed from above, the tip of the rostrum is pointed. The flippers are about one-fifth of the body length, only slightly curved, and pointed at the tip. The triangular dorsal fin is situated at about the middle of the back and leans backward. The total spread of tail flukes is about one-fourth of body length. The length of the rostrum of the skull is about 55 per cent of the condylobasal length, and its breadth at the base is about three-fifths of the length. The antorbital notches are very remarkable. The dental formula is $\frac{22\text{-}25}{21\text{-}24}$. The vertebral formula is C7 + T14 + L17 + Ca44 = 82. The anterior three cervical vertebrae are fused. The phalangeal formula of the flipper is I: 3, II: 9, III: 7, IV: 4, and V: 3.

DISTRIBUTION: They are found in warm regions of the North Pacific and Atlantic Oceans.

MISCELLANEOUS: Gray (1846) had named a species *Lagenorhynchus electra* but had not described its appearance. One specimen of this species was captured in 1963 at Sagami Bay, and several hundred were collected in 1965 at Suruga Bay. Nakajima and Nishiwaki, who immediately studied those specimens, concluded (based on the external morphology and skeletons) that they should not be included in *Lagenorhynchus*. After his study of a juvenile caught in Hawaii in 1964, Norris of the University of

California reached the same conclusion. After discussions on the morphological characteristics, Nishiwaki and Norris established the new genus *Peponocephala* in 1966. Although it was difficult to decide where to place this species, we now include it in family *Globicephalidae* pending further study.

PINNIPEDIA

All seals, sea lions, and walruses are amphibious and spend considerable periods of time out of the water. Thus these animals have adapted to both a terrestrial and an aquatic existence. Pinnipedia have short, thick fur. The tail is very short and flattened, and the limbs are adapted to an aquatic life. The five digits of the end of each limb are covered with a thick web of skin. In the forelimbs, the first digit is usually longest, but in the hindlimbs the first and the fifth digits are generally longer than the others. Although the claws at the ends of the digits are well developed in most species, they are rudimentary in some.

There is no clavical. The ilium is short and lacks its anterior part. The ischiatic bones are not fused in the female but are joined by a very short suture in the male. In the skull, the interorbital widths are short, the facial index is short and wide, there is no lachrymal bone, and the palatine is only slightly distant from the frontal bone. The tympanic bulla is formed by the tympanic and upper tympanic bones. The external acoustic meatus is ossified. The maxillary concha is large, and the rami fill the anterior nasal cavium. The dentition is not replaced, but the first embryonal teeth are degenerated. The molars, unlike the premolars, are not biscuspid, are $P \frac{4}{4}$, $M \frac{1}{1}$ in most cases, and are called cheek or post-canine teeth. There are two pairs of lesser incisors which, at least in the mandible, are degenerated.

There is a bicornuate uterus, a zonal placenta, and one or two pairs of mammary teats on the abdomen.

Superfamily Otarioidea

The distinguishing characteristics of the superfamily Otarioidea are as follows:
38a.
1. Forelimbs oarlike and long (more than one-fourth of body length); locomotion in water accomplished mainly by use of forelimbs.
2. Hindlimbs can be turned forward; locomotion on land accomplished by walking or running.
3. Soft cartilaginous tips extend far beyond claws on each digit of fore-flipper.

4. Distinct claws present on three middle digits and claws on marginal digits of hindflipper rudimentary.
5. All surfaces of all flippers sparsely haired or naked.
6. Mammae have four teats.
7. All species polygamous; males distinctly larger than females.
8. Tympanic bones relatively small, flattened, thin-walled.
9. Mastoid process often prominent.
10. Postcanines of most species have one prominent cusp and sometimes one or two minor cusps.

Otarioidea includes sea lions or walking seals. There are two living families in this superfamily—Otariidae and Odobenidae.

FAMILY OTARIIDAE

Otariidae have the following characteristics:
39a.

1. Body slender and elongated.
2. External ear pinna present (cartilaginous, pointed, conical, up to 50 mm in length.)
3. Tail small but distinct.
4. Five claws of forelimb rudimentary.
5. Testes scrotal.
6. Fifteen thoracic vertebrae.
7. All surfaces of all flippers naked, smooth and leathery.
8. Supraorbital process well developed.
9. Sagittal crest present.
10. Dentention of normal full-growth adult is $I \frac{3}{2}$, $C \frac{1}{1}$, $PC \frac{5(-7)}{5}$.

The body is slender and shaped like an elongated spindle. The forelimbs are longer than the hindlimbs and have degenerated claws. There are sharp-tipped ear pinnae that reach 50 mm in vertical length in some species. The dental formula in adults is $I \frac{3}{2}$, $C \frac{1}{1}$, $PC \frac{5(-7)}{5} = 34(38)$. In the embryonic stage it is $I \frac{2}{3}$, $C \frac{1}{1}$, $PC \frac{3}{3} = 26$. The mandible is not firmly symphysized and contains two or more external foramen. The eyes are large, with well-developed orbital nodules. The septum between the orbits is incomplete.

Adult males are larger than females. On the forelimbs, the outermost or first digit is longest and the remainder are progressively shorter toward the inside. On the hindlimbs, the second to the fourth digits are shorter and equipped with well-developed claws, while those of the larger first and fifth digits are degenerated. The mastoid process of the temporal bone is distinctly protruded, though apparently separated from the typanic bulla, which is not so large as that in Phocidae.

SUBFAMILY OTARIINAE

The following are characteristics of the Subfamily Otariinae:

40a.

1. Pelage has only one layer of coarse hair.
2. First digit of foreflipper longer than second.
3. Marginal digits of hindflippers distinctly longer than middle three.

Eumetopias

The genus *Eumetopias* was named by Gill in 1866. Some of its principal characteristics are these:

41a.

1. Inhabits only the North Pacific.

42a.

2. Conspicuous gap between fourth and fifth postcanines (about the width of two teeth).
3. Width of skull at canines less than 29 per cent of skull length.

Eumetopias jubata

Figure 1–83. *Eumetopias jubata,* known as Steller's sea lion, named by Schreber in 1776.

OTHER COMMON NAME: Northern sea lion.

MORPHOLOGY: Though Steller's sea lion is similar in appearance to *Zalophus californianus*, it is very much larger. Males are often over 3.0 m long and weigh 1,000 kg. A skull of a large male measured 398 mm in total length (condylobasal length) and 232 mm in mastoid width. Females are usually 2.5 m long and weigh about 300 kg. In females, the skull is about 327 mm in length and 158 mm in mastoid width (Scheffer, 1958).

Males are generally cork colored but are darker on the chest and abdomen. Females are comparatively lighter, but pups are blackish. A mane of longer hair grows on the back of the neck, but there is no underfur at any stage.

The parietal bone is slightly depressed. The dental formula is $I \frac{3}{2}$, $C \frac{1}{1}$, $PC \frac{5}{5} = 34$. There is a space between the fourth and fifth post-canines which constitutes 5 to 8 per cent of the skull length and could be filled with two postcanines. In a few cases, there are more than five pairs of postcanines in the maxilla.

DISTRIBUTION: Steller's sea lions are found only in the Pacific, where they are distributed mainly on rocky islands off the coast from the Bering Sea to the southern coast of California on the United States side and along the coast of Sanriku on the Japanese side. Recently they have become abundant on the coast of Hokkaido, especially on the Shiretoko Peninsula, and the Rishiri Islands. Although there have been some occurrences in Korean waters, there are no recent reports from that area. The northern limit of their range appears to be Herschell Island.

On the California coast, fewer adult males are seen during the winter than in summer, indicating that individuals migrate northward in winter and return in early summer. The adult and subadult males of the Aleutian rookeries move north in late summer as far as St. Lawrence Island and Nunivak Island, and some as far as the Bering Strait, returning when the ice begins to form. There is also seasonal movement between the individual islands of the Aleutian chain.

ABUNDANCE: There appear to be 250,000 to 300,000 animals.

FOOD: They consume a wide variety of fish and squids.

REPRODUCTION: There are large breeding colonies off Sakhalin, and on Ion and Yamskye Islands on the eastern coast of Kamchatka and a single breeding colony on Walrus Island in the Probilofs. In addition, there are large breeding colonies on Kodiak, Chicagof, Baranof and the Prince of Wales Islands, off the Alaskan coast, the Scott Island, off British Columbia, and Ano Nuevo Island, off California.

The breeding season begins early in May when the adult bulls arrive and take up their territories. Females arrive two or three weeks later, harems are formed, and the pups are born within a day or two. The bulls continue to control harems of ten to fifteen females from May to August. Mating takes place shortly after parturition, between late May and early July, but the blastocyst is not implanted until October. In any one year, there are a few cows which may miss a pregnancy. These cows may suckle their pup for more than a year. Males are believed to become sexually mature at five, females at three years of age.

Newborn pups are 1 m or slightly longer and weigh approximately 20 kg. They have a thick grayish brown coat which changes to dark brown after six months and to the lighter color of the adult by the end of the second year. The mother may carry her pup by grasping its neck in her mouth. Albino pups with pink flippers and eyelids have been observed and appear to have some difficulty seeing clearly.

BEHAVIOR: These sea lions are very cautious animals. They often haul out on land to rest but quickly escape into the water with the slightest alarm. When an individual is shot, the entire group disappears into the water instantly. Because their groups are always well controlled, Steller's sea lions are difficult to capture. Individuals sometimes venture close to fishing boats, but if they become at all suspicious they will move a distance away from the boat and bark loudly.

CAPTIVITY: Abashiri Aquarium in Hokkaido once captured several females which were tangled in a fishing net. Most died shortly afterward, but one survived and gave birth in captivity. Both mother and pup thrived for a long time, feeding on sole and cod. Maruyama Zoo, Sappolo, Hokkaido, captured a relatively young male and maintained it for a time. Atami Aquarium, Shizuoka Prefecture, also kept a one- or two-year-old pup which had been caught in the Izu Seven Islands. That animal was so violent that the attendants were sometimes in danger. To date, no Steller's sea lions have been trained to perform in a show, though a young female and a five-year-old male which underwent training for research purposes at the Marine Bioscience Facility, Point Mugu, California, learned well. Otaru Aquarium in Hokkaido, Ueno Zoo in Tokyo, and Nagoya Aquarium all had luck in capturing members of this usually difficult-to-catch species. In addition, Higashiyama Zoo in Tokyo captured several and succeeded in keeping them to maturity.

Zalophus

The genus *Zalophus* was named by Gill in 1866. The distinguishing characteristics of its skull are as follows:
42b.
   1. Gap between fourth and fifth postcanines small or absent.
   2. Width of skull at canines less than 23 per cent of skull width.

Zalophus californianus

Figure 1–84. *Zalophus californianus,* known as the California sea lion named by Lesson in 1828. (After Peterson, Richard S. and Bartholomew, George A.: *The Natural History and Behavior of the California Sea Lion.*)

MORPHOLOGY: The body of the California sea lion is slender and contains no underfur. The snout and the ear pinnae are small. Males are dark brown, dotted with lighter areas, have a mane of longer hair on the neck, and when they are mature have a high sagittal crest which may reach 38 mm. The average male is 2.4 m long and weighs about 380 kg. Females are considerably smaller and are straw colored with darker areas on the throat and breast. The limbs of both males and females are dark brown.

The palatine bone is comparatively short, comprising only 37 to 45 per cent of the skull length. The external auditory meatus is narrow, and the tympanic bulla is irregular in shape. The distance from the palatal notch to the incisors is less than 45 per cent of the skull length and the anterior region of the palate is flat or only slightly concave, with the depth of the concavity sometimes reaching 9 mm. The width of the external nasal openings is less than 10 per cent of the skull length (Scheffer, 1958). The dental formula of the adult is $I \frac{3}{2}$, $C \frac{1}{1}$, $PC \frac{5-6}{5}$ $(P \frac{4}{4}, M \frac{1-2}{1}) = 34\text{-}36)$.

DISTRIBUTION: This species is limited to the North Pacific. As its name suggests, it occurs along the California coasts, but distinct populations are also found on the Galapagos Islands and off the Japanese coast. Along the Californian and Mexican coasts, they occur chiefly on such small islands as those in the Santa Barbara group and on San Nicolas, San Clemente, Los Coronados, Guadalupe, San Benito, and Cedros. In addition, there is at least one small rookery off the Sonoran coast in the Gulf of California. Although animals are present in these areas all year around, there is a certain amount of seasonal movement. Many bulls move north in the winter and are reported along the Oregon and Washington coasts and as far north as Vancouver Island, British Columbia. The migrations are not nearly so extensive as those of *Callorhinus ursinus*.

ABUNDANCE: The population of *Zalophus californianus* is as large as 50,000 to 100,000. Although Scheffer (1958) reported that there were from 200 to 300 *Zalophus californianus japonicus* in the coastal waters of Japan, the population is now probably not that large and may even be extinct. There are from 20,000 to 50,000 *Zalophus californianus wollebaeki*.

FOOD: California sea lions are fond of squid, fish, and octopus, but apparently do not eat spined benthic fishes. A mature male in captivity may eat as much as 30 kg of fish per day. From May through July, during the mating season, adult animals, especially males, lose their appetite. This appetite loss occurs even in captive animals.

REPRODUCTION: King (1964) reported that very little work has been done on the activities of this sea lion in the wild, despite their availability for zoos and circuses. However, Peterson and Bartholomew (1966) have recently reported on some extensive studies.

Except on the Galapagos Islands, the breeding season is from the end of May through June. Breeding males usually own about fifteen females, which are loosely organized into harems, and patrol their territories. Females probably mate soon after parturition, remain pregnant 342 to 365 days, and give birth to a single dark-brown pup about 65 cm in length and 9 kg in weight. Lactations begins about two hours after parturition. Pups remain on land for about ten days before taking to the water; nursing continues for five to six months. The nipple is very small and may be seen only when the mother is lying on her side. Pups make a lapping noise when they nurse. Nursing occurs at about two-hour intervals and lasts about ten minutes.

Captive California sea lions have reproduced successfully in many zoological gardens. A female sea lion in the Ueno Zoo gave birth to young three years in a row. The first year, she only nursed the pup for the first two months. The second year, however, she continued to nurse the pup and shared the same enclosure with it until two days before her third parturition.

Another captive female, mated with a male South African fur Seal (*Arctocephalus pusillus*), produced a pup in each of three successive years. The first two died within twenty-four hours, but the third, a male, lived for at least six months and was said to bear a close resemblance to its father. Lactation usually lasts about ten months in captivity. Captive females have been seen to eat the placenta.

BEHAVIOR: California sea lions are prudent and vocal animals. Whenever a large group is asleep on the rocks, there is invariably at least one animal which raises its head periodically to listen or sniff the air. If it senses danger, it will begin a barking which awakens the other animals and becomes contagious. If the danger appears serious enough, a male or an elderly female leads the way into the water, followed closely, sometimes in a stampede, by the rest of the group.

Vocalizations are frequent and undoubtedly play an important part in the maintenance of territories. In situations where one animal is asserting dominance over another, the stronger individual may bark, "oh, oh, oh." Adults may also bark a husky "ga, ga, ga." Pups emit a sound that resembles "ah, ah, ah," but as they grow, their voices become deep and sonorous.

California sea lions appear to have a long memory. In 1950, Ueno Zoo imported a young male, two or three years old, that had had about one year of training. In 1953, they added a female, about the same age, to the training. The two animals performed on exhibit until 1957, when their training was interrupted. Two years later, however, when they were required on short notice to appear for a TV show, they performed perfectly.

LONGEVITY: There are records of captive animals living twelve to fourteen years, and one, a female, was thirty years old when it died.

VARIATIONS: The basic subspecies is *Zolaphus californianus californianus* (Lesson, 1828), the California sea lion, which is distributed in the eastern Pacific from British Columbia (40°N) to Mexico. The fur coloration of this subspecies is reportedly darker than that of the other subspecies.

Zalophus californianus japonicus (Peters, 1866), the Japanese sea lion, is reportedly slightly different from *Zalophus californianus californianus* in morphology and fur coloration (*Zalophus californianus japanicus* is lighter), but these details have not been confirmed. This subspecies is believed to have once lived and bred in the Sea of Japan, but none have been reported in the past twenty years. *Zalophus californianus wollebaeki* (Sivertsen, 1953), the Galapagos sea lion, inhabits the Galapagos Islands some six hundred miles off Equador in the eastern Pacific. It was classified as *Zalophus californianus wollebaeki* by Sivertsen in 1953 but reclassified by Scheffer in 1958. *Zalophus californianus wollebaeki* has a different habitat as well as a shorter and narrower skull than *Zalopus californianus californianus*. Females of this subspecies reach 1.5 to 1.55 m. The ear pinnae are about 30 mm long.

Otaria

The genus *Otaria* was named by Péron in 1816. Its principal characteristics are as follows:

41b.
  1. Inhabits the southern hemisphere.
43a.
  2. Palate very long; distance from palatal notch to incisors greater than 55 per cent of skull length.
  3. Snout broad and upturned; width of skull at canines more than 25 per cent of skull length.
  4. Temporal process present.

Otaria byronia

Figure 1–85. *Otaria byronia,* known as the southern sea lion, named by Blainville in 1820.

OTHER COMMON NAME: South American sea lion.

MORPHOLOGY: The southern sea lion is smaller than the northern sea lion, *Eumetopias jubata,* and resembles *Zalophus californianus* in appearance.

MIGRATION AND ABUNDANCE: In 1958, Scheffer estimated the population as 300,000 to 500,000 animals, but King (1964) gives a figure of about 800,000 animals. The absence of exact information on the Peruvian and Chilean colonies makes any estimate of the total population rather uncertain. Movements of these animals are apparently to and from the feeding grounds. There is no evidence of any true migration.

FOOD: The main foods of the southern sea lions are squid and the crustaceans.

REPRODUCTION: Males become sexually mature and begin to display a mane in their sixth year. Females become sexually mature in the fourth year and probably bear their first pup during the fifth.

The breeding season is from about the end of December to the middle of January. Harems consist of about ten females but are usually so close together that their territorial limits appear to be known only to the harem bulls. Harem bulls will not leave their stations even during high tide when the territory may be covered by water.

Females give birth to a single black pup which is about 80 cm long. The color soon fades to chocolate and, by the end of the first year, is brownish yellow. Cows mate a few days after parturition but continue to suckle their pups for about six months.

After all the available cows have been mated, the harem gradually disintegrates and the bulls, who are quite thin because they have not fed during the breeding season, move out. They spend the next six months feeding and recovering their strength.

BEHAVIOR: Southern sea lions are gregarious animals that are very seldom found singly. Smaller animals often sleep on top of one another in a pile. During the breeding season, they are irritable and the males are pugnacious. A sudden unexplained happening may send the entire herd rushing into the sea in a panic.

When the females return to sea, the pups tend to gather in groups or pods and wander about. They spend much of their time playing and sleeping. During this time, they play at the edge of the water but do not venture any distance out until coaxed to do so by their mothers. Even then, they try to get out of the deeper water by climbing on their mother's backs.

Neophoca

The genus *Neophoca* was named by Gray in 1866. Its principal characteristics are as follows:
43b.
1. Distance from palatal notch to incisors greater than 45 per cent of skull length.
2. Width of skull at canines greater than 23 per cent of skull length.
3. Anterior region of palate deeply concave; depth of concavity at level of canines up to 18 mm.

Neophoca cinerea

Figure 1–86. *Neophoca cinerea,* known as the Australian sea lion, named by Péron in 1816. (After Maxwell, 1967.)

MORPHOLOGY: Adult males are dark brown with a mane of coarse yellowish hair and reach 3.0 to 3.5 m in body length. Younger bulls have a paler area on the neck. Females are rich brown dorsally and yellowish fawn ventrally and reach 2.5 to 3.0 m in length. The skull of the adult is wider than that of *Neophoca hookeri* and has an average length of 308 mm. The sagittal crest is about 30 mm in height.

DISTRIBUTION: Australian sea lions are found along the southwestern coast of Australia from Houtman Rocks to Kangaroo Island. They do not migrate and indeed, do not appear to move very far from their birth place, nearly always returning to the same beach. On land they are noted for their ability to climb cliffs and have been found as far as six miles inland.

ABUNDANCE: This species is not believed to be very abundant. In 1958, Scheffer estimated the population as 2,000 to 10,000.

FOOD: The main food items are reportedly fish and penguins. The males apparently do not fast during the breeding season but catch penguins instead.

REPRODUCTION: When most animals are on shore in October, the breeding season begins with males gathering harems of four or five females. The brown pups are born in December. At birth, they have an abundant under-fur, but they shed that while they are still young.

Neophoca hookeri

Figure 1–87. *Neophoca hookeri,* known as the New Zealand sea lion, named by Gray in 1844. (After Maxwell, 1967.)

OTHER COMMON NAME. Hooker's sea lion.

MORPHOLOGY: Adult males are nearly the same body length as *Zalophus californionus* (2.4 m) but weigh more (about 400 kg). One male's skull was 346 mm long and had a mastoid width of 181 mm. Females weigh about 230 kg and have skulls which are about 126 mm long. The dental formula is I $\frac{3}{2}$, C $\frac{1}{1}$, PC $\frac{5-6}{5}$ = 34-36. At different times, the generic name of this species has been included in *Otaria, Neophoca, Gypsophoca, Euotaria, Zalophus, Eumetopias, Phocarctos,* and even subfamily Arctocephalinae (*Arctocephalus*). Investigation has been quite inadequate, but future study, particularly on real distribution, is expected.

DISTRIBUTION: The New Zealand sea lion is found year round on the Auckland Islands, where there are breeding colonies in Carnley Harbour and at Enderby Island. The most southerly breeding colonies are on Campbell Island, and animals are occasionally found on Macquarie Island. Although Elleman and Morrison-Scott (1951) reported that a species of *Neophoca* occurred in the vicinity of Japan, *Neophoca* is generally known to be a genus of the southern hemisphere.

REPRODUCTION: Adult males haul out on the beaches in early October, take their territories and typical of sea lions, defend them against the surplus bulls. The cows arrive about a month later and are collected into harems of about a dozen. The pups, with fine brown hair, are born near the end of December and January. Mating takes place soon after parturition. After this time, the cows are allowed to go to sea but return at frequent intervals to feed their pups. By the end of January or the beginning of February, most of the cows have mated, most of the pups have taken to the water, the harems begin to break up, and the bulls break their fast and go to sea to feed. Pups are reportedly suckled for about seven months and may remain with their mothers until the following year.

SUBFAMILY ARCTOCEPHALINAE

Some of the characteristics of Arctocephalinae are as follows:
40b.

1. Pelage has two distinct layers: dense, velvety underfur and coarse overhair.
2. First digit of foreflipper shorter than second.
3. Digits of hindflippers approximately equal length.

Arctocephalus

Members of the genus *Arctocephalus* are the southern fur seals whose principal characteristics are the following:
44a.

1. Interorbital region short, usually less than 20 percent of skull length.
2. Tympanic bulla convex.
3. Snout longer, distance from palatal notch to incisors more than 37 percent of skull length.
4. Nasals long and slender, combined width at anterior ends about 40 to 50 percent of nasal length.

All seven species of fur seals in the southern hemisphere belong to a single genus, *Arctocephalus*. The amount of information on those species varies enormously, from species which are well known because of their commercial importance to those about which practically nothing is known. The body color, most of the breeding habits, and the general behavior of all species of *Artocephalus* appears to be very similar.

Arctocephalus australis

Figure 1–88. *Artocephalus australis,* known as the South American fur seal, named by Zimmerman in 1783.

MORPHOLOGY: Adult males of this species are usually 1.8 m long and weigh about 150 kg, while the females are 1.4 m long and weigh 45 kg. The males are dark gray, but the females and most of the immature animals are rather variable in color. Most, however, are gray on the neck and back, have white-tipped hairs which make them appear silvery, and have somewhat yellowish bellies. An adult male skull measured 286 mm in length and 170 mm in mastoid width. The skull of an adult female was 239 mm long and 110 mm in mastoid width (Scheffer, 1958). The snout becomes narrow at the level of the third cheek teeth. The dental formula in the adult is I $\frac{2}{3}$, C $\frac{1}{1}$, PC $\frac{5\text{-}6}{5}$ = 34-36.

DISTRIBUTION: This fur seal occurs on the coasts and offshore islands of the southern parts of South America. There have been many breeding colonies south of Rio de Janeiro, and there are some individuals on the Falkland Islands. They are found on about half of the islands in the Galapagos but are rarely seen in Peruvian waters.

ABUNDANCE: The population of this species is believed to be 100,000 to 130,000.

FOOD: South American fur seals eat fish, crustaceans, and probably cephalopods.

REPRODUCTION: In November, the females are gathered into small harems which consist of an average of three and generally a maximum of five animals. Pups are born soon after the females join the harems, mating takes place soon after parturition, and the harems begin to break up in early January. After July, mothers are seldom seen feeding their pups.

BEHAVIOR: Although South American fur seals inhabit many of the same areas inhabited by the southern sea lion, the two species tend not to mingle. The fur seals live in rocky places, while the sea lions prefer somewhat flat, sandy beaches. They may tolerate each other's presence during the breeding season but in any conflict, the fur seal usually wins.

VARIATIONS: The following three subspecies are classified by location.

Arctocephalus australis australis, known as the Falkland fur seal, was named by Zimmerman in 1783. This species is characterized by a very short interorbital distance (usually less than 20 percent of the total skull length) and by a protrusion in the center of the tympanic bulla. It is distributed on the Falkland Islands, South Georgia, South Orkney and South Scotland.

A. a. gracilis known as the Brazilian fur seal, was named by Nehring in 1887. This seal is said to be the South American mainland subspecies, distributed along the east coast of South America from Brazil to the Strait of Magellan and also on the west coast. King (1964) reported that it is slightly smaller than the animals on the Falkland Islands.

A. a. galapagoensis known as the Galapagos fur seal, was named by Heller in 1904. This species is distributed only in the Galapagos Archipelago. The skull width of the adult male is slightly narrower than that of the mainland and Falkland subspecies. The distance between orbits is also narrower, but the skull becomes wide at the auditory meatus. Sivertsen (1954) reported that the skull is short, 212 mm in a male specimen and 184 mm in a female. This subspecies is the smallest among the forms of *Arctocephalus.*

Arctocephalus pusillus

Figure 1–89. *Artocephalus pusillus,* known as the South African fur seal, named by Schreber in 1776. (After Maxwell, 1967.)

thought to be extinct but was rediscovered by Hubbs and has recovered remarkably in recent years. According to Peterson *et al.* (1968), there are currently about 500 of these fur seals on Guadalupe Island.

Arctocephalus doriferus

Figure 1–91. *Artocephalus doriferus,* known as the Australian fur seal, named by Wood Jones in 1925. (After King, 1964.)

MORPHOLOGY: According to Wood Jones (1925), males are about 6 ft (1.8 m) long and the females are about 5 ft (1.5 m). Both sexes are approximately the same color: grayish brown on the back and a lighter fawn on the ventral surface. The condylobasal length of the male skull is about 250 mm, while that of females is about 200 mm. The front series of cheek teeth (postcanines) have two secondary cusps.

DISTRIBUTION: Australian fur seals range from Eclipse Island, Western Australia, to Sydney, New South Wales, and are found on Kangaroo Island, South Australia, and the Tasmanian coast.

REPRODUCTION: The reproductive behavior is believed to be similar to that of other members of the genus. Males congregate around the end of October and pups are born near the end of December.

VARIATION: Some scientists classify the fur seal population which is found on the shores of southeast Australia and the Tasmanian coast as an independent species, *Arctopcephalus tasmanicus* (Scott and Lord, 1926). Because their ranges overlap and their skull characteristics are only slightly different, *Arctocephalus tasmanicus* is probably a variation of *Arctocephalus doriferus.* At any rate, specimens are very scarce and more studies are needed.

Arctocephalus forsteri

Figure 1–92. *Artocephalus forsteri*, known as the New Zealand fur seal, named by Lesson in 1828. (From Walker, E. P. *et al.: Mammals of the World*. Baltimore, Johns Hopkins Press, 1964, Vol. II.)

MORPHOLOGY: Male New Zealand fur seals are about 1.8 to 2.0 m long and usually weigh 120 to 140 kg. Adult females are about 1.5 to 1.7 m long and weigh around 100 kg. The body is the usual very dark gray color with a brownish ventral surface. The pups are black or silvery gray and are about 50 cm long at birth.

DISTRIBUTION: These fur seals are found on rocky places around the Islands of South New Zealand and on the Islands from Chatham Island to Macquarie Island.

ABUNDANCE: This fur seal has been protected by the New Zealand Government, and the estimated total population is 50,000 to 100,000.

FOOD: At least half of the food of this species consists of squid, crustaceans, particularly *Munida* and noncommercial fish. Shags and penguins are also eaten, the latter being shaken out of their skins in much the same way as they are skinned by the Leopard seal, though with less dexterity.

REPRODUCTION: This fur seal occupies the rookeries for nine months of the year, leaving only for feeding expeditions. The usual harem formation takes place between November and February, when the males gather up to ten cows which they guard until the end of the season. The pups are born about the first week in December and are suckled for about eight months. The females remain with their pups until about the end of May, by which time the young animals are beginning to catch their own food. There is no evidence of any migration.

Arctocephalus gazella

Figure 1–93. *Artocephalus gazella,* known as the Kerguelen fur seal, named by Peters in 1875.

MORPHOLOGY: Adult males of this species are 1.5 to 1.8 m long and commonly have a crest of longer hairs on the top. They are very dark gray on the dorsum and conspicuously yellow on the throat, face, chest. The dark color of the head comes to a clearly marked point between the eyes and extends further posterior to the level of the ears. Females are about 1.3 m long and are brownish gray on the back and sides and cream colored on the chest. An area of russet brown or chestnut which curves ventrally and posteriorly to the midline extends backward from the anterior insertion of the foreflipper as far as the tail.

DISTRIBUTION: These fur seals are found on rough, rocky beaches of isolated islands of the southern Atlantic and Indian Oceans. Colonies are known from the islands of Kerguelen, Amsterdam, Heard, Marion, Bouvet, Tristan, Gough, South Georgia, South Sandwich, South Orkney, and South Shetland. Individuals do wander, but no definite migration is known.

ABUNDANCE: The population of this species is increasing and spreading. The population on Gough and South Georgia Islands has been estimated to be at least 30,000 animals. The present total population numbers about 40,000. Fur seals are now protected on the French islands of Crozet, St. Paul, and Amsterdam, and in certain areas of Kerguelen, on the Norwegian Bouvet Island, and on the British islands, where none may be taken without license.

FOOD: Krill (euphausiid crustaceans) is a large part of the diet, and though feces of South Georgia animals show remains of krill only and are colored bright pink, many animals also eat fish and cephalopods.

REPRODUCTION: Adult males begin to haul out and establish territories at the end of September, and most are established by the end of November. Immature and nonbreeding seals keep away from the breeding area. The harems are small, consisting of only four to five females. The pups are born from the end of November until about the middle of December. At birth, they are about 50 cm long and are clothed in black, wooly fur which is moulted during April and replaced by the gray yearling coat. Lactation probably continues until this moult occurs. The pups tend to congregate in pods and in so doing keep out of the way of the bulls. Mating occurs eight days after parturition.

VARIATION: This species may, in fact, consist of two geographic races or subspecies, one south and one north of the Antarctic convergence. Individuals of the northern group have a narrow skull and five to six normal-sized upper postcanines which do not get exceptionally worn. Members of the southern group have a wider skull, all the postcanines get very worn and smooth on their inner surfaces, and postcanines five and six, particularly the latter, are reduced in size. There are also color differences but no size differences in adults.

Some authors have designated those that breed north of the Antarctic Convergence as *Arctocephalus tropicalis tropicalis* and those to the south as *Arctocephalus tropicalis gazella*.

Callorhinus

The genus *Callorhinus* was named by Gray in 1859. Its principal characteristics are as follows:
44b.

1. Interorbital region long, usually more than 20 percent of skull length.
2. Tympanic bulla concave.
3. Snout shorter, distance from palatal notch to incisors less than 41 percent to skull length.
4. Nasals short and wider, combined width at anterior ends about 80 to 90 percent of nasal length.

Callorhinus ursinus

Figure 1–94. *Callorhinus ursinus,* known as the northern fur seal, named by Linnaeus in 1758. (After Walker *et al,* 1964.)

OTHER COMMON NAME: Alaska or Pribilof fur seal.

MORPHOLOGY: Large males of this species are around 2.5 m long and weigh about 300 kg. One male skull which was 262 mm long had a mastoid width of 147 mm. A female which was 1.45 m long and weighed 63 kg had a skull 199 mm long with a mastoid width of 102 mm. The distance between the palatal notch and the incisors is less than 41 percent of the skull length. The profile of the snout becomes slightly narrow at the third postcanine and gradually narrows from there to the top. The dental formula is I $\frac{2}{2}$, C $\frac{1}{1}$, PC $\frac{5\text{-}6}{5}$ = 34-36.

The ear pinnae are smaller than those of other species of Otariidae, The outer hairs are coarse and cover an abundant underfur of chestnut color. Newborn pups have glossy black, downy hair, which is moulted and replaced by chocolate-colored fur by the end of the first summer. After two years, the coloration achieves the adult pattern, which is dark brown or dark gray on the back and lighter on the underside. About one animal in ten thousand is an albino.

DISTRIBUTION AND MIGRATION: From summer to fall, northern fur seals can be found in their main breeding grounds on the Pribilof Islands in the Bering Sea and on the Commander Islands and Robben Islands in the North Pacific. In 1958, Drofeev of the U.S.S.R. reported that he had observed thousands of this species on the Lovushki Island (48°32′N, 153°15′E), and recently a small breeding colony was discovered to be established on San Miguel Island off Santa Barbara, California. In winter and spring, northern fur seals disperse almost all over the northern Pacific Ocean, usually traveling in small groups of up to ten animals rather than in large herds. Their southern range appears to be 35°N on the Japanese side of the Pacific and 33°10′N on the American side (San Diego).

Rarely, young seals may wander north, but even though several individuals have been found in the Arctic Ocean, less than half a dozen have been recorded from the Arctic coast. The northernmost report was from Letty Harbor, Northwest Territories (69°50′N, 124°24′W). One individual was caught in a freshwater lake in the Yukon.

ABUNDANCE: No other wild animal population in the history of the world has been controlled so successfully and on such a large scale as that of the northern fur seal. By the nineteenth century, the commercial sealing of this species which had begun in the eighteenth century was producing an annual catch of 100,000 animals. In addition to land-based operations, sealers were operating pelagic sealing ships which killed breeding and pregnant females along with the rest of the population. As a consequence, just after the turn of the century, the population had been depleted to such an extent that the countries around the North Pacific became concerned and met to discuss the problem. The result of this meeting was an agreement between Great Britain (including Canada), Japan, Russia, and the United States that, except for the small numbers of animals taken by native hunters, pelagic sealing be prohibited. Although this agreement was broken in 1957, the four original nations met again and agreed on a set of regulations which prohibited pelagic sealing and promised that Canada and Japan would receive 15 percent of the skins from the Pribilofs and subject to some further regulations, a similar percentage of the skins from the Russian Islands, Robben and Commander.

The United States government controls the Pribilof populations and under strict controls, allows the harvesting of from 60,000 to 70,000 bachelors between 41 and 45 in (104–114 cm) long each year from June 20 through the last week in July (or the next to last week in July, depending on the movements of the animals). Killing these bachelors does not affect the structure of the breeding performance of the population because of the polygamous habits of the species. In addition, these young animals have the best-quality fur. Since the bachelors are separated from the breeding animals and pups, it is easy to herd them slowly away from the beach to suitable flat ground, select the animals of the correct size, and allow the others to go back to the beach. The remaining animals are killed with a club, then measured and skinned in only two minutes. The skins are then washed, deblubbered, salted, and packed in barrels. After the Japanese and Canadian skins (each of which has a value of about $20.00) have been dispatched, the rest are sent to a firm in Missouri for processing. During the three months that is required to produce a finished fur, the raw skin goes through 125 different treatments. The long guard hairs are removed, the underfur is straightened from its natural kinked state, dyed to black or shades of brown, and then pelts are dressed to make them light and supple. The carcasses of the seals are converted into meal for chicken food, and the blubber oil is used in soap.

Although at one time the total population of northern fur seals was estimated at no more than 200,000, the biological control programs have been so successful that in 1958, Scheffer estimated the population as 1,500,000 to 1,800,000 animals (including 600,000 pups) on the Pribilof Islands, 40,000 to 60,000 (including 20,000 pups) on the Commander Islands, and 40,000 to 60,000 (including 20,000 pups) on Robben Island.

FOOD: These fur seals feed on pollack, salmon, trout, cod, herring, sardines, silverside, Japanese smelt, sand lance, ocean perch, seal fish, rock fish, and lamprey but seem to be especially fond of squid. When they are hungry, they swallow the fish whole, but when they are full they may eat part of a fish or kill one in cat-and-mouse-like play. Their food consumption is relatively large. An eight year-old male, 180 kg in weight, had 18 kg in its stomach; and a nine-year-old male, 188 kg in weight, had a digestive system 37.88 m in length (Scheffer, 1950). One individual in the San Diego Zoo reportedly ate 4.5 to 5.4 kg per day, and two others who were 23 kg and 29 kg in weight ate 2.7 and 2.9 kg per day, respectively, in winter. Scheffer (1950) estimated that the population of the Pribilof Islands ate 760,000 tons in a year.

REPRODUCTION: The stout males arrive on the islands from the end of May through June and fight to establish their territories. Once they are firmly entrenched, the females arrive and are grouped into harems of fifteen to sixty animals. Females reach sexual maturity and have their first pregnancy when they are four years old. After that, they normally give birth to an offspring every year. Copulation takes place a few days after parturition. Each individual female copulates a few times and then moves to the outskirts of the harem. Each male copulates ten to thirty times a day, and one copulation may last as long as fifteen minutes. After copulation, the rate of implantation in females older than five years is 80 percent and the rate in animals four years old is less. Implantation never occurs in animals less than three years of age.

Newborn males are slightly larger than newborn females. Twenty male pups examined on the Pribilof Islands averaged 5.5 to 5.8 kg, and sixteen female pups averaged 5.0 kg. Even though the mother leaves them for periods of two days to a week to feed at sea, the pups grow rapidly, and by November, males weigh 17 kg and females weigh 16 kg. In general, pup mortality is high. The animals live in close quarters, and pups are often killed by fighting or copulating adults. The hookworm, *Uncinaria lucaci,* also takes a heavy toll.

Females nurse the pups for two to four months and then leave the island in the end of August or in September. After that time, weaning pups gradually begin to venture into the water, usually at night at first, to feed. They lose a considerable amount of weight during weaning and some actually starve before they develop adequate abilities to catch fish. The pups that can swim leave the island in September or November, migrate relatively short distances to the south, and then return to the island for the next breeding season. In the second year, they will migrate as far as the adults do.

Various terms are used to describe the fur seal at different stages of its life: (Russian terms are in parentheses.) The newborn is called a "pup" (Kachiki), the one year old is a "yearling" (kochiki,) the two- or three-year-old male is a "bachelor" (holteaki), the two- or three-year-old female is a "virgin" (no Russian name), the males who are older than bachelors but who do not hold a harem are "idle bulls" (polshikachi), the females of reproductive age are called "breeding cows" (matuki), and the old males who have lost their harems are known as "old bulls" (shikattchi).

BEHAVIOR: Northern fur seals live in the open sea for the majority of the year and do not appear to be strictly limited to waters of a certain temperature. On the contrary, they can be found in waters varying in temperature from 5 to 20°C and are often seen on the boundaries between cold- and warm-water currents where plankton, minerals, and other nutrients support an abundance of various fish and mollusks. Although these fur seals generally feed around dawn, the stomach of specimens taken off Sanriku often contain mictophid fish, deep water fish which migrate vertically only at night.

These animals normally swim near the surface, using their foreflippers. However, when they swim faster, they cut the water, occasionally raising their heads to breathe, and when they swim full speed, they jump for a breath and plunge immediately below the surface. Cetaceans make deep dives and then stay near the surface to breathe several times before making another long dive. In contrast, fur seals normally dive and breathe alternately at regular intervals.

When they want to sleep at sea, fur seals float on the surface, bend their hindlimbs forward, lift one of the foreflippers in the air, and hang the other down into the water somewhat as a keel or centerboard. They then turn their heads back under the axilla on the upper side and in this manner, can sleep even in rough water. In the past, some fishermen let their boats drift at sea and caught sleeping seals with hooks.

Northern fur seals do not form schools or herds at sea. Occasionally, animals group together, but they are only travel mates. If one is shot, the travel mate nearby will flee immediately, a reaction which is quite different from that of dolphins, porpoises, and whales. Distribution appears to be directly related to age and sex. This is especially apparent in such locations as the west coast of Japan where there are few yearlings or older males. Northern fur seals do not mingle or copulate with other species of pinnipeds. Although they have shared islands with *Zalophus californianus, Eumetopias jubata* and some *Phocidae,* each species occupies its own ground.

LONGEVITY: The northern fur seal may live for about twenty-five years. Its age can easily be determined from laminations in the roots of the teeth which are apparently produced by varying rates of growth. The accuracy of this method was proven by tagging, releasing and then later recapturing animals.

FAMILY ODOBENIDAE

The following are the distinguishing characteristics of Odobenidae:
39b.
1. Body thick and robust.
2. External ear pinnae absent (meatus protected by a fold of skin).
3. No free tail.
4. Five small but distinct claws on forelimbs.
5. Testes internal.
6. Normally fourteen thoracic vertebrae.
7. Upper surface of all flippers sparsely haired (at least in young); lower surface naked.
8. Supraorbital process absent.
9. Sagittal crest absent.
10. Upper canines of adult grow more than 50 cm in length.

This family contains only one genus which consists of but one species, *Odobenus rosmarus,* found only in the Arctic.

Odobenus

The genus *Odobenus* was named by Brisson in 1762.

Mammals of the Sea

Odobenus rosmarus

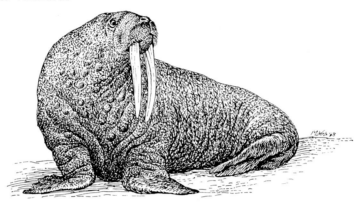

Figure 1–95. *Odobenus rosmarus*, known as the walrus, named by Linnaeus in 1758.

MORPHOLOGY: Adult male walruses are 3.6 to 3.8 m long and weigh 1,500 kg. Females are slightly smaller (3.0 m long and 900 kg in weight) and have two pairs of mammary teats. The body is bulky and heavy, but the head is comparatively small. The snout is blunt with a large array of whiskers on the upper lip. The eyes are small, and there are no ear pinnae. The meatus is protected by a fold of skin. The hindlimbs can be bent forward at the tarsus and the animal can walk on land. The forelimbs each have five digits, each of which has a claw at the end. Both the palms and the plantar surface of the hindlimbs are covered with hair. The brown hair is relatively sparse and gradually drops off the wrinkled skin as the animal gets old. Very old walruses may be nearly naked. The blubber is an average of 5 to 8 cm thick. The functional dental formula in the destinate stage is I $\frac{3(2)}{0}$, C $\frac{1}{1}$, PC $\frac{3(4)}{3(4)}$ = 18 (24). The male has a pair of very long maxillary caspidates, 750 to 950 mm in length, which hang down from the upper jaw. Walrus ivory can be identified by the presence of a granular core of dentine (probably osteodentine) which fills the pulp cavity.

DISTRIBUTION: Walruses are generally found in fairly shallow water around the arctic coasts, stay close to land or ice, and do not go far out to sea. Atlantic walruses are found in both the eastern and western Atlantic. The western populations are found on the Arctic coast of Canada from Hudson Bay to Baffin and Ellesmere Islands, in Hudson strait, in Frobisher Bay, in Foxe Basin, in Baffin Bay, and in Davis Strait. They are also found along the west coast of Greenland, particularly on the Nege and Etah Banks in the Thule district. Less is known about their distribution on the east coast of Greenland, although they are known to inhabit the northeastern coast, particularly in summer. On the European side of the Atlantic, wal-

ruses are occasionally found on ice floes off Iceland and occur off Spitsbergen, Franz Josef Land, Novaya Zemlya, and in the Barents and Kara
Seas as far as the mouth of the Yenisey River. William Caxton reported
that a walrus was taken in the Thames in 1456. King (1964) mentions
twenty to thirty records of walruses having been seen or killed on British
coasts. In addition, there are ten records of walruses off the Norwegian
coast between 1902 and 1954. Though the Atlantic walrus migrates, not
all animals migrate every year. Like the Atlantic walrus, the Pacific walrus
migrates in spring and early summer. All the females and most of the
males move north, primarily on ice floes, following the same path in groups
segregated by sex.

The Pacific walruses are found mainly in the area of the Bering Sea,
and though they are not usually seen east of Point Barrow, they sometimes
move as far east as Herschel and Banks Islands. Their range includes the
Chukchi Sea, Wrangel Island, the East Siberian Sea, and the Laptev Sea.
The ranges of the Pacific and Atlantic animals come very close together
in the region of Severnaya Zemlya and the west side of the Taymyr Peninsula, but it is not known whether there is any interbreeding between
the two groups. In the past, walruses have come as far south as 40°N and
to the waters off Japan. Stragglers were caught in the vicinity of Hakodate,
Nemuro, and Hachinohe. The southernmost catch recorded was from
Shirogane-Mishima (40°, 31′N, 141°322′E) in March, 1937.

ABUNDANCE: Scheffer (1958) estimated the Pacific walrus population as
20,000 to 40,000 and the Atlantic walrus population as 25,000 to 50,000.
Although there are no international regulations to protect the walrus, both
Alaska and Canada have their own laws under which the residents are
allowed to take a certain number under license. There are similar arrangements in Siberia. At the present time, the walrus population is declining,
and several studies are being conducted to determine what can be done
to improve this situation.

FOOD: These animals eat such mollusks as *Mya runcata*, *Sazicava arctica*
and *Cardium groenlandicum*, which they usually obtain by digging the
shells out of the bottom at depths less than 40 fathoms. They seem to
prefer the shallower waters around the coasts where the sea bottom is
gravelly and supports various kinds of mollusks. Stomachs that contain
Cardium are regarded as a great delicacy by the Eskimos. The stomach
contents of a bull walrus may weigh as much as 55 kg. One contained
about 25 kg of *Mya siphons* and 18 kg of the feet of another mollusk
Clinocardium nutali.

Sucking plays a large part in feeding. Although walruses feed mainly
on shellfish, shells are seldom found in stomach contents. Mussels may be

taken into the mouth, the soft parts sucked out and swallowed, and the shell rejected.

REPRODUCTION: In April or early May, females give birth to a single slate gray pup 1.2 m long and 50 kg in weight. Lactation continues for over a year, but even after they are weaned, young animals may stay with their mothers for another year or two. According to King, this is partly due to their natural gregariousness, but it is probably also due to the fact that at this age walruses still have very short tusks and are unable to acquire enough food on their own.

Mating has been observed in April and May, shortly after the birth of the pups. Walruses appear to be polygamous, but there is no evidence of harem formation. The gestation period is almost a year. Sexual maturity occurs in the females at five years and in the males at six years of age.

BEHAVIOR: Walruses are quite gregarious and form large groups. When they are lying leisurely on ice or on the shore, where they spend most of the day, they sometimes rest on their backs with their tusks in the air and sometimes rest on another animal. They do a great deal of rubbing and scratching, much of which is to remove parasites. Although they are usually cowardly and will flee if approached from the windward, on rare occasions they have become excited enough to attack men or overturn Eskimo boats. They can climb up a large pile of ice by using their bulky tusks and may hold them aloft to defend themselves against a polar bear or killer whale. If her pup is attacked, a female will fight vigorously, without concern for herself. When they are swimming, the pups hold firmly to the mothers' necks as they move through the water.

LONGEVITY: Walruses probably live as long as thirty years.

VARIATION: The skulls of Atlantic walruses have shorter tusks, a narrower facial region, and a wider occipital region than those of the Pacific walruses. Therefore, these animals have been classified as two subspecies, *Odobenus rosmarus rosmarus* (Linnaeus, 1758), the Atlantic walrus, and *Odobenus rosmarus divergens* (Illiger, 1815), the Pacific walrus.

Superfamily Phocoidea

The distinguishing characteristics of the superfamily Phocoidea are as follows:

38b.

1. Forelimbs short (much less than one-fourth of body length); locomotion in water accomplished mainly by use of hindlimbs.
2. Hindlimbs cannot be turned forward; locomotion on land accomplished by crawling movements.

3. Claws on tips of digits of forelimbs often large and distinctly functional.
4. Five claws on hindflipper (rudimentary in some species).
5. All surfaces of all flippers distinctly haired.
6. Mammae have two or four functional teats.
7. Most species monogamous; males and females are of similar size in most species.
8. Tympanic bones large, inflated, thick walled.
9. Mastoid processes swollen but not prominent.
10. Postcanines of most species with three or more distinct cusps.

The superfamily includes the single family Phocidae, the true or earless seals.

PHOCIDAE

The neck is short and there are no ear pinnae. On the forelimbs, which are shorter than the hind limbs and directed anteriorly, the first digit is usually the longest and the lengths of the remaining digits decrease medially. On the larger hindlimbs, which are directed posteriorly, the first and fifth digits are longer than the middle three. In most cases, each digit has a well-developed claw. All limbs are covered with fur.

In the skull, the posterior processes of the orbits appear to be in the process of degeneration. The process of the mastoid is large and connected to the expanded tympanic bulla. The premaxillae are prolonged in a posteriodorsal direction and join the nasal bone. The incisors are conical in shape and vary in number among species. The adult dental formula is $I \frac{1\text{-}3}{1\text{-}2}$, $C \frac{1}{1}$, $PC \frac{5\text{-}6}{5} = 28\text{-}36$. There are two radixes in the hind four molars. The scapula is small, and the acromion is hardly developed. The testicles are in the body cavity.

There are thirteen genera in this family: *Erignathus, Halichoerus, Phoca Pusa, Histriophoca, Pagophilus, Monachus, Leptonychotes, Ommatophoca, Hydrurga, Lobodon, Cystophora,* and *Mirounga.*

SUBFAMILY PHOCINAE

The following are additional characteristics of Phocinae.
45a.
1. Three upper, two lower incisors on each side.
2. Hind digits nearly equal in length.
3. Anteromedic.
4. Premaxillary bones prolonged upward, reaching the nasals.

Erignathus

The genus *Erignathus* was named by Gill in 1866. Its principal characteristics are as follows:

46a.

1. Third digit of foreflipper longest.
2. Jugal bone (malar) short and wide: width more than one-third of its greatest diagonal length.
3. No sagittal crest.
4. Mystacial vibrissae smooth, thick, straight and conspicuously bushy.
5. Four mammary teats.
6. Embryonal pelage dark grayish or brownish.
7. Spaces between postcanines almost a tooth wide.

Erignathus barbatus

Figure 1–96. *Erignathus barbatus*, known as the bearded seal, named by Erxleben in 1777.

MORPHOLOGY: Males of this species are about 2.8 m long. Females are 2.6 m and average 400 kg in weight. The fur is cork or brownish gray, is darkest on the center line of the back, and gradually becomes lighter toward the ventral side. There are no dots or patches. In females, there are two pairs of mammary teats. In the forelimbs, the third digits are generally slightly longer than the remainder. The forehead is protruded, and the snout is wide with the characteristic, long, thick whiskers. The total skull length of adult animals is about 230 mm in both sexes. The mastoid width is about 144 mm in males and 131 mm in females. The postcanines are short and wide and are separated by a space which is almost as wide as the tooth. The dental formula is the same as that of genus *Phoca*: $I \frac{3}{2}$, $C \frac{1}{1}$, $P \frac{4}{4}$, $M \frac{1}{1} = 34$.

There is no sagittal crest, and the posterior ends of the palatine are round. There is on acromion on the scapula.

DISTRIBUTION: This species is circumpolar, distributed in the Arctic, the north Atlantic, and the north Pacific Oceans. Isolated stragglers have been reported from Scotland, Normandy, and near Tokyo Bay.

FOOD: Bearded seals feed on benthic forms such as soles, sculpin, flounders, crabs, shrimps, sea snails and mollusks, and on squid.

REPRODUCTION: Breeding takes place from May to July, the gestation cycle is reportedly eleven months, and females give birth on the ice floes in April or May. One pup is born every other year, a pattern which is unusual among Phocidae.

When they are born, the pups are about 1.2 cm long, weigh 40 kg, and are covered with a grayish brown, wooly coat which is shed and replaced by a cork-colored fur in about two weeks. Development of the pup is rapid.

BEHAVIOR: Bearded seals are not gregarious animals and tend to be rather sparsely distributed in any given area. They do not necessarily remain on a certain island for days or weeks, but though they constantly move around, they do not make long migrations. In the summer, small groups are seen in estuaries, and though most groups are small, one pod as large as 1,000 animals was seen in the Sea of Okhotsk.

They sometimes float in the sea with their tails bent down sleeping like dolphins and sometimes are seen swimming entirely submerged, only projecting their nostrils to breathe.

Males bark in a loud and sonorous voice. When bearded seals are on ice floes, they appear quite cautious and will dive into the water at the slightest menace.

MISCELLANEOUS: This species is very important in the life of the Eskimo. The strong, durable, and elastic hide is used for boot soles, heavy ropes, dog harness, kayak construction, and food for the dogs. The intestine is eaten and is sometimes used for window panes. The hind flippers are boiled and eaten, and the blubber is used for lamps. The liver is reportedly very lobate and rather like a kidney in appearance. It frequently contains sufficient concentrations of vitamin A to be poisonous and may cause severe illness if consumed. Dogs will not take fresh liver but may eat them if they are frozen.

VARIATIONS: *Erignathus barbatus barbatus* and *Erignathus barbatus nauticus*.

Erignathus barbatus barbatus

Erignathus barbatus barbatus known as the North Atlantic bearded seal, was named by Erxleben in 1777.

This subspecies may reach a length of 3.0 m. The males are slightly larger than the females.

These animals inhabit the Arctic Ocean from the Laptev Sea westward to the middle of the north Canadian Islands, a range which includes Taymyr Peninsula, Yamal Peninsula, the White Sea, Franz Josef Land, Spitsbergen Isles, Iceland, Greenland, Baffin Island, Hudson Bay, and Ungava Bay. The northernmost range in Novaya Zemlya Island and its adjacent ice field (85°N, 80°E). The southernmost limit is Newfoundland (50°N), but they have visited the coast of France on rare occasions.

Erignathus barbatus nauticus

Erignathus barbatus nauticus, known as the North Pacific bearded seal, was named by Pallas in 1811.

The skull of this subspecies reportedly has a broader and shorter facial region, but skeletal differences are imperfectly distinguished.

Although the Pacific animals are only slightly different morphologically from the basic subspecies, it is set apart by its distribution. It occurs between the northern islands of Canada and the Laptev Sea, a range which includes the Sea of Okhotsk, Bristol Bay in the Bering Sea, the Commander Islands, Point Barrow, Hokkaido, and the Kuril Islands.

ABUNDANCE: The population of *Erignathus barbatus barbatus* is estimated at 50,000 to 100,000 animals and that of the *Erignathus barbatus nauticus* at 25,000 to 50,000 animals.

Halichoerus

The genus *Halichoerus* was named by Nilsson in 1820. The following are its principal characteristics:

46b.
1. Third digit of foreflipper shorter than first and second.
2. Jugal bone (Malar) longer and narrower; width less than one-third of its greatest diagonal length.
3. Mystacial vibrissae beaded, slender, curled, and less bushy.
4. Two mammary teats.
5. Embryonal pelage white.
6. Spaces between postcanines less than a tooth wide.

47a.
7. Snout long; distance from tip of snout to eye almost twice that from eye to eye.
8. Profile of forehead and snout straight or convex.
9. Postcanines large and strong, each usually has a single conical cusp.
10. Width of anterior narial openings of skull more than 30 per cent of mastoid width.
11. Crown pelage usually lighter than back.
12. Polygamous, breed in fall or winter.

Halichoerus grypus

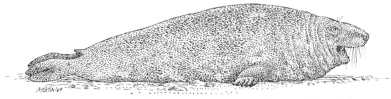

Figure 1–97. *Halichoerus grypus*, known as the gray seal, named by Fabricius in 1791.

MORPHOLOGY: Male gray seals are about 3.0 m long, weigh 300 kg, have well developed sagittal crests as adults, and are marked with three deep lines on the dorsum of the fat neck (a distinct difference between this species and *Phoca vitulina*). Mature adult females are around 2.3 m long and weigh 250 kg.

The fur coloration is subject to much individual variation. When they are wet, animals appear dark slate gray or gray-black, but when they are dried, they are brown or gray. These seals usually have irregular dots or patches, silvery hair, or a whitish-colored face. In most cases, females are basically gray, lighter on the ventral side and frequently marked with dots of grayish brown.

The snout is elongated. The distance from the tip of the snout to the eye is two times the distance from the eye to the ear opening. Individuals are frequently found with ear pinnae more pronounced than is usual for Phocoidae. The claws of the forelimb are long, narrow and curved. The width of the nostril is larger than 30 per cent of the mastoid width and when the nostrils are closed, they form an arc 3 cm in length. The dental formula is $I \frac{2}{3}$, $C \frac{1}{1}$, $PC \frac{5}{5} = 34$.

DISTRIBUTION: In the Arctic Ocean, these seals are widely dispersed from Novaya Zemlya to the Labrador peninsula. On the east coast of the Atlantic, they occur as far south as France. On the west coast, they have been reported north from Atlantic City, New Jersey. They are fairly numerous on the coasts of Great Britain and live in the Baltic Sea, where the most important breeding area is in the Gulf of Bothnia. The are found in the Gulf of Finland and approximately as far south as Bornholm.

ABUNDANCE: The world population was reported by Scheffer (1958) as 25,000 to 50,000 animals.

FOOD: Gray seals feed on a wide variety of available fish, including rock fish, pollack, halibut, lampry, salmon, herring, conger eel, flounder, and other flat fish. In addition, they also feed on some crustaceans and mollusks, including the common mussel.

REPRODUCTION: There are two distinct breeding seasons in the separate populations. Animals in the Baltic Sea and the Gulf of St. Lawrence pup in February and March, while the British and related populations pup between September and December. However, Hickling reported parturition occurs at different times in different localities—May to August in Wales, September to October in Ireland, and September to November in Scotland. On the British coast, newborn pups have been found in nearly every month of the year. The northernmost breeding location is on the Murman coast (70°N).

Although gray seals are polygamous, adult males do not precede females to the breeding grounds and establish territories as otariids do. Instead, they always arrive with the females, sometimes fighting at the shore. Usually, one bull has twenty cows, and several bulls and their harems (one hundred females) join to form a herd. White pups can be seen several days after the arrival of the first group, and groups continue to arrive until the herd is "clouded." Pups are about 9 to 17 kg at birth and gain 0.5 kg every day while they are nursing.

BEHAVIOR: Gray seals do not migrate. They disperse after the breeding season, but the members of the various colonies tend to return to the same breeding ground each year. Young animals are believed to spend their first two years at sea. According to Hickling (1956), a pup born on Farne Island and marked there was found in the Faeroe Isles, a distance of 885 km away, two months later.

Phoca

The genus *Phoca* was named by Linnaeus in 1758. Its principal characteristics are the following:

47b.

1. Snout short; distance between tip of snout and eye much less than twice that between eye and ear.
2. Postcanines small, thin, each with two or more cusps.
3. Width of anterior narial openings of skull less than thirty per cent of mastoid width.
4. Crown pelage not lighter than back.
5. Monogamous (but promiscuous), breeding in spring or summer.

48a.

6. Posterior margin of palate distinctly notched or incised.
7. Adult pelage usually spotted; male and female adult pelage alike.
8. Commonly breeding in harbors and fjords.

49a.

9. Pelage on back smooth to the touch; hairs fine, tips recurved (spots small, often in clusters, not especially ring shaped.
10. Young born on land in spring or early summer.
11. Claws semicircular in cross section, without distinct dorsal ridge or annuli.
12. Skull of old animals of both sexes has low sagittal crest.
13. Face doglike, snout blunt, profile of forehead and snout concave.
14. Length (along axis of tooth row) of second upper postcanine usually 6.8 mm or more, mandibular teeth often crowded out of line or overlapping.
15. First lower postcanines usually with four cusps.
16. Inner side of mandible between middle postcanines convex.

Phoca vitulina

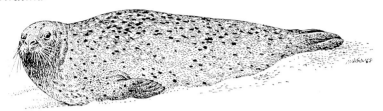

Figure 1–98. *Phoca vitulina,* known as the harbor seal, named by Linnaeus in 1758.

OTHER COMMON NAMES: Common seal, spotted seal.

MORPHOLOGY: Mature adults are 1.5 to 2.0 m long. Males reach a maximum weight of about 150 kg, females about 120 kg. The body is plump and glossy gray or charcoal gray scattered with small black and white dots which are numerous on the dorsal surface but more sparse on the underside.

The outermost digits on the hindlimbs are the longest. Both fore and hindlimbs and webs are covered with fur. The claws are sharp but thin and apparently useless for digging in ice. The male skull length is about 240 mm, and the female's is 222 mm. The mastoid widths are about 140 mm and 124 mm, respectively. The postcanines are large. The ossified nasal septum reaches the posterior end of the V-shaped palatine. The mandibular structure is strong, and the symphysis is short. The dental formula is I $\frac{2}{3}$, C $\frac{1}{1}$, PC $\frac{5}{5}$ = ^{34}.

FOOD: Harbor seals eat various fish, mollusks, squids, octopuses, and, especially at weaning time, crustaceans. In order to eat bivalves, they crush them with their teeth.

REPRODUCTION: The breeding seasons vary by subspecies. *P. v. larga* breeds from March through early May. On the southern Kuril Islands, birth takes place on land in May, in other locations, two or three weeks after. The white pups are born on the ice floes. Both the pups and adults moult. Copulation then takes place in the water. A family—parents and a last year's pup—commonly live together at that time. The pups do not enter the water until they have begun moulting.

When the animals are hauled out, last year's pups often form one group and the middle-sized males and females form another group, while a large male usually stations himself somewhat distant, apparently to keep watch. During the breeding season, males bark loudly and fight.

The other subspecies, *vitulina, concolor, richardi,* and *mellonae,* normally pup on land or on a sandbank between one high tide and the next. Pups shed their embryonal coat of long white hair either in the uterus or immediately after birth and are ready to swim very soon after they are born. Birth takes place in May or June, and the pups are suckled for about three weeks, after which the adults moult and then mate. Pups of all subspecies are close to 1.0 m in body length and about 15 kg in weight at birth. It is said that the pups of *Phoca vitulina richardi* in California are usually seen in early April.

MISCELLANEOUS: In Iceland and Germany, large numbers of yearlings are hunted for their skins, which make very beautiful, though rather stiff, coats. In Alaska, they are shot in an attempt to preserve the salmon, and the carcasses are fed on fox or mink farms. In Hokkaido, Japan, they are caught commercially. The skin is used for hide, oil is extracted from the blubber, the meat is employed as animal food, and the bones and viscera are used in fertilizers. The oil may be used in cheap paints, soaps, and in a process for softening leather.

VARIATIONS AND DISTRIBUTION: Although there is little difference in morphology, the harbor seal is divided into five subspecies by distribution.

Phoca vitulina, vitulina, named by Linnaeus in 1758, is found on Novaya Zemlya Island in the northeast Atlantic, in the Barenz Sea, on the Murman coast, in the Baltic Sea and the coasts of Norway, in Denmark, the Netherlands, Germany, Belgium, France, Spain and Portugal. They are never found in the Bay of Bothnia, the Bay of Finland or the White Sea. This species is very common around the North Sea and on the coasts of Great Britain.

Phoca vitulina concolor, named by Dekay in 1842, is distributed on both coasts of Greenland, on Ellesmere Island (76°N), on Baffin Island, on Southampton Island, in Ungava Bay, and in Labrador. Several animals have come up the St. Lawrence River, and one individual was found in Lake Ontario.

Phoca vitulina mellonae, named by Doutt in 1942, is distributed only in Upper and Lower Seal Lakes (240 m above seal level), 140 km east of Hudson Bay, Canada. The coronoid process of the mandible is long, narrow, and extends more posteriorly than the condyle of the mandible. The coloration of this form is much darker than that of *Phoca vitulina concolor.*

Phoca vitulina richardi, named by Gray in 1864, is distributed on the Pacific coasts of North America from Herschel Island (69°35′N, 139°W) (Dunbar, 1949) to the eastern Bering Sea, and the south of the Aleutians to the coasts of California and Mexico. The southernmost limit is probably Cedros Island (28° 12′N) off Baja California, Mexico.

Phoca vitulina largha, named by Pallas in 1811, is found from the Bering Strait to the coasts of China. Ross (1955) reported that this form is distributed from East Cape (170°W) west along the west coast of the Bering Sea and Kuril Islands, and in all areas of the Sea of Okhotsk.

Breeding grounds occur between 50°N and 63°N. Allen (1938) reported that an individual had been found in the estuary of the Yangtze River and Barabash Nikiforov (1938) reported that this subspecies is found every year on the Commander Islands.

ABUNDANCE: Scheffer (1958) reported that there are 40,000 to 100,000 *Phoca vitulina vitulina;* 40,000 to 100,000 *Phoca vitulina concolor;* about 500 *Phoca vitulina mellonae;* 50,000 to 200,000 *Phoca vitulina richardi;* and 20,000 to 50,000 *Phoca virtulina largha;* therefore, the total number of harbor seals in the world is from 150,000 to 450,000 animals.

Pusa

The genus *Pusa* was named by Scopoli in 1777. Its principal characteristics are as follows:
49b.
1. Pelage on back harsh to touch, hair coarse, tips pointing directly backward (spots large and ring shaped).
2. Young born on ice in spring.
3. Claws more triangular in cross section, with distinct dorsal ridge and annuli.
4. Skull without sagittal crest.
5. Face catlike, snout sharper, old males have disagreeable odor.
6. Length of second upper postcanine usually less than 6.8 mm, mandibular teeth always aligned with jaw, never crowded.
7. Postcanines usually have three cusps.
8. Inner side of mandible between middle postcanines concave.

Pusa hispida

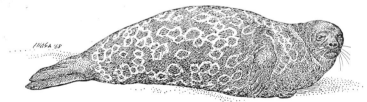

Figure 1–99. *Pusa hispida,* known as the ringed seal, named by Schreber in 1775.

MORPHOLOGY: This is the smallest of the *Phocidae.* Even a large male does not reach 1.4 m in length or 90 kg in weight. The skull length of the male is about 187 mm, and the mastoid width is 115 mm. The larger females are about 1.3 m long and weigh about 90 kg. They have a skull length of about 167 mm and a mastoid width of around 101 mm (Scheffer, 1958). The dental formula in the first stage is $I \frac{3}{2}$, $C \frac{1}{1}$, $PC \frac{3}{3} = 26$ and that in the destinate stage is $I \frac{3}{2}$, $C \frac{1}{1}$, $PC \frac{5}{5} = 34$.

The body is dark brownish gray on the back and whitish on the under-side. There are jet black or slightly grayish irregular spots surrounded by ring-shaped lighter marks on the back and sides of the body but not on the underside. The webs in the hindlimbs are covered with hair. There are two pairs of mammary teats. The embryonal pelage is white, but the pups moult one or two weeks after birth. Animals caught in winter have a great deal of brown.

FOOD: Ringed seals feed on a wide variety of small pelagic amphiods, euphausids and other crustaceans, as well as on small fish. Although they feed largely on planktonic organisms in the ocean, there is some evidence that they pick out the larger animals in a school of *Themisto*, which are ¾ to 2½ in long, and catch them individually. There is little evidence as to depths to which these animals go to feed, but several have been killed in over 30 m of water and they may be able to go as deep as 80 m.

REPRODUCTION: From mid-March to mid-April, females give birth to a single pup on land-fast ice. The newborn pups are usually 80 cm long, weigh about 5 kg, and have a creamy white fur coat which is shed after two or three weeks. They are suckled for nearly two months. Copulation also takes place during mid-March to mid-April. The period of pregnancy is about eleven months.

BEHAVIOR: Ringed seals are found in the open water around the fast ice, even as far as the North Pole, and in fjords and bays but are rarely found in the open sea or on floating pack ice. Their movements are usually only local. In winter, they come up to breathe through round breathing holes which they keep open in the ice.

LONGEVITY: The males do not reach sexual maturity until they are seven years old. Females have the first ovulation in their sixth year. The old male ringed seals may live to be a considerable age. King (1964) reported that a male at least forty-three years old has been taken. Badly decayed teeth may hasten the death of old seals.

MISCELLANEOUS: Many thousands of ringed seals are caught annually from all areas where they occur. They are hunted primarily for their skins, which are used for leather or for their decorative fur. They are particularly useful to the polar Eskimos, who shoot them for kayaks. All parts of the animals are useful to the Eskimo. The flesh is eaten, and the blubber, in addition to serving as food, is used for oil lamps. The liver and intestine are eaten, either boiled or frozen. The white pup skins may be used as underclothes (fur side inside). Skins of adult seals have many uses: as clothes, bags, dog harnesses, tents, and other items.

VARIATION AND DISTRIBUTION: There are six subspecies of ringed seals, distinguished by their different areas of distribution.

Pusa hispida hispida, known as the Common Ringed Seal, was named by Schreber in 1775. This subspecies is found all around the Arctic Ocean (including the North Polar region), on the Northern coasts of Europe, Greenland, and North America, is occasionally reported from Labrador, Hudson Bay and James Bay, and, on rare occasions, migrates as far South as France and Scotland. Naumov (1953) reported that this was the most common and widely distributed seal in the U.S.S.R.

Pusa hispida ochotensis, known as the Okhotsk Ringed Seal, was named by Pallas in 1811. Though this subspecies is found mainly in the Sea of Okhotsk, it migrates southward and is found in the Kuril Islands, in Sakhalin and Hokkaido, on the northeast coast of Korea, and, from March to May, in Abashiri, Hokkaido.

Pusa hispida krascheninikovi, known as the Bering Sea Ringed Seal, was named by Naumov and Smirnov in 1936. These seals are found in the northern sea (but not on the Aleutian Islands) where they mingle with *Pusa hispida hispida* and *Pusa hispida ochotensis*. Some individuals inhabit the Commander Islands, and several have been captured on the Hokkaido coast of Japan. Past records indicated that the subspecies reaches Bristol Bay, but these reports were presumably of animals which had drifted south on floating blocks of ice.

Pusa hispida botnica, known as the Baltic Ringed Seal, was named by Gmelin in 1788. This species has been the subject of much controversy. Scheffer (1958) reported that it was distributed only in Bothnia Bay in the Baltic Sea—including Finland Bay and Lake Ladoga at the neck of the Scandinavian peninsula.

Pusa hispida ladogensis, known as the Ladoga Ringed Seal, was named by Nordquist in 1899. These dark and easily distinguishable animals (Nordquist, 1899) are found in Lake Ladoga, particularly in the deepwater region of the north and sometimes venture as far as Leningrad.

Pusa hispida saimensis

Pusa hispida saimensis, known as the Saimaa Lake Ringed Seal, was named by Nordquist in 1899. Though this subspecies is found primarily in Saimaa Lake on the neck of the Scandanavian peninsula, it is also found in other lakes connected to Saimaa, but there have been no definite reports on their occurrence in Lake Onega to the northeast.

They do not occur in Lake Ladoga because the water falling from Lake Saimaa (76 m above sea level) to Lake Ladoga (70 m above sea level) is so fast that the animals cannot migrate through it.

ABUNDANCE: It is said to be the most valuable of the *Phocidae*. According to Naumov (1933), 10,000 *Pusa hispida hispida* are killed annually, and 50,000 *Pusa hispida ochotensis* are caught in the Bering Sea, where its population is as much as 200,000 to 500,000. The population of *Pusa hispida kroscheninikovi* is estimated as 20,000 to 50,000, and that of *Puca hispida botnica* is estimated as 20,000 to 50,000. According to Scheffer (1958), the present population of *Pusa hispida ladogensis* is 5,000 to 10,000 animals, and about 1,000 of these seals were killed annually in the eighteenth century.

Pusa sibirica

Figure 1–100. *Pusa sibirica,* known as the Baikal seal, named by Gmelin in 1788.

MORPHOLOGY: Though the maximum body length is said to be 1.4 m, the average size is less than that. The captive animals which have been brought to Europe are commonly around 1.1 m. This species has a round head, and spindle-shaped body. The dental formula is I $\frac{2}{3}$, C $\frac{1}{1}$, PC $\frac{5}{5}$ = ^{34}. Fur coloration is yellowish-brown or dark brown mingled with silvery gray on the dorsum, with lighter or cork-like color on the underside. Although this species belongs to the genus *Pusa*, there are no ringlike dots or dapples, except for scarce dots in rare cases. The fur of the pup is ivory.

DISTRIBUTION: This species is strictly limited to Lake Baikal in the U.S.S.R., over 2,000 km from the ocean. Allen (1880) reported them in Lake Oron, but there are none present now.

BEHAVIOR: Bobrinskoi (1944) reported on the movements of the Baikal seal. During the winter, mature males are scattered all over the lake, mature females are on the east shore, and males and females that have not yet attained sexual maturity are on the west shore. Pregnant females remain on the ice, but most other animals spend the winter in the water. They make holes in the ice while it is still thin and keep them open throughout the winter so they will have places to breathe. In April, when spring arrives, the animals haul out onto the ice in groups of one hundred to two hundred animals. Later, in the early summer when the winds drive the ice to the north and the ice melts, these seals haul out onto rocks or beaches, form breeding colonies and mate. Breeding groups break up when the ice begins to form again.

Pusa caspica

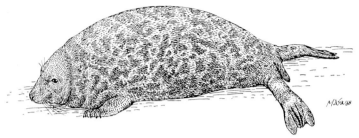

Figure 1–101. *Pusa caspica*, known as the Caspian seal, named by Gmelin in 1788.

MORPHOLOGY: This form is slightly different morphologically from both *Pusa sibirica* and *Pusa hispida*, and though its skull is generally typical of the genus *Pusa*, it is reportedly clearly different from both the above species. The fur is cork or brownish-gray (apparently lighter than that of *Pusa sibirica*) and sometimes has tiny dots which are not ringlike. No detailed report of this species is available.

DISTRIBUTION: As the name suggests, this seal is found only in the Caspian Sea of the U.S.S.R.

Histriophoca

The genus *Histriophoca* was named by Gill in 1873. The following are its principal characteristics:

48b.
1. Posterior margin of palate not distinctly notched or incised, nearly a straight line.
2. Adult pelage unspotted, marked with large bands of dark color; male and female pelage not alike.
3. Commonly breeding on open sea ice.

50a.
4. Only inhabit the Pacific, breed on Pacific-Arctic ice.
5. Forelimbs and neighboring parts of body dark, never any small dark spots on body.
6. Bony nasal septum just fails to reach rear edge of bony palate.
7. Upper tooth row curved.
8. Posterior palatine foramen in, or posterior to, maxillopalatine suture.

Histriophoca fasciata

Figure 1–102. *Histriophoca fasciata*, known as the ribbon seal, named by Zimmerman in 1783.

OTHER COMMON NAMES: Harnessed seal, saddled seal.

MORPHOLOGY: Male ribbon seals reach about 1.6 m in body length and 95 kg in weight and have dark fur (gray with blue and purple mixed). There is a wide necklace-like band around the crown of the head extending to the front of the neck, and there are other circular bands around each of the forelimbs. Two bands are joined at the anus and extend upward around the posterior end of the body. Females are about 1.5 m long, weigh 80 kg, and are dark beige or brownish gray all over with an even darker back and forelimbs. Some are marked with an indistinct ivory band at the rear end of the body. Both sexes of pups are colored like the females and have no dots.

The skull is less than 200 mm long. The nasal septum is ossified and extends to the end of the palatine. When viewed vertically or horizontally, the maxillary tooth row is curved. The forelimbs insert further posterior than those of *Phoca vitulina* and *Pusa hispida*. In the forelimb, the first digit is longest, and the remainder are progressively shorter to the fifth. There is one pair of mammary teats. Except for the first pair, the post-canines have two radices. The cusps of the teeth are simple and angle to the rear. The symphysis of the mandible is comparatively long. The dental formula in the fetal stage is $I\frac{2}{3}$, $C\frac{1}{1}$, $PC\frac{3}{3} = 26$ and that of the destinate stage is $I\frac{2}{3}$, $\overset{\circ}{C}\frac{1}{1}$, $PC\frac{5}{5} = 34$.

DISTRIBUTION: This species is distributed from the northeast area of the Bering Sea to the Sea of Okhotsk, a region which is 5000 km from one end to the other. It is common in Sakhalin, some are found in the northern parts of the Sea of Japan, and some individuals rarely visit the coasts of Korea and the Hokkaido coast of Japan. Information on the movement is scarce, but every year considerable numbers arrive northeast of Hokkaido on drifting ice floes that come from the north and float intact to Sakhalin.

ABUNDANCE: According to Scheffer (1958), there are from 20,000 to 50,000 ribbon seals. In recent years, more than 200 have been brought annually to the market at Abashiri, Japan.

FOOD: Although little is known about their food, the stomach contents of one individual reportedly contained squid.

REPRODUCTION: New pups with white coats, estimated to be less than two weeks old, are often found on ice floes from March to May. Pups shed the white fur after one or two weeks, and in males, the ribbon marks gradually appear. The gestation period is about eleven months and copulation takes place shortly after parturition.

BEHAVIOR: Ribbon seals live away from shore, on ice floes, or on distant islands. They are not gregarious, and usually only a few animals are seen together.

Pagophilus

The genus *Pagophilus* was named by Gray in 1844. Its principal characteristics are as follows:
50b.
1. Only inhabit the Atlantic, breed on Atlantic-Arctic ice.
2. Forelimbs and neighboring parts of body light colored, body sometimes covered with small dark spots.
3. Bony nasal septum reaches rear edge of bony palate.
4. Upper tooth row not curved.
5. Posterior palatine foramen in or anterior to maxillopalatine suture.

Pagophilus groenlandicus

Figure 1–103. *Pagophilus groenlandicus,* known as the harp seal, named by Erxleben in 1777. (After King, 1964.)

MORPHOLOGY: Harp seals are generally white or cork colored and derive their common name from a dark, V-shaped band which crosses the back just above the joint of the forelimbs and runs along the flanks. This mark, which resembles a harp, is distinct on the pale males, less distinct on the more richly colored females, and absent on the snow white pups. Some individuals display dark dots.

Both males and females reach a length of 1.8 m and a weight of 180 kg. The skull length is about 229 mm in the male and 207 mm in the female. The nasal septum is ossified and reaches the posterior end of the palatine bone. The palatine is more than 86 mm long, and the posterior palatine bone is at or near the front of the maxillary palatal symphysis. The posterior margins of the palatine are curved as an arch. The tooth row of the maxillary is straight, and the dental formula is $I \frac{3}{2}$, $C \frac{1}{1}$, $PC \frac{5}{5} = 34$.

DISTRIBUTION: Harp seals are found on the Russian side of the Arctic Ocean, on all coasts of Greenland, and on the northern coasts of Canada and Newfoundland. They are common visitors to Scotland, Germany, and France, and on March 12, 1945, a female and pup were caught on the coast of the United States in Virginia. There is another record of one in the vicinity of 37°N.

ABUNDANCE: According to Scheffer (1958), the population is 20,000 to 50,000.

FOOD: This species feeds mainly on fish but may also eat larger plankton.

REPRODUCTION: Females deliver young on the ice floes from February to March, and the newborn seal is 5.4 to 6.8 kg in weight. In rare cases, twins are born. The mother may leave her pup without nursing for as long as two weeks. When pups grow sufficiently to be able to leave the ice floe in May, they begin to migrate north. The main breeding places are in the White Sea, the east coast of Greenland, and north coast of Newfoundland.

SUBFAMILY MONACHINAE

The primary characteristics of Monachinae are as follows:
45b.
1. Two upper and two lower incisors present on each side.
2. First and fifth hind digits clearly longer than middle three.
3. Anteromedial (inner) wall of orbit defective.
4. Nasal passages not capable of great enlargement; anterior nares horizontal or nearly so, situated on dorsal surface of snout.
5. Female slightly larger than male.
6. Resident or weakly migratory.
7. Monogamous but promiscuous.

Monachus

The genus *Monachus* was named by Fleming in 1822. Its members have the following characteristics:
51a.
1. Postcanines wide and heavy, crushing type.
2. Four mammary teats.
3. Newborn pelage jet black, adult pelage never spotted.
4. Vibrissae smooth.
5. Nasal processes of premaxillary broadly contact nasals.
6. Breed only in subtropical waters.

Monachus schauinslandi

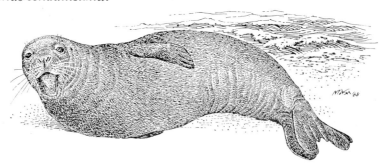

Figure 1–104. *Monachus schauinslandi,* known as the Hawaiian monk seal, named by Matschie in 1905. (After Walker, E. P. *et al.: Mammals of the World.* Baltimore, Johns Hopkins Press, 1964, Vol. II.)

OTHER COMMON NAME: Laysan monk seal.

MORPHOLOGY: Both sexes of adult monk seals are about 2.8 m long, but the females are generally slightly larger than the males. An individual which was 2.9 m long had a skull 279 mm long. Males have a mastoid width of about 135 mm, females about 160 mm. There are two pairs of mammary teats.

The body is cork, blackish brown, or chestnut, and lightens on the ventral side. Fetuses and newborn pups are black, and there are no patches or dots on animals at any stage. Underfur is dispersed or absent.

This species derives its name from the fact that its nearly rounded head is densely covered with short hair and looks like the head of a monk. The snout is wide, and the whiskers are straight and soft. The nostrils are spread apart and have a shallow fold between them. The claws on the digits of the forelimbs are well developed, but those in the hindlimbs are not sharp. In the hindlimbs, the outer digits are longest. The posterior palatine is V shaped. The snout is jutting but flattened, as if it were pressed down. The nostril process of the premaxillary is wide and connected to the nasal bone. The canines are large and sharp at the tip. The postcanines are also large, wide and sharp and are effective in crushing food. Except for the first two, the postcanines have two roots. The rear postcanines are equipped with comparatively well-developed cusps. The dental formula in the destinate stage is $I \frac{2}{2}$, $C \frac{1}{1}$, $P \frac{4}{4}$, $M \frac{1}{1} = {}^{3}{}^{2}$.

DISTRIBUTION: This species is distributed over a range of about 1,600 km. It is found in the Hawaiian Islands from 20°N to 30°N, in the Midway Islands on Pearl and Hermes Reefs, on Lisianski and Laysan Islands, and on French Frigate Shoals.

ABUNDANCE: According to Kenyon and Scheffer, although this species is under the protection of the United States government and out of immediate danger of extinction, the population is still only 1,000 to 5,000 animals.

REPRODUCTION: Although these animals are generally monogamous, there is sometimes intercourse among several animals in a group.

BEHAVIOR: They constantly inhabit the same tropical area, making no extensive migrations.

Monachus tropicalis

Monachus tropicalis, known as the Caribbean monk seal, was named by Gray in 1850.

MORPHOLOGY: Although there are reportedly almost no special morphological differences between this species and *Monachus schauinslandi*, their ranges are clearly separated from each other.

DISTRIBUTION: The Caribbean monk seal, which has inhabited scattered islands in the Caribbean Sea and Gulf of Mexico, has nearly been exterminated. King (1956) and Palmer (1954) reported that a few individuals had been found in Jamaica. The northernmost occurrence reported was from the coast of Texas (28°N), and the southernmost was in Honduras (13°N). The story of the decline of the Caribbean monk seal goes back to August of 1494, when they were first discovered by the crewmen on Columbus' second voyage. Since then, these seals have been taken abundantly, their population has decreased rapidly, and today this species, which once inhabited scattered islands in the Caribbean Sea and the Gulf of Mexico, is extinct or nearly so.

ABUNDANCE: Although Scheffer (1958) reported that this species was extinct, recent evidence indicates that there may still be a few animals in existence.

Monachus monachus

Monachus monachus, known as the Mediterranean Monk Seal, was named by Herman in 1779.

MORPHOLOGY: Although there are reportedly almost no special differences between *schauinslandi* and *tropicalis*, their ranges are clearly separated from each other. Smirnov (1927) and King (1955) reported on the specific differences between the Mediterranean monk seal and the Caribbean species.

DISTRIBUTION: These seals are found on the Anatolian coast of the Black Sea (40°N), in the Adriatic Sea, and on the coasts and islands of the Mediterranean Sea. The southern limit is Cape Blanc (21°N), in Spanish West Africa, and some animals have been found in the vicinity of the Canary Islands.

For that reason, it is reasonable to assume that Mediterranean animals were carried to the Caribbean by wind and currents and later crossed the narrow land mass in Panama to reach the Pacific Ocean. Kellogg (1922) speculated that in the Late Miocene, or slightly earlier, various species of monk seals inhabited the tropical range and Panama must have been a strait of sea.

Leptonychotes

The genus *Leptonychotes* was named by Gill in 1872. Its members have the following characteristics:
51b.
1. Postcanine not crushing type.
2. Two mammary teats.

3. Vibrissae very faintly beaded.
4. Breeding only in Anarctic.

52a.

5. Skull wider; adult skull length not over 50 per cent greater than mastoid width.
6. Postcanines larger, more homodont, not elaborately cusped.

53a.

7. Postcanines strong and functional.
8. Orbits not especially large, zygomatic arches do not drop much.
9. Upper incisors conspicuously unequal, outer about four times larger than inner.
10. Interorbital width less than 18 per cent of skull length.
11. Low sagittal crest in both sexes.
12. Newborn pelage light rusty gray.

Leptonychotes weddelli

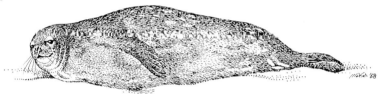

Figure 1–105. *Leptonychotes weddelli,* known as the Weddell seal, named by Lesson in 1826.

MORPHOLOGY: Weddell seals are spindle shaped and fat. A male individual which was 2.8 m long weighed 357 kg and had a skull 290 mm long with a mastoid width of 188 mm. Females are larger, averaging 3.0 m in body length. A 2.9 m female weighed 426 kg and had a skull 287 mm long with a 180 mm mastoid width (Scheffer, 1958). The forelimbs are situated slightly further posterior than those of *Lobodon carcinophagus,* and the hindlimbs are broad.

The fur is dark brownish gray or cork with irregular white to gray dots and is darker on the posterior dorsum, forelimbs, and face.

The zygomatic arch does not extend very far downward, and if the mandible is removed and the upper portion of the skull placed on a table, these arches do not support it. There is a low sagittal crest on the cranium. There are two maxillary incisors in each side, the first being one-fourth of the size of the second. The postcanines are strong and functional. The dental formula is I $\frac{2}{2}$, C $\frac{1}{1}$, PC $\frac{5}{5} = 32$.

DISTRIBUTION: Weddell seals are believed to live further south than any other mammal. Their southern limit is usually 80°S, and they normally inhabit the fringe of the Antarctic continent and its adjacent pack ice. However, Wilson (1907) reported that carcasses and diseased individuals had been found in Antarctica 30 km from the coast and 730 m above sea level. In winter, they migrate north to 30°S in South America, to Australia, to the Tasmanian region, and to both islands of New Zealand.

ABUNDANCE: There are reportedly 100,000 to 300,000 Weddell seals.

BEHAVIOR: These animals live on the permanent fixing ice around the Antarctic continent and make ice holes for entering the water. In winter, when the water temperature is more constant than the air temperature, they stay in the water and use the hole in the ice for breathing.

During the breeding and pupping season, from September to October, Weddell seals form groups of tens of animals, but even though pups show a tendency to be gregarious, adults seem to prefer to live independently the rest of the year.

Ommatophoca

The genus Ommatophoca was named by Gray in 1844. Its members have the following characteristics:

53b.
1. Postcanines small and degenerate, occasionally absent in old animals.
2. Orbits large, zygomatic arches drop well below level of palate.
3. Upper incisors nearly equal, outer cusps slightly larger than inner.
4. Interorbital width greater than 18 per cent of skull length.
5. No sagittal crest.
6. Newborn pelage white.

Ommatophoca rossi

Figure 1–106. *Ommatophoca rossi,* known as the Ross seal, named by Gray in 1844. (After Walker, E. P. *et al.: Mammals of the World,* Baltimore, Johns Hopkins Press, 1964, Vol. II.)

OTHER COMMON NAME: Big-eyed seal.

MORPHOLOGY: The average adult male is 2.2 to 2.3 m long and weighs about 180 kg. One male 2.27 m long and 181 kg in weight had a skull 244 mm long with a mastoid width of 172 mm. Females are slightly larger. A 2.29 m, 215 kg female had a 242 mm skull length with a mastoid width of 170 mm. When the animal draws in the broad short neck, the skin of the neck is folded to cover the posterior crown. The fur is cork or slightly darker, and the hind limbs and top of the head are chocolate color. Newborn pups are white. The orbits are so large that this species has been called the big-eyed seal. The zygomatic arch is curved downward, extending below the base of the palatine. If the mandible is removed and the skull placed on a table, this arch supports the skull. The third incisors are slightly larger than the second. The rear postcanines are small, degenerated, and absent in old individuals. This may be because they feed on soft creatures such as squid and octopus. The dental formula is $I \frac{2}{2}$, $C \frac{1}{1}$, $PC \frac{3}{3}$, $= 24$ at the fetal stage and $I \frac{2}{2}$, $C \frac{1}{1}$, $PC \frac{5}{5}$, $= 32$ in the adult stage.

DISTRIBUTION: The Ross seal is found in the range of the pack ice around the Antarctic continent, but seems to be limited to the western longitude. There have been few reports of its occurrence from the Ross Sea, the Weddell Sea, or from the coasts of South America and New Zealand. There are no reports of this animal from the Southern Indian Ocean or from the coasts of Africa and Australia.

ABUNDANCE: Laws (1953) reported 10,000 animals in the Falkland Islands, and Scheffer (1958) reported 20,000 to 50,000 in the Antarctic.

FOOD: Ross seals feed on Cephalopoda, mainly squid.

Hydrurga

The genus *Hydrurga* was named by Gistel in 1848. The principal characteristics of its members are as follows:

52b.
1. Skull narrow; adult skull length about 75 to 100 per cent greater than mastoid width.
2. Postcanines large; three or more cusps; the central cusp cylindrical, high, pointed, and recurved.

54a.
3. Postcanines sawlike with three cusps, the central cusp cylindrical, high, pointed, and recurved.
4. Posterior edge of mandible gently rounded.
5. Definite sagittal crest present in both sexes.
6. Body long and sinuous (up to 3.9 m), skull massive (up to 416 mm).
7. Skull narrow, adult skull length about 75 per cent greater than mastoid width.
8. Prey on penguins.

Hydrurga leptonyx

Figure 1–107. *Hydrurga leptonyx,* known as the leopard seal, named by Blainville in 1820.

MORPHOLOGY: Leopard seals are spindle shaped and very flexible. The average male is about 3.5 m long and weighs 300 kg, and a 3.2 m, 275 kg specimen had a skull that was 411 mm long and had a mastoid width of 119 mm. Females are far larger. Individuals may reach 4.0 m, and a 3.8 m, 450 kg individual had a skull that was 431 mm long and had a mastoid width of 205 mm.

The body is charcoal gray or slightly blueish gray on the dorsal side, white on the underside from the throat to genital opening, and has black or grey dots scattered abundantly. Those dots sometimes join and form big patches.

The skull of the leopard seal is the second longest of the *Phocidae*, exceeded only by that of the elephant seal. It has a distinct sagittal crest on the cranium. The postcanines are like a saw, and each tooth has three large cusps, the center one of which is cone shaped and slightly longer. It is sharp and slightly bent at the tip. The dental formula is $I \frac{2}{2}$, $C \frac{1}{1}$, $PC \frac{5}{5} = 32$.

DISTRIBUTION: Leopard seals are the most widely distributed of the five species of Antarctic pinnipeds. They are dispersed all over the range of the Antarctic pack ice and the coasts of Australia, New Zealand, South

America, South Africa, and the islands in their vicinity. They occur as far north as Lord Howe Island (31°31'S).

ABUNDANCE: There are reportedly from 100,000 to 300,000 animals.

FOOD: Though their main food item is penguins, leopard seals eat such varied fare as fish, squid, pups of other seals, and decayed carcasses of animals. Some people contend that these feeding habits relate to the large size of the mouth.

BEHAVIOR: These animals are not usually gregarious and are dispersed individually. In the winter, they migrate north to the "no-ice zone" of the subantarctic islands.

Lobodon

The genus *Lobodon* was named by Gray in 1844. The characteristics of its members are as follows:

54b.

1. Postcanines have four to five cusps, with two to three cusps posterior to a large principal cusp.
2. Posterior edge of mandible abruptly rounded, nearly rectangular.
3. No sagittal crest.
4. Body shorter and less flexible, less than 3.0 m long; skull lighter and shorter (up to 306 mm).
5. Feed largely on euphausids.

Lobodon carcinophagus

Figure 1–108. *Lobodon carcinophagus,* known as the crabeater seal, named by Hombron and Jacquinot in 1842.

MORPHOLOGY: Crabeater seals are commonly less than 3.0 m long. Females are slightly larger than males. An indivdual male which was 2.57 m long and weighed 224 kg had a skull which was 306 mm long and had a mastoid width of 167 mm. A female 2.6 m long and 227 kg in weight had a skull that was 286 mm in length with a mastoid width of 157 mm. The skull is comparatively lighter in weight than that of the Antarctic pinnipeds. The fur is cork or brownish gray with whitish dots over the greater part of the animal. The dots are often doubled, causing the dorsal side to appear white. The forelimbs are all dark.

The characteristic tooth structure is apparently a primitive arrangement that has survived in this species longer than in any other mammal. The dental formula in the fetal stage is I $\frac{2}{2}$, C $\frac{1}{1}$, PC $\frac{3}{3}$ = 24 and that in the adult stage is I $\frac{2}{2}$, C $\frac{1}{1}$, PC $\frac{5}{5}$ = 32.

DISTRIBUTION: Although crabeater seals primarily inhabit the coast of the Antarctic continent, they are also found on the coasts of both the north and south islands of New Zealand, on Tasmania, on the southeast coast of Australia, and along the Atlantic coast of South America. From southern spring to summer, they haul out on the pack ice from 55°S to 65°S. Wilson (1907) reported a carcass of this species from a spot 45 km from the coast and 1,000 m above sea level.

ABUNDANCE: According to Bertram (1940), this species is the most abundant of all the Antarctic seals. Scheffer (1958) estimated their numbers as 2,000,000 to 5,000,000.

FOOD: Since these seals feed mainly on krill, the name "crabeater" seems less suitable than the name "krilleater."

BEHAVIOR: This species is circumpolar, pelagic, and gregarious, tending to form large groups. Adult animals make more extensive migrations than the younger animals.

SUBFAMILY CYSTOPHORINAE

The primary characteristics of the subfamily Cystophorinae are as follows:
45c.
1. Two upper and one lower incisor on each side.
2. First and fifth hind digits clearly longer than middle three.
3. Premaxillary bones do not reach the nasals.
4. Nasal passages of adult male capable of great enlargement through combination of inflation and erection; anterior nares vertical or nearly so.
5. Male considerably larger than female.

Cystophora

The genus *Cystophora* was named by Nilsson in 1820. The characteristics of its members are as follows:
55a.
1. Breed on Atlantic-Arctic pack ice.
2. Upper canine about twice as large as the adjacent incisor.
3. Outline of palatine bones nearly a square.
4. Tympanic bulla straight to convex in front.
5. Tip of snout haired.
6. All of the digits have well-developed claws.

Cystophora cristata

Figure 1–109. *Cystophora cristata*, known as the hooded seal, named by Erxleben in 1777. (After Walker, E. P. *et al.: Mammals of the World*. Baltimore, Johns Hopkins Press, 1964, Vol. II.)

OTHER COMMON NAME: Bladdernose seal.

MORPHOLOGY: This species derives its name from an inflatable hood or sacklike projection on the nose of adult males. This hood, which is covered with hair to the tip of the snout, measures about 30 cm in length and 17 to 18 cm in diameter when it is expanded. Males are slightly larger than females. A male 3.5 m long and 408 kg in weight had a skull 275 mm long with a mastoid width of 168 mm. In a female 3.0 m long, the skull was 251 mm long and had a mastoid width of 165 mm.

All the digits are equipped with well-developed claws. The dental formula in the first stage is $I \frac{2}{1}$, $C \frac{1}{1}$, $PC \frac{3}{3} = 22$, and that in the destinate stage is $I \frac{2}{1}$, $C \frac{1}{1}$, $P \frac{4}{4}$, $M \frac{1}{1} = 30$. Most postcanines have a single root, but the fifth maxillary postcanines have two radixes and, in some cases, there are also two roots on the fourth maxillary postcanines. Fetuses have white hair which is moulted before birth, and newborn pups are brownish gray. The fur of adults is chestnut, mingled with dark spots on the dorsal side and lighter ones on the ventral side.

DISTRIBUTION: This species is distributed in the north Atlantic and Arctic seas, where it is found from Newfoundland to Baffin Island, and on southern Greenland, Iceland, and Nova Scotia.

ABUNDANCE: Scheffer (1958) reported the population as 300,000 to 500,000.

REPRODUCTION: The female gives birth to an 11.3 to 13.5 kg pup on the ice floe. Copulation takes place three to four weeks after parturition.

BEHAVIOR: Little is known about its feeding habits, but the hooded seal may feed on various fish.

Mirounga

The genus *Mirounga* was named by Gray in 1827. Its members have the following characteristics:

55b.

1. Breed on land in circumpolar subantarctic seas and a small population off California and Mexico.
2. Upper canine at least five times larger than adjacent incisor.
3. Outline of palatine bones butterfly-shaped.
4. Tympanic bulla concave in front.
5. Tip of snout hairless.

Mirounga leonina

Figure 1–110. *Mirounga leonina,* known as the southern elephant seal, named by Linnaeus in 1758.

MORPHOLOGY: Male southern elephant seals are the largest of all pinnipeds. One large male was 6.5 m long, weighed 3,629 kg, and had a skull 561 mm long with a mastoid width of 293 mm. Females are considerably smaller. One was 3.51 m in body length, 907 kg in weight, 333 mm in skull length, and 202 mm in mastoid width (Scheffer, 1958). The snout (proboscis) of the adult male is long and comb-like, has no hair on the top, and may reach 40 cm in length. When the animal becomes excited, its snout is erected and expanded and appears to be divided into three positions by deep transverse grooves. The forelimbs insert somewhat toward the rear and are comparatively wide apart, so that the chest is very broad. This positioning helps the animal to raise the forepart of the massive body erect.

Fetuses and newborn pups are black, but they moult about ten days after birth. The adult males are dark gray or grayish brown and a little lighter on the underside. Females are about the same color but are slightly darker than the males. The hair is short and stiff.

The maxillary canines are at least five times as large as the second incisor. The dental formula in the first stage is I $\frac{2}{1}$, C $\frac{1}{1}$, PC $\frac{3}{3}$ = 22; that in the destinate stage is I $\frac{2}{1}$, C $\frac{1}{1}$, PC $\frac{4}{4}$, M $\frac{1}{1}$ = 30.

DISTRIBUTION: This species is circumpolar in subantarctic waters and is not believed to occur north of 16°S (St. Helena). It is thought to be migratory, moving in winter toward pelagic feeding grounds at the edge of the pack ice. Breeding colonies are to be found on the islands of South Georgia, Falkland, Gough, Marion, Crozet, Kerguelen, Heard, Macquarie, Campbell, South Shetland, and South Orkney. Individual animals have been recorded from Australia, New Zealand, Tasmania, and South Africa, and also from the coasts of the Antarctic continent.

ABUNDANCE: According to Scheffer (1958), the population is 250,000 to 400,000 in the Falkland area, 50,000 to 100,000 on the Macquarie Islands, 30,000 to 60,000 on Heard Island, and 50,000 to 100,000 on the other subantarctic areas. There are 380,000 to 660,000 animals in all.

Mirounga angustirostris

Figure 1–111. *Mirounga angustirostris,* known as the northern elephant seal, named by Gill in 1866.

MORPHOLOGY: *Mirounga angustirostris* is very similar morphologically to *Mirounga leonina* but is not quite as flexible and connot bend its body backward much over the vertical angle. *Mirounga leonina,* on the other hand, can bend itself far over the vertical into a U or even a V shape. The body color of the two species is quite similar, but their ranges are strictly separated. Both sexes of the northern species are slightly smaller. The snout (proboscis) of the male is very long, hanging down over the mouth about 30 cm when relaxed.

DISTRIBUTION: This species is distributed on the American side of the North Pacific, where they occur on islands off California and Mexico (including Guadalupe, Los Coronados, San Nicholas, San Miguel, and Ano Nuevo). Their northern limit is at Kasaan Bay (55°30′N 132°25′5), Prince of Wales Island in Alaska, which is 3,000 km north of their northernmost breeding place.

ABUNDANCE: According to Scheffer (1958), the population was 8,000 to 10,000 animals. Because the species was thought to be in danger and protected in United States waters, the numbers are presently believed to be increasing.

FOOD: Elephant seals eat various kinds of fish and squid. This species is believed to dive fairly deeply. An individual caught at a distance of 65 km from the coast had many small sharks, squids, and rays in its stomach.

REPRODUCTION: The overall breeding season is from December to the following March, but the peak of breeding is in January and February. A male commonly has a harem of several females, but there may be other males around the group with which the females sometimes copulate. The period of pregnancy is eleven months.

SIRENIA

The stories of mermaids which have long been popular among sea voyagers were probably born in a fertile imagination during long days at sea and given impetus by seamen who saw Sirenians (dugongs or manatees) and "mistook them for maidens."

The sirenian order includes two living families—Dugongidae (dugongs) and Trichechidae (manatees)—each of which consists of a single genus. A third family, Hydrodamalidae (*Hydrodamalis stelleri*), was hunted to extinction in the eighteenth century.

Sirenians are believed to be less abundant today than they were in the past. The oldest sirenians are known from Eocene fossils of Egypt. Additional fossil remains, mostly ancestors of dugongs, have been reported from Egypt, Italy, Austria, Germany, France, Belgium, England, the West Indies, and California. These animals must have inhabited the warm coastal regions of nearly all the continents in ancient times. Although extensive fossil remains of dugongs have been found on the coast of the Atlantic, modern Atlantic Coast sirenians are invariably manatees. The ancestral history of manatees is more obscure.

Sirenians are remarkably adapted to their coastal, estuarine, and riverine aquatic life but do not venture into the open sea. The mammary teats are close to the base of the forelimbs. The hindlimbs have degenerated and have been replaced by a huge, broad, propulsive tail. They have thin layers of hair, relatively thick skin, and almost no subcutaneous fat. The mode of teeth replacement is curious. In most mammals, each milk tooth is replaced by an adult tooth which grows up from beneath its roots. In Sirenians, however, they are replaced by a forward longitudinal movement of teeth in the jaws. Because the teeth are worn by chewing attrition, they have a forward motion. The older teeth reach the front position in the tooth row and are then lost, while the next teeth successively emerge behind, new and sharply ridged.

Although the skeletons of mammalian species generally vary widely in the total number of vertebrae, most have the same number of cervical vertebrae, seven. Two rare exceptions with only six are the South American sloths and the manatees. Sirenians are entirely vegetarian, though it is inevitable that they swallow many small creatures hiding in the weeds. They prefer phanerogamous seaweed, such as shrimp grass, fairly grass, mangrove, and others including *Cabomba, Ancrcharis, Seersia, Utricularis, Nymphaea, Nelumbo,* and *Eichornea.*

Presumably, ancestral sirenians moved into the water partly because they had no functional equipment for defense. Even now they remain still and quiet in the water to avoid enemies. Although sirenians breed in the water, they sometimes show interest in hauling out and can still climb up the river bank or shore.

FAMILY HYDRODAMALIDAE

The characteristics of the family Hydrodamalidae, which is now extinct, were as follows:

56a.
1. Rear margin of tail flukes concave, with a notch in the center.
2. Inhabit only the Bering Sea.
3. Seven cervical vertebrae.
4. No tusk.
5. Adults over 7 m long.

Hydrodamalis

Hydrodamalis stelleri

Hydrodamalis stelleri, known as the northern or Steller's sea cow, was named by Steller in 1774.

The northern or Steller's sea cow is the only representative of this family and was the largest of the Sirenia, reaching a body length of 7.5 to 9.0 m (25 to 30 ft). It was discovered on Capper and Bering Islands, off Kamchatka in the Bering Sea, by the explorer Behring when he was shipwrecked in 1741 on the island which now bears his name. At that time, the Northern sea cow was very abundant in the bays. A scant twenty-seven years later, it was extinct. Its large size and docile nature had made it too easy for man to find and kill and had brought about its rapid extermination.

In July of 1963, Soviet scientists aboard the whale-catcher boat *Buran* in the region of Cape Navarin observed a group of large strange animals which they thought were Steller's sea cows. What a pleasure it would be if this species had survived! Unfortunately, these observations were probably inaccurate. A detailed description is omitted.

FAMILY DUGONGIDAE

The characteristics of the family Dugongidae are as follows:
56b.
1. Rear margin of tail flukes concave in crescent shape.
2. Inhabit Indo-Pacific tropical waters.
3. Seven cervical vertebrae.
4. Large tusk in adult.

Dugong

This family consists of only one genus, Dugong, which includes only one species, *Dugong dugon*.

Dugong dugon

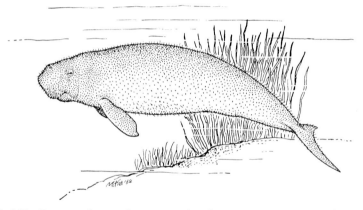

Figure 1–112. *Dugong dugon,* known as the dugong, named by Muller in 1766.

MORPHOLOGY: Although there are very few measurements, dugongs are about 1 m long at birth, and attain a length of about 3 m. One individual which was examined was 2.0 m in length and about 1.3 m in girth.

The shape of the mouth is quite characteristic. The upper lip is very thick and protrudes upward with a terminal disc. The nostrils open at the upper surface of the massive snout. When the face of a pig is viewed from the front, a nostril opening can be seen on the frontal surface of its snout. When the snout of a dugong is viewed from the front, no nostrils are visible. Unlike the nostrils of whales, the nostrils of dugongs cannot close completely. However, there as a functional adaptation to help keep water out. Just beneath the skin, nasal ducts extend about 10 cm posteriorly from the nasal openings. Muscles surrounding them can contract to close the ducts.

There are no ear pinnae, but there are small external openings of the meatus. The forelimbs or flippers have five digits that cannot be seen from the surface. The hindlimbs have vanished. The anus is located two-fifths from the rear of the body. The trunk of the tail is large like that of whales. The tail flukes are broad, and the posterior margin curves in a crescent shape and has no particular notch in the middle. The flukes are boneless, and there is a ridge down the center of their dorsal surface.

Dugongs are blueish-gray on the dorsum, slightly darker on the head, neck, and outer surface of the fins and the tail flukes, and lighter on the ventral surface. The skin resembles that of an elephant. It is wrinkled all over and the hair is dispersed. Hundreds of whiskers which grow around the mouth and are especially thick on the upper lip may be used to find and select foods. A pair of mammary teats at the base of the flippers appear to be the first of a row of mammary teats. The navel is easily recognized at the center of the abdomen.

The skull is extremely thick and osseous. The premaxillary bone is especially heavy and strong, and the second incisors appear tusk-like, another morphological resemblance to elephants. Adult animals completely lack canines, but the young often have lumps of bony tissue where the canines are normally found. In young animals, molars or premolars can be distinguished but are properly called cheek teeth, inclusively. The forward replacement of the cheek teeth is not so remarkable in dugongs as in manatees. The spinal processes of the vertebrae are short, but the transverse processes are well developed. The pelvic bones are attached to the first and the second caudal vertebrae, but neither articularly nor in the condition of sacrals which are widened and firmly fused in most terrestrial animals.

DISTRIBUTION: Dugongs inhabit only regions of seas where there is a lagoon or a coral reef. They are found in the Red Sea, on the coast of East Africa, around the islands of the Indian Ocean, on the southwest coast of Asia, the Philippine Islands, in the Banda Sea, Arafura Sea, and the Coral Sea in north Australia, and other tropical islands in the Pacific. In the vicinity of Japan, they occur in the Okinawa and Amami-Oshima Islands, which appear to be their northern limits. The prospects for the future preservation appear to be most hopeful in the Arafura Sea, where legislative protection has been accomplished with considerable success.

ABUNDANCE: Dugongs are now diminishing in numbers everywhere as a result of excessive pressures from mankind. Even though the slaughter of dugongs has been prohibited in many countries, laws have often been ineffective. The meat is very sweet and tasty and is believed by natives in some countries to be the elixir of permanent youthfulness and immortality. The oil has been considered a precious medicine. For these reasons, some fishermen kill dugongs whenever they find them and do not report the kill to the authorities or scientists. Colin Bertram (1963), who got one of the last survivors in a range of the Gulf of Aqaba, wrote, "it appears that in about 1930, a yearly catch of approximately sixty dugongs was still being taken at Kilakaris, a seaport on the Indian side of the Gulf of Mannar." At that time, they were also said to occur near the north and northwest coasts of Ceylon but were diminishing in numbers. Mohr (1957) says that there have been rapid decreases in their abundance around Madagascar over the last two or three decades.

Glover Allen (1942) quotes records such as these: "apparently plentiful" at Kosseir in the Red Sea in 1870, but by 1932 they were, according to Major Flower "now rare on the (Red Sea) coast of Egypt, rarely north of 25°N latitude, but not uncommon to the south." Since these animals were formerly believed to be extinct in the area, Gohar (1957) listed data from sixteen specimens taken over thirteen years and summarized more recent information from the Red Sea.

FOOD: Dugongs feed primarily on phanerogamous seaweed but may also eat limeweed. Gohar (1957), the director of the Marine Biological Station at Al Gharadapa, has some interesting photographs of dugongs which he uses to explain the way in which the animals seem to use their flippers in shallow waters of lagoons to dig out the sea grass (*Diplanthera uninervis*) which is the exclusive food of the dugongs in that region.

REPRODUCTION: The exact period of gestation is unknown but is probably about one year. The female gives birth to only one pup or calf at a time.

BEHAVIOR: Dugongs spend the greater part of the day quietly on the bottom, rising periodically to breathe and then returning to the bottom without a sound. They feed nocturnally. They do not use the flippers for propulsion but swim with an up-and-down movement of the flukes. Their usual swimming speed is slow, perhaps 2 knots, and their escaping speed is only 5 knots. In Japan, dugongs have been considered a precious animal and protected since before World War II. They are mostly solitary, and though there have been occurrences of a couple or a small group which includes a one-or two-year-old pup, no schools or herds have been seen.

MISCELLANEOUS: Some beautiful legendary stories are told about love affairs of mermaids and men. In the past, sea voyages often took several years and men were away from home for long periods of time. The dugongs are docile, warm-blooded animals whose genital organs bear some resemblance to those of humans. It can be suspected that abnormal relationships have occurred between men and dugongs.

FAMILY TRICHECHIDAE

The following are characteristics of the family Trichechidae:
56c.
1. Rear margin of tail flukes convex in spade shape.
2. Inhabit Atlantic tropical waters.
3. Six cervical vertebrae.
4. Tusk small, even in adults.

Trichechus

This family consists of one genus, *Trichechus*, named by Linnaeus in 1758.

Trichechus manatus

Trichechus manatus, known as the American manatee, was named by Linnaeus in 1758. This group includes both the West Indies and Florida Manatee.

MORPHOLOGY: Although the manatee is generally similar to the dugong in appearance, it has a considerably larger face, larger outer nostrils, which are located more anteriorly and can be opened and shut at will, and thinner whiskers on the upper lip.

Manatees reach a length of about 3.5 m. The average adult is 2.4 to 3.0 m. The body is generally purplish-gray but is darker on the outer or upper surface and lighter on the ventral side of the tail flukes and the forelimbs or flippers. The bones of the flipper from the humerus to the tip of the digits is covered so that only the flippers is seen outwardly. The forelimbs of the manatee are longer than those of the dugong and are tipped by three rough nails. The tips of the flippers can be touched together at the chest, and this species is sometimes seen to take food by "the hand." The hindlimbs have completely vanished, and there is no bone inside. The tail fluke is a large, spade-shaped structure which is quite different from the crescent-shaped fluke of the dugong. If one touches the back of a manatee as it is coming out of the water, he can feel comparatively soft and elastic skin with dispersed hairs 4 to 5 cm in length.

The eyes are round and small and have a closure mechanism which is more nearly like a sphincter than like lids. The body is plump, and slopes gradually to the head, with little or no evidence of a neck. The mammary teats are a single pair positioned close to the base of the forelimbs.

DISTRIBUTION AND VARIATION: This species is distributed from the islands of the West Indies to the east coast of Mexico. Though differences are not very distinct, *Trichechus manatus* is subspecifically divided as follows.

Trichechus manatus manatus (West Indies Manatee) is distributed in the islands of the West Indies, many islands of the Caribbean Sea, along the coast of the Yucatan peninsula, Honduras, Nicaragua, and Panama. In the Caribbean region as a whole, the manatees show a greater tendency to be marine than they do in the Guianas, where great rivers add to its living space.

Trichechus manatus latirostris (Florida Manatee) was named by Harlan in 1823. There are distinct morphological differences between this subspecies and the original species. The manatees of this species appear to have a longer neck, a wider head, and a smaller face. However, when one closely observes both animals in captivity, he gets the impression that they are only slightly different. The range of the subspecies is limited to the coastal waters, lagoons, and downstream waters of rivers in the Florida peninsula. The northernmost record was of an animal caught near Wilmington, North Carolina in 1919. Though there are only a few manatees on the Florida peninsula today, it is clear that there were many in the past. They are now sensibly protected by legislation of the United States government.

ABUNDANCE: The number of manatees is unknown. Conservationists and scientists hope to study them more. Though the population is considered to be more than that of the dugongs, it is evident that this animal is also near extinction.

FOOD: These manatees feed entirely on vegetation but take in small mollusks, crustaceans, and other small creatures with the weeds. Almost any weed appears to be acceptable, and very large quantities of weed must be consumed. In the wild, they most frequently eat water hyacinth and mangroves, which grow in swamps or at the seaside. In captivity, they have been fed lettuce, cabbage, cooked carrots, and potatoes.

REPRODUCTION: Mating takes place in shallow water, and though the actual birth of a "mermaid" calf has only been witnessed in a Florida aquarium, a cow 2.5 to 3.0 m long is thought to give birth to a single calf about 1.0 m long which weighs about 14 kg. The calf is born underwater and is helped to the surface by the mother, who solicitously assists the calf for a while. On occasion, the young manatee even rides on its mother's back. The calf's respiratory rate is rapid at first, but the period of apnea increases until the adult habit of breathing every few minutes is achieved. During the first few hours of life, the calf's tail is curled forward underneath its body and it swims using its flippers instead of its tail (Bertram, 1963).

BEHAVIOR: Though manatee inhabit the rivers and their estuaries and the sea between the mouths of rivers, entering both tidal and fresh water, they are not generally found far inland or in streams with rapid currents. They sometimes inhabit clearer water rivers but, as in the case of the Guiana manatees, usually prefer the muddy places where grass and floating weeds are abundant. They feed entirely upon aquatic vegetation and may most frequently be seen feeding in the quiet of dusk.

A special feature of the manatee's mouth is that its two corners themselves function as active projecting mandibles, pressing in the food with regular cutting movements. The corners of the mouth can be projected and then opposed, dragging in the vegetation with their tough, papillae-covered points. The forelimbs, too, are used actively to sweep and press vegetation toward and into the mouth. Manatees occasionally draw their head and shoulders laboriously from the water by use of the forelimbs pressing against the ground, in order so as to feed on bankside vegetation. If dragged from the water, even onto level ground, they cannot struggle back.

Although manatees are sometimes seen lifting their heads above the surface, presumably to get a better view of the area, they depend mostly on the auditory sense. Allen (1942) made special note of the manatee's good hearing ability. In captivity, they soon learn to respond to a whistle by coming to the side of the pool for food.

Manatees live silent, slow lives. When they breathe, approximately once every minute and a half, they expose their nostrils at the water surface, breathe, and disappear without a ripple or sound.

Families consist of a bull, cow, and one or two calves. In a lagoon or a certain stretch of river, these groups sometimes merge into a loose herd of from ten to fifty or more individuals during the day and scatter at night.

UTILIZATION: In Yucatan, the hide, which may be up to 4 cm thick, as well as the flesh is utilized and brings a good price. Some of the local people believe that the bones of the manatees have marvelous curative properties. The oil has been used as lamp fuel, as a dressing for meat, as a lubricant, and for softening leather.

CAPTIVITY: Some dugongs have been kept in zoos, but manatees are more popular and are kept by aquariums and some private individuals in Florida. They are not difficult to tame or to train to perform some simple tricks by rewarding them cleverly with food. When the water level gets so low that a manatee is stranded, he will turn himself on his back to avoid pressure on the chest and make breathing easier. Because the ribs are not fused firmly to the sternum, the thorax is not rigid. When the water level rises again, the manatee will return to its original position, sometimes to the astonishment of an inexperienced aquarium attendant.

Trichechus senegalensis

Trichechus senegalensis, known as the African manatee, was named by Link in 1788. There are few morphological differences between this animal and other species of manatees. It is found in West Africa from Senegal to the Angora district, in lagoons, coasts, and many rivers. Little scientific information has been collected into convenient form.

Trichechus inunguis

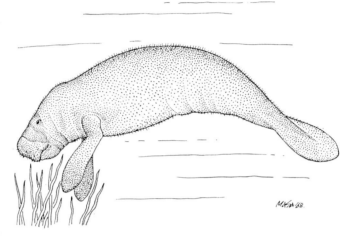

Figure 1–113. *Trichechus inunguis,* known as the Amazonian manatee, named by Natterer in 1883.

Trichechus inunguis, known as the Amazonian manatee, was named by Natterer in 1883.

The Amazonian manatee is a purely freshwater animal, characterized by the absence of nails on the flippers (which are proportionately elongated) and a white breast patch. They are distributed in the Amazon and its tributaries, as well as the Orinoco.

A Brazilian publication in the middle 1940's indicated that there was an export of manatee hides and canned meat from Brazil. This species has been so reduced by hard hunting that they are now incapable of supporting the trade.

REFERENCES

Cetacea

Anderson, J.: *Anatomical and Zoological Research, Comprising an Account of the Zoological Results of the Two Expeditions to Western Yunnan in 1868 and 1875, and a Monograph of the Two Cetacean Genera,* Plantanista *and* Orcella. Piccadilly, Bernard Quaritch. 1878, pp. 355–564.

Anderson, R.M.: Catalogue of Canadian recent mammals. *Bull. Nat. Mus. Canada,* 102(Bio. Ser. 31):238, 1946.

Beddard, F.C.: *A Book of Whales.* Progressive Science Series, 1900.

Bobrinskoi, N.A.: Pinnipedia. In *Mammals of the U.S.S.R. Moscow,* Acad. Sciences U.S.S.R. 1944.

Ellerman, J.R. and Morrison-Scott, T.C.S.: *Checklist of Palaearctic and Indian Mammals, 1758–1946.* London, British Museum of Natural History, 1953.

Ellerman, J.R., Morrison-Scott, T.C.S., and Hayman, R.W.: *Southern African Mammals, 1758–1951, a Reclassification.* London, British Museum of Natural History, 1953.

Eshricht, D.F.: *On the Species of the Genus* Orca *Inhabiting the Northern Seas; Recent Memoirs on the Cetacea.* London, Ray Society, Publication 40, 1862.

Fraser, F.C.: On the development and distribution of the young stages of krill. *Discovery Rep., 14:*1, 1936.

Fraser, F.C.: Whales and dolphins. In Norman, J.R. and Fraser, F.C. (Eds.): *Giant Fishes, Whales and Dolphins.* London, Putnam, 1937 and 1948, pp. 201–349.

Gray, J.E.: *Catalogue of Seals and Whales in the British Museum,* 2nd ed. London, British Museum of Natural History, 1866.

Gray, J.E.: *Supplement to the Catalogue of Seals and Whales in the British Museum.* London, British Museum of Natural History, 1871.

Guldberg, G. and Nansen, F.: *On the Development and Structure of the Whale, Part I on the development of the Dolphin.* Bergen, 1894.

Hall, R. and Kelson, K.R.: *The Mammals of North America,* New York, Ronald Press Co., 1959, pp. 831–1083.

Hamilton, J.E.: A rare porpoise of the South Atlantic, *Phocaena* dioptrica (Lahille, 1912). *Discovery Rep., 21:*227–234, 1941.

Ichihara, T.: The pygmy blue whale, *Balaenoptera musculus brevicauda,* a new subspecies from the Antarctic. In Norris, K.S. (Ed.): *Whales, Dolphins, and Porpoises.* Berkeley, University of California Press, 1966, pp. 79–113.

Jonsgard, A.: Studies on the little piked whale or minke whale (Balaenoptera acutorostrata). *Norwegian Whaling Gazette,* 5, 1951.

Kuroda, N.: *Nippon Jyurui Zusetsu* (Monograph of the Japanese Mammals). Sohgen-sha, 1953. (in Japanese).

Lillie, D.G.: British Antarctic (*Terra Nova*) Expedition, 1910. *Nat. Hist. Repts.* (*Brit. Mus.*) *Zool. 1:*85–124, 1915.

Lütken, C.F.: Geuburt der Wale., Vid. Medd, Dansk, Noturh. For., 1887; *Zool. Jahrb.* 3:802, 1888.

Miller, G.S.: A new river dolphin from China. *Smith. Misc. Coll.,* 68:9, 1918.

Moore, J.C.: New records of the gulf-stream beaked whale, *Mesoplodon gervaisi* and some taxonomic considerations. *Amer. Mus. Nat. Hist., 1993:* 1–35, 1960.

Nishiwaki, M.: *Whales and Pinnipeds.* Tokyo, University of Tokyo Press, 1965 (in Japanese).

Nishiwaki, M. and Yagi,T.: On the age-determination method of the toothed whale by the study of the tooth. *Proc. Acad.* 30:399–404, 1954.

Ogawa, T.: Studies on the Japanese toothed whales. I-IV. *Plants and Animals,* 4, 1936–1937 (In Japanese).

Olsen, O.: the external characters and biology of Bryde's whale. *Proc. Zool. Soc. Lond,* 1913, p. 1073.

Omura, H. and Sakiura, H.: Studies on the little piked whales from the coast of Japan. *Sci. Rep. Whales Res. Inst., 16:7–18,* 1956.

Raven, H.C.: On the structure of *Mespolodon densirostris,* a rare beaked whale. *Bull. Amer. Mus. Nat. Hist.,* LXXX, 1942.

Scammon, C.M.: *Marine Mammals of the North-Western Coast of North American, with an Account of the American Whale Fishery.* San Francisco, Carmany, 1874.

Scoresby, W.: *Journal of a Voyage to the Northern Whale-Fishery.* Edinburgh, Archbold Constable, 1823.

Sergeant, D.E. and Brodie, P.F.: Tagging white whales in the canadian arctic. *J. Fish. Res. Board Canada 26*(8): 2561–2205, 1969a.

Sergeant, D.E. and Brodie, P.F.: Body size in whales, *Delphinapterus leucas. J. Fish. Res. Board Canada 26*(10): 2561–2580, 1969b.

Tomilin, A.G.: *Whales and Whaling in the USSR.* Rybnoe Khozyaistvo USSR, No. 10, 1935 (in Russian).

Pinnipedia

Allen, G.M.: The Mammals of China and Mongolia; Order Pinnipedia. In *Natural History of Central Asia.* Amer. Mus. Natl. Hist. 2:490, 1938.

Allen, J.A.: *History of North American Pinnipeds, A Monograph of the Walruses, Sea-lions, Sea-bears and Seals of North America.* Washington, D.C. U.S. Geol. and Geogr. Surv. Terr. Misc. Publ. 12, 1880.

Barabash-Nikiforov, I.I.: Mammals of the Commander Islands and the surrounding sea. *J. Mammal.* 19:412–429, 1938.

Barrett-Hamilton, G.E.H.: *Report on the Collections of Natural History Made in the Anartic Regions During the Voyage of the* Southern Cross. London, British Museum of Natural History, 1902.

Bertram, G.C.L.: The Biology of the Weddell and Crabeater Seals, with a Study of the Comparative Behavior of the Pinnipedia. *In Sci. Rep. Brit. Graham Land Exped.* (*1934–1937*). Brit. Mus. Nat. Hist., 1940.

Dunbar, M.J.: The Pinnipedia of the Arctic and Subarctic. *Bull. Fish. Res. Bd. Canada,* 85:1–22, 1949.

Ellerman, J.R. and Morrison-Scott, T.C.S.: *Checklist of Palaearctic and Indian Mammals, 1758 to 1946.* London, British Museum of Natural History, 1951.

Hickling, Grace, The Grey Seals of the Farne Islands. *Trans. Nat. Hist. Soc. Northumberland,* Durham and Newcastle upon Tyne, n.s., *11*:230–244, 1956.

Kellogg, R.: Pinnipeds from Miocene and Pleistocene deposits of California and a resume of current theories regarding origin of Pinnipedia. *Bull. Dep. Geol. Univ. Calif.,* 13:23–132, 1922.

Kenyon, K.W. and Scheffer, V.B.: The seals, sea-lions and sea otter of the Pacific Coast, *U.S. Dept. Interior, Fish and Wildlife Service, Cir. 32,* 1955.

King, J.E.: The monk seals (Genus *Monachus*). *Bull Brit. Mus. Nat. Hist.*, 3:201–256, 1955.

King, J.E.: *Seals of the World*, London Trustees of the British Museum of Natural History, 1964.

Laws, R.M.: The seals of the Falkland Islands and dependencies. *Oryx*, 2:87–97, 1953.

Maxwell, Gavin: *Seals of the World*, Boston, Houghton Mifflin, 1967.

McEwen, E.H.: A sporadic occurrence of an Alaskan fur seal. *J. Mammal*, 35:444, 1954.

Naumov, S.P.: The seals of the U.S.S.R., the raw material basis of the marine mammal fishery. In Bobrinskoi, N.A. (Ed.): *Economically Exploited Animals of the U.S.SR.* Moscow, All-Union Cooperative United Publishing House, 1953, pp. 1–105 (in Russian).

Nordquist, O.: Beitrag zur Kenntnis der Isolierten Formender Ringelrobbe (Rhoca Foetida Fabr.) *Acta Soc. Fauna Flora Fenn.* 15:1–44, 1899.

Palmer, R.S.: Seals and sea lions. Order Pinnipedia. In *The Mammal Guide*. Garden City, Doubleday, 1954, pp. 148–166.

Peterson, R.S., and Bartholomew, G.A.: *The Natural History and Behavior of the California Sea Lion*, Special Publication No. 1, American Society of Mammalogists, 1966.

Petersen, R.S., Hubbs, C.L., Gentry, R.L., and Delong, R.L.: The Guadalupe fur seal: habitat, behavior, population size, and field identification, *J. Mammal*, 49:665, 1968.

Ross, T.S., Kaganovskiy, A.G., and Klumov, S.K.: (Ed.): Geographical distribution of fishes and other commercial animals of the Okhotsk and Bering Seas. *Trudy Instituta Okeanologii*, 4:95–115, 1955.

Scheffer, V.B.: *Seals, Sea Lions and Walruses*, Stanford, California, Stanford Univ. Press, 1958.

Scheffer, V.B.: *The Food of the Alaska Fur Seal*, U.S. Dept. Interior, Fish and Wildlife Service, Wildl. Leafl. 329, 1950.

Sivertsen, E.: A survey of the eared seals (family Otariidae) with remarks on the Antarctic seals collected by M/K "Norvegica" in 1928–1929. *Det. Norske Videnskaps-Akademi i Oslo, Sci. Results Norweg. Antarct. Exped.* 1927–1929, *et. seq.*, Lars Christensen, No. 36, 1954.

Smirnov, H.A.: Diagnostical remarks about some seals (phocidae) of the Northern Hemisphere. *Trmso, Mus Aarsh.* 48, 1925; 5:1–23, 1927.

Wilson, E.A.: Mammalia (whales and seals) in National Antarctic Expedition, 1901–04. In *Natural History*. London, British Museum of Natural History, vol. 2, pp. 1–69, 1907.

Sirenia

Allen, G.M.: *Extinct and Vanishing Mammals of the Western Hemisphere with the Marine Species of all the Oceans.* Amer. Com. Int. Wildlife Protection. N.Y. Zool. Park, 11, 1942.

Bertram, C.: *In Search of Mermaids. The Manatees of Guiana.* London, Peter Davis Ltd. 1963.

Berzin, A.A., Tikhomirov, E.A., and Troinin, V.I.: Was Steller's sea cow exterminated? *Priroda,* 52:72–75, 1963 (in Russian).

Gohar, H.A.F.: The Red Sea dugong. *Publ. Mar. Biol. Sta.,* Al-Gharadapa, Red Sea, 9:3–50, 1957.

Mahr, E.: Sirenen Oder Seekuhe. Neue Brehm-Bucherei, A. Ziemens, Verlag. *Wittenberg Lutherstadt.* 1957 (in German).

Chapter 2

THE SEA OTTER

KARL W. KENYON

Figure 2–1. *Enhydra lutris,* known as the sea otter.

INTRODUCTION

The sea otter *Enhydra lutris* is the only member of the family Mustelidae that is limited exclusively to the marine environment. It is also the only fissiped carnivore that is exclusively marine (in the strict sense). Unlike some pinnipeds and cetaceans, which may ascend rivers, there is no authentic record of a wild sea otter entering a freshwater environment.

By comparison with the seals and whales, the sea otter is poorly adapted to inhabit a broad spectrum of marine environments. Its fur appears to be a less efficient insulating mechanism than the blubber of other marine mammals. Even so, the sea otter is well adapted to exist in the narrow environmental zone for which it is specialized. Its habitat includes inshore waters, usually along rocky coasts, which are rich in bottom fauna. No indication has been found that a sea otter is able to obtain pelagic food species in the open sea. Thus, long migratory movements through the open sea are precluded. At Amchitka Island, it was found that the home range of individual sea otters included about five to ten miles of coastal waters.

MORPHOLOGY: The sea otter is the smallest marine mammal. The adult male may reach a length of about 147 cm (58 in) and a weight of up to 45 kg (100 lb). The adult female may grow to 139 cm (55 in) and 33 kg (72 lb). The flattened tail constitutes about 25 percent of the body length.

The forepaws, adapted for grasping food and for grooming the fur, are not generally used in swimming, though an animal may use them as a slight aid when it is gathering food. The retractile claws may be extended for grasping food but are usually retracted during grooming activity so that the fur may be rubbed with the flattened pad that envelops the phalanges. The hind feet are broadly flattened and adapted to the sea otter's unique habit of swimming on its back at the surface. Propulsion at the surface is attained by means of alternate strokes of the hind flippers. Probably because of this manner of swimming, the fifth or outer digit, which dips into the water first on each stroke, is longest. In this respect, the sea otter differs from other mammals.

The fur of the sea otter consists of two layers—the guard hair, about 3.8 cm (1.5 in) long, and a dense underfur layer, about 3.2 cm (1.25 in) long. Dr. Victor B. Scheffer, who studied samples of sea otter pelage, found that each fur bundle contained one guard hair and an average of about seventy underfur roots. Because the sea otter has no blubber, it must rely on a blanket of air trapped in its fur for insulation against its chilly environment. If the fur becomes soiled so that it absorbs water, destroying the insulating air blanket and allowing water to reach the skin, the animal soon chills and dies.

Perhaps to retain needed insulation, the molt is prolonged rather than abrupt. The fur is shed throughout the year, but the amount shed in mid-summer is approximately twice as great as that shed in midwinter. Thus, a unimodal annual molt curve is indicated. In the fur commerce of the eighteenth and nineteenth centuries, sea otter fur was considered to be in prime condition throughout the year. The study of pelage, although on a small sample, indicates that the pelage of the sea otter is approximately twice as dense per unit of area as that of the northern fur seal.

Body fur color is variable, ranging from light buff, which is rare, through shades of brown to nearly black. The guard hairs may be dark in some individuals and light in others. The head, particularly in males, is usually light in color. With age, the head and chest may become grizzled to almost white.

The teeth have no sharp cutting edges. The postcanine or molariform teeth are bunodont, having flattened, rounded cusps adapted to crushing. The canines are also relatively blunt and rounded when compared to those of other carnivores. The lower incisors protrude forward and are adapted to scooping the soft parts of invertebrates from their shells. The sea otter is unique among carnivores in having two instead of three pairs of lower incisors. In the adult, there are thirty-two teeth (dental formula: $I\frac{3}{2}$, $C\frac{1}{1}$, $PC\frac{3}{3}$, $M\frac{1}{2} = \frac{8}{8}$).

DISTRIBUTION: The historical record shows that in the early years of the eighteenth century, the sea otter inhabited the Pacific coast of North America from central Baja California, near Morro Hermoso (27°32′N latitude) (Ogden, 1941), Mexico, northward to Prince William Sound (60°30′N latitude). From this northernmost point, it was found southwestward among the islands and along the coast of Alaska and northeastern Asia. There were large populations in the Pribilof, Aleutian, Commander, and Kuril Islands.

A period of intensive and unregulated exploitation of the sea otter began shortly after 1741 when survivors of the Bering expedition returned with furs and reports of abundant fur-bearing marine mammals in the newly discovered Aleutian and Commander Islands. Impetus was added when members of Captain James Cook's expedition to the North Pacific returned with sea otter furs in 1779.

By 1911, when an international treaty gave the remnant sea otter population protection, the animal was commercially extinct and zoologists feared that the species would not survive. Under a policy of complete protection, however, remnant colonies increased slowly. The seed colonies which ultimately survived were in the Kuril and Commander Islands, U.S.S.R., in the Aleutians and several other remote Alaskan islands, and at one location near Monterey on the California coast. Beginning in the 1940's, some isolated island populations reached maximum size, overpopulated their habitat, and declined. Other less isolated populations continue to expand into nearby unpopulated habitat. Large-scale transplant operations undertaken by state of Alaska biologists in the late 1960's reintroduced the sea otter to isolated and then unpopulated parts of its former range at the Pribilof Islands and in the Alexander archipelago of southeastern Alaska. Today, however, the sea otter has failed to reoccupy most of its former range between Prince William Sound and central Baja California.

ABUNDANCE: No survey count of sea otters ever includes all animals present in the large areas that must be surveyed. Therefore, if a total population estimate is desired, it is necessary to asses the number of otters not counted. Field counts may not be comparable because of variable wind, reflected sunlight or cloud cover, water depths, type of coastline where surveys are made, and observer ability. Therefore, all counts and estimates of sea otters are approximations of varying accuracy. The value of survey counts is that they (a) place a figure on the minimum number of otters in a given area and (b) indicate where otters are abundant, scarce, or absent.

The only American sea otter population that survived south of Alaska is on the California coast between Point Conception and Año Nuevo Island. During recent surveys conducted by biologists of the California Department of Fish and Game and the University of California, 1,014 otters were counted (Peterson and Odemar, 1969).

Aerial surveys in Alaska were conducted by the Bureau of Sport Fisheries and Wildlife from 1959 to 1965. The maximum counts in all areas totaled nearly 18,000 otters. The estimated total number derived from these counts and other observations was 25,000 to 30,000 animals.

Soviet biologists have counted otters in the Kuril and Commander Islands and on the Kamchatka Peninsula. They estimated the total number in these areas at about 5,000 to 6,000. Thus, allowing for reproduction, the total world population in the late 1960's may be about 40,000 animals.

Food and Feeding Behavior: The sea otter prefers benthic mollusks and echinoderms when they are available. In areas where sea otter populations become large and these organisms are depleted, fish (usually sluggish bottom forms) may become an important food source. Under natural conditions, the sea otter does not consume or gather food on land. All food is obtained by diving, usually in water depths from about 1 to 20 fathoms. Where food is scarce in shallow water, it may be sought in deeper areas. Otters are infrequently observed diving for food in water beyond the 30-fathom curve (depth 180 feet). After food is gathered from the bottom, it is stored under the left foreleg and when no more can be held there, under the right foreleg, where a pouch of loose skin enables the otter to carry as many as twenty-five small sea urchins.

The sea otter is exceptional among marine mammals in its habit of using stones as tools. An otter may use a rock, carried to the surface from the bottom, as a base on which to pound the shells of mollusks to break them, or it may use a rock to pound and break the shells of abalones that are firmly attached to the bottom. After the abalone dies and releases its hold on the bottom, the sea otter carries it to the surface for consumption. While eating at the surface, the sea otter frequently rolls over sideways, washing food slime and scraps of food from its chest.

When a large food item such as an octopus is obtained, the otter may,

Figure 2–2. A female sea otter pounds a clam held between her paws against another clam resting on her chest. Also, a rock may be carried to the surface and used as an anvil against which hard-shelled organisms are broken. This captive otter sometimes broke clams by pounding them against the cement edge of her pool. The lines on the head show dry fur where wet outer fur has parted.

after satisfying its appetite, carry the remainder of the prey on its chest until it is ready to eat again.

It has been supposed that sea urchins were an essential sea otter food organism (Barabash-Nikiforov, 1947). It is true that in some areas, sea urchin remains are found in almost every fecal deposit. Stomach examinations, however, revealed that more nourishing organisms, such as mussels, clams, rock oysters, octopus, and fish are by volume and caloric and protein content the more important foods. When they are large and gravid, sea urchins may be an important food source, but when they are immature and during seasons when they are not gravid, their value as food is negligible. The hard parts of the many important foods are not ingested, so that fecal examinations give an incomplete picture of the sea otter's food habits.

In addition to the hard parts of certain foods, sea otters may consume other indigestible material. Kelp, which is often taken fortuitously with other food, passes undigested through the gastrointestinal tract. In areas where food depletion is advanced, hungry otters were observed to eat birds that were found floating dead on the water. Flesh and feathers, however, were passed as feces, showing little or no indication of digestion.

The daily food quantity required by the sea otter is high (see Husbandry). It appears that the sea otter requires a high metabolic rate (and thus a high food intake) to maintain body temperature.

REPRODUCTION: Apparently, the male does not establish a distinct breeding territory. Many males and females may utilize the same home range. Mating may occur at any season and takes place in the water after a searching male finds a female in estrus. The pair may remain together in a limited area for as long as three days. During this period, they dive and feed side by side and sleep together on a rock chosen by the female. Copulation, which in one case lasted for twenty-three minutes, may take place more than once. Toward the end of the mating period, the male may leave the female resting on the favored rock while he dives for food nearby. At this time, the female may desert the male and permanently break the pair bond.

Incomplete studies indicate that the gestation period is approximately one year and consists of unimplanted and implanted periods. It is estimated that the implanted period is about four months. Births occur in all months, but most young are born in the spring or early summer.

Sea otters give birth on land to a single pup covered by a thick, woolly coat. Twin fetuses are recorded but it is doubtful that more than one young ultimately survives. The eyes are open at birth. The young are helpless and may weigh from 1.4 to 2.2 kg (3 to 5 lb) and measure about 61 cm (24 in) in body length.

From birth, the pup nurses from its mother's two abdominal mammae and it is groomed and otherwise attended constantly by her, except while she is diving for food. While the mother is feeding, the newborn pup sleeps quietly on the surface or with uncoordinated movements, squirms about and may attempt swimming or diving movements. From an early age, probably within its first few weeks of life, the young otter's milk diet is supplemented by soft parts of food organisms which its mother passes to it in her forepaws. Near the end of its first year of life, the young otter is still in its mother's company but is capable of diving and obtains some of its own food. There is no available evidence to indicate that the female mates again before she deserts her young after it is a year or more of age. Thus, two years may elapse between pregnancies.

BEHAVIOR AND HABITS: The sea otter is unique among marine mammals in that it sleeps, eats, carries, and nurses it young while resting or swimming on its back at the surface. Infrequently, it swims, belly down, at the surface. Before diving, it usually rises high in the water and rolls forward. Beneath the surface it swims by undulations of the body in the vertical plane, flippers and tail extended, so that propulsion is cetacean-like.

Beneath the surface, the sea otter's escape speed is about 5.7 statute miles per hour. On the surface, while swimming belly up with alternate strokes of the hind flippers, its swimming speed is about 1.7 statute miles per hour.

Figure 2–3. A mother sea otter grooms her pup's fur as the pup nurses from her two abdominal nipples. Nursing usually takes place while the mother floats on her back. However, in fine weather the mother may bring her pup ashore in the late afternoon and then spend the night sleeping on rocks near the water.

Some Alaskan sea otters live in areas where there are no kelp beds (Kenyon, 1969). Where kelp beds are available, the sea otter may seek calm water in which to rest among the floating strands. In areas where wind or water currents might move the sleeping animal, it may anchor its body beneath one or more strands of kelp. During stormy weather, particularly in the Aleutian Islands, otters may haul out to sleep among rocks in sheltered areas near the water.

Grooming, during which the fur is scrubbed, licked, and rubbed dry with the forepaws, is an important activity. One captive sea otter spent 48 percent of the daylight hours in grooming activity. In the wild, grooming is reduced because feeding activity requires more time than it does in captivity.

Sea otters may be scattered and solitary or they may gather in pods of more than 100 animals to rest on the open sea, in sheltering kelp beds, or on land. Although segregation of sexes is variable, females with young usually segregate themselves from males, and numbers of males may haul out together apart from areas frequented by females (Kenyon, 1969).

PARASITES, DISEASE, AND PREDATION: Aside from fortuituous infestations by a nasal mite, *Halarachne miroungae*, there is no authentic record of

external parasites on sea otters. *Halarachne miroungae* is found commonly
in the nasal passages of the harbor seal, *Phoca vitulina.* Cross-infestation
on hauling-out areas used by both species probably accounts for the sea
otter's infestation by this seal parasite.

The sea otter is infested by a number of internal parasites. Jellison and
Neiland (1965, pp. 8–9) list eleven species of helminths. In general, it
appears that these parasites have little detrimental effect on the host.
Rausch (1953), however, considered two species, *Micropallus pirum* and
Terranova decipiens, to be pathogenic, and one animal found dead in the
wild was believed to have died from dense populations of these two species
(Fay, 1962).

The problems caused by parasite infestation which resulted when otters
were fed fresh fish were eliminated when fish were held frozen for several
days before feeding. A trematode, *Orthosplanchnus fraterculus,* was
abundant in the gall bladder and bile ducts of most sea otters examined.
Apparently this parasite has little or no pathological effect.

Enteritis was found to be the terminal symptom in many otters that
were found dead or dying on beaches at Amchitka Island in the 1954–63
period. All of these animals were emaciated and exhibited inflammation
and lesions in parts of the small intestine. Several animals showing symptoms of enteritis (black, tarry feces and general malaise) were taken from
the beaches and placed in an enclosure having a pool and dry sheltered
areas. When offered an ample supply of filleted fish, some of these animals
ate greedily and regained health. It was indicated that a large, local otter
population had depleted food resources and that starvation and accompanying lowered resistance allowed enteritis to develop. It was presumed
that a *Clostridium* organism may have been the causative agent.

Field observations reveal that sea otters are rarely killed by killer whales
(*Orcinus orca* (Nikolaev, 1965, p. 231)) and the bald eagle (*Haliaeetus
leucocephalus* (Jones, 1961)). The tooth of a great white shark (*Carcharo-
don carcharias*) was removed from a dead sea otter (Orr, 1959), indicating
that shark bite was the cause of death. Many reports from field observers
indicate, however, that predation (except by man) is an unimportant cause
of sea otter mortality.

HUSBANDRY: If the sea otter's basic requirements are satisfied, it adapts
readily to captivity. The most important requirements are (a) an abundant
supply of clean water, preferably sea water, and (b) an abundant supply
of fresh mollusk or fish flesh for food. Free air circulation, clean dry areas
adjacent to the water, and moderate temperatures are also important. The
greatest barriers to the successful holding of captive sea otters are the
problems encountered in transporting them from the place of capture to a
properly prepared enclosure at the final destination. If more than a few

hours (eight to twelve) elapse during transit and if careful preparations for care in transit are not made, the chances of ultimate survival at the destination are poor.

If the period of transit is prolonged and an otter must be fed in a dry cage or in one having an inadequate supply of water, the fur becomes soiled with food and excrement. Also, under these conditions, the animal will exhibit excitement and distress. When the otter is again introduced to water, its fur no longer retains an insulating airblanket but becomes wet. When water reaches the skin, chilling occurs and unless special care is rendered to warm, wash, and dry the animal, it soon dies. Animals having fur soiled during prolonged travel (one to three days) were often so upset that even with special care they failed to survive.

Although rapid air transport is the most ideal way of carrying sea otters over long distances, care must be taken to keep cabin temperatures low. If the fur is dry, sea otters show distress when air temperatures are above 40°F. Sea otters died from heat prostration when cabin temperatures were near 70°F., even though water was poured on them. Traveling cages having water compartments in them and cabin temperature between 35° and 45°F. have proved most successful. Since sea otters always exhibit distress when deprived of water, transportation in dry cages should be limited to a minimum.

Newly captured sea otters often take food soon after being placed in a pool. A variety of fresh sea food is readily accepted. A monotonous diet of filleted rockfish and squid, however, has kept an otter at the Tacoma Aquarium in excellent condition for the past four years. The daily requirement of this animal, a 30 kg (65 lb) male, is 6.8 kg (15 lb) of food (two-thirds filleted rockfish and one-third squid). This quantity (nearly one-quarter of body weight) furnishes approximately 5,300 calories daily and remains constant throughout the year (Kenyon, 1969).

MEDICINE: Tranquilizers—promazine hydrochloride (Sparine®, Wyeth) and propiopromazine hydrochloride (Tranvet®, Diamond)—were useful in speeding the adjustment of newly captured sea otters to conditions in captivity. A tranquilizer was particularly useful in calming mother otters having small, helpless young when they were first placed in a holding enclosure. The disadvantage of tranquilizer use is that it inhibits normal attention to bodily needs, such as grooming, drying the fur, and eating. In general, captives did better when they were not given tranquilizers. If circumstances or the temperament of individual otters indicated tranquilizer use, a small dose, 0.5 to 1 mg of Sparine per pound of body weight, was adequate.

Certain fish contain an enzyme (thiaminase) that inhibits the proper utilization of vitamin B. To assure health, captive otters are given a vitamin

B-complex (100 mg) pill daily. The pill is readily eaten when embedded in a piece of fish.

Minor cuts or scratches on the paws of several captive otters developed infections. If the otter's condition was otherwise good, these infections were cured after one or sometimes two injections of 600,000 units of Bicillin (Wyeth) or Penicillin.

Experiments with Nembutal® (sodium pentobarbital, Abbot) as an anesthetic proved unsatisfactory. Otters that were given the normal dose for dogs died (Kirkpatrick *et al.*, 1955).

REFERENCES

Sea Otter

Barabash-Nikiforov, I.I.: *Kalan* (The Sea Otter). Jerusalem, Israel Program for Scientific Translations, 1962.

Fay, F.H.: Personal communication, 1962.

Jellison, William, L. and Neiland, Kenneth A.: *Parasites of Alaskan Vertebrates.* Norman, Oklahoma, University of Oklahoma Research Institute, Project 1508, 1965.

Jones, R.D.: Personal communication, 1961.

Kenyon, K.W.: The sea otter in the eastern Pacific Ocean. In *North American Fauna*, No. 68. Washington, U.S. Government Printing Office, in press, 1969.

Kirkpatrick, C.M., Stullken, Donald E., and Jones, R.D.: Notes on captive sea otters. *J. Arctic Inst. N. Amer.*, 8(1):46–59, 1955.

Nikolaev, A.M.: On the feeding of the kurile sea otter and some aspects of their behavior during the period of ice. In Pavlovskii, E.N., Zenkovich, B.A. *et al.: Marine Mammals.* Moscow, Izdatel'stvo "Nauka," 1965.

Ogden, Adele: *The California Sea Otter Trade, 1784–1848.* Berkeley, University of California Press, Publications in History, 1941, vol. 26.

Peterson, R.S. and Odemar, M.W.: Population growth of the sea otter in California; results of aerial censuses and behavioral studies. A paper read to the 49th Annual Meeting of the American Society of Mammalogists, June 17, 1969.

Rausch, Robert: Studies on the Helminth fauna of Alaska. XIII. Disease in the sea otter, with special reference to helminth parasites. *Ecology, 34*(3): 548–604, 1953.

Chapter 3

THE CENTRAL NERVOUS SYSTEM

Norbert J. Flanigan

CETACEA

At first, it might seem unusual to include a discussion of the central nervous system (C.N.S.) in a consideration of the problems involved in maintaining a colony of marine mammals. The nervous system is usually regarded as quite sophisticated and perhaps the last system to yield to our understanding and to treatment. Cetaceans have always intrigued man, and it now appears that their nervous systems might well prove to be their most interesting feature. In this chapter, then, we will consider the history and the present knowledge of the central nervous system of cetaceans. We shall find many questions which remain unanswered and, indeed, some questions which remain unasked. We shall indicate some areas in which research is progressing, as well as some areas into which research must be directed.

Since the smaller cetaceans are more likely to be exhibited at oceanaria than the larger forms, the smaller species are of greater interest to the reader. But the literature is not so plentiful that we can disregard the information gained from larger forms. In some instances, we would expect slight differences in the nervous systems, differences related to modes of life. Provided that we recognize these differences, the information thus gained seems valid; therefore, we will consider information from species of all sizes.

The size of cetaceans has greatly intrigued man, both commercially and scientifically. Much early knowledge of cetacean anatomy was gained from dissections of beached whales. When one considers the tremendous size of these animals, the relative lack of communications, and the difficulty of travel—a specimen might be "well along" before an interested anatomist would be aware of it and reach it—and when one considers the impracticality of fixation and preservation, one can appreciate that these early dissections were both monumental and heroic, even in the most literal interpretations!

Why details of the central nervous system were so seldom included in early descriptions is understandable. By the time a worker had concerned himself with external anatomy, musculature, the heart, and perhaps some major vessels and the viscera, there was little time for deeper structures as part of routine dissection. The effort and time that might be required for a peripherocentrad dissection of an unpreserved behemoth often precluded the acquisition of a central nervous system suitable for study. Skeletal anatomy might be noted in the fresh dissection, but was most likely arrived at from the beached and bleached skeletons which found their way into museums. These, too, meant that the central nervous system was not available for study.

This is not to say that there have been no early reports on the cetacean central nervous system; the earliest reporters, Ray (1671) and Tyson (1680), described the brain briefly. This is also not to say that there have been no detailed descriptions of general brain anatomy but that there have been relatively few. The following citations constitute the literature for almost a century: Gervais (1871), Beauregard (1883), Guldberg (1885), Kükenthal and Ziehen (1889), Pettit (1905), Langworthy (1932), Wilson (1933), Ries and Langworthy (1937), Grünthal (1942), Kojima (1951), Breathnach (1955), and Pilleri (1962–1967). Descriptions were sometimes based upon a single species, often upon a single specimen, certainly a far cry from the vast literature on the more readily available land mammals.

This situation still exists today to some extent in the study of even the smaller cetaceans. Well-fixed specimens are still relatively rare; although we perfuse specimens, the blood supply to the C.N.S. presents problems. Certainly the history has been that one seldom secures a suitable brain and spinal cord from a specimen which has spent any time on the dissecting table. Even in his definitive work on the comparative anatomy of several species of smaller cetaceans, Slijper (1936) did not consider the C.N.S., although his review of the peripheral anatomy in itself still stands as a significant contribution.

Just as man has been intrigued by the body size of these animals, he has also been impressed by brain size, both absolute and relative. There is a considerable literature (as summarized in Wirz, 1950) on brain-to-body ratios in mammals. Again, one would expect that data from these largest of mammals would constitute a significant part of this literature. But their very size has militated against the acquisition of a sufficient number of observations upon which to base generalizations. Because of their commercial value, only a relatively few specimens of larger species have been accurately weighed in total. A dissection permitting the separate weighing of the central nervous system has not been attempted in such specimens. Although the largest species might have proved most interesting, there have been some recent attempts to begin acquiring a significant amount of data from the smaller cetaceans (Ridgway *et al.*, 1966).

The principal differences in the brains of the two types of cetaceans (Breathnach, 1960, and Slijper, 1962) lie in the relative shapes of the cerebral hemispheres, the relative lack of development of the olfactory apparatus, and in whichever of the cranial nerves is the largest. In mystacocetes, the cerebral hemisphere is about as wide as it is long; in odontocetes, the width greatly exceeds the length. In mystacocetes, the olfactory apparatus is much reduced when compared with other mammals; in odontocetes, the adult olfactory structures are lacking. In mystacocetes, the trigeminal nerve is the largest of the cranial nerves; in odontocetes, the honor falls to the eighth cranial nerve, especially in its auditory (cochlear) component. Since these differences are restricted and well recognized, it seems not unreasonable to consider the mystacocete information in the literature to apply to odontocetes as well.

We shall adopt a practical approach to a description of the cetacean brain—an approach which readily permits a comparison with the brains of other mammals. This method is to recall the development of the vertebrate brain, in which we identify a stage in which five consecutive vesicles, or sac-like protrusions, are evident. We can then conveniently trace all adult brain structures to their origin in one of these five vesicles. Table 3-I lists the vesicles and their principal derivatives in the adult. In order to give some coherence to our presentation, we shall use this arbitrary sequence. There are unfortunate complications in this process and in this method. The five vesicles are at first arranged in linear order, and in some vertebrates this linear order is maintained into adulthood. The basic vertebrate pattern is readily seen in an adult fish, amphibian, or reptilian brain. In the mammalian embryo, however, the developing brain undergoes several flexures. The basic linear sequence is lost. Only in the median sagittal section of the adult mammalian brain can this original linearity be seen (Fig. 3–1). Further, the flexures of the cetacean brain vary from the general mammalian pattern of flexures. This variance in axes, together with the rarity of well-fixed central nervous tissue, account for the "cetacean gap" in comparative neuroanatomy.

There have been attempts to relate the flexure difference to development of the skull. Ogawa and Arifuku (1948), followed by Kojima (1951), adopted the term "telescoping" to these changes in the disposition of the brain stem. The term was admittedly borrowed from, but is not to be confused with, Miller's (1923) "telescoping of the cetacean skull." While

TABLE 3–1

DERIVATIVES OF THE VERTEBRATE NEURAL TUBE

Primary Divisions	*The Five Vesicles*	*Adult Derivatives*	*Characteristics of the Cetacean Brain*
Prosencephalon	Telencephalon (*endbrain*)	Cerebral cortex (pallium)	Complex pattern of gyri and sulci.
		Basal ganglia (corpora striata)	
		Rhinencephalon	In adult, peripheral olfactory apparatus is reduced in mystacocetes, absent in odontocetes
	Diencephalon (*twixbrain*)	Pars optica hypothalami	
		Epithalamus	
		Thalamus	Medial geniculate body greatly developed.
		Hypothalamus	
		Tuber cinereum	
		Mammillary bodies	Mammillary "substance" not superficially evident as a "body."
		Posterior lobe of hypophysis	Pars intermedia absent in adult.
Mesencephalon	Mesencephalon (*midbrain*)	Corpora quadrigemina	Inferior colliculi greatly developed.
		Tegmentum	
		Crura cerebri	
Rhombencephalon	Metencephalon (*afterbrain*)	Cerebellum	
		Pons	
	Myelencephalon (*spinal brain*)	Medulla oblongata	
Myelon		Spinal cord	

the latter does also imply a change in position, Miller applied his term only to components of the skull. There is no relation between the phylogenetic use of the term by Miller and the ontogenetic changes in brain axes.

Taxonomy is considered earlier in this book and will be kept to a minimum here, although indirectly, the size of cetaceans does enter into this consideration. The smaller cetaceans, in general, are the odontocetes or toothed whales, which are of principal concern. The larger form are the mystacocetes, or baleen whales. The prominent exception to size and taxonomy is the sperm whale, large but toothed. Nor will the terms "porpoise" and "dolphin" be aired here. In general, the common terminology of the original investigators will be used, especially where it is in apparent agreement with modern usage.

It is not thought necessary or useful to include the details ordinarily covered in neuroanatomy. The reader interested in this will undoubtedly wish to consult the original literature in the bibliography. (Breathnach (1960) is an excellent beginning for such a study.) Every effort has been made to keep these listings current and comprehensive. The entries have been limited to the nervous system. No attempt has been made to cover the overlapping anatomy of other systems or to cover the whole field of comparative anatomy. Nor is it likely that in the immediate future, the practitioner who is charged with the care of cetaceans will be concerned with neurosurgery. Surgery on those animals has only recently become practical (Nagel *et al*, 1964 and Ridgway and McCormick, 1967) and is still in the definitely experimental stage. While a knowledge of the nervous system is not yet needed for this purpose, it is thought useful for the

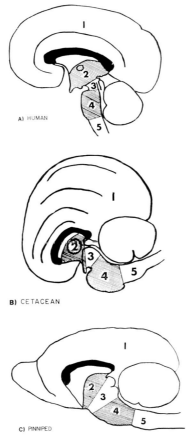

Figure 3–1. The varying axes of representative mammalian brains. The significance of the peculiar cetacean variation is explained in the text. These axes are as follows: (1) telencephalon, (2) diencephalon, (3) mesencephalon, (4) metencephalon, and (5) myelencephalon. No cortical detail has been included, except for the single gyrus parallel to the corpus callosum in the human and the several such gyri ("tiering" of Turner, 1891) in the cetacean. The telencephalic corpus callosum is indicated in solid black and the diencephalon and metencephalon are cross-hatched for contrast. Each figure is shown in proper proportion but the three figures do not indicate relative sizes. A rarity of well-fixed specimens and a hesitancy to interpret the brain as seen in sections have been the principal obstacles in cetacean neuroanatomy.

general practitioner to be aware of our current and prospective knowledge of this system, particularly of the *central* nervous system. There is no attempt to cover the peripheral nervous system.

Following the presentation of the principles of comparative anatomy of the cetacean central nervous system, an example of functional anatomy will be considered. The embryological-morphological approach serves descriptive anatomy well. Quite obviously, it breaks down when one emphasizes the functional aspects—to which knowledge of the cetacean can contribute much.

The Telencephalon

The telencephalon is a fortuitous site at which to begin the study of the cetacean brain because it is the telencephalic derivatives, the cerebral hemispheres, and the cerebral cortex that have contributed most to the size and complexity of the mammalian brain and to the comparative status of the cetacean brain.

Based upon classical studies, the odontocete brain, if not that of the mystacocete as well, presents the following incompatibilities: (a) a general level of gross development comparable to the carnivore or ungulate, (b) a complex pattern of gyri and sulci perhaps second only to that of man and, (c) a primitive, incomplete, or inadequate pattern of microscopic anatomy, apparently insufficient to account for the complex behavior patterns seen in these animals.

The behavioral conclusions must necessarily be limited to odontocetes because, although we have anatomical information about both odontocetes and mystacocetes, we have derived most of our knowledge of behavior from the smaller forms commonly kept in captivity. We shall review the literature which has led to the anatomical conclusion and then attempt modern interpretations. We shall consider the general size and shape of the cerebral hemispheres, the external anatomy of gyri and sulci, the rhinencephalon or older cortex and the "modern" or neocortex, and finally, the microscopic anatomy.

Cetacean cerebral hemispheres are characteristically short and wide, not elongate as in most mammals. It is not improbable that these dimensions are a reflection of skull adaptations in the vicinity of the blowhole, although there is no experimental evidence for a causal relation. Edinger (1955) has suggested that paleontology does not support such a view. There is evidence that lateral expansion of the brain preceded the "phylogenetic migration" of the blowhole from the rostral snout to the dorsum of the head. Langworthy (1931), among others, mentions that the lateral expense of hemisphere can represent a reduction in frontal and "prefrontal" hemisphere. There is no behavioral evidence for a reduction in the functions commonly attributed to these areas, and this question seems best answered by detailed physiological mapping of the cetacean cortex. Lilly has long advocated this, and the anesthesia techniques of Nagel *et al.* (1964), Ridgway (1965), and Ridgway and McCormick (1967) give promise that this mapping can soon begin.

The complexity of cetacean cerebral convolutions was one of the first features noted (Ray, 1671, and Tyson, 1680) in the study of these brains. Mention of similarities to the human brain have been a part of almost all of the studies cited in our introduction. The number of gyri and sulci exceeds even that of man. If one then accepts the rather commonly held teleology that an increase in convolutions provides for a total increase in gray matter (and thereby an increase in behavioral capacity?), this gross anatomy, indeed, supports the concept of an animal approaching the capacities of the primates, including man.

The terminology of Guldberg (1885) has most often been used to name the gyri and sulci, to permit comparison with other mammals. The pattern is particularly revealing when seen from both the mesial and lateral aspects the cortex is seen to be arranged in multiple layers (the "tiers" of Turner, 1891). From the mesial aspect (Fig. 3–1B) three tiers are seen to lie above the corpus callosum and parallel to it. From the lateral aspect (Fig. 3–1B) three tiers are circumferentially arranged around an almost vertical lateral fissure (of Sylvius).

These tiers are not readily recognized in the undisturbed hemisphere. Only when one has removed the blood vessels and meninges and checked the relative depths of the fissures and sulci do the principal gyri stand out. When one consults the illustrations in the literature, this anatomy is emphasized in line drawings and in specimens properly shadowed in photography. It is not at all evident in many illustrations, and one can get the impression from the literature that the tiers are an inconstant feature of the cetacean brain.

In the primitive vertebrate brain, the morphological "end" brain (telencephalon) probably functioned solely in olfaction, as a rhinencephalon or "nose brain." In modern vertebrates in which the derivatives of the five vesicles are still linearly arranged even in the adult, the telencephalon and rhinencephalon are probably synonymous. In the mammal, however, the neocortex has been added to the primitive cortex, forming the greater bulk of the cerebral hemisphere, and is the site of localization of "higher" functions. The neocortex can be identified principally by its microscopic anatomy which will be considered later. While it is true that the "older" cortex can be distinguished by a simpler microscopic anatomy, the problem for mammals is to distinguish that which is rhinencephalic in origin from that which is olfactory in function. It would be expected that knowledge of cetaceans would make a significant contribution to this problem.

Broca (1878) established a classification of mammals based upon relative olfactory development, "osmatic," having a sense of smell, or "anosmatic," lacking this sense. Turner (1890) further distinguished relative capacities within the osmatic group as "microsmatic" and "macrosmatic." Alone among mammals, odontocetes constitute the anosmatic group. Mystacocetes were placed in the microsmatic group.

It might have been expected that study of the toothed whales, in comparison with studies of the baleen whales and other mammals, especially those widely studied in the laboratory, would give significant clues to the correlation of olfactory function and structure, if indeed close correlation exists. Broca himself (1879) examined the brain of the dolphin with this in mind, as did Zuckerkandel (1878), Addison (1915), Grünthal (1942), Breathnach (1953), and Breathnach and Goldby (1954).

The proposed relation between olfactory function and rhinencephalic structure was questioned by many observers, especially Brodal (1947) and Pribram and Kruger (1954). Based upon the relative development of those structures known (or thought) to be olfactory, mammals were subdivided into elaborate categories, yet there was little evidence for a structural and functional relation. Filimonoff (1965) has arrived at the same conclusions in a detailed study of the dolphin. He has shown that absolutely all of the cortical rhinencephalic structures in osmatic mammals are found in the anosmatic dolphin. There have been many suggestions in the literature as to the function(s) which might have replaced olfaction in this anatomy. Since our knowledge of cetaceans does not contribute to this answer, such conjectures lie outside our province.

The microscopic anatomy of the cetacean cortex was observed in limited numbers of sections by Major (1878), Kükenthal and Ziehen (1889), Bianchi (1905), and Riese (1925). The general conclusion presented by these observers was that of a cortex more primitive than in other mammals—that the number of cell layers was less than in other mammals or that the cell layers were not readily distinguishable from one another. Rawitz (1910) presented the early exception to this view, considering the organization to be similar to that of other mammals.

Later observers used samples from more regions of the cortex. Rose (1926) had no difficulty in finding the number of cell layers typical of other mammals, but Langworthy (1923) held the opposing view, that of a primitive organization varying strikingly from other mammals. It is unfortunate that his conclusions were so forcefully and positively stated, since one premise must be questioned. He freely and precisely identified his "functional areas" of the cortex, yet he admitted a lack of experimental evidence for functional localization. In fact, he and his coworkers failed in a crude attempt to acquire some initial evidence for functional localization.

The paper by Grünthal (1942) is often cited in contrast to these earlier studies and opinions. However, this is misleading because he did not concern himself with the neocortex. His cytoarchitectonic studies included brain stem, thalamus, basal ganglia, and allocortex but not neocortex, which is the usual criterion for these comparisons. Kojima (1951), who studied thirty-eight samples of cortex from sperm whales, described the giant pyramidal cells as quite widespread, not confined to a restricted area. He had difficulty in distinguishing granular and agranular components and difficulty in distinguishing layer IV from layer V and finding a definitive layer VI. Most of the previously cited investigators also remarked on the relative sparsity of cortical neurons when compared with that of other mammals, but did not quantitate their estimates.

The number of cortical neurons has also been considered. Tower (1944) plotted the density of neurons vs. brain size. Using tissue from fourteen cortical regions of two adult fin whale brains, he found that both the whale and the elephant data supported the contention that the density of mammalian cortical neurons decreases with brain size. He did not pretend to be aware of any structural or functional differences in these regions, taking only average numbers of cells. It is curious that being able to identify only four layers with certainty, he apparently had no difficulty identifying neurons, per se, and made no mention of neuron types. Hawkins and Olszewski (1957), using a small portion of the tissues used by Tower, plotted the number of neurons not against brain size but in relation to the number of neuroglial (supporting) cells. Comparing the whale with man, they found that this "glia-nerve cell index" increased with absolute brain size rather than with an animal's position on the phylogenetic scale, as had been proposed by others.

Morgane (1965) feels that past difficulties were due to lack of proper fixation. In well-perfused dolphin brains, he finds the cortical layers as easily identifiable as in primates, and areas that do differ from one another architectonically. It is unfortunate that thus far he has reported only in abstract form. It is to be hoped that the planned atlas (Morgane *et al.*, in press), based upon both cellular and fiber stains, will be the definitive work in this field. There simply has not been for the cetacean brain, the volume of materials, the variety of techniques, or the embryonic and the degeneration studies comparable to the information available from other mammals. Cetacean anatomy has suffered from lack of such comparisons and these are the kinds of studies now needed.

The Diencephalon

The second vesicle, the diencephalon, is represented in the adult essentially by the thalamus, its subdivisions, and related structures. These surround the third ventricle and dorsoventrally are the pineal, epithalamus, thalamus proper, hypothalamus, and pituitary. We shall consider these in an arbitrary sequence based both upon the relative sizes of the structures and upon the relative amounts of information available for mammals generally. This sequence is the thalamus proper, the hypothalamus and pituitary, and the pineal and epithalamus. A cursory glance at the gross anatomy of this region tells very little, even when viewed in the opportune midsagittal section. Some structures can be seen when the overlying hemisphere has been dissected away, but diencephalic anatomy lies largely in the domain of the neuroanatomist's microscope.

The thalamus receives impulses from all ascending sensory systems and its neurons radiate to the cerebral cortex. It has been thought of as the great antechamber to the cortex and this is, in fact, the derivation of the name. For the other mammals commonly studied in the laboratory, it has been shown that many of the (extrinsic) thalamic nuclei radiate only to specific areas of the cortex. In return, neurons of these areas of the cortex project back to the specific thalamic nuclei. A similar relation exists between nonspecific (intrinsic) thalamic nuclei and more generalized cortical areas. As one ascends the mammalian scale, reaching the primates, Rose (1926) found an increase in the associational cortex (linked to the intrinsic thalamic nuclei) and a corresponding decrease in relay cortex (linked to extrinsic thalamic nuclei). We have seen that there is little agreement as to structural specialization in the cetacean cortex. We could hope, then, that if significant differentiation were found in the thalamus, this might be supporting evidence for a cortical organization not otherwise evident. An appropriately developed thalamus might well be taken as an indicator of a level of cortical organization.

The first real description of the internal anatomy of the cetacean thalamus was that by Hatschek and Schlesinger (1920) in their description of the microscopic anatomy of the brain stem of the common dolphin. Additional data was furnished by Langworthy (1932), Jelgersma (1934), and Grünthal (1942). The definitive work has been that of Kruger (1959) whose observations were detailed enough to compare *Tursiops truncatus* to other mammals. He found that the nuclear anatomy warranted comparing the odontocete thalamus with that of primates. Here, then, is possible support of the behavioral observations of Lilly and others who would rank cetaceans with or near the primates in other respects. Here, too, is the suggestion that cortical anatomy needs reinvestigation. We must determine either that the cetacean cortex is structurally similar to other mammals or be prepared to accept function as more complex than structure.

The mammalian hypothalamus (a center for autonomic control) and the hypophysis (the pituitary, or "master" endocrine gland) have attracted study by both the neuroanatomist and endocrinologist. The two regions lie together structurally and are related functionally. In cetaceans, the latter has a slightly larger literature, although the usual method of study— the experimentally produced hormone deficiency—has not been available with animals of this size and rarity. The gross anatomy of the pituitary has most recently been covered by Hanström (1944) and the microscopic anatomy by Drager (1953). The cell types of other mammals are found in cetaceans, and though experimental evidence is lacking, there is no reason to think that the endocrine system is basically different. Curiously, cetaceans have no pars intermedia (as noted by all observers). Hormones have been identified chemically in tissue samples and there is evidence that the hormone ordinarily produced by the mammalian pars intermedia is, in the cetacean, produced by the pars distalis.

The pineal organ is absent in cetaceans or rudimentary in those species where it has been described. Fuse (1936) has reviewed the literature on this topic and his own observations support this general view. One should not be surprised that very little attention has been paid to this structure in cetaceans; relatively little attention has been paid to it in mammals as a whole, and there is no agreement as to function. It is not strange, then, that so little is known in cetaceans. Gersch (1938) has described a microscopic anatomy of the pineal in the humpback whale similar to that of other mammals. The deeper habenular nuclei are apparently well developed in all cetaceans. All observers of the thalamus so report them. As mentioned in the comment on the rhinencephalon, this state of development in the anosmatic dolphin is evidence against the inclusion of these structures in a functional rhinencephalon.

Literature on the hypothalamus is limited to incidental mention in general descriptions of the brain stem and in already-cited studies of the rhinencephalon. In the latter, the much reduced mammillary "structures" have been noted by all observers. They are grossly not large enough to be dignified with the term mammillary "bodies" as is common for other mammals. There is no reason to suspect an autonomic nervous system which functions differently in those animals but, again, neither is there an experimental literature to support this.

The Mesencephalon

The midbrain is a prominent structure in the adult brain of lower vertebrates, where it is the gross optic lobe, but often functions also as a motor center. The midbrain is much reduced in the mammal. Both the vision center and motor center of the mammal reside in the neocortex of cerebral hemisphere. The primitive plan of the midbrain is retained in the paired superior colliculi as a visual reflex center and the paired inferior colliculi as an auditory reflex center. The cetacean inferior colliculi are appropriately oversized as we find the auditory portion of the eighth-nerve greatly increased over the average mammalian size. Since sensory systems are considered in another chapter, we give this only passing mention.

The Metencephalon

The fourth vesicle of the mammalian brain gives rise to the dorsal cerebellum and the ventral pons. The inferior olive forms a functional part of the pontocerebellar system and is usually considered as such, although morphologically it has been displaced caudally into the medulla oblongata. A broad statement of the function of the mammalian cerebellum—coordination of motor activity—is so widely accepted that it is seldom, if ever, challenged. The term "cerebellum" means "little brain," i.e., little when compared by early anatomists with the larger cerebral hemispheres. As one would expect, early descriptions of mammalian brains included the cerebellum and it has been well covered in general works on the cetacean brain. Guldberg (1885), Wilson (1933), Jelgersma (1934), Ogawa (1954), and Pilleri (1966) give excellent general coverage.

There were, however, two unfortunate aspects to the study of the vertebrate cerebellum. First, the gross terminology of its lobes, lobules, and fissures has been overburdened with several sets of fanciful terms which tell nothing of functional relations. Most workers decry such usage, yet they usually propagate old sets of terms and often add new ones! This we shall not do for the cetacean brain. But one does recognize the plight of preceding authors, since it is impossible to consider previous terms without repeating them. We shall simply abandon detailed terms and concern ourselves with the principles of cerebellar organization.

The second problem has been the difficulty in homologizing the subdivisions of the various mammalian cerebelli. This has extended to, rather than been based upon, a lack of agreement as to the comparative embryology of this metencephalic derivative. Only fairly recently has the viewpoint (and terminology!) of Larsell come into fairly wide acceptance. The cetacean cerebellum is in agreement with Larsell's findings. The definitive works on the development of the cetacean cerebellum, based upon gross and microscopic anatomy, are the works of Jansen (1950, 1953), Jansen and Korneliussen (1964, 1965), and Korneliusseen (1967).

One tends, perhaps, to marvel that whereas in many areas we find the cetacean brain at variance with the mammalian pattern, here, in a widely disputed area, there is agreement. One must remember that it is the mammalian plan that has been rethought, not the concept of cetacean anatomy which has been altered. Fortunately, Korneliussen has utilized microscopic anatomy in her studies on the development of the cetacean cerebellum. Microscopic anatomy in the adult has been rather neglected (Obersteiner, 1912; Brunner, 1919; and Addison 1930, 1934), often covering just a brief mention of the reported presence of a few outsized cells. With improved fixation and with the importance of this region in the motor system (see Functional Neuroanatomy), the metencephalon looms as an important area of investigation.

The Myelencephalon

The fifth vesicle, the myelencephalon, is the medulla oblongata of the adult and as such is perhaps the least anatomically distinguished region of the mammalian brain. Due to the pattern of flexures, it is rather elongated and arched in the cetacean. This does not alter its basic anatomy. For all mammals thus far investigated, this is the site of the so-called "vital centers" for control of heartbeat, rate of respiration, etc. Its functional importance is great and it is to be expected that cetaceans fit the mammalian pattern. De Graaf, in his review of the neuroanatomy of the cetacean brain stem (1967), presents a fairly typical nuclear pattern for this region.

The Spinal Cord

That portion of the original dorsal, tubular nerve cord which is destined to become spinal cord is first called the myelon. For convenience in description, the anatomist typically divides the body into several parts and these parts into several further subdivisions. It is too easy to forget that these are artifact and that the totally functioning body or a totally functioning system is dependent upon the integrity of all of its components. The remainder of the central nervous system, the spinal cord, might well be considered in this context. Often overlooked, usually considered the least glamorous portion of the system, we tend to forget that it acts as the great "mediator" between the brain and the body. Unfortunately, we often think of its function in only a negative way—when we see the effects of transection of a human spinal cord.

Until very recently, only a few papers have given more than passing consideration to either the gross or microscopic anatomy of the cetacean spinal cord. Cunningham (1887), Hatscheck (1896), Rawitz (1903), and Hepburn and Waterston (1904) presented conclusions based upon very few gross cords. In land-living tetrapods, the mammalian spinal cord is typically larger in cross-section at the brachial and lumbar regions, representing innervation to and from the paired limbs. The reduced cetacean anterior limbs and the absence of posterior limbs might be expected to be reflected in appropriately reduced brachial and lumbar regions of the cord. There was no unanimity among these early observers but a general consensus that the brachial swelling is prominent and the lumbar swelling less so (but not absent, as might have been anticipated). In several cords of various species of porpoises, I find it difficult to make a case for a grossly prominent lumbar swelling (Flanigan, 1963, 1966).

The earlier microscopic work was unfortunately based upon a limited number of sections observed. One should not, however, fault these investigations, for when one checks the literature, one finds that many detailed atlases of the human spinal cord, which have long been accepted as the standard, were also based upon observations of limited numbers of sections and upon composite drawings of idealized sections. One cannot really blame these observers. The cetacean material was necessarily limited. To overcome this shortage of material, I used a spinal cord of *Lagenorhynchus obliquidens* in complete serial section (Flanigan, 1966). Additional specimens and additional species are being added.

Undoubtedly, the most consistent observation of the cetacean spinal cord has been of the relative size difference between the dorsal (sensory) horn and the ventral (motor) horn. The large motor horn might be expected, knowing the large volume of body musculature. The dorsal horn, when compared with the ventral horn and when compared with the ratios in other mammals, is much smaller. This led to the supposition by many that the animal had a reduced sensory capacity over the body. This is not supported by recent observations of behavior in which animals responded to body caressing and often sought it (Lilly, 1961). Slijper (1962) makes perhaps the obvious but overlooked conclusion, i.e. that the cross-section anatomy of the cord represents not a reduced sensory capacity but merely a proportional increase in musculature and musculature innervation. Confirmation of the extensive development of the nucleus dorsalis of Clarke, by which proprioceptive innervation (see Functional Neuroanatomy) would bypass the apex of the dorsal horn, fits this anatomy (Flanigan, 1966).

An unsolved problem in the cetacean cord is the situation found in the tetrapod cord in which there is a patterned innervation of axial and appendicular muscle, that is, medial groups of motor neurons innervate axial muscles and lateral groups of ventral horn cells innervate limb musculature. This has been confirmed both by stimulation studies and by degeneration studies in the common laboratory mammals and in man. With the reduced anterior appendage and its function as a steering organ rather than a propelling one, and with the absence of posterior appendages, one might expect a rather radical reduction of lateral motor cells in the brachial region and an absence of lateral cells in the lumbar region. I have seen medial and lateral nuclei at the rostral level and a single grouping at the caudal level. Cells have not been counted.

Romanes (1945) presented complex nuclear patterns in the fetal whale spinal cord. My own observations were based upon adult porpoise material and the two observations cannot really be compared. It is not improbable that embryonic cell numbers are later reduced. Our real deficiency lies in the lack of studies in a complete series of embryos of at least one species. Work has been begun (Flanigan and Ridgway, unpublished) in attempts to create deliberate peripheral lesions in musculature to trace degeneration into the spinal cord.

Functional Neuroanatomy: The Motor System

The anatomist uses the term "functional" anatomy merely to remind himself that anatomy is not studied for purely descriptive purposes. It can be so but should not be so. Our purpose is to understand the body as a functioning whole—we divide and subdivide purely for our convenience in study. When we subdivide the body or nervous system on a functional rather than on an anatomic basis, it is seen that the anatomical approach almost immediately breaks down.

It was convenient to begin our discussion of the cetacean C.N.S. from the embryological-anatomical point of view. At any point along the way, we might have adopted a functional point of view. This happened in our discussion of the spinal cord, and it became evident that the functional subsystem overrides the anatomical system. This is what we recognize in the term functional neuroanatomy.

It seems useful to take as an example of functional neuroanatomy a neurological subsystem which is not covered elsewhere in this book and which to my knowledge simply has not yet been covered anywhere else. A chapter of this book has been devoted to a consideration of at least some of the sensory systems. Consideration of the cetacean motor system has been much neglected. Yet knowledge gained from the cetacean motor system can make significant contributions to our understanding of the motor system of other mammals, including man.

The locomotor capacities of these animals has long been known. Their behavioral capacities in captivity are now marvelled at. In contrast to land mammals, especially tetrapods, what remains of the cetacean limbs is used not for propulsion but for guidance. The propulsive muscles are the dorsal and ventral body-fluke muscle masses. While admitting a well-developed muscular system, we have not pursued investigation of neuro-muscular mechanisms. Closely associated with motor innervation of muscle is its proprioceptive innervation (the "position" sense) necessary to proper functioning of the total system. Only fairly recently have we gained some knowledge of the afferent innervation of muscle and of the gamma efferent reflex system which manages the proprioceptors. This system was first studied in the frog, only recently extended to some of the common laboratory mammals, and there is the suggestion that this would be a very intriguing investigation in cetaceans.

When this system is working normally, it contributes to postural reflexes. Teleologically, we understand the maintenance of posture appropriate to the biped (man), the usual land-living tetrapod, and even the inverted tetrapod, the sloth. What is posture in a cetacean? What is its equivalent?

As mentioned earlier when discussing the telencephalon, the mapping of cortical areas will have great significance. Perhaps the most intriguing of these areas will be the motor area. In addition to the purely comparative interest (i.e. Where does the motor area of the cetacean lie in comparison with other mammals?), how much, if any, premotor area exists when the motor area is definitely known? Will the area from which we can elicit motor activity following stimulation agree with the area in which we can find the giant pyramidal cells of Betz?

We are familiar with deficiencies in the motor systems of man and of the common laboratory mammals. We are familiar with the characteristics of the upper motor neuron paralysis and the lower motor neuron paralysis, although all species thus far investigated vary in their capacities to overcome these deficiencies. Before postulating how further knowledge of the motor systems of cetaceans might contribute to our general knowledge, we must admit that we have never really seen a cetacean exhibiting the characteristics of either motor neuron syndrome. At least to my knowledge, this has not been reported in the literature, although in his book, Lilly (1961) did mention an animal which landed on its head or back and thereafter listed to one side. There was no attempt to correlate the pathology with the direction of list. It is not likely that one would come upon a paralyzed specimen in the wild. The habitat is such that survival would be difficult, if not impossible. Anesthesia techniques have only recently opened up the possibility of creating deliberate lesions in these specimens and this has already been mentioned in our consideration of the spinal cord, where the lower motor neuron is being investigated.

We should perhaps remember that rather than attempting to predict what our ultimate findings will be, we must first produce and describe the phenomena of upper and lower motor neuron paralysis in these animals. Will the upper motor neuron paralysis be "typically" spastic? One might expect that the lower motor neuron paralysis would definitely be flaccid in type, but how would a mammal confined to the water react to this? Could such an animal survive? One could anticipate that we shall need some very good postoperative nursing techniques and postoperative handling techniques to permit animals to survive the effects of such lesions for a significant length of time for study.

Need we emphasize that our discussion of functional neuroanatomy has asked questions rather than answered them? This is where we are. This is where we are going—to some answers—to many more questions.

Pinnipedia

When the volume of the literature on the central nervous system of cetaceans was compared with that for the common laboratory mammals, the former was found to be relatively small. This fact was attributed to the scarcity of cetacean specimens and to technical difficulties in their preparation. The even shorter list for pinnipeds must be looked at in quite a different light. Pinnipeds have been available, both in the vast numbers taken commercially and in the smaller number of familiar performing animals. What appears to have happened is that a few well-described specimens seem to have satisfied our curiosity that the C.N.S. is not markedly different from the mammalian pattern. The period during which general descriptions of the anatomy of the brain appeared would seem to support this view. Murie (1874), Vrolik (1882). Kükenthal and Ziehen (1889), Fish (1898), and Hepburn (1913) cover representative species, and their descriptions were accomplished essentially before this century.

The gross anatomy of the cerebral hemisphere, especially the pattern of gyri and sulci, has been quite well covered in the general works listed above. Hepburn considered the animal as basically a water-living carnivore and apparently expected the convolution pattern to resemble those forms. He found the pattern to be more complex. Murie (1874) called attention to the "squarish" shape of the hemisphere and also ranked pinnipeds above the carnivores. Fish (1903) and Anthony and Friant (1937) presented further information. Hepburn noted also that once one passed the superficial cortical anatomy, the deeper anatomy showed little variance from other mammals. In both microscopic anatomy and physiology of the cortex, knowledge of the pinniped is more extensive than that of the cetacean. This can perhaps be attributed simply to the lack of circulatory peculiarities—that there is no significant blockage in fixation and that the microscopic pattern was early recognized as typically mammalian (Haig, 1913), at least for the motor area. Rioch (1937) confirmed the typical six cortical layers of the mammal. The identification of the motor cortex by Rioch has special significance in that he established its location by physiological methods, i.e. cortical stimulation under anesthesia. Further stimulation studies of motor cortex were reported by Langworthy, *et al.* (1938). Alderson, *et al.* (1960), have reported sensory studies, both tactile and auditory.

In a surprisingly few papers, there has been a significant contribution to the general picture of pinniped neuroanatomy. Haig (1913) is the most thorough, presenting a sufficient number of illustrations of representative sections through the brain stem for comparison with other mammals. Ogawa (1928, 1937), Fuse (1928, 1940) and Tani (1941) included the pinnipeds in comparative studies with other water-living mammals. Three investigators have presented significant descriptions of the pinniped spinal cord. Haig (1913) included sections from representative regions of the cord in his general study of the nervous system. Hatschek (1896) wrote principally on the cord, and Wilcox (1966) had considerably more microscopic material at his disposal. However, none has shown clear-cut evidence for nuclear organization or pattern. This must wait upon serial section studies. Wilcox did note the shortness of this cord and I have confirmed this in dissections. Although the mammalian spinal cord is commonly shorter than the length of the vertebral column, that of *Zalophus Californianus* is remarkably short, ending at T-9. This is not the shortest on record, but it can have a practical aspect. Complete serial sections can be obtained with a less than usual volume of tissue; this work is now in progress.

Conclusions concerning either the status of the pinniped central nervous system or of our knowledge of it are difficult to arrive at. We cannot assume that a small volume of literature precludes a complete knowledge of this anatomy. We cannot be that smug! All living forms contribute to our knowledge. The contribution of pinnipeds to knowledge of diving physiology, for example, is significant. Yet we do not fully understand neural mechanisms even in this well-researched specialty. We can conclude, as we do for all forms of life, that our studies of function must not be tied too closely to anatomical substrates.

REFERENCES

Cetacea

Addison, W.H.F.: On the rhinencephalon of *Delphinus delphis*, L. *J. Comp. Neurol.*, 25:497–522, 1915.

Addison, W.H.F.: Aberrant cells in the cerebellar cortex of the porpoise (*Phocaena*). *Anat. Rec.*, 45:204, 1930.

Addison, W.H.F.: Unusual large nerve cells in the cerebellar cortex of several aquatic mammals. *Psychiat. neurol. Bl.*, 38:587–595, 1934.

Alpers, A.: *Dolphins, the Myth and the Mammal,* 2nd ed. Cambridge. Riverside Press, 1961.

Andrews, R.C.: The California gray whale (*Rhachianectes glaucus* Cope), its history, habits, external anatomy. osteology and relationship. *Mem. Amer. Mus. Nat. Hist.,* (NS) *1*:229–288, 1916.

Andrews, R.C.: The sei whale (*Balaenoptera borealis* Lesson), history, habits, external anatomy, osteology and relationship. *Mem. Amer. Mus. Nat. Hist.,* (NS) *1*:291–388, 1916.

Anthony, M.R.: Sur un cerveau de foetus de Mégaptère. *C. R. Acad. Sci.,* (*Paris*), *181*:681–683, 1925.

Baer, K.E.: Ueber den Braunfisch (*Delphinus phocoena*). *Isis von Oken,* Heft 1–6, 1826.

Beauregard, D. H.: Recherches sur l'encéphale des Balaenides. *J. Anat. Physiol.,* *19*:481–516, 1883.

Biach, P.: Vergleichend-anatomische Untersuchungen über den Bau des Zentralkanales bei den Säugetieren. *Arb. Neurol.,* 13:399–454, 1906.

Bianchi, V.: Il mantello cerebrale del delfino. *Atti Accad. Sci. fis. mat. Napoli,* *12*:1–18, 1905.

Breathnach, A.S.: The olfactory tubercule, prepyriform cortex and precommisural region of the porpoise (*Phocaena phocaena*). *J. Anat.,* 87:90–113, 1953.

Breathnach, A.S.: The surface features of the brain of the humpback whale (*Megaptera novaeangliae*), *J. Anat.* 89:343–354, 1955.

Breathnach, A.S.: The cetacean central nervous system. *Biol. Rev.,* 35:187–230, 1960.

Breathnach, A.S. and Goldby, F.: The amygdaloid nuclei, hippocampus and other parts of the rhinencephalon in the porpoise (*Phocaena phocaena*), *J. Anat.,* 88:267–291, 1954.

Broca, P.P.: Le grand lobe limbique, et la scissure limbique dans la série des Mammifères. *Rev. Anthropol.,* *1*:385–498, 1878.

Broca, P.P.: Recherches sur les centres olfactifs. *Rev. Anthropol.,* 2:385–455, 1879.

Brodal, A.: The hippocampus and the sense of smell. *Brain,* 70:179–222, 1947.

Brunner, H.: Bemerkungen zum Aufbau des Hirnstammes der Cetaceen mit besondere Berücksichtigung der unteren Oliven. *J. Phychol. Neurol.,* 24:138–165, 1918.

Brunner, H.: Die Zentralen Kleinhirnkerne bei den Säugetieren, *Arb. Neurol.,* 22:200–277, 1919.

Bruns, V.: Sistens disquisitiones anatomico-physiologicas de nervis cetaceorum cerebralibralibus. Dissertation, Tubingae (praes. Rapp), 1836.

Carte, A. and Macalister, A.: On the anatomy of *Balaenoptera rostrata. Philos. Trans.,* *158*:201–262, 1868.

Cunningham, D.J.: The spinal nervous system of the porpoise and dolphin. *J. Anat. Physiol.,* *11*:209–228, 1877.

De Graaf, A.S.: *Anatomical aspects of the cetacean brain stem.* Assen, the Netherlands, Royal Van Gorcum 1967.

Doeschotte, G.T.: Ueber die Retina von Walembryonen. *Anat. Anz., 51:*200–205, 1918.

Drager, G.A.: The innervation of the porpoise pituitary gland with special emphasis on the adenohypophysis. *J. Comp. Neurol., 99:*75–89, 1953.

Edinger, T.: Hearing and smell in cetacean history. *Mschr. Psychiat. Neurol., 129:*37–58, 1955.

Filimonoff, I.N.: On the so-called rhinencephalon in the dolphin. *J. Hirnforsch., 8:*1–23, 1965.

Flanigan, N.J.: The cetacean spinal cord. *Anat. Rec., 145:*319, 1963.

Flanigan, N.J.: The anatomy of the spinal cord of the Pacific white-sided dolphin (*Lagenorhynchus obliquidens*): A preliminary report. China Lake, Calif., Naval Ordnance Test Station, (NOTS TP 3300), 1963.

Flanigan, N.J.: Neuroanatomy of the dolphin spinal cord. *Anat. Rec., 151:*350, 1965.

Flanigan, N.J.: The anatomy of the spinal cord of the Pacific striped dolphin, *Lagenorhynchus obliquidens.* In Norris, K.S. (Ed.): *Whales, Dolphins and Porpoises.* Berkeley, Univ. of California Press, 1966.

Fraser, F.C. and Purves, P.E.: Hearing in cetaceans, *Bull. Brit. Mus. Nat. Hist., 2:*103–114, 1954

Friant, M.: Le cerveau du Marsouin (*Phocoena communis* Cuv.) et les charactéristiques fondamentales du cerveau des Cétacés. *Acta Anat., 17:*61–71, 1953.

Friant, M.: Le cerveau du Baleinoptère (*Balaenoptera sp.*) *Acta Anat., 23:*242–250, 1955.

Friant, M.: Un cerveau de foetus de Rorqual (*Balaenoptera musculus* L.). *C.R. Acad Sci. (Paris), 244:*236–238, 1957.

Friant, M., Un stade de l'évolution cérébrale du rorqual *Balaenoptera musculus. Hvalrad. Skr., 42:*4–15, 1958.

Fuse, G.: Einige strukturelle Besondherheiten am Hirnstamm bei den im Wasser lebenden Säugern (Seehund, Seebär und und Delphin). *Arb. anat., 13:*333–354, 1928.

Fuse, G.: Ueber strukturelle Eigenheiten am vorderen Zweihügel des Seiwals (*Balaenoptera borealis* LESS.). *Arb. anat., 17:*203–227, 1935.

Fuse, G.: Ueber die Epiphyse bei einigen Wasserbewohnenden Saügetieren. *Arb. anat., 18:*241–341, 1936.

Fuse, G.: Beitrage zur Anatomie des Nucleus ruber tegmenti beim *Delphinus delphis* L., *Arb. anat., 21:*219–235, 1938.

Fuse, G.: Ueber einen bisher unbekannten, dem Nucleus olivaris corporis quadrigemini anterioris gleichstellbaren Kern bei einigen Delphinen. *Arb. anat. Inst. Sendai, 21:*349–357, 1938.

Fuse, G.: Einiges Vergleichend-anatomisches über ein bisher nicht genügend dargesttelltes bzw. gewürdigtes Grausystem in und an der spinalen Quintuswurzel (Nuclei intra-et extratrigeminales) bei einigen Wassersäugetieren

(Seehund, Seebär, Seeotter, Delphin und Seiwal), *Arb. Anat. Inst. Sendai,* 23:165–223, 1940.

Gans, A.: Die Pyramidenbahn der *Phocaena. Anat. Anz.,* 49:281–284, 1916.

Geiling, E.M.K., Tarr, L.N., and Tarr, A.: The hypophysis cerebri of the finback (*Balaenoptera physalus*) and sperm (*Physeter megalocephalus*) whale. *Bull. Johns Hopk. Hosp.,* 57:123–129, 1935.

Geiling, E.M.K., Vos, B., Jr., and Oldham, F.K.: The pharmacology and anatomy of the hypophysis of the porpoise, *Endocrinology,* 27:309–316, 1940.

Gervais, P.: Remarques sŭr l'anatomie des Cétacés de la division des Balénides, *Nouv. Arch. Mus. Hist. Nat. (Paris),* 7:65–146, 1871.

Gersch, I.: Note on the pineal gland of the humpback whale. *J. Mammal., 19:* 477–480, 1938.

Gierlich, N.: Zur vergleichenden Anatomie der aus dem Grosshirn stammenden Faserung. 3. Der anteil des Cerebellum sowie motorischen Kernlager des Hirnstammes und des Rückenmarks an dem pes pedunculi bei *Phocaena* und *Delphinus delphis. Anat. Anz.,* 49:285–288, 1916.

Gihr, M. and Pilleri, G.: Hirn-Körpergewichts-Beziehungen bei Cetaceen. In Pilleri, G. (Ed.): *Investigations on Cetacea.* Berne, Pilleri, 1969, vol. 1, pp. 109–120.

Gorry, J.D.: Studies on the comparative anatomy of the ganglion basale of Meynert. *Acta Anat.,* 55:51–104, 1963.

Gorry, J.D. and Pilleri, G.: The structure and comparative anatomy of the Nucleus basalis Meynert of *Delphinus delphis* LINNAEUS. *Acta anat.,* 53:268–275, 1963.

Grünthal, E.: Ueber den Primatencharakter des Gehirns von *Delphinus delphis. Mschr. Psychiat. Neurol.,* 105:249–274, 1942.

Guldberg, E.: Ueber das Zentralnervensystem des Bartenwale. *Chria. Vid-Selsk. Forh.,* 1:1–154, 1885.

Guldberg, G.A.: Ueber die Groessenund Gewichtsverhaeltnisse des Gehirns bei den Bartenwalen und ihren Vergleich mit dem Gehirn der übringen Cetaceen und anderen Säugethiere, *Medellelser Naturhist. Forening i Kristiana* 1885, pp. 53–56.

Guldberg, G. and Nansen, F.: *On the Development and Structure of the Whale. Part 1:* On the development of the dolphin. Bergen, 1894.

Hall, E.R. and Kelson, K.R.: Cetacea. In: *Mammals of North America,* New York City, Ronald Press, 1959, pp. 806–840.

Hanström, B.: Zur Histologie und vergleichenden Anatomie der Hypophyse der Cetaceen. *Acta Zool.,* 25:1–25, 1944.

Harkmark, W. and Jansen, J.: On the development of the cetacean hypophysis. *Hvalrad Skr.,* 1961.

Harris, G.W.: The hypophysial portal vessels of the porpoise (*Phocoena phocoena*). *Nature* (London), 159:874–875, 1947.

Harris, G.W.: Hypothalamo-hypophysial connexions in the Cetacea. *J. Physiol.,* 111:361–367, 1950.

Harrison, R.J. and King, J.E.: *Marine Mammals.* London, Hutchinson University Library, 1965.

Haswell, W.A.: On the brain of Grey's whale (*Kogia greyi*). *Proc. Linn. Soc. N.S. Wales,* 8:437–439, 1883.

Hatschek, R.: Ueber das Rückenmark des Delphins (*Delphinus delphis*). *Arb. neurol.,* 4:286–312, 1896.

Hatschek, R.: Sehnervenatrophie bei einem Delphin. *Arb. neurol.* 10:223–229, 1903.

Hatschek, R. and Schlesinger, H.: Der Hirnstamm des Delphins (*Delphinus delphis*). *Arb. neurol.* 9:1–117, 1902.

Hawkins, A. and Olszewski, J.: Glial/nerve cell index for cortex of the whale. *Science,* 126:76–77, 1957.

Hepburn, D. and Waterston, D.: The pelvic cavity of the porpoise (*Phocoena communis*) as a guide to the determination of a sacral region in Cetacea. Rep. 71st Meeting, British Association for the Advancement of Science, 1901 pp. 680–681.

Hepburn, D. and Waterston, D.: A comparative study of the grey and white matter, of the motor-cell groups, and of the spinal accessory nerve, in the spinal cord of the porpoise (*Phocaena communis*). *J. Anat. Physiol.,* 38: 105–118, 295–311, 1904.

Hofmann, F.: Die obere Olive der Säugetiere, nebst Bemerkungen über die Lage der Cochlearisendkerne. *Arb. neurol.,* 14:76–328, 1908.

Hosokawa, H.: On the extrinsic eye muscles of the whale, with special remarks upon the innervation and function of the musculus retractor bulbi. *Sci. Rep. Whales Res. Inst.,* 6:1–33, 1951.

Hosokawa, H. and Sekino, T.: Comparison of the size of cells and some histological formations between whales and man. *Sci. Rep. Whales Res. Inst.,* 13:269–301, 1958.

Howell, A.B.: *Aquatic Mammals: Their Adaptations to Life in the Water.* Springfield, Thomas, 1930.

Hulke, F.R.S.: Notes on the anatomy of the retina of the common porpoise (*Phocaena communis*). *J. Anat. Physiol.,* 2:19–25, 1865.

Hunter, J.: Observations on the structure and oeconomie of whales. *Philos. Trans. Roy. Soc. London,* 16:306–351, 1787.

Jacobs, M.S.: Retino-hypothalamic connexions in Cetacea. *Nature (London),* 203:778–780, 1964.

Jacobs, M.S. and Jensen, A.V.: Gross aspects of the brain and a fiber analysis of cranial nerves in the great whale. *J. Comp. Neurol.,* 123:55–71, 1964.

Jacobs, M.S. and Piliero, S.J.: Comparison of cranial nerves in three forms of dolphin. *Anat. Rec.,* 151:365, 1965.

Jansen, J.: The morphogenesis of the cetacean cerebellum, *J. Comp. Neurol.,* 93:341–400, 1950.

Jansen, J.: On the whale brain with special reference to the weight of the brain of the fin whale (*Balaenoptera physalus*). *Norsk Hvalfangst. Tid.,* 9: 480–486, 1952.

Jansen, J.: Studies on the cetacean brain; The gross anatomy of the rhomben-cephalon of the fin whale (*Balaenoptera physalus*, L.). *Hvalrad. Skr.*, 37:1–35, 1953.

Jansen, J. Jr., and Jansen, J.: A note on the amygdaloid complex in the fin whale (*Balaenoptera physalus*, L.). *Hvalrad. Skr.*, 39:1–14, 1953.

Jansen, J. and Janson, J.K.S.: The nervous system of Cetacea. In Andersen, J.T. (Ed.): *The Biology of Marine Mammals.* New York, Academic Press, 1969, pp. 175–252.

Jansen, J. and Otnes, B.: A note on the hypothalamus of Cetacea. *Hvalrad. Skr.*, 1959.

Jelgersma, G.: Zentralnervensystem der Cetaceen *Munchen. Med. Wchr.*, 1905.

Jelgersma, G.: *Das Gehirn der Wasser Säugetiere.* Leipzig, J.A. Barth, 1934.

Kaneko, K.: Ueber eine Faserverbindung zwischen dem Ganglion Habenulae und dem Zentralhöhlengrau bei einegen Zetazeen: den Fasciculus habenulocentralis (Fuse). *Arb anat.* 20:97–102, 1937.

Kellogg, R.: The history of whales. Their adaptation to life in the water. *Quart. Rev. Biol.*, 3:29–76, 174–208, 1931.

Kellogg, R.: Adaptation of structure to function in whales. (Cooperation in Research) *Publ. Carnegie Inst,* No. 501 p. 649–682, 1938.

Kellogg, W.N.: *Porpoises and Sonar.* Chicago, University of Chicago Press, 1961.

Kesteven, H.L.: Some features in the anatomy and later development of the head of *Delphinus delphis* Linne. *Rec. Aust. Mus.*, 21:59–80, 1941.

Kojima, T.: On the brain of the sperm whale (*Physeter catodon* L.). *Sci. Rep. Inst.* Tokyo, 6:49–72, 1951.

Kolmer, W.: Ueber das hautige Labyrinth des *Delphinus.* *Anat. Anz.* 32:295–300, 1908.

Kooy, F.H.: The inferior olive in Cetacea. *Folia neuro-biol.*, 11:647–664, 1920.

Korneliussen, H.: Fiber spectra of spinal nerve roots in Cetacea. *J. Comp. Neurol.*, 123:325–334, 1964.

Korneliussen, H.K.: Cerebellar corticogenesis in Cetacea, with special reference to regional variations. *J. Hirnforsch.*, 9:152–185, 1967.

Korneliussen, H.K. and Jansen, J.: The morphogenesis and structure of the inferior olive of Cetacea. *J. Hirnforsch.*, 7:301–314, 1964.

Korneliussen, H.K. and Jansen, J.: On the early development and homology of the central cerebellar nuclei in Cetacea. *J. Hirnforsch.*, 8:47–56, 1965.

Kraus, C. and Gihr, M.: Architectonical and volumetrical investigations on the thalamus of the Cetacea in comparison with the human brain. *Experientia*, 23:973–976, 1967.

Kraus, C. and Gihr, M.: Vergleichende morphometrische Untersuchungen über den thlamus der Cetaceen. *J. Hirnforsch.*, 10:441–449, 1968.

Kraus, C. and Pilleri, G.: Zur Feinstruktur des grossen Pyramidzellen in der V. Cortexschicht der Cetaceen (*Delphinus delphis* und *Balaenoptera borealis*). *Z. Mikranat. Forschung.*, 80:89–99, 1969.

Kraus, C. and Pilleri, G.: Quantative Untersuchungen über die Groshirnrinde der Cetaceen. In Pilleri, G. (Ed): *Investigations on Cetacea. Berne*, Pilleri, 1969, vol. 1, pp. 127–150.

Kraus, C. and Pilleri, G.: Zur Histologie der Grosshirnrinde von *Balaenoptera borealis*. In Pilleri, G. (Ed.): *Investigations on Cetacea*. Berne, Pilleri, 1969, vol. 1, pp. 151–170.

Krompecher, St. and Lipak, J.: A simple method for determining cerebralization. Brain weight and intelligence. *J. Comp. Neurol., 127*:113–120, 1966.

Kruger, L.: The thalamus of the dolphin (*Tursiops truncatus*) and comparison with other mammals. *J. Comp. Neurol., 111*:133–194, 1959.

Kruger, L.: Specialized features of the cetacean brain. In Norris, K.S. (Ed.): *Whales, Dolphins, and Porpoises*. Berkeley, University of California Press, 1966, pp. 232–254.

Kükenthal, W. and Ziehen, T.: Vergleichend-anatomische und entwickelungs-geschichtliche Untersuchungen an Walthieren, III. Das Centralnerven-system der Cetaceen. *Denkschr. Med. Naturw. Ges. Jena, 3*:77–198, 1889.

Langworthy, O.R.: Factors determining the differentiation of the cerebral cortex in sea-living mammals (the Cetacea), A study of the brain of the porpoise, *Tursiops truncatus. Brain, 54*:225–236, 1931.

Langworthy, O.R.: Central nervous system of the porpoise (*Tursiops truncatus*). *J. Mammal., 12*:381–389, 1931.

Langworthy, O.R.: A description of the central nervous system of the porpoise (*Tursiops truncatus*). *J. Comp. Neurol, 54*:437–499, 1932.

Langworthy, O.R.: The brain of the whalebone whale, *Balaenoptera physalus. Bull. Johns Hopkins Hospital, 57*:143–147, 1935.

Legendre, R.: Notes sur le systeme nerveux central d'un dauphin. *Arch. anat. micro., 13*:377–400, 1912.

Legendre, R.: Notes sur le système nerveux central d'un dauphin (*Delphinus delphis*). *Bull. Mus. Hist. Nat. (Paris), 18*:6–8, 1912.

Leszlenyi, O.: Vergleichend-anatomische studien über die Lissaurersche Rand-zone des Hinterhorns. *Arb. neurol. 19*:252–304, 1912.

Lilly, J.C.: Electrode and cannulae implantation in the brain by a simple percutaneous method. *Science, 127*:1181–1182, 1958.

Lilly, J.C.: Some considerations regarding basic mechanisms of positive and negative types of motivations. *Amer. J. Psychiat., 115*:498–504, 1958.

Lilly, J.C.: *Man and Dolphin*. New York, Doubleday, 1961.

Lilly, J.C.: Consideration of the relation of brain size to capability for language activity as illustrated by *Homo sapiens* and *Tursiops truncatus* (bottlenose dolphin). *Electroenceph. Clin. Neurophysiol., 14*:424, 1962.

Lilly, J.C.: In: Mountcastle, V. (Ed.): *Interhemispheric relations and cerebral dominance*. Baltimore, Johns Hopkins Press, 1962, p. 112.

Lilly, J.C.: Critical brain size and language. *Persp. Biol. Med., 6*:246–255, 1963.

Lilly, J.C.: Animals in aquatic environments: adaptation of mammals to the oceans. In Dill, D.B. (Ed.): *Handbook of Physiology-Environment*. Washington, The American Physiological Society, 1964, pp. 741–747.

Lilly, J.C. and Miller, A.M.: Operant conditioning of the bottlenose dolphin with electrical stimulation of the brain. *J. Comp. Physiol. Psychol.,* 55:73–79, 1962.

Major, H.C.: Observations on the structure of the brain of the white whale (*Delphinapterus leucas*). *J. Anat. Physiol.,* 13:127–138, 1879.

Mann, F.G.: Ojo y vision de los Ballenos. *Biologica, 4:23–81, 1946.*

Matsumoto, Y.: Contributions to the study on the internal structure of the cetacean brain stem. *Acta Anat., (Nippon)* 28:167–177, 1953, in Japanese.

McBride, A.F. and Hebb, D.O.: Behavior of the captive bottle-nose dolphin, *Tursiops truncatus. J. Comp. Psysiol. Psychol., 41*:111–123, 1947.

McCormick, J.G.: *The behavior and physiology of sleep and anesthesia in the Atlantic bottle-nosed dolphin (Tursiops truncatus).* Thesis, Princeton University, 1967.

McCormick, J.G. and Ridgway, S.H.: An anesthetic procedure for psychophysiological studies of the bottle-nosed dolphin. Movie presented at Eastern Psychological Association Meetings, Boston, Massachusetts, 1967.

McFarland, W.L.: Ventricular configuration in the brain of the dolphin (*Tursiops truncatus*). *Anat. Rec., 151:385, 1965.*

McFarland, W.L.: Ventricular system in the brain of the dolphin, *Tursiops truncatus. Anat. Rec., 145*:474–475, 1966.

McFarland, W.L., Morgane, P.J., and Jacobs, M.S.: Ventricular system of the brain of the dolphin, *Tursiops truncatus,* with comparative anatomical observations and relations to brain specializations. *J. Comp. Neur., 135*:275–368, 1969.

Miller, G.S.: The telescoping of the cetacean skull. *Smiths. Misc. Coll.,* 76 (5): 1–62, 1923.

Mishima, K.: A contribution to the neuroanatomical study of the aquatic mammals, especially on the cerebellar cortex of *Balaenoptera physalus. Hiroshima J. Med. Sci.,* 6:217–233, 1958.

Morgane, P.J.: Lamination characteristics and areal differentiation in the cerebral cortex of the bottlenose dolphin (*Tursiops truncatus*). *Anat. Rec., 151*:390–391, 1965.

Morgane, P.J., Jacobs, M.S., Yakovlev, P.I., McFarland, W.L., and Piliero, S.J.: Surface configurations and nomenclature of sulci and gyri of the brain of the bottlenose dolphin, *Tursiops truncatus:* In preparation, 1970.

Morgane, P.J., McFarland, W.L., Jacobs, M.S., Piliero, S.J., and Yakovlev, P.I.: The gross and microscopic structure of the brain of the dolphin, *Tursiops truncatus. Anat. Rec., 151*:491, 1965.

Morgane, P.J., Yakovlev, P.I., Jacobs, M.S., McFarland, W.L., and Piliero, S.J.: *An atlas of the brain of the dolphin, (Tursiops truncatus).* Pergamon Press, In press.

Murie, J.: On the organization of the caaing whale. *Trans. Zool. Soc. London,* 8:235–301, 1873.

Nagel, E.L., Morgane, P.J., and McFarland, W.L.: Anesthesia for the bottle-nose dolphin. *Science, 146*:1591, 1964.

Nakai, J. and Shida, T.: Sinus-hairs of the sei-whale (*Balaenoptera borealis*). *Sci. Rep. Whales Res. Inst.,* 1:41–47, 1948.

Nishiwaki, M.: Taxonomical considerations on genera of Delphinidae. *Sci. Rep. Whales Res. Inst.* 17:93–103, 1963.

Nishiwaki, M.: Revision of the article Taxonomical consideration on genera of Delphinidae in No. 17, *Sci. Rep. Whales Res. Inst.,* 18:171–172, 1964.

Obersteiner, H.: Die kleinhirnrinde von *Elephas* und *Balaenoptera*. *Arb. neurol* 20:145–154, 1913.

Ogawa, T.: Ueber den Nucleus ellipticus und den Nucleus ruber beim Delphin, *Arb. anat.* 17:55–61, 1935.

Ogawa, T.: Beitrage zur vergleichenden Anatomie des Zentralnervensystems der Wassersäugetiere: Ueber die Kleinhirnkerne der Pinnipedien und Zetazeen, *Arb. anat.* 17:63–136, 1935.

Ogawa, T.: Ueber den Tractus tectocerebellaris bei den Säugetieren. *Arb. anat.,* 20:53–78, 1937.

Ogawa, T.: On the cardiac nerves of some Cetacea with special reference to those of *Berardius bairdii Stejneger. Sci. Rep. Whales Res. Inst.,* 7:1–22, 1952.

Ogawa, T. and Arifuku, S.: On the acoustic system in the cetacean brains. *Sci. Rep. Whales Res. Inst.,* 2:1–20, 1948.

Ogawa, T. and Shida, T.: On the sensory tubercles of lips and of oral cavity in the sei and the fin whale. *Sci. Rep. Whales Res. Inst.,* 3:1–16, 1950.

Osen, K.K. and Jansen, J.: The cochlear nuclei in the common porpoise, *Phocoena phocoena. J. Comp. Neurol., 125*:223–257, 1965.

Palmer, E. and Weddell, G.: The relationship between structure, innervation and function of the skin of the bottlenose dolphin (*Tursiops truncatus*). *Proc. Zool. Soc. London, 143*:553–568, 1964.

Pettit, A.: Descriptions des encephales de *Grampus griseus* Cuv., de *Steno frontatus* Cuv., et de *Globicephalus melas* Traill, provenant des compagnes du yacht Princesse-Alice. *Result. Camp. sci. Monaco, 31*:1–58, 1905.

Pilleri, G.: Die zentralnervöse Rangordnung der Cetacea. *Acta Anat., 51*:241–258, 1962a.

Pilleri, G.: Intelligenz und Gehirnentwicklung bei den Walen. *Panorama,* Sandoz-Basel, 1962b.

Pilleri, G.: Zur vergleichenden Morphologie und Rangordnung des Gehirns von *Delphinapterus* (Beluga) *leucas* Pallas. *Rev. Suisse, Zool., 70*:569–586, 1963.

Pilleri, G., Morphologie des Gehirnes des Blauwals: *Jahrb. Naturhist. Mus. Bern,* p., 187–203, (1963–1965).

Pilleri, G.: Zur Morphologie des Auges vom Weisswal, *Delphinapterus leucas,* Pallas, 1776. *Hvalrad. Skr., 47*:1–16, 1964.

Pilleri, G.: Morphologie des Gehirnes des southern right whale *Eubalaena australis* Desmoulins. *Acta Zool.,* Stockholm, *46*:245–272, 1964.

Pilleri, G.: The brain of the southern sei whale (*Balaenoptera borealis* LESSON), *Experientia, 21*:703–708, 1965.

Pilleri, G.: Morphologie des Gehirnes des Seiwals (*Balaenoptera borealis* LESSON). *J. Hirnforsch, 8*:221–267, 1966a.

Pilleri, G.: Zum Hirnbau und verhalten des Buckelwals, *Megaptera novaeangliae* Borowski, *Acta Anat., 64*:256–262, 1966b.

Pilleri, G.: A brain anatomist goes whaling. *Ciba Symposium, 14*:57–65, 1966c.

Pilleri, G.: Ueber die Anatomie des Gehirnes des Gangesdelphins, *Platanista gangetica. Rev. Suisse Zool., 73*:113–118, 1966d.

Pilleri, G.: On the anatomy of the brain of the humpback whale, *Megaptera novaeangliae. Rev. Suisse Zool., 73*:161–165, 1966e.

Pilleri, G.: Morphologie des Gehirnes des Buckelwals, *Megaptera novaeangliae. J. Hirnforsch., 8*:437–491, 1966.

Pilleri, G.: Zum Hirnbau und Verhalten des Pilotwals, *Globicephala melaena*, Frôdskaparrit. *Ann. Soc. Sci. Faroensis, 15*:103–112, 1966.

Pilleri, G.: Die zentralnervose Rangstufe des Blauwals, *Sibbaldi musculus. Experientia, 22*:849–854, 1966.

Pilleri, G.: Retinalfalten im Auge von Wassersäugetieren. *Experientia, 23*:54–58, 1967.

Pilleri, G.: Considérations sur le cerveau et le comportement du *Delphinus delphis. Rev. suisse Zool., 74*:655–657, 1967.

Pilleri, G. and Gihr, M.: On the brain of the Amazon dolphin *Inia geoffrensis. Experientia, 24*:932–934, 1968.

Pilleri, G., Kraus, C., and Gihr, M.: The structure of the cerebral cortex of the Ganges dolphin *Susu (Platanista) gangetica. Z. Mikr. anat. Forschung, 79*:373–388, 1968.

Pilleri, G. and Wandeler, A.: Zur Entwicklung der Körperform der Cetacea, *Rev. Suisse de Zool., 69*:737–758, 1962.

Pilleri, G. and Wandeler, A.: Ontogenese und funktionelle Morphologie des Auges des Finnwals, *Balaenoptera physalus* (Linn.). *Acta Anat., 57S*:1–74, 1964.

Pressey, H.E. and Cobb, S.: Observations on the spinal cord of *Phocaena. J. Comp. Neurol., 47*:75–83, 1928.

Pribram, K.H. and Kruger, L.: Functions of the "olfactory brain," *Ann. N. Y. Acad. Sci., 58*:109–138, 1954.

Purves, P.E.: Anatomy and physiology of the outer and middle ear in cetaceans. Pütter, A.: Die Augen der Wassersäugethiere. *Zool. Jahrb., 27*:99–404, 1902. In Norris, K.S. (Ed.): *Whales, Dolphins and Porpoises.* Berkeley, University of California Press, 1966, pp. 320–380.

Quiring, D.P.: Weight data on five whales. *J. Mammal, 24*:39–45, 1943.

Radinsky, L.: Relative brain size; a new measure. *Science, 155*:836–838, 1967.

Rapp, W.: Nervensystem. In *Die Cetaceen, zoologisch-anatomisch dargestellt,* Stuttgart, 1837, pp. 115–123.

Rawitz, B.: Das Zentralnervensystem der Cetaceen., I. Das Rückenmark von

Phocoena communis Cuv., und das Cervicalmark von *Balaenoptera rostrata* Fabr. *Arch. mikr. Anat., 62*:1–40, 1903.

Rawitz, B.: Beiträge zur mikroskopischen Anatomie der Cetaceen, III. Die Papilla nervi optici von *Phocoena communis* Cuv. *Internat. Mschr. Anat. Physiol., 21*:23–30, 1905.

Rawitz, B.: Das Zentralnervensystem der Cetaceen. II. Die Medulla oblongata von *Phoceana communis* (Cuv.) Less., und *Balaenoptera rostrata* Fabr. *Arch. mikr. Anat., 73*:182–260, 1908.

Rawitz, B.: Das Zentralnervensystem der Cetaceen. III. Die Furchen und Windungen des Grosshirns von *Balaenoptera rostrata* Fabr. *Arch. mikr. Anat., 75*:225, 239, 1910.

Rawitz, B.: Zur Kenntniss der Arkitektonik der Grosshirnrinde des Menschen und einiger Säugetiere. III. Die Hirnrinde von Schwein, Schaf. Pferd, Zahnwal, Bartenwahl, Beutelratte, IV. Allgemeine Betrachtungen. *Z. Anat. Entwicklungsgesch, 82*:122–141, 1927.

Ray, J.: An account of the dissection of a porpess. *Phil. Trans. Roy. Soc. Lond., 6*:2274–2279, 1671.

Reysenbach de Haan, F.W.: Hearing in whales, *Acta. Otolaryng.*, Suppl., *134*:1–114, 1957.

Reysenbach de Haan, F.W.: Some aspects of mammalian hearing underwater. *Proc. Roy. Soc., 152*(B): 54–62, 1960.

Reysenbach de Haan, F.W.: Listening underwater: Thoughts on sound and cetacean hearing. In Norris, K.S. (Ed.): *Whales, Dolphins and Porpoises.* Berkeley, Univ. of California Press, 1966.

Ridgway, S.H., Flanigan, N.J., and McCormick, J.G.: Brain-spinal cord ratios in porpoises: Possible correlations with intelligence and ecology. *Psychon. Sci., 6*:491–492, 1966.

Ridgway, S.H. and McCormick, J.G.: Anesthetization of porpoises for major surgery. *Science, 158*:510–512, 1967.

Ries, F.A. and Langworthy, O.R.: A study of the surface structure of the brain of the whale (*Balaenoptera physalus* and *Physeter catdodon*). *J. Comp. Neurol, 68*:1–47, 1937.

Riese, W.: Formproblems des Gehirns. Ueber die Hirnrinde der Wale, Ein Beitrag zum Forschungsproblem, *J. Psychol. Neurol., 31*:257–279, 1925.

Riese, W.: Ueber die Stammganglien der Wale, *J. Psychol. Neurol., 32*:21–28, 1925.

Riese, W.: Ueber anatomische und funktionelle Differenz im optischen System. *J. Psychol. Neurol., 32*:281–290, 1926.

Riese, W.: Ueber den Bau und die Leistungen des akustichen Systems der Wale. *J. Psychol. Neurol., 34*:194–201, 1926.

Riese, W.: Ueber das Vorderhirn des Walfötus (*Megaptera boops*). *Anat. Anz., 65*:255–260, 1928.

Riese, W.: Ueber die Entwicklung des Walhirns. *Proc. Acad. Sci., 39*:97–109, 1936.

Rochon-Duvigneaud, A.: L'oeil des Cetaces. *Nouv. Arch. Mus. Hist. nat. Paris,* (Series 7), *16:57–90, 1940.*

Romanes, G.J.: Some features of the spinal nervous system of the foetal whale (*Megaptera nodosa*). *J. Anat. London, 79:145–156, 1945.*

Rose, M.: Der Grundplan der Cortextektonik beim Delphin. *J. Psychol. Neurol., 32:161–169, 1926.*

Schulte, H.v.W.: Anatomy of a fetus of *Balaenoptera borealis* Lesson. *Mem. Amer. Mus. Nat. Hist., 1:389–502, 1916.*

Schulte, H.v.W. and M. de F. Smith: The external characters, skeletal muscles and peripheral nerves of *Kogia breviceps* (Blainville) *Bull. Amer. Mus. Nat. Hist. 38:7–72, 1918.*

Seki, Y.: Observations on the spinal cord of the right whale. *Sci. Reps. Whales Res. Inst., 13:231–251, 1958.*

Sinclair, J.G.: The terminal olfactory complex in the porpoise. *Texas J. Sci., 3:251, 1951.*

Slijper, E.J.: Die Cetaceen vergleichend anatomisch und systematisch, Ein Beitrag zur vergleichenden Anatomie des Blutgefäss-, Nerven- und Muskelsystems, sowie des Rumpfskelettes der Säugetiere, mit Studien über die Theorie des Aussterbens und der Foetalisation. *Capita Zooligica, 7:1–590, 1936.*

Slijper, E.J.: *Whales.* Translated by A.J. Pomerans, London, Hutchinson and Company, 1962. (From Slijper, E.J., *Walvissen*, D.B. Centen's Uitgeversmaatschappji, Amsterdam, 1958).

Stannius, H.: Ueber die Augennerven des Delphins (*Delph. phocoena*), *Arch. f. Anat. Physiol.,* 378–387, 1842.

Stannius, H.: Ueber den Bau des Delphin Gehirnes. *Abhandl. a.d. Gebiete d. Naturwiss. 1:1–16, 1846.*

Straus, W.L., Jr.: Note on the spinal cord of the finback whale (*Balaenoptera physalus*), *Bull. Johns Hopkins Hospital, 57:317–329, 1935.*

Sverdrup, A. and Arnessen, K.: Investigations on the anterior lobe of the hypophysis of the finback whale. *Hvalrad Skr., 36:1–15, 1952.*

Takahashi, D.: Zur vergleichenden Anatomie des Seitenhorns im Rückenmark der Vertebraten, *Arb. neurol. 20:62–83, 1913.*

Tani, M.: Ueber das Corpus geniculatum laterale bei den Wassersäugetieren. *Arb. anat. 24:39–84, 1941.*

Tiedemann, F.: Hirn des delphins mit dem des menschen verglichen. *Z. Phys., 20:251–263, 1829.*

Tower, D.B.: Structural and functional organization of the mammalian cerebral cortex: The correlation of neurone density with brain size *J. Comp. Neurol., 101:19–52, 1944.*

Turner, W.: The convolutions of the brain. *J. Anat. Physiol.,* 1890.

Tyson, E.: Phocoena, or the anatomy of a porpess dissected at Gresham Colledge, with a preliminary discourse concerning anatomy and a natural history of animals, London, printed for Benjamin Tooke, (1680); reprinted in: *Dublin's Philosophical Journal, 2:48–60, 192–207, 1826.*

Valeton, M.T.: Beitrag zur vergleichenden Anatomie des hinteren Vierhügels des Menchen und einiger Säugetiere. *Arb. neurol. 14:*29–75, 1908.

Valsö, J.: Die hypophyse des Blauwals (*Balaenoptera sibbaldii*), Makroskopische und mikroskopische Anatomie. *Z. Anat. Entwicklungsgesch, 105:*715–719, 1936.

Vermeulen, H.A.: On the vagus and hypoglossus areas in *Phocaena communis. Proc. Acad. Sci. Amsterdam, 18:*965–980, 1916.

Wilson, R.B.: The anatomy of the brain of the whale (*Balaenoptera sulfurea*). *J. Comp. Neurol., 58:*419–480, 1933.

Wirz, K.: Studien über die Cerebralization: Zur Quantitativ en Bestimmung der Rangordnung bei Säugetiere. *Acta Anat., 9:*134–196, 1950.

Wislocki, G.B.: The hypophysis of the porpoise (*Tursiops truncatus*). *Arch. Surg. 18:*1403–1412, 1929.

Wislocki, G.B. and Geiling, E.M.K.: The anatomy of the hypophysis of whales, *Anat. Rec. 66:*17–41, 1936.

Zuckerkandl, E.: *Ueber das Reichcentrum.* 8. Ueber die Bedeutung der bisher beschriebenen Rindentheile und über das Gehirn des Delphins, Stuttgart, p. 87–109, 1887.

Pinnipedia

Alderson, A.M., Diamantopoulos, E. and Downman, C.B.B.: Auditory cortex of the seal (*Phoca vitulina*). *J. Anat., 94:*506–511, 1960.

Anthony, R. and Friant, M.: Recherches sur le neopallium de l'otarie. *Anat. Anz. 85:*139–158, 1937.

Beddard, F.E.: On the structure of Hooker's sea lion (*Arctocephalus hookeri*). *Zool. Soc. Trans., 12:*369–380, 1887.

Brunner, H.: Die Zentralen Kleinhirnkerne bei den Säugetieren. *Arb. Neurol. 22:*200–277, 1919.

Fish, P.A.: The brain of the fur seal, *Callorhinus ursinus;* with a comparative description of those of *Zalophus californianus, Phoca vitulina* and *Monachus tropicalis. J. Comp. Neurol., 8:*57–95, 1898.

Fish, P.A.: The cerebral fissures of the Atlantic walrus. *Proc. U.S. Nat. Mus., 26:*675–688, 1903.

Fuse, G.: Einige strukturelle Besondherheiten am Hirnstamm bei den im Wasser lebenden Säugern (Seehund, Seebär und Delphin). *Arb. anat. 13:*333–354, 1928.

Fuse, G.: Einiges Vergleichend-anatomisches über ein bisher nicht genügend dargesttelltes bzw. gewürdigtes Grausystem in und an der spinalen Quintuswurzel (Nuclei intra-et extratrigeminales) bei einigen Wassersaügetieren (Seehund, Seebär, Seeotter, Delphin und Seiwal). *Arb. anat. 23:*165–223, 1940.

Haig, H.A.: A contribution to the histology of the central nervous system of the Weddell seal (*Leptonychotes weddellii*). *Trans, Roy. Soc. Edinburgh, 48:*849–866, 1913.

Harrison, R.J., and King, J.E.: *Marine Mammals,* London, Hutchinson University Library, 1965.

Hatschek, R.: Ueber das Rückenmark des Seehundes (*Phoca vitulina*) im Vergleiche mit dem des Hundes, *Arb. neurol.* 4:313–340, 1896.

Hepburn, D.: Observations on the anatomy of the Weddell seal (*Leptonychotes weddelli*) IV. The brain, *Trans. Roy, Soc., Edinburgh,* 48:827–847, 1913.

Hofmann, F.: Die obere Olive der Säugetiere, nebst Bemerkungen über die Lage der Cochlearisendkerne, *Arb. neurol, Inst. Univ. Wien,* 14:76–328. (1908).

Howell, A.B.: Contribution to the comparative anatomy of the eared and earless seals (genera *Zalophus* and *Phoca*), *Proc. U.S. Nat. Mus.,* 73:(Art 15); 1–142, 1928.

Jelgersma, G.: *Das Gehirn der Wasser Saügetiere,* J.A. Barth, Leipzig, 288 p., 1934.

King, J.E.: *Seals of the world.* London, Trustees of the British Museum of Natural History, 1964.

Kükenthal, W., and Ziehen, T.: Vergleichend-anatomische und entwickelungsgeschichtliche Untersuchungen an Walthieren. III. Das Centralnervensystem der Cetaceen. *Denkschr. Med. -naturw. Ges. jena,* 3:77 198, 1889.

Laszlonyi, O.: Vergleichend anatomische studien über die Lissauersche Randzone des Hinterhorns. *Arb. neurol,* 19:252–304, 1912.

Langworthy, O.R., Hesser, F.H., and Kolb, L.D.: Physiological study of cortex of hair seal. *J. Comp. Neurol.,* 69:351–369, 1938.

Lassek, A.M., and Karlsberg, P.: The pyramidal tract of an aquatic carnivore (seal). *J. Comp. Neurol.,* 106:425–431, 1956.

Murie, J.: Researches upon the anatomy of the Pinnipedia I. On the walrus (*Trichechus rosmarus,* Linn). *Trans. Zool. Soc. London,* 7:411–464, 1871.

Murie, J.: Researches upon the anatomy of the Pinnipedia. III. Descriptive anatomy of the sea lion (*Otaria jubata*). *Trans. Zool. Soc. London,* 8:501–582, 1874.

Ogawa, T.: Beiträge zur vergleichenden Anatomie der Hinterstrangkerne der Wassersaugetiere: Ueber den medianen unpaarigen Burdachschen Kern. (Necleus Burdachii medianus impar) beim Seehunde (*phoca vitulina L.*). *Arb. anat.,* 13:80–89, 1928.

Ogawa, T.: Beiträge zur vergleichenden Anatomie des Zentralnervensystems der Wassersäugetiere. Ueber das vierte oder sub-kortikale graue Lager, stratum griseum quartum a. sub-corticale im Kleinhirn des Seebären (*Callorhinus ursinus,* Gray). *Arb. anat.* 16:83–96, 1934.

Ogawa, T.: Beiträge zur vergleichenden Anatomie des Zentralnervensystems der Wassersäugetiere: Ueber die Kleinhirnkerne der Pinnipedien und Zetazeen. *Arb. anat.* 17:63–136, 1935.

Ogawa, T.: Ueber den Tractus tectocerebellaris bei den Säugetieren, *Arb. anat.,* 20:53–78, 1937.

Rioch, D. McK.: A physiological and histological study of the frontal cortex of the seal (*Phoca vitulina*) *Biol. Bull. Woods Hole,* 73:591–602, 1937.

Spitzka, E.C.: Zur Monographie Dr. Theodor's ueber das Seehundsgehirn. *Anat. Anz.*, 5:173–176, 1890.

Tani, M.: Ueber das Corpus geniculatum laterale bei den Wassersäugetieren. *Arb. anat.* 24:39–84, 1941.

Turner, W.: Comparison of the convolutions of the seal and walrus with those of Carnivora and of apes and man. *J. Anat. Physiol.*, 22:554–581, 1888.

Vrolik, W.: *Specimen anatomica–zoologicum de Phocis, speciatim de Phoca*, Trajecti ad Rhenum, 1822.

Wilcox, H.H.: Observations on the spinal cord of the California sea lion. *Proc. Third Ann. Conf. on Biol. Sonar and Diving Mammals*, Stanford Research Institute, 1966, pp. 41–54.

Chapter 4

OBSERVATIONS ON THE ANATOMY OF SOME CETACEANS AND PINNIPEDS

ROBERT F. GREEN

This chapter is designed to introduce the reader to the general anatomy of cetaceans and pinnipeds. Because the cetacean most frequently seen in captivity is the Atlantic bottlenosed dolphin (or porpoise), *Tursiops truncatus*, the majority of my observations have been on this species. Unless otherwise stated, discussions of cetacean anatomy will primarily relate to the bottlenosed dolphin. Of the Pinnipedia, the California sea lion, *Zalophus Californianus*, and the harbor seal, *Phoca vitulina*, are most frequently encountered. Since my experience has most frequently involved the California sea lion, this species will be featured, along with frequent comparisons with *Phoca vitulina* and *Mirounga angustirostris* (northern elephant seal). Other species are discussed primarily from the literature.

CETACEAN ANATOMY

The cetaceans or whales have undergone many modifications in their anatomy in becoming highly adapted to a totally aquatic existence (Kellogg, 1931, 1938). While remaining viviparous, homeothermic air breathers, they have significantly altered their mode of locomotion to become excellent swimmers and divers. The casual observer might think whales to be more closely related to fish than to mammals. This probably occurs because they have similar body form and both live in the water. Closer examination, however, reveals whales to be true mammals and not fish-like at all. While there are many variations in form, most cetaceans have a fusiform or spindle-shaped body which offers a minimum of resistance in moving through the water (Fig. 4–1). The head is more or less tapered to the snout, and the neck is not outwardly visible in most species.

Most of the propulsive force in swimming is achieved by way of the laterally expanded, flattened, caudal lobes called flukes. This organ con-

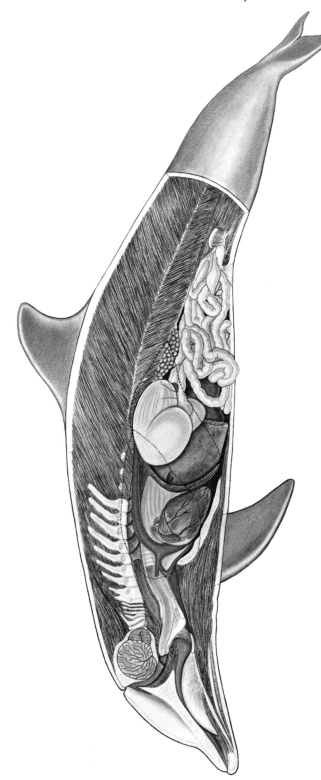

Figure 4–1A. Sagittal view of the Atlantic bottlenosed dolphin (porpoise), *Tursiops truncatus* (drawn by Barbara Stolen Irvine from dissections by Robert F. Green). See opposite page for labeling.

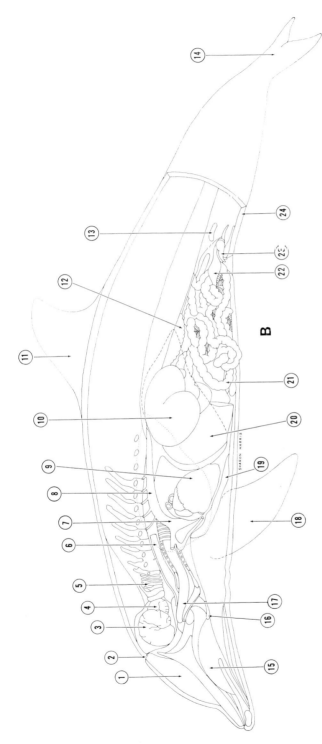

Figure 4–1B. Outline drawing of Fig. 4–1A with labels (outline drawn by Sharon Harris). (1) Melon, (2) Blowhole, (3) Cerebrum, (4) Cerebellum, (5) Cervical Vertebrae, (6) Esophagus, (7) Aortic Arch, (8) Dorsal Aorta, (9) Heart, (10) Stomach, (11) Dorsal Fin, (12) Kidney, (13) Pelvis, (14) Flukes, (15) Tongue, (16) Hyoid Bone, (17) Larynx, (18) Right Flipper, (19) Sternum, (20) Liver, (21) Intestine, (22) Urinary Bladder, (23) Penis, and (24) Blubber (hypodermis).

tains neither bone nor cartilage for support, except for the distal caudal
vertebrae in the tail stock. Most cetaceans also possess a single dorsal fin
which is similar in structure to the flukes. This organ is strengthened by
subcutaneous fibers which extend vertically from the base to the tip. Both
the dorsal fin and the flukes are well vascularized (Fig. 4–2) and are
important to the animals' temperature regulatory ability (Scholander and
Schevill 1955; also see Chap. 10).

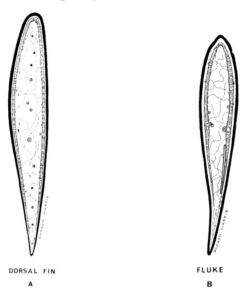

DORSAL FIN   FLUKE
A   B

Figure 4–2. Cross section of dorsal fin and fluke of the Atlantic bottlenosed dolphin
(porpoise), *Tursiops truncatus*.

The pectoral appendages have the same basic structure as the forelimbs
of terrestrial mammals but have become modified as paddle-like flippers.
The pelvic appendages have completely disappeared and the pelvic girdle
persists as a pair of rod-like bones imbedded in the lateral trunk musculature just above and behind the genital area (Fig. 4–14, 4–15). These
bones are not attached to the vertebral column, and there is no evidence
of a sacrum. In most whales, the skin is quite smooth and noticeably free
of hairs. Some species have a few bristles about the head and lips.

There are no external ears, and each external auditory meatus is reduced to a tiny pinpoint opening in most odontocetes. Some mystacocetes,
however, have large external auditory openings. The external genital
organs are recessed in a genital fold or slit. In both males and females,
the gonads are located in the pelvic cavity. The nipples of the mammae
are likewise recessed in slits on either side of the female urogenital slit.

The rorquals, and to some degree the gray whales (see Chap. 1), have
a series of parallel longitudinal grooves or folds on the ventral surface of

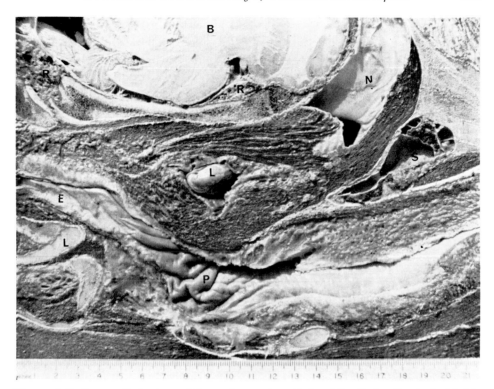

Figure 4–3. Parasagittal view of the gular region of the Atlantic bottlenosed dolphin (porpoise), *Tursiops truncatus*, sectioned 1 cm off the midline. (B) Brain, (E) Esophagus, (L) Larynx, (N) Nasal passage, (P) Pharynx, (S) Pterygoid sinus. Photograph by Robert F. Green.

the throat and thoracic region. These grooves extend from the lower jaws posterior as far as the umbilicus and laterally to the pectoral limbs. While the full significance of these grooves is not known, several functions have been suggested. They may allow distension of the skin during breathing and eating; they may function to help reduce drag; and since the skin in the grooves is thinner and more vascularized, they may aid in temperature regulation (Harrison and King, 1965).

Although color of whales is quite variable, black and white are the main colors. Some species are totally black and others totally white. Most animals are dark on the dorsal surface and light on the ventral surface. This pattern helps to camouflage the animals so that they blend well with the sea surface when viewed from below or above. The beluga, which spends much of its life near the Arctic ice, is completely white.

Integument

The cetacean skin is generally quite smooth and hairless and consists of epidermal, dermal, and hypodermal layers. The smoothness of the skin is achieved by the absence of hairs, by an overall compactness of the layers, and by variation in thickness over the various body regions. Newborn animals have a few bristles on the head and snout which are soon lost. The position of these hairs is marked by pits which (because they are intricately and copiously innervated) are regarded as specialized sense organs (Palmer and Weddell, 1964).

The epidermis, which is usually less than 1 cm thick, is composed of a poorly defined stratum corneum and a better defined stratum germinativum. The cells in the corneum are flattened parallel to the surface and only partly keratinized. Numerous dermal ridges lying parallel to the long axis of the body project into the deeper epidermis. Dermal papillae project still further into the epidermis from the upper surface of the ridges.

The dermis, which is as thin or thinner than the epidermis, is composed of masses of connective tissue fibers. These fiber are less dense and interspersed with adipose tissue where the dermis merges with the hypodermis. The hypodermis is the thickest of the three skin layers and is composed of adipose cells interspersed with bundles of connective tissue fibers (see Chap. 5).

The skin is quite well vascularized, with arterioles passing to the base of the epidermis, there giving rise to numerous branches which pass through the dermal ridges to supply the capillaries in the papillae. Blood can pass from the capillaries by way of venules or through a dermal plexus of smaller vessels, some of which lie in close proximity to the arterioles.

Muscular System

Space does not permit more than a brief statement concerning the musculature of cetaceans. There have been no less than a hundred papers written on the myology of various species, applying a wide variety of names to the various muscles.

For the reader interested in detailed descriptions of musculature the following are recommended: Stannius (1849) on *Delphinus* (*Phocaena*) *phocaena*, Murie (1865) on *Physalus antiquorum* (*Balaenoptera physalus*), Carte and MacAlister (1868) on *Balaenoptera rostrata*, Struthers (1871) on *Balaenoptera muscullus*, Murie (1871a) on *Grampus rissoanus* (*Grampus griseus*), Murie (1871b) on *Lagenorhynchus albirostris*, Murie (1874) on *Globicephalus melas*, Boenninghauss (1902) on *Phocaena communis* (*Phocoena phocaena*), Hein (1914) on *Monodon*, Schulte (1916) on *Balaenoptera borealis*, Schulte and Smith (1918) on *Kogia breviceps*, Howell (1927) on *Neomeris phocaenoides* (*Neophocoena*), Howell (1930) on *Monodon monoceros*, Huber (1934) on *Tursiops truncatus*, Lawrence and Schevill (1956) on the anatomy of the delphinid nose, and Lawrence and Schevill (1965) on the gular musculature of the delphinids.

Skeletal System

A typical odontocete skeleton is illustrated in Fig. 4–4, while that of a mystacocete, *Balaena mysticetus,* reproduced from the early works of Eschricht and Reinhardt (1866), may be seen in Figs. 4–5 and 4–6.

CRANIUM

Even to the untrained eye, the cetacean skull appears quite modified in comparison to other mammals (Figs. 4–4 to 4–9). The external nares have migrated posteriorly to lie above the internal nares. The proximal ethmoid is exposed from above, and the palatine forms a part of the narial wall. The rostrum is most often developed into a slender beak.

The maxillae form the major part of the beak and are divided into superior facial and inferior palatine parts by the tooth row. The frontal process of the maxilla is a thin layer of bone spread over the anterior frontal bone and covering most of the lacrimal, reaching the nasal bones and external nares on its medial edge.

The premaxillae are elongated bones fitting between the maxillae and extending posteriorly along the length of the snout to bound the external nares laterally. Ventrally, the premaxillae appear as strips of bone on either side of the midline of the snout, extending posteriorly about one-half the length of the snout. The nasal septum, which is attached posteriorly to the mesethmoid crest and the superior edge of the vomer, extends forward between the median faces of the premaxillae.

The parietal bones fit between the frontal, the supraoccipital, the squamosal, and the lateral margin of the alisphenoid. They are curved ventrally, helping to form the cranial floor lateral to the alisphenoid. The interparietal is an irregular-shaped bone situated between the frontals, the parietals, and the exoccipital.

The frontal bone forms the greater part of the roof and anterior wall of the cranial vault. Except for the stout supraoccipital process, which forms most of the roof of the orbital fossa, this bone is generally thin. The anterior edges of the bone extend under the frontal process of the maxillae. Posteriorly, the bone makes contact with the parietals and interparietals. Inferiorly, it sutures with the outer margin of the alisphenoid.

The malar (zygomatic) bones can best be visualized in the ventral view where they are situated beneath the anterior lateral edge of the frontal process of the maxillae in front of the frontal bones. Each forms part of the pterygopalatine fossa and the anterior part of the orbital fossa.

The vomer is a flat plate of bone attached posteriorly to the ventral surface of the basisphenoid and anteriorly to the interpalatine suture. The palatines are situated along the midline just anterior to the pterygoids.

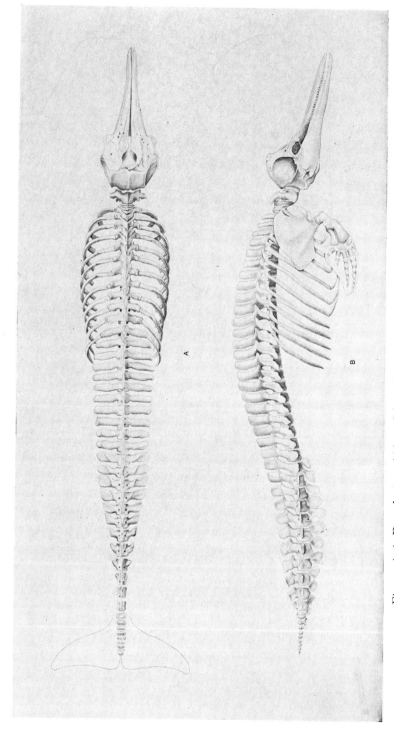

Figure 4–4. Dorsal view (A) and lateral view (B) of an odontocete skeleton *Delphinus* (*Sousa*) *sinensis* (drawn by Barbara Stolen Irvine after Flower, 1870).

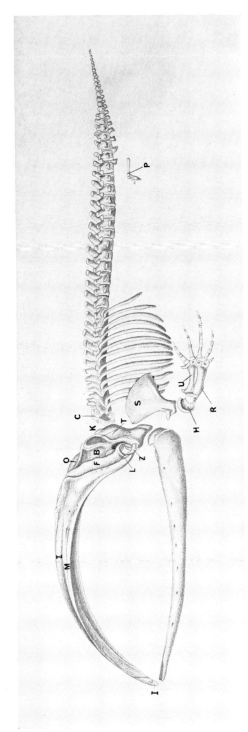

Figure 4–5. Lateral view of a mystacocete skeleton, *Balaena mysticetus* (drawn by Barbara Stolen Irvine after Eschricht and Reinhardt, 1861). (B) Left parietal bone, (C) Cervical vertebrae, (F) Frontal bone, (H) Humerus, (I) Intermaxillary bone, (K) Right occipital condyle, (L) Left lacrimal bone, (M) Maxilla bone, (O) Occipital bone, (P) Pelvis, (R) Radius, (S) Scapula, (T) Left temporal bone, (U) Ulna, (Z) Zygomatic arch.

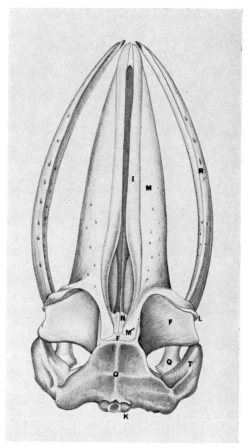

Figure 4–6. Dorsal view of mystacocete skull, *Balaena mysticetus* (drawn by Barbara Stolen Irvine after Eschricht and Reinhardt, 1861). (F) Orbital process of frontal bone, (F¹) Middle piece of frontal bone, (I) Intermaxillary bone, (K) Right occipital condyle, (L) Lacrymal bone, (M) Maxilla, (M¹) Posterior process of maxilla, (N) Nasal bone, (O) Occipital bone, (Q) Condyle of mandible, (R) Mandible, (T) Lateral process of temporal bone.

The tympanoperiotic (ear capsule) bones vary considerably in their attachment to the cranium. In the Delphinidae, the periotic part of the mastoid is neither wedged into, nor integrated with, the squamosal, and the periotic is separated from the bones of the cranium by an appreciable gap (Purves, 1966).

HYOID

The hyoid is well developed, appearing as a pair of U-shaped arcs of bone and cartilage passing below and slightly anterior to the larynx. The most posterior arc is formed of basihyal and thyrohyal segments. The

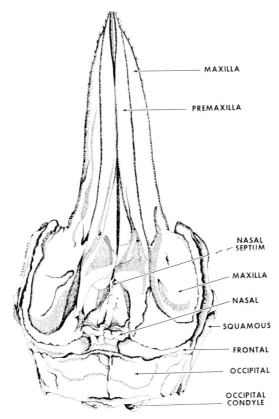

MAXILLA

PREMAXILLA

NASAL SEPTUM

MAXILLA

NASAL

SQUAMOUS

FRONTAL

OCCIPITAL

OCCIPITAL CONDYLE

Figure 4–7. Dorsal view of the skull of an Atlantic bottlenosed dolphin (porpoise), *Tursiops truncatus.* (Drawn by Sharon Harris.)

anterior arc is formed of cartilaginous ceratohyals which connect the basihyals to well ossified rod-like stylohyals. The stylohyals attach to the cranium by cranium by cartilaginous ceratohyals which connect the basihyals to well ossified rod-like stylohyals. The stylohyals attach to the cranium by cartilaginous tips. These tips may be separate elements and are sometimes called tympanohyals (Lawrence and Schevill, 1965).

Vertebral Column

The neck is generally shortened with varying degrees of fusion of the cervical vertebrae. In some species (rorquals, narwhals, white whales and river dolphins) all seven bones remain unfused. In other species (right whales and bottlenosed whales) all the bones fuse to form a single osseous unit.

The remainder of the vertebral column is modified by extension, es-

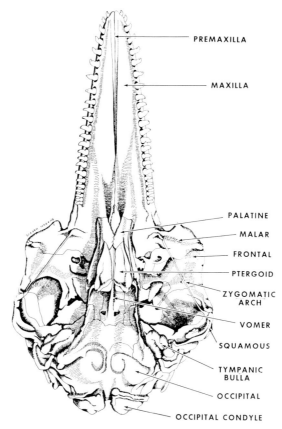

PREMAXILLA

MAXILLA

PALATINE

MALAR

FRONTAL

PTERGOID

ZYGOMATIC
ARCH

VOMER

SQUAMOUS

TYMPANIC
BULLA

OCCIPITAL

OCCIPITAL CONDYLE

Figure 4–8. Ventral view of the skull of an Atlantic bottlenosed dolphin (porpoise), *Tursiops truncatus*. (Drawn by Sharon Harris.)

pecially in the lumbar area. The total number of vertebrae is quite variable (see Chap. 1), with the more recent types having the greater number (Slijper, 1962). The caudal vertebrae have well-formed haemal arches (chevron bones), each of which articulates with two vertebral bodies. In addition to forming the haemal arch, the chevron bones also provide a greater surface area for attachment of caudal muscles.

PECTORAL GIRDLE

The pectoral girdle is made up of left and right scapular bones and the median sternum. The scapulae are broad, flattened, fan-shaped bones. The structure of the sternum, the number of ribs that attach to it, and the number of double-headed ribs varies among species (see Chap. 1). In general, the thorax and pectoral girdle are structured with enough

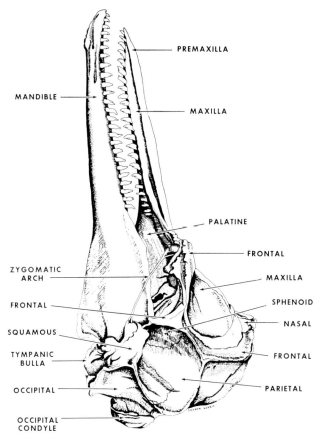

PREMAXILLA

MANDIBLE

MAXILLA

PALATINE

FRONTAL

ZYGOMATIC
ARCH

MAXILLA

FRONTAL

SPHENOID

NASAL

SQUAMOUS

TYMPANIC
BULLA

FRONTAL

OCCIPITAL

PARIETAL

OCCIPITAL
CONDYLE

Figure 4–9. Lateral view of the skull of an Atlantic bottlenosed dolphin (porpoise), *Tursiops truncatus*. (Drawn by Sharon Harris.)

flexibility that the thorax can collapse considerably during a deep dive (Ridgway *et al.* 1969).

Flipper

The forelimbs or flippers have the same basic structure as the pectoral appendages of other mammals but have developed into flat, fin-shaped paddles. The humerus, radius, and ulna have become so shortened that the elbow is located at the body surface (Felts and Spurrell, 1965, 1966).

The humerus has a large globular head where it attaches to the scapula, while the distal end is flattened where it joins the ulna and radius. The carpals are identifiable as separate bones, while the metacarpals are not identifiable from the proximal phalanges, especially in the three middle digits. While *Tursiops* has the usual five digits, some of the cetaceans have a reduction from the basic plan (see Chap. 1).

PELVIC GIRDLE

The pelvic girdle is highly reduced and only the remnants of a pubic bone remain. This short, rod-like bone is embedded in the lateral body musculature, oriented in a longitudinal direction. The bones do not attach to the vertebral column and are generally larger in the male than in the female, serving as an attachment for genital muscles.

Respiratory System

Cetaceans breathe through the external nares which have migrated to a position high on top of the head (Fig. 4–1). This opening, called the blowhole, is bipartite in the baleen whales and appears as two long, narrow slits which have an elevated margin when open. In toothed whales, the blowhole is single and is usually crescentic with the concavity directed rostrally. In the gangetic dolphin, the blowhole appears as a single longitudinal slit at the dorsum of the head.

NASAL SACS

In odontocetes, the nasal passageway consists of a pair of simple tubes which pass through the skull just anterior to the cranium and posterior to the rostrum. The upper end of the passageway opens to the surface through the blowhole, which can be opened and closed by means of a dense fibrous mass called the "plug." There are four pairs of sacs associated with the upper end of the passageway. These sacs are considered to be continuous with the passageway and widen it to a diameter far greater than that of the nares or the blowhole (Lawrence and Schevill, 1956).

The paired premaxillary sacs lie between the melon and the premaxillary bones which form the upper surface of the rostrum. These sacs open into the nasal passageway at the upper margin of the bony nares and are lined by an extension of the integument which covers the nasal plug above. The vestibular sacs lie lateral and somewhat posterior to the lips of the blowhole. They, like the premaxillary sacs, are continuous with the main canal. The U-shaped tubular sacs are somewhat horizontally oriented, surrounding the slit-like openings between the posterior wall of the nasal passageway and the top of the nasal plug. The small connecting sacs are located lateral to and internal to the tubular sacs with which they communicate. The nasal passageway of baleen whales is paired like that of toothed whales, but is much less modified and is partly roofed over by the nasal bones. The well-developed eustachian tubes pass from the air-containing cavity of the ear forward along the basioccipital crest and into the nasopharynx (also see Chap. 10).

LARYNX

The cetacean larynx is composed of a cartilagenous framework held together by a number of muscles (Fig. 4–10). In *Tursiops*, as in the odontocetes in general, the epiglottal and arytenoid cartilages have elongated to form a tube or beak which projects anteriorly and superiorly from the floor of the pharynx with the distal end resting within the internal nares (Fig. 4–3). This beak-like tube has been named the "aryteno-epiglottideal" tube by Hosokawa (1950) and has been decribed in a number of species (Howes, 1879; Dubois, 1886; Benham, 1901; Hosokawa, 1950; and Purves, 1966).

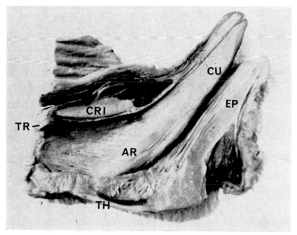

Figure 4–10. Sagittal view of the larynx of an Atlantic bottlenosed dolphin (porpoise), *Tursiops truncatus.* (Photograph and dissection by Robert F. Green.) (AR) Arytenoid cartilage, (CRI) Cricoid cartilage, (CU) Cuneiform cartilage, (EP) Epigiottal carti-lage, (TH) Thyroid cartilage, (TR) 1st tracheal cartilage.

In *Tursiops*, the thyroid cartilage is formed of left and right lamina which fuse at their ventral margins to form part of the lateral wall and floor of the chamber. Each lamina has two well-developed processes, the anteriorly directed hyoideal cornu and the posteriorly directed cricoid cornu.

Some odontocetes have a typical, complete, signet-ring cricoid, while others have a fissure in the ventral part with the posterior ventral margins projecting caudally as lateral cornu. This latter arrangement is the con-dition of the cricoid in *Tursiops*.

The epiglottal cartilage is quite elongated, forming a deep, wide trough in which the arytenoids lie. When observed laterally, the base is wide and robust, while the cranial apex is long and narrowed. The concaved posterior surface is smooth and deep. The inferior caudal edge articulates with the anterior margin of the body of the thyroid cartilage.

The arytenoid cartilage articulates with the anterior margin of the cricoid. The cranial process is thin and tongue-like, with the smooth, flat, medial surface of each cartilage lying along the midline. The caudal processes are much shorter and are robust. The body of the cartilage has a somewhat laterally directed process to which the thyroarytenoid muscle attaches. This attachment is just anterior and medial to the cricoarytenoid articulation. The medial border of the arytenoid is flat and smooth and has no vocal process.

While most descriptions of the cetacean larynx do not mention the corniculate and cuneiform cartilages, Howes (1879) reports the arytenoid of *Phocoena* to be composed of two separate pieces and believes that the upper part, which is prolonged into the nasal passage, represents an elongated cuneiform cartilage. In *Tursiops*, the arytenoid is composed of four separate cartilages. I interpret the cranial process and the superior anterior half of the caudal process as cuneiform cartilage and the posterior half of the caudal and posterior half of the corpus as the true arytenoid. The two small cartilages at the anterior margin of the terminal end of the caudal process represent the corniculate (Santorini) cartilage.

Hosokawa (1950) has stated that every species of whale has more or less its own muscular structure. After dissecting a number of odontocete larynges, I am of the opinion that each animal has its own highly individual pattern of larynageal muscular structure.

The laryngeal muscles are classified into two groups, the extrinsic muscles and the intrinsic muscles. The following extrinsic muscles are identifiable in *Tursiops*. The hyoepiglottal muscle has its origin to the middorsal surface of the basihyal bone and its insertion to the inferior one-half of the anterior surface of the epiglottal cartilage along the midline. This muscle functions to retract the larynx and to enlarge the orifice at the distal end of the tube. The thyrohyoid muscle has its origin on the medial 4 to 5 cm of the basihyal bone and its insertion to the lateral surface of the thyroid cartilage just behind the cranial notch. The sternothyroid muscle has its origin on the medial anterior sternum and its insertion to the thyroid cartilage along the margin of the caudal notch. The occipitothyroid muscle has its origin on the basioccipital plate anterior to the hypoglossal canal and its insertion to the outer surface of the anterior corner of the thyroid cartilage and over the lateral walls of the pharynx. The thyropharyngius muscle has its origin along the dorsal surface of the posterior cornu of the thyroid cartilage, passing through the lateral walls and across the roof of the pharynx.

The following intrinsic muscles are found in *Tursiops:* the cricohyoid muscle has its origin on the lateral surface of the thyroid cartilage about the edge of the caudal notch and its insertion of the lateral surface of the caudal cricoid cornu. The cricoarytenoid dorsalis muscle originates along the dorsal surfaces of the cricoid cartilage, passing forward and laterally to insert on the arytenoid cartilage. The interarytenoid muscle runs transversally between the dorsal posterior margins of the cranial process of the arytenoid cartilage with the posterior fibers covered by the anterior end of the cricoarytenoid muscles. The thyroarytenoid muscle has its origin in the inner surface of the body of the thyroid cartilage and inserts to the lateral surface of the muscular process of the arytenoid.

TRACHEA

Due to the abbreviated neck, the cetacean trachea is short but robust with a large lumen to facilitate the rapid and complete exchange of lung air. There are numerous complete, heavy rings which surround the trachea. Many of these rings anastomose, making the trachea a sturdy but resilient structure.

LUNGS

The lungs are elongated and primarily situated dorsally in the thorax. They extend forward of the first rib (6 to 8 cm in the case of *Tursiops truncatus*) and as far posterior as the second or third lumbar vertebrae. The majority of the lung tissue is located in the dorsal thorax, and the ventral or sternal margins of the lung are quite thin. Because of the oblique orientation of the diaphragm, the lungs have a triangular appearance when viewed from the side (Fig. 4–11).

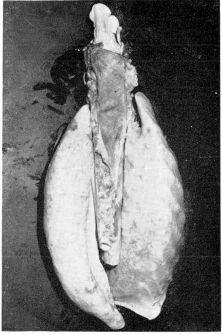

Figure 4–11. Dorsal view of the lungs and larynx of an Atlantic bottlenosed dolphin (porpoise), *Tursiops truncatus*. (Photograph and dissection by Robert F. Green.)

Externally, the lungs show little or no lobulation and are somewhat asymmetrical, due in part to a separate right bronchus (accessory) that branches a short distance anterior to the bifurcation of the trachea into two main bronchi (Fig. 4–13). Some whales lack the accessory bronchus, but in these species, the main bronchus on the right side is larger than the one on the left. The main bronchi, the stem bronchi, and the bronchioles are supported by an extensive network of cartilage rings which anastomose at irregular intervals. The microanatomy of cetacean lungs is discussed in Chapter 5.

Digestive System

Most odontocetes have numerous peg-shaped, single-rooted teeth which are generally much alike (homodont) (Fig. 4–9). Since these teeth are modified for holding and not for chewing, the jaw musculature is considered weak when compared to that of other mammals. The lower jaw is attached in such a way as to move only in one plane, and the coronoid process is either highly reduced or completely missing.

Instead of teeth, adult mystacocetes have a series of elongated, triangular-shaped plates on each side of the upper jaw. These plates are quite flat and thin, averaging less than 7 mm in thickness, and range between 2 to 4 m in length and 25 to 30 cm in width. They are usually shorter at the front and rear on each side and may number as many as 300 to 400 (see Chap. 1). The inner edge of the plates are frayed to form a fringe which acts as a strainer. The plates continue to grow throughout the life of the animal to replace that part which is worn out.

The odontocete tongue is short and robust with a freely movable tip. Even though whales are usually considered to have little or no gustatory sense, Slijper (1962) reports that taste buds have been described in some species. Other researchers have not found taste buds in *Tursiops truncatus* (see Chap. 5 and Chap. 7).

The mouth cavity is generally long and narrow anteriorly, widening posteriorly to pass into the highly muscular pharynx. Posteriorly, the pharynx passes into the esophagus which passes through the thoracic cavity and the diaphragm before entering the first of three main compartments of the stomach. This compartment, called the forestomach, is nonglandular and is lined with white and yellow noncornified squamous epithelium. This chamber is formed as a sacculation of the esophagus (Fig. 4–12).

The second compartment, the main stomach, has a softer velvety lining and is considered homologous to the fundic stomach of other mammals. This is where most of the digestive enzymes are secreted. The next stomach cavity, the pyloric or connecting stomach, also has a velvety lining but is more tubular than saccular in form in most species. There is some enzyme secretion into this part of the stomach. The pyloric stomach passes to the duodenum which also has a large dilation just beyond the pyloric sphincter. This chamber, called the duodenal ampulla (Fig. 4–12), is often mistaken for a compartment of the stomach. The large common bile duct and pancreatic duct drain into the duodenal ampulla.

The intestines are quite long. In Odontoceti there is no caecum and no gross delineation into small and large intestines. In Mystacoceti there is usually a caecum and a more obvious large intestine. In the pigmy whale and beaked whales, the large intestine is also more prominent than in other odontocetes.

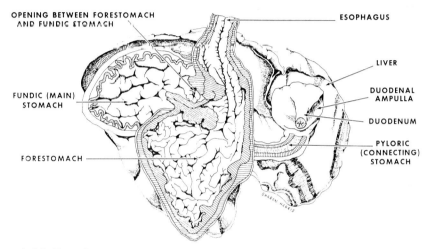

Figure 4–12. Dorsal view of the stomach and liver of an Atlantic bottlenosed dolphin (porpoise), *Tursiops truncatus*. (Drawn by Sharon Harris from dissection by Robert F. Green.)

The liver is generally bilobed and may weigh as much as one ton in larger species. There is no gall bladder, and the hepatic ducts are well developed. The pancreas is generally mammal-like, having from one to several ducts leading from it.

Cardiovascular System

Although the circulatory system is of the basic mammalian plan, there are numerous modifications; modifications which initially might appear to contribute significantly to the animal's diving ability. It is thought, however, that no single feature accounts for this ability, since many of the same vascular modifications are found in terrestrial mammals of one kind or another (Harrison and Tomlinson, 1956).

HEART

The heart is four chambered, following the general mammalian plan. The ventricles contain a slightly greater number of trabeculae than in terrestrial mammals and the right ventricle is comparatively thicker walled. The organ is highly muscular, but in many species represents only about 0.5 per cent of body weight. In very large species, the heart may represent a smaller proportion of the body weight. In the smaller, more active species, the relative heart size is much greater. The largest heart-to-body-weight ratio reported is in the Dall porpoise (*Phocoenoides dalli*), where the heart weight averages over 1.3 per cent of the body weight (Ridgway and Johnston, 1966; Ridgway, 1966).

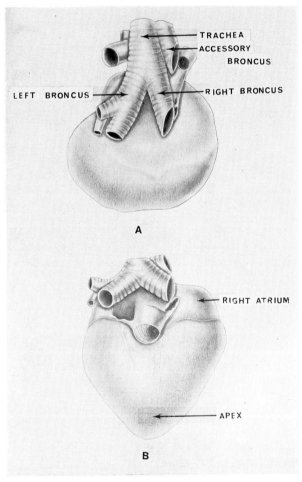

Figure 4–13. Dorsal view (A) and ventral view (B) of the heart of an Atlantic bottlenosed dolphin (porpoise), *Tursiops truncatus*. (Drawn by Barbara Stolen Irvine.)

The orientation of the heart within the body may be seen in Figure 4–1. Illustration of dorsal and posterior views of a *Tursiops truncatus* heart are shown in Figure 4–13. In larger whales, the heart becomes broader and the apex is not so pronounced.

BLOOD VESSELS

The most obvious modifications in the system are those in peripheral vessels, the most spectacular being the retia mirabilia. These vascular beds are not restricted to cetaceans but are found in numerous nonaquatic forms as well. The retia were first reported in cetacea by Tyson who in 1680 described the thoracic retia which lie on the dorsal thoracic wall along either side of the vertebral column. It was Owen (1866, 1868) who first named these vascular anastomoses retia mirabilia (see Table 4–1).

TABLE 4–1

DISTRIBUTION OF THE MAJOR *Retia Mirabilia* IN THE ATLANTIC
BOTTLENOSED DOLPHIN (PORPOISE), *Tursiops truncatus*

Retia mirabilia	
Cranial region:	*Rete basis cranii*, a well-developed network below the brain, extending along the optic nerve, around the tympanoperiotic (ear) bones and posterior to join the rete in the neck.
Cervical region:	*Rete cervicale dorsale*, lateral and dorsal to the cervical vertebrae.
	Rete cervicale ventrale, lateral and ventral to the cervical vertebrae.
Thoracic region:	*Rete thoracicum*, the most extensive of the retia, dorsal to the lungs, extending from the anterior thoracic cavity, posterior to the level of the 1st lumbar vertebrae.
Spinal canal:	*Rete spinale*, lateral and dorsal to the spinal cord.
Lumbar region:	*Rete lumbale*, a posterior extension of the *rete thoracicum*, between the transverse processes of the lumbar vertebrae.
Pelvic region:	*Rete pelvicum*, superior and medial to the pelvis.
	Rete genitale feminum, dorsal to the ovaries and uterus in the mesometrium.
	Rete genitale masculinum, dorsal and lateral to the testes.
Caudal region:	*Rete caudale*, posterior extension of the *rete spinale* in the chevron (haemal) canal.

There seems to be little agreement as to the structure or composition of these vascular plexuses. While Murie (1874), Wilson (1879), Ommanney (1932), and Walmsley (1938) reported the retia to be both arterial and venous, Hunter (1787) and Stannius (1849) reported them to be arterial only. Fawcett (1942) found the thoracic retia in *Tursiops* and *Kogia* to be composed almost totally of arteries with few thin-walled veins (see Chap. 5). The arteries have thick muscular walls and are imbedded in fat with no restricting fibrous sheath. Burne (1952) published beautiful color plates of his dissections of the thoracic retia in *Phocaena sp.* Nakajima (1961) and Nagel *et al.* (1968) have recently made extensive studies of the retia. Nagel *et al.* studied *Tursiops*, and Nakajima studied *Grampus* and *Tursiops*.

DeKock (1959) described the neck arteries in the pilot whale,

Globicephala melaena, and the porpoise, *Phocaena phocaena*. In both species, he found the short, paired innominate arteries to rise from the summit of the arch. They branch into subclavian, internal carotid and external carotid arteries. This branching is so abrupt that the common carotid is eliminated.

Just beyond their origin, the internal carotids enlarge to form the carotid sinuses. They then taper until they are approximately one-third their original diameter as they enter the skull. While it is generally accepted that cetaceans receive virtually all their cranial blood flow through vertebral arteries and not by the internal carotids (Burne, 1952, Bourdelle and Grasse, 1955), DeKock believes there is no evidence of actual dysfunction. He interprets the presence of a lumen in the vessel well within the tympanic cavity, together with an extremely heavy muscular coat and generous innervation of the adventitia, to indicate a local blood-flow control mechanism, possibly of intermittent function. Galliano *et al.* (1966) described the internal carotid as gradually tapering to form a solid cord. They could not demonstrate by angiography that the internal carotids supplied the brain. From gross dissections, they do appear to supply an arterial network (corpus cavernosum) within the middle ear.

The external carotid, which is several times larger than the internal, retains its diameter for some distance into the neck. A small artery branches from its base to supply the carotid body. The external carotid sends branches into the tongue, the mandible, the maxilla, and the external opthalmic retia (Slijper 1936).

A fibrous sheath, containing a dense retia mirabilia extends from the point of origin along the entire length of the internal and external carotids. The openings into these small arteries feeding the retia mirabilia can be seen piercing the arterial walls. A network of veins also surrounds the carotids.

The subclavian arteries are relatively thin-walled vessels with no retia accompanying them. Two major vessels emerge from each subclavian just before it penetrates the body wall to pass into the flipper—the internal thoracic, which passes posteriorly along the ventral wall to terminate in the pelvic retia; and the transverse scapular, which passes anteriorly for a short distance before sending the omooccipital branch superior to terminate in the basicranial and occipital retia.

Leaving the left ventricle, the aorta makes the characteristic left arch before passing superiorly and caudally to lie just under the centra of the thoracic vertebrae. Beyond the subclavians, the aorta continues caudally through the thoracic cavity to pass through the diaphragm. There are numerous segmental branches from the thoracic segment of the aorta.

Just posterior to the diaphragm, the aorta sends out single coeliac and superior mesenteric branches. Just beyond this point, the paired suprarenal and renal arteries leave the aorta.

At a point just posterior to the kidneys, the aorta sends out paired genital arteries and a single posterior mesenteric artery. Just beyond the posterior mesenteric, the aorta gives off a pair of well-developed common iliac arteries and continues posteriorly as the caudal artery passing through the hemal canal formed by the caudal vertebrae and the chevron bones associated with them (Figs. 4–4, 4–5).

There is considerable variation in the arrangement of the abdominal postcaval vein. Slijper (1936) has described five main patterns with the primary differences being in the number of branches posterior to the renal arteries and the arrangement of the tributaries surrounding the aorta. In those species in which the postcaval vein is bifurcated, the branches may vary considerably in size. Numerous small veins pass from the thoracic body wall and the intervertebral venous system into the postcaval vein or veins, whichever the case may be (Harrison and Tomlinson, 1956; Slijper, 1936).

The renal veins emerge from a mesial slit located toward the rostral end of each kidney. These veins are often duplicated at their proximal ends but usually fuse into a single vessel before passing into the postcaval vein. There is a poorly developed superficial subcapsular plexus over a part of each kidney. The vessels composing the plexus drain into the main renal veins at the mesial slit.

Most of the blood returning from the cranium to the heart is by way of thin-walled intravertebral vessels. These vessels vary considerably from species to species but appear to be well developed in most. Other vessels drain the ventral cranium by way of an extensive venous plexus around the ear bones, which is in turn drained by jugular veins.

The intravertebral vessels are connected to the precaval vein by right and left costocervical veins. These vessels leave the spinal canal through the third costal foramen on either side of the anterior thoracic cavity. There are also several smaller vessels which exit from other costal foramina and are associated with the thoracic retia. The most anterior of these vessels on the right side is a rather large vein and may be the remains of the arch of the azygous vein.

Urogenital System

The cetacean kidneys are located on the dorsal wall of the abdominal cavity lateral to the lumbar vertebrae (Fig. 4–1). They are held snugly in place by the peritoneum which is reflected from the dorsal body wall to form a mesial longitudinal mesentery which supports the distal intestine.

The two kidneys are approximately equal in size and lack the bean-shape characteristic of most mammalian kidneys. The left kidney is often slightly more caudal than the right.

The kidneys are extensively lobulated due to their being divided into numerous small units or renules. Each renule contains its own cortex, medulla, papilla, calyx, and blood supply. Each four to six renules share a common duct leading to the proximal ureter. The renal blood vessels and subcapsular plexus associated with the kidneys are discussed in the circulatory system section elsewhere in this chapter.

The renal blood vessels connect to the kidney on the mesial surface near the rostral end, with no depression or hilum present. Each ureter exits from the posterior end of its kidney to pass caudally to the urinary bladder. The ureters lie between the peritoneum and the fascia covering the dorsal lumbar muscles. Before reaching the urinary bladder, each ureter passes ventral to the hypogastric artery. The ureters then pass through the lateral walls of the bladder, opening into the cavity a short distance anterior to the outlet of the organ.

The urinary bladder is situated in a midventral position in the pelvic cavity. The dorsal surface is covered with peritoneum which is reflected to form weak ligaments along the apical and lateral margins. The ventral surface of the posterior end of the bladder rests upon a fibrous membrane which extends between the pelvic bones.

The obliterated urachus persists as a rounded, cord-like structure projecting forward from the apex of the bladder a few centimeters toward the umbilicus. In several latex-injected specimens, the latex passed 1 cm or so into the lumen of this structure.

In the male, the urethra passes posteriorly for a short distance before passing through the prostate gland. The elongated, cylindrical testes are attached to the dorsal body wall just lateral and caudal to the kidneys (Fig. 4–14). The tunica vaginalis is smooth and grayish-white in color and in addition to covering the testes, covers much of the epididymus as well. The tunica albuginea is a tough, thick membrane, covering the glandular part of the testis. There appears to be no tunica vaginalis cavity, as the two membranes fuse together.

When the tunica albuginea is removed, the organ is seen to consist of many irregular-shaped lobules, each bounded by delicate septal membranes. There appears to be no distinct mediastinum testis, but numerous small channels in the septa form a rete testis. These channels then unite to form a short, flattened vas efferentia which passes into the extensively convoluted epididymus. This organ is differentiated into a head, a body, and a tail. Distally, the tail enlarges to become the highly convoluted vas deferens. Ping (1926) has reported the vas deferentia to enlarge distally in *Neomeris phocoenoides* (*Neophocoena phocoenoides*) to form ejaculatory ducts, which pass separately to the floor of the urethra.

Meek (1918) has described another pair of openings which lead into a blind tube lying between and behind the distal vas deferentia. From its position, this tube would appear to be the uterus masculinus (sinus pocularis) and could very well be the median sac that Ping (1926) called the vesicular seminalis. Most descriptions of the accessory reproductive organs in male cetaceans include only the prostate gland.

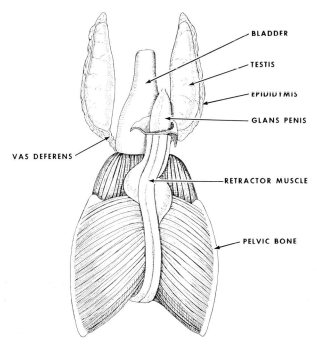

Figure 4–14. Ventral view of the reproductive organs of a male Atlantic bottlenosed dolphin (porpoise), *Tursiops truncatus*. (Drawn by Barbara Stolen Irvine from dissections by Robert F. Green.)

The testes vary in size according to species, age, and degree of sexual activity. In the blue whale, the largest member of the order, the testes may be 75 cm long and weigh 45 kg; while in *Delphinus*, one of the smaller species, they are 4 or 5 cm long and weigh only a few grams. There appears to be a definite rutting season in some species (Ridgway and Green, 1966), with the testes increasing dramatically in size during the peak of sexual activity. In a 100 kg *Lagenorhynchus obliquidens*, each testes may weigh 750 gm during the peak of the breeding season, while Nishiwaki (Chap. 1) indicates that the testes may weigh as much as 1000 kg in a mature breeding right whale.

Ridgway and Green (1966) have shown that the well-developed ischiocavernosal muscles (Fig. 4–14), which pass from the pelvic bones dorsal along the crurae, and the less well developed bulbocavernosal muscles are much enlarged during the rutting season in *Lagenorhynchus obliquidens* and *Delphinus delphis bairdii*.

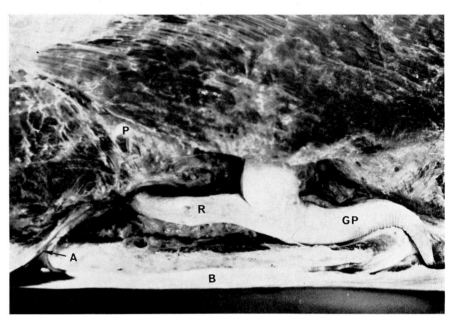

Figure 4–15. Lateral view of the pelvic region of a male Atlantic bottlenosed dolphin (porpoise), *Tursiops truncatus*. (Photograph and dissection by Robert F. Green.) (A) Anus, (B) Blubber, (GP) Glans Penis, (P) Pelvis, (R) Retractor Penis Muscles.

The cetacean penis has its origin by crura from the median surfaces of the pelvic bones. These crura fuse into a long, firm, rope-like body which is round to oval in cross section. From its origin between the pelvic bones, the corpus penis passes cranially a short distance before forming a distinct sigmoid flexure lying in a horizontal plane. The distal end of the organ protrudes through the body wall into the penial slit, located along the midventral line between the umbilicus and the anus (Fig. 4–15). This slit is formed by an infolding of the skin in this region. The distal penis or terminal cone is similar to the glans penis found in some terrestrial mammals, except that it is not enlarged. Cetaceans can protrude from two-thirds to four-fifths of the penis upon erection. A flat retractor penis muscle attaches to the ventral surface of the penis just behind the terminal cone, passing just above the ligamentum intercruale to the rectal wall.

In the female, the ovaries are located somewhat posterior to the kidneys and are held in place by the broad ligament (Fig. 4–16). Each ovary is

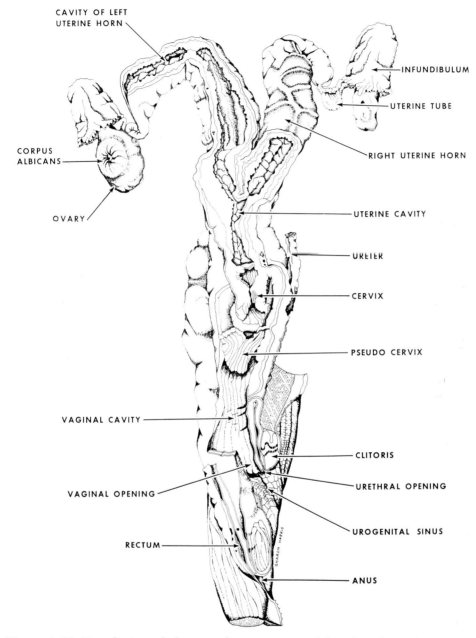

CAVITY OF LEFT
UTERINE HORN

INFUNDIBULUM

UTERINE TUBE

CORPUS
ALBICANS

RIGHT UTERINE HORN

OVARY

UTERINE CAVITY

URETER

CERVIX

PSEUDO CERVIX

VAGINAL CAVITY

CLITORIS

URETHRAL OPENING

VAGINAL OPENING

UROGENITAL SINUS

RECTUM

ANUS

Figure 4–16. Dorsal view of the reproductive organs of female Atlantic bottlenosed dolphin (porpoise), *Tursiops truncatus*. (Drawn by Sharon Harris from dissection by Robert F. Green.)

more or less covered by a large fallopian funnel at the outer end of the very short, slender fallopian tube. The fallopian tubes join the anterior ends of the horns of the bicornuate uterus. The uterine horns join to form the much-shortened body of the uterus, which is delineated from the vagina by the presence of a true cervix.

In many species, there are numerous folds in the anterior vaginal wall just caudal to the true cervix. These lateral folds form a spermathecal recess or recesses which may function to keep semen from being washed out of the vagina following copulation. The opening into the thick-walled, tubular vagina is housed within a midventral genital slit. This slit also houses the urethral orifice, the clitoris, and the anus.

The elongated, oval mammary glands are located just below the blubber along each side of the genital slit. The slits which house the nipples are just lateral to the larger, longer midventral genital slit. The nipples protrude quite noticeably during the period of suckling but otherwise are drawn within the general contour of the body.

PINNIPED ANATOMY

The pinnipeds have undergone extensive anatomical modification in becoming well adapted to a marine existence. Since they spend much time on land, however, they are not as extensively modified as the cetaceans.

The pinniped body, which is more or less spindle shaped, has fewer external protuberances than fully terrestrial mammals, allowing for ease of movement through the water (Fig. 4–17).

Though both the otariids and phocids have dog-like heads, there are several differences between them. The otariids have a slender lobular external ear, while the phocids have none. While the nostrils in the otariids are directed rostrodorsally at about 15 to 20 degrees above the cranial axis, the nostrils in the photids are at a 45-degree angle to the same axis. The otariid mystacial pad is quite narrow when compared to the wider phocid pad, and there are no suprarorbital vibrissae above the otariid eye and only a few above the phocid eye. The limbs have developed into paddle-like "fin feet" which are characteristic of the order. The feet of various species have many structural similarities but also exhibit major anatomical and functional differences (Backhouse, 1961).

In water, ortariids move chiefly by way of a skulling motion of the broad, oar-like foreflippers. In these appendages, the first digit is strongly developed and is strengthened along the leading edge by the addition of fibrous tissue. There is also additional fibrous tissue between the digits, each of which has been lengthened by cartilaginous extensions. The nails have been reduced to small circular nodules located at or near the ends of the terminal phalanges.

The hindflippers are also lengthened by cartilaginous extensions extending beyond the bony framework. The soles are naked and are held together more or less straight out behind the animal when it is swimming. All digits of the hindflippers have slender, almost straight nails.

The phocid forelimb is covered with fur on both surfaces and has no cartilaginous extensions beyond the bony framework. In most species, the digits are approximately the same length. While the animal is swimming, it holds the foreflippers close to the body except when changing direction or when swimming very slowly. The hindflippers are also covered with fur on both surfaces with expandable skin between the digits. The hindlimbs and some lateral movement of the trunk provide the propulsive force for swimming, especially in the lumbar region.

On land, the otariids support their weight mainly on the foreflippers which extend laterally with the manus bent at 90 degrees to the wrist. The pes is also bent at right angles to the shank but is directed more anteriorly than laterally.

Since the chin is contained within the body contour and is almost totally immovable, the sacral vertebrae are forced to assume an almost vertical position so as to allow the foot to assume the plantigrade position (Howell, 1928).

On land, the phocids move from place to place by shifting their weight alternately from the sternum to the pelvis by a quite clumsy "hitching" movement (Matthews 1952; Backhouse 1961). Some phocids, notably the gray seal, *Halichoerus grypus*, use a well-developed grip of the terminal phalanges of the foreflipper to pull themselves over the rocks, etc. Figure 4–18 shows the gripping capability of the northern elephant seal, *Mirounga angustirostris*.

The anatomy of the pinniped forelimbs has been extensively described by Duvernoy (1822), Humphrey (1868), Murie (1870), Lucae (1887), Miller (1887), Howell (1928), Mori (1958), and Backhouse (1961).

Both the phocids and the otariids have a small, flattened tail which rests in a depression between the hind limbs and is not used in swimming.

The other pinniped family, the Odobenidae, is represented only by the familiar walrus which has locomotor capabilities similar to those of sea lions (see Chap. 1).

Integument

The pinniped skin has undergone numerous adaptive changes, allowing for long periods of immersion. The epidermis is rather thick (0.5 to 1.0 mm) and well pigmented. The stratum corneum contains nucleated, non-cornified cells which extend almost to the surface, producing a soft outer layer. Since the stratum granulosum is missing, the corneum contains more permanent cells which are not continually flaking off.

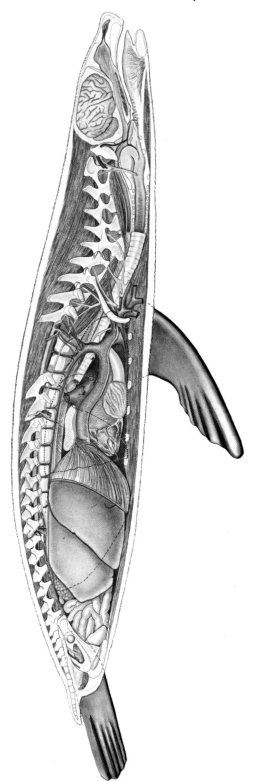

Figure 4-17A. Sagittal view of a California sea lion, *Zalophus californianus.* See opposite page for labeling. (Drawn by Barbara Stolen Irvine from dissections by Warren G. Simison.)

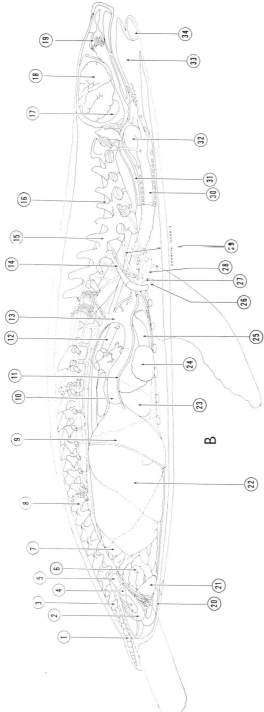

Figure 4–17B. Outline drawing of Fig. 4–17A with labels. (Outline drawn by Sharon Harris.: (1) Caudal vertebrae, (2) Ischium, (3) Sacrum, (4) Acetabulum, (5) Ilium, (6) Intestines, (7) Kidney, (8) Lumbar vertebrae, (9) Diaphragm, (10) Postcaval vein, (11) Phrenic nerve, (12) Left bronchus, (13) Azygos vein, (14) First rib, (15) Seventh cervical vertebrae, (16) Subdural vein, (17) Cerebellum, (18) Cerebrum, (19) Olfactory epithelium, (20) Penis, (21) Urinary bladder, (22) Liver, (23) Heart, (24) Right auricle, (25) Aorta, (26) Subclavian vein, (27) Subclavian artery, (28) Jugular vein, (29) Vertebral artery, (30) Trachea, (31) Esophagus, (32) Larynx (33) Tongue, (34) Mandible.

The dermis consists of a thin, more superficial, papillary layer containing numerous dilated venules and capillaries with few collagenous fibers. The deep dermis is a thick reticular layer composed of dense, fibrous connective tissue. The innermost part of this reticular layer contains elastic fibers and bundles of smooth muscle cells.

The blubber, situated beneath the dermis, is permeated with numerous blood vessels which extend into the upper layers of the dermis. The pinniped skin, including the blubber, is easier to separate from the under-lying muscles than is the cetacean skin.

Figure 4–18. A young male elephant seal, *Mirounga angustirostris*, gripping a piece of hose.

The hairs of the pinniped fur are arranged in groups, with a single, flattened guard hair in front of a number of shorter, finer underhairs. Each hair is formed in a separate follicle, but each group of hairs emerges through a single piliary canal.

The number of shorter underhairs varies from species to species, with from two to five in the phocids to as many as nineteen or more in the fur seals. None of the seals appear to have arrector pili muscles associated with the hair follicles. Harrison and King (1965) have an excellent illustrated discussion of pinniped hair.

The skin and fur is waterproofed by a thin film of oil secreted by the numerous large sebaceous glands which secrete into the hair canals. There is also a single apocrine sweat gland secreting into each hair canal. The function of this gland is not clearly understood, but it has been suggested that its secretion is a waste product and may produce the musky smell characteristic of many of the seals (King, 1964).

Muscular System

For the reader who is interested in pinniped musculature, the following works are recommended: Duvernoy (1822) on *Phoca,* Humphrey (1868) on *Phoca,* Lucae (1887) on the seal and otter, Miller's (1887) general discussion of the myology of Pinnipedia, Howell (1928) on *Zalophus* and *Phoca,* Mori (1958) on *Zalophus,* and Murie (1872) on *Otaria.*

Skeletal System

The pinniped skull has a rather large, rounded cranium, with an elongated narrow interorbital region between the large orbits. The snout is short, and the lacrimal bones, the nasolacrimal ducts, and the cranial sinuses are missing.

The otariid and odobenid skulls have small, flattened tympanic bullae, large mastoid processes, alisphenoid canals, and elongated frontals. The phocid skulls have larger inflated bullae, small mastoid processes, no alisphenoid canal, and nasals which protrude posteriorly between the frontal bones along the sagittal plane (Fig. 4–19). The otariid skull has well-developed postorbital processes and sagittal crests, which do not occur in the phocid skulls.

MANDIBLE

The form of the mandible is chiefly influenced by the form of the skull. The *Zalophus* mandible is stouter than the *Phoca* mandible due to a heavior dentition and musculature. There is, however, much specific and generic variation exhibited by the two families (Howell, 1928).

TEETH

The number of teeth in pinnipeds is considered reduced when compared to most mammals. While incisors and canines are well differentiated, the teeth posterior to the canines are referred to collectively as postcanines because of their lack of specialization. As in other mammals, the dental formulae are important taxonomically (see Chap. 1).

HYOID

The pinniped hyoid is of the usual carnivore type, with basihyal, epihyal, stylohyal, and tympanohyal elements. Even though this bone is quite variable in shape, it is generally more robust in the Otariidae.

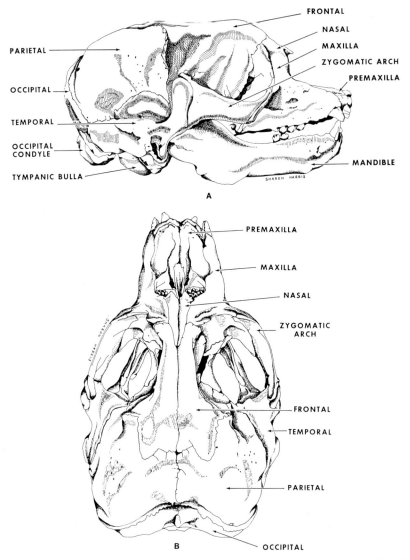

Figure 4–19. Lateral view (A) and dorsal (B) of the skull of a young male elephant seal, *Mirounga angustirostris*. (Drawn by Sharon Harris.)

FORELIMBS

The forelimb skeleton is generally much the same in all pinnipeds, with shortened humerus, radius and ulna. The deltoid ridge, olecranon process, and anterior distal radius are quite well developed. These modifications increase the surface area for insertion of the more proximal muscles of the foreflipper.

Vertebral Column

The pinniped vertebral column reflects the differences in otariid and phocid locomotion. There are typically seven cervical, fifteen thoracic, five lumbar, three sacral and ten to twelve caudal vertebrae (see Chap. 1).

Fay (1967) has reported the number of thoracic vertebrae to vary from fourteen (observed in three walruses) to sixteen (observed in two ringed seals *Pusa hispida* and one fur seal *Callorhinus ursinus*). Fay also suggests that the number of ribs is more variable than previously recognized.

The ortariids have their main muscular power concentrated at the front of their body, with the cervical and thoracic vertebrae having longer, better-developed transverse processes and neural spines. The phocids have smaller, less-developed cervical and thoracic vertebrae, but since their muscle power is concentrated at the posterior end, they have lumbar vertebrae with larger transverse processes and more widely spaced zygapophyses than those of the phocids. Since the pinniped tail is not specialized for swimming, the caudal vertebrae have remained small and have poorly developed processes.

Sternum

The sternum is made up of eight to nine pieces. Whereas the otariids have a long bony extension of the manubrium, the phocids and the walrus have a long cartilaginous extension.

Pectoral Girdle

The pinniped pectoral girdle is incomplete, since there are no clavicles. The scapulae are well developed with differences between *Zalophus* and *Phoca* which appear to be related to differences in locomotion. In *Zalophus*, the spinous process is located quite posterior, forming a large supraspinous fossa almost twice the area of the infraspinous fossa. A second smaller bony ridge runs approximately parallel to the spinous process, increasing the area of the supraspinous fossa. The spinous process is smaller and more medially placed in *Phoca* with more equal supraspinous and infraspirous fossae. In *Phoca*, the inferior (posterior) angle of the scapula extends more caudally than in *Zalophus*. The angle of the scapular spine in relation to the glenoid fossa is approximately the same in both *Zalophus* and *Phoca* (Howell, 1928).

The humeri of *Zalophus* and *Phoca* are not much alike except that both are short, robust bones with marked development of the deltoid crest. Differences which exist are related to differences in muscular attachment, leverage, etc. The ulnas are quite different when compared to other mammals, having a quite large, broad olecranon process. The radii have a much expanded distal half.

The carpal elements consist of scapholunar, ulnar, first, second and third carpales, unciform and pisiformis. There has been much reduction in the carpus in the *Phoca* to allow for extreme abduction of the manus.

In both *Zalophus* and *Phoca*, the longest digit is the first digit or pollex. This is due in part to the length of the first metatarsal, especially in *Zalophus*. The distal phalanges in *Zalophus* are quite enlarged and flattened.

PELVIC GIRDLE

The pinniped pelvis is composed of a shortened ilium joined to elongated ischial and pubic bones. The acetabulum is much nearer the iliac crest in *Phoca* than in *Zalophus*. This difference may be more apparent than real, since the iliac crest in the earless seals is bent laterally almost to 90 degrees to the longitudial axis. The elongation of the ischium and pubis are more obvious in *Zalophus* than in *Phoca*, resulting in increased leverage in *Zalophus*. Other differences in the pelvis of these two forms are related to areas of muscular attachment.

POSTERIOR APPENDAGES

The femur is very short, broad, and flat, due in great part to the reduced function of the bone in both *Zalophus* and *Phoca*. In *Zalophus*, the tibia is straight and robust with moderate constriction along the middle of the shaft. In *Phoca*, the tibia is more curved and more constricted in the middle of the shaft. While the anterior tibial fossa is slight in both *Zalophus* and *Phoca*, the posterior fossa is well developed, especially in *Phoca*. The tibia and fibula are fused at their proximal ends and are bound by ligaments at their distal ends.

The foot, which makes up slightly less than 50 percent of the length of the leg, contains the following tarsal elements: astragalus, calcaneus, centrale; first, second, and third tarsales; cuboid, and a median sesamoid. These bones differ somewhat between *Zalophus* and *Phoca*, with major differences in the astragalus. In *Phoca*, the astragalus has an elongated caudal process which extends beyond the caudal margin of the caleaneum. This process is grooved to receive the tendon of the flexor hallucis longus muscle which by its tension prevents the foot of *Phoca* from being bent at right angles to the shank as that of *Zalophus* does.

In *Zalophus*, the four lateral metatarsals are approximately the same size and the fifth or most lateral one is slightly more robust. The first metatarsal (hallux) is wider and flatter than the other four. In *Phoca*, there is more interlocking of metatarsals at the proximal ends with some decrease in mobility at the tarsal-metatarsal joints.

There are fourteen phalanges, three in each digit except the hallux, which has two. In both *Zalophus* and *Phoca*, the first and fifth digits are longer than the other three. In *Zalophus*, the middle three digits have better-developed nails than those on the first and fifth digits. In *Phoca*, which has generally better-formed nails, the first and fifth digits have the longer nails.

Respiratory System

The pinniped nostrils are situated somewhat terminal, with differences in position and orientation existing in the families. These differences have already been described. When the animal dives, the nostrils are closed by relaxation of the nasolabialis and maxillolabialis muscles (King, 1964). The turbinate bones are finely divided and highly convoluted, almost completely filling the nasal cavity.

LARYNX

The pinniped larynx is not as modified as the cetacean larynx and more nearly resembles the larynx in carnivores.

The most extensive works on the organ are by Kelemen and Hassko (1931), Schneider (1962), and Odend'hal (1966).

The cricoid cartilage forms much of the roof and posterior lateral surfaces of the laryngeal cavity. The lamina forming the roof has median cranial extensions which give the arch the appearance of being constricted anteriorly while widening posteriorly. From the side, the cricoid appears triangular in form, with the superior surface at 90 degrees to the posterior margin. The demarcation of the cricoid lamina from the cricoid arch is at the point where caudal thyroid cornu articulate with the lateral wall of the cricoid.

The thyroid cartilage forms the anterior lateral walls of the laryngeal cavity. The two lamina are only connected by way of the very small pars interlaminaris which serves as a point of insertion of the vocal cords. There are no cranial cornu, but well-developed caudal cornu articulate with the lateral cricoid cartilage. The caudal thyroidal notch is better developed than the indistinct cranial notch.

The large, well-developed arytenoid cartilage occupies most of the laryngeal cavity. Dorsally, there is a large notch formed between the process of santorini and the dorsomedial process. The very small interarytenoid cartilage is found in this notch. The process of santorini is composed mostly of elastic cartilage and forms part of the opening to the larynx. The dorsomedial processes of the two arytenoids articulate with each other at a point just cranial to the cricoid lamina. The vocal cords run from the pars interlaminaris of the thyroid to the ventral edge of the arytenoids.

The epiglottis is very small and composed mainly of elastic cartilage with a small oval base composed solely of hyalin cartilage.

There are two lateral saccules at the entrance into the larynx lying between the thyroid and arytenoid cartilages. A smaller dorsomedial pouch lies just below the cranial extension of the cricoid lamina. The laryngeal cavity enlarges posteriorly between the arytenoid cartilages before joining the trachea. A smaller part of the cavity lies ventral to the arytenoids and posterior to the vocal cords.

Possibly unique among the pinnipeds is the extremely elastic pharyngeal walls found in the walrus (*Odobenus rosmarus*) (Fay, 1960). In fact, the walls are so elastic they can be expanded as large pouches or diverticuli. Ostia into the pouches are located lateral to, or just posterior to, the glottis. From the ostia, the pouches extend dorsally and posteriorly to lie between the muscle layers of the neck and back. It is suggested by Fay (1960) that

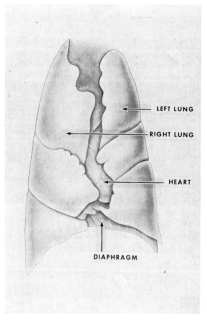

Figure 4–20. Ventral view of the lungs, heart, and part of the diaphragm of a California sea lion, *Zalophus californianus*. (Drawn by Barbara Stolen Irvine from dissections by Warren G. Simison.)

some of the larger otariid and phocid seals may also have pharyngeal pouches.

The lumen of the trachea is held open by supporting cartilages which vary from species to species. They are incomplete dorsally in *Zalophus californianus*, but are generally complete in *Phoca vitulina*. The rings have been reduced to small ventral bars in species noted for swallowing large organisms as a part of their diet.

The trachea divides just dorsal to the heart, after which the bronchi pass immediately into each lung. In *Zalophus*, the division is more anterior with the longer bronchi lying close together until they pass into the lungs.

The lungs are composed of multiple lobes (three on each side) as shown in Figure 4–20. They are situated high in the thoracic cavity to aid in buoyance and equilibrium in the water. This position is achieved by a rather obliquely oriented diaphragm which is attached anteriorly to the back of the ziphisternum and to the dorsal body wall at the level of the second lumbar vertebrae.

The phocid lungs are more nearly symmetrical, while the otariids have a larger right lung, much like cetaceans. Upon close examination, they are found to be lobulated by the intervention of connective tissue septa. There are numerous myoelastic valves in the bronchioles which, like the trachea and bronchi, are extensively supported by cartilaginous rings.

Digestive System

The pinniped abdominal cavity is somewhat ovoid, being slightly wider anteriorly and narrowing posteriorly to the well-defined pelvic cavity. The liver and stomach occupy the wide anterior end of the cavity, while the extensively coiled intestine fills most of the posterior end.

The greater omentum is attached to the greater curvature of the stomach with its free margin reflected over the ventral margin of the more anterior intestines. The well-defined lesser omentum has gastric and heptic connections. The *gastrosplenic* omentum is also well formed.

The digestive tract is rather uncomplicated when compared to those of other marine mammals. The rather long esophagus is easily dilated to allow for passage of food. The stomach normally has a single chamber (Fig. 4–21), with its long axis generally parallel to the long axis of the body. There is a suggestion of sacculation or compartmentalization in some species. The esophagus enters the stomach just to the right of the fundic end, resulting in a lesser curvature which is about two-thirds as large as the greater curvature.

The duodenum begins at the pyloric valve, which is readily identifiable, and continues for some 12 to 13 in. This segment of the small intestine is

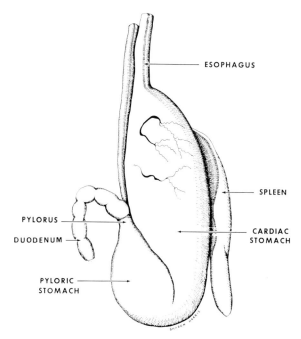

Figure 4–21. Ventral view of the stomach, spleen, and duodenum of a California sea lion, *Zalophus californianus*.

attached by a dorsal mesial mesentery and, due to its characteristic C shape, has proximal and distal ends ten to fifteen cm apart.

The remainder of the small intestine is also supported by the dorsal mesentery, which generally corresponds to the entrance of the superior mesenteric vessels. The end of the small intestine and the beginning of the colon is marked by a diverticulum which is quite varied and probably represents a caecum.

There are no taenia coli or sacculations visible in the colon.

LIVER

The liver (3 to 3.5 percent body weight in adults) is highly lobed and somewhat elongated (Fig. 4–22). The gall bladder is located in a depression at the mesial surface of the right lobe of the liver just to the right of the ligamentum teres. Three hepatic ducts join the cystic duct to form the common bile duct, which in turn joins the pancreatic duct just before passing into the duodenal wall near the pyloric end.

The pancreas is well developed, with the pancreatic duct emerging from the cephalic end to join the common bile duct.

The elongated, flattened spleen is located along the left side of the abdominal cavity between the stomach and the dorsal body wall, supported

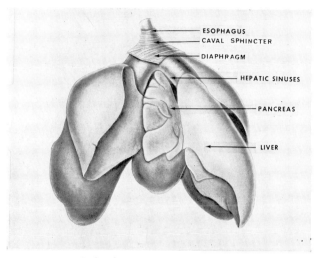

Figure 4–22. Ventral view of the liver, pancreas, and diaphragm of a California sea lion, *Zalophus californianus*. (Drawn by Barbara Stolen Irvine from dissections by Warren G. Simison.)

by the greater omentum and the dorsal mesentery. Since the kidneys are located more posteriorly, there is no close association between them and the spleen.

Cardiovascular System

Even though the pinniped vascular system has much the same pattern as other mammals, it exhibits several marked modifications. Some of these modifications are found in pinnipeds only, some are present in other marine or aquatic mammals, and a few are seen in a less marked form in terrestrial forms (Harrison and Kooyman, 1968). Most of the modifications in pinniped circulation are in the venous system rather than in the arteries. These changes generally achieve an increase in venous capacity.

The major veins, especially those in the abdomen, are large and thin walled. Harrison and Tomlinson (1956) report the blood volume of a young *Phoca* to the 60 percent greater than the blood volume of an adult man, and Simpson *et al.* (1970) reported blood volume in the northern elephant seal to be about 20 percent of body weight (see Chap. 10).

Postcaval Vein

The postcaval vein is often duplicated in the region of the kidneys, with the right limb usually the larger. The single postcaval vein in *Zalophus* is probably the right branch. Each limb receives branches from a plexus of vessels draining the hindflippers (Fig. 4–23), the pelvic region, and the abdominal wall. Each limb also receives tributaries from the subcapsular renal plexus and the extradural vertebral vein. Anastomoses between the two limbs are usually small or completely lacking. King and Harrison (1961) report finding various-sized connecting vessels in the Hawaiian monk seal.

After the two limbs fuse, the common postcaval vein drains into the right side of the hepatic sinus. Barnett *et al.* (1958) have discussed and illustrated the main patterns of distribution of the postcaval vein in pinnipeds.

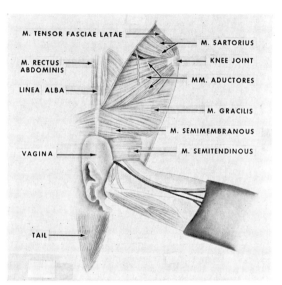

Figure 4–23. Ventral view of the pelvic and flipper areas of a female California sea lion, *Zalophus californianus*. (Drawn by Barbara Stolen Irvine from dissections by Warren G. Simison.)

POSTCAVAL SPHINCTER

Some of the pinnipeds have a muscular sphincter around the vena cava, just cranial to the diaphragm. This sphincter was first described by Burow (1838) in *Phoca* and has since been described in a number of species by Burne (1909), Harrison and Tomlinson (1956, 1964), and Harrison and Kooyman (1968). Harrison *et al.* (1963) have discussed this structure and have shown that it can control the flow of blood from the abdomen to the right atrium. The sphincter is better developed in *Phoca* than in *Zalophus* (Fig. 4–17), in which it appears to be made up of a number of muscle slips reflected from the diaphragm.

HEPATIC VEINS

The numerous hepatic veins have dilated to form a large saccular hepatic sinus located posterior to the diaphragm and anterior to the liver (Fig. 4–22). The walls of this sinus are somewhat thicker than the walls of the postcaval vein. Harrison and Tomlinson (1956) report the capacity of this sinus to vary with age and to hold at least 1,000 ml of blood in an adult common seal. The sinus is extraordinarily large in the elephant seal and in adults can hold several liters of blood.

JUGULAR VEINS

The internal jugular veins are quite reduced, serving mostly to drain extracranial tissues. Much of the intracranial blood returns to the heart by way of extradural veins, the dorsal cervical plexus, and connecting vessels between the dorsal cervical plexus and the external jugular (Figs. 4–24, 4–25). The external jugular begins as a small vessel but enlarges rather abruptly after receiving the connecting vessels from the dorsal cervical plexus.

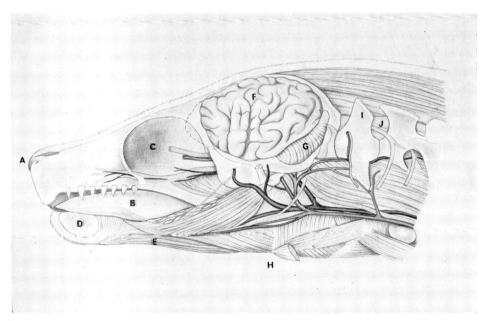

Figure 4–24. Lateral view of the head of a California sea lion, *Zalophus californianus*. (Drawn by Barbara Stolen Irvine from dissections by Warren G. Simison.) (A) Nostril, (B) Tongue, (C) Orbit, (D) Mandible, (E) Hyomandibular muscle, (F) Cerebrum, (G) Cerebellum, (H) Hyoid, (I) First cervical vertebrae, (J) Spinal cord.

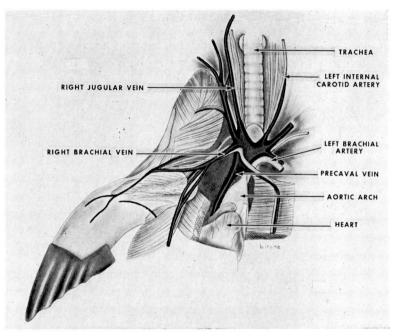

Figure 4–25: Ventral view of the neck and bronchial region of a California sea
lion, *Zalophus californianus*. (Drawn by Barbara Stolen Irvine from dissections by
Warren G. Simison.)

AZYGOUS VEINS

In *Phoca*, the azygous system begins in the abdominal cavity with right
and left branches. In the thoracic cavity, the right branch becomes much
enlarged, while the left branch becomes reduced. The left branch drains
the anterior intercostal spaces before joining the right vein just before it
turns ventrally to pass into the precaval vein. The left branch is almost
totally missing in *Zalophus*.

EXTRADURAL VEIN

Most of the blood returning from the intracranial sinuses does so by way
of hypocondylar veins which pass out of the cranium through the hypocondylar canals, where they join to form a large, flat, thin-walled extradural
vein. This vessel is situated between the spinal dura mater and the roof
of the vertebral canal.

Anteriorly, the extradural vein communicates with the dorsal cervical
plexus as well as with the dorsal musculature by way of segmental veins
and with thoracic musculature by way of intercostal veins. Posteriorly, the
extradural vein communicates with renal, pelvic, and segmental lumbar
and sacral veins.

Urogenital System

While some aspects of the anatomy of pinnipeds have been well described, there are few descriptions of the urogenital organs. The most important papers on the reproductive system have been summarized by Harrison, *et al.* (1952). Theirs is by far the most complete treatment of reproduction in the pinnipeds.

MALE

In the male, the short crura meet at the midline to form a single corpus cavernosum penis which is directed cranially, lying flat along the ventral body wall (Fig. 4–26). In a young adult *Zalophus californianus*, the penis measured 12.5 cm from the point where the crura merge to the orifice at the distal end. The penis is composed primarily of corpus cavernosum penis with a weakly developed cavernosum urethra surrounding the urethra. In cross section, the urethra is seen in a groove along the underside of the rounded, fused corpus cavernosum penis.

The distal end of the corpus cavernosum is ossified to form a comparatively large os penis which extends to the extreme tip of the glans. The glans is compressed laterally with the orifice opening near the midventral tip.

The well-developed retractor penis muscles run along the ventral surface of the penis to insert at the level of the preputial fold. The muscles pass posteriorly beyond the base of the penis, separating to attach to the lateral and dorsal surfaces of the distal intestine.

Zalophus, like other otariid seals, has scrotal testes which lie just lateral

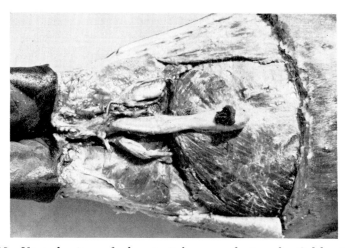

Figure 4–26. Ventral view of the genital area of a male California sea lion, *Zalophus californianus*. (Photograph and dissection by Robert F. Green.)

to the base of the penis. They contain very weakly developed mediastina. The epididymides are quite large with little differentiation into head, body, and tail.

FEMALE

In a young adult female *Zalophus californianus,* the vagina measured approximately 15 cm from the hymenal ridge to the cervix. The cavity tapers slightly from its opening inward to the cervix (Fig. 4–23). The membranous lining projects into the cavity by way of a number of wide longitudinal ridges. The urethra passes along the ventral wall of the vagina to penetrate the urinary papilla.

The uterus is bicornuate with the corpus (approximately 12 cm) nearly as long as the cornu (14 to 15 cm). The uterus is divided through most of its length by a well-developed septum and has a lining raised into a number of prominent ridges.

The ovaries are situated at the tips of the cornu in large, flattened bursae. The uterine tubes pass from the ends of the cornu around the bursae so the fimbriated funnels lie close to the point of origin of the tubes.

KIDNEY

The pinniped kidney is of the lobulated or reniculated type, similar to the type found in cetaceans. The extent to which the reniculi are separated from each other varies from species to species. Marked separation occurs in *Phoca,* where the external fibrous capsule extends deep between the reniculi. In *Zalophus,* however, the thin, fibrous capsule is confined to the outer surface except for a few anchor strands.

In most pinnipeds, the kidneys are shaped much like the kidneys of terrestrial carnivores, with the ureters leaving the medial border. In *Lobodon* and *Ommatophoca,* however, the kidneys are even more cetacean-like with the ureters leaving the ventral aspect of the caudal end of each kidney (King, 1964).

In many pinnipeds, the interlobular vessels drain by communicating renicular vessels into a subcapsular renal plexus which drains into the limbs of the postcaval vein by way of several tributaries. According to Harrison and Kooyman (1968), this is the only way blood leaves the kidney, since there are no renal veins. I have personally found no evidence of a perirenal plexus in *Zalophus californianus* but have found large, single renal veins emerging at the hilum alongside the renal arteries.

The bladder is quite elongated and narrow, tapering cranially to the elongated urachus which passes forward to the level of the umbilicus. In the male, the urethra passes from the blunt caudal end of the bladder to pass into the penis as the urethra penis. The weakly developed prostate is located just posterior to the neck of the bladder along the proximal urethra. The vas deferentia enter the urethra in the same area as the prostate gland. Their distal ends appear not to be differentiated into ejaculatory ducts, and they fuse to enter the lumen of the prostatic urethra as a single duct.

In the female, the urethra passes forward below the vagina to open into the urinary papilla near the hymenal ridge.

❖   ❖   ❖

I thank Barbara Stolen Irvine and Sharon Harris for illustrating my material and Dr. Warren G. Simison for his work on the pinniped dissections. The editorial assistance of Mr. Steve Leatherwood and the typing of Miss Victoria Vargas and Mrs. Maria Ridge is much appreciated. I also thank the staff of the Marine Bioscience Facility at Point Mugu, California, for their continued support.

REFERENCES

Barnett, C.H., Harrison, R.J. and Tomlinson, J.D.W.: Variations in the venous systems of mammals. *Biol. Rev.,* 33:442–487, 1958.

Backhouse, K.M.: Locomotion of seals with particular reference to the forelimb. *Symp. Zool. Soc. London,* 5:59–75, 1961.

Benham, W.B.: On the Larynx of certain whales (*Cogia, Balaenoptera* and *Ziphius*). *Proc. Zool. Soc. London,* 1:278–300, 1901.

Boenninghaus, G.: Der Rachen von *Phocaena communis. Zool Jahrb.,* 17(1–2): 1–98, 1902.

Bourdelle, E. and Grasse, P.: Ordre des Cetaces. *Traite' de Zoologie.,* 17:374–375, 1955.

Burne, R.H.: Notes on the viscera of a walrus (*Odobaenus rosmarus*). *Proc. Zool. Soc. London,* pp. 732–738, 1909.

Burne, R.H.: *A Handbook of Cetacean Dissections.* London, British Museum of Natural History, 1952.

Burow, A.: Uber das Gefassystem der Robben. *Muller's Arch. Anat. Phys.,* pp. 230–258, 1838.

Carte, A. and MacAlister, A.: On the anatomy of *Balaenoptera rostrata. Phil. Trans. Roy. Soc. London,* p. 158, 1868.

DeKock, L.L.: The arterial vessels of the neck in the pilot whale (*Globicephala melaena*) Traill and the porpoise (*Phocaena phocaena L.*) in relation to the carotid body. *Acta Anat.,* 36:274–292, 1959.

Dubois, E.: Ueber den Larynx in *Studen uber Saugethiere.* Jena, M. Weber and G. Fischer, 1886.

Duvernoy, G.L.: Recherches Anatomique sur les organes du movement de phoque common, *Phoca vitulina L. Mem. Mus. Hist. Nat.,* (Paris), 9:49–70, 165–189, 1822.

Eschricht, D.F. and J. Reinhardt: On the Greenland right whale (*Balaena mysticetus*). In Flower, W.H. (Ed.): *Recent Memoirs on the Cetacea.* London, Ray Society, 1866, vol. 40.

Fawcett, D.W.: A comparative study of blood vascular bundles in Florida manatee, and certain cetaceans and edentates. *J. Morph.,* 7:105–123, 1942.

Fay, F.H.: Structure and fuction of the pharyngeal pouches of the walrus (*Odobenus rosmarus L.*). *Mammalia,* 24:361–371, 1960.

Fay, F.H.: The number of ribs and thoracic vertebrae in pinnipeds. *J. Mammal.,* 48:144, 1967.

Felts, W.J.L. and Spurrell, F.A.: Structural orientation and density in cetacean humeri. *Amer. J. Anat.,* 116:171–203, 1965.

Felts, W.J.L. and Spurrell, F.A.: Structural orientation and development characteristics of cetacean (odontocete) radii. *Amer. J. Anat.,* 118:103–134, 1966.

Flower, W.H.: Description of the Skeleton of the Chinese White Dolphin (*Delphinus sinensis, Osbeck*). *Trans. Zool. Soc. London,* 7(2):151–160, 1870.

Galliano, R.E., Morgane, P.J., McFarland, W.L., Nagel, E.L., and Catherman, R.L.: The anatomy of the cervicothoracic arterial system in the bottlenose dolphin (*Tursiops truncatus*) with a surgical approach suitable for guided angiography. *Anat. Rec.,* 155:325–338, 1966.

Harrison, R.J. and King, J.E.: *Marine Mammals.* London, Hutchinson University Library, 1965.

Harrison, R.J. and Kooyman, G.L.: General physiology of the pinnipedia. In Harrison, R.J., Hubbard, R.C., Peterson, R.S., Rice, C.E., and Schusterman, R.J. (Eds.): *The Behavior and Physiology of Pinnipeds.* New York, Appleton-Century-Crofts, 1968.

Harrison, R.J., Matthews, L.H., and Roberts, J.M.: Reproduction in some pinnipedia. *Trans. Zool. Soc. London,* 27(5):437–541, 1952.

Harrison, R.J. and Tomlinson, J.D.W.: Observations on the venous system in certain Pinnipedia and Cetacea. *Proc. Zool. Soc. London,* 126:205–233, 1956.

Harrison, R.J. and Tomlinson, J.D.W.: Anatomical and physiological adaptations in diving mammals. In *Viewpoints in Biology,* London, Butterworth, 1963, pp. 115–162.

Hein, S.A.A.: The larynx and its surrounding in monodon. *Verhand. Kor. Adkad. Wetensch.,* 2–18(3):4–54, 1914.

Hosokawa, H.: On the cetacean larynx, with special remarks on the laryngeal sack of the sei whale and the aryteno-epiglottideal tube of the sperm whale. *Sci. Rep. Whales Res. Inst.,* 3:23–62, 1950.

Howell, A.B.: Contribution to the anatomy of the Chinese finless porpoise, *Neomeris phocaenoides. Proc. U. S. Nat Mus.,* 70–13:1–43, 1927.

Howell, A.B.: Contributions to the comparative anatomy of the eared and earless seals (Genera *Zalophus* and *Phoca*). *Proc. U. S. Nat. Mus.,* 73:1–143, 1928.

Howell, A.B.: Myology of the narwhal (*Monodon monoceros*). *Amer. J. Anat.,* 46(2):187–215, 1930.

Howes, G.B.: On some points in the anatomy of a porpoise. *J. Anat. Physiol.,* 14:467–474, 1879.

Huber, E: Anatomical notes on Pinnipedia and Cetacea. *Carnegie Inst.* Washington, 447:105–136 1934.

Humphrey, G.M.: On the myology of *Phoca communis. J. Anat.* 2:290–322, 1868.

Hunter, J.: Observations on the structure and oeconomy of whales. *Phil. Trans. Roy. Soc. London,* 77:371, 1787.

Kelemen, G. and Hassko, H.: Das Stimmorgan des Seelorven. (The voice organ of the sea lion). *Z. Anat. Entwicklungsgesch,* 95:497–511, 1931.

Kellogg, R.: The History of Whales—Their Adaptation to Life in the Water. *Quart. Rev. Biol.,* 3:29–76, 174–208, 1931.

Kellogg, R.: Adaptation of Structure to Function in Whales. *Carnegie Inst.* Washington, 501:649–682, 1938.

King, J.E. and Harrison, R.J.: Some notes on the Hawaiian monk seal. *Pacific Sci.,* 25:282–293, 1961.

King, J.E.: *Seals of the World.* London, Trustees British Museum of Natural History, 1964.

Lawrence, B. and Schevill, W.E.: The functional anatomy of the delphinid nose. *Bull. Mus. Comp. Zool.,* 114:103–152, 1956.

Lawrence, B. and Schevill, W.E.: Gular musculature in delphinids. *Bull. Mus. Comp. Zool,* 133:5–58, 1965.

Lucae, J.C.G.: Die Robbe and Die Otter in Ihrem Knocken and Muskelskelet. *Abh. senckenb. naturf. ges.,* 8:277–378, 1872.

Matthews, L.H.: *British Mammals.* London, William Collins Sons & Co., Ltd., 1952.

Meek, A.: The reproductive organs of the cetacea. *J. Anat.,* 52:186–210, 1918.

Miller, W.C.S.: The myology of the Pinnipedia. *Challenger Rep.,* 26(67):139–234, 1887.

Mori, M.: The skeleton and musculature of *Zalophus. Okajimas Foli Anat., 31:* 203–284, 1958.

Murie, J.: On the anatomy of a fin whale (*Physalus antiquorum,* Gray) captured near Gavesend. *Proc. Zool. Soc. London,* 1865.

Murie, J.: On *Phoca groenlandica* mull. Its modes of progression and its anatomy. *Proc. Zool. Soc. London,* pp. 604–508, 1870.

Murie, J.: On Risso's grampus *Grampus rissoanus* (Desm). *J. Anat. Phys., 5:* 115–138, 1871a.

Murie, J.: Notes on the white-beaked bottlenosed *Lagenorhynchus albirostris,* Gray. *J. Linn. Soc. London,* 11(50):141–153, 1871b.

Murie, J.: Researches upon the anatomy of the pinnipedia. *Trans. Zool. Soc. London,* 7:527–596, 1872.

Murie, J.: On the organization of the caaing whale *Globicephala melas. Trans. Zool. Soc. London,* 8:235–301, 1874.

Nagel, E.L., Morgane, P.L., McFarland, W.L., and Galliano, R.E.: Rete mirabile of dolphin: Its pressure-damping effect on cerebral circulation. *Science,* 161:898–900, 1968.

Nakajima, M.: In regard to the rete mirabile of the Cetacea. *Toho Med. Acad. J.,* 8(4), 1961.

Oden'hal, S.: The anatomy of the larynx of the California sea lion (*Zalophus californianus*). *Proceedings of the Third Annual Conference on Biological Sonar and Diving Mammals,* Menlo Park, California, Stanford Research Institute, 1966, pp. 41–48.

Ommanney, F.D.: The vascular networks (*Retia mirabilia*) of the fin whale (*Balaenoptera physalus*). *Discovery Rep.* 5:327–363, 1932.

Owen, R.: *On the Anatomy of the Vertebrates.* London, Longmans Green, 1866, 1868, vols. 2 and 3.

Palmer, E. and Weddell, G.: The relationship between structure, innervation and function of the skin of the bottlenose dolphin (*Tursiops truncatus*). *Proc. Zool. Soc. London,* 143:553–568, 1964.

Ping, C.: On the testis and its accessory structure in the porpoise. *Anat. Rec.,* 32: 113–117, 1926.

Purves, P.E.: Anatomical and Experimental Observations on the Cetacean Sonar System. In Busnel, R.G. (Ed.): *Les Systems Sonars Animaux, Biologie et Bionique I.* France Laboratoire de Physiologe Acoustique, 1966.

Purves, P.E.: The anatomy and physiology of the outer and middle ear in cetaceans. In Norris, K. (Ed.): *Whales, Dolphins, and Porpoises.* Berkeley, University of California Press, 1966.

Ridgway, S.H. and Johnston, D.G.: Blood oxygen and ecology of porpoises of three genera. *Science, 151*(3709):456–458, 1966.

Ridgway, S.H.: Dall Porpoise, *Phocoenoides dalli* (True): Observations in captivity and at sea. *Norsk Hvalfangst Tid.,* 55:97–110, 1966.

Ridgway, S.H. and Green, R.F.: Evidence for a sexual rhythm in male porpoises, *Lagenorhynchus obliquidens* and *Delphinus delphis bairdi. Norsk Hvalfangst Tid.,* 56:1–8, 1967.

Ridgway, S.H., Scronce, B.L., and Kanwisher, J.: Respiration and deep diving in the bottlenosed porpoise. *Science, 166*:1651–1654, 1969.

Schneider, R.: Vergleichende untersuchurgen am Kehlkiph der Robben. (Comparative Investigations on the Larynges of the Seals). *Gegenbaur Morph. Jahrb., 103*:177–262, 1962.

Scholander, P.F. and Schevill, W.E.: Counter-current vascular heat exchange in the fins of whales. *J. Appl. Physiol., 8*(3):279–282, 1955.

Schulte, H. Von W.: Anatomy of a foetus of *Balaenoptera borealis. Mem. Amer. Mus. Nat. Hist., 1*:289–502, 1916.

Schulte, H. von W. and Smith, M.: The external characteristics, skeletal muscles and peripheral nerves of *Kogia breviceps* (Blainville). *Bull. Amer. Mus. Nat. Hist., 38*(2):7–72, 1918.

Slijper, E.J.: Die Cetaceen Vergleichend-Anatomisch und Systematisch. *Cap. Zool., 7*:1–590, 1936.

Slijper, E.J.: *Whales.* New York, Basic Books, 1962.

Simpson, J.G., Gilmartin, W.G., and Ridgway, S.H.: Blood volume and other hematologic parameters in young elephant seals, *Mirounga angustirostris. Amer. J. Vet. Res.,* (in press) 1970.

Stannius, F.H.: Beschreinbung der Muskeln des Tummlers (*Delphinus phocaena*). *Arch. Anat. Physiol., Wiss. Med.,* 1:1–41, 1849.

Struthers, J.: On some points in the anatomy of a great fin whale (*Balaenoptera musculaus*). *J. Anat. Phys.,* 6, 1871.

Tyson, E.: *Phocaena,* or the anatomy of a porpess dissected at Gresham Colledge. London, 1680. Reprinted in *Dublin's Phil. J.,* 2:48–60, 192–206, 1826.

Walmsley, R.: Some observations on the vascular system of a female fetal Finback. *Cont. Embryol. Carneg. Inst.,* 164(27):107–178, 1938.

Wilson, H.S.: The rete mirabile of the narwhal. *J. Anat. Phys.,* 14:377–398, 1879.

Chapter 5

COMPARATIVE MICROSCOPIC ANATOMY
OF SELECTED MARINE MAMMALS

John G. Simpson and Murray B. Gardner

Our initial naive intention was to compile the definitive work on the microscopic anatomy and histopathology of marine mammals. With this in mind, we assiduously began collecting and studying tissue and searching the literature. We rapidly became aware that our undertaking was presumptuous. Information on these subjects is limited, and varieties of fresh tissues from normal and diseased marine mammals are scarce. Moreover, we realized the limitations of generalizing on the basis of relatively restricted tissue sampling. Thus, we became more humble and realistic and submit that this chapter will present mostly our own observations and illustrations, together with a guarded appraisal of comparative features. We include a general discussion and appropriate references pertaining to the major organ systems (except the central nervous system) of certain marine mammals and comments regarding selected pathologic processes, mostly of cetaceans but with some mention of pinnipeds.

This material is intended primarily for persons who are concerned with pathologic processes in marine mammals and who may also desire information pertaining to the normal microscopic anatomy of these species. We will not ordinarily dwell on elaborate microscopic detail but will highlight those features that are unique or particularly interesting in comparison to man and other terrestrial mammals. We also include some of our findings on the ultrastructure of the cetacean lung and stomach, not heretofore reported.

The majority of the tissues available to us were from odontocetes. Certain species of Odontoceti comprise the principal whale and porpoise populations kept in captivity and are therefore of particular interest from a veterinary medicine viewpoint. Generalizations regarding the microscopic anatomy of cetaceans which are based upon study of Odontoceti, do not, of course, necessarily apply equally to the Mystacoceti (baleen whales). We recognize this limitation and will cite observations from the literature pertaining to histologic differences between the toothed and baleen whales.

Most of us who have done a large number of necropsies on marine mammals would, we suspect, admit that an uncomfortable number of cases do not reveal a good, defensible cause of death. This seems particularly true of animals that die shortly after coming into captivity. The necropsy may reveal a variety of findings, ranging from no significant lesions in any organ in some animals to severe respiratory or hepatic pathology in others. Some cadavers present gross features which suggest antemortem disease (e.g. pulmonary congestion), but upon histologic examination tissues merely reveal terminal changes. Often times, we ritualistically attribute these undiagnosed cases to "shock" or "stress" and try to forget them. In fact, the exact mechanism of death in these cases is not understood. This situation is not limited to marine mammals; it occurs in all species. There is much to be learned, and it is our hope that the material presented here, limited as it is, will contribute to some better understanding of disease in marine mammals.

RESPIRATORY SYSTEM

Compared to land mammals, several striking modifications in microscopic anatomy exist in cetacean and pinniped lungs. Both are diving mammals, and there are many similarities in lung structure. In fact, the differences noted between species are more a matter of degree than a basic difference in architecture. To some extent, it appears that these structural variations can be correlated with diving depth and duration of time spent underwater. This section will be divided as follows: (a) proximal conducting airways, (b) terminal airways and alveolar parenchyma, (c) pathology, (d) fine structural studies, and (e) literature review and comments.

Proximal Conducting Airways

In Cetacea, the larynx, trachea, bronchi, and distal divisions, diminishing to a diameter of 0.5 to 1.0 mm, comprise the proximal air conducting airways. In the larynx, a few mucous glands may lie between the epithelium and underlying cartilage (Fig. 5–1). A ciliated pseudostratified columnar epithelium (Fig. 5–2) arises abruptly from the squamous epithelium in the larynx and extends throughout the air-conducting pathways. This epithelium rests upon a basal layer of cuboidal cells and a narrow basement membrane. In the submucosa of the larger conduits, large, thin-walled, flattened veins course primarily in a longitudinal direction.

Compared to those of terrestrial mammals, the larger air-conducting pathways of Cetacea show several modifications ideally suited for rapid and vigorous exchange of air. A generous peripherally extending cartilagi-

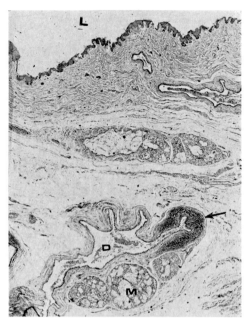

Figure 5–1. Larynx of an Atlantic bottlenosed porpoise. (L) Tracheal lumen, (M) Mucous gland, (D) Part of mucous gland duct system, (Arrow) Aggregation of lymphoid tissue. Note that in this portion of the larynx the mucosa consists of stratified squamous epithelium. (Hematoxylin and Eosin, ×25)

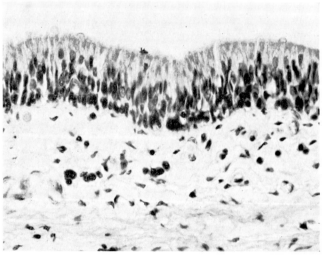

Figure 5–2. Tracheal mucosa of an Atlantic bottlenosed porpoise. A ciliated pseudostratified columnar epithelium lines the trachea and bronchi. There is an absence of goblet cells. A few lymphoreticular cells are present in the submucosa but there are no mucous glands. (H and E, × 500)

nous armature furnishes added structural support. Circumferential cartilaginous rings nearly surround the trachea and large bronchi with none of
the large membranous portion present in humans. Cartilaginous support,
in the form of plates and rings, extends into the smaller airways to the
junction with alveolar ducts or sacs. Additional airway support and resil-
iency is provided by abundant elastic tissue. There are dense layers of longitudinally oriented elastic fibers, an inner layer just beneath the mucous
membrane and an outer layer encircling and connecting the cartilages
(Fig. 5–3). The elastic layers extend into the smallest airways. A few in-

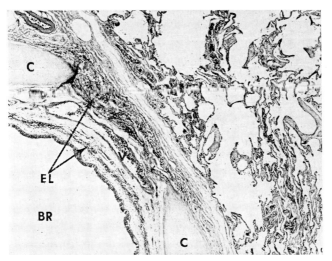

Figure 5–3. Bronchus and parenchyma of an Atlantic bottlenosed porpoise. Two
layers of elastic tissue (EL) are present in the bronchial wall. The inner layer in
the submucosa runs longitudinally. The outer layer connecting the cartilagenous
rings (C) has both longitudinal and circularly oriented fibers. A large thin walled
vein (V) lies between the two elastic layers. There is no circular smooth muscle
layer. (BR) bronchial lumen. (Elastic × 40)

conspicuous circular smooth muscle fibers lie in the bronchial submucosa,
but these are not as prominent as in humans. Thin-walled, cavernous veins
are unusually prominent throughout the submucosa of the proximal bronchi (Fig. 5–4). Mucous glands are fewer in number than in terrestrial
mammals and are often indetectable. Surface goblet cells are not usually
apparent. Lymphoid aggregates are sparse and without nodule formation.
Cilia, however, are present throughout the air-conducting pathways.

Variations in this uniform structure were noted in some Cetacea that we
examined. In one Atlantic bottlenosed porpoise, mucous glands were surprisingly plentiful in the trachea and bronchi (Fig. 5–5). In the bronchus
of one sperm whale, the apical cytoplasm of many lining cells contained
para-aminosalicylic acid–(PAS) positive droplets, probably representing
mucous secretory material (Fig. 5–6). A single, small lymphoid nodule is

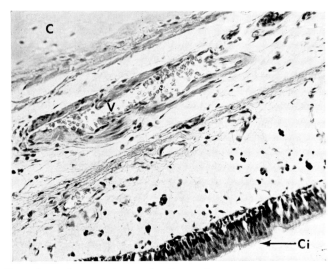

Figure 5–4. Bronchus of an Atlantic bottlenosed porpoise. A large vein (V) lies in the submucosa between cartilage (C) and respiratory type mucous membrane. Cilia (Ci) are seen to good advantage. Notice the paucity of lymphoreticular cells and the absence of goblet cells and mucous glands. (H and E, × 75)

also seen in this bronchus. In both the gray whale and the Amazon River porpoise, large, circular, smooth muscle bundles were noted in several 1 mm sized bronchi.

In the Pinnipedia, especially the seals, the air-conducting pathways show histologic features more like those seen in terrestrial mammals. In sea lions, the cartilaginous support extends as far peripherally as it does in the Ceta-

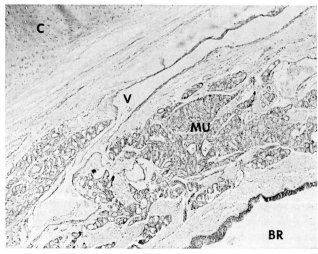

Figure 5–5. Main stem of the bronchus of an Atlantic bottlenosed porpoise. A collection of mucous glands (MU) resides within the submucosa, an unusual feature in Cetacea. (V) Cavernous venous channel, (C) Cartilage ring, (BR) Bronchial lumen. (H and E, × 45)

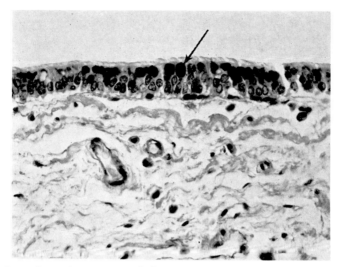

Figure 5–6. Bronchus of a sperm whale. The dark globules (PAS positive, arrow) in the apical cytoplasm of some mucosal lining cells represent aggregates of mucous droplets. Cilia are also clearly visible. (Periodic Acid-Schiff, × 500)

cea; but in seals, cartilage is not found distal to the small bronchi. In general, the Pinnipedia exhibit plentiful, large mucous glands and surface goblet cells, dense lymphocytic accumulations including nodules, a thick basement membrane, and large, circular smooth muscle bundles in their large and small bronchi (Fig. 5–7). In sharp contrast to those of Cetacea, the elastic layers of pinnipeds are considerably less prominent.

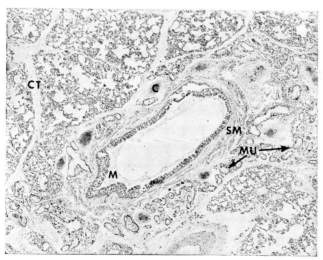

Figure 5–7. Bronchus and parenchyma of an elephant seal. Numerous mucous glands (MU) are present in the bronchial wall and a layer of mucus (M) coats the lining cells. A circular smooth muscle layer (SM) can be seen in the submucosa. The cartilage rings (C) are small. The parenchyma is divided into small lobules by numerous connective tissue septae (CT). (H and E, × 35)

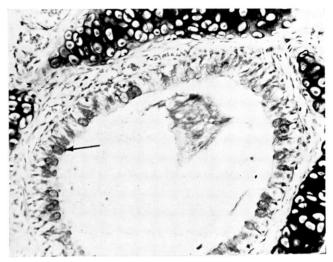

Figure 5–8. Small bronchus of a Steller's sea lion. Numerous mucus-containing goblet cells (arrow) are seen in this small bronchus. A small plug of mucous is also present in the lumen. (Trichrome, ×250)

Minor variations were noted in the four species of Pinnipedia that we examined. For example, in one small (1 mm) bronchus of a Steller's sea lion, surface goblet cells seemed unusually abundant (Fig. 5–8), but there were no submucosal glands in the wall. At a comparable site in a Cali-

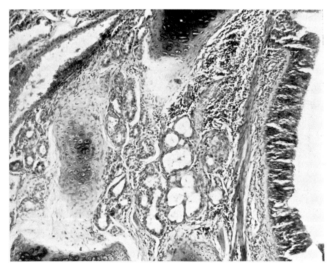

Figure 5–9. Bronchus of a California sea lion. In the submucosa of this small bronchus there are pale mucous glands, a circular smooth muscle layer and numerous diffuse lymphocytes. The heavy lymphocytic component may be in response to a parasitic worm infestation present in a significant percentage of California sea lions. (H and E, × 125)

fornia sea lion, however, surface goblet cells were inconspicuous and mucous glands numerous (Fig. 5–9).

Terminal Airways and Alveolar Parenchyma

Several remarkable features are noted in the cetacean lung at the level of the smallest airways, beginning at a caliber of about 0.5 mm. These features undoubtedly facilitate the adaptation of these animals to deep diving, prolonged breathholding, and rapid exchange of air upon surfacing. Compared to terrestrial mammals, there is a striking increase in the amount of supportive structures, namely cartilage, collagen, smooth muscle, and elastic tissue in the peripheral portions of the lung. A dense, elastic visceral pleura (Fig. 5–10), up to 1 mm or greater width (3 to 4 mm in larger whales), covers the nonseptate, nonsegmented lung. Discrete circular myoelastic bundles lead to prominent sphincter-like narrowings (in smaller cetaceans) in the terminal bronchioles which probably function as valves. The large Cetacea we examined do not possess such prominent myoelastic sphincters in the terminal bronchi. Instead, they show particularly thick longitudinal myoelastic bundles supporting tubular alveolar ducts. The alveolar septae have a thick core of collagen and elastica measuring 15 to 50μ in width and are surmounted at their free ends by prominent clastic knobs, suggesting a sphincter-like function also at this site. Each alveolar septum has a double blood supply, one capillary running along each side of the thick septum (Fig. 5–11).

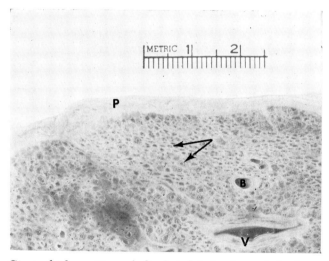

Figure 5–10. Giant thick section of fixed inflated pilot whale lung. The visceral pleura (P), 3 mm in thickness is uniformly thick and elastic. The lung is nonseptate. Air bubbles (arrows) lie within air sacs which measure about 1.0 x 1.0 mm. Surrounding each air sac, individual alveoli can be seen even at this very low magnification. Higher magnifications of this lung are seen in Figures 5–13 and 5–15. (B) Bronchus, (V) Vein. (× 1.8)

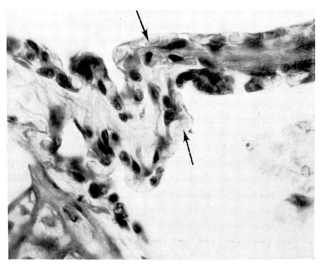

Figure 5–11. Alveolar septum of a pilot whale. A single alveolar septum, 20μ in width, is shown with a capillary containing RBC's (arrows) running along each side. The septum has a dense collagenous core. (H and E, × 1000)

The sphincteric narrowings in the terminal bronchioles are most prominent in porpoises. These narrowings, up to eight to ten in number, cause a compartmentalization of the small airways into a series of chambers (Fig. 5–12). The myoelastic sphincters lie in the intervals between successive cartilaginous rings and are composed primarily of circular smooth muscle fibers within which radial elastic fibers ramify and connect the inner and outer longitudinal elastic layers. Sphincters guard the openings into smaller bronchioles and into the alveolar sacs (Fig. 5–13). The mucous membrane in the most distal terminal bronchioles is composed of a single layer of small cuboidal cells without mucous or cilia, occasionally lying in close juxtaposition to a capillary (Fig. 5–14). Despite the absence of alveolar outpouching from these terminal airways, the portion of terminal bronchioles containing flattened mucosa has been referred to as a "respiratory bronchiole" (Wislocki, 1929). Several features suggest to us that these are in fact not areas of oxygen-carbon dioxide exchange. The small surface area of this flattened epithelium does not seem adequate for any significant amount of respiratory function. Capillaries, which would have to be present for gaseous exchange, are not consistently found in intimate contact with the flattened mucosa. In porpoises, the distal bronchioles, 0.2 to 0.3 mm in diameter, open singly or dichotomously into saccular air spaces from whose circumference 10 to 20 elongated alveoli exit (Figs. 5–12, 5–13). In porpoises and smaller whales, the alveolar septae generally measure about 10 to 20μ in thickness (Fig. 5–15). The elastic fibers at the mouth of each air sac connect with elastic fibers in the bron-

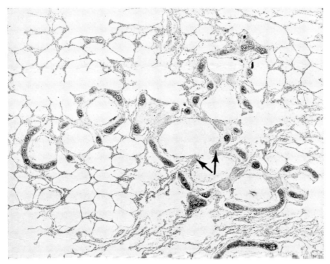

Figure 5–12. Terminal bronchiole of an Hawaiian spinning dolphin. Circular smooth muscle spincters (arrows) divide the terminal bronchioles into a series of compartments. They guard the branch points of tributary bronchioles as well as the opening into the alveolar sacs. The sphincters lie between the cartilagenous rings which extend also to the opening into the air sacs. (H and E, × 35)

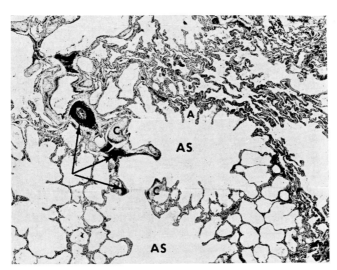

Figure 5–13. Terminal bronchiole and alveolar parenchyma of a pilot whale. Prominent circular smooth muscle sphincters (arrows) with intermingled elastic fibers guard the opening of a terminal bronchiole with two air sacs (AS). The air sacs are approximately 1 mm in diameter. They give rise to 10 to 20 elongated alveoli which measure about 0.1 to 0.2 mm in length. Cartilage (C) extends to the termination of the bronchioles. (Trichrome, × 40)

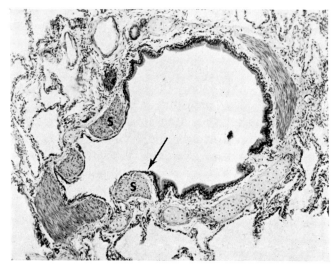

Figure 5–14. Terminal bronchiole of the Pacific white-striped dolphin. This is a small bronchus, 0.4 mm in diameter, just proximal to an air sac. At this point, a prominent circular smooth muscle sphincter (S) resides, and the mucosa changes from columnar to flat cuboidal (arrow). (H and E, × 125)

chiolae terminal muscle sphincter (Fig. 5–13). Individual elastic fibers lie within the alveolar septae and form prominent knobs at the free ends (Fig. 5–15).

Several histologic differences are apparent in the lungs of larger and deeper-diving Cetacea, e.g. sperm whale, killer whale, gray whale, and fin

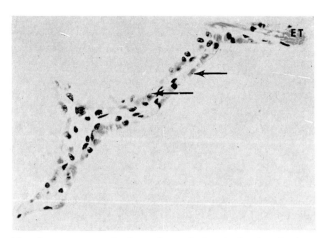

Figure 5–15. Alveolar septum of the pilot whale. A knob of elastic tissue (ET) lies at the free end of the alveolar septum. Note the double capillary supply, one channel along each side of the septum (arrows). Also compare to Figure 5–11. (H and E, × 500)

whale. In these species, there are thicker alveolar septae, measuring 30 to
50μ, and an even greater abundance of elastic tissue (Fig. 5–16). The distal bronchioles are shorter and the periodic muscular-elastic narrowings
are less frequent and less conspicuous than those of porpoises. More prominent longitudinal bands of elastic tissue with some intermingled smooth
muscle fibers (as judged by trichrome stain) extend from the distal bronchioles along long tubular alveolated passageways, which constitute the
alveolar ducts and correspond to the more dilated alveolar sacs seen in the
porpoise lung. The elastic tissue knobs (sphincters) at the mouth of each
alveolus are also more prominent in these larger species (Figs. 5–16 and
5–17).

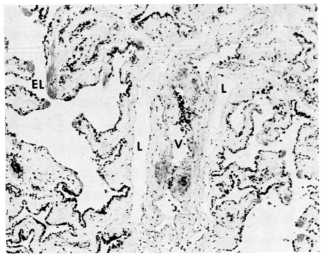

Figure 5–16. Alveolar parenchyma of the sperm whale. The alveolar septae are
quite stout, measuring 40 to 60μ in width. Their double capillary blood supply is
well seen. Prominent elastic bands (EL) lie at the tips of the alveolar septae. A
vein (V) running in the center of the field is focally narrowed by a smooth muscular
sphincter (S). Dilated lymphatic channels (L) surround this vein. (Trichrome,
× 125)

In the cetacean lung, pulmonary arterial branches are inconspicuous,
thin walled, and few in number in comparison with the venules. The arteries and arterioles generally reside close to the airways and can be identified by a prominent internal elastic membrane. Venous branches run
some distance apart from the airways. In contrast to arterioles, the caliber
of the small peripheral venules is often uneven, due to the existence of
isolated circular smooth muscle valves (Fig. 5–16). A loosely textured connective tissue cuff containing lymphatic spaces encircles the venous channels.

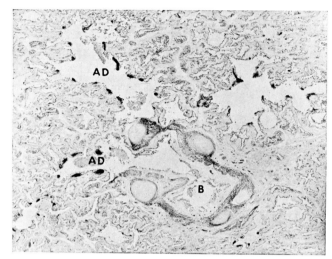

Figure 5–17. Respiratory bronchiole and alveolar parenchyma of the fin whale. An abundance of black staining elastic tissue outlines branching alveolar ducts (AD) and extends between and around cartilage rings of a terminal bronchiole (B). Note the lack of prominent smooth muscle sphincters in the terminal bronchiole. (Elastic, × 35)

A peculiar anatomic feature is found in the Dall porpoise—a triangular fat pad attached to the peripheral margin of the relatively thin visceral pleura. This fat pad is quite vascular with a number of thick-walled arterioles and spacious veins, some with sphincters (Figs. 5–18, 5–19).

The histology of the pinniped lung, especially in seals, differs less from

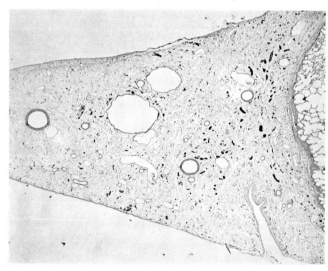

Figure 5–18. Pleural fat pad of the Dall porpoise. A triangular fat pad is attached to the rather thin layer of visceral pleura. Within the adipose tissue run numerous small and large vascular channels. (H and E, × 10)

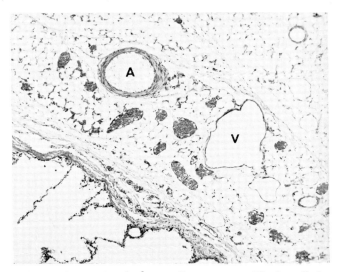

Figure 5–19. Pleural fat pad of the Dall porpoise. Thick-walled arteries (A), thin-walled veins (V), and numerous congested capillaries lie within the mature adipose tissue. (H and E, × 75)

that of solely terrestrial mammals. Compared to cetaceans and sea lions, seals have much less elastic tissue and cartilage and comparatively small rudimentary valve-like sphincters. Thin, fibrous septae delineate lung lobules to a much greater degree than in humans (Fig. 5–20). In the seals, as in humans, the short, cartilage-free respiratory bronchiole appears to become

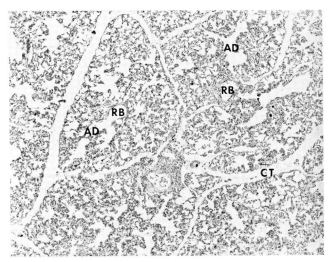

Figure 5–20. Alveolar parenchyma of the elephant seal. The respiratory bronchioles (RB) and alveolar ducts (RD) contain neither cartilagenous support or smooth muscle sphincters. The parenchyma is divided by numerous fine connective tissue septae (CT). Elastic tissue is not apparent. The alveolar septae are thin and contain but a single capillary. (H and E, × 35)

a long alveolar duct. In the sea lion, by contrast, cartilage rings still surround the respiratory bronchioles and extend to the mouth of the alveolar sacs, as in porpoises (Fig. 5–21). Seal alveoli have but a single capillary, and the alveolar septum is about the same width as in humans, averaging about 8μ in width. Sea lions have a slightly thicker alveolar septum. The California sea lion has only a single capillary within each alveolar septum. We have been confounded by the apparent presence of a double alveolar capillary supply (as in Cetacea) in the Steller's sea lion (Fig. 5–22). Such a difference in alveolar capillary supply in two species so closely related is indeed surprising. In summary, (from the standpoint of microanatomical pulmonary adaptations) sea lions fall in an intermediate position between man and seal on the one hand and porpoises and whales on the other.

Lung Pathology

After careful gross examination of many thousands of whales on factory ships in the Antarctic, Cockrill (1960b) concluded that large whales in their natural environment are remarkably free of overt lung disease. Because his method of examination precluded routine histologic study, incidental small lesions were probably overlooked. Furthermore, the animals examined very likely represented a biased selection of relatively healthy animals because diseased individuals would be less likely to be found in pelagic herds. We also found no pulmonary histopathology in our limited study of lungs from various whales. We have, of course, been able to examine only a miniscule fraction of their total lung tissue. Lack of inflammation together with the paucity of tracheal lymphoid cells and mucous glands probably bears testimony to the clean, relatively microbe-free environment in which these animals live.

Lung disease in the more extensively studied porpoises appears to be reasonably common under natural conditions and is often due to nematode infestation. Porpoises probably ingest parasitic nematodes in infected fish. Under ordinary circumstances, nematodes in the lung may not result in any obvious adverse systemic effect upon the cetacean host. Acute bacterial bronchopneumonia, by contrast, is probably rare under natural conditions but more likely to be seen in captivity. This type of pneumonia is likely to have a much more devastating effect. Its onset often seems to be determined by recent transportation ("shipping fever") and confinement. It is likely due to the aspiration of dirty water, something more apt to occur in captivity or under adverse circumstances. In captivity, the animals must also be exposed to unfamiliar pathogens to which they have acquired relatively little resistance. In recent years, acute lung disease has become a frequent occurrence, especially in the Amazon River porpoise sub-

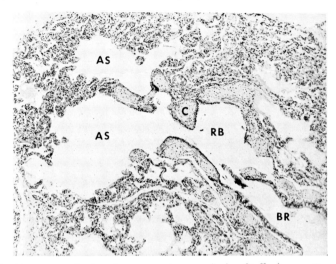

Figure 5–21. Airways and alveolar parenchyma of the Steller's sea lion. A bronchus (BR) lined by numerous mucous-containing goblet cells terminates in a respiratory bronchiole (RB) lined by cuboidal epithelium. This in turn divides and empties into air sacs (AS). Cartilage support (C) extends to the mouth of the air sacs. There is an absence of smooth muscle sphincters. Elastic tissue is inapparent. (H and E, × 75)

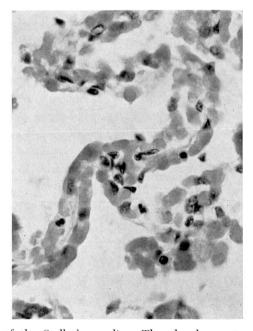

Figure 5–22. Lung of the Steller's sea lion. The alveolar septum appears to contain two distinct capillaries. The thickness of the septum here is approximately 20μ. (H and E, ×750)

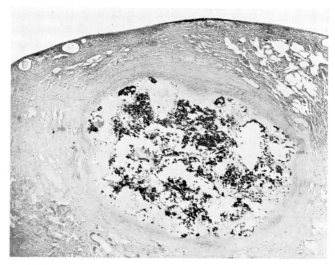

Figure 5–23. Calcified nodule of the lung of an Atlantic bottlenosed porpoise. A 1 mm-sized walled off and calcified nodule lies just beneath the pleura. This is an old granuloma probably due to prior parasitic invasion, a common finding in our experience. (H and E, ×10)

sequent to extended transportation. The present method of shipping these animals in plastic-lined boxes containing only a few inches of water provides an ideal situation for aspiration of excreta, contaminated water, and aerosols.

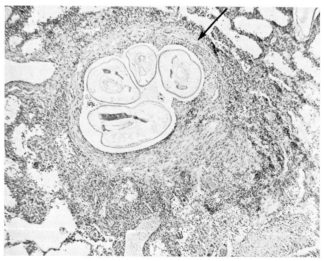

Figure 5–24. Parasitic granuloma of the lung of a Dall porpoise. A cross-sectioned helminthic parasite lies in the center of an intense inflammatory reaction. A proliferation of fibrous connective tissue (arrow) has begun to wall off the parasite from the surrounding lung. (H and E, ×55)

Nematode infestation may elicit several different histopathologic expressions, depending upon site of involvement and the stage of evolution
of the inflammatory process. In the air passages, the worms cause little if
any inflammatory reponse; however, in one Atlantic bottlenosed porpoise
(Fig. 5–23), calcific debris in the lumina and submucosa of the respiratory
bronchioles was possibly due to prior parasitic infestation. Parasitic invasion into the alveolar parenchyma is usually but not invariably accompanied by an inflammatory response. Recent infection incites a subacute
granulomatous inflammatory response characterized mainly by lymphocytes and plasma cells and usually few or no giant cells. A few polymorpho-
nuclear leucocytes and eosinophils may also be present. Walling-off of the
organisms occurs by fibrosis (Fig. 5–24) and ultimately results in a fibrotic
calcified nodule within which parasitic remnants may occasionally be
identified (Fig. 5–25). At other times, focal scars (Fig. 5–26), nonspecific
chronic inflammatory foci (Fig. 5–27), and peculiar, sharply demarcated
zones of eosinophilic-staining, noncellular, intra-alveolar material (Fig. 5–
28) can be seen in the absence of demonstrable parasites. A relationship of
these lesions to prior parasitic invasion, however, seems a most likely possibility. Testi and Pilleri (1969) have documented in detail the pathogenesis of verminous pneumonitis in the common dolphin (*Delphinus delphis*). There are, in addition, other reports of both parasitic and nonparasitic pulmonary disease in Cetacea (Brown *et al.*, 1960; Slijper,
1962; Miller *et al.*, 1963; Ridgway, 1965; Woodard *et al.*, 1969). Cowan
(1966) found black nematode worms, 1.5 cm in length, in the bronchi of
fifty-four of fifty-five pelagic pilot whales examined after grounding on a
Newfoundland beach. He suggests that the peculiar microanatomy of the
cetacean lung, in particular the bronchiolar sphincters, tends to promote
retention of intraluminal matter and thus to keep disease processes localized.

In captive porpoises (also pinnipeds) we have seen cases of erysipelas
(*Erysipelothrix insidiosa*) complicated by septicemic spread to lungs and
other viscera. Both pulmonary nocardiosis (Cowan, 1968) and aspergillosis
(Carrol *et al.*, 1968) have also been reported in porpoises.

In one Atlantic bottlenosed porpoise, apparently drowned after head
trauma, the bronchiolar sphincters were so profoundly contracted as to
completely obliterate the lumen (Fig. 5–29). This appearance dramatically
demonstrated the functional ability of the sphincters to essentially seal off
the terminal airways.

We have noted intracellular, golden-brown, coarse pigment granules
(Fig. 5–30) near large blood vessels in areas of chronic inflammation. Since
these granules stain for iron, they represent hemosiderin, probably of endogenous origin. We have not observed exogenous black anthracotic pig-

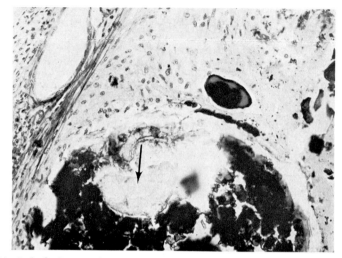

Figure 5–25. Calcified granuloma of the lung of an Atlantic bottlenosed porpoise. Near the margin of this heavily calcified nodule one can identify what appears to be a parasitic remnant (arrow). Epithelioid cells lie immediately above and fibrous tissue to the left. (H and E, ×250)

ment in cetacean lung, even in those porpoises living for some years in confinement near urban centers.

To our knowledge, neither bronchial mucosal dysplasia and/or metaplasia, nor tumors of the cetacean lung, benign or malignant, have ever been reported.

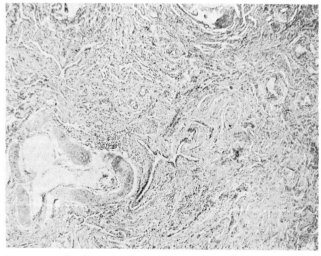

Figure 5–26. A scar on the lung of an bottlenosed porpoise. This is a collapsed and fibrotic area of lung with some slight, nonspecific chronic inflammation. The etiology is not apparent. (H and E, ×55)

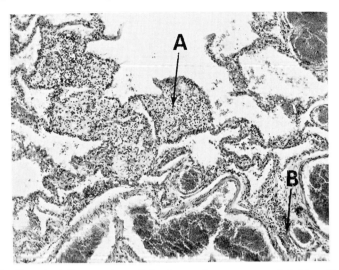

Figure 5–27. Chronic inflammation of the lung of a common dolphin. Alveolar septae are thickened and contain chronic inflammatory cells (arrow A). Golden brown intracellular pigment granules are noted (arrow B) adjacent to several large vessels. This area is shown at a higher magnification in Figure 5–30. The etiology of this chronic interstitial pneumonitis is not apparent. (H and E, ×125)

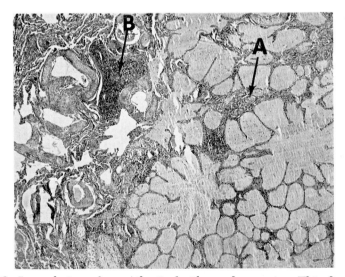

Figure 5–28. Lung lesion of an Atlantic bottlenosed porpoise. This figure shows a sharply demarcated zone of markedly proteinaceous alveolar exudate containing a paucity of intact cells. Septal chronic inflammation and thickened small vessels (arrow A) are confined to this area. A peribronchial lymphoid nodule (arrow B) is noted at the periphery of this lesion. Parasitic remnants are not observed. (H and E, ×35)

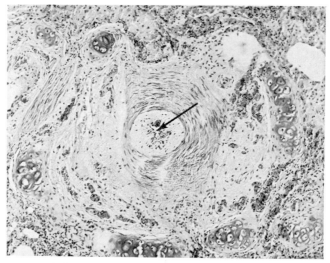

Figure 5–29. Terminal bronchiole of an Atlantic bottlenosed porpoise. A profound constriction of the smooth muscle sphincter in this terminal bronchiole has essentially occluded the lumen (arrow). This porpoise died by drowning, which must account for this finding. (H and E, ×125)

Inflammatory and parasitic diseases also affect the respiratory tract of pinnipeds. The California sea lion, an important animal because of its widespread display in zoos and in trained animal acts, is host to an often lethal parasitic pneumonitis (Fig. 5–31). The worm responsible is a nema-

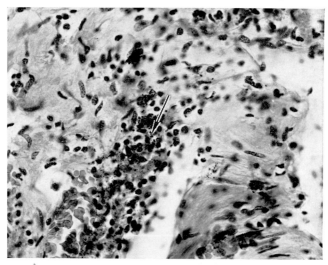

Figure 5–30. Pigment deposition in the lung of a common dolphin. This is a higher magnification of the area seen at arrow B in Figure 5–27. The golden-brown, coarse pigment granules (arrow) are mostly intracellular. Iron stains indicate that they are hemosiderin granules of endogenous origin. We have not seen black anthracotic pigment in the cetacean lung tissues that we have examined. (H and E, ×125)

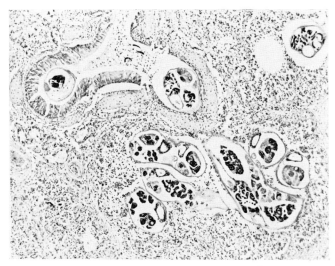

Figure 5–31. Nematode infestation of the lung of a California sea lion. Numerous round worms are present in the airways and alveolar spaces. There is an intense acute inflammatory response. This has been a very frequent finding in California sea lions. (H and E, ×75)

tode, *Parafilaroides decorus*, which measures about 80μ in cross section. The life cycle of this parasite requires a fish as an intermediate host (Dailey, 1970; also see Chap. 9). This appears to be an insidious disease in that an animal may be asymptomatic for a long period of time (months, and possibly years), and then in a period of a month or so may rapidly deteriorate and die with an extensive acute bronchopneumonia which may be due to bacterial superinfection.

Lung mites may also be present in airways of pinnipeds. We have found *Orthohalarachne* species in California sea lions, sometimes coexisting with the lung worm, *Parafilaroides decorus*. The lung mites do not appear to incite significant lung pathology. In our experience, nonspecific acute bronchopneumonia without visible worms has been a rather common finding at necropsy in California sea lions, Steller's sea lions, and harbor seals. A mixed flora of both gram-positive and gram-negative organisms is invariably recovered upon culture of these lungs. Whether these are primary or secondary pathogens remains to be determined.

Fine Structure

With the light-microscope study of even the best-prepared lung tissue from experimental animals, it is difficult to distinguish between alveolar epithelial and endothelial cell nuclei and impossible to resolve cytoplasmic structure. Investigators (Slijper, 1962) have remarked on the conspicuous absence of free alveolar cells or intra-alveolar debris in the cetacean lung.

Considering the technical difficulties in procural and prompt fixation of lung tissues for electron microscope study, it is not surprising that the cetacean alveolar fine structure has not yet been described. Based upon electron microscopic studies in other mammals (Low, 1953; Rhodin, 1963), one might expect to also find in Cetacea the customary two types of alveolar cell, one forming the ultrathin cytoplasmic lining membrane, suitable for gaseous exchange (type 1); the other, so-called "granular pneumatocyte" (type 2) (Macklin, 1954), bearing cytoplasmic dense lamellar inclusions thought to represent storage sites of the lipoprotein, surfactant (Avery and Said, 1965; Buckingham *et al.*, 1966). Because of the profound ability of the cetacean alveoli to maintain stability despite exaggerated pressure changes resulting in complete collapse at depths of approximately 100 m (Ridgway *et al.*, 1969), the fine structural features of the alveolar wall in these species assume added interest. Using the electron microscope, we therefore examined pulmonary biopsies from a pilot whale and from a Pacific white-striped porpoise.

Our findings confirm that there is indeed a mammalian-type alveolar lining cell in the cetacean lung (Figs. 5–32, 5–33, 5–34). The ultrathin alveolar lining cell (type 1) cytoplasm extends over the interior of the alveoli and rests on a basement membrane about 150 mμ in width. The capillary air barrier, present on each side of the alveolar septum, averages from 300 to 600 mμ in width, the same thickness as in other mammals. In our biopsy material, type 2 alveolar cells seem especially numerous and not particularly confined to the alveolar corners or apices. These show a microvillus surface and numerous dense concentric lamellar inclusions. Considerable membranous debris of similar configuration lies free in the alveolar spaces. An occasional intra-alveolar macrophage is laden with engulfed debris. Pulmonary endothelium shows no unusual characteristics. The alveolar septal core contains many well-formed collagen fiber bundles, numerous microfibrils, and elastic lamellae. Fibroblasts with long, thin cytoplasmic streamers are the only cells identified within the septal core; no smooth muscle cells are seen.

The presence of frequent type 2 alveolar cells and the detection of membranous debris in alveolar spaces is consistent with an ample production of surface-active lipoprotein and suggests that Cetacea, like other mammals, possess this important physicochemical attribute which must contribute to their marked alveolar stability.

Discussion and Review of Literature

One of the first definitive descriptions of the microscopic anatomy of porpoise lungs was by Fiebiger (1916). Among previous reports, we would also call particular attention to the thorough study of the Atlantic bottlenosed porpoise lung by Wislocki (1929) and to the comparative histologic study of three species of Odontoceti and three species of Mystacoceti by Murata (1951). Wislocki (1929) accurately described the bronchiolar sphincters and cartilaginous support and emphasized the respiratory function of the terminal air passageways. According to Murata's observations, the lung of Mystacoceti differs from the Odontoceti in possessing

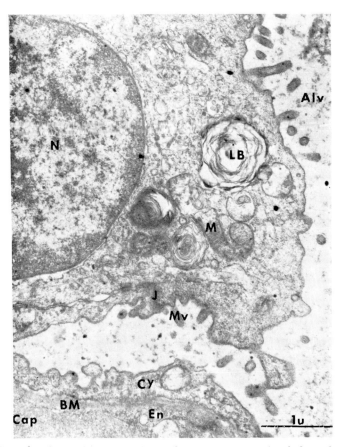

Figure 5–32. Alveolar cell, type II (granular pneumatocyte) of the pilot whale. The alveolar cell, Type II, protrudes into the alveolar lumen (Alv) with a surface showing numerous microvillous projections (Mv). Within the cytoplasm are many concentric lamellar bodies (LB) believed to represent storage sites of the lipoprotein "surfactant." The alveolar lining cell, Type I, covers the rest of the alveolar surface with a broad but flat layer of cytoplasm (Cy) in which there are few organelles and no lamellar bodies. Both Type I and II alveolar cells rest upon a basement membrane (BM) which adjoins the capillary endothelial cell cytoplasm (En). The total blood-air barrier is relatively thin, in the order of 0.5mm thickness, as in other mammals. (N) Nucleus of alveolar Type II cell, (M) Mitochondrion, (J) Junction of alveolar Type I and II cells, (Cap) Capillary lumen. (Uranyl acetate–lead citrate stain, ×20,600)

a less-developed series of bronchiolar smooth muscle sphincters and a greater amount of smooth muscle fibers accompanying the elastic bands along the wall of alveolar ducts. We concur with these observations. In the Odontoceti lungs, Murata designated as "alveolar duct" the funnel-like

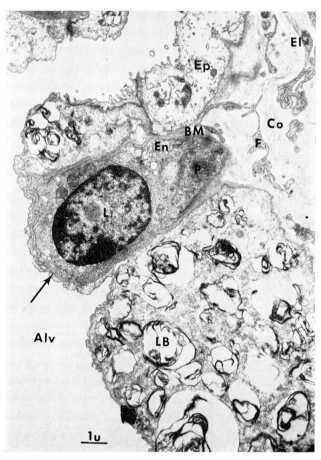

Figure 5–33. Alveolar wall of the Pacific white-striped porpoise. A large alveolar wall cell (Type II) full of lamellar bodies (LB) lies on both sides of the pulmonary capillary. A narrow bridge of interconnecting cytoplasm (arrow) overlies the capillary and seemingly constitutes at this site part of the ultrathin blood-air barrier for gaseous exchange. This finding suggests that there may not be such a sharp distinction between Types I and II alveolar cells. The cytoplasm of the Type I epithelial lining cells (EP) is swollen and hydropic, probably an artifact of fixation. In the alveolar septum there are many fibroblast cell processes (F). Collagen fibers (Co) and elastic tissue bands (El). No smooth muscle cells are identified in the alveolar septae. (Alv) Alveolar lumen, (L) Mononuclear blood cell, probably a lymphocyte, in pulmonary capillary lumen, (En) Pulmonary capillary endothelium, (P) Tubulated rods in endothelial cytoplasm, (BM) Basement membrane. (Uranyl acetate and lead citrate stain, ×8,600)

opening at the termination of sphinctered terminal bronchiole. Wislocki (1929) preferred to consider this site as part of the "air sac." The discrepancy in nomenclature seems to arise from whether one recognizes at this site smooth muscle fibers within the thick elastic bands. Even with special stains, we found this virtually impossible to do. In peripheral lung sections from Mystacoceti that we have studied (gray whales and fin whale) the tubular-shaped branching conduits from which single alveolar outpouchings and alveolar sacs arise are, we believe, analogous to alveolar ducts in other mammalian lungs. Belanger (1940) states that the larger

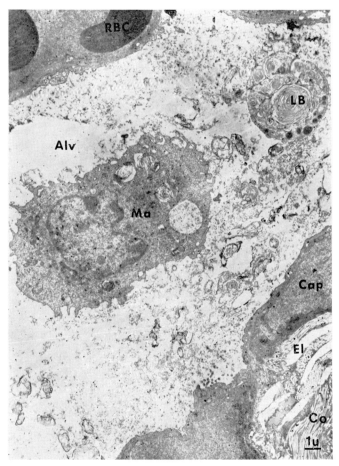

Figure 5–34. Alveolar lumen of a pilot whale. Within the alveolar lumen (Alv) there is a macrophage (Ma), a conglomerate of lamellar bodies (LB), and considerable membranous debris. This material could represent the elusive morphologic counterpart of the pulmonary "surfactant." (Cap) Capillary, (RBC) Red blood cell in capillary, (EL) Elastic tissue bands in alveolar septum, (CO) Collagen fibers in alveolar septum. (Uranyl acetate-lead citrate stain, ×5,800)

Cetacea lack respiratory bronchioli and that the terminal bronchioles open directly into several alveolar ducts.

As pointed out by Murata and in agreement with our findings, there is in the lung of Mystacoceti a greater degree of branching and intercommunication of alveolar ducts, whereas in the lung of Odontoceti, the terminal bronchioles lead into more simply branched and isolated respiratory units. This feature of Mystacoceti would seem to indicate a higher degree of evolutionary development than the more simple reptilian-like pattern of odontocete lungs. Wislocki and Belanger (1940) pointed out that the myoelastic sphincteric system seen in the bronchioles of many cetacean species is not common to all porpoises and whales. Locoste and Baudrimont (1933) found that this feature was lacking in the harbor porpoise and that the sphincters were also absent in many of the large whales. The absence of the bronchiolar sphincters in larger whales was also mentioned by Harrison and Tomlinson (1963). Engle (1966) has noted the histological similarity between the lung structures of certain whales and the larger crocodiles. Baudrimont (1955) discussed in detail the pulmonary venous sphincters of the common dolphin. He emphasizes the reservoir function of the pulmonary veins, together with the inferior vena cava, and hepatic and portal veins, during periods of immersion. Slijper (1962) aptly summarized cetacean pulmonary structure and function.

Descriptions of pulmonary mircoanatomy in Pinnipedia and Sirenia are limited. Wislocki (1935) found the lungs of Sirenia to be quite similar to those of Cetacea (double capillaries in alveolar septae, a cartilaginous armature extending to the the terminations of the smallest bronchioles, etc.) but different in several other respects. They have giant air sacs and do not have myoelastic sphincters in the bronchioles. The histology of the manatee lung has also been described by Belanger (1940). Belanger also noted the marked lobulation of the lung and a single capillary within the alveolar septum of the harbor seal. Harrison and Tomlinson (1963) described bronchiolar valves in the common seal, elephant seal, Weddell seal, gray seal, and the Hawaiian monk seal.

CARDIOVASCULAR SYSTEM

The way of life of the Cetacea calls for more extreme cardiovascular adaptability than does that of any other mammalian species. In studying the histology of the cetacean heart and vessels, one sees little difference from other mammals to account for this talent. On close inspection, however, several unusual features of microscopic anatomy are noted which may relate to these profound physiologic adaptations.

Our study of cetacean tissue was confined to the heart and aorta of the pilot whale, Atlantic bottlenosed porpoise, Pacific white-sided porpoise, Amazon River porpoise, and the aorta only from the beluga. We have not examined the heart from any species of large whale. A limited amount of pinniped cardiovasculature was studied.

We were impressed with two unusual features in those hearts examined. The first of those features is a relatively thick, pale endocardium which is a prominent feature of the cetacean hearts. The definite thickening of the endocardium is noted in all four chambers, particularly in the atria, where it may reach 1 mm (Fig. 5–35); in the ventricles it is most striking along the outflow tracks (Fig. 5–36). This thickening is due to a layer of collagen containing numerous elastic fibers molded to the inner surface of the heart. If seen in the human heart, this degree of endocardial fibroelastosis would be considered an abnormal finding, but in the Cetacea, and in certain other large mammals, it undoubtedly represents a normal phenomenon. The elastic tissue may function, in a sense, like a rubber band tending to withstand cardiac dilatory forces in these large volume chambers.

The second unusual feature is the large size of the Purkinje's cells and the prominent demarcation of these cells from the underlying myocardium (Figs. 5–37, 5–38). These specialized cardiac cells that convey the electrical impulse coordinating each heartbeat lie within the subendocardium and ramify over the inner surface of both ventricles. Whether these unusually large and distinct Purkinje's cells confer some selective advantage for the conduction of the cardiac impulse in these animals is

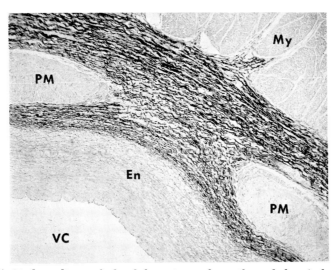

Figure 5–35. Endocardium of the left atrium of a pilot whale. A layer of black-staining elastic tissue, 0.7 mm in thickness lies just beneath the fibrous endocardium (En) and encases prominent pectinate muscles (PM). (VC) Ventricular cavity, (My) Myocardium. (Elastic, ×55)

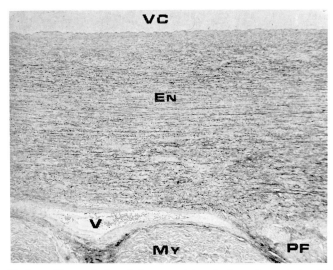

Figure 5–36. Endocardium of the right ventricle of the pilot whale. The fibroelastic endocardium (En) at this site measures 1 mm in thickness. Elastic fibers are stained black. (VC) Ventricular cavity, (V) Thebesian vein, (My) Myocardium, (PF) Purkinje fibers. (Elastic, ×55)

not known. One might suspect, as did White *et al.* (1953), that some valuable lessons in cardiac electrophysiology and adaptability to stress might be learned from monitoring these aquatic mammals. The cetacean heart would also be a suitable model for attempting to dissect out or isolate

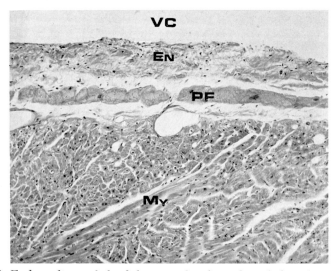

Figure 5–37. Endocardium of the left ventricle of a pilot whale. The Purkinje fibers (PF) lie in the subendocardium. Compared to those of man, they are unusually large and delineated from the myocardium. (En) Endocardium, (VC) Ventricular cavity, (My) Myocardium. (H and E, ×125)

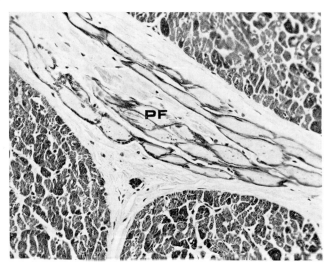

Figure 5–38. Subendocardium of the left ventricle of a pilot whale. A prominent bundle of Purkinje fibers (PF) lies within a fibrous trabecula just deep to the endocardium. Note the relatively large size, vacuolar appearance, and clear demarcation of these specialized impulse-conducting fibers. (Trichrome, × 250)

Purkinje's fibers for research purposes. These cardiac features were not seen in the four pinniped species that we examined.

The myocardial histology is otherwise remarkably similar to that of the human heart. Even in large whales, the myocardial cells are about the same dimension, 10 to 20μ in width, as in man. Fibrous trabeculae are thin and epicardial fat is sparse. The valvular histology is also comparable to man (Fig. 5–39), except that in the Cetacea a slight increase in the elastic tissue and mucoid ground substance is present in the valve core.

We have seen little cardiac disease. Small fibrous scars, probably of no functional significance, are occasionally noted in the myocardium of porpoises (Figs. 5–40, 5–41). A focal, circumscribed microscopic deposit of cartilage is seen just beneath the epicardium of an elephant seal heart (Fig. 5–42).

The coronary arteries are richly elastic. Rarely, a tiny fibrous intimal plaque is noted (Figs. 5–43, 5–44), but there is no overt lipid deposition, elastic fraying, or calcification. However, we have not used fat stains for detection of minor degrees of fat deposition. The intramyocardial coronary arterial branches do not differ in appearance from those in man. Coronary venules are large and prominently elastic, more so than in man.

The ascending aorta is strikingly thick walled and elastic (Figs. 5–45, 5–46), whereas the distal aorta is much thinner walled. Tiny vasa vasora penetrate deeply into the middle third of the aortic wall. We have seen no aortic atherosclerosis, medial scars, or calcification.

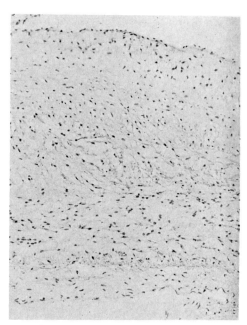

Figure 5–39. Atrioventricular valve of the harbor seal. The total thickness of this valve is slightly less than 1 mm. It is composed of a loose textured connective tissue core with an ample mucopolysaccharide (myxoid) extracellular matrix. This appearance is quite similar to that of the A-V valves in man. (H and E, ×135)

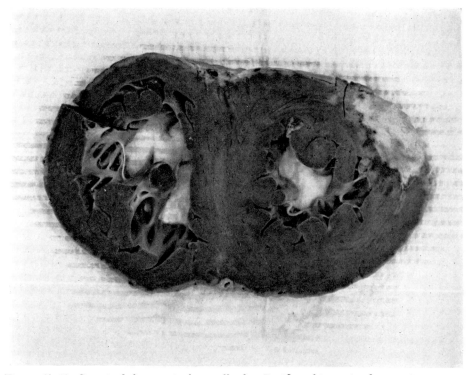

Figure 5–40. Scar in left ventricular wall of a Pacific white-striped porpoise.

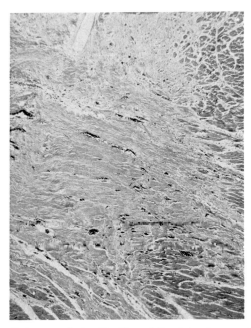

Figure 5–41. Myocardial scar of the Pacific white-striped porpoise. This is a micro-scopic section of the lesion seen grossly in Figure 5–40. (H and E, ×55)

Venous valves, composed of circular smooth muscle bundles, are another special adaptive feature in the vascular system of Cetacea. They were noted in the lung (Fig. 5–16) and in the portal triads of the liver (Figs. 5–85, 5–86). According to Slijper (1962), a venous sphincter occurs in the

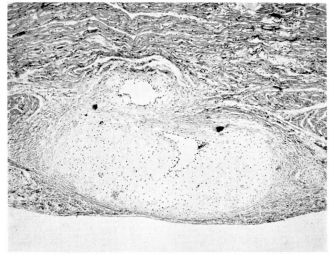

Figure 5–42. Subepicardial deposit of cartilage of the elephant seal. (Trichrome, ×75)

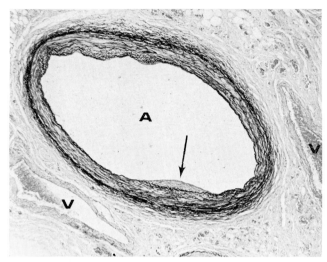

Figure 5–43. Left anterior descending coronary artery of the Amazon River porpoise. This large, elastic coronary artery (A) is seen here in the epicardium. Its inner surface is smooth except for a tiny fibrous intimal hillock (arrow). This is shown under higher magnification in the next illustration. Coronary venous branches (V) lie adjacent to the artery. Elastic fibers stain black. (Elastic, ×55)

common hepatic vein at its junction with the inferior vena cava just below the diaphragm. Harrison and Tomlinson (1963) have described muscular postcaval sphincters in seals (see Chap. 4). These sphincters are thought to regulate storage of blood in the venous system during diving.

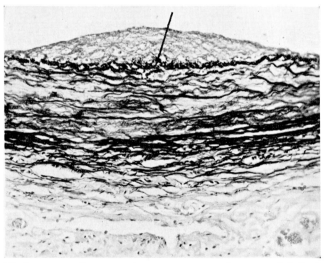

Figure 5–44. Higher magnification of Figure 5–43. The intimal hillock is composed of pale-staining fibrous tissue. A small amount of fat would probably be seen with special fat stains. The inner elastic lamellae (arrow) is intact. There is no medial degeneration and no calcification. (×250)

Figure 5–45. Ascending aorta of a beluga whale. This shows approximately the inner one-third of the ascending aorta which measured 5 to 6 mm in thickness. The intimal surface at the top is smooth and thin and there is no atherosclerotic change. The medial wall is richly endowed with elastic fibers which appear as dark streaks. Between the elastic lamellae lie abundant collagenous connective tissue stroma and smooth muscle cells which are inapparent at this magnification. There is no degeneration or calcification of the medial wall. (Trichrome, ×75)

Rete mirabile are highly developed in cetaceans (Fig. 5–47). These vascular networks occur in many regions of the body and consist primarily of a spongework of uniform-sized small arteries possessing prominent medial musculature. A few small veins and moderately numerous nerve trunks are interspersed in the intervening adipose tissue. Direct arterial venular anastomoses have not been seen. Retia are present in pinnipeds but are not as well developed as in cetaceans. A pericardial venous plexus or retia consisting of relatively thick-walled veins and nerve bundles has been reported in the harbor seal, northern elephant seal, and gray seal (Harrison and Tomlinson, 1956). These investigators state that a similar pattern is also found in some Cetacea.

The retia mirabilia are thought to function as shock absorbers, adjusting to marked pressure changes and facilitating changes in blood distribution during diving and resurfacing (Nakajima, 1961; Nagel *et al.*, 1968). The presence of nerve trunks within the retia is consistent with some degree of neurovascular control.

There are but a few notations on the histology of the cetacean cardio-

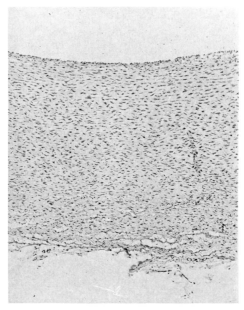

Figure 5–46. Ascending aorta of the harbor seal. This is a section of the entire thickness of the ascending aorta which measures only about 1 mm in thickness. Compare with Figure 5–45. The elastic lamellae are unstained but the numerous smooth muscle cell nuclei in the intervening stroma are well seen. The intimal surface at the top is perfectly smooth, showing no atherosclerotic changes. (H and E, ×75)

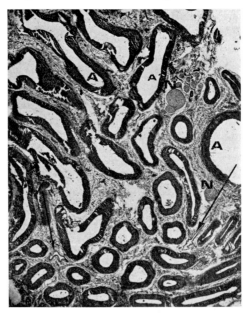

Figure 5–47. Thoracic *retia mirabilia* of the Atlantic bottlenosed porpoise. Small arteries (A), veins (arrows), and nerves (N) are situated within a loose connective tissue stroma. (H and E, ×15)

vascular system. Truex (1961) described the coronary collateral circulation of several large whales in some detail. He observed lipid-containing fibrous intimal plaques in the distal branches of the coronary arteries within the myocardium of four male sperm whales. He also found nematode worms in the right ventricle and coronary veins of two sperm whale hearts. One male sperm whale contained a large interventricular septal infarction, which might have been caused by nematode obstruction of the tributary veins.

Roberts *et al.* (1965) have undoubtedly done the most work in recent years on comparative atherosclerosis in the Cetacea and have utilized special stains for fat. In the Pacific white-striped porpoise aorta, they observed involvement of 10 to 30 percent of the intima with fibrous plaques which overlayed small collections of lipid in the deeper intima. They did not find plaques complicated by thrombi, ulceration, or hemorrhage, nor were there myocardial infarctions. The coronary arteries were generally less involved than the aorta. However, in one old female killer whale, they did observe extensive atherosclerotic changes with ulceration and thrombi in the anterior descending coronary artery and aorta.

Cowan (1966) described the pathologic findings in fifty-five pilot whales grounded in a Newfoundland "catch." In the myocardium, he found these three types of lesions: focal inflammation and scarring (20 to 25 percent of animals), basophilic degeneration of myocardial fibers (60 percent of animals), and sarcocystic infestation (8 percent of animals). Fibrous intimal plaques were noted in the coronary arteries and aorta of about 20 percent of the animals. The degree of intimal involvement, however, was minimal, and there were no complicated plaques.

Filaroid worms are found commonly in the hearts of seals and sea lions. In the harbor seal and California sea lion, these nematodes have been identified as *Dipetalonema spirocauda* (Taylor *et al.*, 1961). Fox reported finding fibrinous pericarditis in a California sea lion (1923) and unspecified degenerative and inflammatory cardiac lesions in pinnipeds (1921). Recently, Stout (1969) found lesions which resemble early proliferative atherosclerosis of man in aortas of California sea lions and harbor seals. In addition, aortitis (Kelly and Jensen, 1960) and spontaneous arterial lesions (Prathap *et al.*, 1966) have been described in pinnipeds.

URINARY SYSTEM

The basic mammalian renal microstructure is altered in Cetacea and Pinnipedia by the subdivision of the kidney into many separate lobules or reniculi. Each reniculus is a complete renal unit in miniature, possessing a separate cortex, medulla, and medullary pyramid, and a private calyx

(Figs. 5–48, 5–49). The complete kidney is made up of many such reniculi (less than a hundred in the Gangetic porpoise (Slijper, 1958) to several thousand in the fin whale, according to Beauregard and Boulart (1882)), separated only by thin connective tissue septae (Fig. 5–50). In each reniculus, the cortex completely encompasses the medulla, thereby greatly increasing the total cortical surface area. The cortical thickness in each reniculus is less than that of the human kidney, measuring about 2 mm or roughly six layers of glomerulae. In the larger gray whale, the cortical

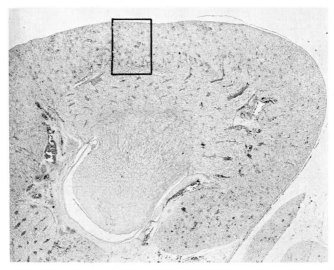

Figure 5–48. Kidney reniculus of the Atlantic bottlenosed porpoise. The cetacean and pinniped kidney is made up of several hundred such reniculi, each of which represents a separate, complete renal unit with cortex, medulla, and individual papillae. The area within the box is seen under higher magnification in the next figure. (H and E, ×10)

thickness is still only about 4 mm. Glomerulae do not differ appreciably in size and cellularity from those in man. The macula densa portion of the juxtaglomerular apparatus is easily discernible, but the juxtaglomerular cells are no more conspicuous than in healthy humans (Fig. 5–51). Proximal and distal tubules, collecting ducts, and renal vessels are essentially identical in appearance to those in man. A discontinuous coarse band of connective tissue containing a few smooth muscle fibers runs along the corticomedullary junction on the medullary side of the arcuate vessels (Fig. 5–52). Cave and Aumonier (1962) conferred upon this fibromuscular band the fanciful name of intrarenicular sporta perimedullaris musculosa. Its functional significance is unknown, although these investigators (Cave and Aumonier, 1961) suggested that the sporta has a "milking" action on

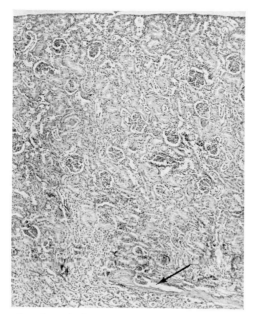

Figure 5–49. Area outlined with box in Figure 5–48. The glomerular and tubular structure is quite similar to that in man. An arcuate artery (arrow) traverses the reniculus at the corticomedullary junction. (H and E, ×75)

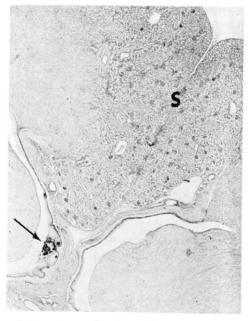

Figure 5–50. Kidney of the Atlantic bottlenosed porpoise. Two adjacent reniculi are separated by a narrow connective tissue septum (S). Focal calcium deposition (arrow) is present in the transitional epithelial lining of one calyx. (H and E, ×25)

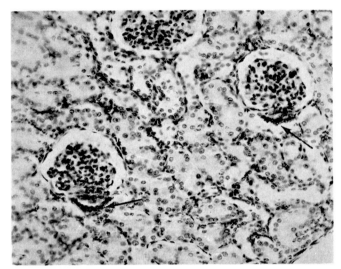

Figure 5–51. Kidney of an Atlantic bottlenosed porpoise. In the juxtaglomerular zone, the lamina densa (arrows) is particularly well seen. There does not, however, appear to be an overabundance of juxtaglomerular cells. (H and E, ×250)

the ducts of Bellini. This structure is not found in pinniped or human kidneys.

There is no significant difference in the renal histology between marine or freshwater porpoises or between the one species of Mystacoceti that we

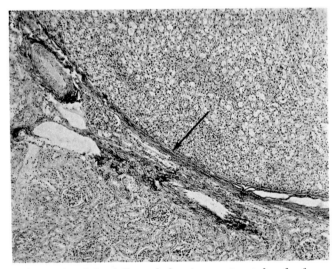

Figure 5–52. Kidney of a false killer whale. A prominent band of connective tissue (arrow) surrounds the renicular pyramid at the corticomedullary junction. This fibrous tissue extends from the ureteric calyx and runs near to but apparently separate from the arcuate vessels. This structure has been called the *intrarenicular sporta perimedullaris musculosa*. Its functional significance is unknown. (H and E, ×75)

have examined (gray whale) and the Pinnipedia (except for lack of a sporta). It would be of immense interest to compare the juxtaglomerular cell granularity and tubular lining cell ultrastructure of porpoises living in fresh and salt water and to compare the effect upon these structures of changes to salt or fresh water, respectively.

According to Harrison and Tomlinson (1956), all venous drainage in the pinniped kidney is by way of a stellate plexus on the cortical surface rather than, as in most other mammals, via veins which accompany arteries in the internal kidney. Two routes of venous return are available in cetaceans. One is peripheral, similar to that in most Pinnipedia, and the other is central, as in most mammals. According to Cave and Aumonier (1967), certain species (Atlantic bottlenosed porpoise, long-beaked dolphin, harbor porpoise) mainly utilize the intrinsic or central route, while other species (sperm whale) utilize the extrinsic route and yet others (beluga) use both pathways equally (also see Chap. 4).

The calyces, renal pelvis, ureter, and bladder of the cetaceans and pinnipeds are lined by a nonkeratinized transitional epithelium about six cells in average thickness. Occasional epithelial cells contain mucous droplets. The submucosa of the urinary bladder has parallel lamellae of loose connective tissue, and the muscularis is composed of fascicles of smooth muscle which run in a generally circular direction (Fig. 5–53) and do not show the same thickness or degree of multidirectionality as seen in the human bladder.

We observed surprisingly little renal disease in pinnipeds and cetaceans.

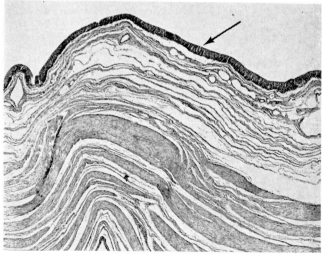

Figure 5–53. Urinary bladder of the Atlantic bottlenosed porpoise. Transitional epithelium (arrow) lines the inner surface. The loose-textured walls are composed largely of concentric smooth muscle layers. (H and E, ×40)

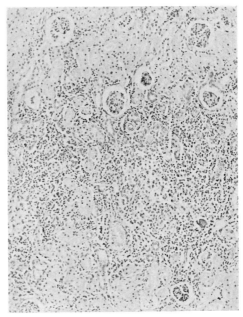

Figure 5–54. Kidney of a Steller's sea lion. An interstitial focus of chronic inflammation with normal parenchyma adjacent to it. (H and E, ×125)

In an Atlantic bottlenosed porpoise, calcific debris was embedded in the calyceal mucosa without inflammatory change, and a Steller's sea lion had a diffuse interstitial chronic inflammatory infiltrate of nonspecific nature (Fig. 5–54). We encountered one instance of acute necrotizing cystitis in an Atlantic bottlenosed porpoise (Fig. 5–55). Necropsy of several adult

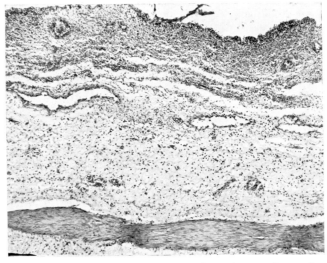

Figure 5–55. Acute cystitis of the urinary bladder of an Atlantic bottlenosed porpoise. The epithelial lining is denuded and is the site of an acute inflammatory reaction. (H and E, ×20)

Atlantic bottlenosed porpoises dying from a disease characterized by massive liver degeneration revealed greenish-brown stones, measuring approximately 0.3 x 0.5 cm, in the calyces and calyceal branches of the ureter. Since the calyces were not dilated and the renal tissue was histologically normal, these stones were apparently not causing any obstruction. Similar stones were also found in the collecting ducts of the kidneys of a twelve-year-old male Atlantic bottlenosed porpoise which died of a clostridial myositis. Here, too, the stones appeared to be incidental. Another finding was an ectopic adrenal on the kidney of an aged California sea lion (Fig. 5–56). Fox (1923) reported finding chronic interstitial nephritis in this species.

A study of two thousand whales flensed at Saldanha Bay, South Africa, revealed kidney pathology in only two whales (Bryde's whales) (Uys and Best, 1966). No parasites were found in these lesions. There has been a report of arteriosclerotic changes in the kidney of a fin whale diagnosed

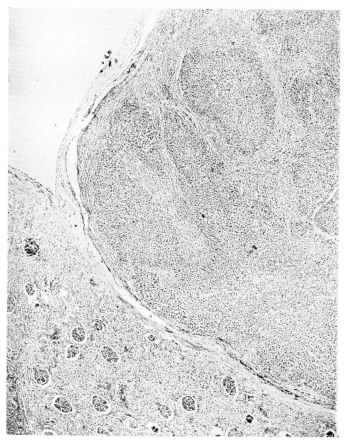

Figure 5–56. Ectopic adrenal gland of the California sea lion. The adrenal tissue is enclosed within the capsule of the kidney. There were no evident clinical signs of adrenal abnormality in this animal. (H and E, ×35)

as having "granuloma malignum" (Stolk, 1962). Miller and Ridgway
(1963) found a renal abscess in the kidney of a recently captured Pacific
white-striped porpoise, and Addison (1950) discovered a renal abscess as
part of a generalized septic disease in an immature fin whale.

DIGESTIVE SYSTEM

The structures and organs to be considered in this section include the
intestinal tract from mouth to anus, the liver, and the pancreas. Like
ruminants, cetaceans have a compartmentalized stomach (see Chap. 4)
while pinnipeds are monogastric. In the Pacific white-sided porpoise, for
example, we recognize a forestomach which histologically resembles the
esophagus, a fundic stomach which is glandular, and a connecting stomach
which empties into the pylorus. Beyond the pylorus is the duodenal
ampulla. The intestinal tract of one Pacific white-sided porpoise was
studied in detail. Sections were taken surgically at one foot intervals
throughout the entire 10 m length of bowel while the animal was under
anesthesia. In addition, a biopsy of the second or parietal stomach (also
main stomach or fundic stomach) was prepared for electron microscopy.

The cetacean tongue is entirely smooth surfaced, without papillae or
taste buds. Papillae have, however, been reported in Irrawaddy River
dolphins and in the gangetic dolphin (Sonntag, 1922). The tongue of the
beluga has been described in detail by Kleynenberg, *et al.* (1964). In
the tongue of porpoises, the squamous mucosa is moderately thick (0.8
to 1.0 mm) and covered by a layer of flattened parakeratotic cells, five or
six cells deep. The submucosa is anchored by well-developed rete pegs
which interdigitate with submucosal papillae. Numerous veins and aterioles
are present in the submucosa. The anterior region of the tongue is free
of glands, but tubuloalveolar glands and ducts are present at the base of
the tongue (Figs. 5–57, 5–58). Nerves lie in close proximity to the
glandular lobules and are generally more prominent at the tongue base
than in the anterior tongue. The musculature, as in man, consists of interlacing fascicles of skeletal muscle cells intersecting each other more or less
at slight angles.

In the sea lion, the tongue is more like that of man, containing numerous
mucous glands, papillae, and taste buds at the base (Fig. 5–59). Some
lymphoid nodules also appear at the base of the tongue (lingual tonsils).
Kubota (1968) described the tongue of the northern fur seal as having
vallate papillae, few fungiform papillae, but no foliate papillae.

Gut-associated lymphocytes (e.g. Peyer's patches) are by no means
lacking in Cetacea. In the oropharynx of the Atlantic bottlenosed porpoise,
tonsil-like lymphoid nodules with germinal centers lie in immediate

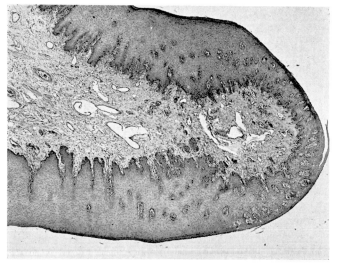

Figure 5–57. Tip of tongue (sagittal section) of an Atlantic bottlenosed porpoise. (H and E, ×35)

juxtaposition to invaginated crypts of squamous mucosa (Fig. 5–60). Submucosal lymphoid nodules are present in the pyloric stomach, in a short segment of small intestine about 5 m distal to the pylorus, and in the terminal colon. In the lamina propria of both the small and large

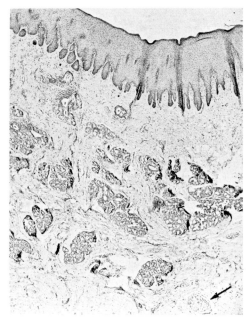

Figure 5–58. Tongue base of an Atlantic bottlenosed porpoise. This view shows the dorsal surface and submucosal glands. Nerves (arrow) are seen in close proximity to the glands. Note the absence of papillae and taste buds. (H and E, ×35)

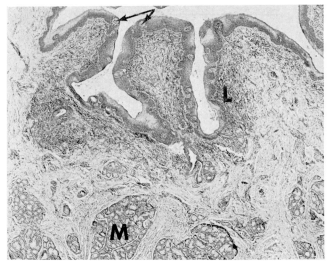

Figure 5–59. Tongue base of a California sea lion. Features to be noted include taste buds (arrows) along the surface of the papillae, submucosal lymphocytic aggregations (L), and mucous glands (M). (H and E, ×35)

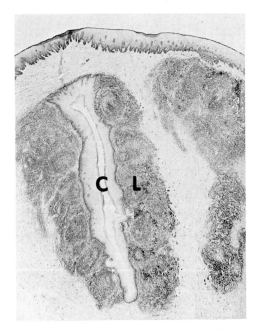

Figure 5–60. Tonsil of an Atlantic bottlenosed porpoise. Invaginated crypts (C) of squamous mucosa are encased by dense nodular lymphoid masses (L). (H and E, ×20)

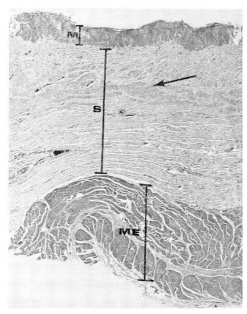

Figure 5–61. Distal esophagus of an Amazon River porpoise. (M) Squamous mucosa, (S) Submucosa, (ME) Muscularis externa. The arrow points to smooth muscle bundles which belong to the muscularis mucosa. Note the absence of glands. (Trichrome, ×20)

bowels, from pyloric stomach to anus, there are numerous diffusely distributed lymphocytes, plasma cells, eosinophils, and globular leukocytes. Lymphocytes are frequently seen transgressing the mucosal lining. The odontocetes that we studied lack a cecum and appendix. The seals and sea lions, by contrast, have both cecum and appendix which are the site of prominent lymphoid nodularity.

The esophagus in the porpoise is devoid of submucosal glands. The squamous mucosa is slightly thinner than that over the tongue (Fig. 5–61). A thick muscularis mucosa consisting of a number of longitudinal smooth muscle bundles runs from midesophagus to pylorus. In the sea lion and seal, in contrast to the porpoise, the entire esophagus is richly endowed with mucous glands (Fig. 5–62).

As in man, the outer esophageal wall of cetaceans and pinnipeds is composed of several tangentially oriented layers of skeletal muscle in the upper third, giving rise gradually in the middle third to an inner circular and outer longitudinal smooth muscle layer. Throughout the intestinal tract, the myenteric nerve plexi seem particularly prominent.

The first subdivision of the cetacean stomach (the forestomach) is lined by a keratinized, thick (1 to 1.5 mm in porpoises) squamous mucosa thrown up into large folds (Fig. 5–63). The muscularis mucosa is

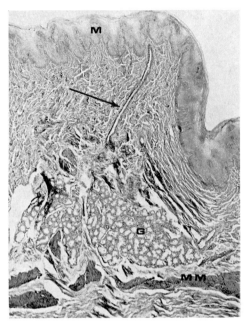

Figure 5–62. Distal esophagus of the California sea lion. (M) Squamous mucosa, (G) Esophageal gland, (Arrow) Duct from gland, (MM) Muscularis mucosa. (Trichrome, ×20)

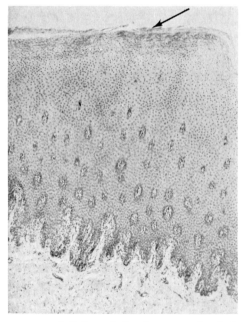

Figure 5–63. Squamous mucosal lining of the forestomach of the Atlantic bottlenosed porpoise. The thick squamous mucosa is covered with a flattened layer of keratin scales (arrow). No glands are present in the submucosa. (H and E, ×75)

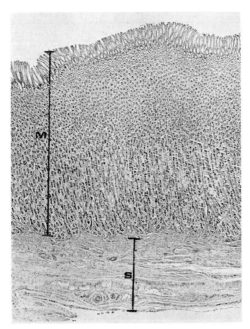

Figure 5–64. Fundic stomach of an Atlantic bottlenosed porpoise. The fundic mucosa (M) is typical in appearance. Though not evident, muscle bundles (the muscularis mucosa) run immediately beneath the mucosa. The submucosa (S) consists of a connective tissue matrix which contains vessels and nerves. The muscularis externa is not shown here. (H and E, ×25)

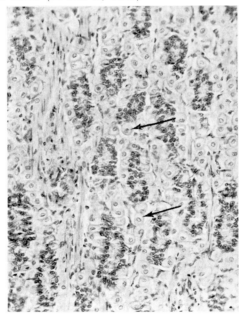

Figure 5–65. Fundic stomach of an Atlantic bottlenosed porpoise. Light pink stainin parietal cells (arrows) are abundant. These cells tend to lie peripherally to the darker staining chief cells which are closer to the lumina of the gastric glands. (H and E, ×250)

particularly thick in the forestomach and is interspersed with collagen. The forestomach is completely devoid of glands.

Gastric glands occur in the second subdivision of the porpoise stomach. The mucous membrane is thick (1 to 3 mm) and contains closely packed, simple, branched tubular glands oriented perpendicular to the surface (Fig. 5–64). As in man and other mammals, three cell types can be identified with hematoxylin and eosin stain. These are the mucous secreting neck cells, pepsinogen-secreting chief or zymogenic cells, and (HCl) secreting parietal or oxyntic cells. Parietal cells seem relatively abundant in both the porpoise and the sea lion (Fig. 5–65). The abundance of parietal

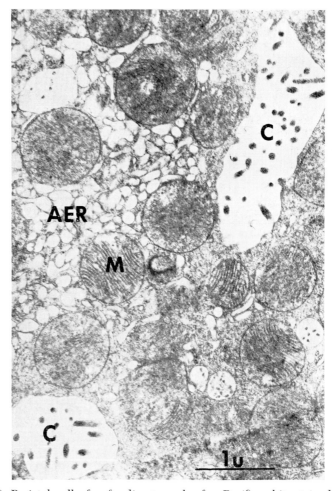

Figure 5–66. Parietal cell of a fundic stomach of a Pacific white-striped porpoise. A few microvilli protrude into the intracellular canaliculus (C). The mitochrondria (M) are spherical and uniform with abundant, densely compact cristae. The labyrinthine agranular endoploxmic reticulum (AER) gives the appearance in tissue section of vesicles and short tubules. (×29,250)

cells in the porpoise has been noted by other workers (Harrison *et al.*, 1966).

Under the elctron microscope, the parietal cells (Figs. 5–66, 5–67, 5–68) are characterized by an extensive tubular labyrinth of smooth endoplasmic reticulum, numerous uniform oval mitchondria with densely packed cristae, and intracellular canaliculi. The microvilli protruding into the canaliculi seem to be somewhat blunt and sparse compared to man (Lillibridge, 1964) and certain other mammals and to amphibia (Ito, 1961). This feature was also noted by other investigators (Johnson and Harrison, 1969). This observation may be related to the functional activity of these

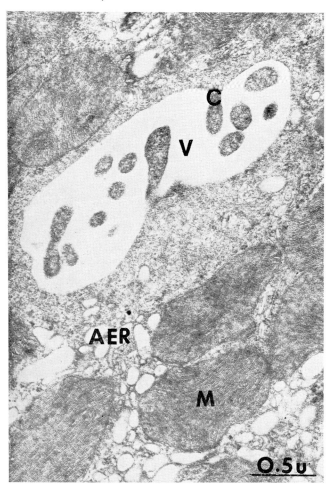

Figure 5–67. Parietal cells of the fundic stomach of a Pacific white-striped porpoise. A few blunt microvilli (V) extend into an intracellular canaliculus. Mitochondria (M) contain numerous tightly compact cristae. The labyrinthine agranular endoplasmic reticulum (AER) is vesicular and tubular in appearance and closely approaches the canaliculus. (×47,250)

cells at the moment of biopsy (Seder and Friedman, 1961). The secretory product of parietal cells is apparently transported via the channels of agranular endoplasmic reticulum to the canaliculi and then to the lumen of the gastric gland.

Electron microscopic study of the chief cells (Fig. 5–69) reveals a fine structure similar to that in man. The cytoplasmic apices contain a collection of membrane-bound vesicles containing the secretory (zymogen or pepsinogen) granules. The base of the chief cells is replete with ribosome-coated endoplasmic reticulum (rough or granular endoplasmic reticulum), the site of protein synthesis. The Golgi apparatus, a system of smooth

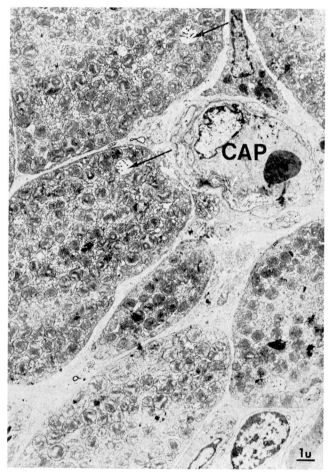

Figure 5–68. Parietal cells of fundic stomach of a Pacific white-striped porpoise. Portions of six parietal cells surround a capillary (CAP). The cytoplasm of these HCl-secreting cells is characterized by numerous mitochrondria, extensively vesiculated agranular endoplasmic reticulum, and intracellular canaliculi (arrows). (×6,750)

membranous cisterns involved in the "packaging" of the secretory protein, pepsinogen, lies in the supranuclear zone. Focal areas of cytoplasmic degradation give rise to membranous profiles (myelin figures), a commonly observed feature in both parietal (Winborn and Bochman, 1968) and chief cells.

In the third subdivision or pyloric stomach, the mucosa consists solely of mucous type cells. Lymphoid nodules appear in the submucosa, and the lamina propria from this point onward contains many lymphocytes, plasma cells, and eosinophils (Fig. 5–70).

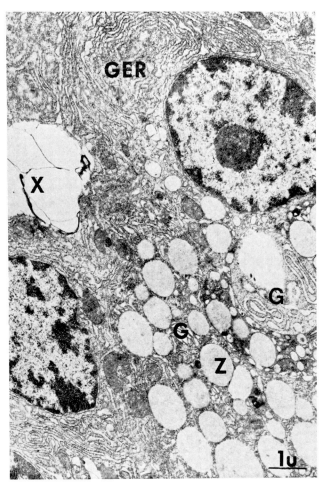

Figure 5–69. Chief cells of the fundic stomach–Pacific white-striped porpoise. The cytoplasm of these protein (pepsinogen)-secreting cells contains an apical accumulation of pepsinogen-secreting granules (Z). In the basilar position of the cells, an extensive network of granular endoplasmic reticulum (GER) is present. Portions of the Golgi zone are seen at (G). Membranous debris is present in areas of focal cytoplasmic degradation (X). (×14,175)

Mammals of the Sea

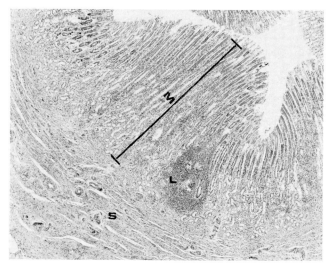

Figure 5–70. Pyloric stomach of an Atlantic bottlenosed porpoise. The mucosa in this third region of the stomach is characterized by rather straight glands whose cells are of the mucous secreting type. At this level, lymph nodules (L) and diffuse white cell infiltrates begin to appear in the lamina propria and submucosa. (M) Mucosa, (S) Submucosa. (H and E, ×35)

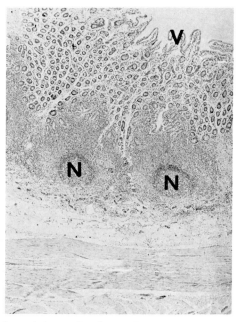

Figure 5–71. Ileum of an Atlantic bottlenosed porpoise. Only at this site, 5 m distal to the pylorus, were lymphoid nodules (N) detected in the small bowel. The mucosal villi (C) are rather short. (H and E, ×35)

The bowel of the Pacific white-striped porpoise from pylorus to about 30 cm above the anus is a tube of uniform caliber without cecum or appendix. According to Slijper (1962), the gangetic dolphin and the Mystacoceti possess a cecum. The mucosa throughout the bowel is similar to the mucosa found in the small bowel of man (Fig. 5–71). Although villi are virtually absent in the proximal duodenum, they begin to appear at a distance of about 30 cm below the pylorus and extend distally to the relatively short (e.g., approximately 30 cm) colon where the surface then becomes flattened resembling the large bowel of man (Fig. 5–72). It is interesting that Kleynenberg *et al.* (1964) reported finding an absence of typical villi in the intestine of the beluga. Plica circulares are well developed (Fig. 5–73) throughout the bowel. Only two types of mucosal cells can be identified with hematoxylin and eosin stain: absorptive cells with a striated border and distended mucous goblet cells. Brunner's glands are lacking in the duodenum. Peyer's patches are occasionally seen. Paneth cells are completely absent in both porpoises and sea lions. In the terminal 15 to 30 cm of colon, goblet cells occur almost exclusively along with numerous lymphoid nodules.

Breakdown of the food into smaller digestible fragments occurs in the

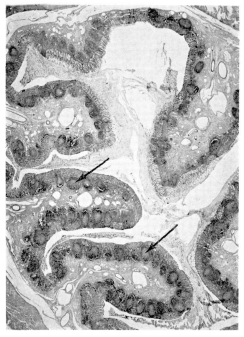

Figure 5–72. Terminal colon of an Atlantic bottlenosed porpoise. There is a plethora of lymphoid nodules and germinal centers (arrows) lying in the submucosa. This section is taken about 30 cm anterior to the anal-rectal junction. (H and E, ×9)

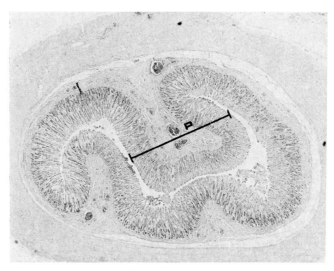

Figure 5–73. Small intestine of an Amazon River porpoise. The plica circulares (P) result from an infolding of the intestinal mucosa and submucosa. (H and E, ×20)

forestomach, where the inner wall is appropriately thick and protected by a skin-like layer of keratin. Enzymatic digestion takes place in the fundic stomach, which is endowed with abundant HCl- and pepsinogen-secreting cells, and in the small intestine. The fact that only the last 30 cm of colon resembles the large bowel or rectum of man implies that there is probably little intestinal storage of nondigestible residue. It appears that

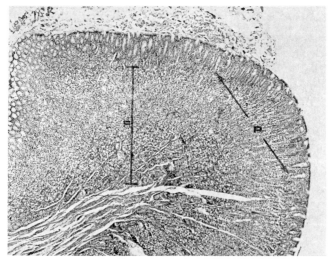

Figure 5–74. Stomach of a California sea lion. The fundic stomach contains three cell types. These are the mucous-secreting cells of the gastric pit (P) area and the chief and parietal cells of the fundic glands (F). (H and E, ×35)

Cetacea, as other mammals, possess a fully developed gut-associated lymphatic system as part of their immunologic defenses.

The pinniped stomach, a single chamber, can be divided into cardiac, fundic, and pyloric portions. It contains the same types of cells and glands as those in other monogastric mammals (Fig. 5–74). The small and large intestines of the pinniped species are also basically similar to those of land mammals. Villi begin in the proximal duodenum and terminate at the cecum (Fig. 5–75). We found Brunner's glands in the duodenum of an elephant seal (Fig. 5–76) but did not find them in the California sea lion.

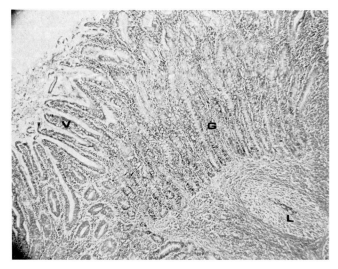

Figure 5–75. Distal ileum of the California sea lion. At this location the cells of the villi (V) and intestinal glands (G) are, to a large extent, of the mucuos secreting type. A lymph nodule (L) is seen in the submucosa. (Giemsa, ×50)

The mucosa from the cecum distally is composed of straight tubular glands whose cells are entirely of the goblet type. Lymph nodules in the sub-mucosa and lymphocytes and plasma cells in the lamina propria are numerous (Figs. 5–77, 5–78).

Incidental Pathology

One might anticipate that parasitic infestation would be a common finding in the intestinal tract. Indeed, roundworm attachment to the mucosa of the parietal stomach with associated inflammation was noted in all adult pelagic pilot whales examined by Cowan (1966). We observed worm infestation in captive Cetacea much less frequently. This lack of infestation can be attributed at least partially to the routine use of anthelminthics in

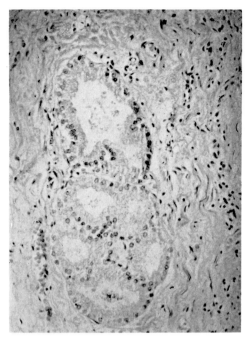

Figure 5–76. Brunner's glands of the elephant seal. These glands were found in the submucosa of the proximal duodenum. (H and E, ×160)

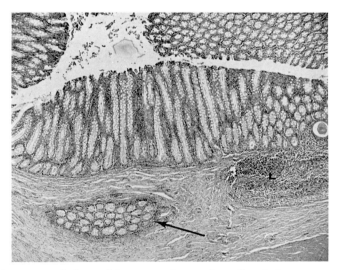

Figure 5–77. Cecum of the California sea lion. The cells of the intestinal glands are of the goblet type; the arrow points to a cross section of intestinal glands which appear to (but do not actually) lie within the submucosa. A lymph nodule (L) extends from the submucosa into the mucosa. (H and E, ×35)

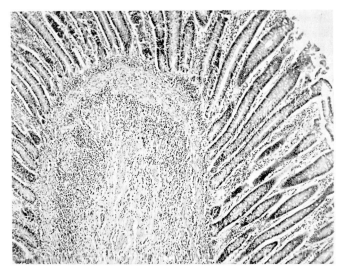

Figure 5–78. Colon of a Steller's sea lion. The glands (crypts of Lieberkuhn) contain large numbers of goblet cells, and the crypt fundi extend all the way to the submucosa. In this section, the white cells of the submucosa are diffusely distributed rather than formed into a nodule. (H and E, ×75)

captive cetaceans and also to the feeding of frozen fish in which some parasites have become inactivated. Figure 5–79 shows several nematodes imbedded in the mucosa of the pyloric stomach of an Atlantic bottlenosed porpoise without an inflammatory response. A fluke, *Braunina cordiformis*, is seen within the fundic stomach of another Atlantic bottlenosed porpoise. The parasite has become well walled off by a fibrous capsule (Fig. 5–80). We have seen nonparasitic ulceration of the esophagus (Fig. 5–81) and first stomach compartment in both captive and stranded small odontocetes; this occurrence has also been reported by others (Geraci *et al.*, 1966). Gastroenteritis and gastrointestinal foreign bodies in Cetacea are occasionally found at necropsy (Stolk, 1953a; Brown *et al.*, 1960; Amemiya, 1962; Ridway, 1965; Nakajima *et al.*, 1966).

Another incidental finding in an Atlantic bottlenosed porpoise was a dilated, pus-filled epithelial-lined sac at the anal-rectal junction, accompanied by chronic inflammation and focal squamous metaplasia of the gland mucosa (Fig. 5–82).

We necropsied two young California sea lions that died from peritonitis subsequent to perforation of an intestinal ulcer. One of these animals had been in captivity for over a year and the other was a feral animal that died on shore. No parasites were found in association with either of these ulcers. We have also seen crypt abscesses in the intestine (Fig. 5–83). Gastroenteritis and ulceration of parasitic and nonparasitic origin in pinnipeds has

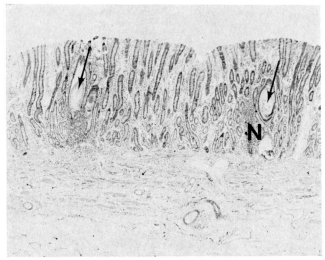

Figure 5–79. Worms in mucosa of pyloric stomach of an Atlantic bottlenosed porpoise. Roundworms (arrows) are present within the mucosal glands. There is no inflammation. Lymphoid nodules (N) are normally found in this segment of the stomach. (H and E, ×35)

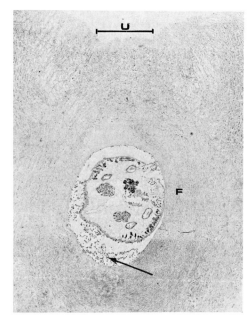

Figure 5–80. *Braunina cordiformis* in the fundic stomach of an Atlantic bottlenosed porpoise. The small objects (arrow) next to the fluke are ova. The parasite is well walled off by fibrous tissue (F) which extends up to the stomach lumen and forms a healed ulcer (U). (H and E, ×25)

Figure 5-81 Esophageal ulcer of an Atlantic bottlenosed porpoise. Although difficult to identify at this magnification, there is some inflammatory cell infiltration in the submucosa adjacent to the area of ulceration. (H and E, ×17)

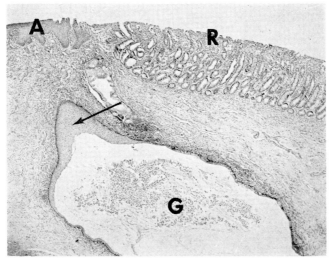

Figure 5–82. Anal-rectal junction of an Atlantic bottlenosed porpoise. This section is taken of the junction of anus (A) and rectum (R). A dilated perirectal sac (G) exhibits acute inflammatory cells in the lumen and a focus of squamous metaplasia (arrow) near its ductular outlet. (H and E, ×35)

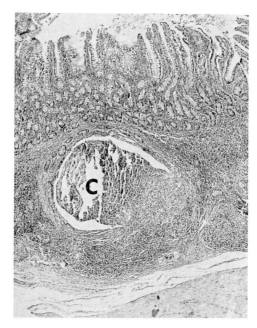

Figure 5–83. Crypt abscess of the ileum of the California sea lion. A dilated mucosal crypt (C) filled with acute inflammatory cells lies in the submucosa of the ileum surrounded by normal nodular lymphoid elements. (H and E, ×35)

been reported by others (Fox, 1923; Schroeder *et al.*, 1935; Herman, 1941; Keyes, 1965; and Hubbard, 1968).

Liver and Pancreas

The microscopic appearance of the pancreas (Fig. 5–84) in cetaceans and pinnipeds is generally similar to that of man. We frequently noted a paucity of islets in cetacean pancreas. One investigator (Hill, 1926) reported numerous islets in the pancreas of a porpoise, but they were quite small (only a few cells). In the pancreas of a Pacific white-sided porpoise, we observed helminths imbedded in the pancreatic duct with associated fibrosis and chronic inflammation (Fig. 5–85).

A striking feature in the liver of certain cetaceans is the presence of prominent muscular sphincters in the portal vein branches (Figs. 5–86, 5–87). These sphincters are observed in Atlantic bottlenosed porpoises, common dolphins, harbor porpoises, and Hawaiian spinning dolphins but are not noticable in the Amazon River porpoise, the Dall porpoise, the beluga, the gray whale, or the sea lion. They possibly contribute to the pooling of blood in venous reservoirs during prolonged diving. In the California sea lion, the biliary ductules in the portal tracts are lined with

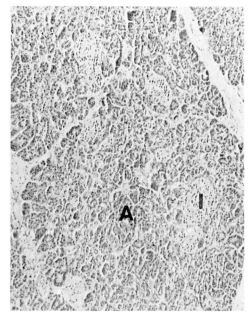

Figure 5–84. Pancreas of an Atlantic bottlenosed porpoise. The exocrine acinar (A) and endocrine islet tissue (I) are normal in appearance. (H and E, ×125)

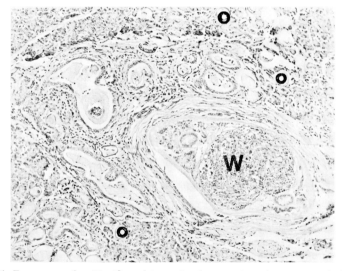

Figure 5–85. Pancreas of a Pacific white-striped porpoise. A parasitic helminth (W) is obstructing the pancreatic duct, resulting in small ductular proliferation and inspissated secretion, and periductular fibrosis. Parasitic ova (O) are embedded in the pancreatic parenchyma. There is only a slight chronic inflammatory response. (H and E, ×125)

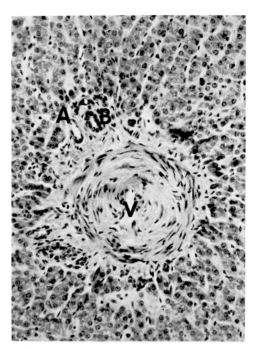

Figure 5–86. Liver portal tract of an Atlantic bottlenosed porpoise. The portal venous branch (V) bears a prominent circular smooth muscle sphincter. In comparison, the adjacent bile ductule (B) and hepatic arterial branch (A) are relatively inconspicuous. (H and E, ×250)

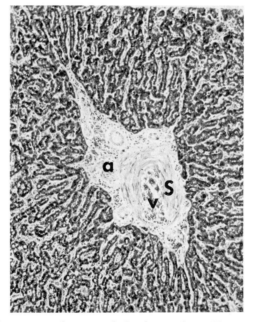

Figure 5–87. Portal venous sphincter of the liver of an Hawaiian spinning dolphin. In this liver portal triad, the portal venous branch (V) is asymmetrically encased with a prominent, thick, circular smooth muscle bundle (S). The hepatic artery branch (A), by contrast, is quite small. (H and E, ×125)

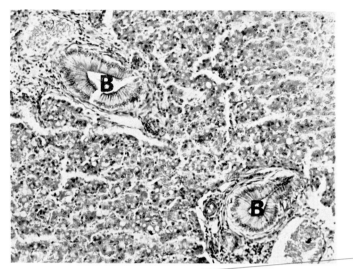

Figure 5–88. Liver and portal tract of a California sea lion. Unusually tall columnar epithelium lines the biliary ductules (B) in the portal space. This has been a characteristic feature in the liver of the California sea lion. (H and E, ×150)

unusually tall mucous-secreting columnar cells (Fig. 5–88). The liver of one Amazon River porpoise (Fig. 5–89) showed a pattern of bile stasis suggesting extrahepatic biliary obstruction most likely due to roundworm infestation. Biliary stones have, to our knowledge, never been found in the

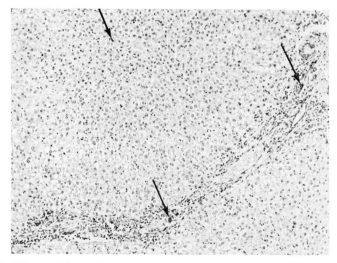

Figure 5–89. Liver with cholestasis of an Amazon River porpoise. Bile plugs are noted in the biliary ductules within the portal tract (arrows) as well as in the biliary canaliculi between liver cells in the adjacent lubule. The portal tract is fibrotic and infiltrated by acute and chronic inflammatory cells. A slight degree of fatty change is present. This picture is probably due to the extra hepatic obstruction of bile flow. (H and E, ×125)

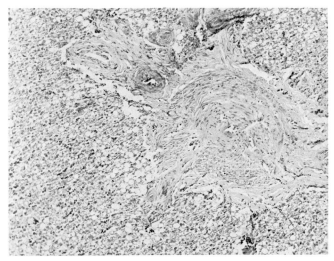

Figure 5–90. Liver of an Atlantic bottlenosed porpoise. This section, which includes a portal triad containing a venous sphincter, shows marked fatty metamorphosis of hepatocytes. (H and E, ×125)

cetacean common bile duct. Perhaps this can be attributed to the absence of a gall bladder in these animals. A slight degree of fatty change in the liver is a relatively common necropsy finding in sick Cetacea, probably due in part to poor nourishment. Cockrill (1960b) described the storage of fats in the liver of pregnant Cetacea.

We recently studied five Atlantic bottlenosed porpoises that died in an epidemic fashion within a period of several weeks. These were adult

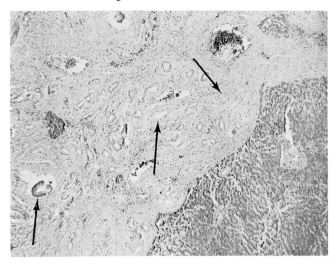

Figure 5–91. Liver of a California sea lion. Marked portal fibrosis and bile duct (arrows) proliferation (biliary hyperplasia) is seen throughout the liver. (H and E, ×100)

animals kept in the same tank. The only abnormal necropsy finding was a fatty degeneration of hepatocytes together with limited inflammatory cell infiltration (Fig. 5–90). Bacterial cultures from liver tissue were sterile. The cause of this hepatic pathology has not been determined.

The liver illustrated in Figure 5–91 is from a California sea lion which had performed in an animal act for twelve years and was reported to have had periodic epileptiform convulsions. Liver pathology, including cirrhosis, has been reported in cetaceans (Stolk, 1953b; Stolk, 1954b; Brown *et al.*, 1960; Cockrill, 1960; Uys and Best, 1966; Woodard *et al.*, 1969).

INTEGUMENTARY SYSTEM

The cetacean skin, in constant contact with water, must be uniquely adapted to carry out those functions common to the integument of all animals, such as protection, heat regulation, and sensory perception. In addition, the agile aquatic behavior of Cetacea demands a minimum of frictional resistance and a maximum of body streamlining. We will see how the structure of cetacean skin is modified to fulfill these functional requirements.

Cetacean skin possesses a thick epidermis essentially without hair, accessory glands, or keratin (Fig. 5–92). The thickness of the epidermis varies, depending on species and location sampled. The ventral body wall tends to have the thickest epidermal layer. Giacometti (1967) reported epidermis measuring 3.0 mm thick in the fin whale, and Slijper (1958) reported epidermis approximately 5 to 7 mm in thickness in the larger whales. The cellular strata are rather simplified compared to man. Most of the epidermis is made up of uniform polyhedral prickle cells. Only in the most superficial strata, eight to ten cells in depth, is there some flattening of cells, giving the appearance of parakeratosis (Fig. 5–93). The basal or germinative layer is a single cell thick. In pigmented areas, melanin granules are numerous (Fig. 5–94), both in the basal layer and throughout the stratum spinosum. Dendritic-like cells of Langerhans are outlined by their melanin content in the basal portion of the epidermis. Throughout the stratum spinosum the cells often show a clear, distended infranuclear cytoplasm (Fig. 5–95).

A stratum granulosum, stratum lucidum, and nonnucleated, keratinized stratum corneum are absent in the Cetacea. The epidermis is anchored to the underlying dermal connective tissue by uniformly long, moderately thick downward extensions, the rete pegs (Fig. 5–95). Dermal papillae interdigitate in regular fashion with the rete pegs and constitute long longitudinal ridges in the cetacean skin. The papillae extend upward almost four-fifths of the distance to the surface and are covered by a thin epi-

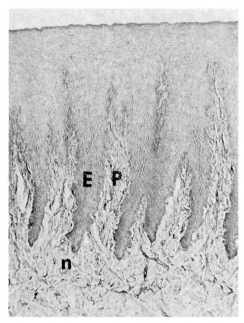

Figure 5–92. Glabrous skin of the ventral midbody of an Amazon River porpoise. At this site the epidermis measures about 1.0 mm in thickness. Characteristic features include alternating long epidermal rete pegs (E) and dermal papillae (P), and an absence of surface keratin. A nerve ending (N) is seen in the superficial dermis. (H and E, ×75)

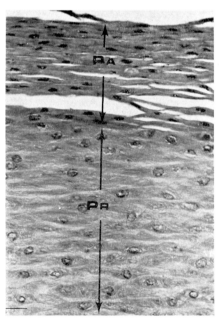

Figure 5–93. Epidermis of the Upper Jaw of an Atlantic bottlenosed porpoise. (PA) Parakeratotic layer, (PR) Prickle cell layer. (H and E, ×225)

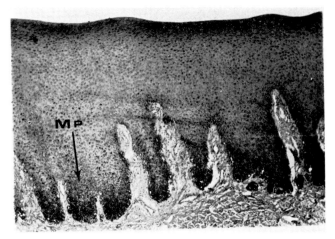

Figure 5–94. Skin of the upper jaw of an Atlantic bottlenosed porpoise. (Mp) Melanin pigmentation. It is most prominent in the lower portion of the epidermis. (H and E, ×50)

dermal layer, 0.1 to 0.3 mm in thickness. Such a complex, serrated interface between dermis and epidermis is characteristic of the smooth (glabrous) skin occurring in the nonhirsute areas of man and animal (Montagna, 1967).

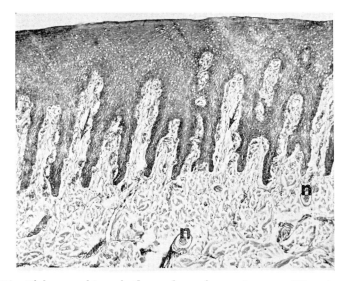

Figure 5–95. Glabrous skin of the vulva of an Amazon River porpoise. The epidermis measures about 0.8 mm in thickness at this site. Note the clear cytoplasm of cells of the stratum spinosum. Long rete pegs interdigitate with dermal papillae extending upward to where they are covered by no more than 0.15 to 0.35 mm of epidermis. Within the papillae lie prominent thin vascular channels (arrows). Nerve endings (N) are observed in the upper dermal layer. (H and E, ×75)

The dermis blends gradually with the adipose layer or blubber. There is no sharp demarcation at this site because fat extends to some extent up to the epidermis and heavy collagen bundles ramify throughout the subcutaneous blubber. Compared to man, the dermal collagen is of a denser, more heavily textured appearance. The dermis is of relatively greater density in the dorsal fins, flippers, and tail flukes than in the body proper. Collagen fiber bundles interlace at more or less right angles in a three-dimensional array (Fig. 5–96). Most of the bundles run parallel or slightly tangential to the surface. Many fine elastic fibers accompany the collagen bundles and extend vertically to the apex of each dermal papilla. Numerous blood vessels and nerve endings also lie in the dermis. The amount of elastin and fat varies among species and the thickness of the subcutaneous blubber increases during the winter (Sokolov, 1962b).

Muscular arterioles and thin-walled venules run parallel to the surface in the superficial and deeper layers of the dermis (Fig. 5–96). A vertically directed thin-walled arteriole runs up the center of each dermal papilla and connects through anastomotic channels with tributary veins on each side.

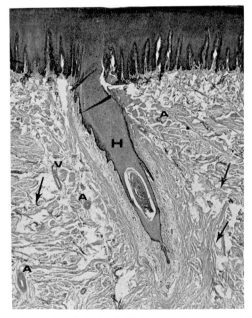

Figure 5–96. Skin and vestigeal hair follicle on the snout of an Atlantic bottle-nosed porpoise. The epidermis is slightly over 1 mm in thickness and the rete pegs are long and fairly sharp. A single vestigeal hair follicle (H) without attached sebaceous glands or smooth muscle is present but there is no mature hair formation. The interlacing bands of dermal collagen (A) (arrows) are permeated by pale adipose cells, small muscular arterioles (AA) and venules (V). (H and E, ×20)

There is a uniquely structured arteriovenous plexus in the tail fluke and flippers. These thick, muscular-walled ventral and dorsal central arteries are surrounded or baffled by a plexus of veins running alongside (Fig. 5–97). In our material, we did not encounter direct communications between these vessels. We observed this structure in a number of species including *Tursiops truncatus, Langenorhynchus obliquidens, Phocoenoides dalli,* and *Delphinus sp.* and suspect that it is present in all Cetacea. These vascular arrangements function in body temperature regulation (Scholander and Schevill 1955; Bel'Kovich 1965). Incidentally, these veins in the tail flukes and flippers serve as most useful sites for venipuncture.

The skin of Cetacea is richly innervated. Numerous nerve endings resembling small, onionskin-like configurations are present in the superficial portion of the dermis, particularly in the jaw region, flukes, vulva, and perineum (Fig 5–95). Special silver staining shows numerous nerve fibrils in the dermis extending up into the epidermis (Palmer and Weddell, 1964). The nerve endings are considered to be largely proprioceptive. One might speculate that sensitivity to hydrodynamic pressure facilitates the delicate body adjustments which allow for minimizing frictional resistance.

As befitting a mammal, a few residual hair follicles arise in the rostral

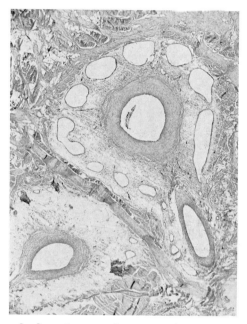

Figure 5–97. Skin and dermal arterial-venous plexus of the tail fluke of an Atlantic bottlenose porpoise. This muscular artery is surrounded by thin venous channels in such a way as to suggest a functional relationship. Direct communication between artery and venules has not been seen but might be found on serial sectioning. (H and E, ×25)

area of all Cetacea (Figs. 5–96, 5–98). We did not find accessory glands associated with these hair follicles. In at least one species, the Amazon River porpoise, hair follicles are relatively well developed and hair shafts are produced. These follicles are well innervated, and Palmer and Weddell (1964) suggest that they act either as "speedometers" or for sensing low-frequency vibrations.

In summary, Cetacea have essentially a nonhirsute, friction-reducing glabrous skin throughout, with no waterproofing or oily superficial covering. Structural modifications permitting temperature homeostasis and low water resistance to swimming are apparent.

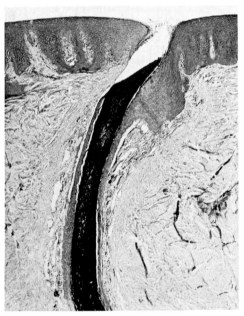

Figure 5–98. Skin of the lower jaw of an Amazon River porpoise. A single residual hair follicle with hair stub is noted. No associated sebaceous or sweat glands are present. (Trichrome, ×30)

In contrast to cetaceans, the pinnipeds are covered with a generous pelage and display glabrous skin only in select areas, as for instance on the ventral surface of the flippers (Fig. 5–99). Where a pelage is present, the epidermis is thin. An outer layer of keratin is present and the epidermal-dermal interface is relatively smooth (Figs. 5–100, 5–101). The dermis contains sebaceous glands and tubular sweat glands. Compared to other mammals, the skin of seals is reported to be highly vascular (Montagna, 1967). A number of investigators have described pinniped integument (Sokolov, 1962a; Montagna and Harrison, 1956; Harrison and Kooyman, 1968).

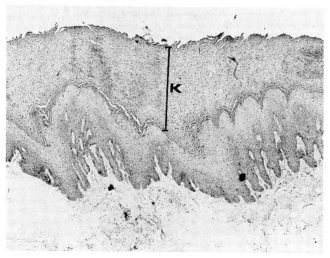

Figure 5-99. Skin of ventral flipper of a California sea lion. In this area of skin, there are no hair follicles or glands, and a thick keratin (K) layer is present. (Giemsa, ×45)

Numerous skin abnormalities, due to parasites, trauma, and microorganisms, occur in marine mammals. There is one report of a dermatomycosis (*Trichophyton sp.*) in a cetacean (Hoshina and Sugiura, 1956). Many of the skin lesions of marine mammals have not been etiologically defined. We have seen two neoplasms in the dermis of California sea lions.

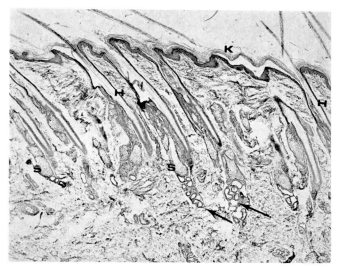

Figure 5-100. Hirsute skin of the lower jaw of a California sea lion. Characteristic human-like features include a thin but keratinized epidermis (K-Keratin layer) and a relatively smooth dermal interface interrupted by numerous hair follicles (H) with associated sebaceous (S) and tubular sweat glands (arrows). (H and E, ×35)

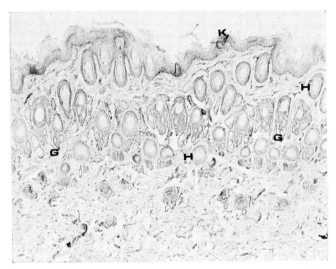

Figure 5–101. Skin of the abdomen of a harbor seal. Numerous hair follicles and associated glands are present, but hair shafts do not protrude through the keratinized epidermis at this particular site. (H and E, ×35)

One was a fibroma from the ventral neck region (Fig. 5–102), and the other was an adenocarcinoma found in both the neck and the lung (Figs. 5–103, 5–104). A dermal fibroma (Stolk, 1953c) and a benign melanotic

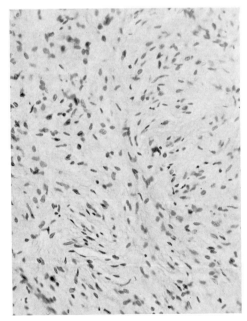

Figure 5–102. Fibroma of neck of a California sea lion. The tumor is composed of uniform fibroblasts with a moderate amount of collagenous stroma. (H and E, ×250)

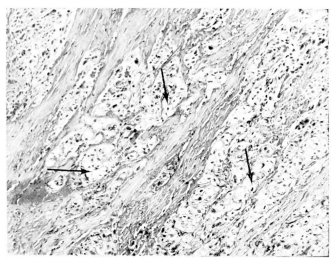

Figure 5–103, Tumor of the neck of a California sea lion. The neoplastic cells (arrows), which are characterized by clear, distended cytoplasm and pyknotic nuclei, can be seen infiltrating muscle. Moderate numbers of mitotic figures are present. (H and E, ×150)

tumor of the lip (Uys and Best, 1966) have been reported in cetaceans. Porpoises in captivity commonly show a variety of skin lesions. One type appears as a pinpoint hole sometimes surrounded by rings, somewhat akin to the appearance of a stone dropping into a still pool of water. This lesion

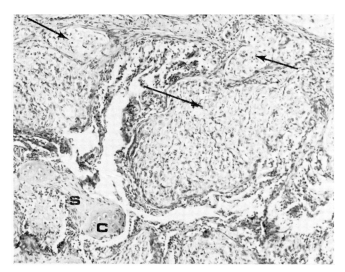

Figure 5–104. Lung of a California sea lion. This lung is from the same animal whose neck tissue is shown in Figure 5–103. Neoplastic cells (arrows) resembling those in the neck can be seen invading lung parenchyma. In the lower left, a bronchiolar cartilage (C) and smooth muscle sphincter (S) are seen, (H and E, ×150)

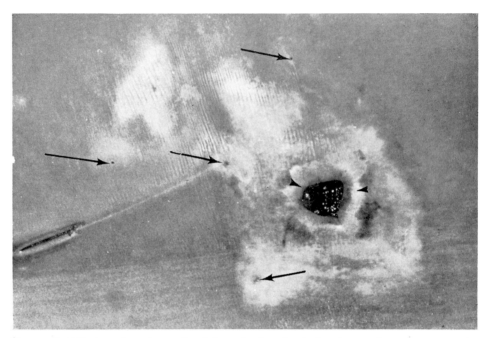

Figure 5–105. An ulcer (arrowheads) and pinpoint holes (arrows) are seen on the skin of an Atlantic bottlenosed porpoise. Depigmentation of the skin frequently occurs in association with these lesions.

may be single or in a group, flat or slightly raised, and sometimes ulcerated (Figs. 5–105, and 5–106). Although it has not been confirmed, we suspect that this particular lesion is of parasitic origin. Numerous small (1 mm) pigmented dots or specklings with an irregular outline sometimes called "tattoos" (Figs. 5–107, 5–108) are occasionally seen in Atlantic bottlenosed porpoises. They do not appear to be pathologically significant, and no causative agent has been identified. Another characteristic skin lesion of porpoises is rhomboid or irregularly outlined plaques thought to be caused by erysipelas. *Erysipelothrix insidiosa* has been recovered from subcutaneous fat in an Atlantic bottlenosed porpoise with erysipelas septicemia and associated cutaneous lesions (Simpson *et al.*, 1958). Similar lesions can sometimes be produced by vaccination against erysipelas. These artificially produced lesions are, in our experience, rather square in outline and sometimes ulcerated. Histologic sections show nonspecific ulceration and inflammation. A skin lesion around the genital openings of Atlantic bottlenosed porpoises, common dolphins, pilot whales, and Dall porpoises (and possibly other species) is caused by a trematode infection. The affected skin has a raised, irregular outline. These lesions are generally self limiting and do not appear to cause the host any particular distress.

Purity and salinity of water (in marine species) are particularly

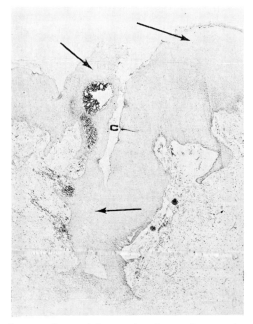

Figure 5–106. Skin lesion of an Atlantic bottlenosed porpoise. The pinpoint holes (see Fig. 5–105) consist of an invaginated crypt (C) formed by epidermis. Within the involved epidermis, necrosis of cells is seen (arrows) and there is vascular congestion. The dermis which surrounds the lesion is also congested and contains some inflammatory cell infiltrates. (H and E, ×35)

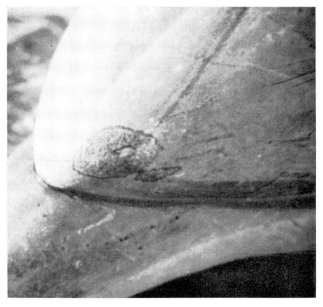

Figure 5–107. Skin lesion of an Atlantic bottlenosed porpoise. This circumscribed, pigmented lesion, is commonly called a "tattoo."

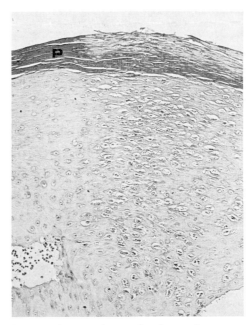

Figure 5–108. Skin lesion of an Atlantic bottlenosed porpoise. Each one of the pinpoint dots seen grossly, is characterized histologically by a focus of epidermal cells with clear cytoplasm and fragmented nuclei. The parakeratotic layer (P) also shows degenerative change. (Trichrome, ×150)

important factors determining integumentary health. It has been demonstrated in the Atlantic bottlenosed porpoise that immersion in fresh water for extended periods of time (up to a month) will cause "ballooning" degeneration of epidermal cells (Maderson, 1967) (Fig. 5–109). This process is usually reversible if the animal is put back into salt water. Ballooning degeneration can also result when sea water is greatly diluted. Ocean water is normally about 3.4 percent salt by volume. When the salt concentration drops below about 1 percent, patchy necrosis and ulceration of the epidermis will result.

Abscesses of the vestigial hair pits on the rostrum of porpoises are frequently seen, particularly where the water is not clean. Abscesses also occur on other parts of the body and can become quite large (3.0 to 4.0 cm across). Often no opening to the outside is seen. If lanced when mature, they contain a center of liquefactive necrosis. Fissures, which may extend quite deeply into the dermis, are occasionally seen around the blowhole of whales and porpoises. These fissures develop gradually, and as they progress, the epidermal edges will become necrotic and an exudate will be produced in the dermal furrow. In the Atlantic bottlenosed porpoise, these areas will also become darkly pigmented. Though it has been suggested that these are due to sunburn, we have seen the condition in animals kept

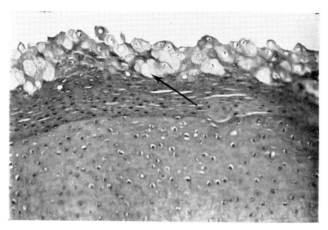

Figure 5–109. Epidermis of the upper jaw of an Atlantic bottlenosed porpoise. Note ballooning of cells (arrow) of the parakeratotic layer. This animal had been in fresh water for three weeks. (H and E, ×170)

exclusively in covered areas. The condition is seen in those animals which tend to remain for long periods of time in a resting position with their blowhole area out of the water and most likely results from drying. It has also been seen in killer whales maintained in fairly shallow tanks.

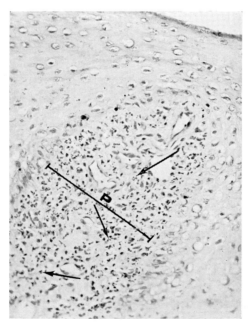

Figure 5–110. Skin lesion of an Atlantic bottlenosed porpoise. A very common lesion of the skin of porpoises, particularly when kept in water which is contaminated, appears grossly as small elevated mounds (1 to 4 cm diameter) or as ulcers. Histologically, one of the first changes noted is inflammatory cell infiltration of the dermal papillae (P). Neutrophils (arrows) are particularly prominent. (H and E, ×250)

Porpoises kept in markedly impure water frequently suffer from septic skin lesions (Fig. 5–110). The lesions often arise from small cuts or abrasions and fail to heal because of opportunistic bacteria which thrive on porpoise flesh. We have cultured a variety of bacteria, including *Staphylococcus, Streptococcus, Proteus, Pseudomonas,* and coliforms, from these sores. The significance of these bacteria as primary etiologic agents is questionable. Common sites of ulceration include the edges of flukes, flippers, and fins, and the tip of the rostrum. In some instances, entire tips of tail flukes and triangular blocks of tissue from edges of fins and flukes become necrotic for no obvious reason and drop off (or have to be surgically removed). The shape of these necrotic areas suggests a vascular infarct, though the pathogenesis has not been determined. One Atlantic bottlenosed porpoise kept at the Marine Bioscience Facility had recurrent inflammatory and ulcerative episodes involving the tail fluke. Each time the condition occurred, a portion of the fluke would become necrotic. This condition persisted for approximately a year, and just prior to death as the result of the rupture of a pulmonary vessel, the tail fluke was much reduced in size. A biopsy of the tail fluke lesion taken during an exacerbation revealed a nonspecific inflammatory process and thrombi of small vessels (Fig. 5–111).

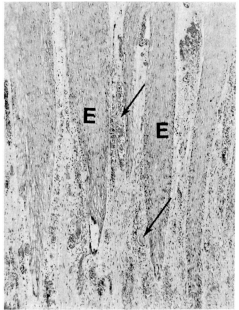

Figure 5–111. Skin of the tail fluke of an Atlantic bottlenosed porpoise, showing intravascular coagulation. Platelet thrombi (arrows) are present in the dilated vessels of the dermal papillae. There is extensive epidermal ulceration and inflammatory change present in the affected area. (E) Rete pegs of the epidermis. (H and E, ×75)

Figure 5–112. Focal areas of hair loss with pigmentation or depigmentation (lesions within block) are common in captive sea lions. They probably result from repeated friction (rubbing against side of pool).

A very common pathologic lesion on the skin of the California sea lion is irregular areas of hair loss. The hairless areas may look inflamed or may be pigmented (Fig. 5–112). These lesions may occur on any hirsute area of the body and may become extensively distributed. The animal does not appear to experience any adverse systemic effects from the depilation. A variety of causes, including erysipelas, mycotic infections, and mechanical abrasion, have been proposed. No definitive cause(s) has been established. Biopsies reveal a nonspecific inflammatory process. We call these lesions alopecia erythematosa or alopecia pigmentosa, depending upon the features manifested.

We have found budding, septae hyphae in focal, circumscribed, but not hairless skin lesions of California sea lions (Fig. 5–113). Wilson *et al.* (1969) reported on a skin lesion of the California sea lion caused by a pox virus. Demodectic mange has been observed in the California sea lion (Kenney, 1969). Abscesses containing yellowish, purulent material are sometimes found in the body and head of the California sea lion. We have recovered a beta hemolytic *Streptococcus* in pure culture from these abscesses.

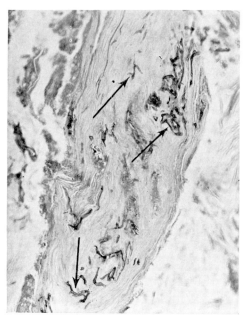

Figure 5–113. Mycotic skin lesion of a California sea lion. Budding, septate, hyphae (arrows) are found in the keratin of hair shafts. (PAS, ×250)

LYMPHOID ORGANS

We examined lymph nodes and spleen from a number of cetacean species including the Atlantic bottlenosed porpoise, the Hawaiian spinning dolphin, the common dolphin, the Amazon River porpoise, and the pilot whale. Lymph nodes sampled include mesenteric, periaortic, cervical, and parotid. The microscopic anatomy was typically mammalian, and the cellular pattern in many instances was one of lymphoid hypoactivity (Fig. 5–114). Follicles were usually inconspicuous or absent and when present failed to show active germinal centers. A few plasma cells could usually be identified in the medullary cords, especially with a PAS stain. Occasionally, heightened lymph node activity could be found in clinically ill cetaceans (Fig. 5–115). The customary absence of lymphoid hyperplasia or plasma cellular proliferation indicates that the immunogenic mechanisms of these mammals are usually relatively quiescent. This may be attributed to the age and health of the animals sampled and to the usual lack of potent immunogenic stimuli.

Bacterial infection can call forth a plasma cellular response as in other mammals. This has been witnessed in the acutely inflamed mediastinal lymph node of an Amazon River porpoise with pneumonia (Fig. 5–116). In a pilot whale, a number of eosinophils were noted in the capsule of a

Figure 5–114. Periaortic lymph nodes of an Atlantic bottlenosed porpoise. The cortex is thin and virtually devoid of lymphoid nodules. The medullary sinusoids are dilated but show no unusual histologic activity. (H and E, ×55)

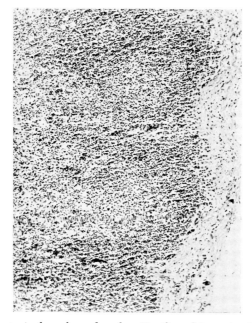

Figure 5–115. Mesenteric lymph node of a Pacific white-striped porpoise. Germinal centers are active. The cortical sinus is filled by lymphocytes. This animal died from erysipelas septicemia. Compare this lymph node with that of Figure 5–114. (H and E, ×250)

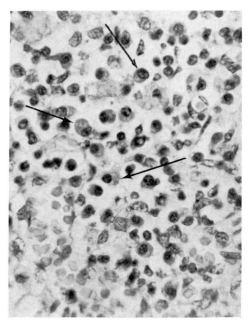

Figure 5–116. Mediastinal lymph node of an Amazon River porpoise. Plasma cells (arrows) are present in large numbers in the medullary sinuses. This animal died as a result of purulent pneumonia. (H and E, ×850)

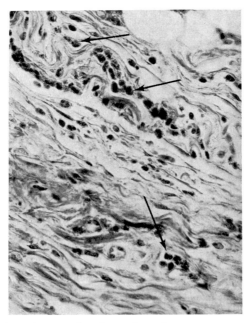

Figure 5–117. Lymph node capsule of a pilot whale. Eosinophils (arrows) are seen within the collagenous stroma. This was an incidental finding at necropsy. (Trichrome, ×500)

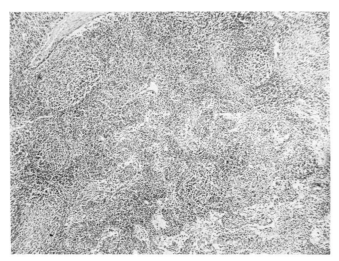

Figure 5–118. Mesenteric lymph node of a California sea lion. Cortical lymphoid nodules are rather inactive in appearance. Under higher magnification, plasma cells are only infrequently seen. The sinusoids are not dilated nor is there any evidence of unusual histiocytic activity. (H and E, ×55)

lymph node (Fig. 5–117). Stolk (1962) described granuloma malignum (Hodgkin's disease) in the fin whale. The lymph nodes we have examined from pinnipeds (Fig. 5–118) have not differed significantly from those of cetaceans. We have never seen primary disease of lymphatic organs in cetaceans or pinnipeds. We have noted enlargement of regional nodes in instances of pneumonias or enteric inflammation in both pinnipeds and cetaceans.

In cetaceans, the gut-associated lymphocytic system is well developed. Tonsils (Fig. 5–60) have already been mentioned in the section on the digestive system. Of interest is the report by Stolk (1953a) of tonsillitis in a sperm whale. Throughout the lamina propria of the small bowel, lymphocytes, plasma cells, and eosinophils occur in abundance. Lymphoid follicles corresponding to Peyer's patches in man with germinal centers were found at a site about 45 cm distal to the pylorus, and in larger numbers in the rectum.

The splenic follicles are generally as inactive in appearance as those in the lymph nodes (Fig. 5–119). A few plasma cells can usually be identified near the fibromuscular trabeculae. Lymphoid depletion and neutrophilic infiltrates were seen in the spleen of an Amazon River porpoise (Fig. 5–120), the result, presumably, of septicemia. Pigment (hemosiderin) deposition in splenic histiocytes was not particularly marked in any of the cetacean species examined, and no suggestion of extramedullary hematopoesis or amyloidosis has been seen.

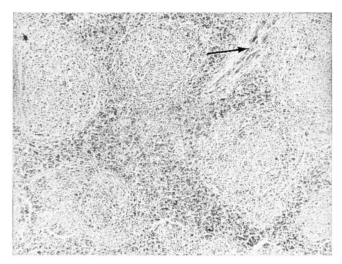

Figure 5–119. Spleen of a common dolphin. Splenic lymphoid follicles show relatively inactive appearing germinal centers. Under higher power, relatively few plasma cells are seen. The central arterioles are small and never hyalinized. A prominent band of smooth muscle is present at the lower right (arrow). (Trichrome, ×75)

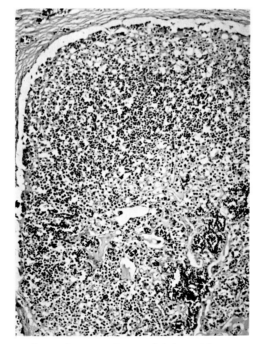

Figure 5–120. Spleen of an Amazon River dolphin. This animal died as a result of purulent pneumonia and septicemia. The splenic pulp revealed a paucity of cells and almost no lymph nodular formation. (Trichrome, ×125)

The thymus was examined in several Atlantic bottlenosed porpoises and in one Amazon River porpoise. An interesting subtle variation in mammalian structure was noted in one thymus, that is, the occurrence of lymph nodal architecture intimately embedded in the thymic cortex without fibrous demarcation (Fig. 5–121). Prominent Hassall's corpuscles were noted in the thymic tissue of the Atlantic bottlenosed porpoise (Fig. 5–122).

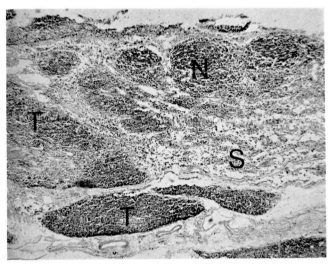

Figure 5–121. Thymus of an Atlantic bottlenosed porpoise. Note the lymph nodal histologic pattern intimately imbedded in the thymic cortex. Cortical lymphoid nodules (N) and medullary sinusoids (S) show little, if any, fibrous demarcation from the adjacent thymic lobules (T). (H and E, ×55)

The presence of eosinophils in the lymph nodes of marine mammals, particularly pinnipeds, is not uncommon. This probably reflects the ubiquitous presence of parasites in these animals.

We have examined lymphatic tissue from California sea lions, harbor seals, Steller's sea lions, and elephant seals and find it generally similar to that of porpoises. Figure 5–123 shows the thymus of a young elephant seal. The gland is well vascularized and Hassall's corpuscles are prominent. Figure 5–124 illustrates the reactivity of elephant seal splenic tissue to an inflammatory process. This animal had acute pancreatitis and a generalized septicemia. Within the red pulp, hemosiderin, megakaryocytes, and plasma cells are prominent, and there is necrosis within the germinal centers. Figure 5–125 is from a normal California sea lion spleen. Red and white pulp and cortical sinuses are well developed.

In a pathologic survey of pilot whales, Cowan (1966) found the following conditions in the spleen: multiple fibrous and granulomatous nodules

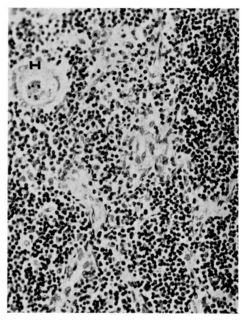

Figure 5–122. Thymus of an Atlantic bottlenosed porpoise. (H) Hassall's Corpuscle. (H and E, ×350)

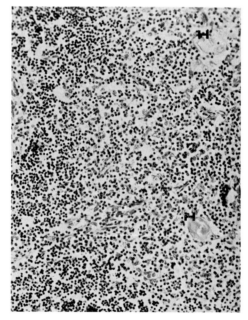

Figure 5–123. Thymus of an elephant seal. (H) Hassall's corpuscle. (H and E, ×250)

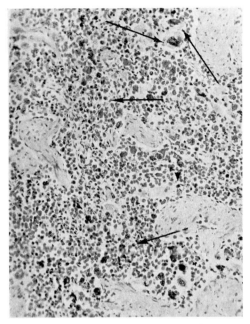

Figure 5–124. Spleen of an elephant seal. At necropsy, this animal was found to have had acute pancreatitis and was septicemic. The dark-staining granular material is hemosiderin. Megakeryocytes (arrows) and plasma cells (arrowheads) were distributed throughout the red pulp. (H and E, ×250)

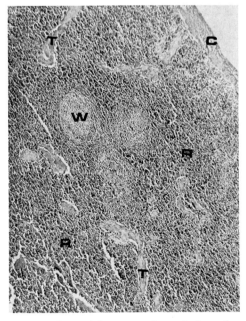

Figure 5–125. Normal spleen of a California sea lion. (R) Red pulp, (W) White pulp, (T) Trabeculae, (C) Capsule. (H and E, ×55)

(3 to 4 mm diameter) in three animals, amyloid-appearing material in the follicles of four animals, and bands of scar tissue in one animal. In lymph nodes, he also noted pathologic alterations such as edema, mild reticular hyperplasia, intrasinusoidal infiltration by mixed inflammatory cells, and in one animal, tiny foci of necrosis with multinucleated giant cells. Recently, Griner (1970) has identified lymphosarcoma in two harbor seals.

THYROID AND ADRENAL GLAND

The overall histologic pattern of the thyroid gland in Cetacea and pinnipeds is much like that of the human. The parenchyma is lobulated and consists of follicles which are variable in size but for the most part somewhat smaller than usually seen in the human (Fig. 5–126). The interlobular septae consist of connective tissue and vessels. The follicles ordinarily contain the usual pink colloid substance, as seen in the human. The follicular lining cells are cuboidal to low columnar (Fig. 5–127) and often show a few intracytoplasmic vacuoles. Numerous epithelial cells are often noted between the follicles and are, for the most part, probably tangentially cut sections through normal follicles (Fig. 5–128). It is possible, however, that there may be some parafollicular cells present which are thought to secrete calcitonin. We found no lymphocytes in normal glands. Blood vessels within the connective tissue septae are not particularly thick walled or unusual in their appearance. Harrison (1969b)

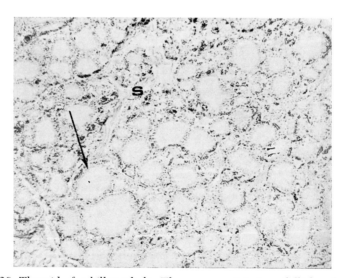

Figure 5–126. Thyroid of a killer whale. The arrow points to a follicle whose diameter is 165μ. Connective tissue septae (S) divide groups of follicles into lobules. The thyroid is well vascularized and dark-staining erythrocytes can be seen within interfollicular capillaries. (H and E, ×75)

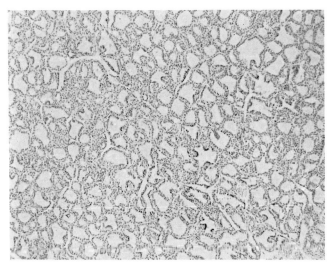

Figure 5–127. Thyroid of a California sea lion. The thyroid acini are uniformly small and lacking in colloid. The lining cells are cuboidal and show slight papillary infolding. The appearance is that of a fairly active gland. (H and E, ×75)

reported that the average follicular diameter in a group of young Pacific white-striped porpoises was 0.2 mm and that in young North Pacific pilot whales and Atlantic pilot whales was 0.25 mm. Harrison *et al.* (1962) found the average follicular diameter in a group of neonatal harbor seals to be 0.070 mm and those of a group of adults to be 0.129 mm. They also noted under the electron microscope large Golgi apparati and secretion

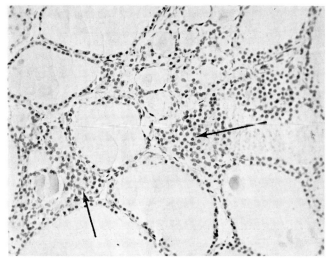

Figure 5–128. Thyroid of a Pacific white-striped porpoise. Areas of what appear to be parafollicular cells (arrows) may actually be tangentially cut follicular walls. (H and E, ×250)

droplets in thyroid cells of young seals. The fine structural appearance
indicated active secretion.

We have seen no evident pathology in the thyroid of cetaceans and
pinnipeds examined. Cowan (1966) reported a simple colloid goiter in
four pilot whales and granulomata in the thyroid of two pilot whales.

The adrenal glands of cetaceans and pinnipeds are also similar to those
of other mammals. The major variation among different species appears
to be in amount of connective tissue and degree of surface lobulation. The
fibrous capsule is somewhat thick and surrounded by numerous nerve
trunks and vessels in a connective tissue stroma (Figs. 5–129, 5–130,
5–131). In some but not all specimens, the zona glomerulosa, fasciculata,
and reticularis are well defined. In Cetacea, the cortex is separated into
pseudolobules by connective tissue fibers projecting at a right angle from
the capsule. The connective tissue septae are more prominent in some
specimens than others. This pseudolobulation is not evident in pinniped
adrenals. Generally, the zona fasciculata is the thickest layer of the cortex.
There appears to be a significant variation in degree of thickness of the
three zones in different specimens. This is probably related to the func-

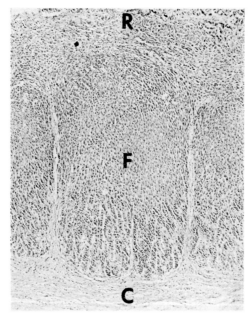

Figure 5–129. Adrenal cortex of an Atlantic bottlenosed porpoise. The fibrous capsule
(C) invaginates into the cortex to delineate pseudo nodules. An outer zona glomerulosa
is not apparent in this photo. Most of the cortex consists of straight cords of the
zona fasciculata (F). At the corticomedullary junction, the sinusoidal pattern of the
reticularis zone (R) is seen. The cortical cells are conspicuously lacking in stored
lipid. There is no lipofusion pigment present in the reticularis zone. (H and E, ×75)

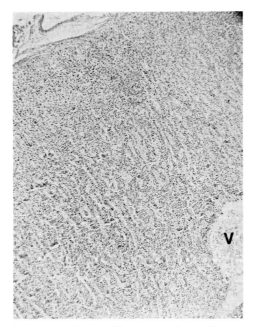

Figure 5–130. Adrenal cortex of the California sea lion. There is no pseudolobulation and the entire cortex appears to consist of a zona fasciculata pattern. The cells are compact and lacking in stored lipid. The central vein (V) is seen at the lower right. There is no lipofuscin pigment in the inner cortical cells. (H and E, ×55)

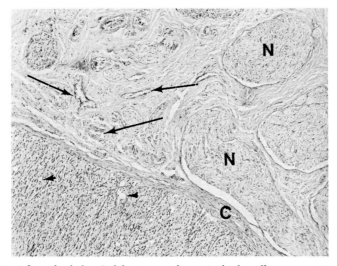

Figure 5–131. Adrenal of the California sea lion. A thick collagenous stroma surrounds the adrenal gland. This stroma contains numerous nerve trunks (N) and vessels (arrows). Just below the adrenal capsule (C) fat vacuoles (arrowheads) can be seen in the cortex. (H and E, ×75)

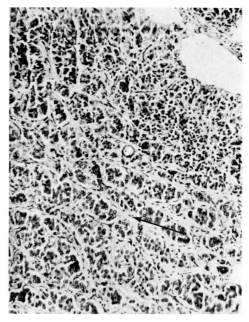

Figure 5–132. Adrenal medulla of the Dall porpoise. Thin connective tissue septae (arrow) divide the parenchymal cells in numerous cords. (Trichrome, ×75)

tional state of the gland. Harrison (1969b) found that the zona glomerulosa constituted about two thirds of the cortical thickness in pinnipeds. We have not found this to be so. In both Pinnipedia and Cetacea, the zona fasciculata appears to be the thickest layer. In one specimen (Fig. 5–130),

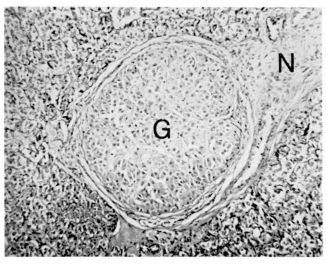

Figure 5–133. Adrenal medulla, Atlantic bottlenosed porpoise. A prominent sympathetic ganglia (G), approximately 500 microns in diameter, and nerve trunk (N) are present in the medulla. (H and E, ×70)

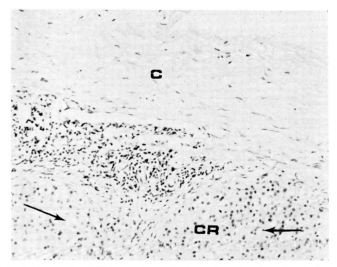

Figure 5–134. Subcapsular inflammation of the adrenal of a Steller's sea lion. The majority of these infiltrating cells are lymphocytes and they tend to be distributed around small vessels. There is some fatty deposition in cortical cells (arrows). (C) Capsule, (CR) Cortex. (H and E, ×100)

the whole cortex seems composed of the fascicular layer. We did not observe lipofusion pigment, which is seen in adrenals of older humans. The adrenal medulla is particularly well illustrated with a trichrome stain (Fig. 5–132). The cells of the medulla tend to stain more basophilic, and

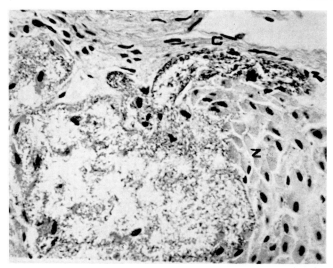

Figure 5–135. Adrenal cortical lesion in an Hawaiian spinning porpoise. This was an incidental finding at necropsy. There was essentially no inflammatory response. It may have been a postmortem change, although the general freshness of the tissue as seen histologically would seem to make this possibility unlikely. (C) Capsule, (Z) Zona glomerulosa. (H and E, ×300)

the increase in connective tissue stroma of the medulla is better defined than by hematoxylin and eosin. Amoroso *et al.* (1965) noted that in adult male harbor seals, but not in the females, the cortex is sharply separated from the medulla by fibrous tissue. The medulla is relatively more vascular than the cortex and contains prominent nerve trunks and sympathetic ganglia (Fig. 5–133). The parenchymal cells of the medulla are cuboidal and form nests or cords separated from each other by vascular, thin connective tissue septae.

Adrenal pathology encountered has been incidental. It is not uncommon to find focal inflammatory cell infiltration in cortices of animals which have died from pneumonia or septicemic disease (Fig. 5–134). An interesting but unclassified lesion was seen in the adrenal cortex of a Hawaiian spinning dolphin (Fig. 5–135), and an adrenal teratoma was found at necropsy in a Pacific white-striped porpoise (Fig. 5–136). Griner (1970) found an adrenal cortical carcinoma in an elephant seal.

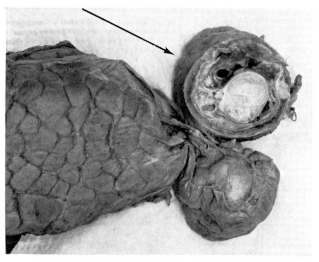

Figure 5–136. Adrenal teratoma (arrow) found incidentally in a Pacific white-striped porpoise at necropsy.

REPRODUCTIVE SYSTEM

The microscopic anatomy of reproductive organs in cetaceans and pinnipeds is generally similar to that of terrestrial mammals. The material available to us for study represents specimens taken more by chance than by design and thus does not constitute a systematic sampling throughout the complete sexual cycle. Cyclic changes in the uterus and ovaries of whales were studied by MacKintosh and Wheeler (1929), Matthews (1948), Harrison (1949 and 1969a), and Slijper (1962). Bonner (1955), Rand

(1955), Harrison (1951 and 1969a), Craig (1964), and Amoroso *et al.* (1965) made similar studies on pinnipeds.

Female Organs

OVARY

The typical mammalian ovarian histology is illustrated in Figure 5–137. The lining germinal epithelium, tunica albugenia, cortex, and medulla are clearly evident. The porpoise ovary has a fairly prominent basophilic cortical stroma composed of compact intertwining connective tissue cells. Follicles in varying stages of development and involution are present within the cortex. In young adult porpoises and sea lions, our impression is that there are fewer developing and atretic follicles than are seen in young adult human females. In a normal, mature Atlantic bottlenosed porpoise, the cortex measured approximately 2 mm in thickness. Corpora lutea can reach rather large size. Chittleborough (1954) described corpora lutea weighing as much as 2185 gm in humpback whales (and ovaries weighing up to 3900 gm), and Slijper (1963) observed football-sized corpora lutea of pregnancy in rorquals. According to Dempsey (1941), one of the principal architectural peculiarities of the whale ovary is the relatively marked lengthening of the smallest arterioles and capillaries supplying the corpora lutea. Dempsey (1941), Slijper (1962), and Harrison (1969a) have reported that the remnants of the corpus luteum (the corpus albicans) never completely disappear from the cetacean ovary. This observation may be used to roughly approximate the age of whales and porpoises, since it is believed that Cetacea only produce one ovum at a time (except in occasional instances of multiple births). According to Harrison (1949), spontaneous ovulation probably occurs several times yearly in the pilot whale and false killer whale. Slijper (1962) has stated that the corpora albicantia in larger whales are composed almost exclusively of thickened elastic walls from arteries which previously supplied the corpus luteum. Compared to the cortex, the medulla of the cetacean ovary is less cellular but more vascular and collagenous (Fig. 5–138).

The ovaries of pinnipeds have few differences from those of cetaceans. We have noted in our material that the tunica albugenia of the seals and sea lions appears to be relatively thinner than that of cetaceans (Fig. 5–139). In four species of adult seals, Harrison (1950) reported finding typically mammalian subsurface crypts invaginated into the cortex. The crypts were lined by germinal epithelium which was directly continuous with epithelium surrounding the primary oöcytes. Craig (1964) found that the ovaries of the fur seal alternate in function, each one ovulating every two years. An ovary with numerous corpora albicantia from an adult California

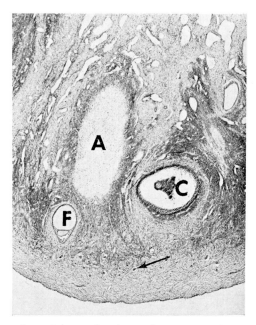

Figure 5–137. Ovary of an Atlantic bottlenosed porpoise. A ripening Graffian follicle (F), a follicle cyst (C) and a corpora albicans (A) are seen. Many primordial ova (arrow) are present in the dense cortical stroma. (H and E, ×40)

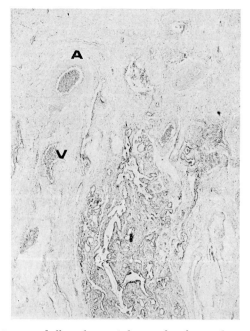

Figure 5–138. Ovarian medulla of an Atlantic bottlenosed porpoise. The medulla is densely collagenous and contains moderate numbers of veins (V) and arteries (A). This section includes a portion of the infundibulum (I) of the oviduct. (H and E, ×35)

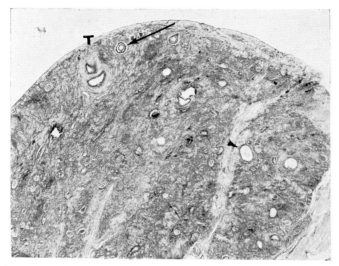

Figure 5–130. Ovary of a California sea lion. The tunica albugenia (T) appears relatively thin. Both developing (arrow) and atretic (arrowhead) follicles are seen in the cortex. (H and E, ×25)

sea lion showed an involuting corpus luteum with a connective tissue lined cyst in the center (Fig. 5–140).

We have found no ovarian pathology in our necropsies on cetaceans and pinnipeds. Rewell and Willis (1949) reported a mucinous cystadenoma and a granulosa cell tumor in blue whales and granulosa cell tumors in fin whales. An ovarian carcinoma in a fin whale was described by Stolk (1950).

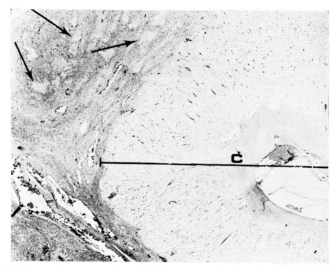

Figure 5–140. Corpus leuteum of a California sea lion. The corpus leuteum (C) occupies a sizeable portion of cortex. The cortical stroma contains numerous corpora albicantia (arrows) indicating prior ovulations. (H and E, ×20)

UTERUS

The uterus of cetaceans, like that of humans, is composed of an endo-metrium, myometrium, and serosa (Fig. 5–141). The endometrial surface is lined by a single layer of cuboidal to columnar ciliated epithelium (Fig. 5–142). MacKintosh and Wheeler (1929) found ciliated epithelium lining

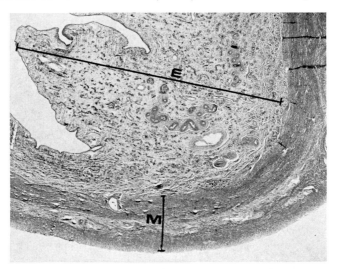

Figure 5–141. Uterus of an Atlantic bottlenosed porpoise. This cross section demonstrates the endometrium (E) and myometrium (M) which consists of inner circular and outer longitudinal smooth muscle layers. The thin serosal coat is not evident in this section. (Trichrome, ×20)

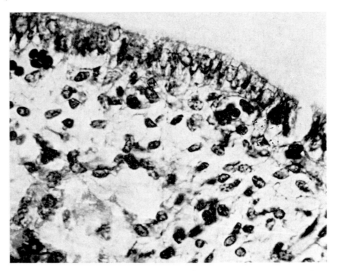

Figure 5–142. Endometrium of an Atlantic bottlenosed porpoise. These endometrial lining cells tend to be rather columnar in shape. Cilia are present but are rather blurred in this photo. The specimen was obtained during anestrous. (Trichrome, ×800)

the endometrium of blue and fin whales. The uterine glands are tubular and lined by cuboidal to slightly columnar epithelium. The glands in the resting uterus are generally unbranched and extend to the myometrium (Fig. 5–143).

Rather large arterioles are seen in the loose-textured endometrial stroma (Fig. 5–144). According to Matthews (1948), the mucosa of the baleen whale becomes greatly thickened, and superficial capillaries become congested in the progestational stage. At ovulation, the uterine glands become complex and the mucosal surface forms grossly visible indentations. Har-

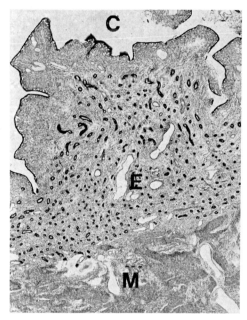

Figure 5–143. Uterus of an Atlantic bottlenosed porpoise. Simple tubular glands without evidence of proliferation or secretion extend into the endometrial stroma (E). The uterine cavity (C) is empty and is lined by a single layer of germinal epithelium. (M) myometrium. (H and E, ×35)

rison (1949) felt that these indentations were less prominent in the pilot whale than in the baleen whales studied by Matthews. Matthews (1948) described well-marked cyclic changes in the baleen whales from anestrus through ovulation, pregnancy, and lactation. He refers to a prominent stratum compactum (the outermost area of the endometrium) which increases greatly in thickness after ovulation but which regresses slowly until the end of pregnancy, at which time it quickly involutes. Wislocki (1933) noted that placentation in the bottlenosed porpoise is a diffuse epithelial-chorial type.

The cervix in Cetacea is composed of mucous membrane, connective tissue, lamina propria, and an underlying smooth muscle and vascular

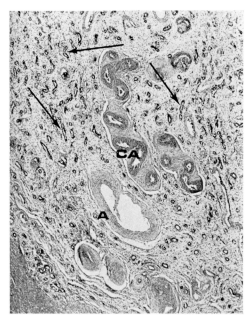

Figure 5–144. Endometrium of an Atlantic bottlenosed porpoise. An artery (A) and what appears to be a coiled arteriole (CA) are seen in the endometrial stroma. Numerous uterine glands (arrows) are also present. (Trichrome, ×45)

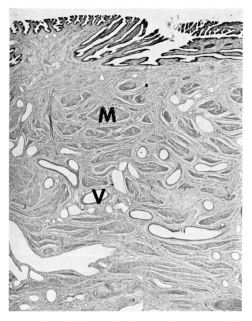

Figure 5–145. Endocervix of an Atlantic bottlenosed porpoise. Erectile tissue composed of vascular sinusoids (V) and smooth muscle bundles (M) is present in the wall beneath the corrugated columnar mucosa. (H and E, ×25)

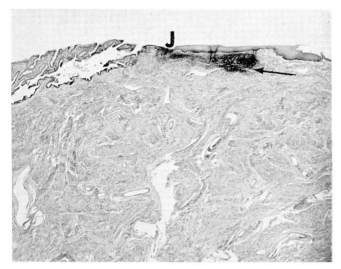

Figure 5–146. Cervix of an Atlantic bottlenosed porpoise. A lymphocytic infiltrate (arrow) lies immediately beneath the squamo-columnar junction (J). (H and E, ×15)

area which appears to be erectile tissue (Figs. 5–145, 5–146). We have found no pathology in uterine or cervical tissue of cetaceans and pinnipeds. Rewell and Willis (1949) reported finding a uterine fibromyoma in a whale (species not given), and Uys and Best (1966) found multiple fibromyomata in the uterus of four sperm whales.

Pinniped uteri are also typically mammalian. Figures 5–147 and 5–148 show the endometrium of a California sea lion three days after aborting a near-term fetus. Figure 5–147 is from the right horn of the uterus; figure 5–148 is from the left horn where the fetus was carried. In a yearling California sea lion, uterine glands are inconspicuous (Fig. 5–149), while in a young anestrous adult, the formation of straight, epithelial-lined tubular glands can be seen in the endometrium (Fig. 5–150).

Murphy (1967) described the coiled arteries in the connective tissue surrounding the uterine glands in the harbor seal. Harrison, *et al.* (1952), described the pinniped uterine histology in detail. A number of authors have investigated the uterus of fetal and juvenile pinnipeds (Harrison 1951, 1960; Craig, 1964; Amoroso, *et al.*, 1965; Murphy 1968). A feature of interest in the uteri of fetal and newborn pinnipeds, particularly in phocids, is a precocious hyperplasia of uterine glands, probably due to stimulation from maternal hormones. This precocious development is temporary, and according to Harrison *et al.* (1952), involution is well along a week after birth. As the animal matures, the uterine glands become inconspicuous until estrus and pregnancy. Rand (1955) has observed that uterine glands in phocids appear inactive until after implanta-

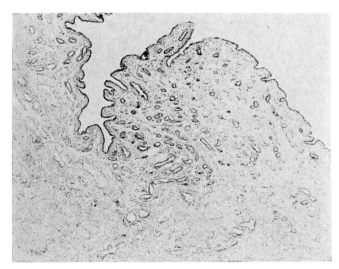

Figure 5–147. Endometrium of the right horn of a California sea lion. The animal had recently aborted a near-term fetus from the opposite horn. (H and E, ×45)

tion of the blastocyst, which is several months subsequent to impregnation. Harrison, *et al.* (1952) reported that delayed implantation seems to be universal among pinnipeds. Harrison and Young (1968) investigated

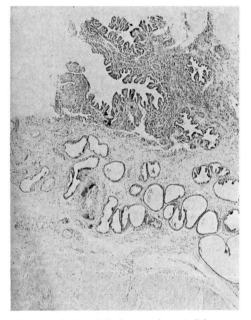

Figure 5–148. Endometrium of the left horn of a California sea lion. A near-term fetus had recently been aborted from this horn. Note the papillary projections of the endometrium and the dilated uterine glands. There is a modest infiltration by acute inflammatory cells into the endometrium just beneath the germinal epithelum. (H and E, ×45)

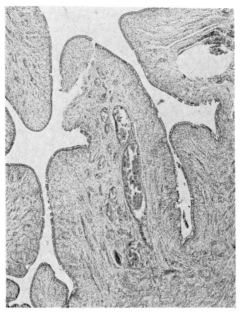

Figure 5–149. Endometrium of a California sea lion. No uterine glands are evident in the endometrium of this yearling animal. (H and E, ×50)

placentation in the California sea lion, the common seal, the gray seal, the Weddell seal, and the crabeater seal. They found in all species that the placental band is annular in shape and has marginal blood clots. Electron microscopic study confirmed an endothelial-chorial relationship of uterus and placenta.

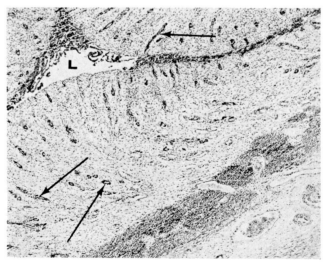

Figure 5–150. Endometrium of a California sea lion. In this young adult female (4 or 5 years), straight, tubular glands (arrows) are seen developing in the endometrium. (L) uterine lumen. (H and E, ×75)

MAMMARY GLANDS

In cetaceans, one pair of glands is found on either side of the genital groove. Mammary glands are paired in pinnipeds, but the number of pairs varies among species (see Chap. 1). Figure 5–151 shows mammary tissue from a near-term pregnant Dall porpoise. Connective tissue septae which lack fat (in this example) divide the parenchyma into lobules. Secretory material in some of the alveoli indicates that this animal was probably producing colostrum. MacKintosh and Wheeler (1929) listed four stages which

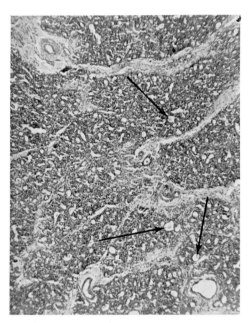

Figure 5–151. Mammary gland of a Dall porpoise. The tubuloalveolar glands are divided into lobules by connective tissue septae. This animal, which was pregnant and near term, displayed a secretion (arrows) in alveolar spaces. (H and E, ×75)

could be identified histologically in mammary glands of adult blue and fin whales:

1. Lactating. Milk is actively being secreted.
2. Intermediate. Glandular lobules are better developed than in resting state but not developed as well as in lactating stage.
3. Resting. Complete involution of gland.
4. Virgin. Gland of animal never pregnant.

Slijper (1962) noted that the "presence of myoepithelial cells in the mammary glands of Cetacea was established by W. A. Smit."

We have no pinniped mammary specimens in our collection. Amoroso *et al.* (1965) described mammary tissue in several species of young pinnipeds. They noted an epithelial-lined tubuloalveolar gland arrangement similar to that of other mammals.

Mastitis has been recorded in a lactating blue whale by Cockrill (1960a), and Fox (1941) reported an adenocarcinoma and a myosarcoma in the mammary gland of a sea lion.

Male Reproductive Organs

PENIS

Figure 5–152 shows a cross section of the penis of an Atlantic bottle-nosed porpoise taken just proximal to the penile tip. The epidermis is quite thick, with prominent epidermal pegs. The underlying connective tissue dermis contains many nerve trunks and vessels. The tunica albu genia is a thick musculoelastic layer surrounding the relatively small corpus cavernosis penis, which is not clearly divided into bilateral compartments as it is in man. Matthews (1950) noted that the corpora cavernosa peni are fused together into one compartment throughout most of the penile length in all Cetacea. The erectile corpus cavernosa penis is more fibrous than in humans but is similarly composed of thin-walled vascular spaces, arterioles, and venules with smooth muscle bundles interspersed in the intervening loose connective tissue stroma. The corpus spongiosum has an outer poorly developed vascular plexis, a thick middle connective

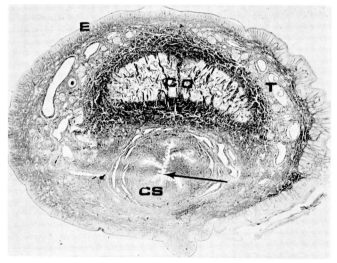

Figure 5–152. Penis of an Atlantic bottlenosed porpoise. The cross section shows the epidermis (E), the tunica albugenia (T), which is approximately 2 mm thick, a fused corpus cavernosum (CC), corpus spongiosum (CS), and the urethra (arrow). (Trichrome, ×3)

tissue layer containing vessels and nerve fibers, and a central urethra. The urethra is lined by urothelium that varies in appearance from transitional to stratified columnar. There are no submucosal glands present nor is there any evidence of bulbourethral glands (Cowper's glands). An os penis does not exist in cetaceans. Slijper (1962) stated that the whale penis forms more from an abundance of connective tissue than from erectile vascular tissue.

The penis of the pinnipeds is more typically mammalian than the cetacean penis. An os penis (baculum) or penile bone replaces the distal corpus cavernosum penis in pinnipeds.

PROSTATE GLAND

In the porpoise, as in man, the prostate gland has a tubuloalveolar pattern (Fig. 5–153). The glandular acini are of rather uniform size and are divided into lobules by fibroelastic septae. Unlike in humans, there is no smooth muscle in these septae. The glandular epithelium is generally columnar in appearance. The cell nuclei tend to be basal in location, and the cytoplasm faintly basophilic. The collecting ducts are lined by a low cuboidal layer of epithelial cells. Flattened nuclei beneath the glandular mucosa (Fig. 5–154) are probably myoepithelial cells. We have not seen prostatic concretions (corpora amalacia). Harrison (1969a) described an underdeveloped prostate in fetal and infant delphinids which developed into a large, active gland in the adult.

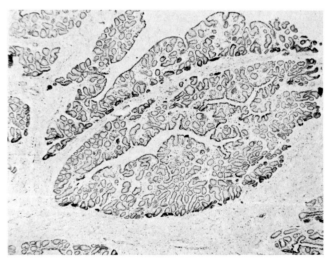

Figure 5–153. Prostate of an Atlantic bottlenosed porpoise. The prostatic glandular acini are small and uniform. There is no secretion seen and no corpora amylacea are present. (H and E, ×40)

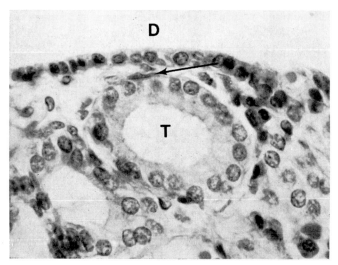

Figure 5–154. Prostate of an Atlantic bottlenosed porpoise. Cuboidal epithelium lines a prostate duct (D), while columnar epithelial cells line secretory tubules (T). Flattened nuclei (arrow) at the base of secretory epithelial cells probably belong to myoepithelial cells.

We do not have a pinniped prostate in our collection. Amoroso *et al.* (1965) reported that the prostate in the gray seal and harbor seal is larger at birth than it is at six months to a year after birth. It enlarges again by adulthood and in the harbor seal is reportedly twenty times heavier than at birth. According to Harrison (1969a), the prostate in the harbor seal is not fully developed until after sexual maturity has been reached. The description of the histology of the gray seal prostate by Amoroso *et al.* (1965) noted that it is composed predominately of secreting alveoli imbedded in a dense fibromuscular stroma, and that the epithelium lining the alveoli is generally tall and columnar but in some places is pseudostratified.

TESTICLES

Our impression gained from random pinniped and cetacean necropsies is that both groups of animals manifest spermatogenesis only seasonally. Slijper (1962) stated that "while small quantities of semen may be produced by whales throughout the year, a marked increase occurs during the mating season." Harrison, *et al.* (1952) found a peak of testicular activity during October in the crabeater seal and the Weddell seal. Activity regressed after this peak and did not accelerate until the following October-centered period.

The testes of both cetaceans and pinnipeds are similar in microstructure. They consist of irregularly lobulated groupings of seminiferous tubules surrounded by a fibrovascular capsule, the tunica albugenia (Figs. 5–155,

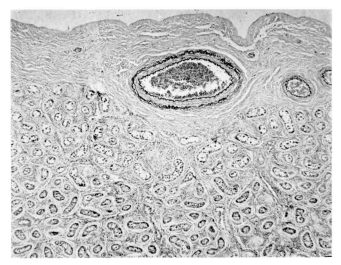

Figure 5–155. Testicle of an Amazon River porpoise. The wavy dark layers in the small artery are elastic lamellae. The tunica albugenia measures approximately 300μ, and the seminiferous tubules average 35 to 40μ in diameter. (Elastic, $\times 35$)

5–156). The fibrous interlobular septae contain vessels, nerves, and collecting ducts (Fig. 5–157). In a quiescent gland, the tubules are lined by a single layer of rather basophilic epithelial cells which rest on a basement membrane. Towards the center of the lumen, sertoli cells have a larger, paler staining nucleus and string pale retriculated cytoplasm. No spermatozoa are seen in the tubules (Fig. 5–158). Within the intertubular spaces (the interstitium) of cetacean testes, identification of cell types other than

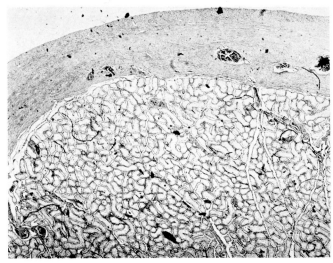

Figure 5–156. Testicle of a California sea lion. The thickness of the tunica albugenia is approximately 1.8 mm and the diameter of the tubules average 100 to 300μ. (H and E, $\times 10$)

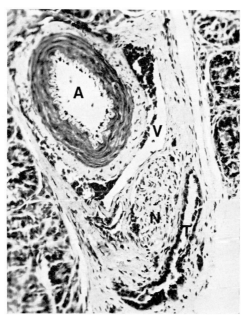

Figure 5–157. Interlobular Area of the testicle of a pygmy sperm whale. An artery (A), vein (V), nerve (N), and straight tubule (T) are seen in the connective tissue stroma. (Trichrome, ×250)

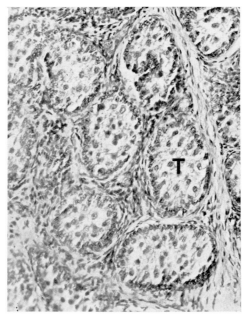

Figure 5–158. Testis of an Atlantic bottlenosed porpoise. The seminiferous tubules (T) are small and lined only by supporting sertoli cells. Spermatogenesis is absent in this testis. Interstitial Leydig cells are difficult to distinguish from fibroblasts. (H and E, ×250)

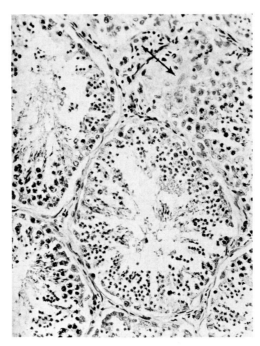

Figure 5–159. Testis of the common dolphin. Active spermatogenesis is present in these large tubules. Prominent interstitial cells (arrow) lie between the tubules. In our experience, interstitial cells are usually not this prominent in cetacean testicles. (H and E, ×250)

endothelial or connective tissue cells is ofen difficult (Fig. 5–159). In our experience, Leydig cells are more easily discerned in pinnipeds. Murphy (1969) found Leydig cells most prominent in fur seals whose testicles showed peak spermatogenic activity. These testicles were obtained in the month of July.

We have not seen Reinke crystaloids in any marine mammalian interstitial cells. Figure 5–160 shows spermatogenesis in the testis of a California sea lion which was approximately three years of age. Sertoli cells, primary spermatocytes, and mature spermatozoa can be identified within the lumen. This testis was removed during the month of August. Figures 5–161 and 5–162 demonstrate the efferent ducts and epididymis of a porpoise, and the epididymis of a sea lion is illustrated in Figure 5–163. Stereocilia are seen on the columnar epithelium of the efferent duct (Fig. 5–164).

Some naturally occurring pathologic lesions in porpoises' testes are shown in Figures 5–165 and 5–166. Uys and Best (1966) have described caseous necrosis with an associated tuberculoid inflammatory reaction in the right testis and epididymis of a blue whale. Testicular abscesses in a whale were reported by Addison (1949).

✿ ✿ ✿

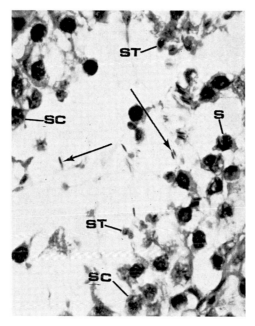

Figure 5–160. Spermatogenesis in a California sea lion. Spermatozoa (arrows), a primary spermatocyte (S), a few spermatids (ST), and sertoli cells (SC) are seen in the lumen of the seminiferous tubule. (H and E, ×850)

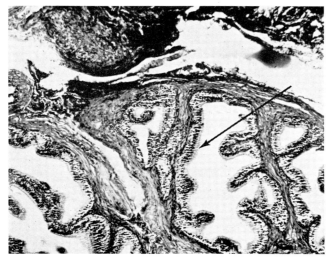

Figure 5–161. Efferent ducts of the northern right whale dolphin. Stereocilia (arrow) lines the pseudostratified columnar epithelium of the ducts. (H and E, ×50)

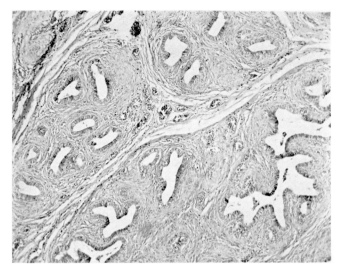

Figure 5–162. Epididymis of an Amazon River porpoise. The convoluted tube (the ductus epididymis) is cut numerous places when a cross section is made. The duct is lined by rather low ciliated, pseudostratified columnar epithelium. A thin layer of smooth muscle surrounds the duct. The majority of interductal stroma is collagenous connective tissue. (Elastic, ×100)

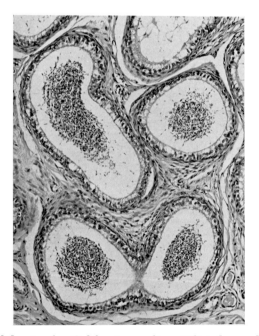

Figure 5–163. Epididymis of a California sea lion. Ciliated pseudostratified columnar epithelium lines the ducts, which are surrounded by a thin layer of smooth muscle. Spermatozoa are seen in the lumina. (H and E, ×150)

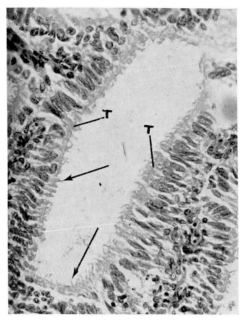

Figure 5–164. Efferent duct of an Atlantic bottlenosed porpoise. Stereocilia (arrows) project from the terminal bars (T) of columnar epithelial cells. Basal cells are also present, and thus the lining of the efferent duct is of the pseudostratified columnar type. (H and E, ×500)

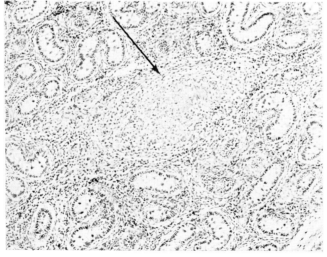

Figure 5–165. Granuloma in the testis of an Amazon River porpoise. A granuloma lies in the interstitium (arrow), displacing the seminiferous tubules. The etiology is not apparent. (H and E, ×125)

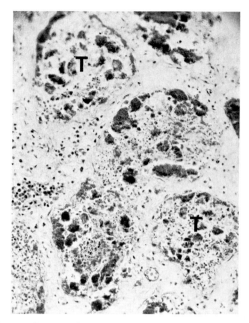

Figure 5–166. Orchitis of an Atlantic bottlenosed porpoise. The tubules (T) are dilated and filled by necrotic debris. Interstitium is thickened by fibrous proliferation and inflammatory cells (plasma cells, neutrophils, lymphocytes, and macrophage) have infiltrated tubules and interstitial tissue. (Trichrome, ×250)

The material which we had available came from several sources. The majority of Atlantic bottlenosed, Pacific white-striped, Dall porpoise, and pinniped tissue was obtained from animals at the Marine Bioscience Facility, Point Mugu, California. Mr. W. G. Gilmartin prepared the specimens from Point Mugu for histological examination, and we are most grateful for his cooperation and skill. Many of the whale specimens were kindly loaned to us by Dr. James Roberts who collected these tissues in many different areas of the world. In addition, we had access to a collection of whale specimens from the Department of Pathology, University of Southern California School of Medicine. These were made available to us through a study funded by Mr. Bruce McNeil and collected by Dr. John Waken and Dr. Edward Arquilla. We appreciate the skill of Mr. Lloyd Matlovsky of the University of Southern California and Los Angeles County General Hospital who took the photomicrographs used in this chapter, and the patience of Dr. Howard P. Charman of the School of Medicine, University of Southern California who reviewed the manuscript.

REFERENCES

Addison, F.H.: Antarctic whaling expedition. Ministry of Food Report (unpublished), 1949–50.

Amemiya, I.: The dolphin that swallowed a football. *International Zoo Yearbook*, 4:34, 1962.

Amoroso, E.C., Bourne, G.H., Harrison, R.J., Matthews, L.H., Rowlands, I.W., and Sloper, J.C.: Reproductive and endocrine organs of foetal, newborn and adult seals. *J. Zool.*, 147:430–486, 1965.

Avery, M.E. and Said, S.: Surface phenomenon in lungs, in health and disease. *Medicine*, 44:503–526, 1965.

Baudrimont, A.: Structure of the pulmonary veins and functional circulation of the lung of the common dolphin, *Delphinus delphis* L. Bull. *Microscopie Appl.* 5:57–58, 1955.

Beauregard, H. and Boulart, R.: Recherches sur les Appareils Genito-Urinaires des Balaenides. *J. de l'anat. et Physiol.*, 18:158, 1882.

Belanger, L.F.: A study of the histological structure of the respiratory portion of the lungs of aquatic mammals. *Amer. J. Anat.*, 67:437–461, 1940.

Bel'Kovich, V.M.: Particular features of thermoregulation in an aquatic environment (from the example of mammals). *Bionika (Bionics)*, pp. 215–219, 1965.

Bonner, W.N. Reproductive organs of foetal and juvenile elephant seals. *Nature (London)*, 176:982–983, 1955.

Brown, D.H., McIntyre, R.W., Delli Quadri, C.A., and Schroeder, R.J.: Health problems of captive dolphins and seals. *J. Amer. Vet. Med. Assn.*, 137:534–538, 1960.

Buckingham, S., Heineman, H.O., Sommers, S.C., and McNary, W.F.: Phospholipid synthesis in the large pulmonary alveolar cell. *Amer. J. Path.*, 48:1027–1041, 1966.

Carroll, J.M., Jasmin, A.M., and Baucom, J.N.: Pulmonary aspergillosis of the bottlenose dolphin (*Tursiops truncatus*), *Amer. J. Vet. Clin. Path.*, 2:139–140, 1968.

Cave, A.J.E. and Aumonier, F.J.: The visceral histology of the primitive cetacean, *Caperea (Neobalaena)*, *J. Roy. Micro. Soc.*, 80:25–33, 1961.

Cave, A.J.E. and Aumonier, F.J.: Morphology of the Cetacean reniculus *Nature (London)*, 193:799–800, 1962.

Cave, A.J.E. and Aumonier, F.J.: The reniculus of *Tursiops truncatus, Stenella longirostris* and other Cetaceans. *J. Roy. Micro. Soc.*, 86:323–393, 1967.

Chittleborough, R.G.: Studies on the ovaries of the humpback whale, *Megaptera Nodosa (Bonnaterre)*, on the western Australian coast. *Aust. J. Mar. Freshw. Res.*, 5:35–62, 1954.

Cockrill, W.R.: Pathology of the Cetacea—Part I. *Brit. Vet. J.*, 116:133–144, 1960a.

Cockrill, W.R.: Pathology of the Cetacea—Part II. *Brit. Vet. J.*, 116:175–190, 1960b.

Cowan, D.F.: Pathology of the pilot whale. *Arch. Path.*, 82:178–189, 1966.

Cowan, D.F.: Lung diseases in whales and dolphins. Proc. 2nd Conference on Diseases of Aquatic Mammals. Boca Raton, Fla., 1968.

Craig, A.M.: Histology of reproduction and the estrus cycle in the female fur seal, *Callorhinus ursinus*. *J. Fish Res. Bd. Canada*, 21:773–811, 1964.

Dailey, M.D.: Transmission of *Parafilaroides decorus* (Nematoda: Metastrongyloidea) in the California sea lion (*Zalophus californianus*). *Proc. Helm. Soc. Washington*, 37:215, 1970.

Dempsey, E.W. and Wislocki, G.B.: The structure of the ovary of the humpback whale (*Megaptera nodosa*). *Anat. Rec.*, 80:243–251, 1941.

Engle, S.: The respiratory tissue of the blue whale and the fin whale. *Acta. Anat.*, 65:381–390, 1966.

Fiebiger, J.: Ueber Eigentuemlichkeiten im Aufbau der Delphin vs. Lunge und Ihre Physiolugische Bedeutung. *Anat. Anz.*, 58:540–564, 1916.

Fox, H.: Comparative pathology of the heart as seen in the animals at the Philadelphia Zoological Gardens. *Trans. Coll. Phys.*, 3rd Series, 43:130–145, 1921.

Fox, H.: *Disease in Captive Wild Mammals and Birds.* Philadelphia, Lippincott, 1923, p. 339.

Fox, H.: Report of the Penrose Research Laboratory, 1941.

Geraci, J.R. and Gerstmann, K.E.: Relationship of dietary histamine to gastric ulcers in the dolphin, *J. Amer. Vet. Med. Assn.* 149(7):884–890, 1966.

Giacometti, L.: The skin of the whale (*Balaenoptera physalus*). *Anat. Rec.*, 159:69–76, 1967.

Griner, L.A.: Personal communication, 1970.

Harrison, R.J.: Observations on the female reproductive organs of the ca'aing whale *Globiocephala melaena* Traill. *J. Anat.*, 83:238–253, 1949.

Harrison, R.J.: Observations on the seal ovary. *J. Anat.*, 84:400, 1950.

Harrison, R.J.: Changes in the reproductive tract of foetal and adult seals. *J. Anat.*, 85:428–429, 1951.

Harrison, R.J., Matthews, H.L., and Roberts, J.M.: Reproduction in some Pinnipedia. *Trans. Zool. Soc. Lond.*, XXVII(5):437–531, 1952.

Harrison, R.J. and Tomlinson, J.D.W.: Observations of the venous system in certain Pinnipedia and Cetacea. *Proc. Zool. Soc. Lond.*, 126:205–233, 1956.

Harrison, R.J.: Reproduction and reproductive organs in common seals (*Phoca vitulina*) in the Wash, East Anglia. *Mammalia*, 24:372–385, 1960.

Harrison, R.J., Rowlands, I.W., Whitting, H.W., and Young, B.A.: Growth and structure of the thyroid gland in the common seal (*Phoca vitulina*). *J. Anat.* 96:3–15, 1962.

Harrison, R.J. and Tomlinson, J.D.W.: Anatomical and physiological adaptations in diving mammals. In *Viewpoints in Biology.* London, Butterworths, 1963, pp. 115–162.

Harrison, R.J., Johnson, F.R., and Tedder, R.S.: Underwater feedings, the stomach and intestine of some delphinids. *J. Anat.*, 101:186–187, 1966.

Harrison, R.J. and Kooyman, G.L.: General physiology of the pinnipedia. In Harrison, R.J., Hubbard, R.C., Peterson, R.S., Rice, C.E., and Schusterman,

R.J. (Eds.): *The Behavior and Physiology of Pinnipeds*. New York, Appleton-Century Crofts, 1968, pp. 258–263.

Harrison, R.J. and Young, B.A.: Functional characteristics of the Pinniped placenta. In Zoological Society of London: *Comparative Biology of Reproduction in Mammals*. New York, Academic Press, 1968, pp. 47–67.

Harrison, R.J.: Reproduction and reproductive organs. In Andersen, H.T. (Ed.): *The Biology of Marine Mammals*. New York, Academic Press, 1969, vol. 1, pp. 253–342.

Harrison, R.J.: Endocrine organs: hypophysis, thyroid and adrenal. In Andersen, H.T. (Ed.): *The Biology of Marine Mammals*. New York, Academic Press, 1969, vol. 1, pp. 349–388.

Herman, C.M.: The effect of Higueronia on the nemathelminthic gastric ulcers of California sea lions, *Rev. Med. Trop.*, 8:45–47, 1942.

Hill, W.C.O.: A comparative study of the pancreas, *Proceedings of the General Meetings for Scientific Business of the Zoological Society of London*. 1926, pp. 581–631.

Hoshina, T and Sugiura, Y.: On a Skin Disease and a Nematode Parasite of a Dolphin, *Tursiops truncatus* (Montagu, 1821). *Sci. Rep. Whales Res. Inst.*, 11:133–138, 1956.

Hubbard, R.C.: Husbandry and laboratory care of Pinnipeds. In Harrison, R.J., Hubbard, R.C., Peterson, R.S., Rice, C.E., and Schusterman, R.J.: *The Behavior and Physiology of Pinnipeds*. New York, Appleton-Century Crofts, 1968, pp. 299–358.

Ito, Susumo: The endoplasmic reticulum of gastric parietal cells. *J. Biophys. Biochem. Cytol.*, 11:333–347, 1961.

Johnson, F.R. and Harrison, R.J.: Ultrastructural characteristics of the dolphin stomach. *J. Anat.*, 10:173, 1969.

Kelly, A.L. and Jansen, D.: Chronic aortitis in the California sea lion, *Zalophus californianus*. *Nature (London)*, 186:731, 1960.

Kenney, D.W.: Personal communication, 1965 and 1969.

Keyes, M.C.: Pathology of the northern fur seal. *J. Amer. Vet. Med. Assn.* 147:1090–1095, 1965.

Kleynenberg, S.Y. and Yablokov, A.V.: *Beluga—Results of Monographic Investigation of the Species*. Moscow, Academy of Sciences of the U.S.S.R., 1961.

Kubota, K.: Comparative anatomical and neurohistological observations on the tongue of the northern fur seal (*Callorhinus ursinus*). *Anat. Rec.*, 161(2):257–266, 1968.

Lacoste, A. and Baudrimont, A.: Dispositifs D'Adaptation Fonctionnelle A La Plongee Dans L'Appareil Respiratoire Du Marsouin (*Phocoena communis. less.*). *Arch. Anat., Histol. Embroyol.*, 17:1–48, 1933.

Lillibridge, C.B.: The fine structure of normal human gastric mucosa. *Gastroenterology*, 47:209–298, 1964.

Low, F.N.: The pulmonary alveolar epithelium of laboratory mammals and man. *Anat. Rec.*, 117:241–264, 1953.

MacKintosh, N.A. and Wheeler, J.F.C.: *Discovery Rep.*, 1:257–540, 1929.

Macklin, C.C.: The pulmonary alveolar mucoid film and the pneumatocytes. *Lancet,* 1:1099–1104, 1954.

Maderson, P.F.A.: Unpublished data from Marine Bioscience Facility, Pt. Mugu, Calif., 1967.

Matthews, L.H.: Cyclic changes in the uterine mucosa of balaenopterid whales. *J. Anat.,* 82:207–232, 1948.

Matthews, L.H.: *Atlantide Rep.,* 1:223, 1950.

Miller, R.M. and Ridgway, S.H.: Clinical experiences with dolphins and whales. *Small Animal Clinic.* 3:189–193, 1963.

Montagna, W. and Harrison, R.J.: Adaptations in the skin of the common seal (*Phoca vitulina*). *J. Anat.,* 90:597, 1956.

Montagna, W.: Comparative anatomy and physiology of the skin. *Arch. Derm.,* 96:357–63, 1967.

Murata, R.: Histological studies on the respiratory portions of the lungs of Cetacea. *Sci. Rep. Whales Res. Inst.,* 6:33–47, 1951.

Murphy, H.D.: Some comparative histological features in Pinnipeds. Presented at the Fourth Annual Conf. Biol. Sonar and Diving Mammals, Menlo Park, California, Stanford Research Institute, 1967.

Murphy, H.D.: Miscroscopic studies on the testis of the northern fur seal *Callurhinus ursinus* (Part II). Unpublished report, San Jose, California, San Jose State College, 1969.

Nagel, E.L., Morgane, P.J., McFarland, W.L., and Galliano, R.E.: Rete mirabile of dolphin: its pressure-damping effect on cerebral circulation. *Science,* 161:898–900, 1968.

Nakajima, Masayuki: In regard to the rete mirabile of the Cetacea. *Toho Med. Acad. J.,* 8:4, 1961.

Nakajima, M., Sawaura, K., Fujimoto, A., and Oda, T.: Foreign bodies in the stomachs of the captive dolphins. *Enoshima Marineland Rep.* (Enoshima, Japan) 2:1–6, 1966.

Palmer, E. and Weddell, G.: The relationship between structure, innervation, and function of the skin of the bottlenosed dolphins (*Tursiops truncatus*). *Proc. Zool. Soc. London,* 143:553–568, 1964.

Prathap, K., Ardlie, N.G., Paterson, J.C., and Schuartz, C.J.: Spontaneous arterial lesions in the Antarctic seal. *Arch. Path.,* 82:287–296, 1966.

Rand, R.W.: Reproduction in the female cape fur seal, *Arctocephalus pusillus. Proc. Zool. Soc. London,* 124:717–740, 1955.

Rewell, R.E., and Willis, R.A.: Some tumours found in whales, *J. Path. Bact.,* 61:454–456, 1949.

Rhodin, J.A.G.: *An Atlas of Ultrastructure.* Philadelphia, Saunders, 1963, pp. 88–93.

Ridgway, S.H.: Medical care of marine mammals, *J. Amer. Vet. Med. Assn.* 147:1077–1085, 1965.

Ridgway, S.H., Scronce, B.L., and Kanwisher, J.: Respiration and deep diving in the bottlenose porpoise. *Science,* 166:1651–1654, 1969.

Roberts, J.C., Boice, R.C., Brownell, R.L., and Brown, D.H.: Spontaneous atherosclerosis in pacific toothed and baleen whales. In Roberts, J.C. and Straus, S.: *Comparative Atherosclerosis*. New York, Harper and Row, 1965, pp. 151–155.

Scholander, P.F., and Schevill, W.E.: Counter-current vascular heat exchange in the fins of whales. *J. Appl. Physiol., 8:*279–282, 1955.

Schroeder, C.R. and Wegeforth, H.B.: The occurrence of gastric ulcers in sea mammals of the California coast, their etiology and pathology. *J. Amer. Vet. Med. Assn., 87:*333–342, 1935.

Seder, A.W. and Friedman, M.H.F.: Correlation of the fine structure of the gastric parietal cells (Dogs) with functional activity of the stomach. *J. Biophys. Biochem. Cytol., 11:*349–363, 1961.

Simpson, C.F., Wood, F.G., and Young, G.: Cutaneous lesions on a porpoise with erysipelas. *J. Amer. Vet. Med. Assn., 133*(11): 1958, pp. 558–560.

Slijper, E.J.: Organ weights and symmetry problems in porpoises and seals. *Arch. Neerl. Zool., 13:*97, 1958.

Slijper, E.J.. *Whales*. New York, Basic Books, 1962.

Sokolov, V.E.: Adaptations of the mammalian skin to the aquatic mode of life. *Nature* (*London*), *195:*464–466, 1962a.

Sokolov, V.E.: The structure of the skin covering of some cetaceans II. *Nauchn. Dokl. Vysshei, Shkoly. Biol., 3:*45–55, 1962b.

Sonntag, C.F.: The comparative anatomy of the tongues of the mammalia— VII, Cetacea, Sirenia, and Ungulata. *Proc. Zool. Soc. London*, 1922, pp. 639–657.

Stolk, A.: Tumors in whales. *Amsterdam Natur., 1:*28–33, 1950.

Stolk, A.: Some inflammations in whales. *Proc. Kon. Akad. V. Wetensch., 56:*364–368, 1953.

Stolk, A.: Some tumors in whales II, *Proc. Kon. Ned. V. Wetensch., 56:*360–377, 1953.

Stolk, A.: Hepatic cirrhosis in the blue whale, *Balaenoptera musculus*. *Proc. Kon. Ned. Akad. V. Wetensch., 56:*375, 1953.

Stolk, A.: A new case of hepatic cirrhosis in the blue whale *Balaenoptera musculus* (L.). *Proc. Kon. Akad. V. Wetensch., 57:*258–260, 1954.

Stolk, A.: Tumors in Whales III, *Proc. Kon. Ned. Akad. V. Wetensch., 65:*250–267, 1962.

Stout, C.: Atherosclerosis in exotic Carnivora and Pinnipedia, *Amer. J. Path., 57:*673–687, 1969.

Taylor, A.E.R., Brown, D.H., Heyneman, D., and McIntyre, R.W.: Biology of filaroid nematode, (*Dipetalonema spirocauda*) from the heart of captive harbor seals and sea lions, together with pathology of the hosts. *J. Parasitol., 47:*971–976, 1961.

Testi, F. and Pilleri, G.: Verminous pulmonitis induced by nematoda (*Halocoercus, Pseudaliidae*) in the Dolphin (*Delphinus delphis* L.). In Pilleri, G. *Investigations on Cetacea*. Waldau-Berne, Switzerland, G. Pilleri 1969.

Truex, R.C., Nolan, F.G., Truex, R.C., Jr., Schneider, H.P., and Perlmutter,

H.I.: Anatomy and pathology of the whale heart with special reference to the coronary circulation. *Anat. Rec., 141*:325–354, 1961.

Uys, C.J. and Best, P.B.: Pathology and lesions observed in whales flensed at Saldanha Bay, South Africa. *J. Comp. Path., 76*:407–412, 1966.

White, P.D., King, R.L., and Jenks, J., Jr.: The relation of heart size to the time intervals of the heart beat, with particular reference to the elephant and the whale, *New Eng. J. Med., 248*:69–70, 1953.

Wilson, T.M., Cheville, N.F., and Karstad, L.: Seal pox, *Bull. Wildlife Dis. Ass., 5*:412–418, 1969.

Winborn, W.B. and Bochman, D.E.: Origin of lysosomes in parietal cells. *Lab. Invest., 19*:256–264, 1968.

Wislocki, G.B.: On the structure of the lungs of the porpoise (*Tursiops truncatus*). *Amer. J. Anat., 44*:47–77, 1929.

Wislocki, G.B.: On the placentation of the harbor porpoise (*Phocoena Phocoena (Linnaeus)*). *Biol. Bull., 65*:80–98, 1933.

Wislocki, G.B.: The lungs of the manatee (*Trichechus latirostris*) compared with those of other aquatic mammals. *Biol. Bull., 68*:385–396, 1935.

Wislocki, G.B. and Belanger, L.F.: The lungs of the larger Cetacea compared to those of smaller species. *Biol. Bull., 78*:289–297, 1940.

Woodard, J.C., Zam, S.G., Caldwell, D.K., and Caldwell, M.C.: Some parasitic diseases of dolphins. *Path. Vet., 6*:257–272, 1969.

Chapter 6

BEHAVIOR OF MARINE MAMMALS

Melba C. Caldwell and David K. Caldwell

CETACEA

This section deals primarily with personal observations made on the smaller species of toothed whales. Much of the material relates to the Atlantic bottlenosed dolphin, *Tursiops truncatus*, the species most commonly maintained in captivity in the United States. Additional detailed personal observations are included on the Amazon dolphin, *Inia geoffrensis;* the Pacific white-striped dolphin, *Lagenorhynchus obliquidens;* and the eastern Pacific pilot whale, *Globicephala scammoni.* Brief mention is made from firsthand observation of the eastern Pacific common dolphin, *Delphinus delphis bairdi;* the Risso dolphin or grampus, *Grampus griseus;* the killer whale, *Orcinus orca;* the spotted dolphin, *Stenella plagiodon;* and the false killer whale, *Pseudorca crassidens.*

Much of the following information on small cetaceans was gathered on a "catch-as-catch-can" basis. The behavioral work done by both ourselves and others is still in the naturalistic stage. Some areas, however, have been extended into investigations of normative behavior, and the fields of both communication and echolocation have received a good hard look; but age, sex and individual differences in even these latter well-studied areas have received too little attention in Cetacea.

A good recent summary of various behavioral aspects of cetacean biology was presented by Evans and Bastian (1969).

The generally large baleen whales have had a great deal of excellent work devoted to their anatomy and life history because of the plethora of dead specimens at whaling stations and aboard whaling factory ships at sea. However, the likelihood of their being maintained at length in captivity is remote, with the possible exception of the little piked or minke whale, *Balaenoptera acutorostrata.* This species is relatively small, and will eat fish, thus making it practical to keep in a large tank or enclosure (see Kimura and Nemoto, 1956). General information on the biology of

419

baleen whales can be found in Chapter 1, in Slijper (1962), and in the several extensive works on different species of baleen whales done by various writers for the British Discovery Committee (*Discovery Reports*). We have summarized certain aspects of their social behavior elsewhere (Caldwell and Caldwell, 1966).

Regarding the larger toothed whales, information on sperm whales is comprehensive and dependable, chiefly because of the excellent original studies of Clarke which are referred to in the recent review of sperm whale behavior by Caldwell, *et al.* (1966). The work done by Sergeant (1962) on the north Atlantic pilot whale is a classic and will be difficult to equal for other smaller species of toothed whales. Until this is done, this section should serve as a guide to the present state of knowledge on the behavior of the bottlenosed dolphin, the species most likely to be maintained in captivity.

The following behavior studies served to provide much of this information.

1. *Small-group normative behavior in previously established but naive groups:*

For approximately two years, we observed an undisturbed cetacean community tank at Marineland of the Pacific. This community contained from five to nine Atlantic bottlenosed dolphins and two Pacific white-striped dolphins. None had received more than the most rudimentary training, and some had not been trained at all. The group was observed and recorded biweekly, for a minimum two-hour period beginning at approximately 0800 hours. Because the public is not admitted at this site until 1000 hours, we had two hours in which to observe normative behavior and record concurrent vocalizations. Our primary objectives were to correlate these and determine the pattern of developing vocalizations of the two males born in the tank during the study period. Additional observations were made intermittently when new animals were added or when individuals were removed from the community for use elsewhere at Marineland. Air and hydrophone recordings were also made when the tank was lowered for routine medical examinations of the animals.

Over a period of approximately two years, we intermittently observed an undisturbed community tank at Marineland of Florida which contained from three to nine Amazon dolphins, which had had no training other than to feed from the hand. As in the group noted above, general behavior was studied and an attempt made to correlate concurrent vocalizations. No new animals were added during this period; the losses were either due to removal elsewhere or death.

2. *Behavior of small groups freshly introduced to captivity:*

One group of five Atlantic bottlenosed dolphins was studied at Florida's Gulfarium.

One group of two spotted dolphins was studied at the Gulfarium.

Two groups of three juvenile Atlantic bottlenosed dolphins were studied at Marineland of the Pacific.

Three groups, numbering three, four, and five Atlantic bottlenosed dolphins were studied at Marineland of Florida.

One group of four juvenile eastern Pacific common dolphins was studied intermittently at Marineland of the Pacific for approximately thirty-four days.

3. *Behavior of small groups exposed to light but routine duties:*

At Marineland of Florida, sporadic observations were made over a one-year period of a community tank containing Atlantic bottlenosed dolphins of varying numbers of from three to nine, one or two Risso dolphins, and one Pacific white-striped dolphin. Also during this time, for brief periods, the community included one eastern Pacific pilot whale and from one to four spotted dolphins. Some of the animals in the community did nothing in the way of duties, and the others either jumped for food, were fed underwater by a diver, or both, at intervals of approximately ninety minutes throughout the day, every day.

4. *Behavior of freshly captured and naive individuals in isolation and/or with one or two other individuals:*

The following numbers of Atlantic bottlenosed dolphins were recorded and observed: Marineland of Florida, 36; Marineland of the Pacific, 5; Florida's Gulfarium, 2; United States Navy Marine Bioscience Facility, Point Mugu, California, 1. Duration of observation varied from thirty minutes to about two weeks before captive training procedures began. We regard the taking of food directly from a trainer's hand as the end of the naive period. This varied with individual animals and individual trainer techniques, but the period may be as short as an hour after captivity or as long as several weeks. Usually it is about one or two days.

5. *Behavior of individuals in training, under experimental procedures, or performing animals:*

This is the most frequently encountered type of individual, as most institutions begin training or experimental procedures as quickly as possible on incoming animals. This is usually purely a matter of economics, as only the larger oceanaria or research facilities can afford a backlog of naive animals. We have worked for brief periods, mostly recording, at the following institutions with these kinds of subjects: Florida's Gulfarium, Ft. Walton Beach (Atlantic bottlenosed dolphins, spotted dolphins); Aquarium of Niagara Falls, New York (Atlantic bottlenosed dolphins, Amazon dolphins; Amazon river dolphin, *Sotalia fluviatilis*); U. S. Navy Marine Bioscience Facility, Point Mugu, California (Atlantic bottlenosed dolphins); Steinhart Aquarium, San Francisco, California (Amazon dolphins, Pacific white-striped dolphins); Sea World, San Diego, California (Amazon dolphins); Fort Worth, Texas, Zoo (Amazon dolphins); Marineland of the Pacific, Los Angeles, California (Atlantic bottlenosed dolphins; eastern Pacific bottlenosed dolphins, *Tursiops gilli;* Pacific white-striped dolphins, eastern Pacific common dolphins, eastern Pacific pilot whales, false killer whales, Amazon dolphins). Most of our work in this category, however, consists of observations of the Atlantic bottlenosed dolphin at Marineland of Florida, St. Augustine, where we have had the opportunity of following some of these individuals through capture to polished performers. Ontogeny of the vocalizations have also been studied in two infants born here in captivity, a male and a female. Additional information was obtained from the Miami (Florida) Seaquarium, Ocean World at Ft. Lauderdale, Florida, and the Aquatarium at St. Petersburg, Florida.

Small Group Normative Behavior

EFFECTS OF GROUP SIZES

No effects directly attributable to overcrowding have been noted in the community tanks at Marineland of Florida and Marineland of the Pacific. Both are large tanks but at times have housed up to thirteen individuals. There is probably more crowding in some of the smaller holding tanks in which up to five already integrated individuals are sometimes housed when first captured (in a tank some 21 ft (6.4 m) in diameter and about 5 to 6 ft (1.5 to 1.8 m) deep). Since most of the odontocetes are intensely social in the wild, clean-water maintenance would probably become a husbandry problem before behavioral effects of overcrowding manifested themselves.

At times, mature males may inflict injury or even death to others. This is an individual problem that has to be guarded against by attendants. Juveniles or females rarely cause problems of this nature, but a highly territorial female in a small enclosure may fight newcomers. Problems of integration of newcomers have already been discussed (Caldwell, Caldwell, and Townsend, 1968), but the gist of the matter is that newly introduced animals and maturing males should be observed closely. Alert attendants will pick up signs of incipient trouble.

Various aspects of cetacean aggressive behavior which bear on this discussion recently were summarized by Norris (1967).

Isolation of these social animals may also introduce a husbandry problem. Unless the dolphin is to be involved in some experimental or training procedure whereby it will receive considerable human contact (which often seems to satisfy the social needs of the animal as much as contact with another dolphin) isolation may bring about behavioral problems. Trainers have told us that such problems usually manifest themselves in the dolphin's becoming very aggressive and unwilling to accept a tank-mate. When placed in isolation, newly captured animals, especially juveniles, often whistle constantly for hours or even days, a behavior which suggests emotional unrest. Still another related husbandry problem may come when a long-term resident of a tank is removed to complete isolation in a strange tank, even though the animal previously lived alone or with only one other companion. For example, at Marineland of Florida, an adult female that had spent her entire captive life (ten years) with the same animal, a male, in one of the holding pens in the Stadium where dolphins perform their trained acts was removed to a small isolated and unattached holding tank prior to being sent to perform elsewhere for a short period. This animal had been performing well and showed no behavioral problems prior to this move. Upon being placed in isolation, she refused to perform and for two days and three nights remained in the center of the small tank bobbing up and down in one spot and vocalizing constantly. She refused to eat and paid no attention to her usual training props when they were offered or placed in the tank with her, except to violently flip them out of the tank if they happened to come near her snout. She was then returned to the Stadium. At the next show, within the hour, she performed perfectly (said to be even better than normal) and ate heartily. After her return to familiar surroundings and tankmate, there were no further manifestations of the unusual behavior observed while she was in isolation.

SEXUAL AND AFFECTIONAL INTERACTION

Primate studies in both the field and laboratory are so well advanced and cetacean studies so rudimentary that comparisons between the two groups may be dangerous. However, in primate papers we find area after area in which behavioral comparisons fall immediately into place, while we truly have to work at finding meaningful behavioral correlates in other groups. It is possible that the long time span for development of sexual and physical maturity in both groups lends itself to more analagous effects, particularly in the area of learned behaviors.

In the odontocetes, we prefer the Harlows' (1965) synthesis of affectional bonds in nonhuman primates, a process involving a natural progression of social experiences that are rewarding, beginning with the initial infant rewards of mother-infant interaction, normally proceeding through the "roughhouse" of juvenile peer-group play, then to heterosexual relationships involving effective copulation, and ultimately to the parental role from which the mother must receive strong rewards to compensate for her curtailment of freedom.

As in the primates (Harlow and Harlow, 1965, p. 323), reflex penile erection occurs in male *Tursiops* within forty-eight hours of birth. Unlike infant primates, however, whose inadequate posture makes intromission impossible or extremely unlikely (Harlow, 1967), dolphin infants necessarily possess highly developed physical control, and the young males attempt copulation (usually with the mother) within a few weeks. The mammary glands are located one on each side of the genital area and doubtless serve to direct the infant's attention on this area (Fig. 6–1). Also, the infant's nosing in this area undoubtedly stimulates the mother. The mother's response may range from passive acceptance to active solicitation of the infant by nosing his genital area (Fig. 6–2) which elicits an erection. The young male then continues his copulatory attempts as he develops, and may achieve what appears to be an effective copulatory pattern within a few months (Fig. 6–3). This is significant in an animal such as *Tursiops* which has not been known to achieve sexual maturity before seven years, as it permits a long learning period for sexual patterns.

Figure 6–1. Infant *Tursiops truncatus* in typical nursing position which also probably affords sexual stimulation to the mother since her genital aperture is immediately adjacent to the nipples. (Photograph courtesy of Marineland of Florida, by William A. Huck, prepared by Frank Miller.)

Figure 6–2. Adult female *Tursiops truncatus* soliciting her male infant by nosing his genital region. (Photograph courtesy of Marineland of Florida.)

Figure 6–3. Juvenile male *Tursiops truncatus* (below) effectively affecting intromission with his mother at the age of three months. (Authors' photograph made at Marineland of the Pacific, by William A. Huck.)

Although we considered these seven-year-old males sexually mature in the past, there is some evidence that these males would more properly be termed adolescent until some fourteen to fifteen years of age. Our data on reproductive capacity are limited, but suggest some conclusions. Several males, both wild-caught and long-term captive, all necropsied in April-May 1968, showed a threefold to fourfold acceleration in testis size and an even greater increase in spermatozoa production between animals of about 2.3 to 2.4 m (7½ to 8 ft) in length and those of approximately 2.5 to 2.6 m (8 ft 3 in to 8 ft 6 in). We suspect that sufficient data will result in a curve very similar to that shown by Sergeant (1962: Figs. 19–20) for the north Atlantic pilot whale; and that whereas eight- to twelve-year-old males in captivity with constant exposure to females may well produce offspring, males over fifteen years old probably impregnate most of the females in the wild.

Captive males not only engage in frequent copulation with females of the same or different species, but they also frequently masturbate, especially the juveniles. This may be accomplished by rubbing the genital area against the dorsal fin, the tip of the fluke, or the flipper of a female, usually resulting in an erection. Even the appendages of a dead animal of either sex on the bottom of the tank have been used. Sometimes the edge of a sea turtle's shell is utilized, with the male inserting his erected penis under the edge of the turtle's shell as they both swim slowly around the tank. At Marineland of the Pacific, a juvenile *Tursiops* used the frame of one of the observation windows as a source of stimulation for several days, and the management was greatly relieved when he found other sources of stimulation and discontinued the practice. (This sort of behavior can be a great source of embarrassment to the management of a public exhibit and thus can present a husbandry problem.) There is also some evidence that penile erection is, at least in part, under purely voluntary control in dolphins (males have been known to use the penis as a manipulatory organ). As an in-house joke, one trainer at Marineland of Florida taught a dolphin to have an erection on cue and then carry a hoop around by his penis. The cue for the behavior was the trainer's raising his arm, which proved to be an unfortunate choice. When this animal, along with his hoop, was transferred into a tank available to the paying public, the behavior created quite a stir whenever an innocent, friendly tourist raised his arm to wave at the seemingly smiling creature (see also section on play, below).

As females do not demonstrate penile erection, our indices of sexual arousal are more difficult for accurate interpretation. The female dolphin has a well-developed clitoris and, unlike most other mammals, copulates through ventral-surface to ventral-surface contact. The tactile stimulation of copulation with concurrent clitoral stimulation could be expected to be rewarding to the females (also see section on play, below). The frequent manifestation of what appears to be sexual interplay of both adolescent and mature female dolphins with other dolphins of both sexes and all ages indicates that this is true.

Masturbation is frequent in females of any age (McBride and Kritzler, 1951, p. 262), and there is much clitoral tactile stimulation practiced between females in which the snout, flippers, flukes, or dorsal fin of the partner are used. Since the roles of the participants are reversed at intervals, the likelihood of this behavior's being involved with submissive behavior is pretty much ruled out. A female may also actively masturbate on an appendage of a male (Fig. 6–4). Because the female initiates and solicits much of the sexual interaction of any kind, we may speculate that she is also sexually receptive much of the time.

We have no knowledge of estrus periods for the dolphin female. Previous data from Marineland of Florida (Tavolga, 1966; Tavolga and Essapian,

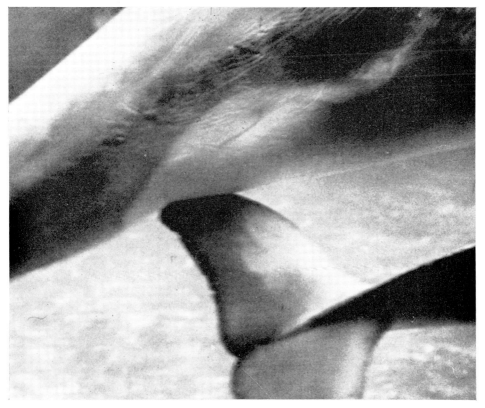

Figure 6–4. Adult female *Tursiops truncatus* (above) masturbating by purposefully positioning herself alongside a swimming juvenile male so that his fluke tip is inserted into her genital aperture. (Authors' photograph made at Marineland of the Pacific.)

1957; McBride and Kritzler, 1951) indicate a spring pairing period with a
postulated eleven- to twelve-month gestation period (McBride and Hebb,
1948; Essapian, 1963). With the exception of one September and one
October birth, this pattern has continued to exist at this site over the years,
and judging from the size of these two calves and the fact that one animal
was stillborn and the other lived only one day, both were probably premature. Other localities do not show this same peak pattern (Fig. 6–5),
and except for pointing out the disparity, insufficient data make further
speculation meaningless. There does not appear to be any striking discrepancy at any oceanarium between animals impregnated in the wild
but delivering in captivity, and those conceiving in captivity.

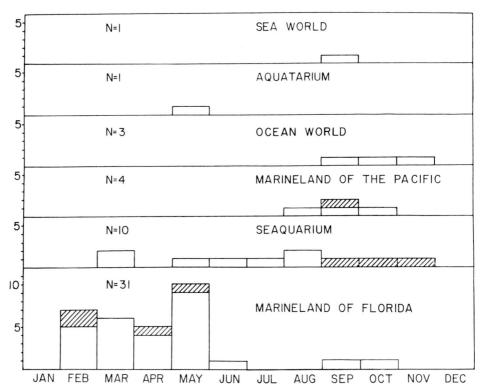

Figure 6–5. Numbers of live captive births of *Tursiops truncatus* by month at five
different oceanaria. Open areas indicate births of young conceived in captivity; cross-
hatched areas indicate births conceived in the wild. All mothers were originally
captured in Florida. Those females at Aquatarium, Seaquarium, and Marineland of
Florida were captured, or were from stock captured, near those sites, as were the
males siring the young. Those mothers at Marineland of the Pacific were captured
near Miami and the young were sired by a male captured near St. Augustine. The
females and males siring their young at Ocean World were captured in the central
Florida Keys. The female at Sea World was from Florida (probably southern) and
the male siring her calf from Gulfport, Mississippi.

PARENTAL BEHAVIOR

Maternal behavior in captive Atlantic bottlenosed dolphins has been well covered in the literature (e.g. McBride and Kritzler, 1951; Tavolga and Essapian, 1957) and what little is known for different species in the wild summarized (Caldwell and Caldwell, 1966). Although the period of intensive care involving constant body contact is measured in weeks, as the infant is precocial, the social bond between mother and female offspring is measured in years. There is a strong social bond between mother and male offspring for at least two years, the longest that we have been able to observe this relationship. Staff members at Marineland of Florida tell us, however, that under stress the offspring may return to its mother over a period of several years. We know of no cases of separation of mother and offspring in oceanaria before two years of age, as the bond is so close that psychological damage to the offspring might have occurred. However, we have seen animals as young as an estimated nine months to a year that have been brought in from the wild to various oceanaria. Trainers there preferred such animals, even though these young individuals take considerable extra care and attention (some even have to be bottle fed). When such an infant is successfully reared, it is said to make a good trained animal, probably because it establishes rather close bonds with its human trainer. At other oceanaria, an animal some 1½ to 2 years of age (about 6½ to 7 ft, 2.0 to 2.1 m, in tip of upper jaw to fluke notch length) is preferred because it is fully weaned but is not yet old enough to have established strong behavioral patterns which must be overcome before intensive training can begin. Trainers usually have individual preferences as to sex as well as size of animals for initial training. This is, however, a matter of the trainer's thoughts about the desirability of one sex or another when the animal reaches adult size. In the beginning, the sex seems to have little effect on the ability of an animal to be trained, probably because the young animal is primarily involved with establishing an animal-trainer relationship to replace its more normal offspring-mother relationship.

Males normally take no part in rearing individual animals. Their role is apparently one of defense of the school and its territory. A single short-term occurrence of a male's adopting a protective role toward an infant has been reported (Essapian, 1963). The females in a community tank normally have to protect the infants from the male's aggression.

PLAY

Because it is so varied and occupies much of a captive dolphin's time, this area has been extensively covered for several dolphins and porpoises (e.g. McBride and Hebb, 1948; Brown and Norris, 1956; Norris and

Prescott, 1961; Caldwell and Caldwell, 1964, 1966; Caldwell and Caldwell, 1968b). Almost any object placed in a tank immediately becomes the object of close scrutiny. After the initial fear aroused by the strange object is allayed (the time ranging from a few seconds to many days, according to the animal and its experience), any number of activities may be instigated, using the object as a toy for either solitary or group play. Although juveniles are more playful than adults, play is common throughout life.

Since the streamlined dolphins have a limited number of means by which to manipulate playthings (primarily with the mouth, snout, flippers, dorsal fin, and flukes), it is not surprising that they have developed what appear to be games that utilize the genital region, although some of these "games" may actually represent sexual stimulation in the form of masturbation (see section on sexual behavior, above). One adroit male *Tursiops* at Marineland of Florida enjoyed the rare ability of carrying a pelican feather around the tank by curving his erect penis around it. Another game that somewhat embarrassed the same establishment was perfected by two adult female Atlantic bottlenosed dolphins. In it, they learned to push a small, hollow rubber ball about 15 cm in diameter to the bottom of the tank where they could manipulate it and pick it up by the muscles of the vaginal region (Fig. 6–6). Holding the ball in this manner, they carried it around the tank or pushed it to the bottom again where they obviously received some sexual stimulation from prolonged rubbing against it. When not manipulating the ball in this manner, they often carried it under the flipper to be utilized again shortly after.

Figure 6–6. Adult female *Tursiops truncatus* manipulating a small partly inflated rubber ball with the muscles of her genital region. (Photograph courtesy of Marineland of Florida.)

Play may even be initiated with humans. A familiar sight at Marineland of Florida is a dolphin tossing a rubber ring or a small rubber ball to the tourists standing at tankside, who in turn vie among themselves for the privilege of catching and returning the offered plaything (Fig. 6–7). The bright, shiny coins that the interaction-seeking visitors throw into the display tanks make wonderful playthings for the dolphins but a husbandry problem for the curators. Unfortunately, although they will often play with a small coin for hours, there is a strong tendency for dolphins to swallow any small foreign object and as much as 97 cents, mostly in pennies of recent date and probably the shiniest the tourist had, was recovered from one animal's stomach at necropsy. Some individual dolphins are more likely to swallow foreign objects than others and even though deaths in captivity are sometimes attributed to the ingestion of large foreign objects, the stomachs of wild animals also sometimes contain a variety of inedibles. The tendency to swallow foreign objects by dolphins often seems to be related to competitive behavior when two or more animals are playing with the same object. For example, the exchange of a coin between two

Figure 6–7. Adult *Tursiops truncatus* engaged in play activity with tourists, in which an inflated rubber ring was tossed back and forth. (Photograph courtesy of Marineland of Florida.)

animals may go on for some time before one appears to be afraid that the second may take it away. Apparently rather than allow this, the first may swallow the object more rapidly than might be the case if the animal were playing alone. Such competitive behavior may extend to a dolphin-human relationship. According to Prescott (1968), a Hawaiian spinner dolphin, *Stenella* sp. at Marineland of the Pacific was given a small towel to play with when it was placed in a large fish tank with no other dolphin companions. For a time, all went well, with the human attendants removing the towel each night for fear that the animal might swallow it. This led to the animal swallowing, or partly swallowing, the towel on its own in an apparent effort to keep possession at all times. Usually, the animal would regurgitate the towel and use it again as a plaything, but when it did not, the animal died of a digestive tract blockage.

In our communication studies, we have been made to feel extremely foolish on more than one occasion by getting excited over wildly different sounds coming through our earphones until we were able to correlate the sounds with a young *Tursiops* resting in the tank, blowing bubbles, and obviously just playing with the many different sounds that his noisemakers could produce.

Social Facilitation and Observational Learning

Except possibly for the big males, cetaceans spend much time in swimming either in actual body contact or in close proximity. In times of real or fancied danger, or at night, the distance between animals is reduced even more (Caldwell and Caldwell, 1964, p. 13).

The high degree of social facilitation evidenced by cetaceans can be used to solve practical problems in captive animals. An animal that is feeding will frequently induce new captives to feed. Sick animals may be stimulated or occasionally supported by others. A newly acquired spotted dolphin, in quasi-shock from capture and transport, was supported and walked by human divers with no effect in a shallow tank for about thirty minutes, but after being placed in a deep tank with several *Tursiops*, it was swimming normally in a few minutes.

We have been able to offer only qualitative, and consequently weak, evidence of mimicry and observational learning in cetaceans (Caldwell *et al.*, 1965; Brown *et al.*, 1966), but recent quantitative studies clearly demonstrate its efficacy in cats (John *et al.*, 1968). In the same paper, the authors review the literature for other species as well. In cetaceans, only reward techniques are used and there is great variation in an individual animal's learning rate, but there is some evidence that training time is reduced when a naive animal is allowed to observe a trained individual.

FOOD AND FEEDING

A newborn dolphin begins to nurse within a few hours after birth. There appears to be an innate tendency to mouth the mother. One infant that we watched learning to nurse consistently directed its mouthing toward the wrong areas of the mother's body, mostly far anterior to the mammae. The mother gave no assistance toward directing the infant's efforts until the placenta was passed. After this she slowed her pace when the calf nosed her body, turned on her side and maintained position, thus aiding the infant's nursing efforts. Within a few minutes, the infant was nursing successfully, if inexpertly.

Nursing continues for as long as eighteen months, although infants begin to mouth, then take, an occasional whole fish for approximately a year before nursing is discontinued completely. Chances of a motherless six-month-old's living in captivity should be fairly good, with considerable human attention. In the wild, it would probably be abandoned and lost to predators, since we have no evidence of a captive orphan's being reared by a foster mother.

We have not seen any indication of a hungry female's sharing food with her offspring. There is some indication, however, that where fish are plentiful, mothers in the wild may speed up an infant's learning to eat fish. Two dolphin mothers at Marineland of Florida have shown this tendency even in captivity where the animals are not overfed. On occasion, when these two mothers were completely gorged, they would shake the heads from small food fish which they did not want and proffer the bodies to the infants. When the young took the fish, mouthing them, there were none of the attempts to retrieve them that characterized the play that dolphins devise.

These observations gain some reinforcement from the following: A freshly captured six-foot (1.8 m) male at Marineland of Florida had refused food for several days, although he appeared hungry and took fish in his mouth. An animal this small is probably not fully weaned, and the head trainer, Fred Lyons, remembered having seen the mothers shake heads from the fish before proffering them to the young. Consequently, he cut the heads from several fish before offering them to the animal. No luck. In desperation, he manually broke off some heads so that the fish would look like those proffered by the mothers. Instant success. Not really believing his own cleverness, he switched back to the cut bodies. These were taken but dropped. Back to the torn heads and success. After several hours, the animal was taking anything offered, including fish tails, but this technique did appear to get the animal over the initial hump of learning to eat dead fish for the first time in captivity.

The problem of getting freshly captured cetaceans to make the transition from live to dead fish is not unusual. Contrary to expectations, this is more apparent in young animals, 1.8 to 2.1 m (6 to 7 ft) in length, than in the older ones. Some newly captured adults may take dead fish from a trainer's hand in a matter of minutes after being placed in a tank. The ubiquitous and previously mentioned Fred Lyons, who has "dolphin ESP," had the responsibility of getting two especially valuable 2.1 m (7 ft) male dolphins to eat. After they had been eight days without food despite heroic measures, Lyons had an inspiration. He lowered the water in the tank to approximately two feet and, standing in the tank with them, began to harass the animals by hitting them with fish either in his hand or by throwing fish at them. When the dolphins were thoroughly antagonistic and on the verge of turning on him (which an angered dolphin may do, despite the comments of many writers), he held a fish in his hand, slapping at an animal with it. Then, admittedly with more determination than good sense, he held the fish extended toward the circling animal. In turn, each animal promptly bit with a vengeance. Lyons kept this up for thirty to sixty minutes, and at the end of this period the animals were eating vigorously—not only proffered dead fish, but were picking up previously rejected ones from the bottom of the tank.

PROPULSION

Slijper (1962) has reviewed the mechanisms of propulsion in Cetacea. Work done in the meantime regarding speeds attained by these animals will be of interest to those maintaining the smaller species in captivity. Lang and his coworkers have conducted studies of swimming speeds from three different aspects—anatomy (Lang, 1966b), laboratory performance (Lang and Daybell, 1963; Lang and Pryor, 1966; Lang, 1966a) and open ocean trials (Lang and Norris, 1966; Lang and Pryor, 1966). He found that swimming speeds for most aquarium species are about what can be postulated mathematically and that the muscular expenditure about equals that of champion human athletes. Average top speeds naturally vary with the duration of the swim, decreasing with increased swimming time. Maximum speeds recorded for trained Pacific coast dolphins are 7.7 m/sec (15 knots or 17.2 mph) for the white-striped dolphin, 8.3 m/sec (16.1 knots or 17.2 mph) for the eastern Pacific bottlenosed dolphin and 11.0 m/sec (21.4 knots or 24.6 mph) for the pelagic spotted dolphin (*Stenella attenuata*).

Newly introduced captives spend up to several days endlessly circling the tank. If the new animal is a juvenile or adolescent, it usually whistles constantly. The longer they are captive, the less they tend to swim steadily and gradually they begin to manipulate and play with objects.

An interesting problem is raised by the direction in which captive dolphins swim. Attendants can usually predict with great accuracy the direction in which a new captive will swim in any given tank. We have tried to relate this to direction of current flow or to clockwise vs. counter-clockwise but no pattern seems to fit consistently. It is an interesting problem, as we feel that a solution possibly could shed light on migration. The determined directionality poses both husbandry and training problems. In small tanks, the animals may develop a kink in their back that almost always ends in death, and breaking this directionality is one of the more difficult problems that a trainer may face.

Some form of leaping or jumping seems to be a normal component of behavior in all of the odontocetes. Spinning on the horizontal body axis is typical of some. When these patterns are reinforced, they make spectacular displays, particularly if three or four animals are trained to perform in synchrony.

ACTIVITY CYCLES AND SLEEP

There has been only one quantitative study that sheds any light on the normal diurnal cycle of bottlenosed dolphins. Powell (1966) did a study of the vocalizations of this species, an index of activity. His subjects, on a roughly average daytime feeding cycle of three times a day, showed a periodicity in vocalizations, with an early morning peak and a secondary peak in the afternoon. This activity was modified by shifting the feeding schedule to three times a night, which fairly well destroyed vocal periodicity.

Powell's work may have been slightly skewed unavoidably by the sharp increase in echolocation and competitive protest squawks that occur during feedings, but the total picture of a twice daily increased activity of vocalization during daylight hours was clear. The postfeeding decrease in vocal activity is also clear, as it was in naive common dolphins (Caldwell and Caldwell, 1968a). We have found at times, however, that dolphins tend to be less vocal at night, even though they appear to be just as active in their swimming and play.

There are only a few early passing references to sleep in dolphins. McBride and Hebb (1948) stated that Atlantic bottlenosed dolphins sleep under lights and with lowered water levels. This is not true of the animals presently in this same tank at Marineland of Florida. Lilly (1964, p. 745) stated that dolphins sleep with only one eye closed, but McCormick (1967) found this to be variable. In one thirty-hour observation period, three adult-sized Pacific white-striped dolphins were not seen sleeping (Caldwell and Caldwell, 1964, p. 13), nor were several juvenile Atlantic bottlenosed dolphins who were observed during the same period.

The primitive Amazon dolphin, conversely, does give every appearance of a fairly deep sleep (Caldwell, *et al.*, 1966, p. 18). We also have seen individuals of this species engaged in apparent deep sleep both day and night at Marineland of Florida. The "lighter sleep" of marine cetaceans, when they appear to doze, lasts only for a moment, unless the animals are of advanced age.

McCormick (1967) has done observational work on sleep in six Atlantic bottlenosed dolphins and one male and one female Pacific white-striped dolphin. He calls attention to "cat-napping" on the tank bottom and "surface sleep," the former being more subject to easy arousal. Our observations on this pattern of lying on the bottom lend credence to this in some animals, but there are also, in our experience, more that do not. On occasion, however, one animal that demonstrates this pattern may induce a tankmate to follow the same pattern, frequently in synchrony. The entire problem of cetacean sleep has so many variations, involving age, sex, and individual situations, that even brainwave studies on one of two animals will not solve the problem; it should, however, give us a beginning.

INTERSPECIFIC INTERACTION

Cetaceans of almost all the species that are kept in captivity have at one time or another been maintained together in one tank. Attendants should keep the same wary eye on them for evidence of aggressiveness that they would keep on members of the same species. The likelihood of male-male aggressiveness between species is of about the same order of magnitude as it is in conspecifics. All cetacean males tend to be more tolerant of females of their own or another species. This tolerance occasionally may extend to active care giving (Caldwell and Caldwell, 1966). For over a year, Marineland of Florida had two inseparable male Risso's dolphins in a tank of mixed species. One was moved, and the larger, who occasionally became aggressive toward the large male bottlenosed dolphins, particularly during feeding, gave an indication of actively warding off the large males when his newly acquired female companions were trying to feed. On the other hand, this same animal attacked the largest female *Tursiops* on occasion. These attacks have contained no component of sexual behavior. The introduction of a new animal into an established community may result in husbandry problems.

All of the dolphin species that we have studied in captivity appear to establish an individual microterritory even within a small tank and often even in isolation. The establishment of a microterritory is apparently un-related to sexual considerations but may be related to some factor in the dolphin-human relationship, such as the point where the trainer comes to feed the animal, or it may have no obvious significance. When two or more animals are in the tank, these preferred microterritories do not appear to be especially vigorously defended, if at all, and when the animals are active, they swim freely through each other's microterritory. However, an isolated animal or individuals in a group of any size tend to return to their own microterritory when at rest. In a large community tank, when it is deep enough, the territory may take form in any of the three spatial dimensions of the water mass. Frequently the microterritories overlap, and this may occur in any dimension of the water mass. When an animal occupies a microterritory deep in the water mass, we have found no aggressiveness on the part of an animal holding a microterritory in the upper water levels above when the deeper-territoried animal rises to breathe. While in a community tank of mixed species, some animals undoubtedly tend to establish a microterritory that best approximates a natural ecological preference. We have found that *Tursiops truncatus* in large tanks at Marineland of Florida, Marineland of the Pacific, and Florida's Gulfarium tend to establish microterritories throughout the water mass. While social dominance undoubtedly is involved in holding an established microterritory, we have found no clear correlation between the known or suspected dominance of an individual and the physical position of the microterritory that is established within the water mass (al-though we feel that there is a slight tendency for a dominant individual to establish its microterritory centrally in the tank and near the surface). Husbandry problems resulting from microterritories in an established community have not been observed, but it is something to be aware of as related to overcrowding. The shortage of space for the establishment of microterritories could cause an animal social difficulties in having no place to retreat to when at rest. This could result in such husbandry problems as inappetence or fear to perform.

Performing or Experimental Animals

Selection of Animals

The two prime requirements for animals in these categories are good health and alertness. For show animals, either performing or for simple aquarium display, individuals with no major physical disfigurements are preferred. On the other hand, experimental animals need not be pretty, and sometimes one that is multilated and healed from the loss of a flipper or an eye, for example, may be even more desirable for special experiments.

Trainers have different preferences in animals according to the training requirements, physical makeup of the training area, and previous experience of the trainer. Some trainers prefer males because females appear to have periods of heat when they are least tractable and because they may become pregnant. On the other hand, large males tend to become more aggressive, and in a tank that is likely to have both sexes, such an animal may not be desirable in the long run. Several adult males apparently can be maintained successfully provided there are no females for them to fight over.

If an animal is to be trained to do an intricate routine where a long life is especially desirable, then a young animal (2.0 to 2.1 m (6½ to 7 ft) in the case of *Tursiops*) is preferable at the start since that animal will have a longer useful life span. On the other hand, older and larger animals are showy and thus better for simple display or for simple acts (such as a high jump) that require little training and hence do not mean a large investment in training time and effort, and consequently are more expendable. Because very young animals (5 to 6½ ft or 1.5 to 2.0 m in the case of *Tursiops*) are more playful and not as highly motivated for food reward, they do not usually learn as quickly. Younger, and thus smaller, animals also eat less per day and consequently can physically handle fewer food rewards, with the result that their potential for work is reduced, since the two usually are closely interrelated. There is also the possibility that a small animal will not be able to throw off the diseases of captivity as readily as the larger, stronger animal. Even so, as noted under the topic of parental behavior (above), some trainers feel the affectional bonds between animal and trainer that tend to develop by starting with a young animal are worth the extra effort in the long run.

TRAINING PROCEDURES

As far as we know, the only method successfully used in training dolphins is positive reinforcement, using food reward. There is some evidence that negative reinforcement may lead to neurosis, but as the animals encounter negative reinforcement in the wild (and certainly do from others of their own species in captivity), the idea of negative reinforcement would have been explored further but for the difficulty of punishing an animal in the water when the trainer is several feet away on dry land. The one case of physical punishment inflicted on an animal that we know of was one in which the animal was so heavily punished (actually beaten) that it did indeed become very aggressive. If any negative reinforcement is to be used, it probably will have to be in the form of light punishment and especially in the form of nonphysical punishment (such as a time-out period with or without the trainer turning his back), since dolphins tend to sulk very readily when attempts at punishment are made and will not work at all during the rest of the session. It should also be mentioned that some animals will do considerable work without food reward but literally will accept a pat on the head from the trainer or some other simple interaction such as the trainer splashing water at the dolphin.

Training is an arduous task, requiring six to eight weeks to build up a few simple responses except in very unusual cases where only two or three weeks may be required. A year or more of intensive training is not unusual for obtaining polished performances involving several complicated maneuvers on the part of the animal.

Once the animal is trained, there is always the battle to prevent deterioration of performance. Sub-par performance has to be met by the trainer with stony indifference and total lack of reward to the animal, or the entire training period can be lost. On the other hand, a well-trained animal that had not been rewarded for a poor performance may retain the ability to perform a trained sequence for many years without doing it in the interim.

At Marineland of Florida, an adult female with an eight-month-old calf was called upon to fill in when needed in the Stadium show. The required routine consisted of jumping hurdles and through a hoop, tail walking, jumping and pulling a ball suspended several feet over the water, and carrying various props. The routine required several minutes and a number of different signals were used by her trainer. She had once performed the routine as a regular part of the show, but eight years had transpired since she had done it. However, she did another act in the show in the interim before the birth of her calf and lived in a holding tank in the Stadium where she could see through her gate as other animals were performing her old routine. The first time she was tried on the original routine after the eight-year interim, she did it well in private. She also did it well in private the next day. The third day she was returned to the public show and has performed the routine well for over a year.

EFFECTS OF CAPTIVITY AND TRAINING

Captivity alone is an abrupt transition for cetaceans. Most that can adapt to captivity at all can be trained for simple tasks. The Atlantic bottlenosed dolphin has proven to be adaptable and long living, as well as easily procured. Somewhat unexpectedly, the pilot whale, Risso dolphin, and killer whale have done well in captivity, and one false killer whale at Marineland of the Pacific was a truly exceptional animal, while others have been kept elsewhere with average success. The harbor porpoise (*Phocoena phocoena*), the Pacific white-striped dolphin and the common spotted dolphin of the western Atlantic have a usual captive life span of only one or two years but are beautiful animals and warrant simple training procedures. The Dall porpoise, *Phocoenoides dalli*, probably the most beautiful and active of all well-known marine mammals, almost always dies very quickly in captivity, although one was kept for twenty months at the Navy Marine Bioscience Facility (Ridgway, 1966). Other species, such as the Amazon dolphin, the beluga, *Delphinapterus leucas* (e.g. Ray, 1966); and the pygmy killer whale, *Feresa attenuata* (e.g. Pryor, *et al.*, 1965) are in general so difficult to obtain that they are subjected to little if any training but often do very well as purely exhibit animals.

Statistics on life span of performing versus exhibit animals are meager, but there are some indications that both reproductive capacity and life span are reduced in regularly performing animals even though they probably receive more intensive care.

OTHER MARINE MAMMALS

There is a tremendous disparity in almost all behavioral aspects of the thirty-two (see King, 1964) or thirty-three (see Rice and Scheffer, 1968) species of the order Pinnipedia, due mainly to the differences in degree of freedom from land (or ice) that particular species have adopted. Consequently, it has been impossible in this section to make many generalizations. Even so, little purpose would be served by an attempt at detailing every aspect of each type of behavior for every species. The best alternative seemed to be to concentrate on those pinnipeds and other marine mammals most likely to be maintained in captivity, to mention the extremes of variability possible between species, and to provide the reader with a bibliography that will at least direct him to the literature available on anything else he might need to know. This is the approach we have tried to follow. Evans and Bastian (1969) recently have summarized many aspects of the known behavior in this category.

Group Sizes and Effects

This discussion includes those factors leading to aggregation or dispersal of individuals of a species. In effect, it boils down to an analysis of the space requirements of each individual at any given moment. An unfortunate general lack of published information on the subject of group size at sea forces us to rely mainly on data on animals on land.

If breeding is to occur, some degree of sociability must occasionally be

present in every mammal. It might better be phrased that during reproduction periods, there must be either a reduction in space requirements
or a change in territorial behavior of the males for copulation to occur.
Even pinnipeds that are extremely solitary for most of the year become
gregarious during the breeding season (e.g. northern fur seal, Kenyon
and Wilke, 1953; Ross seal, Scheffer, 1958; elephant seal, Bartholomew,
1955; leopard seal, Hamilton, 1939). In animals with a harem system, such
as the fur seal or sea lion, this change requires a great deal of the neural
system, since apparently the same hormone that activates the reproductive
system of males also increases aggression and territorial defense (see Guhl,
1961, for review).

These changes in behavior are vital, since a harem system dictates that
a male becomes belligerent toward the males with which it was peaceably
feeding or playing even a month prior to the increase in testis size. The
description by Kenyon (1960) of a steady increase in territoriality in bulls
arriving early on the fur seal breeding grounds fits well with the demonstrated correlation of increase in testis weight and territorial behavior in
ring-necked pheasants (Collias and Taber, 1951). In addition, a harem
master must now not only tolerate females but must actively seek them
out and try to keep them in his territory (Alaska fur seal, Scammon, 1874;
southern sea lion, Wynne-Edwards, 1962). Since male sea lions react
toward man or other large species (during breeding season) as they would
toward another male of their own species (Peterson and Bartholomew, 1967;
Eibl-Eibesfeldt, 1961), this increased aggressiveness could well show up in
captivity in an otherwise tractable animal.

The social order of all pinnipeds is determined by the place of copulation, and those species that copulate on land typically observe a harem
system, (Bertram, 1940). In the harem system of the much-studied
Northern fur seal, there is during the breeding season a progressive increase
in hostility between the mature bulls that have arrived first on the breeding
grounds (Elliott, 1887a). The hostility and territoriality become even more
pronounced after the arrival of the females (Bartholomew, 1953).

Pinnipeds engage in the ritualized fighting that characterizes most
animal species; rarely is another animal killed (California sea lion, Peterson
and Bartholomew, 1967; Weddell seal, Poulter, 1968a; Steller's sea lion,
Orr and Poulter, 1967). The ritual battle may last several days and the
two combatants may become so exhausted that a third male may easily take
over the disputed territory (Scammon, 1874). Again, as in other animals,
the original holder of a territory rarely loses. Hewer (1960) observed that
he had never seen an intruder gray seal win, and Peterson and Bartholomew (1967) said that they never saw a temporary intruder California sea
lion establish himself as a territorial bull.

Site tenacity is apparent in some species. According to Elliott (1884) Eskimos believed that fur seal bulls occupied the same spot year after year, describing one unusually marked bull that occupied the same rock for three years. Elliott could not quite bring himself to believe it. Scammon (1874), however, reported a story by native hunters of a bull, recognizable by its having only one flipper, which occupied the same spot for seventeen years, and Scammon was too wise in the use of native observations to discount the story. Kenyon (1960) reaffirmed that mature bulls do indeed tend to reoccupy the same site that they establish in early maturity. As a result, the best bulls do not necessarily have the best territory, preferring a familiar one instead. Rice (1960) found that twenty of the nonmigratory Hawaiian monk seals tagged a previous year had shown no movement between atolls when checked the following year.

Female animals usually become more aggressive after giving birth (Lorenz, 1966) a phenomenon which may simply be due to an increased tendency to withdraw, as Hersher *et al.* (1963) observed in sheep and goats. They proposed the rather interesting theory that defense of the young in these species may only constitute territorial defense. Pinniped females follow the usual mammalian pattern of increased aggressiveness with young. A Steller's sea lion with calf may attack males, other females, or young other than her own (Orr and Poulter, 1967). California sea lions are more aggressive with pups (Peterson and Bartholomew, 1967), and harp seals with pups stake out and defend territories (Sergeant, 1965). Male fur seals need a minimum of four square feet (1.23 sq m) of territory, while females, even those with pups, need only two square feet (0.61 sq m). These territorial limitations probably represent maximum population figures for adults (Elliott, 1887a).

Population density affects the age of sexual maturity of female harp seals. In densely populated areas, the age is five and one-half years; in times of overkill, it is only four years. Indications are that this phenomenon also occurs in other species (Sergeant, 1966). Davis (1964) outlined the adverse effects of overcrowding on reproductive rates in animals and did not include an advance in age of sexual maturity of females among his causative factors. Sergeant's observation is therefore of considerable interest. Scheffer (1955) also demonstrated a correlation between decrease in body size with increase in population density in the Alaska fur seal. Except during the breeding season, the leopard seal is so solitary, both in and out of water, that only three or four are normally found in thirty to forty miles of cruising (Hamilton, 1939).

Group reaction is evident in pinnipeds. Peterson and Bartholomew (1967) postulated that the highly contagious alarm reaction that is characteristic of sea lion populations is learned by one generation and

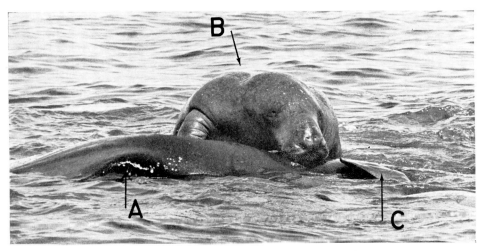

Figure 6–8. Precopulatory behavior of Florida manatees in the Banana river, near Cape Canaveral. (A) posterior portion of central animal is lifted slightly out of water by an animal (not seen here) pushing from underneath, (B) attending animal climbing onto the back of the central animal, (C) attending animal with flipper across the back of the central animal in an embrace. See text for more detailed discussion. (Photo by R. McDonald.)

wise position, sometimes pushed its head and the anterior part of its body under the ventral portion of the central animal until the latter often was lifted well out of the water (Fig. 6–9) with often violent tail slapping on the part of the central and/or attending animals and other splashing caused by the active movements of the animals in interacting with one another. Although we could not tell for certain, it appeared that on occasion, one of the animals, as demonstrated by the position of an embracing flipper, had achieved an upside-down position belly to belly under the central animal. No matter how violent the interaction, the aggregation stayed in essentially the same spot near the shore, and even when disturbed, moved only about twenty-five feet down the shore and resumed the behavior.

Although we saw no erections, the motion of some of the attending animals suggested that their ventral side, in the region of the genital aperture, was being swung toward and under the region of the genital aperture of the central animal. Only the one animal seemed to be the center of attention, and no other groups of a central and attending animal or animals were formed. On occasion, other individuals were seen within a fifty-foot radius of the central activity, and it is presumed that these animals sometimes joined the main group when that aggregation grew in numbers.

Figure 6–9. Precopulatory behavior of seven Florida manatees in the Banana river, near Cape Canaveral. See text for more detailed discussion. (1) central animal, (2) attending animal approaching and nuzzling central animal at right angles, (3, 7) attending animals attempting to push under central animal, (4) attending animal embracing central animal with flippers, (5, 6) attending animals trying to climb onto the back of the central animal. Figures in foreground show proximity of aggregation of manatees to shore. (Photo by R. McDonald.)

Parental Behavior

Pupping times for all pinnipeds are shown by King (1964). In the wild, all southern-hemisphere seals pup in spring or summer. Although the seasons are, of course, reversed, the spring and summer months are also the norm in the northern hemisphere, with the exceptions of the northern elephant seal, gray seals, and the tropical monk seal. These exceptions may have evolved to reduce food competition in the young of sympatric species (McLaren, 1966; Sergeant, 1968). The sea otter may pup any month of the year (Elliott, 1887c; Scheffer, 1940). Rice (1964) noted that Hawaiian monk seals and bearded seals pup only every second year. Wirtz (1968) found, on the other hand, that Hawaiian monk seals sometimes pup every year. The Pacific walrus gives birth every three years (Buckley, 1958). Although there may be an occasional exception, during parturition, the pinniped mother normally gives no assistance and has no interest in the placenta. The umbilical cord breaks during usual movements of mother or pup (Slijper, 1956).

The variable nursing periods are discussed under the section on Food and Feeding in this chapter. Few pinnipeds in the wild nurse any pup other than their own, but Fogden (1968) cited excepitons in the gray seals and northern elephant seals, and Poulter (1968a) mentioned adoption of Weddell seals. Adoption of strange pups by captive harbor seals is also reported (Finch, 1966). Female sea lions not only refuse to accept strange young but may become aggressive toward them (California sea lion, Bonnet, 1929; Steller's sea lion, Orr and Poulter, 1967). Pinniped mothers appear to recognize their pup by the characteristic voice and odor.

The extent of maternal care varies from minimal in the fur seal to the long-term intensive care given by the walrus. The Alaska fur seal pup receives no licking or grooming, is retrieved for only the first few hours following birth, and receives maternal protection only during the six days between its birth and the onset of the mother's estrus period (Bartholomew, 1959). Female sea lions have a much more highly developed retrieving pattern and aggressively defend their young (Peterson and Bartholomew, 1967; Orr and Poulter, 1967; Scheffer, 1945). Hediger (1955) saw a captive female grab a newborn which failed to breathe by the nape of the neck, dip it repeatedly in deep water, and put it on the ground, where breathing started immediately.

Harp seals with pups stake out and defend small territories (Sergeant, 1965), normally accepting a male only after the pup has been weaned (Sergeant, 1967). The monk seal with pup also refuses to accept a male. If one approaches, she threatens until he leaves (Kenyon and Rice, 1959). Ringed and Baikal seals build birth lairs for their pups on the ice under snow (Ognev, 1962). The tunnel, roughly ten feet long with an entrance to the water, provides the pup with a protected environment in which it receives a longer period of maternal care than most seals (McLaren, 1958b). Should the pup be washed into the water by a wave, the mother may attempt to push it back up onto the ice (Millais, 1904).

There seems to be no factual basis to the reports that pinniped mothers teach their young to swim. Pups apparently take to the water at the appropriate age for the species; this may vary from the day of birth for the harbor seal and walrus to ten weeks for the southern elephant seal (Bertram, 1940; Buckley, 1958). Walruses have the longest lactation and dependency periods of all pinnipeds—minimally eighteen months. Mothers and young have close ties and neither leaves if the other is threatened (Clark, 1887; Buckley, 1958).

Observers of pinniped behavior indicate that the male poses a threat to the pups. He may inadvertently crush them when moving about. The only recent exception is Eibl-Eibesfeldt's report (1955, 1961) that male Galapagos sea lions herded swimming pups back to shore, behavior which he interpreted as parental protection. There is also an early observation of the male Steller's sea lion herding young in the water during times of danger (Allen, 1884). There is no doubt that territorial bulls of all species defend that territory, and any established resident of the territory will gain all of the protection incidental to this defense.

For those interested in the role of hormones in parental behavior, an excellent review is available by Lehrman (1961). The sea otter reportedly is an attentive mother (Scheffer, 1940), and the Florida manatee is adequate in its own typically sluggish way (Moore, 1957).

PLAY

The amount and direction of play in the young of various mammalian species provides a good index of the complexity of adult behavior patterns. Play appears characteristic of most young and even some adult pinnipeds and adds to their attractiveness as exhibit animals. At least two species body surf frequently, apparently for the sport of it (California sea lions, Bonnot 1929, Peterson and Bartholomew, 1967; and Galapagos sea lions, Eibel-Eibesfeldt, 1961). Captive sea lions toss bits of wood in their ponds and one has been reported to stow its toys (Hediger, 1955).

Harbor seals demonstrate extensive investigatory behavior and have been reported to drop 30 ft from the rocks to hurriedly gather around a strange boat (Millais, 1904). Those with which we worked at Marineland of the Pacific immediately investigated and manipulated any strange object which was introduced into their tanks. A male walrus there showed similar curiosity about a hydrophone which was lowered into his tank. Juvenile fur seals spend much time playing in tide pools (Peterson, *et al.*, 1968), and bachelor groups of fur seals play "King-of-the-Mountain" frequently and for long periods of time (Elliott, 1884). Play in elephant seals is limited to the young animals, and objects are rarely manipulated (Bartholomew, 1952).

Although play is negligible in even young Florida manatees (Moore, 1956), one juvenile female at Marineland of Florida spent some time pushing around both a large and a small freshwater turtle. Sea otters are characterized by much playfulness and curiosity (Gilmore, 1956). They manipulate objects in play as well as in food gathering, and the young will duck other young and sometimes even mature males (Limbaugh, 1961).

ACTIVITY CYCLES AND SLEEP

Light-dark cyclic activity in pinnipeds varies with species, as well as with sex, age, and sexual state (breeding cycle) of the animal. The Alaska fur seal has received so much intensive study that we have a clearer idea of its circadian rhythm than we do of other pinnipeds. It is on the breeding grounds, where extensive behavioral observations can and have been made, that the most extensive studies have been done on this species. For the six-week or longer breeding season, harem bulls sleep only for brief, intermittent periods (Bartholomew, 1953). Another report (Baker *et al.*, 1963) indicates unabated activity on the rookery day and night but does not indicate which individuals contribute to the activity.

Elliott (1884) gave such a detailed description of which individuals sleep and the duration and the type of sleep that an expert in the field of sleep research could probably make an educated guess as to what phase of sleep the animal was in. On the basis of hundreds of observations, Elliott reported that he never saw a harem bull on its territory sleep for over five minutes but that away from it, it might sleep fitfully for up to an hour. In his descriptions, he hesitantly introduces the words "nightmares" and "dreamland" which coincide closely with behavioral and electroencephalographic analysis of the D-state occurring in all mammalian species (Hartman, 1967, p. 14). It is during these sleep episodes that humans and at least some other animals are believed to be dreaming (Hartman, 1967, p. 18). Since D-state deprivation appears the most hazardous form of sleep deprivation in mammals, the apparently sleepless harem bulls may be catching minimal amounts of at least this absolutely necessary type of sleep. Pups are the only group that sleep quietly; although the cows sleep a good deal, their sleep is also restless.

Activity levels in the male California sea lion on rookeries are slightly higher at night (Bonnot, 1929; Peterson and Bartholomew, 1967). During daylight hours, male Galapagos sea lions may doze in the water for a few seconds but remain alert even then (Eibl-Eibesfeldt, 1961).

Bartholomew (1955) describes the incredible inertness of the northern elephant seal when it is hauled out and sleeping. He took heart beat and rectal temperatures on these sleeping animals without disturbing them and also reported that he saw up to three yearling sea lions using their backs as a couch—also without disturbing the seals. All seals appear able to sleep in the water. Fur seals sleep at the surface on their back or sides (Elliott, 1884; Baker *et al.*, 1963). Captive sea lions and some seals can sleep underwater (Hediger, 1955), and the harbor seal sleeps either at the surface or underwater (Millais, 1904). A walrus may sleep with its head under the water, coming up for air at intervals, or with its head out of water, sometimes long enough for ice to congeal around the neck (Clark, 1887). Walruses are apparently extremely sensitive to overheating and appear to fall asleep in the water while being chased by hunters. Solitary and adult walruses in the water are reportedly very alert, much more so than the juveniles (Scoresby, 1820).

Sea otters are diurnal by nature but may move about at night, particularly when the moon is bright (Barabash-Nikiforov, 1962). They may rest on patches of seaweed at night but are perfectly capable of sleeping on their backs, even while holding one of their young (Elliott, 1887c). Manatees are also diurnal in nature with an increase of activity at noon (Moore, 1956).

MIGRATION

Although most pinnipeds migrate to some extent, the distance is extremely variable, depending on species. Rice (1960) reported that the Hawaiian monk seals he studied did not migrate at all but later (1969) stated that subsequent tagging studies had shown inter-island movements and one movement of several hundred miles. Kenyon and Wilke (1953) reported that some northern fur seals may make an annual round trip of over 5000 miles. Norris (1967) recently outlined briefly the migratory patterns of marine mammals. He summed up this review with the statement that ". . . our knowledge of the functional orienting mechanisms used is nearly nonexistent."

We have often speculated about the effects of captivity on animals during migratory seasons. Because all adult harp seals migrate, whereas many of the one- to four-year-old group do not, Sergeant (1968) suggests that the gonadotropic hormones initiate migration. Captivity, then, could be a more frustrating factor to these adults.

Understanding of migratory patterns in animals is so sketchy (e.g. Storm, 1967) that speculations on their past causes or origins are indeed weak. Rigidly fixed food habits and breeding-site tenacity must have played a large part in the evolution of such energy-consuming behavior as a long yearly migration. The frustrated student is tempted to reach for explanations along the lines of continental drift combined with site tenacity, as Carr (1967) has done in sea turtles, or in a study of advancing and retreating climatic zones which might have affected the past and present proximities of feeding and breeding grounds. Carr, however, stands on firmer ground in both direction of migration and evolutionary age of his species.

FOOD AND FEEDING

Some members of the non-cetacean group of marine mammals herein under discussion are vegetarians (e.g. the manatee), but most are epipelagic carnivores. A few (e.g the walrus and bearded seal) are bottom feeders. All apparently obtain and consume their food in the water.

Nursing periods in pinnipeds are extremely variable, extending from one to two weeks in the crabeater seal to seventy-five weeks in the walrus;

a chart of nursing periods of many species is available (Bertram, 1940). Most mammalian newborn do not find the mother's teat immediately but, much like dogs (Rheingold, 1963) and dolphins, undergo an initial period of fumbling efforts and mouthing of different parts of the mother's body. Seals and sea lions, and presumably the other pinnipeds, also go through this same learning procedure (Harrison, *et al*, 1952; Bertram, 1940; Peterson and Bartholomew, 1967). Pinniped milk is extremely rich in fat content (see Chap. 11). Pup growth, consequently, is very rapid. It is not unusual for the mother to begin foraging for food at sea soon after the pup is born, but the nursing pups may go without food for several days with no ill effects (Alaska fur seal, Bartholomew, 1959; California sea lion, Peterson and Bartholomew, 1967). Alaska fur seal feeding excursions may last five to fourteen days but average eight (Baker *et al.*, 1963). Until they are weaned at three or four months pups of this species take no nourishment other than milk. The Galapagos sea lion may continue to nurse intermittently until the nursing immature animal is as large as its mother (Orr, 1967). Although most observations of suckling are made on land, the harbor seal has been seen nursing both on land and in the water (Venables and Venables, 1955).

All pinnipeds are carnivorous, with the diet, according to Scheffer, (1958) varying with the species and ranging from small crustaceans to sea birds. The leopard seal actively works at capturing penguins by lying in wait for them at their jumping-off places (Hamilton, 1939) or when the penguins return to the rookeries from feeding (Poulter, 1968b). King (1964) has detailed the natural food habits of each species under the description of that species. Keyes (1968) details the diets of captive pinnipeds at thirty-four institutions, based on data acquired from questionnaires.

Pinnipeds have a higher metabolic rate than land mammals of similar size (Scheffer, 1958). A 100 kg seal eats 5 to 7 kg of food a day (Walker, 1964). Eating often but little in nature, sea lions train readily to bits of food reward (Hediger, 1955). However, they are also known to have gone without food for a month in captivity without permanent harm (Scammon, 1874). Keyes (1968) also reported spontaneous fasting in captivity. Since breeding fur seal bulls go without both food and water for six weeks (Bartholomew, 1953, 1959), and breeding bull elephant seals fast for three months (LeBoeuf and Peterson, 1969), these fasting periods in captivity may be perfectly normal.

All pinnipeds take in and regurgitate sand, gravel, or stone, presumably as a part of the natural process. Sand has even been found in the stomachs of elephant seals that were still nursing (Matthews, 1929). Stones are almost always found in the stomachs of animals taken on the Pribilof Is-

lands but rarely in those taken at sea (Wilke and Kenyon, 1952). Dis-
gorged bones and fish otoliths are commonly found on both breeding and
hauling grounds (Wilke and Kenyon, 1952, 1954). Also, small stones or
gravel were found in six of twenty-five sea otter stomachs examined (Barabash-Nikiforov, 1962). Perhaps those maintaining these animals become
unduly concerned when they swallow objects.

Sea lions have not endeared themselves to fishermen. They do not
hesitate to rob and tear up fishing nets (Bonnot, 1951). Several species
are reported to take fish from lines (e.g. gray seals, Millais, 1904; Steller's
sea lions, Kenyon, 1952; harbor seals, Scheffer and Sperry, 1931), and one
young harbor seal was caught in the mouth trying to take shrimp from a
surf fisherman's line (Caldwell and Caldwell, 1969). Eskimos make use
of this pinniped trait and catch walrus by baiting hooks with chunks of
blubber (Scheffer, 1958).

Sergeant (1968) presents a nice analysis of species distribution by
ecological factors, with food one of the primary parameters. In those
sympatric species with overlapping food habits, the pupping seasons may
be different (McLaren, 1966).

Food and feeding in captive sea otters was discussed by Shidlovskaya
(1962) and Barabash-Nikiforov (1962). One of the major problems reported by them was an unwillingness by the otters to eat frozen fish. The
animals ate fresh fish readily, apparently preferring it in captivity to crustaceans, contrary to reports in wild individuals (Wilke, 1957; Ebert, 1968).
From observations of Limbaugh (1961), made both above and underwater, sea otters practice food sharing with the young and possibly even
between adults.

Manatees are strictly vegetarians and in captivity are fed on such foods
as lettuce or cabbage (Moore, 1951). In the wild, the Florida manatee
consumes vast quantities of floating water hyacinths and a juvenile female
at Marineland of Florida was fed hyacinths for a short period to adjust
it to eating in captivity. She also eats small herring readily and reportedly
takes ground beef patties.

LOCOMOTION

All pinnipeds are well adapted to spending much, if not most, of their
time in the water. Electrical stimulation of the motor cortex of the brain
of harbor seals induces strong swimming movements but little or no movement related to terrestrial locomotion (Rioch, 1937; Langworthy *et al.*,
1938). Swimming speeds are difficult to estimate, but the Alaska fur seal
is capable of brief bursts of 19 to 28 km/hour (10 to 15 mph). Earlier
reports that they are taught to swim by the mothers are apparently er-

roneous. They learn on their own when about one month old (Scheffer and Kenyon, 1952). Most seals become skillful body surfers. King (1964) discussed types of pinniped locomotion on land in relation to anatomy. Although both the otariids and the phocids are capable of movement on land, the anatomy of the former group enables it to navigate more effec tively. Maximum speeds and types of locomotion on land were discussed for several species by O'Gorman (1963). The crabeater seal is probably the fastest pinniped on land, moving at 19 km/hr across ice (11.8 mph). Captive harbor seals are often noted swimming upside down. Like some cetaceans, it is postulated that this may be a mechanism for better viewing of the bottom while searching for food that has been missed in mid-water.

DIVING

Species differences on diving ability are probably extensive and figures are available for only a few species. These figures are usually based on the depths at which a pinniped is caught on a fishing hook when taking fish or bait from fishing lines. By this method, Alaska fur seals have been recorded at 60 to 80 fathoms (108 to 144 m) (Kenyon, 1952) and fur seals at 200 ft (60 m) (Scheffer and Kenyon, 1952). California sea lions have been trained to dive to depths of at least 250 m in the open ocean off California (Ridgway, 1969). Both Scheffer (1958) and King (1964) briefly discussed the physiological aspects of diving.

TRAINING

For decades, the California sea lion has been a favorite in trained animal acts. Although it may take a year to train a polished performance in one of these animals, the good memory makes a performing life of eight to twelve years possible (King, 1964). Other species of pinnipeds have been trained to a lesser degree.

The trainer usually prefers to begin work with as young an animal as possible but must always weigh the benefits of raising very young animals against the difficulties. Hediger (1955) considered good training no more than disciplined play and there is no question that the more curiosity and manipulation that an animal exhibits, the greater the variety that can be introduced into its performances. Because young mammals are more playful, less fearful, and more easily socialized than older ones, there is much to be said in their favor as show animals even though the initial training time is slow.

We strongly believe that observational learning plays a significant part in the education of the advanced mammals. Caution in this area has quite correctly been advocated (Beach, 1947) and until recently, information on the extent of the process in marine mammals has been too anecdotal to stand on its own (Caldwell *et al.,* 1965; Brown *et al.,* 1966, Appendix 5). Recently, however, good methodology has been applied to a study of observational learning in cats which provides solid evidence for its existence in that species (John *et al.,* 1968). Significantly, investigations indicate that chimpanzees will, by observation, learn a puzzle solution from an older animal but will ignore a younger animal's solving of the same problem (Yerkes, 1943). Even jackdaws ignore alarm signals of a low-ranking bird but attend to those of birds of higher rank (Lorenz, 1966). Discrimination in the "attending" process is shown, therefore, not only in what the animal will learn by observation but also in the individual from which the animal will accept a lesson or a signal. If a young mammal in training is exposed to one that is more dominant and trained, training time should be reduced.

In the only controlled experiment of which we are aware on learning in pinnipeds, Schusterman (1966) found that the interreversal learning curve of two California sea lions was superior to that of rats and squirrels and within the proficiency range achieved by cats, rhesus monkeys, and chimpanzees.

Handling of large captive animals can frequently be a problem; should the need arise, a useful method has been worked out for immobilizing and handling seals without drugs (Stirling, 1966; also see Chap. 11).

❊   ❊   ❊

We thank Dale W. Rice of the United States Bureau of Commercial Fisheries Marine Mammal Biological Laboratory, Seattle, Washington, for his critical review of a final version of the section on Other Marine Mammals.

Many people have been especially generous in allowing us to study dolphins at the oceanaria and aquaria under their charge and/or answering our many questions about animals in their care. To them we extend special thanks, and acknowledge them here in the same order that their establishments are listed earlier in this chapter: J. B. and Marjorie Siebenaler; Winfield Brady and Stephen Spotte; F. G. Wood, William E. Evans, Bill A. Powell, C. Scott Johnson, Ralph Penner and Sam H. Ridgway; Earl S. Herald, Robert P. Dempster and Thomas Green; Kent Burgess and David W. Kenney; Lawrence Curtis and Gary T. Hill; John H. Prescott, David H. Brown and Ray Cribbs; B. C. Townsend, Jr., W. Fred Lyons, David A. Nelson, Henry M. Lightsey, Cecil M. Walker, Gary C. Ammons, Gerald E. Foreman, Joseph E. Petty, Thomas G. DeVoe and many others at Marineland of Florida who have contributed brief comments; Burton Clark,

Paul S. Hirschman, and Carl Selph. The list could go on to include every employee at every establishment we visited, but those mentioned have been especially helpful in providing access to animals and/or behavioral notes drawn from their own personal experiences.

Financial support which in part has permitted our gathering information for this chapter has come from the following in the form of grants and contracts: Office of Naval Research contracts Nos. N00014-67-C-0358 and N00014-67-C-0358-P001; National Institute of Mental Health grant No. MH-07509-01; National Science Foundation grant No. GB-1189; Los Angeles County Museum of Natural History Foundation; and Marineland, Inc.

REFERENCES

Cetaceans

Brown, David H., Caldwell, David K., and Caldwell, Melba C.: Observations on the behavior of wild and captive false killer whales, with notes on associated behavior of other genera of captive Delphinids. *Los Angeles County Mus., Cont. in Sci.*, 95:1–32, 1966.

Brown, David H., and Norris, Kenneth S.: Observations of captive and wild Cetacea. *J. Mammal.*, 37(3):120 145, 1956.

Caldwell, David K., and Caldwell, Melba C.: The dolphin observed. *Nat. Hist.*, 77(8):58–65, 1968b.

Caldwell, David K., Caldwell, Melba C., and Rice, Dale W.: Behavior of the sperm whale, *Physeter catodon* L. In Norris, K.S. (Ed.): *Whales, Dolphins, and Porpoises.* Berkeley: University of California Press, 1966, pp. 677–716.

Caldwell, Melba C., and Caldwell, David K.: Experimental studies on factors involved in care-giving behavior in three species of the cetacean family Delphinidae. *Bull. S. Cal. Acad. Sci.*, 63(1):1–20, 1964.

Caldwell, Melba C., and Caldwell, David K.: Epimeletic (care-giving) behavior in Cetacea. In Norris, K.S. (Ed.): *Whales, Dolphins, and Porpoises.* Berkeley: University of California Press, 1966, pp. 755–788.

Caldwell, Melba C., and Caldwell, David K.: Vocalization of naive captive dolphins in small groups. *Science*, 159:1121–1123, 1968a.

Caldwell, Melba C., Caldwell, David K., and Evans, William E.: Sounds and behavior of captive Amazon freshwater dolphins, *Inia geoffrensis*. *Los Angeles County Mus., Cont. in Sci.*, 108:1–24, 1966.

Caldwell, Melba C., Caldwell, David K., and Siebenaler, J.B.: Observations on captive and wild Atlantic bottlenosed dolphins, *Tursiops truncatus*, in the northeastern Gulf of Mexico. *Los Angeles County Mus., Cont. in Sci.*, 91:1–10, 1965.

Caldwell, Melba C., Caldwell, David K., and Townsend, B.C., Jr.: Social behavior as a husbandry factor in captive odontocete cetaceans. In *Proc. Second Symposium on Diseases and Husbandry of Aquatic Mammals.* Marineland Research Laboratory, Marineland, Florida, 1968, pp. 1–9.

Essapian, Frank S.: Observations on abnormalities of parturition in captive bottlenosed dolphins, *Tursiops truncatus,* and concurrent behavior of other porpoises. *J. Mammal., 44*(3):405–414, 1963.

Evans, William E. and Bastian, Jarvis: Marine mammal communication: social and ecological factors: In Andersen, H.T. (Ed.): *The Biology of Marine Mammals.* New York, Academic Press, 1969, pp. 425–475.

Harlow, H.F.: Personal communication, 1967.

Harlow, Harry F., and Harlow, Margaret K.: The affectional systems. In Schrier, A.M., Harlow, H.F., and Stollnitz, F. (Eds.): *Behavior of Non-human Primates, Modern Research Trends.* New York, Academic Press, 1965, vol. 2, pp. 287–334.

John, E. Roy, Chesler, Phyllis, Bartlett, Frank, and Victor, Ira: Observation learning in cats. *Science, 159:*1489–1491, 1968.

Kimura, Seiji, and Nemoto, Takahisa: Note on a minke whale kept alive in aquarium. *Sci. Rep. Whales Res. Inst., 11:*181–189, 1956.

Lang, Thomas G.: Hydrodynamic analysis of cetacean performance. In Norris, K.S. (Ed.) *Whales, Dolphins, and Porpoises.* Berkeley, University of California Press, 1966a, pp. 410–432.

Lang, Thomas G.: Hydrodynamic analysis of dolphin fin profiles. *Nature, 209*(5028):1110–1111, 1966b.

Lang, Thomas G., and Daybell, Dorothy A.: Porpoise performance tests in a sea-water tank. Naval Ordnance Test Station, China Lake, Calif. NAVWEPS Rept. 8060, *NOTS Tech. Publ. 3063,* 1963.

Lang, Thomas G., and Pryor, Karen: Hydrodynamic performance of porpoises (*Stenella attenuataa*). *Science, 152:*531–533, 1966.

Lang, Thomas G., and Norris, Kenneth S.: Swimming speed of a Pacific bottle-nosed porpoise. *Science, 151:*588–590, 1966.

Lilly, John C.: Animals in aquatic environments: adaptation of mammals to the ocean. In *Handbook of Physiology; Adaptation to the Environment.* Washington, Amer. Physiol. Soc., 1964, vol. 1, pp. 741–747.

McBride, Arthur F., and Hebb, D.O.: Behavior of the captive bottlenosed dolphin, *Tursiops truncatus. J. Comp. Physiol. Psychol., 41*(2):111–123, 1948.

McBride, Arthur F., and Kritzler, Henry: Observations on pregnancy, parturition, and post-natal behavior in the bottlenose dolphin. *J. Mammal., 32*(3):251–266, 1951.

McCormick, James G.: *The Behavior and Physiology of Sleep and Anesthesia in the Atlantic Bottle-nosed Dolphin (Tursiops truncatus).* Princeton University, Master's thesis, 1967.

Norris, Kenneth S.: Aggressive behavior in cetacea. In Clemente, C.D., and Lindsley, D.B. (Eds.): *Aggression and Defense.* Berkeley, University of California Press, 1967, pp. 225–241.

Norris, Kenneth S., and Prescott, John H.: Observations on pacific cetaceans of Californian and Mexican waters. *Univ. Calif. Pub. Zool., 63*(4):291–402, 1961.

Powell, Bill A.: Periodicity of vocal activity of captive Atlantic bottlenose dolphins: *Tursiops truncatus. Bull. S. Calif. Acad. Sci.,* 65(4):237–244, 1966.

Prescott, John H.: Personal communication, 1968.

Pryor, Taylor, Pryor, Karen, and Norris, Kenneth S.: Observations on a pygmy killer whale (*Feresa attenuata* Gray) from Hawaii. *J. Mammal.* 46(3):450–461, 1965.

Ray, Carleton: Round table: practical problems (Comments on *Delphinapterus*.) In Norris, K.S. (Ed.) *Whales, dolphins, and porpoises.* Berkeley, University of California Press, 1966, pp. 649–673.

Ridgway, Sam H.: Dall porpoise, *Phocoenoides dalli* (True): observations in captivity and at sea. *Norsk Hvalfangst Tid.* 55(5):97–110, 1966.

Sergeant, David E.: The biology of the pilot or pothead whale *Globicephala melaena* (Traill) in Newfoundland waters. *Bull. Fish. Res. Bd. Canada,* 132:i-vii, 1–84, 1962.

Slijper, E.J.: *Whales.* London, Hutchinson, 1962.

Tavolga, Margaret C.: Behavior of the bottlenose dolphin (*Tursiops truncatus*): social interactions in a captive colony. In Norris, K.S. (Ed.): *Whales, dolphins, and porpoises.* Berkeley, University of California Press, 1966, pp. 718–730.

Tavolga, Margaret C., and Essapian, Frank S.: The behavior of the bottle-nosed dolphin (*Tursiops truncatus*): mating, pregnancy, parturition and mother-infant behavior. *Zoologica,* 42(1):11–31, 1957.

Other Marine Mammals

Allen, Joel A.: The seals and walruses. In Goode, G.B. *et al.* (Eds.): *The Fisheries and Fishery Industries of the United States.* Washington, D.C., U.S. Govt. Printing Office, 1884, Section I, pp. 33–113. (Extracted from J.A. Allen: *History of North American Pinnipeds,* 1880.)

Backhouse, Kenneth M.: The grey seal (*Halichoerus grypus*) outside the breeding season; a preliminary report. *Mammalia,* 24(3):307–312, 1960.

Backhouse, Kenneth M.: and Hewer, H.R.: Delayed implantation in the grey seal, *Halichoerus grypus* (Fab.). *Nature,* 178(4532):550, 1956.

Baker, Ralph C., Wilke, Ford, and Baltzo, C. Howard: *The Northern Fur Seal.* U.S. Bur. Comm. Fish., Circular 169:1–22, 1963.

Barabash-Nikiforov, I.I.: The sea otter (*Enhydra lutris* L.) biology and economic problems of breeding. In *The Sea Otter.* Jerusalem, Israel Program for Scientific Translations, 1962.

Bartholomew, George A., Jr.: Reproductive and social behavior of the northern elephant seal. *Univ. Calif. Pub. Zool.,* 47(15):369–472, 1952.

Bartholomew, George A., Jr.: Behavioral factors affecting social structure of the alaska fur seal. *Trans. 18th N. Amer. Wildlife Conf.,* 1953, pp. 481–502.

Bartholomew, George A., Jr.: The northern elephant seal. *Zoonooz,* 28:6–9, 1955.

Bartholomew, George A., Jr.: Mother-young relations and the maturation of pup behaviour in the Alaska fur seal. *Animal Behavior,* 7(3–4):163–171, 1959.

Bartholomew, George A., Jr.: (In discussion to paper by Leakey, 1967). In Clemente, C.D. and Lindsley, D.B. (Eds.): *Aggression and Defense.* Berkeley, University of California Press, 1967, pp. 11–32.

Beach, Frank A.: Do they follow the leader? *Nat. Hist.,* 56(8):356–359, 379–383, 1947.

Beach, Frank A.: Characteristics of masculine sex drive. *Nebraska Symp. Motivation,* 4:1–32, 1956.

Beach, Frank A. and Jordan, Lisbeth: Sexual exhaustion and recovery in the male rat. *Quart. J. Exp. Psychol.,* 8(3):121–133, 1956.

Bertram, G.C.L.: The biology of the Weddell and crabeater seals. *British Graham Land Exped. 1934–37, Sci. Rep.,* 1(1):1–139, pls. 1–10, 1940.

Bonnot, Paul: Report on the seals and sea lions of California. *Calif. Dept. Fish and Game, Fish. Bull.,* 14:1–62, 1929.

Bonnot, Paul: The sea lions, seals and sea otter of the california coast. *Calif. Fish and Game,* 37(4):371–389, 1951.

Brown, David H., Caldwell, David K., and Caldwell, Melba C.: Observations on the behavior of wild and captive false killer whales, with notes on associated behavior of other genera of captive delphinids. *Los Angeles County Mus., Cont. in Sci.,* 95:1–32, 1966.

Buckley, John L.: The Pacific walrus. *U.S. Fish and Wildlife Serv., Spec. Sci. Rept. Wildlife,* 41:1–29, 1958.

Caldwell, David K. and Caldwell, Melba C.: The harbor seal, *Phoca vitulina concolor,* in Florida. *J. Mammal.,* 50(2):379–380, 1969.

Caldwell, Melba C., Caldwell, David K., and Siebenaler, J.B.: Observations on captive and wild Atlantic bottlenosed dolphins, *Tursiops truncatus,* in the northeastern Gulf of Mexico. *Los Angeles County Mus., Cont. in Sci.,* 91:1–10, 1965.

Carr, Archie: Adaptive aspects of the scheduled travel of *Chelonia.* In Storm, R.M. (Ed.): *Animal Orientation and Navigation.* Corvallis, Oregon State University Press, 1967, pp. 35–55.

Clark, A. Howard: The Pacific walrus fishery. In Goode, G.B. *et al.* (Eds.): *The Fisheries and Fishery Industries of the United States.* Washington, U.S. Govt. Printing Office, Section V., vol. 2, pp. 313–318.

Collias, Nicolas E., and Taber, R.D.: A field study of some grouping and dominance relations in ring-necked pheasants. *Condor,* 53:265–275, 1951.

Davis, David E.: The physiological analysis of aggressive behavior. In Etkin, W. (Ed.): *Social Behavior and Organization Among Vertebrates.* Chicago, The University of Chicago Press, 1964, p. 53–74.

Ebert, Earl E.: A food habits study of the southern sea otter, *Enhydra lutris nereis. Calif. Fish and Game,* 54(1):33–42, 1968.

Eibl-Eibesfeldt, Irenäus: Ethologische Studien am Galapagos-Seelöwen, *Zalophus wollebacki* Sivertsen. *Z. Tierpsychol.,* 12:286–303, 1955.

Eibl-Eibesfeldt, Irenäus. *Galapagos; the noah's ark of the pacific.* Garden City, Doubleday, 1961.

Elliott, Henry W.: The habits of the fur seal. In Goode, *et al.* (Eds.): *The Fisheries and Fishery Industries of the United States.* Washington, U.S. Govt. Printing Office, 1884, Section I, pp. 75–113.

Elliott, Henry W.: The fur-seal industry of the Pribylov group, Alaska. In Goode, G.B. *et al.* (Eds.): *The Fisheries and Fishery Industries of the United States.* Washington, U.S. Govt. Printing Office, 1887a, Section V, vol. 2, pp. 321–393.

Elliott, Henry W.: The sea-lion hunt. In Goode, G.B. *et al.* (Eds.): *The Fisheries and Fishery Industries of the United States.* Washington, U.S. Govt. Printing Office, 1887b, Section V, vol. 2, pp. 467–474.

Elliott, Henry W.: The sea-otter fishery. In Goode, G.B. *et al.* (Eds.): *The Fisheries and Fishery Industries of the United States.* Washington, U.S. Govt. Printing Office, 1887c, Section V, vol. 2, pp. 483–491.

Evans, William F. and Bastian, Jarvis: Marine mammal communication: social and educational factors. In Andersen, H.T. (Ed.) *The Biology of Marine Mammals.* New York, Academic Press, 1969, pp. 425–475.

Finch, Virginia A.: Maternal behavior in the harbor seal. *Proc. Third Annual Conf. on Biol. Sonar and Diving Mammals,* Stanford Research Institute, 1966, pp. 147–150.

Fogden, S.C.L.: Mother young relations amongst pinnipeds, *Univ. California, Santa Cruz; Ann. Rep.,* 1966–1967, Biological Investigations in Año Nuevo State Reserve, Appendix *C*:1–8, 1968.

Gilmore, Raymond M.: The sea otter. In *Our Endangered Wildlife.* Washington, National Wildlife Federation, 1956, pp. 7–8.

Guhl, A.M.: Gonadal hormones and social behavior in infrahuman vertebrates. In Young, W.C. (Ed.): *Sex and Internal Secretions.* Baltimore, Williams and Wilkins, 1961, vol. 2, pp. 1240–1267.

Hamilton, J.E.: The leopard seal *Hydrurga leptonyx* (DeBlainville). *Discovery Rep.,* 18:239–264, pls. 7–13, 1939.

Harlow, Harry F., and Harlow, Margaret K.: The affectional systems. In Schrier, A.M. *et al.* (Eds.): *Behavior of Nonhuman Primates; Modern Research Trends.* New York, Academic Press, 1965, pp. 287–334.

Harrison, R.J., Matthews, L.H., and Roberts, J.M.: Reproduction in some Pinnipedia. *Trans. Zool. Soc. London,* 27(5, no. 1):437–540, 4 pls, 1952.

Hartmann, Ernest: *The Biology of Dreaming.* Springfield, Thomas, 1967.

Hediger, H.: *Studies of the Psychology and Behaviour of Captive Animals in Zoos and Circuses.* London, Butterworths Sci. Publ., 1955.

Hersher, Leonard, Richmond, Julius B., and Moore, A. Ulric: Maternal behaviour in sheep and goats. In Rheingold, H.L. (Ed.): *Material Behavior in Mammals.* New York, John Wiley, 1963, pp. 203–232.

Hewer, H.R.: Behaviour of the grey seal (*Halichoerus grypus* Fab.) in the breeding season. *Mammalia,* 24(3):400–421, 1960.

John, E. Roy, Chesler, Phyllis, Bartlett, Frank, and Victor, Ira: Observation learning in cats. *Science, 159*:1489–1491, 1968.

Kenyon, Karl W.: Diving depths of the Steller sea lion and Alaska fur seal. *J. Mammal., 33*(2):245–246, 1952.

Kenyon, Karl W.: Territorial behavior and homing in the Alaska fur seal. *Mammalia, 24*(3):431–444, 1960.

Kenyon, Karl W. and Rice, Dale W.: Life history of the Hawiian monk seal. *Pacific Sci., 13*:215–252, 1959.

Kenyon, Karl W. and Scheffer, Victor B.: The Seals, sea lions, and sea otter of the Pacific coast. *U.S. Fish and Wildlife Serv., Fish. Leaf, 344*:1–28, 1953.

Kenyon, Karl W. and Wilke, Ford: Migration of the northern fur seal, *Callorhinus ursinus. J. Mammal, 34*(1):86–98, 1953.

Keyes, Mark C.: The nutrition of pinnipeds. In Harrison, R.J. *et al.* (Eds.): *Behavior and Physiology of Pinnipeds.* New York, Appleton-Century-Crofts, 1968, pp. 359–391.

King, Judith E.: *Seals of the World.* London, Brit. Mus. Nat. Hist., 1964.

Langworthy, Orthello R., Hesser, Frederick H., and Kolb, Lawrence C.: A physiological study of the cerebral cortex of the hair seal (*Phoca vitulina*). *J. Comp. Neur., 69*(3): 351–369, 1938.

Leakey, Louis S.B.: Development of aggression as a factor in early human and pre-human evolution. In Clemente, C.D. and Lindsley, D.B. (Eds.): *Aggression and Defense.* Berkeley, University of California Press, 1967, pp. 1–33.

LeBoeuf, Burney J., and Peterson, Richard S.: Social status and mating activity in elephant seals. *Science, 163*:91–93, 1969.

Lehrman, Daniel S.: Hormonal regulation of parental behavior in birds and infrahuman mammals. In Young, W.C. (Ed.): *Sex and Internal Secretions.* Baltimore, Williams and Wilkins, 1961, vol. 2, pp. 1268–1382.

Limbaugh, Conrad: Observations on the California sea otter. *J. Mammal, 42*(2): 271–273, (1961).

Lorenz, Konrad: *On Aggression.* New York, Harcourt, Brace and World, 1966.

McLaren, Ian A.: Some aspects of growth and reproduction in the bearded seal, *Erignathus barbatus. J. Fish Res. Bd. Canada, 15*(2):219–227, 1958a.

McLaren, Ian A.: The biology of the ringed seal (*Phoca hispida* Schreber) in the eastern Canadian Artic. *Bull. Fish. Res. Bd. Canada, 118*:1–97, 1958b.

McLaren, Ian A.: Taxonomy of harbor seals in the western North Pacific and evolution of certain other hair seals. *J. Mammal, 47*(3):466–473, 1966.

Matthews, L. Harrison: The natural history of the elephant seal with notes on other seals found at south Georgia. *Discovery Rep., 1*:233–256, pls. 19–24, 1929.

Millais, J.G.: *The Mammals of Great Britain and Ireland.* London, Longmans, Green, 1904, vol. 1.

Moore, Joseph C.: The status of the manatee in the Everglades National Park, with notes on its natural history. *J. Mammal, 32*(1):22–36, 1951.

Moore, Joseph C.: Observations of manatees in aggregations. *Amer. Mus. Novitates, 1811*:1–24, 1956.

Moore, Joseph C.: Newborn young of a captive manatee. *J. Mammal*, 38(1): 137–138, 1957.

Norris, Kenneth S.: Some observations on the migration and orientation of marine mammals. In Storm, R.M. (Ed.): *Animal Orientation and Navigation.* Corvallis, Oregon State University Press, pp. 101–125, 1967.

O'Gorman, Fergus: Observations on terrestrial locomotion in Antarctic seals. *Proc. Zool. Soc. London*, 141(4):837–850, pls. 1–4, 1963.

Ognev, S.I.: *Mammals of U.S.S.R. and Adjacent Countries.* III. Carnivora (*Fissipedia and Pinnipedia*). Jerusalem, Israel Program for Scientific Translations, 1962.

Orr, Robert T.: The Gelapagos sea lion. *J. Mammal.*, 48(1):62–69, 1967.

Orr, Robert T. and Poulter, Thomas C.: Some observations on reproduction, growth and social behavior in the Steller sea lion. *Proc. Calif. Acad. Sci.*, 4th Ser., 35(10):193–226, 1967.

Peterson, Richard S. and Bartholomew, George A. Jr.: *The Natural History and Behavior of the California Sea Lion.* Amer. Soc. Mammal., Spec. Publ. No. 1, 1967.

Peterson, Richard S. and Gentry, Roger L.: Biological investigations in Año Nuevo state reserve, Annual Rep., 1966–1967. Univ. Calif. Santa Cruz, 1968.

Peterson, Richard S., Hubbs, Carl L., Gentry, Roger L., and DeLong, Robert L.: The Guadalupe fur seal: habitat, behavior, population, size and field identification, *J. Mammal.*, 49(4):665–675, 1968.

Poulter, Thomas C.: Marine mammals. In Sebeok, T.A. (Ed.): *Animal Communication.* Bloomington: Indiana University Press, 1968a, pp. 405–465.

Poulter, Thomas C.: Underwater vocalizations and behavior of pinnipeds. In Harrison, R.J. *et al.* (Eds.): *Behavior and Physiology of Pinnipeds.* New York, Appleton-Century-Crofts, 1968b, pp. 69–84.

Prescott, John H.: Personal communication, 1968.

Rheingold, Harriet L.: Maternal behavior in the dog. In Rheingold, H.L. (Ed.): *Maternal Behavior in Mammals.* New York, John Wiley, 1963, pp. 169–202.

Rice, Dale W.: Population dynamics of the Hawaiian monk seal. *J. Mammal.*, 41(3):376–385, 1960.

Rice, Dale W.: The Hawaiian monk seal. *Nat. Hist.*, 73(2):48–55, 1964.

Rice, Dale W.: Personal communication, 1969.

Rice, Dale W. and Scheffer, Victor B.: *A List of the Marine Mammals of the World.* U.S. Bur. Comm. Fish., Spec. Sci. Rept., Fish., 579:i–iv, 1–16, 1968.

Ridgway, S.H.: Personal communication, 1969.

Rioch, David McK.: A physiological and histological study of the frontal cortex of the seal (*Phoca vitulina*). *Biol. Bull.*, 73:591–602, 1937.

Scammon, Charles M.: *The Marine Mammals of the North-Western Coast of North America, Described and Illustrated: Together with an Account of the American Whale Fishery.* San Francisco. John H. Carmany, 1874.

Scheffer, Theo. H., and Sperry, Charles C.: Food habits of the Pacific harbor seal, *Phoca richardii. J. Mammal*, 12(3):214–226, 1931.

Scheffer, Victor B.: The sea otter on the Washington coast. *Pacific Northwest Quart.*, Oct., 1940, pp. 370–388.

Scheffer, Victor B.: Growth and behavior of young sea lions. *J. Mammal,* 26:390–392, 1945.

Scheffer, Victor B.: Body size with relation to population density in mammals. *J. Mammal, 36(4)*:493–515, 1955.

Scheffer, Victor B.: *Seals, Sea Lions and Walruses; A Review of the Pinnipedia.* Stanford, Stanford University Press, 1958.

Scheffer, Victor B. and Kenyon, Karl W.: The fur seal herd comes of age. *Natl. Geographic Mag., 101(4)*:491–512, 1952.

Scheffer, Victor B. and Kenyon, Karl W.: Baculum size in pinnipeds. *Z. Saügetierkunde, 28(1)*:38–41, 1963.

Schevill, William E., Watkins, William A., and Ray, Carleton: Analysis of underwater *Odobenus* calls with remarks on the development and function of the pharyngeal pouches. *Zoologica, 51(3)*:103–106, pls 1–5, phonograph record, 1966.

Schusterman, Ronald J.: Serial discrimination-reversal learning with and without errors by the California sea lion. *J. Exper. Analysis of Behavior, 9(5)*:593–600, 1966.

Scoresby, William Jr.: *An Account of the Artic Regions, with a History and Description of the Northern Whale-Fishery.* Edinburgh, Archibald Constable, 1820, vol. 1.

Sergeant, David E.: Migrations of harp seal *Pagophilus groenlandicus* (Erxleben) in the northwest Atlantic. *J. Fish. Res. Bd. Canada, 22(2)*:433–464, 1965.

Sergeant, David E.: Reproductive rates of harp seals *Pagophilus groenlandicus* (Erxleben). *J. Fish. Res. Bd. Canada, 23(5)*:757–766, 1966.

Sergeant, David E.: Personal communication, 1967.

Sergeant, David E.: Feeding ecology of marine mammals. *Proc. Second Symposium on Disease and Husbandry of Aquatic Mammals.* Marineland, Florida, Marineland Research Laboratory, 1968, pp. 89–96.

Shidlovskaya, N.K.: Directions for the feeding and care of the male sea otter. In *The Sea Otter.* Jerusalem, Israel Program for Scientific Translations, 1962, pp. 225–227.

Slijper, E.J.: Some remarks on gestation and birth in Cetacea and other Aquatic Mammals. *Hvalrad. Skr., 41*:1–62, 1956.

Stirling, Ian: A technique for handling live seals. *J. Mammal, 47(3)*:543–544, 1966.

Storm, Robert M. (Ed.): *Animal Orientation and Navigation.* Corvallis, Oregon State Universtiy Press, 1967.

True, Frederick W.: The siernians or sea cows. In Goode, G.B. *et al.* (Eds.): *The Fisheries and Fishery Industries of the United States.* Washington, U.S. Govt. Printing Office, 1884, Section I, pp. 114–136.

Venables, U.M. and Venables, L.S.V.: Observations on a breeding colony of the seal *Phoca vitulina* in Shetland. *Proc. Zool. Soc. London, 125*:521–532, 1955.

Walker, Ernest P.: *Mammals of the World.* Baltimore, Johns Hopkins Press, 1964.

Wilke, Ford and Kenyon, Karl W.: Notes on the food of fur seal, sea-lion and *Management, 21*(2):241–242, 1957.

Wilke, Ford and Kenyon, Karl W.: Notes on the food of fur seal, Sea-Lion and harbor porpoise, *J. Wildlife Management, 16*(3):396–397, 1952.

Wilke, Ford and Kenyon, Karl W.: Migration and food of the northern fur seal. *Trans. 19th North Amer. Wildlife Conf.* 1954, pp. 430–440.

Wirtz, William O., II: Reproduction, growth and development, and juvenile mortality in the Hawaiian monk seal. *J. Mammal, 49*(2):229–238, 1968.

Wynne-Edwards, V.C.: *Animal Dispersion in Relation to Social Behavior.* Edinburgh, Oliver and Boyd, 1962.

Yerkes, R.M.: *Chimpanzees: A Laboratory Colony.* New Haven, Yale University Press, 1943.

Chapter 7

SENSES AND COMMUNICATION

David K. Caldwell and Melba C. Caldwell

CETACEA

This section, like the one on cetacean behavior, will be devoted mainly to the smaller toothed whales, i.e. that group of animals that might reasonably be expected to be maintained in captivity. Also, since the senses and the communication system are so integrally related, they are considered together here.

Acoustic System

There is strong evidence that the acoustic system of most toothed whales is their primary sensory modality. For that reason and because acoustic data are easier to gather and to quantify than most other sensory data, work in this area has proceeded much more rapidly than investigation of the other senses.

Sound Reception

The potential methods by which cetaceans receive sound have been investigated rather fully anatomically (see review by Tavolga, 1965) but comparatively little experimentally. Norris (1964, p. 334) postulated that the lower jaw may function as an acoustic receiver, and the work of Bullock and others, recording from the auditory centers, indicates that this may be so (Grinnel, 1967). This group also found, however, that though a stimulus in the lower frequency range (15 to 30 kHz) directed towards the external auditory meatus was "quite effective," stimuli in the higher frequencies (50 to 100 kHz) directed toward the melon and jaw were much more effective. It seems reasonable to postulate that evolving toothed whales retained the useful original pathways for sounds in the lower frequencies which were significant in their original terrestrial environment but evolved new pathways to process the higher frequency ranges associated with echolocation.

466

In our experience, attempts to place suction cups over the external auditory meatus of Atlantic bottlenosed dolphins, *Tursiops truncatus*, elicited violent reactions, much more violent than when the cups were placed over the eyes. This is contrary to a report by Norris *et al.* (1961) that their animals, trained to take eye cups, did not fight the simultaneous use of eye and ear cups. We do not know whether Norris' group had a better animal or a better trainer.

One Atlantic bottlenosed dolphin was able to discriminate 100 percent accurately between a steel ball, 5.40 cm in diameter and one 6.35 cm in diameter (Norris, *et al.*, 1967), and Evans and Powell (1967) demonstrated that even when the object reflectivity is made equal, this species can discriminate between different targets.

The effective upper limit of hearing in the Atlantic bottlenosed dolphin has been experimentally established as 150 kHz (Johnson, 1967; Schevill and Lawrence, 1953). Regarding the lower limit, Johnson's (1967) data indicate that below about 200 Hz, the sound pressure would have to be increased to such a degree that normal hearing would probably not be effective, but he does indicate a response at as low as 75 Hz with a threshold of +37 dB.

SOUND EMISSIONS

Cetacean sound emissions have been received and studied both in the field and in the laboratory (see Evans, 1967, for complete review by species, vocalization type, and locality). Most species appear to produce a pulsed sound similar to that produced by most mammals, and many (especially the Delphinidae) clearly produce a second type of sound which is a *quasi*-pure tone and which may best be described as a "whistle." Though both types of sounds are produced within the human hearing range, they may extend above it at times. The pulsed sound is variable in duration, repetition rate, and dominant frequency. Many of these variable pulsed sounds appear emotionally induced and sound much the same as the vocalizations of other mammalian species which are typically described as "barks," "grunts," "squeaks," and "squawks" (Caldwell and Caldwell, 1967).

Pulsed sounds both above and within the human audible range are also used in echolocation (Norris, *et al.*, 1961; Busnel and Dziedzic, 1967). These sounds are different qualitatively than emotionally induced sounds but to date are undifferentiated quantitatively. Generally speaking, in sounds used for echolocation, the repetition rate is slower, the pulses are sharper, and the sound has a distinctly "controlled" quality. This sound has frequently been referred to as a "creaking door" or "rusty hinge."

Both the pulsed "squeaks," "squawks," etc., and the whistle type of phonation are postulated as emotional and communicative of the vocalizing animal's physiological state. Additionally, they give information on location and identity. Both can be reinforced and elicited on command, and are therefore not completely under involuntary control. We find experimentally that *Tursiops truncatus* can be made to discontinue an ongoing vocalization by the introduction of an unusual sound stimulus. The animal appears to stop its own phonations in order to listen without interference to the incoming stimulus.

Sound emissions up to 196 kHz (the upper limit of their equipment) have been reported for *Tursiops truncatus* by Schevill and Lawrence (1953). Norris and Evans (1967) demonstrated directionality in the beaming of high-frequency sound, falling off as frequencies are lowered progressively below 100 kHz, in the rough-toothed dolphin, *Steno bredanensis*. Those authors also found sound emissions of 208 kHz in this species, but it was not determined at that time whether the animal was using these frequencies. Directionality in hearing has been demonstrated for the harbor porpoise, *Phocoena phocoena* (Dudok van Heel, 1959), and was found to be better for a 6 kHz than a 3.5 kHz signal.

We do not yet know whether a calf is born with the ability to echolocate. Working with recording gear effective only to 20 kHz, we were unable to elicit echolocation pulses from a young male Amazon dolphin, *Inia geoffrensis*, and we suggested that this primitive species may have to learn to echolocate (Caldwell, *et al.*, 1966). Conversely, a young male Atlantic bottlenosed dolphin, first recorded at the age of twenty-six days, emitted pulsed sounds within the audible range almost every time that he passed the hydrophone. To us, these sounded like very good low-intensity echolocation runs.

The mechanism or mechanisms by which cetacean sounds are made are still very much a question of debate (Norris, 1964, 1968, 1969; Norris and Evans, 1967). It appears that both soft and skeletal parts are involved. It also appears that some ecological correlates may be drawn between the degree of concavity of the upper surface of the skull and the habitat (and consequent need for efficiency of vocalization—especially echolocation) most frequented by the various odontocetes.

Communication by Sound

It is apparent that the whistle sounds emitted by one animal have a noticeable effect on other animals. This effect has been studied closely only in the whistle component, a more discrete and easily quantifiable unit than the pulsed sound. Several studies indicate the stimulus value of a whistling animal upon another animal either in the same tank (Caldwell and Caldwell, 1968, using the eastern Pacific common dolphin, *Delphinus delphis bairdi*) or in a separate tank with acoustic contact (Lilly and Miller, 1961; Lang and Smith, 1965; all using *Tursiops truncatus*). Additional work introduced previously taped sounds of other dolphins (Dreher, 1966, using *Tursiops truncatus*). A whistle stimulus tend to elicit a whistle from a second animal. This has been noted in the wild as well as in captivity and has been termed a "call-answer sequence" by Evans (1967) and "chorusing" by Dreher and Evans (1964). The whistles are characteristic to the animal (Caldwell and Caldwell, 1965), and we postulate that their function is to transfer information relative to the identification, localization, and level of arousal of the emitter to the other herd members.

We have followed the developing vocalizations of three infant *Tursiops truncatus* (two males and one female) from birth to up to two years, and those of one other male of the same species beginning on the twentieth day following birth. The whistle is present on the day of birth, albeit a trifle ragged. Though it appeared to become smoother in the one animal that we recorded regularly for two years, this was the only change that we found. Generally speaking, however, there appears to be a tendency in maturing animals, especially females, to repeat whistles without a time break, thus making the whistle appear more complex. Up to six months of age, all four of the youngsters we observed had a simple whistle contour corresponding to the simplicity of contours 1, 2, 3, 9, or 17 of Dreher and Evans (1964, Chart I). Adult animals, conversely, usually have repetitive many-looped whistles such as those in contours 7, 14, 15, and 16 of Dreher and Evans. We should note, however, that many juvenile *Tursiops truncatus*, captured at lengths of about six to seven feet (1.8 to 2.1 m, tip of snout to fluke notch), can maintain an unbroken, many-looped whistle or on the next breath emit only one of the simple, single-looped "signature" whistles that had gone to make up the unbroken, many-looped whistle of the previous sequence.

When we have found an animal that emits more than one contour, we have been unable to find any behavioral correlate with the secondary whistle, which appears as fixed and as peculiar to the individual animal as the primary "signature" whistle.

The most important thing to remember about the acoustic communication system of cetaceans is that the animal is intensely aware of and easily conditioned to any sound that it can perceive, and it both perceives and discriminates a wide range of sound.

There is yet another means of communication that may involve sound, vision, a combination of sound and vision, or in some instances even the tactile sense. Captive *Tursiops truncatus* often vigorously slap the surface of the water with their flukes; wild animals may do the same (Norris and Prescott, 1961). The result is a loud sonic report which can be heard both in and out of water, and the context is most frequently one in which the animal seems disturbed by some outside stimulus. In the case of trained animals, it may be precipitated by the trainer's wanting it to perform some routine that it does not want to perform. Anthropomorphically, it indicates displeasure. To the trainer, the lifted flukes are also a visual clue to retreat because the animal is likely either to splash him with water or even to hit him if they are working closely enough together. *Tursiops* in captivity may also squirt or splash water at a bystander with their snouts. This form of communication is frequently accompanied by the pulsed sound, made from the blowhole out of water, that is sometimes referred to as a "Bronx cheer." These sounds are usually quite successful in drawing the attention of the animal's trainer. Snapping jaws both in and out of water also provide a means for a combined visual and sonic communication, indicating displeasure.

The normal blow or exhalation in Atlantic bottlenosed dolphins is fairly quiet, but under excitement it becomes louder and more explosive. These loud, explosive exhalations doubtless also are communicative in nature; an explosive blow by an animal in one tank is frequently followed by the same type of exhalation by animals in adjacent tanks which are neither in visual contact nor subjected to the same stressful stimuli. Dolphins may also emit a large bubble of air while still underwater. This makes an audible sound that behaviorally appears to indicate begging or inquisitiveness.

Finally, it should be noted that total silence is a form of vocal communication (Caldwell and Caldwell, 1967). An abruptly quiet tank often results when some danger is present, and is just as worthy of the observer's attention as a loud sound. It also must be so for the dolphins.

Visual System

Slijper (1962) reviewed the problems inherent to vision adapted for use in air and water and discussed the work that has been done on the anatomy of the eyes of many cetacean species. He also described briefly the anatomy of that part of the brain presumed to process visual information.

That at least some odontocetes use vision is supported by behavioral observations in captivity. Eye movements are noticed both in water and out. Since an animal's eye may move even when its head remains stationary by choice or by circumstance, that animal is obviously visually attending a person or an activity. The acuity of that vision, however, is unknown.

The fact that a potentially injuring stimulus or bright lights can cause an animal to close its eyes indicates a sensitivity to light. In the later instance even if the eyelids do not close, the pupil may contract and then dilate again after the bright light is removed.

Figure 7–1. Adolescent male *Tursiops truncatus* showing position of eye that would seem to permit forward and downward stereoscopic vision. (Photograph courtesy of Marineland of Florida by William A. Huck.)

The primary plane of movement by the eyeball appears to be dorso-ventral, but the animals are also capable of rotating their eyes in an anterior-posterior direction. When an animal is viewed head on (i.e. *Tursiops truncatus* (Fig. 7–1), *Stenella plagiodon*, *Lagenorhynchus obliquidens*, *Grampus griseus* and *Globicephala scammoni* in our own experience), it is apparent that its anatomy would permit stereoscopic vision in a forward and perhaps partly downward direction but not in other directions. On the other hand, while *Inia geoffrensis* probably have forward stereoscopic vision, their downward vision is obstructed by their large protruding cheeks and is replaced by an upward field (Fig. 7–2).

These animals often swim on their backs near the bottom, apparently to see better and to retrieve objects on the bottom (Caldwell *et al.*, 1966). The question of binocular or stereoscopic vision in dolphins has been mentioned by Kellogg and Rice (1966). We agree that until controlled experiments are done, a question still exists regarding its validity. However, based on behavioral correlates, it is our impression that the small toothed whales that we have studied are capable of and use stereoscopic vision. From the head-on aspect, we have observed that movement of the two eyes is not independent as it is in some lower vertebrates but rather is coordinated as one might expect in normal mammals.

Figure 7–2. Adult female *Inia geoffrensis* showing position of eyes that would seem to permit forward and upward stereoscopic vision. (Photograph courtesy of Marineland of Florida by William A. Huck.)

When a light is thrown on the eyes of *Tursiops truncatus*, they shine brightly in the dark (Fig. 7–3). Slijper (1962) observed this in other cetaceans. While there are a number of exceptions to the hypothesis, eye shine in general may be positively correlated with superior night vision. It might also be of special value for increased visual acuity in murky water such as that often inhabited by *Tursiops* or in deeper offshore waters where light penetration from the surface is reduced.

The visual mode has received almost no experimental attention in cetaceans, and as Kellogg and Rice (1966) pointed out, most of the information that we have is circumstantial or inferential and frequently contradictory. It is so contradictory, in fact, that the work of two psychologists who did attempt study in the field remains unpublished. Kellogg and Rice's work in visual discrimination tests with *Tursiops truncatus* indicates poor vision out of water but very good vision underwater. As these authors suggest, the results of the tests out of water, indicating very poor vision, are surprising. In practice, trained animals respond differentially to simple hand cues out of water. They accurately catch and throw balls to variable locations even though they complete the entire sequence with the head out of water. *Tursiops* have also been reported to respond to colors (or hues) when their heads were out of water (e.g. Norris, 1966). The neuroanatomist, Breathnach (1960), also suggested that vision in cetaceans may be more acute and discriminatory than was

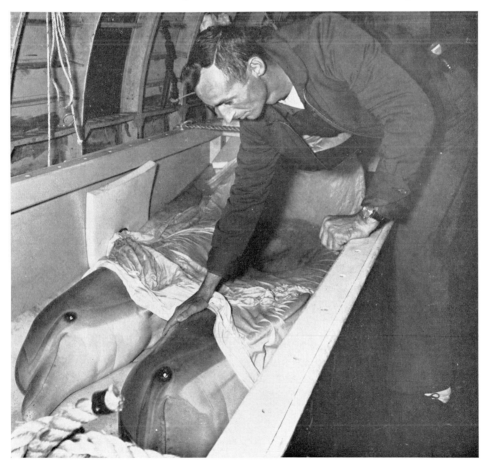

Figure 7–3. Two adult *Tursiops truncatus* in shipping box out of water. Note eye shine resulting from the photographer's flash. (Photograph courtesy of Marineland of Florida.)

previously thought. Additional experimental work is needed, particularly in distance and color vision.

We have detected few discrete visual communication signals in cetaceans other than those of body position and speed of motion. They are incapable of the many facial expressions so often seen in other mammals, and do not have the control of appendages and body parts such as ears, lips, or rear limbs that many other mammals have and use as visual signals. Threat may be expressed by facing an offending animal, by opening the mouth and exposing the teeth, and/or by slightly arching the back and holding the head downward. Submission is expressed, as is frequently the case in animals, by displaying the opposite of threat signals. Sexual solicitation frequently involves swimming ahead of the other animal, looking back, and rolling over to display the genital area.

Because dolphins are complex animals with complex signals, we may never recognize more than a few of the more pronounced signals. Many humans, both juvenile and adult, are unable to recognize or give signals to others of their own species when a play versus threat or play versus fight is initiated; the learning of such ambiguous signals in other species involves a tremendous outlay of time and attention to detail. As noted by Evans and Bastian (1969), and we agree, color patterns may provide a form of visual signaling.

Tactile Sense

In this area there is an anomaly between what the anatomy and histology of an animal would lead one to expect and what the animal actually demonstrates behaviorally. Compared with that of other mammals, the tactile thalamic region (ventrobasal complex) in *Tursiops truncatus* is distinctly reduced (Kruger, 1959, 1966). It has even been stated that the skin of the dolphin is so thick (see Chap. 5) that it is not adapted to the reception of delicate shades of stimuli (Langworthy, 1931).

Conversely, behavioral observations lead to the conclusion that the sense of touch is one of the most important senses in dolphins. Unfortunately, because that sense has proven difficult to instrument, behavioral observations will have to suffice until someone works out a methodology for quantifying it.

Except for the large bulls, which spend considerable time withdrawn from the others, all *Tursiops* that we have observed in captivity seek out body contact. Even the bulls initiate some body contact but it is not clear whether this is purely sexual solicitation. With more limited data at our disposal, we have found the same tendency towards body contact to exist in all of the captive dolphins that we have studied (*Stenella plagiodon, Stenella* sp., *Delphinus delphis, Lagenorhynchus obliquidens, Orcinus orca, Grampus griseus, Globicephala scammoni, Globicephala macrorhyncha, Pseudorca crassidens, Sotalia fluviatilis, Phocoenoides dalli, Delphinapterus leucas,* and *Inia geoffrensis*).

This body contact seems highly rewarding and runs the gamut from gentle rubbing and mouthing (Fig. 7–4) to violent head banging and

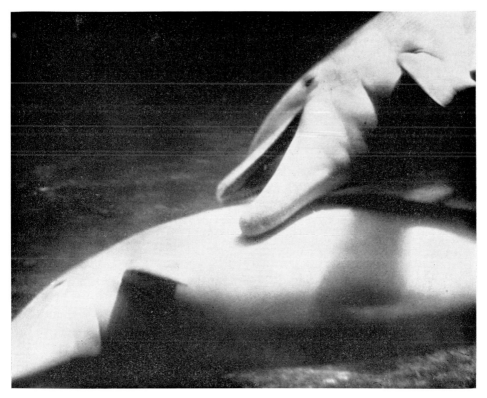

Figure 7–4. Subadult *Tursiops truncatus* gently mouthing the side of an adult. (Authors' photograph made at Marineland of the Pacific.)

biting (Caldwell and Caldwell, 1967, Figs. 1, 15, and 17). Undisturbed Atlantic bottlenosed dolphins frequently swim with flippers touching the flippers or body of another (Figs. 7–5, 7–6). One may nose the genital area of a tankmate while both swim leisurely (Fig. 7–7), and several animals often swim together so closely that all are in contact with one another (Fig. 7–8). When circumstances permit, two or more species (or even genera or families) may come into physical contact, apparently for rewarding body contact. Brushes secured bristle-up on the floor of the tank become worn from the animals' rubbing against them. Captive animals rub on almost any projection in their tank and many animals, especially

Figure 7–5. Two adult female *Tursiops truncatus* gently touching flippers as they swim together. (Authors' photograph made at Marineland of the Pacific.)

tame ones, return again and again for gentle stroking and patting from their human attendants.

Venipuncture of the flukes causes obvious pain; the dolphin's reaction is frequently violent and is accompanied by protest vocalizations.

The vibrissae in the primitive Amazon dolphin are functionally developed and have been postulated as tactile organs in food finding (Layne and Caldwell, 1964). The pits on the snouts of *Tursiops truncatus*, from which the embryonic hairs are almost lost, never close throughout the life of the animal. If the pits were nonfunctional, they would be expected to close. Palmer and Weddell (1964) noted the copious innervation of the pit in a female of unstated age that they believed to be an adult. From the histologic picture, they regarded the pits as a "specialized sense organ derived from the hair follicle present at birth by a secondary adaptation." Our sections through the hair follicles of a twenty-one-year-old

Figure 7–6. Juvenile *Tursiops truncatus* swimming with its flipper in contact with its mother's side. (Photograph courtesy of Marineland of Florida.)

Figure 7–7. Adult *Tursiops truncatus* nuzzling the genital region of a second adult as they slowly swim together. (Photograph courtesy of Marineland of Florida.)

Figure 7–8. *Tursiops truncatus,* left to right: juvenile male, his mother, unrelated adolescent female, unrelated adult female. All swimming slowly in tight formation with some part of the body in contact with the adjacent animal. The two central animals are each in contact with two animals. (Authors' photograph made at Marineland of the Pacific.)

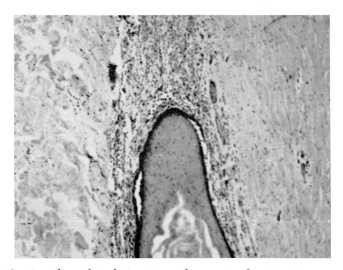

Figure 7–9. Section through a hair pit on the snout of a twenty-one-year-old adult female *Tursiops truncatus* showing a rudimentary hair within the pit and its accompanying vessels and nerves. Hematoxylin and eosin. (Photograph by James C. Woodard.)

female Atlantic bottlenosed dolphin (Fig. 7–9) were interpreted by Woodard (1969) as follows: "The section reveals a rudimentary hair with its accompanying vessels and nerves, but it cannot be said whether or not there is a sensory function associated with the pits." However, because the pit is still open, even in an older animal, we feel that experimental study of this possible sensory site is indicated.

Chemoreception

OLFACTORY SENSE

Even though taste and smell are closely related subjectively in humans and are often difficult for us to distinguish, the apparatuses are very distinctly different. The sense of smell serves in distance chemoreception while the sense of taste serves in contact chemoreception. The anatomy of odontocete brains indicates that they can taste but cannot smell. Apparently, when the blowhole migrated to the top of the head, the neural pathways for smell had to be sacrificed. Mysticetes, on the other hand, still retain a group of cells in the brain which have been interpreted as representing the nucleus of the lateral olfactory tract (Jansen and Jansen, 1953).

GUSTATORY SENSE

Kruger (1959, p. 177) commented upon the "excellent development" of the nucleus ventralis medialis in *Tursiops* which suggested to him "that the sense of taste is probably present and perhaps is well developed, but the conclusion remains tenuous because of the uncertainty of the relationship of this element of the gustatory pathways." Breathnach (1960) also noted the high degree of differentiation within the hypoglossal nucleus of Cetacea.

Behaviorally, captive odontocetes exhibit strong individual preferences for certain food fish and may switch back and forth between preferences at intervals, usually of a minimum of several weeks. This behavior occurs even when fish is cut into small pieces, and individual *Tursiops* have been observed to refuse food rather than eat a nonpreferred species of fish. This can, therefore, present a serious husbandry problem—especially among those trained animals that will not perform well, or at all, without a food reward to their liking. The fact that the fish are cut into pieces is further evidence that the dolphin is relying on taste or texture (which may be an important correlated factor in palatability) rather than simply the size of the fish.

In the Atlantic bottlenosed dolphin, we have been unable to demonstrate

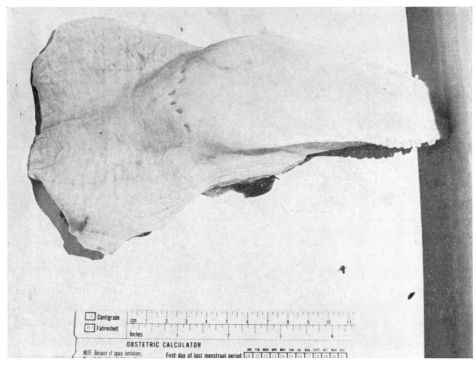

Figure 7–10. Tongue of adult female *Tursiops truncatus,* showing location of large papillae near tip and seven large pits near base. Small pits mentioned in text are concentrated on the basal and lateral surfaces of tongue and extend down oral tract behind tongue. Enlargements of these three areas are shown in Figures 7–11, 7–13, and 7–15. (Photograph courtesy of Marineland of Florida by William A. Huck.)

histologically external taste receptors. However, the following three sites on the tongue which appeared to be potential taste centers were examined with that possibility in mind: (a) the large symmetrically placed pits arranged in the posteriorly directed V toward and near the base of the tongue (Figs. 7–10, 7–11), which in turn have concentrations of smaller pits within their concavities (Fig. 7–11), (b) the smaller pits concentrated on the basal and lateral surfaces on the tongue and extending partly down the oral track behind the tongue (Figs. 7–11, 7–13), and (c) the large papillae on the anteriolateral part on the tongue (Figs. 7–10, 7–15), which tend to disappear or to be overgrown in very large adults. Woodard (1969) interpreted his histological preparations from these pits and papillae as follows: "Both the large (Fig. 7–12) and small (Fig. 7–14) pits appear to be normal exocric glands of the tongue. Sections reveal depressions in the lingual epithelium. These are compound tubular alveolar exocrine secretory glands with a merocrine type of secretion. They are mixed glands with both serous and mucous secreting cells. These organs probably represent

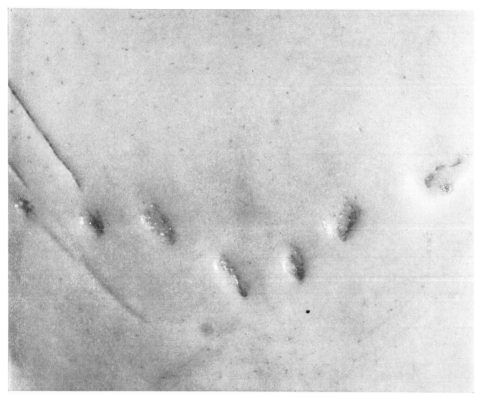

Figure 7–11. Enlargement of series of large pits near base of tongue shown in Figure 7–10. Note concentrations of small pits within the concavities of larger ones, and additional small pits like those shown in Figure 7–13 on the surfaces around the larger. (Photograph courtesy of Marineland of Florida by William A. Huck.)

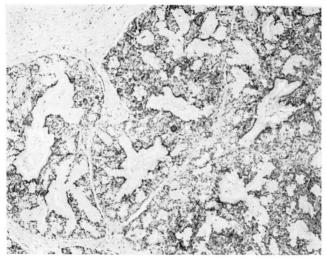

Figure 7–12. Section through one of the large pits (upper left) at the base of the tongue (as in Figs. 7–10 and 7–11) of an adult male *Tursiops truncatus*. Hematoxylin and eosin. (Photograph by James C. Woodard.)

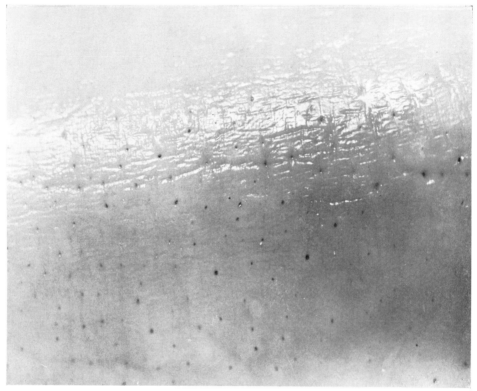

Figure 7–13. Enlargement of small pits on surface of tongue shown in Figure 7–10. Pits figured here are located on the left (upper in photograph) edge of tongue about midway between the papillae and the large pits. Similar small pits may be seen near the large pits in Figure 7–11. (Photograph courtesy of Marineland of Florida by William A. Huck.)

digestive secretory glands (possibly lingual salivary glands) rather than sensory organs. Sections of the papillae reveal parakarytotic oral epithelium with a dense underlying dermal core containing blood vessels. No special sensory function is indicated for these papillae."

It should be noted that the tongue of at least some cetacean species is not as immovable as it has been depicted by Slijper (1962). We have observed considerable tongue movement by a killer whale, *Orcinus orca* (Fig. 7–16), and have seen it frequently in *Tursiops truncatus*. We have seen animals of these two species stick out their tongues for no apparent reason as they swam around the tank. In the latter species, sticking the tongue out can become a husbandry problem during training (especially when younger animals are involved). Much as some humans do when solving a problem, young *Tursiops* have sometimes been observed to stick part of their tongue out of the side of their mouth while learning a new

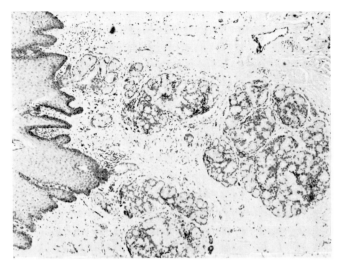

Figure 7–14. Section through one of the small pits of the tongue (as in Figures 7–11 and 7–13) of an adult male *Tursiops truncatus*. Hematoxylin and eosin. (Photograph by James C. Woodard.)

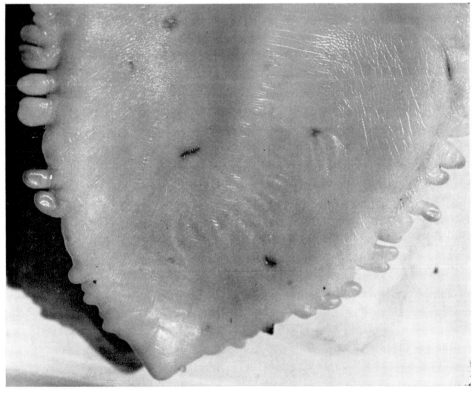

Figure 7–15. Enlargement of papillae of tongue shown in Figure 7–10. The apparent pits and the black spots are small lesions or cuts, and are not the pits shown in Figures 7–11 and 7–13. (Photograph courtesy of Marineland of Florida by William A. Huck.)

Figure 7–16. Adolescent female *Orcinus orca* with tongue extended in response to a grating sound made by an observer running his finger across the teeth of a pocket comb held against the observation window of the whale's tank. The whale apparently could see the comb and after being attracted by the sound usually pressed her tongue against the glass immediately opposite the comb. (Authors' photograph made at Sea World, San Diego, California.)

routine. In one case, an animal that was learning to jump and grasp a ball got his tongue stuck between his teeth and the ball as he fell back onto the water. The forces involved resulted in a perfect series of punctures diagonally across the center of his tongue, corresponding to his tooth arrangement. He apparently got a very sore tongue, as evidenced by his refusing food for several days and failure to perform the trick for several more. The tooth marks demonstrated that his tongue could be moved considerably out of its alignment. Whether a moveable tongue in odontocetes functions in chemoreception or touch is speculative, but there seem to be behavioral correlates for both.

Other Sensory Media

We do not know the loci for the reception of information about temperature, current, and salinity. The skin of the Atlantic bottlenosed dolphin is richly innervated and everywhere contains highly specialized end organs (Palmer and Weddell, 1964), but their function or functions are totally unknown and the resolution of the problem still awaits electrophysiological studies. According to Jansen (1953), the lobulus simplex is homologous with the posterior quadrangular lobule of the human cerebellum and is enormously developed in cetaceans, probably due to the high development of tactile nerves (Jansen, 1950). Slijper (1962) regarded this as evidence that the tactile receptors must be sensitive to water pressure and flow. It is theorized that depth changes may be perceived in the region of the ear. There is no reason to assume that the vestibular tract works greatly different in cetaceans than in other mammals.

The frequent presence of nematode parasites in the acoustic sinuses (Reysenbach de Haan, 1957, p. 34) indicates that stranded cetaceans should be examined for these parasites which may contribute to orientation difficulties. However, to date, we have not found this parasite in any of the singly stranded *Tursiops truncatus, Kogia breviceps, Physeter catodon,* and *Ziphius caviorstris* we have examined. Fluke eggs found in the brain of a stranded common dolphin, *Delphinus delphis bairdi,* were credited with causing disorientation and death (Ridgway and Johnston, 1965).

Behaviorally, cetaceans are apparently able to perceive changes in the salinity of the water. For example, in the Amazon River system, the freshwater *Inia geoffrensis* normally does not venture into saline waters although physically it is certainly able to do so. The reverse situation has been observed for the marine *Tursiops truncatus,* which ventures upstream in large rivers usually only as far as the influence of the tides, even when other physical conditions of the stream would permit it to continue upstream many more miles. Other factors, such as the presence or absence of food fish, which are much more susceptible to salinity changes, may play a part in the movements of the dolphins. However, the behavioral evidence seems to be that some direct mechanism for salinity determination is present.

Sensory Coordination

Both of us received our early training in animal behavior in the ethologically oriented approach. We continue to rely heavily on looking for simple sensory cues that tend to elicit behavior, but for some years we have had to concede that dolphins and other odontocetes just do not react as do insects and birds to seemingly all-or-none signals. A particular odor, color, shape, or sound does not automatically elicit the initiation of courtship or feeding. A single cue may increase the probability of a behavior's occurring, but somewhere in the brain all simultaneously incoming stimuli are being processed and balanced one against the other. It is the summation of all internal and incoming stimuli, plus individual experience, that determines the final behavior, and it is the wise dolphin handler that early discontinues the practice of predicting what any one animal will do at any given moment that a particular stimulus is presented.

Researchers are tediously probing the many factors, in which the sensory pathways play a leading part, that lead to final behavior. The game of entering a dolphin's world is far from won, but the odds are improving daily.

OTHER MARINE MAMMALS

Acoustic System

SOUND RECEPTION

Almost all of the natural history observations of pinnipeds and sea otters indicate an excellent sense of hearing. Møhl (1968) reviewed the scattered literature on the anatomy of the pinniped ear and noted that the mechanism probably works in much the same manner as the mechanisms of other mammals. Although the external ear is either essentially absent (Odobenidae and Phocidae) or greatly reduced (Otariidae), the ear bones are massive (Scheffer, 1958). The meatus is open in air, closed underwater.

Students of various species in the wild note that the mother appears to recognize her own infant by its voice, even among hundreds or even thousands of distant pups (harp seal, Sergeant, 1965; California sea lion, Peterson and Bartholomew, 1967; Galapagos sea lion, Eibl-Eibesfeldt, 1961; Alaska fur seal, Elliott, 1884; harbor seal, Evans, 1967; Hawaiian monk seal, Kenyon and Rice, 1959). These observations are reinforced by the facts that the California sea lion vocalizes at birth (Peterson and Bartholomew, 1967) and the young harp seal vocalizes constantly (Sergeant, 1967). Eskimos imitating walrus sounds obtain a response from other walruses a mile distant (King, 1964).

In some species, it may be up to the pup to recognize the voice of the mother, who vocalizes when emerging from the water (Steller's sea lion, Orr and Poulter, 1967; Alaska fur seal, Bartholomew, 1959). As demonstrated in elephant seals (Bartholomew and Collias, 1962) and Galapagos sea lions (Orr and Poulter, 1967), this recognition may involve a call-answer contact sequence between mother and pup. Bonnot (1928) noted that when a drowning California sea lion pup cried out, several females approached and nosed it but left it because it was not their own.

Sea lion rookeries are so noisy and animals can be approached so closely that observers have occasionally postulated that these animals could not hear very well. However, this behavior is apparently not the result of poor hearing, but of a process of habituation to the constant low-frequency roar of the surf and their fellows. A sharp sound usually is noted instantly

(Bonnot, 1928; Peterson and Bartholomew, 1967), but hunters of both the harbor and ribbon seal shoot one animal at a time and pause between shots (Wilke, 1954), doubtless permitting habituation to even the sharp report of a rifle.

There have been a few excellent studies on psychoacoustics in pinnipeds. Møhl (1964) found that harbor seals (*Phoca vitulina*) react to signals of moderate intensity up to 160 kHz. Later, he was able to get responses in water up to 180 kHz but found that the animals lost pitch discrimination above 60 kHz (Møhl, 1968). Harbor seals are capable of directional hearing underwater, though it is not perfect. Their hearing in air is good but extends to only 12 kHz.

Underwater directional hearing in the California sea lion was investigated on a simple left versus right basis by Gentry (1966). Two transducers were placed in the water at angles varying from 5 to 40 degrees from the median, and a tone emitted from only one. Reward depended upon the unblindfolded animal's chosing the correct emitter. On a 3.5 kHz tone, the animal did only slightly better than chance until an angle of 15 degrees was reached, but with a 6 kHz signal at only 10 degrees, performance was significantly better than chance. Directional hearing also improved when the frequency was raised in 1 kHz increments from 1.5 kHz to 6.0 kHz (with one exception—2.5 kHz).

Electrode implants into the cortex of three harbor seal pups recorded activity to auditory stimuli in an area smaller than the auditory cortex of other carnivores (Alderson *et al.*, 1960). The pups were only eight to twelve days old, however, and the authors did not know how this affected the results.

Sound Emissions

Most of the pinnipeds are extremely vocal. Evans (1967) listed those species recorded underwater. Sea lions can be heard for miles at sea (Scammon, 1874), and the underwater sounds of a Steller's sea lion can be heard from three to five miles away (Poulter, 1968a). During the breeding season, the barks of a Galapagos sea lion male were counted for a brief period as he routinely patrolled the beach. The barks were emitted in series, averaging 5.5 per series. The elapsed time between series (not barks) averaged only 4.3 seconds (Orr, 1967). This surely must represent some kind of record for vocal maintenance of territory among mammals. Orr was able to recognize the different voices of the bulls with territories and harems after only six days of observations.

The anatomy of the sea lion larynx was described by Odend'hal (1966). The bark has been experimentally determined to originate in the vocal cords (Eiseman *et al.*, 1965); the clicks rise in frequency in an animal breathing an oxygen-helium mixture, indicating their production within the respiratory passages (Brauer *et al.*, 1966).

In the laboratory, it has been found that the most dominant male of a group of six sea lions did the most barking. When he was removed, the next most dominant animal became the most frequent barker (Schusterman and Dawson, 1968). However, a bull intruding into another's territory is silent (Peterson and Bartholomew, 1967).

Female California sea lions bark less frequently and have higher-pitched barks than males (Poulter, 1968b; Peterson and Bartholomew, 1967). The same distinction is true of the northern fur seal (Poulter, 1966b), the Steller's sea lion (Poulter, 1968a), and the northern elephant seal (Bartholomew and Collias, 1962). In addition to the long-distance threat bark, female sea lions emit three aggressive vocalizations which indicate increasing levels of aggressiveness—a squeal, a belch, and a growl. Vocalizations in the elephant seal carry the two dominant biological messages of threat and attraction (Bartholomew and Collias, 1962). The clap threat of the male becomes lower pitched with increase in body size. Poulter (1968a) found that older Steller's sea lions also have lower-pitched signals.

Walruses are credited with three underwater calls: the rasp, a series of clicks, and an amazing bell-like sound associated with sexual activity (Schevill *et al.*, 1966). We observed the walruses at Marineland of the Pacific, where underwater visibility is excellent, during a period when they were learning to make an underwater clicking sound by clicking their teeth. It was learned by one animal overnight and by another in an adjacent tank in acoustic but not visual contact within a week. If this proves to be the same sound recorded by Schevill *et al.*, (1966), and it appears very much as though it is, the sound might better be termed a phonation than a call. It would, however, be communicative, even if it only indicated the presence of another animal. Lindsey (1937) also reported a staccato tooth clicking in the Weddell seal.

The Florida manatee emits a squeaky sound underwater which carries about 30 m (Schevill and Watkins, 1965). Caribbean animals that were probably of the same species were recorded earlier (Kellogg, 1955) and the same squeaks were found.

The role of the vocalizations of pinnipeds out of water is well established as constituting social signals, emotionally induced as either call or threat and recognized by herd members for what they are. Lindsey (1937), who observed and recorded the vocalizations of the Weddell seal both in air and underwater, noted that when an animal was disturbed it emitted a trill. When they were exposed to a playback of recorded sounds. the seals tended to respond to these presumed threat trills with more trills (Watkins and Schevill, 1968). The duration of the trill of the respondent also tended to approximate the duration of that of the playback.

The voice of the emitter is probably characteristic to the animal and individually recognizable to associated herd members. It is interesting that a clap threat of a dominant male elephant seal scatters all of the low-ranking males in the vicinity but will not cause a male of intermediate rank to move unless the threat is directed toward that individual animal (Bartholomew and Collias, 1962).

An echolocation function has been ascribed to the underwater clicks of sea lions (Poulter, 1963, 1966a, 1967; Shaver and Poulter, 1967) and postulated as possible for other pinnipeds (Poulter, 1968a). Poulter seems to stand alone in his conviction that the click sounds emitted underwater have an echolocation function. Schevill (1968) covered the opposition literature, and the evidence against echolocation in pinnipeds is impressive (see e.g. Schusterman, 1967, for detailed experimental evidence).

Blind pinnipeds in excellent physical condition are reported (Bonnot, 1928; Hickling, 1962; King, 1964; Poulter, 1968a). The evidence for echolocation is indeed weak and the evidence against it appears good, but the animals are responding to some cue that we ourselves do not understand. It could be any of the well-known sensory modes but in a more highly developed degree than we are accustomed to considering.

Visual System

Many factors must be considered when speaking of "vision." These include light versus dark adaptations, near and distance perception, object movement and size, the frequently underrated "attention" factor, habituation, and color and hue discrimination. In marine mammals these also have to be considered in two media, air and water.

Scheffer (1958; also see King, 1964) briefly reviewed the anatomy of the eye in pinnipeds. He noted that perhaps most of the seals are nocturnal and mentioned that those of the higher latitudes, such as the Weddell and ringed seal, spend as much as four months of each year in total darkness. Elliott (1884) observed that fur seals may see better at night, but the California sea lion appears to have better vision in air during daylight (Peterson and Bartholomew, 1967). The California sea lion tested by Evans and Haugen (1963) found fish underwater in darkness but used a more complicated search pattern than in daylight. Blindfolded, it failed to find the fish. Considerable information about the mechanism of the air-water adaptation of the seal eye is included in Walls (1963), who considered the seal "eye-minded" and noted that the average seal, unlike the elephant seal and Weddell seal, will take flight from a man 150 yd away. If we disregard the elephant seal, which is so lethargic that it ignores almost everything (Bartholomew, 1952), the extent and type of experience with man would probably affect the animal's attentiveness and reaction even if the man could be seen clearly.

The California sea lion is the pinniped whose sensory system has been studied most extensively both in the wild and in the laboratory. In the wild, the animal appears to see any object that moves and subtends the horizon extensively (Peterson and Bartholomew, 1967); it does not react at all to stationary objects (Bonnot, 1928). On the snow, both seal hunters (Wilke, 1954) and walrus hunters (Clarke, 1887) wear white for concealment. Early seal hunters easily drove both individual surly bulls and entire herds of sea lions to slaughterhouses by alternately opening and closing an umbrella in their faces (Elliott, 1887b; Scammon, 1874). A puzzling fact in Elliott's report is that after a sea lion drive, the animals were kept in groups of twenty-five to forty in a pen composed only of flimsy stakes driven at 10- to 30-foot (3 to 9 m) intervals to which a piece of fluttering white cloth was attached. A thin line or two was strung between the poles. The weak corral contained the animals although they were alert, active, and obviously uncomfortable with the situation and would escape were it not for this pseudo-enclosure.

B. C. Townsend, Jr., of Marineland of Florida offers a significant observation that demonstrates that universal applicability of observations made in the wild are no less subject to distortion than observations in the laboratory. At the time that Townsend was Assistant Curator to F. G. Wood, Jr., at the Marineland Research Laboratory, a pet male California sea lion had pretty much the run of the laboratory building. After about a month in captivity, when first shown dry photographs of a fish it showed no response; but if a photograph of a fish was in a pan of water, the sea lion tried to grab and eat it (Fig. 7–17). After initial exposure to the picture underwater, the animal began to show interest in even the dry photographs. It also was much enamoured of a prized mounted specimen of a 30-inch striped mullet that had grown up in one of the large tanks at Marineland (Fig. 7–18). The sea lion eventually succeeded in getting to the fish, which meant climbing up onto a bookcase, and today the specimen looks a little ragged from the toothmarks.

Kohler (1927) demonstrated visual recognition of photographed objects in chimpanzees. Among other signs of proper identification of photograph with object (particularly food, as with the sea lion), one of the male chimpanzees always gave the familiar greeting gesture to a photograph of another chimpanzee. Primates are notably visual animals, however, and photographs are almost always ignored throughout the rest of the animal kingdom.

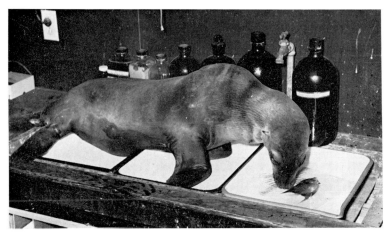

Figure 7–17. Young, tame, male California sea lion, *Zalophus californianus*, closely examining a photograph of a queen angelfish, *Holacanthus ciliaris*, in a pan of water. Sea lion captive about one month. (Photograph courtesy of Marineland of Florida.)

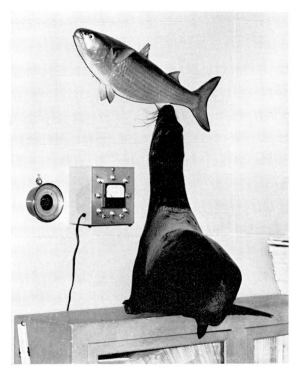

Figure 7–18. Same sea lion shown in Figure 7–17 closely examining a large mounted striped mullet, *Mugil cephalus*. Sea lion captive about one month. (Photograph courtesy of Marineland of Florida.)

Wild sea lions of the same species have been described as having vision of a "low order" and "limited" by extremely competent observers (Peterson and Bartholomew, 1967). The singularity of the visual recognition in air of a photograph by a captive sea lion again points up the impact of attending (which frequently involves learning) on an animal's reactions (Horn, 1965). Although no so-called "formal" training is involved, the act of existing constitutes formal training enough.

Good underwater visual discrimination of size has been shown in the California sea lion (Schusterman *et al.*, 1965) and in the harbor seal (Feinstein and Rice, 1966). The sea otter has good underwater vision at close range, roughly equal to that of man (Gentry and Peterson, 1967).

VISUAL SIGNALS

The gestures, particularly by breeding bulls, are the most frequently mentioned visual signals in pinnipeds. Even this consists of such gross elements as rising to full height, forward lunging, open-mouth thrusts, head shaking, and recurved neck posture (see e.g. Peterson and Bartholomew, 1967; Bartholomew, 1953). As in most mammalian groups, these signals with their accompanying vocalizations are usually sufficient to prevent outbreaks of actual fighting, but occasionally animals are wounded.

Poulter (1968a) revealed an incident which is indicative of the extent of the ritualization of fighting in the Weddell seal. One of his sled dogs thrust its head into the open mouth of a threatening female Weddell seal, sniffed around, and withdrew without a tooth scratch. A sea lion, threatened with a similar open-mouth gesture by a bull elephant seal, thrust its head partially into the open mouth. Instead of biting down, the elephant seal returned to a resting position (Bartholomew, 1952).

The female sea lion, as opposed to other pinnipeds, does the sexual soliciting. Significantly she also has an estrus display (in addition to the pink and slightly edematous vulva); she approaches the bull with submissive postures and languorous movements and lies prone in front of him (Peterson and Bartholomew, 1967). A courtship display is also characteristic of the harp seal (Sivertsen, 1941).

Visual cues of both sex and age are apparent in some pinniped species. Sexual dimorphism occurs both in size and color pattern. The proboscis and enlarged canine teeth of the male elephant seal must be a vivid visual cue to others of the species, and the enlarged tusks of the male walrus another. The various stages of moult occurring during growth in those species with infantile coloration are good visual indicators. Seals and sea lions both indicate emotion also by the position of their whiskers (Hediger, 1955).

Tactile Sense

Vibrissae have been described in detail for the northern fur seal by Scheffer (1962), and we follow his terminology in the use of the word vibrissa for an overgrown facial hair situated on either side of the snout and above each eye. Vibrissae grow throughout life and do not molt.

All pinnipeds have abundant mystacial vibrissae; these may be used as probes by the bottom feeders as the walrus and bearded seal (King, 1964). Sea otters also have coarse bristling vibrissae (Barabash-Nikiforov, 1962). The vibrissae of the Florida manatee superficially resemble those of the walrus. Histologically, Woodard (1969) tells us that manatee vibrissae (Figs. 7–19, 7–20) are typical sinus hairs. Trautmann and Fiebiger (1952) have also referred to sinus hairs as tactile hairs, and the vibrissae of the manatee must serve some tactile sensory function.

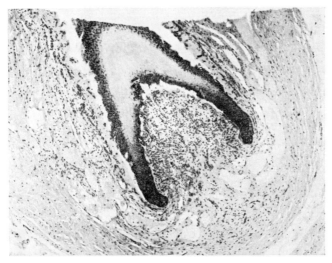

Figure 7–19. Longitudinal section through base of a sinus hair from the anterior portion of the snout of a juvenile male Florida manatee, *Trichechus manatus latirostris* (×40). (Photograph by James C. Woodard.)

No extensive experimental work has been done on these tactile organs in marine mammals. There are, however, a few potentially significant observations reported. Evans and Haugen (1963) called attention to the fact that if target fish brushed the vibrissae or face of their blindfolded sea lion, they were located; otherwise not. The long chest hairs of sea otters, called vibrissae, may aid in catching fish (Reshetkin and Shidlovskaya, 1962).

A study of the role of the vibrissae in the pinnipeds seems a fertile field. In visual cliff tests, glass is placed over what appears visually as open

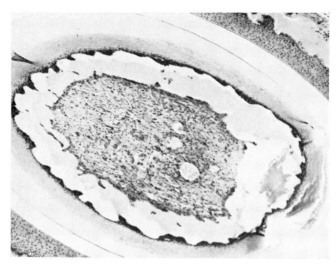

Figure 7–20. Cross section of same sinus hair shown in Figure 7–19, distal to the section shown in that figure (×40). (Photograph by James C. Woodard.)

space (Marler and Hamilton, 1966; Walk, 1965). Rats, like most animals, will not approach the seeming precipice. They do, however, if their vibrissae first touch the glass. Tactile information afforded by the vibrissae apparently takes precedence over visual information in this species. Electrode implants in cats show the exquisite sensibility of the receptors connected with the interosseus nerve to vibratory stimuli. They respond to slight jarring of the floor some distance away and even to loud sound (Hunt and McIntyre, 1960). Tweaking the vibrissae causes bradycardia in some species.

Behaviorally, some pinniped species are more thigmotactic than others (King, 1964). Some, like the elephant seal, crowd closely together and ignore a man walking across their backs. The Laysan monk seal reacts adversely, however, to being touched by even its own species (King, 1964). Unlike most mammals, the fur seal pup receives only minimal tactile stimulation from the mother; there is no licking or grooming (Bartholomew, 1959). Even the act of retrieving lasts for only a few hours postpartum. Tactile stimulation of the male California sea lion by an female in estrus is part of the courtship procedure (Peterson and Bartholomew, 1967).

Chemoreception and Chemical Signalling

Olfactory Sense

The pinnipeds in general are classified as microsomatic, with olfactory lobes and nerves being reduced (Scheffer, 1958; Rioch, 1937). Smell, however, continues to play the important role of final identification of the pup by the mother after she has localized it by its voice (see e.g. Bartholomew, 1953, on Alaska fur seals; Kenyon and Rice, 1959, on Hawaiian monk seals; Sergeant, 1965, on harp seals; Peterson and Bartholomew, 1967, on California sea lion). Male California sea lions sniff the genital region of a soliciting female prior to copulation (Peterson and Bartholomew, 1967).

Sea otters, when they were being hunted, were credited with a good sense of smell (Scammon, 1874); reportedly they could smell smoke for four to five miles and would not land on a beach where a man had walked until several tides had washed away the scent (Elliott, 1887c).

Many seals are reported to have a musky odor, postulated as originating in the glands opening into each hair canal. Increased activity in those glands at moulting and breeding seasons suggests a sexual scent gland function (King, 1964). The odor of the male may be particularly strong, as in the harp seal (Sergeant, 1967) and the ringed seal (McLaren, 1958).

GUSTATORY SENSE

The number of taste buds is reduced in those pinnipeds which have been examined (King, 1964). They apparently are sufficiently functional, however, to prevent their acceptance of horse meat or beef (Poulter, 1968b).

Other Sensory Modalities

As in the Cetacea, little is known about reception of information relative to pain, currents, or other mechanoreceptors. Pinnipeds, in general, are restricted to colder waters, the 20°C summer isotherm in either hemisphere serving as an effective barrier (King, 1964). Monk seals constitute the only exception other than an occasional stray. We can guess that the temperature receptors must be highly sensitive since overheating is lethal. In earlier days, many fur seals died during overland drives if they were driven over two miles or faster than 0.5 mph (Elliott, 1887a).

Bartholomew (1966) reviewed the heat regulation problems in pinnipeds and the behavioral and physiological adaptations by which they cope with them. Fur seals enter the water when air temperature rises to 12°C (Bartholomew, 1966). Steller's sea lions begin a herd movement toward the water when sand temperature is between 18° and 21°C; between 21° and 24°C the last animal has entered the water (Peterson and Gentry, 1968).

Early work with electrode implants in hair seals failed to show evidence of an antigravity system (Langworthy *et al.*, 1938).

Evans and Bastian (1969) recently have discussed a number of factors bearing on sensory communication in various noncetacean marine mammals.

✿   ✿   ✿

Although we have studied marine mammals and their behavior at many sites, three have been particularly productive of data pertinent to this section. These institutions and the individuals there who have been particularly helpful to our research in senses and communication are as follows: Marineland of Florida, St. Augustine (B. C. Townsend, Jr., W. Fred Lyons, David A. Nelson, Gary C. Ammons, and Gerald E. Foreman); Marineland of the Pacific, Los Angeles, California (John H. Prescott and David H. Brown), and Florida's Gulfarium, Ft. Walton Beach (J. B. and Marjorie Siebenaler). At our request, Dr. James C. Woodard, comparative animal pathologist at the University of Florida, School of Medicine, prepared a number of histological slides, and his comments about them are included above. To all others who have cooperated with us in many ways, we are especially grateful.

Financial support which in part has permitted our gathering information for this chapter has come from the following in the form of grants and contracts: Office of Naval Research contracts Nos. N00014-67-C-0358 and N00014-67-C-0358-P001, National Institute of Mental Health grant No. MH-07509-01, National Science Foundation grant No. GB-1189, American Philosophical Society grant No. 3755-Penrose, Los Angeles County Museum of Natural History Foundation, and Marineland, Inc.

REFERENCES

Cetacean Senses and Communication

Breatnach, A.S.: The cetacean central nervous system. *Biol. Rev.*, 35:187–230, 1960.

Busnel, R.G. and Dziedzic, A.: Résultats métrologiques expérimentaux de l'echolocation chez le *Phocaena phocaena*, et leur comparison avec ceux de certaines chauves-souris. In Busnel, R.G. (Ed.): *Les Systèms Sonars Animaux, Biologie et Bionique.* Jouy-en-Josas, France, Laboratoire de Physiologie Acoustique, 1967, vol. 1, pp. 307–355.

Caldwell, Melba C. and Caldwell, David K.: Individualized whistle contours in bottlenosed dolphins (*Tursiops truncatus*). *Nature (London)*, 207 (4995): 434–435, 1965.

Caldwell, Melba C. and Caldwell, David K.: Intraspecific transfer of information via the pulsed sound in captive odontocete cetaceans. In Busnel, R.G. (Ed.): *Les Systèms Sonars Animaux, Biologie et Bionique.* Jouy-en-Josas, France, Laboratoire de Physiologie Acoustique, 1967, vol. 2, pp. 879–936.

Caldwell, Melba C. and Caldwell, David K.: Vocalization of naive captive dolphins in small groups. *Science*, 159:1121–1123, 1968.

Caldwell, Melba C., Caldwell, David K., and Evans, William E.: Sounds and behavior of captive Amazon freshwater dolphins, *Inia geoffrensis*. *Los Angeles County Mus., Cont. in Sci.*, 108:1–24, 1966.

Dreher, John J.: Cetacean communication: small-group experiment. In Norris, K.S. (Ed.): *Whales, Dolphins and Porpoises.* Berkeley, University of California Press, 1966, pp. 529–543.

Dreher, John J. and Evans, William E.: Cetacean communication. In Tavolga, W.N. (Ed.): *Marine Bio-acoustics.* New York, Pergamon Press, 1964, vol. 1, pp. 373–393.

Dudok van Heel, W.H.: Audio-direction finding in the porpoise (*Phocaena phocaena*). *Nature (London), 183*:1063, 1959.

Evans, William E.: Vocalization among marine mammals. In Tavolga, W.N. (Ed.): *Marine Bio-acoustics.* New York, Pergamon Press, 1967, vol. 2, pp. 159–186.

Evans, William E. and Bastian, Jarvis: Marine mammal communication: social and ecological factors. In Andersen, H.T. (Ed.): *The Biology of Marine Mammals.* New York, Academic Press, 1969, pp. 425–475.

Evans, William E. and Powell, Bill A.: Discrimination of different metallic plates by an echolocating delphinid. In Busnel, R.G. (Ed.): *Les Systèms Sonars Animaux, Biologie et Bionique.* Jouy-en-Josas France: Laboratoire de Physiologie Acoustique, 1967, vol. 1, pp. 363–383.

Grinnell, A.D.: Discussion to Norris, Evans and Turner (1967). In Busnel, R.G. (Ed.): *Les Systèms Sonars Animaux, Biologie et Bionique.* Jouy-en-Josas, France: Laboratoire de Physiologie Acoustique, 1967, vol. 1, pp. 442–443.

Jansen, Jan: The morphogenesis of the cetacean cerebellum. *J. Comp. Neur., 94*:341–400, 1950.

Jansen, Jan: Studies on the cetacean brain: the gross anatomy of the rhombencephalon of the fin whale (*Balaenoptera physalus* (L)), *Hvalrad. Skr. 37:* 1–35, 1953.

Jansen, Jan, Jr. and Jansen, Jan: A note on the amygdaloid complex in the fin whale (*Balaenoptera physalus* (L.)), *Hvalrad. Skr., 39*:1–14, 1953.

Johnson, C. Scott: Sound detection thresholds in marine mammals. In Tavolga, W.N. (Ed.): *Marine Bio-acoustics.* New York, Pergamon Press, 1967, vol. 2, pp. 247–260.

Kellogg, Winthrop N. and Rice, Charles E.: Visual discrimination and problem solving in a bottlenose dolphin. In Norris, K.S. (Ed.): *Whales, Dolphins, and Porpoises.* Berkeley, University of California Press, 1966, pp. 731–754.

Kruger, Lawrence: The thalamus of the dolphin (*Tursiops truncatus*) and comparison with other mammals. *J. Comp. Neur., 111*(1):133–194, 1959.

Kruger, Lawrence: Specialized features of the cetacean brain. In Norris, K.S. (Ed.): *Whales, Dolphins and Porpoises.* Berkeley, University of California Press, 1966, pp. 232–254.

Lang, Thomas G. and Smith, H.A.P.: Communication between dolphins in separate tanks by way of an electronic acoustic link. *Science, 150*(3705): 1839–1843, 1965.

Langworthy, Orthello R.: Central nervous system of the porpoise *Tursiops truncatus. J. Mammal, 12*(4):381–389, 1931.

Layne, James N. and Caldwell, David K.: Behavior of the Amazon dolphin,

Inia geoffrensis (Blainville), *in captivity. Zoologica,* 49(2):81–108, 4 pls, 1964.

Lilly, John C. and Miller, Alice M.: Vocal exchanges between dolphins. *Science,* 134(3493):1873–1876, 1961.

Norris, Kenneth S.: Some problems of echolocation in cetaceans. In Tavolga, W.N. (Ed.): *Marine Bio-acoustics.* New York, Pergamon Press, 1964, vol. 1, pp. 317–336.

Norris, Kenneth S.: In Round Table: Practical Problems. In Norris, K.S. (Ed.): *Whales, Dolphins, and Porpoises.* Berkeley, University of California Press, 1966, pp. 670–671.

Norris, Kenneth S.: The evolution of acoustic mechanisms in odontocete cetaceans. In Drake, E.T. (Ed.): *Evolution and Environment.* New Haven, Yale University Press, 1968, pp. 297–324.

Norris, Kenneth, S.: The echolocation of marine mammals. In Andersen, H.T. (Ed.): *The Biology of Marine Mammals.* New York, Academic Press, 1969, pp. 391–423.

Norris, Kenneth S. and William E. Evans: Directionality of echolocation clicks in the rough-toothed porpoise *Steno bredanensis* (Lesson). In Tavolga, W.N. (Ed.): *Marine Bio-acoustics.* New York, Pergamon Press, 1967, vol. 2, pp. 305–316.

Norris, Kenneth S., Evans, William E., and Turner, Ronald N.: Echolocation in an Atlantic bottlenose porpoise during discrimination. In Busnel, R.G. (Ed.): In *Les Systèms Sonars Animaux, Biologie et Bionique.* Jouy-en-Josas, France: Laboratoire de Physiologie Acoustique, 1967, vol. 1, pp. 409–437.

Norris, Kenneth S. and Prescott, John H.: Observations on Pacific cetaceans of Californian and Mexican waters. *Univ. of California Publ. in Zool.,* 63(4): 291–402, 1961.

Norris, Kenneth S., Prescott, John H., Asa-Dorian, Paul V. and Perkins, Paul: An experimental demonstration of echo-location behavior in the porpoise *Tursiops truncatus* (Montagu). *Biol. Bull.,* 120(2):163–176, 1961.

Palmer, Elisabeth and Weddell, G.: The relationship between structure, innervation and function of the skin of the bottlenose dolphin (*Tursiops truncatus*). *Proc. Zool. Soc. London,* 143(4):553–568, 7 pls, 1964.

Reysenbach de Haan, F.W.: Hearing in whales. *Acta Oto-laryng. Suppl. 134:* 1–114, 1957.

Ridgway, S.H. and D.G. Johnston: Two interesting disease cases in wild cetaceans. *Amer. J. Vet. Res.,* 26:771–775, 1965.

Schevill, William E. and Lawrence, Barbara: Auditory response of a bottlenosed porpoise, *Tursiops truncatus,* to frequencies above 100 Kc. *J. Exp. Zool.,* 124(1):147–165, 1953.

Slijper, E.J.: *Whales.* London, Hutchinson, 1962.

Tavolga, William N.: Review of marine bio-acoustics: state of the art, 1964. Port Washington, N.Y., U.S. Naval Training Device Center, Technical Rpt.: NAVTRADEVCEN 1212–1, 1965.

Woodard, James C.: Personal communication, 1969.

Other Marine Mammals

Alderson, Ann, Diamantopoulos, M.E., and Downman, C.B.B.: Auditory cortex of the seal (*Phoca vitulina*). *J. Anat.*, 94:506–511, 1960.

Barabash-Nikiforov, I.I.: The otter (*Enhydra lutris L.*)— biology and economic problems of breeding. In *The Sea Otter*. Jerusalem, Israel Program for Scientific Translations, 1962, pp. 1–174.

Bartholomew, George A., Jr.: Reproductive and social behavior of the northern elephant seal. *Univ. of California Publ. Zool.*, 47(15):369–472, 1952.

Bartholomew, George A., Jr.: Behavioral factors affecting social structure in the Alaska fur seal. *Trans. 18th N. Amer. Wildlife Conf.*, 1953, pp. 481–502.

Bartholomew, George A., Jr.: Mother-young relations and the maturation of pup behavior in the Alaska fur seal. *Animal Behaviour*, 7(3–4):163–171, 1959.

Bartholomew, George A., Jr.: Interaction of physiology and behavior under natural conditions. In Bowman, R.I. (Ed.): *The Galapagos*. Berkeley, University of California Press, 1966, pp. 39–45 .

Bartholomew, George A., Jr., and Collias, Nicholas E.: The role of vocalization in the social behaviour of the northern elephant seal. *Animal Behaviour*, 10(1–2):7–14, pl. 3, 1962.

Bonnot, Paul: The sea lions of California. *Calif. Fish and Game*, 14(1), 1928.

Brauer, Ralph W., Jennings, Richard A., and Poulter, Thomas C.: The effect of substituting helium and oxygen from air on the vocalization of the California sea lion, *Zalophus californianus*. *Proc. Third Annual Conf. on Biol. Sonar and Diving Mammals, Stanford Research Institute*, 1966, 68–73.

Clarke, A. Howard: The Pacific walrus fishery. In Goode, G.B. *et al.* (Eds.): *The Fisheries and Fishery Industries of the United States*. Washington, U.S. Govt. Printing Office, 1887, Section V, vol. 2, pp. 313–318.

Eibl-Eibesfeldt, Irenaus: *Galapagos, the Noah's Ark of the Pacific*. Garden City, Doubleday, 1961.

Eiseman, B., Dilbone, R., and Slater, J.: Devocalizing sea lions. *J. Amer. Vet. Med. Ass.*, 147:1086–1089, 1965.

Elliott, Henry W.: The habits of the fur seal. In Goode, G.B. *et al.* (Eds.): *The Fisheries and Fishery Industries of the United States*. Washington, U.S. Govt. Printing Office, 1884, Section I, pp. 75–113.

Elliott, Henry W.: The fur-seal industry of the Priblylov group, Alaska. In Goode, G.B. *et al.* (Eds.): *The Fisheries and Fishery Industries of the United States*. Washington, U.S. Govt. Printing Office, 1887a, Section V, vol. 2, pp. 321–393.

Elliott, Henry W.: The sea-lion hunt. In Goode, G.B. *et al.* (Eds.): *The Fisheries and Fishery Industries of the United States*. Washington, U.S. Govt. Printing Office, 1887b, Section V, vol. 2, pp. 467–474.

Elliott, Henry W.: The Sea-otter fishery. In Goode, G.B. *et al.* (Eds.): *The Fisheries and Fishery Industries of the United States*. Washington, U.S. Govt. Printing Office, 1887c, Section V, vol. 2, pp. 483–491.

Evans, William E.: Vocalization among marine mammals. In Tavolga, W.N. (Ed.): *Marine Bio-acoustics*. New York, Pergamon Press, 1967, vol. 2, pp. 159–186.

Evans, William E. and Bastian, Jarvis: Marine mammal communication: social and ecological factors. In Andersen, H. T. (Ed.): *The Biology of Marine Mammals*. New York, Academic Press, 1969, pp. 425–475.

Evans, William E., and Haugen, Ruth M.: An experimental study of the echo-location ability of a California sea lion, *Zalophus californianus* (Lesson). *Bull. S. Calif. Acad. Sci., 62*(4):165–175, 1963.

Feinstein, Stephen H. and Rice, Charles E.: Discrimination of area differences by the harbor seal. *Psychon. Sci., 4*(11):379–380, 1966.

Gentry, Roger L.: Underwater directional hearing by a California sea lion. *Proc. Third Annual Conf. on Biol. Sonar and Diving Mammals*, Stanford Research Institute, 1966, pp. 116–126.

Gentry, Roger L. and Peterson, Richard S.: Underwater vision of the sea otter. *Nature (London), 216*(5114):435–436, 1967.

Hediger, H.: *Studies of the Psychology and Behaviour of Captive Animals in Zoos and Circuses*. London, Butterworths Scientific Publications, 1955.

Hickling, Grace: *Grey Seals and the Farne Islands*. London, Routledge and Kegan Paul, 1962.

Horn, Gabriel: Physiological and psychological aspects of selective perception. In Lehrman, D.S., Hinde, R.A., and Shaw, E. (Eds.): *Advances in the Study of Behavior*. New York, Academic Press, 1965, vol. 1, pp. 155–215.

Hunt, C.C. and McIntyre, A.K.: Characteristics of responses from receptors from the flexor longus digitorum muscle and the adjoining interosseous region of the cat. *J. Physiol., 153*:74–87, 1960.

Kellogg, Winthrop N.: *Sounds of Sea Animals*. Talkways Records Album No. FX6125; Sci. Ser., Vol. II, New York, Florida Talkways Records and Service Corp., 1955.

Kenyon, Karl W. and Rice, Dale W.: Life history of the Hawaiian monk seal. *Pacific Sci., 13*:215–252, 1959.

King, Judith E.: *Seals of the World*. London, Brit. Mus. Nat. Hist., 1964.

Köhler, Wolfgang: *The Mentality of Apes*. New York, Harcourt, Brace, 1927.

Langworthy, Orthello R., Hesser, Frederick H., and Kolb, Lawrence C.: A physiological study of the cerebral cortex of the hair seal. *J. Comp. Neurol., 69*(3):351–369, 1938.

Lindsey, A.A.: The Weddell seal in the Bay of Whales. *J. Mammal., 18*(2):127–144, 1937.

Marler, Peter, and Hamilton, William J., III: *Mechanisms of Animal Behavior*. New York, John Wiley, 1966.

McLaren, I.A.: The biology of the ringed seal (*Phoca hispida* Schreber) in the eastern Canadian Arctic. *Bull. Fish. Res. Bd. Canada, 118*:1–97, 1958.

Møhl, Bertel: Preliminary studies on hearing in seals. *Vidensk. Medd. Dansk Naturh. Foren., 127*:283–294, 1964.

Møhl, Bertel: Hearing in seals. In Harrison, R.J. *et al.* (Eds.): *The Behavior and Physiology of Pinnipeds.* New York, Appleton-Century-Crofts, 1968, pp. 172–195.

Odend'hal, Stewart: The anatomy of the larynx of the California sea lion (*Zalophus californianus*). *Proc. Third Annual Conf. on Biol. Sonar and Diving Mammals.* Stanford Research Institute, 1966, pp. 55–67.

Orr, Robert T.: The Galapagos sea lion. *J. Mammal, 48*(1):62–69, 1967.

Orr, Robert T. and Poulter, Thomas C.: Some observations on reproduction, growth, and social behavior in the Steller sea lion. *Proc. Calif. Acad. Sci.,* 4th ser., *35*(10):193–226, 1967.

Peterson, Richard S. and Bartholomew, George A., Jr.: *The Natural History and Behavior of the California Sea Lion.* Amer. Soc. Mammal., Spec. Publ., 1 1967.

Peterson, Richard S. and Gentry, Roger L.: Biological investigations in Año Nuevo State Reserve, annual rep., 1966–1967. Univ. Calif. Santa Cruz, 1968.

Poulter, Thomas C.: Sonar signals of the sea lion. *Science, 139*(3556):753–755, 1963.

Poulter, Thomas C.: The use of active sonar by the California sea lion, *Zalophus californianus* (Lesson). *J. Audit. Res., 6:*165–173, 1966a.

Poulter, Thomas C.: Recording the underwater signals of seals of the Arctic. Final Rep. on Phase III, Subcontract ONR-371, March 22–May 6, 1966, 1966b.

Poulter, Thomas C.: Systems of echolocation. In Busnel, R.G. (Ed.): *Les Systèms Sonars Animaux, Biologie et Bionique.* Jouy-en-Josas, France, Laboratoire de Physiologie Acoustique, 1967, vol. 1, pp. 157–186.

Poulter, Thomas C.: Marine mammals. In Sebeok, T.A. (Ed.): *Animal Communication.* Bloomington, Indiana University Press, 1968, pp. 405–465.

Poulter, Thomas C.: Underwater vocalization and behavior of pinnipeds. In Harrison, R.J. *et al.* (Eds.): *The Behavior and Physiology of Pinnipeds.* New York, Appleton-Century-Crofts, 1968, pp. 69–84.

Reshetkin, V.V. and Shidlovskaya, N.K.: Acclimatization of sea otters. In *The Sea Otter.* Jerusalem, Israel Program for Scientific Translations, 1962, 175–224.

Rioch, David Mck.: A physiological and histological study of the frontal cortex of the seal (*Phoca vitulina*). *Biol. Bull., 73:*591–602, 1937.

Scammon, Charles M.: *The Marine Mammals of the North-Western Coast of North America,* etc. San Francisco, John H. Carmany, 1874.

Scheffer, Victor B.: *Seals, Sea Lions, and Walruses.* Stanford, Stanford University Press, 1958.

Scheffer, Victor B.: Pelage and surface topography of the northern fur seal. Washington, U.S. Govt. Printing Office, *North Amer. Fauna, 64,* 1962.

Schevill, William E.: Sea lion echo ranging? *J. Acous. Soc. Amer., 43*(6):1458–1459, 1968.

Schevill, William E. and Watkins, William A.: Underwater calls of *Trichechus* (Manatee). *Nature (London), 205*(4969):373–374, 1965.

Schevill, William E., Watkins, William A., and Ray, Carleton: Analysis of underwater *Odobenus* calls with remarks on the development and function of the pharyngeal pouches. *Zoologica, 51*(3):103–106, 5 pls, phonograph record, 1966.

Schusterman, Ronald J.: Perception and determinants of underwater vocalization in the California sea lion. In Busnel, R.G. (Ed.): *Les Systèms Sonars Animaux, Biologie et Bionique.* Jouy-en-Josas, France, Laboratoire de Physiologie Acoustique, 1967, vol. 1, pp. 535–617.

Schusterman, Ronald J. and Dawson, Ronald G.: Barking, dominance, and territoriality in male sea lions. *Science, 160*(3826):434–436, 1968.

Schusterman, Ronald J., Kellogg, Winthrop N., and Rice, Charles E.: Underwater visual discrimination by the California sea lion. *Science, 147*(3665): 1594–1596, 1965.

Sergeant, David E.: Migrations of harp seals *Pagophilus groenlandicus* (Erxleben) in the northwest Atlantic. *J. Fish Res. Bd. Canada, 22*(2):433–464, 1965.

Sergeant, David E.: Personal communication, 1967.

Shaver, H.N. and Poulter, Thomas C.: Sea lion echo ranging. *J. Acous. Soc. Amer., 42:*428–437, 1967.

Sivertsen, E.: On the biology of the harp seal. *Hvalra. Skr. 26,* 1941.

Trautmann, Alfred and Fiebiger, Josef: *Fundamentals of the Histology of Domestic Animals.* Ithaca, N.Y., Comstock, 1952.

Walk, Richard D.: The study of visual depth and distance perception in animals. In Lehrman, D.S., Hinde, R.A., and Shaw, A. (Eds.): *Advances in the Study of Behavior.* New York, Academic Press, 1965, vol. 1, pp. 99–154.

Walls, Gordon L.: *The Vertebrate Eye and Its Adaptive Radiation.* New York, Hafner, 1963.

Watkins, William A. and Schevill, William E.: Underwater playback of their own sounds to *Leptonychotes* (Weddell Seals). *J. Mammal., 49*(2):287–296, 1968.

Wilke, Ford: Seals of northern Hokkaido. *J. Mammal., 35*(2):218–224, 1954.

Woodard, James C.: Personal communication. 1969.

Chapter 8

EVOLUTION AND CYTOGENETICS

Deborah Duffield Kulu

ORIGINS OF THE CETACEA

Although it is generally recognized that the Cetacea derived from primitive land mammals early in the Tertiary, theories as to their exact origin differ widely, due in part to an often limited and sketchy fossil record. In many instances, intermediate forms which would indicate a specific direction of development and differentiation have yet to be found; and geological deposits yield advanced forms but not the less-specialized, primitive forms antecedent to them. This apparent lack of intermediate and antecedent fossil evidence may well be due both to the cosmopolitan distribution of the evolving cetaceans and to the lack of systematic fossil collection in the past.

The earliest fossil to be positively identified as a member of the whale group was *Protocetus atacus*, found in Egyptian deposits of the Middle Eocene. This primitive cetacean had dentition and certain cranial characteristics typical of the very earliest group of carnivores, the Hyaenodontidae (Creodonts). It also manifested skeletal modifications typical of later cetaceans and this lead Winge (1921) to suggest that *Protocetus* arose from the early carnivores and was itself directly ancestral to at least one of the three suborders of cetaceans, the Archaeoceti (zeuglodonts). The Archaeoceti were widespread during the Middle Eocene but extinct by the Upper Oligocene. The remaining two suborders of cetaceans, the Odontoceti (toothed whales) and the Mystacoceti (baleen whales), although evolving along separate lines, presumably had their common origin in a very early, relatively undifferentiated zeuglodont.

A number of the characteristics found in many primitive cetaceans tend to support the argument that the Cetacea derived from a primitive carnivore. Many retain characteristics already developed in the hyaenodont-creodonts after their derivation from the insectivore-creodont stock which ultimately gave rise to all mammals. Some of the more primitive

503

cetaceans have well-differentiated heterodont dentition similar to that of the flesh-eating carnivores and skeletal characteristics such as hyaenodont-like sagittal and occipital crests, hyaenodont-like zygomatic processes, and an axis of the type found in modern carnivores. Early modifications to the marine environment are equally in evidence. Even the most primitive cetacean shows the characteristic thickening of the inner wall of the tympanic bone, elongation of the rostrum and body, development of flipper-like fore limbs, vestigial hind limbs, and migration of the nostrils to the top of the head.

After comparing various characteristics of the whales with those of the Carnivora on the one hand and the Ungulata on the other, Weber (1886) determined that although there were characteristics typical of the carnivores, as indicated by paleontological studies, there were also a number of characteristics which would indicate a close affinity with the ungulates. For this reason, he and other authors have, for lack of definitive evidence, maintained that the Cetacea evolved from stock intermediate between the Carnivora and Ungulata.

Following Bouvier (1889) and Flower (1884), who emphasized a common descent with the Ungulata, Anthony (1926) compared both anatomical and ecological characteristics of the various groups and concluded that the Cetacea are most closely related to the odd-toed ungulates, the Perissodactyl. Although his evaluation seems to ignore the evidence which points to skeletal similarities between the earliest Cetacea and a carnivore-like ancestor, Anthony's theory is supported in part by work done by Ommanney (1932) on the anatomy of the fin whale urogenital system.

Makino (1948) took a different approach. Comparing the number and morphology of the chromosomes of animals representative of the carnivores, the odd-toed ungulates, the even-toed ungulates, and the cetaceans (*Phocoenoides dalli*), he found the chromosomes of the Dall's porpoise similar only to those of the pig, an even-toed ungulate (Artiodactyl). Assuming that the chromosomes of the Cetacea would be most like the chromosomes of the stock from which they arose, Makino proposed that these findings supported a closer relationship between the Cetacea and the even-toed ungulates. It must be stressed, however, that the apparent similarity may be coincidental, since the rest of the Artiodactyl studied (ten additional species including cow, sheep, goat, etc.) showed little or no correspondence to the porpoise in chromosome number and morphology. Similarity in chromosome composition does not by itself support the argument for an affinity between such extremely diversified and specialized groups as the Cetacea, the Carnivora, and the Ungulata.

Another argument for relating the origin of the Cetacea to the even-toed ungulates was presented by Boyden and Gemeroy (1950). When these researchers compared the protein structure of the Cetacea, Carnivora, and Ungulata by employing a precipitin test to determine the percentage of reaction between antibody produced against the sera of a given group and the sera of other groups, they reported a correspondence of approximately 11 percent between all cetacean and Artiodactyl serum proteins but only a 2 percent or less correspondence between the serum proteins of either the Cetacea or the Artiodactyl and those of the Carnivora.

In general, the evidence supporting any one of these arguments does not by itself adequately establish the specific origin of the Cetacea. Considering the correlations between the earliest cetaceans and the very early carnivores on the one hand, and those between the modern cetaceans and the ungulates on the other, it is at present perhaps best to postulate that the Cetacea evolved from ancestral insectivore creodont stock just antecedent to the separation of the carnivore and ungulate lines. A great deal more evidence—paleontological, anatomical, physiological, and cytological—must be gathered before a definite conclusion can be drawn.

CETACEAN EVOLUTION

There is still some controversy as to whether the three main groups of Cetacea evolved from a common ancestor (or from closely related land mammals). The degree of structural correlation among the three suborders suggests that they shared a common origin, although they must have differentiated soon after their entry into the water and evolved along three independent lines of specialization. As no definite intersuborder transitional forms have been found (although, in most instances, there is a fairly well-established sequence of evolving forms within each group), until the fossil record is more complete, it will be necessary to treat each of the three suborders as separate and distinct lines of descent.

One of the main groups of features distinguishing the three suborders is the relative arrangement of the cranial bones. The zeuglodonts differ markedly from both of the living suborders in that they retain many of the cranial characteristics of the land mammals from which they must have evolved. The earlier zeuglodont skull bore differentiated teeth in the same numbers as typical eutherian dentition and showed little or none of the anterioposterior shortening or "telescoping" that is distinct in even the earliest mystacocetes and odontocetes.

Though the skulls of both the living suborders are charactertistically telescoped, the extreme changes in the relationships of the bones of the skull appear to have occurred in two different directions. In the Mystacoceti, the skull has been shortened largely because of the forward overthrust of posterior cranial elements, whereas the odontocete skull, with a few exceptions (notably the physeterids and ziphiids), has been shortened due to the backward thrust of anterior cranial elements. A detailed description of representative fossil skulls and skeletal remains is available in Winge (1921) and Kellogg (1928).

Although there appear to be too many structural similarities between the two living suborders to support the postulation of biphyletic origin, they must have separated very early in their evolution. This is suggested not only by skeletal differences but by differences in the chemical composition of their oil, protein structure (myoglobin), and anatomies.

Archaeoceti

The Archaeoceti or Zeuglodontia are known from a series of fossils extending in geological time from the Middle Eocene to the Upper Oligocene, when they became extinct.

The earliest fossil, *Protocetus atacus*, exhibited a typically zeuglodont skull but had the dentition of a carnivore and, as mentioned earlier, is thought to provide a link between the later zeuglodonts and the stock from which the Cetacea arose. The zeuglodonts themselves appear to be a specialized branch which diverged from the earliest ancestral forms and developed along distinctive lines until the suborder became largely extinct in the Upper Eocene. One controversial fossil of the Oligocene, *Patriocetus*, thought to be an advanced zeuglodont, has slight telescoping of the skull reminiscent of the earlier mystacocetes and is perhaps representative of a line of zeuglodonts which earlier gave rise to the forerunners of the mystacocetes, although it could not itself represent the ancestral connection between the two groups because it existed concurrently with the primitive mystacocetes. It has not been determined whether *Patriocetus* actually represents a mystacocete precursor, belongs to the earliest odontocetes (the archaic toothed whales), or is just a rather specialized zeuglodont.

Fossils of the late Middle and Upper Eocene indicate that the zeuglodonts developed along two major lines which differ principally in size and gross skeletal characteristics. Within these two groups, at least four distinct series are distinguishable on the basis of changes occurring in the relation of skull components, the dentition, and other skeletal characteristics. One line of descent, which appears to have terminated in the Upper Eocene, produced the gigantic *Basilosaurus* (*Zeuglodon*), a snake-like cetacean which reached a length of 17 to 22 m and, due to its specialized vertebral column, must have moved in a serpentine manner. This animal did exhibit a horizontal fluke typical of the Cetacea, although the fluke was probably quite small. The other major series were comprised of smaller zeuglodonts such as *Prozeuglodon* and *Dorudon* which were more characteristically porpoise-like in shape. These shorter zeuglodonts had a vertebral column developed in the same manner as that found in the fastest and most powerful of the modern cetaceans and probably propelled themselves in the manner of present whales with upward and downward movements of the fluke. This smaller line of zeuglodonts outlasted the Zeuglodons, extending into the Oligocene. In general, the zeuglodonts retained a well-defined sternum, independent cervical vertebrae (although the neck was shortened), and short fin-shaped limbs still movable at the elbow. A detailed description of the structural characteristics of the various zeuglodonts can be found in Kellogg (1928).

Mystacoceti

Although fragments of certain early Eocene forms (*Archaeodelphis*) may prove antecedent to the mystacocete line, the earliest fossil baleen whales known at present were found in the Upper Oligocene, considerably later than the first toothed whales. The presence in these earliest known mystacocetes, the Cetotheres, of already characteristic telescoping and skeletal reorganization makes it reasonable to expect that extension of the fossil record will produce connectant types which will push the Mystacoceti (as well as the other groups) further into the Eocene and more clearly indicate the exact relationship between the three suborders.

That the baleen whales derived from toothed ancestors is suggested not only by paleontological evidence but also by the fact that teeth are still found in mystacocete embryos. (The teeth are absorbed as the fetus develops the whalebone characteristic of this suborder.) While they have become highly specialized in many ways, the baleen whales have retained certain relatively primitive characteristics which have been lost in the higher families of the odontocetes.

Since fossil evidence for this group is rather meager, it is difficult to establish the exact lines of descent of the families within this suborder. Kellogg (1928) indicates that the most primitive of the modern baleen whale families is the Balaenidae (right whales). Early fossils of already specialized balaenids are found in the Lower Miocene and although later development in the Miocene is not immediately traceable, several very advanced balaenids thought to have been directly ancestral to the living right whales are found in Pliocene deposits. At least two lines of descent are distinguishable within the balaenid fossil record. One line gave rise to the larger right whales, *Balaena* and *Neobalaena*. The other developed in a somewhat different direction and gave rise to the pygmy right whale.

Another group of mystacoceles, the Cetotheres, representing a line of development slightly different from the balaenids, appear in Oligocene fossils. At least in the early part of their development, this group of true baleen whales appear more similar to their terrestrial ancestors with regard to certain skeletal characteristics than the most primitive balaenids. The Cetotheres developed along two distinct lines; one line exhibited skull modifications reminiscent of the balaenids, while the other resulted in the type of telescoping characteristic of modern rorquals and gray whales. The Cetotheres flourished in the Miocene and gradually disappeared during the Upper Miocene and Pliocene as modern forms developed and took their place. They were extinct by the end of the Pliocene.

The gray whales have remained the least specialized of all the living Mystacoceti. Cranial characteristics indicate that they derived from early Cetotheres, and the modern representative, the California gray whale, appears little modified from the primitive representatives of this family. The Balaenopteridae (rorquals), though evolved from the same Cetotherian line, became more specialized and were highly differentiated and widespread by the Upper Miocene. Extinct balaenopterines very similar to the present species appear throughout Miocene and Pliocene deposits. There are two modern genera: the *Balaenoptera*, including the blue, fin, sei, Bryde's and little piked whales, and the highly specialized *Megaptera* or humpback whale.

Odontoceti

Fossil remains of several distinctive toothed whales are found in Upper Eocene deposits. The skulls of these small archaic whales indicate that they had developed along slightly different lines than the zeuglodonts. Although it is possible to postulate the sequence by which they might have derived from a primitive zeuglodont, there is no fossil evidence to support this speculation. The archaic toothed whales appear to have died out in the Oligocene after reaching a rather high degree of specialization.

The fossils of this group exhibit various skeletal modifications, but all show some degree of "telescoping." *Agorophius* and *Xenorophus*, basic among these fossils, have the same type of "telescoping" found in the odontocetes, although they also appear to be modified in ways characteristic of the archaic whales alone. It is possible that *Archaeodelphis* and *Patriocetus* (previously mentioned) belong with this group, although these fossils are thought to exhibit skull characteristics more typical of mystacocete development.

Kellogg (1928) suggests that *Agorophius* represents a step through which the odontocetes must have passed during their development and that it is perhaps a distantly related precursor of the Squalodonts, a group of primitive but well-defined odontocetes found in the Lower Miocene. It is further postulated that the archaic toothed whales (including *Agorophius*) were the predecessors of at least two distinct lines of odontocete development. One line gave rise to the squalodonts which were themselves probably the ancestors of the Platanistidae and beaked whales. Another line of the Eocene archaic whales was more than likely directly ancestral to the delphinids and although, due to the scarcity of Oligocene fossils, there is no direct fossil evidence to support this postulate, the appearance of several well-differentiated, characteristically modern delphinid odontocetes by the Lower Miocene would suggest that they had indeed derived from an earlier period. Such rapid development and diversification is difficult to explain if, as previously thought, the delphinids (and physeterids) had developed solely from such well established odontocetes as the Miocene squalodonts.

It is possible to identify four modern odontocete families whose primitive representatives, constructed along the same general lines as the modern genera, appeared with the squalodonts in the Lower Miocene; the Platanistidae, the Ziphiidae, the Delphinidae (in which Winge includes the now distinguished families Monodontidae and Phococnidae), and the Physeteridae. Many of the Miocene representatives, especially those that died out by the end of the Miocene or early Pliocene, were characterized by extreme elongation of the rostrum, and the true short-snouted odontocetes of the family Delphinidae did not appear until the late Miocene.

The Squalodontidae or shark-toothed porpoises were first found in Lower Miocene deposits, and though the group radiated rapidly in the Miocene, it was reduced to a single representative by the Pliocene. There are at least three lines of descent distinguishable within the squalodonts. One is represented by the relatively short-snouted *Prosqualodon* of the Lower Miocene which traces its ancestry with the other primitive squalodonts to the archaic toothed whales. *Prosqualodon* had advanced from the very early toothed whales, developing skull characteristics and the simplification of dentition typical of higher odontocetes, and it is quite possible that the archaic toothed whales ancestral to this line were also ancestral to some of the delphinid odontocetes. The representative of the second line, *Squalodon*, is typical of the more highly specialized, longer-snouted squalodonts. This fossil representative appears later in the Lower Miocene and, in addition to a characteristic arrangement of skull elements, shows a retention of heterodont dentition and an increase in tooth number. The third line of descent is represented by *Neosqualodon*, an extinct form similar to *Squalodon* but representing the extreme in increased and elaborated heterodont dentition. The Miocene squalodonts appear to represent a line of devel-

opment which at this stage was neither antecedent to the higher odontocetes nor particularly well adapted to the Pliocene environment, at which
time they became extinct.

The Platanistidae, which includes both extinct forms and the present
freshwater dolphins, is the least specialized of the modern families. Even
though fossil evidence from this family rests on a few Miocene and Pliocene
skull fragments, certain trends in their development can nevertheless be
established. The teeth have lost their heterodonty, becoming simple and
conical. The degree of telescoping indicates that these odontocetes probably had their origin in the earliest squalodonts, and available evidence
does suggest a definite affinity between squalodont and primitive platanistid skulls. The Platanistidae, like most of the primitive Cetacea, retained such characteristics as a well-developed sternum and independent
cervical vertebrae. The family developed through such forms as *Pontistes*
and *Pontoporia*, evolving mainly towards simplification of the dentition
and increase in the number of teeth.

Pontoporia-like animals seem to have developed in two directions. One
line gave rise to the modern *Inia* (South America boutu), *Lipotes* (the
Chinese freshwater dolphin), and the modern *Pontoporia* (La Plata dolphin); these genera differing from each other in certain tooth and
skull characteristics. Another line developed by way of the extinct
Saurodelphis, a strongly telescoped Lower Pliocene porpoise. The arrangement and development of certain of the cranial bones of this specimen
are reminiscent of the modern *Platanista gangetica* (susu or Ganges River
dolphin), although the two are not thought to be closely related. The
Platanista may more probably be traced back to a *Pontoporia*-like ancestor,
though the jaws of this modern cetacean are more elongated and slender
than those of any other representative of this family.

The origin of the modern ziphiids and physeterids (the beaked and
sperm whales, respectively) is the subject of some debate. A lack of early
fossil material again clouds the issue. Winge (1921) suggests that a group
he designates as the Physeteridae, which includes not only the modern
physeterids but the ziphiids as well, originated from the most primitive
delphinids. Later authors, following Miller (1923) and Kellogg (1928),
dispute this claim and separate the Ziphinidae from the Physeteridae. The
earliest ziphiid, *Diochotichus*, appeared concurrent with the squalodonts
in the Lower Miocene. *Diochotichus* was clearly antecedent to the modern
ziphiids, even though its facial depression was less modified, its cervical
vertebrae were free, and its teeth were found in both jaws (teeth have
disappeared from the upper jaw of most later ziphiids). Moreover, this
primitive whale still shared several important characteristics with the
squalodonts from which it supposedly developed. In general, it appears

that all the earlier ziphiids were much closer to the squalodonts than to the physeterids or delphinids. It is interesting to note that the line of primitive squalodonts giving rise to the early ziphiids seems to have been already differentiated from that which gave rise to the platanistids.

By the Upper Miocene, ziphiids appearing similar to modern forms were becoming abundant. They shared many skull characteristics with present ziphiids, including the loss of functional teeth in the upper jaw. Apparently there were three lines of modification among the fossil ziphiids and these lead to the three major genera of modern ziphiids—*Mesoplodon, Ziphius,* and *Hyperoodon. Mesoplodon* has remained perhaps the most primitive of the three. (The first *Mesoplodon* fossils appeared in Upper Miocene deposits.) The living genus *Ziphius* appears to have originated from whales very similar to *Mesoplodon* and deviates from the latter principally in the modification of various cranial elements. The *Hyperoodons* are thought to have originated from the third line of the primitive ziphiids and to have evolved in a different direction than *Mesoplodon* and *Ziphius.* Another ziphiid genus, *Berardius,* appears to be closely related to *Hyperoodon.*

Perhaps the most outstanding specialization in odontocete evolution has been the development in the Physeteridae of the spermaceti (fat) cushion and reservoir. It is currently believed that the earliest sperm whales developed from cetacean stock well before the Miocene, but other than the already diversified and specialized fossils found in the Middle Miocene, there is no fossil evidence to suggest the exact origin of this interesting family.

The various fossil physeterids differed from one another in the exact relationship of the cranial elements, but the skulls of even the oldest Miocene physeterids were modified for carrying the developing spermaceti cushion in a large supracranial basin. The early physeterids had teeth in both the upper and lower jaws, although the teeth that are found in the upper jaw of later species are atrophied, nonfunctional, and buried in the gum. The reduction of upper dentition had begun by the Middle Miocene, but fossils with functional teeth in both jaws were still found until the end of the Miocene. The culmination of the development of this group is the living genus *Physeter* in which the spermaceti cushion has reached an enormous size. This modification has affected the shape of the head and the position of the eye and, together with the dorsal hump, gives the sperm whale its unusual appearance.

Although there is little paleontological evidence regarding this small group of odontocetes, the modern genus, *Kogia,* is thought to represent an offshoot of the early physeterid line, since it still retains some of the characteristics found in primitive physeterids.

The fossil record being what it is, it is difficult to pinpoint the actual ancestor of the Delphinidae. Some authors argue that the delphinids are descendent from a primitive platanistid or squalodont, while others maintain that they developed from a primitive archaic toothed whale. Whatever their actual derivation, delphinid species (all exhibiting the highly telescoped delphinoid-type skull, conical teeth which are characteristically modified in the various genera, and in most instances, fusion of the cervical vertebrae) were abundant by the Lower Miocene. This group encompasses a large variety of forms and illustrates the tremendous plasticity of the odontocete skull in its response to the stresses of the marine environment. There are various accounts of the interrelationships between the delphinids, but because many of the genera were first identified from the same Miocene deposits and there is insufficient fossil material to establish the actual lines of descent, only the possible relationships as proposed by Winge will be presented here.

There are several fossil remains of a group of extinct delphinids. The earliest of these dates back to the Lower Miocene and the group culminates in the extinct *Eurhinodelphis,* where the transformation of the snout into a long, slender rooting tool reached its greatest development. Another line of odontocetes appears to have branched from the most primitive of this extinct group of delphinids and to have specialized along the line of the modern monodonts. The monodonts are represented by the beluga (*Delphinapterus*), first present in the Upper Miocene, and the narwhal (*Monodon*), initially found in the Pliocene. Though they both retain, along with *Eurhinodelphis,* the primitive characteristic of independent cervical vertebrae (lost in the higher odontocetes), *Delphinapterus* has numerous small, conical teeth in both jaws which marks it as the more primitive of the two. With the exception of the specialized "ramming-tooth" now restricted to the male, the teeth of *Monodon* seem to be in the process of atrophy. The monodonts are currently separated from the delphinids and comprise the family Monodontidae.

The rest of the delphinids are distinguishable from these earlier genera by a partial-to-complete coalescence of the cervical vertebrae with the axis and the atlas invariably fused. This diversified group is thought to have originated from the lower eurhinodelphids. The most primitive genus of this higher group is *Steno,* which retains a long, though not exaggerated, rostrum and teeth with fluted enamel, presumably reminiscent of a less-reduced state. Near *Steno* are *Stenella* (*Prodelphinus*), *Sotalia,* and *Delphinus.*

Higher delphinids differ from these four genera in exhibiting a shorter and more depressed "face" which becomes flatter and broader as the rostrum shortens. The genera closest in appearance to the prodelphis type are *Tursiops* and *Lissodelphis*, both of which have a flattened foreface that is still of considerable length. A further step towards reduction of the rostrum has been achieved by *Lagenorhynchus*, which Winge suggests might also be joined by *Cephalorhynchus* and *Feresa*.

There are two groups of higher odontocetes in which the shortening and broadening of the "face" has been fully exploited. The first and more primitive of these includes the varied genera *Orcinus, Orcella, Grampus, Pseudorca,* and *Globicephala.* This group is thought to be more primitive than the second on the basis of the dentition. Winge suggests that the second group, which includes *Phocoena, Neomeris (Neophocoena),* and *Phocoenoides,* originated either among the most primitive of the *Globicephala* group or the most primitive of the *Tursiops-Lagenorhynchus* group. The *Phocoena* group are characteristically broad-faced odontocetes which are differentiated from the other odontocetes in the peculiar form of their teeth, many of which have compressed crowns that have become fan or leaf shaped with notches at the margins. This group has been relegated to its own family, the Phocoenidae, by recent authors.

CETACEAN CYTOGENETICS

Cytogenetic studies have proven helpful in clarifying the relationships between living members of controversial taxa. Animals derived from the same ancestral stock would be expected to have similar chromosomal constitutions. In many instances, closely related species, genera, and even families have been found to retain relatively unmodified chromosome numbers and morphology or to exhibit chromosomal changes traceable to a common karyotype characteristic of the more primitive representatives of that genus, family, tribe, etc. Although still limited, chromosomal comparisons among both cetaceans and pinnipeds indicate that reconsideration of some of their more controversial groupings is necessary.

Chromosome preparations are obtained by tissue culture, usually of skin, kidney, or blood. Direct examination of other tissues, such as bone marrow, is also possible. After slides are prepared and stained, the chromosomes are selected under a microscope, photographed, and examined. The following determinations are important in comparing chromosome complements: (a) establishing the total or modal number of chromosomes found in each cell and (b) describing the arrangement of these into various groups of chromosome pairs (karyotyping) to aid specifically in comparisons of the morphological characteristics of the chromosomes. The following cetacean karyotypes have been described:

Species	Modal Chromosome Number	References
Odontoceti:		
Delphinus delphis (common dolphin)	44	Kulu (in press)
Globicephala scammoni (Pacific pilot whale)	44	Walen (1965)
		Kulu (unpub.)
Inia geoffrensis (Amazon freshwater dolphin)	44	Kulu (in press)
Lagenorhynchus obliquidens (white-sided dolphin)	44	Duffield (1967)
Orcinus orca (killer whale)	44	Kulu (in press)
Phocoenoides dalli (Dall's porpoise)	44	Makino (1947)
		Kulu (in press)
Physeter catodon (sperm whale)	42*	Atwood (1965)
Pseudorca crassidens (false killer whale)	44	Kulu (unpub.)
Tursiops truncatus (Atlantic bottlenosed dolphin)	44	Walen (1965)
		Duffield (1967)
Stenella sp. (Prodelphinus)	44	Kulu (unpub.)
Steno bredanensis (rough-toothed dolphin)	44	Kulu (unpub.)
Mystacoceti:		
Balaenoptera borealis (sei whale)	44	Kasuya (1966)
Balaenoptera physalus (fin whale)	44	Benirschke (unpub.)
		Arnason (1969)
Eschrichtius gibbosus (gray whale)	44	Benirschke (unpub.)

* This count may need further evaluation because very few cells could be counted and variation in the counts indicates that several of these cells were incomplete or broken.

Although it is beyond the scope of this chapter to present all the karyotypes available, it is interesting to note that the karyotypes for many of the species listed appear to be the same. For example, a single karyotypic

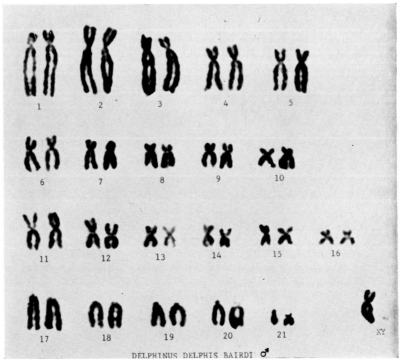

Figure 8–1. Karyotype of *Delphinus bairdi*.

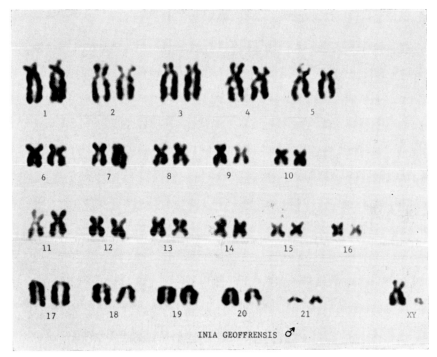

Figure 8–2. Karyotype of an *Inia geoffrensis*.

pattern is applicable to *Delphinus, Globicephala, Inia, Lagenorhynchus, Phocoenoides, Pseudorca, Stenella,* and *Steno.* Figure 8–1 (*Delphinus delphis*), Figure 8–2 (*Inia geoffrensis*), and Figure 8–3 (*Phocoenoides dalli*) illustrate this basic karyotype and the striking similarity to be found between the aforementioned species.

Figure 8–4 and 8–5 illustrate the chromosomes of *Balaenoptera physalus* and *Eschrichtius gibbosus,* respectively. These have only recently been obtained, and although they are not arranged in the karyotypic pattern illustrated in Figures 8–1, 8–2, and 8–3, the overall similarity of their chromosome morphology to that of the other species is obvious. It is not possible to compare the karyotypes of *Balaenoptera borealis* and *Physeter catodon* to those of the above from the literature currently available.

The karyotype of *Orcinus orca* is presented in Figure 8–6. The morphology of the chromosomes is notably different from that of the other species which have been reported. Interpretation of the significance of this observation must await the results of additional chromosome studies on many more species. However, it is striking that not only several members of the same family, the Delphinidae, but also species representative of different families of the same and even of different suborders, the Odontoceti and Mystacoceti, are so similar with regard to chromosome

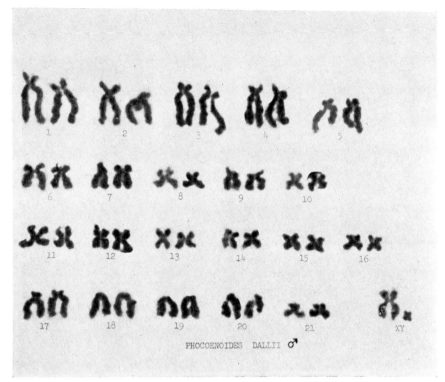

PHOCOENOIDES DALLII ♂

Figure 8–3. Karyotype of *Phocoenoides dalli.*

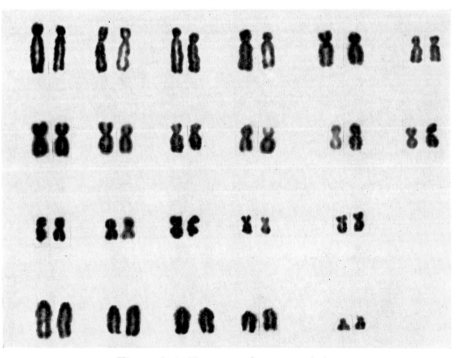

Figure 8–4. Karotype of a gray whale.

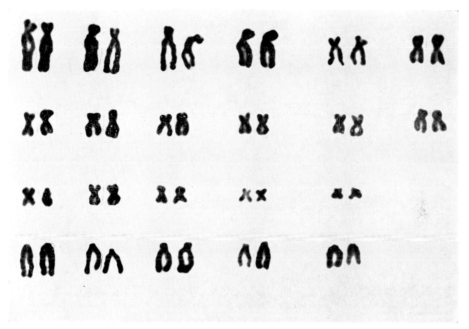

Figure 8–5. Karyotype of a fin whale.

morphology and karyotype; while *Orcinus,* thought to be a relatively advanced delphinid of the same rank as *Pseudorca* and *Globicephala,* exhibits such a radical departure from the basic pattern. This suggests that further karyotypic evidence and more detailed karyotypic comparisons may necessitate the reassessment of the classification of at least one cetacean species and may allow further elucidation of the evolutionary relationships of the modern cetacean suborders and families.

ORIGINS OF THE PINNIPEDIA

There continues to be a great deal of controversy about the exact origin of the Pinnipedia. The earliest fossil pinnipeds uncovered to date are found in Miocene deposits in the Northern Hemisphere. They are already well differentiated and representative of modern genera, suggesting that the order derived much earlier, perhaps during the Eocene or Oligocene. Beyond this point, however, there is considerable disagreement. Howell (1930), McLaren (1960), and King (1964, 1966), for example, interpret available fossil, anatomical, and physiological evidence to indicate that the families comprising this order were of biphyletic origin, developing from two closely related but already differentiated ancestral carnivore (canoid) stocks. Using the same evidence, however, Simpson (1945), Hopkins (1949), and Scheffer (1958) concluded that the families were of monophyletic origin, deriving from the same ancestral carnivore.

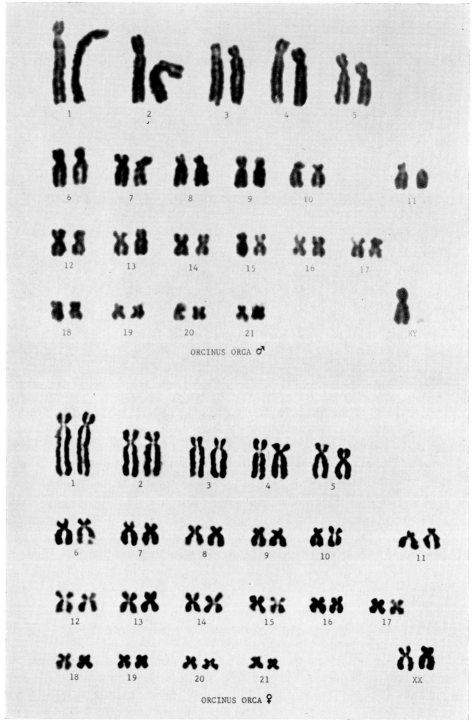

Figure 8–6. Karyotype of two killer whales; male at the top female below.

No one of the three pinniped families, the Phocidae (hair seals), the Otariidae (sea lions and fur seals), or the Odobenidae (walruses), is clearly ancestral to the other two. The Odobenidae have generally been considered more closely related to the Otariidae than to the Phocidae (although some authors argue that they are actually intermediate between the two families), and it is the divergence of the phocids from the otariids that has given rise to speculation concerning separate origins.

There have been a variety of approaches to the problem. Winge (1941) suggests that the pinnipeds are most nearly alike in structure to the bears and argues that all pinnipeds are undoubtedly derived from primitive ursids. He postulates that both the Phocidae and the Odobenidae evolved from early otariids, the Odobenidae retaining many characteristics in common with the Otariidae while the Phocidae became more divergent. Mivart (1885) pointed out that there were numerous resemblances not only between the otariids and ursids but also between the phocids and otters (luterine carnivores). These resemblances led several authors to suggest that the Otariidae and Odobenidae developed from bear-like carnivore ancestors and the Phocidae from otter-like carnivore ancestors. Simpson (1945) reconciles these divergent views by observing that the Pinnipedia are most likely offshoots from an early undifferentiated carnivore (canoid) line which subsequently gave rise to both the luterines and the ursids.

The evidence supporting monophyletic or biphyletic origin of the pinnipeds was initially based on the correlation of certain skeletal characteristics between the Pinnipedia and the ursids on the one hand and the Pinnipedia and the luterines on the other, and there is considerable disagreement concerning the correct interpretation of this data. McLaren (1960), for example, argues that the presence in the earliest phocid fossils and in the most primitive of the modern phocids of characteristics typical of early luterines is indicative of a phocid-luterine ancestry separate from the otariids, while other authors maintain that these similarities are merely the result of convergent evolution.

The study of pinniped parasites has added another dimension to the controversy. Newell (1947) found two genera of nasal mites in the Pinnipedia, one limited to the phocids and the other to the otariids and odobenids. He interpreted this as evidence for biphyletic origin. Hopkins (1949), on the other hand, found that the Pinnipedia are infested with a unique group of anoplurid lice distinct from the anoplurids found in the other canoid carnivores and argues that on this basis, the entire pinniped order must have initially differentiated as a single group from one ancestral canoid carnivore.

Comparative serological studies have not to date added significantly to the question of monophyletic versus biphyletic origin, although they have more closely pinpointed the origin of the Pinnipedia as a group. Studies by Leone and Wiens (1956) and Pauley and Wolfe (1957) indicate that with respect to serum proteins, the Pinnipedia show more resemblance to canoid carnivores than to feloid (feline) carnivores. The species available for these comparisons were not representative of the three pinniped families; however, more recent work by Sarich (1969) using a representative species of each family supports the earlier conclusions. Using immunological comparison (as did Leone and Pauly), Sarich indicates that the Pinnipedia derived from canoid carnivores after the separation of the feloid and canoid carnivore lines and suggests that the canoid-pinniped separation occurred later than has previously been thought. As the question of biphyletic versus monophyletic pinniped derivation concerns the possible evolution of the Pinnipedia from one or more "canoid" ancestral forms, these studies, although interesting in their own right, do not shed light on the specific question of whether the Pinnipedia derived solely from ursid-like ancestors or biphyletically from ursid-like and otter-like canoids.

An important factor in this controversy has been the distribution of early pinnipeds. According to Scheffer (1958), the fact that the earliest otariids are represented by the North Pacific fossils *Allodesmus* and *Desmatophoca* indicates that the Otariidae probably originated in the well-protected, food-rich kelp reefs of that area. *Allodesmus* is suggestive of both the Odobenidae and the modern otariid genus *Eumetopias*, although it lacks any distinctive connectant features that would establish it as an intermediate form in the evolution of the otariids from the primitive ursids. (Another North Pacific genus, the Miocene *Arctocephalus* closely resembles the modern otariid of that name.) Scheffer points out that the Odobenidae probably originated with the Otariidae in the North Pacific, although the first fossil Odobenidae, *Prorosmarus*, was found in Atlantic deposits of the Upper Miocene. He suggests that the early odobenids migrated from the Pacific to the Atlantic in the Oligocene when there were sea connections between the two bodies of water. Though there is very little fossil evidence for this family, the earlier forms showed definite otariid affinities, especially with regard to the teeth. Typically modern Odobenidae are found by the Pliocene. The earliest phocid, *Leptophoca*, is known from a Miocene fossil found in the Northern Atlantic, but by the end of the Miocene, the phocids were well established in both the northern Atlantic and Pacific oceans and appear to have migrated to southern waters even later.

Davies (1958), assuming a monophyletic origin, suggests that all Pinnipedia ultimately had their origin in Northern Atlantic waters. He postulates that the earliest otariids migrated through the Bering Sea to the North

Pacific where the first well-differentiated fossils are found during the late Eocene and Middle Oligocene. The Odobenidae are thought to have derived from the Northern Pacific otariid line, moving back into the Arctic seas before the Bering Sea connection closed. The earliest phocids are found in a different region of the North Atlantic and do not appear with the walruses until the Plio-Pleistocene.

McLaren (1960) disputes Davies' conclusions and suggests that biphyletic origin of the phocids and the Otariidae-Odobenidae better explains the available fossil evidence. He suggests that the phocids evolved from otter-like ancestors in the extensive freshwater systems of central Tertiary Asia and that they invaded the Atlantic in the Miocene. He further suggests that there were two simultaneous radiations from the Asiatic system— one leading to the establishment of the southern phocids, the other to the northern phocids. The Otariidae and the Odobenidae, he argues, developed from littoral bear-like ancestors inhabiting the Pacific coast of North America. The Odobenidae subsequently migrated to the Atlantic, while the Otariidae remained in the North Pacific and gradually extended their range into southern Pacific waters. To support his theory, McLaren (1960) discusses two controversial fossils found in the lacustrine deposits of Europe. The earliest, *Potamotherium*, (known by fragments alone) appears to have characteristics both of the Phocidae and of the advanced luterine line it is thought to represent. Whether these similarities to the Phocidae are convergent or whether this animal represents a true link between otter-like ancestors and modern phocids is still an undecided question. Another fossil from this region, *Semantor*, is also characteristic of both the Phocidae and the otters. Thenius (1949) maintains that *Semantor* is merely an advanced otter and that any similarity to the Phocidae is due to convergence, while Savage (1957) and McLaren (1960) support the theory that it is representative of a line of intermediate forms indicative of the evolution of the Phocidae from early luterines. Again, the basic problem in the interpretation of the position of these fossils lies in the relative importance of the various characteristics in question and whether the resemblances are superficial or in fact reliable indications of phylogenetic affinity. In any case, *Semantor* itself is from deposits too late to be directly ancestral to any phocid.

The evidence presented in support of each of these theories is often conflicting as well as complicated by the relative importance assigned to adaptations found in each family. Until additional fossil material or other evidence has been found, it is likely that the exact relationship of these families will remain obscure.

The establishment of the various genera, species, and subspecies of this order is thought to be a result of the following four principal evolutionary stages: invasion of new territory, geographical or ecological isolation, dispersion, and stabilization of the species. A discussion of these various stages is found in Scheffer (1958). The family Otariidae is currently represented by the northern and southern fur seal and sea lion genera. The family Odobenidae is represented by a single species, *Odobenus rosmarus*. The family Phocidae is represented by three subfamilies including the Phocinae (northern true seals), the Monachinae (monk and Antarctic seals) and the Cystophorinae (hooded and elephant seals). However, King (1966) suggests that it is best represented by only two subfamilies which comprise the northern hair seals (Phocinae), extended to include the hooded seal; and the southern hair seals (Monachinae), including the elephant seal. Based on characteristics of their teeth and the presence of a proboscis, the elephant and hooded seals were earlier included in the separate subfamily, the Cystophorinae.

As has been noted, there is disagreement among authors not only as to the exact relationship of the pinniped families—the Phocidae, the Odobenidae, and the Otariidae but also as to the exact arrangement of the genera within certain of these families. The most that can be said at this point is that although the taxonomic relationships of the families and genera comprising the Pinnipedia remain controversial, it is possible to distinguish three families in this order and within two of these families it is possible to arrange the genera into two or more subgroups based upon correlation of various characteristics. Whether these are superficial groupings or representative of evolutionary affinities must await additional evidence.

PINNIPED CYTOGENETICS

The majority of the work on pinniped cytogenetics has been done by Fay *et al.* (1967), who compare and discuss the karyotypes in terms of pinniped phylogeny. The following table indicates the pinniped karyotypes available.

Species	Modal Chromosome Number	References
Phocidae:		
Phoca vitulina (harbor seal)	32	Fay (1967) Kulu (unpub.)
Pusa hispida (ringed seal)	32	Corfman (1964)
Erignathus barbatus (bearded seal)	34	Fay (1967)
Leptonychotes weddelli (Weddell seal)	34	Fay (1967)
M.rounga angustircstris (northern elephant seal)	34	Kulu (unpub.)
Odobenidae:		
Odobenus rosmarus (walrus)	32	Fay (1967) Kulu (unpub.)
Otariidae:		
Eumetopias jubata (Steller's sea lion)	36	Fay (1967)
Callorhinus ursinus (northern fur seal)	36	Fay (1967) Kulu (unpub.)
Zalophus californianus (California sea lion)	36	Hungerford (1964)

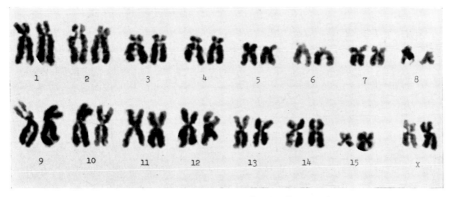

Figure 8–7. Karyotype of a harbor seal.

Representative karyotypes are presented in Figures 8–7 through 8–11. Figure 8–7 illustrates the chromosome complement of the female harbor seal, *Phoca vitulina*. The X chromosome has been identified by autoradiography and is indicated in the karyotype. The karyotype of this species appears to be virtually the same as that of the closely related phocid, *Pusa hispida* (ringed seal). The modal chromosome number for both species is 32. The karyotype of another phocid, the northern elephant seal (*Mirounga angustirostris*) is presented in Figure 8–8. The modal chromo-

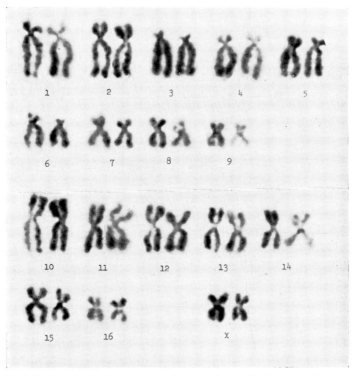

Figure 8–8. Karyotype of a northern elephant seal.

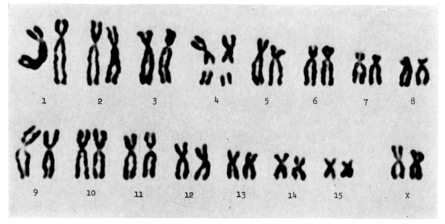

Figure 8–9. Karyotype of a walrus.

some number of this species is 34. In both chromosome number and morphology, this karyotype is very similar to that presented by Fay *et al.* (1967) for the bearded seal, *Erignathus barbatus,* and the Weddell seal, *Leptonychotes weddelli.* Fay suggests that the similarity in karyotype of the bearded seal and the Weddell seal supports the conclusion by Scheffer (1958) and King (1966) that *Erignathus,* although currently classified in the subfamily Phocinae with *Phoca* and *Pusa,* is closely related to the

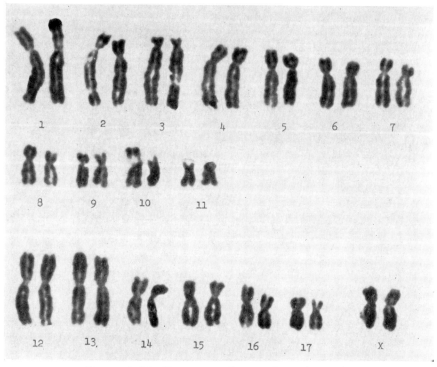

Figure 8–10. Karyotype of a northern fur seal.

members of the subfamily Monachinae (*Leptonychotes*). The similarity
between these karyotypes and that of the elephant seal would suggest
that this latter species is also closely related to the Monachinae—a relationship already proposed by King (1966).

The karyotype of the walrus, *Odobenus rosmarus* (female), is presented
in Figure 8–9. (The X chromosome has been identified by autoradiography
and is indicated in the figure.) The modal chromosome number of 32 corresponds most closely with that of the phocids *Phoca* and *Pusa*. However,
Fay *et al.* (1967) point out that in the relative numbers of metacentric
and submetacentric chromosomes, the karyotype is more similar to those
of the otariids. The similarities between the walrus and the Phocidae have
been minimized by many taxonomists who consider the walrus to be a
specialized branch of the Otariidae. In some characteristics, the walrus is
like the phocids, in some it is like the otariids, and in still others it appears
intermediate between the two. Fay *et al.* (1967) maintain that the cytogenetic evidence suggests an intermediate position for the walrus between the Phocidae and the Otariidae.

Figure 8–10 illustrates the karyotype of the northern fur seal. *Callorhinus ursinus* (female). The modal chromosome number of this species
is 36. The karyotypes of two other otariids, the California sea lion and the
Steller's sea lion, seem to vary only slightly from that of the northern fur
seal (Fay *et al.*, 1967). The X chromosome of this species has also been
identified by autoradiography and is indicated in Figure 8–11.

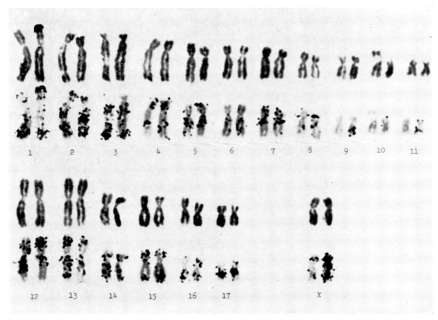

Figure 8–11. Karyotype of a northern fur seal in which the X chromosomes have
been identified by autoradiography.

Detailed consideration of the implications of cytogenetic comparison must await the karyotyping of more species. However, it can be noted that the similarity between the karyotypes of members of the three pinniped families in regard to both chromosome number and morphology suggests not only a monophyletic origin for the Pinnipedia, but also that taxonomic reassessment of this order, especially at the subfamily level, is necessary.

✳   ✳   ✳

I thank Dr. R. S. Sparkes and Iris C. Veomett of the Department of Pediatrics, University of California School of Medicine, Los Angeles, for their considerable time and valuable assistance in the preparation of the karyotypes presented in this chapter.

REFERENCES

Anthony, R.: Les Affinites des Cetaces. *Ann. Inst. Oceanographique,* 3:1, 1926.

Arnason, U.: The karotype of the fin whale. *Separat Hereditas,* 62:273–284, 1969.

Atwood, R.P. and Razavi, L.: Chromosomes of the sperm whale. *Nature (London),* 207:328, 1965.

Bouvier, E.L.: Les Cetaces Souffleurs. *These d'Agregation de Pharmacie,* Paris, 1889.

Boyden, A. and Gemeroy, D.: The relative position of the Cetacea among the order of mammalia as indicated by precipitin tests, *Zoologica,* 35:145+, 1950.

Corfman, P.A. and Richart, R.M.: Chromosomes of the ringed seal. *Nature (London),* 204:502–503, 1964.

Davies, J.L.: The Pinniped: an essay in zoogeography. *Geog. Rev.,* 48:474–493, 1958.

Duffield, D.A., Ridgway, S.H., and Sparkes, R.S.: Cytogenetic studies of two species of porpoise. *Nature (London),* 213:189–190, 1967.

Fay, F.H., Rausch, V.R., and Feltz, E.T.: Cytogenetic comparison of some pinnipeds ('Mammalia: Eutheria). *Canad. J. Zool.,* 45:773–778, 1967.

Flower, W.H.: Evolution of the Cetacea. *Nature (London),* 29:170, 1884.

Hopkins, G.H.E.: Host associates of the lice of mammals. *Proc. Zool. Soc. London,* 119:389–604, 1949.

Howell, A.B.: *Aquatic Mammals.* Springfield, Thomas, 1930.

Hungerford, D.A. and Snyder, R.L.: Karyotypes of two more mammals. *Amer. Nat.,* 98:125–127, 1964.

Kasuya, T.: Karyotypes of a Sei whale. *Sci. Rep. Whales Res. Inst.,* 20:83–88, 1966.

Kellogg, R.: Pinnipeds from Miocene and Pleistocene deposits of California. *Univ. Calif. Berkeley Publ. Geol. Sci.,* 13:23–132, 1922.

Kellogg, R.: The history of whales. *Quart. Rev. Biol.* 3:174+, 1928.

King, J.E.: *Seals of the World*. London, Brit. Mus. Nat. Hist., 1964.

King, J.E.: Relationships of the hooded and elephant seals (Genera Cystophora and Mirounga). *J. Zool.*, *148*:385–398, 1966.

Leone, C.A. and Wiens, A.L.: Comparative serology of Carnivores. *J. Mammal.*, *37*:11–23, 1956.

Makino, S.: The chromosomes of the Dall's porpoise, *Phocoenoides dallii* (True) with remarks on the phylogenetic relations of the Cetacea. *Chromosoma*, *3*:220–231, 1948.

McLaren, I.A.: Are the pinnipeds biphyletic? *Sys. Zool.*, *9*:18–28, 1960.

Miller, G.S.: The telescoping of the cetacean skull. *Smiths. Misc. Coll.*, *76*:5, 1923.

Mivart, St. G.: Notes on pinnipeds. *Proc. Zool. Soc. London*, pp. 484–500, 1885.

Newell, I.M.: Studies on the morphology and systematics of the Family Halarachnidae Oudemans, 1906 (Ascari, Parasitoidea). *Bull. Bingham Oceanogr. Coll.*, *10*:235–266, 1947.

Ommanney, F.D.: The urogenital system of the fin whale (*Balaenoptera physalus*) with appendix of the dimensions and growth of the kidney of the blue and fin whales. *Discovery Rep.*, *5*:363–466, 1932.

Pauly, L.K. and Wolfe, H.R.: Serological relationships among members of the order Carnivora. *Zoologica*, *42*:159–167, 1957.

Sarich, V.M.: Pinniped origins and the rate of evolution of carnivore albumins. *Syst. Zool.*, *18*:286–95, 1969.

Savage, R.J.G.: The anatomy of Potamotherium, an Oligocene lutrine. *Proc. Zool. Soc. London*, *129*:151–244, 1957.

Scheffer, V.B.: *Seals, Sea Lions and Walruses: A Review of the Pinnipedia*, Stanford, Stanford University Press, 1958.

Simpson, G.G.: The principles of classification and a classification of mammals. *Bull. Amer. Mus. Nat. Hist.*, *85*:1–350, 1945.

Thenius, E.: Uber die Systematische und Phylogenetische Stellung der Genera Promeleslind, Semantor. *S. B. Ost. Akad. Wiss.*, Abst. 1, Band 158, Heft 4:323–335, 1949.

Walen, K.H. and Madin, S.H.: Comparative chromosome analyses of the bottlenosed dolphin (*Tursiops truncatus*) and the pilot whale (*Globicephala scammonii*). *Amer. Nat.*, *99*:349–354, 1965.

Weber, M.: *Studien uber Saugetiere, Bin Beitrag Zum Frage nach dem Ursprung der Cetacean*. Jena Fischer, 1889.

Winge, H.: Review of the Interrelationships of the Cetacea. *Smith. Misc. Coll.*, *72*:1–97, 1921.

Winge, H.: Interrelationships of the mammalian genera. In Deichmann, E., Allen, G.M., and Jensen, A.S. *et al.* (Eds.): *Mammals*. Kobenbovn, C.A. Reiteel. 1941, pp. 241–249.

Chapter 9

A CHECKLIST OF MARINE MAMMAL PARASITES

Murray D. Dailey and Robert L. Brownell, Jr.

Parasites of marine mammals have been described as early as 1758 by Linneaus in his *Systema Naturae*. Since this time, a deluge of new animals has been described in a myriad of sources. Several attempts to present a comprehensive study on parasites of marine mammals have been made by Price (1932), Baylis (1932), Delyamure (1955), Tomilin (1957), and King (1964). These publications have, unfortunately, concentrated only on certain taxonomic groups or geographical areas, or presented lists without references.

In this chapter, we present a comprehensive checklist of reported parasites from marine mammals throughout the world. Needless to say, the list is obsolete even before going to press, due to the large number of new parasites reported each month. However, it is hoped that the present information will be useful as a guide for all those working with marine mammals where parasites and parasitic diseases are encountered.

In order to make this list more useful, a departure from the standard reference citation has been used. The first citation following the parasite represents the morphological description while the second indicates a report of the parasite from a particular host. In some instances, they are the same and only one citation is used. Parasites listed as "new host record" are in the author's collections.

The taxonomy of marine mammal hosts follows that of Rice and Scheffer (1968). Hosts having no reported parasites are omitted.

PINNIPEDIA

Otaria byronia (South American Sea Lion)

Cestoda

Diphyllobothrium scoticum, (Raillet et Henry, 1912); Rennie and Reid, 1912

Phyllobothrium delphini, (Bosc, 1802); Markowski, 1952

528

Nematoda

Anisakis patagonica, Linstow, 1880
Contracaecum osculatum, (Rudolphi, 1802); Delyamure, 1955
Uncinaria hamiltoni, Baylis, 1933
Contracaecum rectangulum, (Linstow, 1907); King, 1964
Porrocaecum dicipiens, (Krabbe, 1878); Baylis, 1916
Anisakis similis, (Rudolphi, 1802); King, 1964

Acanthocephala

Corynosoma strumosum, (Rudolphi, 1802); King, 1964
Corynosoma semerme, (Forssell, 1904); King, 1964
Corynosoma australe, Johnston and Best, 1937
Corynosoma hamanni, (Linstow, 1892); King, 1964

Acarina

Orthohalarachne magellanica, (Finnegan, 1934); Newell, 1947

Anoplura

Antarctophthirius microchir, (Trouessart and Neumann, 1888); Enderlein, 1906

Eumetopias jubata (Steller's Sea Lion)

Cestoda

Anophryocephalus ochotensis, Delyamure and Krotov, 1955
Diphyllobothrium pacificum, (Nybelin, 1931); Margolis, 1956
Diplogonoporus fasciatus, (Krabbe, 1865); Stunkard, 1948
Diplogonoporus tetrapterus, (Von Seibold, 1848); Stunkard, 1948
Adenocephalus pacificus, (Nybelin, 1931); King, 1964
Pyramicocephalus phocarum, (Fabricius, 1780); Monticelli, 1890

Nematoda

Anisakis simplex, (Rudolphi, 1809); Baylis, 1920
Anisakis tridentata, Kreis, 1938
Contracaecum osculatum, (Rudolphi, 1802); Baylis, 1920
Porrocaecum decipiens, (Krabbe, 1878); Baylis, 1916
Parafilaroides nanus, Dougherty and Herman, 1947
Parafilaroides prolificus, Dougherty and Herman, 1947
Parafilaroides sp., Dougherty and Herman, 1947
Anisakis similis, (Baird, 1853); Baylis, 1920
Uncinaria hamiltoni, Baylis, 1933

Acanthocephala

Bolbosoma bobrovi, Krotov and Delyamure, 1952
Corynosoma strumosum, (Rudolphi, 1802); King, 1964
Corynosoma villosum, van Cleave, 1953

Acarina

Orthohalarachne attenuata, (Banks, 1910); Newell, 1947
Orthohalarachne zalophi (zoo), (Oudemans, 1916); Newell, 1947

Anoplura

Antarctophthirius microchir, (Trouessart and Neumann, 1888); Ferris, 1916

Zalophus californianus (California Sea Lion)

Trematoda

Stephanoprora denticulata, (Rudolphi, 1802); Price, 1932
Pricetrema zalophi, (Price, 1932); Ciurea, 1933
Zalophotrema hepaticum, Stunkard and Alvey, 1929
Stictodora ubelakeri, Dailey, 1969
Heterophyes heterophyes (zoo), King, 1964
Schistosoma mansoni (zoo), King, 1964
Schistosoma haematobium (zoo), King, 1964

Cestoda

Diphyllobothrium pacificum, New host record

Nematoda

Dirofilaria immitis (zoo), (Leidy, 1856); Faust, 1937
Parafilaroides decorus, Dougherty and Herman, 1947
Dipetalonema odendhali, Perry, 1967
Uncinaria sp., New host record
Anasakis similis (zoo), (Baird, 1853); Herman, 1942
Contracaecum osculatum (zoo), (Rudolphi, 1802); Herman, 1942
Dujardinia sp. (zoo), Herman, 1942
Porrocaecum sp. (zoo), Herman, 1942

Acanthocephala

Corynosoma obtuscens, Lincicome, 1943
Corynosoma osmeri, Fujita, 1921

Acarina

Orthohalarachne diminuata, Doetschman, 1941
Demodex sp., New Host Record (Kenney, 1968)

Anoplura

Antarctophthirius microchir, (Enderlein, 1906); Ferris, 1916

Neophoca cinerea (Australian Sea Lion)

Cestoda

Diphyllobothrium arctocephalinum, Johnston, 1937

Nematoda

Contracaecum osculatum, (Rudolphi, 1802); Baylis, 1920

Acanthocephala

Corynosoma australe, Johnston, 1937

Anoplura

Antarctophthirius microchir, (Trouessart and Neumann, 1888); Enderlein, 1906

Neophoca hookeri (New Zealand Sea Lion)

Nematoda

Porrocaecum decipiens, (Krabbe, 1878); Baylis, 1920

Anoplura

Antarctophthirius microchir, (Trouessart and Neumann, 1888); King, 1964

Arctocephalus australis (South American Fur Seal)

Trematoda

Zalophotrema hepaticum, Stunkard and Alvey, 1929

Cestoda

Adenocephalus pacificus, Nybelin, 1931
Diphyllobothrium glaciale, (Cholodkovsky, 1915); Markowski, 1952
Phyllobothrium delphini, (Bosc, 1802); Markowski, 1952

Nematoda

Contracaecum corderoi, Lent and Freitas, 1948
Contracaecum osculatum, (Rudolphi, 1802); Baylis, 1920
Porrocaecum sulcatum, (Rudolphi, 1819); Baylis and Daubney, 1923
Anisakis similis, (Baird, 1853); Baylis, 1920
Contracaecum rectangulum, (Linstow, 1907a); Baylis, 1920

Acanthocephala

Corynosoma semerme, (Forssell, 1904); Lühe, 1911

Acarina

Orthohalarachne magellanica, (Finnegan, 1934); King, 1964

Arctocephalus doriferus (Australian Fur Seal)

Cestoda

Diphyllobothrium arctocephalinum, Johnson, 1937

Nematoda

Contracaecum osculatum, (Rudolphi, 1802); Baylis, 1920
Porrocaecum decipiens, (Krabbe, 1878); Baylis, 1916

Acanthocephala

Corynosoma australe, Johnston and Best, 1937

Arctocephalus pusillus (South African Fur Seal)

Cestoda

Diphyllobothrium arctocephalinum, Johnston, 1937
Phyllobothrium delphini, (Bosc, 1802); Markowski, 1952

Nematoda

Contracaecum osculatum, (Rudolphi, 1802); Baylis, 1920

Acanthocephala

Corynosoma villosum, van Cleave, 1953

Acarina

Orthohalarachne attenuata, (Banks, 1910); Newell, 1947
Orthohalarachne diminuata, (Doetschman, 1944); Newell, 1947

Anoplura

Proechinopthirius zumpti; King, 1964

Artocephalus tasmanicus (Tasmanian Fur Seal)

Cestoda

Diphyllobothrium arctocephalinum, Johnston, 1937

Nematoda

Anisakis sp.; King, 1964

Acarina

Orthohalarachne reflexa, Tubb, 1937

Arctocephalus tropicalis (Kerguelen Fur Seal)

Cestoda

Diphyllobothrium sp.; King, 1964
Phyllobothrium delphini, (Bosc, 1802); Markowski, 1952

Nematoda

Contracaecum osculatum, (Rudolphi, 1802); Baylis, 1920
Porrocaecum decipiens, (Krabbe, 1878); Baylis, 1916

Acanthocephala

Corynosoma strumosum, (Rudolphi, 1802); King, 1964

Callorhinus ursinus (Northern Fur Seal)

Trematoda

Pricetrema zalophi, (Price, 1932); Neiland, 1961
Cryptocotyle jejuna, (Nicholl, 1907); Neiland, 1961
Phocitrema fustforme, Goto and Ozaki, 1930

Cestoda

Adenocephalus septentrionacis, (Nybelin, 1931); Delyamure, 1955
Diphyllobothrium pacificum, Keyes, 1965
Diphyllobothrium glaciale, (Cholodkovski, 1914); Stunkard, 1948
Diphyllobothrium krooyi, Delyamure, 1955
Diplogonoporus tetrapterus, (Siebold, 1948); Stunkard, 1948
Diphyllobothrium macrocephalos, (Linstow, 1905); Stiles and Hassall, 1912

Nematoda

Contracaecum osculatum, (Rudolphi, 1802); Keyes, 1965
Contracaecum callotariae, King, 1964
Porrocaecum decipiens, (Krabbe, 1878); Stiles and Hassall, 1899
Porrocaecum callotariae, King, 1964
Uncinaria lucasi, Stiles, 1901
Dipetalonema spirocauda, (Leidy, 1858); Anderson, 1959

Acanthocephala

Corynosoma strumosum, (Rudolphi, 1802); van Cleave, 1953
Corynosoma semerme, (Forssell, 1904); van Cleave, 1953
Corynosoma villosum, van Cleave, 1953
Bolbosoma bobrovi, Krotov and Delyamure, 1952
Bolbosoma nipponicum, Yamaguti, 1939

Acarina

Orthohalarachne attenuata, Newell, 1947
Orthohalarachne diminuata, (Doetschman, 1944); Newell, 1947

Odobenus rosmarus (Walrus)

Trematoda

Odhneriella rossica, Skrjabin, 1915
Orthosplanchnus fraterculus, Odhner, 1905
Microphallus orientalis, Yurakhno, 1968

Cestoda

Diphyllobothrium cordatum, (Leuckart, 1863); Gedoelst, 1911
Diphyllobothrium latum, (Linnaeus, 1758); Delyamure, 1955
Diphyllobothrium romeri, Zschokke, 1903

Nematoda

Anisakis bicolor, King, 1964
Anisakis rosmari, (Baylis, 1916); Baylis, 1920
Anisakis alata (zoo), (Hsü, 1933); King, 1964
Contracaecum osculatum, (Rudolphi, 1802); Baylis, 1920
Porrocaecum decipiens, (Krabbe, 1878); Baylis, 1916
Trichinella spiralis, (Owen, 1835); Roth and Madsen, 1953

Acanthocephala

Corynosoma clavatum, King, 1964
Corynosoma semerme; (Forssell, 1904); Cameron, *et al.,* 1940

Corynosoma strumosum, (Rudolphi, 1802); van Cleave, 1953
Corynosoma validum, (van Cleave, 1953); King, 1964

Phoca vitulina (Harbor Seal)

Trematoda

Phocitrema fusiforme, Goto and Ozaki, 1930
Cryptocotyle lingua, (Creplin, 1825); Ransom, 1920
Echinostoma acanthoides, Rudolphi, 1819
Pseudamphistomum truncatum, (Rudolphi, 1819); Delyamure, 1955
Rossicotrema venustum, Ransom, 1920
Zalophotrema hepaticum, (Stunkard and Alvey, 1929); King, 1964

Cestoda

Diplogonoporus tetrapterus, (Siebold, 1848); Delyamure, 1955
Diphyllobothrium cordatum, (Leuckart, 1863); Delyamure, 1955
Diphyllobothrium hians, (Diesing, 1850); Delyamure, 1955
Diphyllobothrium schistochilos, (Germanos, 1895); King, 1964
Diphyllobothrium latum, (Linnaeus, 1758); Delyamure, 1955
Diphyllobothrium osmeri, Neiland, 1962
Schistocephalus solidus, (Müller, 1776); Delyamure, 1955

Nematoda

Contracaecum osculatum, (Rudolphi, 1802); Baylis, 1920
Porrocaecum decipiens, (Krabbe, 1878); Stiles and Hassall, 1899
Parafilaroides qymnurus, (Railliet, 1899); Dougherty, 1946
Otostrongylus circumlitus, (Railliet, 1899); Bruyn, 1933
Skjabinaria spirocauda (zoo), (Leidy, 1858); Lubimov, 1927
Dirofilaria spirocauda (zoo), (Leidy, 1858); Taylor, *et al.*, 1961
Anisakis similis, (Baird, 1853); King, 1964
Phocascaris netsiki, Lyster, 1940

Acanthocephala

Corynosoma falcatum, van Cleave, 1953
Corynosoma strumosum, (Rudolphi, 1802); Ball, 1930
Corynosoma magdaleni, Montreuil, 1958
Corynosoma semerme, (Forssell, 1904); Neiland, 1962

Acarina

Halarachne miroungae, Ferris, 1925

Anoplura

Echinophthirius horridus, (Olfers, 1816); Ferris, 1934

Pusa hispida (Ringed Seal)

Trematoda

Orthosplanchnus arcticus, Odhner, 1905
Phocitrema fusiforme, Gato and Ozaki, 1930
Pseudamphistomum truncatum, (Rudolphi, 1819); Lühe, 1908

Cestoda

Anophryocephalus anophrys, Baylis, 1822
Trigonocotyle skrjabini, Delyamure and Krotov, 1955
Diphyllobothrium hians, (Diesing, 1850); Delyamure, 1955
Diphyllobothrium latum, (Linnaeus, 1758); Delyamure 1955
Diphyllobothrium lanceolatum, (Krabbe, 1865); Delyamure, 1955
Diplogonoporus fasciatus, (Krabbe, 1865); Delyamure, 1955
Diplogonoporus tetrapterus, (Siebold, 1948); Delyamure, 1955
Pyramicocephalus phocarum, (Fabricius, 1780); Delyamure, 1955
Schistocephalus solidus (larva), (Müller, 1776); Delyamure, 1955

Nematoda

Anisakis rosmari, (Baylis, 1916); King, 1964
Contracaecum osculatum, (Rudolphi, 1802); Baylis, 1920
Porrocaecum decipiens, (Krabbe, 1878); Baylis, 1916
Phoconema decipiens, Johnston, *et al.,* 1966
Phocascaris netsiki, Lyster, 1940
Halocercus qymnurus, King, 1964
Otostrongylus circumlitus, (Railliet, 1899); Bruyn, 1933
Otostrongylus andreewaae, King, 1964
Dipetalonema spirocauda, (Leidy, 1858); Taylor, *et al.,* 1961
Parafilaroides arcticus, Delyamure and Alekseev, 1966
Uncinaria lucasi, Stiles, 1901
Trichinella spiralis (larva), (Owen, 1835); King, 1964
Skrjabinaria spirocauda, (Leidy, 1858); Delyamure, 1955
Ascaris dehiscens, King, 1964

Acanthocephala

Bolbosoma nipponicum, Yamaguti, 1939
Corynosoma reductum, (Linstow, 1905); van Cleave, 1953
Corynosoma strumosum, (Rudolphi, 1802); van Cleave, 1953
Corynosoma semerme, (Forssell, 1904); van Cleave, 1953
Corynosoma hadweni, van Cleave, 1953

Anoplura

Echinopthirius horridus, (Olfers, 1816); Ferris, 1934

Pusa caspica (Caspian Seal)

Trematoda

Pseudechinostomum advena, Shchupakov, 1936
Cryptocotyle lingua, (Creplin, 1825); Delyamure, 1955

Nematoda

Anisakis schupakovi, Mozgovoi, 1951
Eustrongylides excisus, King, 1964

Acanthocephala

Corynosoma strumosum, (Rudolphi, 1802); van Cleave, 1953

Pusa sibirica (Baikal Seal)

Nematoda

Contracaecum osculatum baicalensis, Mozgovoi and Ryjukov, 1950

Anoplura

Echinophthirius horridus, (Olfers, 1816); King, 1964

Erignathus barbatus (Bearded Seal)

Trematoda

Opisthorchis tenuicollis, (Rudolphi, 1819); Stiles and Hassall, 1896
Orthosplanchnus arcticus, Odhner, 1905
Orthosplanchnus fraterculus, Odhner, 1905
Microphallus orientalis, Yurakhno, 1968

Cestoda

Diphyllobothrium cordatum, (Leuckart, 1863); Delyamure, 1955
Diphyllobothrium hians, (Kiesing, 1850); Wardle, McLeod, and
  Stewart, 1947
Diphyllobothrium latum, (Linnaeus, 1758); Delyamure, 1955
Diphyllobothrium lanceolatum, (Krabbe, 1865); Delyamure, 1955
Diphyllobothrium macrocephalus, (Linstow, 1905); Delyamure, 1955
Diphyllobothrium schistochilus, (Germanos, 1895); Delyamure, 1955
Diplogonoporus tetrapterus, (Siebold, 1848); Johnson, *et al*, 1966
Pyramicocephalus phocarum, (Fabricius, 1780); Kenyon, 1962
Polypocephalus tortus, King, 1964

Nematoda

Contracaecum osculatum, (Rudolphi, 1802); Delyamure, 1955
Phocanema decipiens, Johnson, *et al.*, 1966

Porrocaecum decipiens, (Krabbe, 1878); Baylis, 1916
Trichinella spiralis, (Owen, 1835); King, 1964

Acanthocephala

Corynosoma validum, van Cleave, 1953
Corynosoma strumosum, (Rudolphi, 1802); Delyamure, 1955
Corynosoma semerme, (Forssell, 1904); King 1964
Corynosoma hadweni, van Cleave, 1953

Anoplura

Echinophthirius horridus, (Olfers, 1816); King, 1964

Halichoerus grypus (Gray Seal)

Trematoda

Cryptocotyle lingua, (Creplin, 1825); King, 1964
Metorchis albidus, (Braun, 1893); King, 1964
Opisthorchis tenuicollis, (Rudolphi, 1819); Stiles and Hassall, 1896
Pseudamphistomum truncatum, (Rudolphi, 1819); King, 1964
Echinostoma acanthoides, (Rudolphi, 1819); King, 1964

Nematoda

Anisakis similis, (Baird, 1853); Baylis, 1920
Contracaecum osculatum, (Rudolphi, 1802); Baylis, 1920
Porrocaecum decipiens, (Krabbe, 1878); Baylis, 1916
Dioctophyme renale, (Goeze, 1782); King, 1964

Acanthocephala

Corynosoma strumosum, (Rudolphi, 1802); van Cleave, 1953
Corynosoma semerme, (Forssell, 1904); King, 1964
Corynosoma hadweni, van Cleave, 1953
Corynosoma falcatum, van Cleave, 1953
Corynosoma magdaleni, Montreuil, 1958

Anoplura

Echinophthirius horridus, (Olfers, 1816); King, 1964

Pagophilus groenlandicus (Harp Seal)

Trematoda

Orthosplanchnus arcticus, Odhner, 1905
Pseudamphistomum truncatum, (Rudolphi, 1819); King, 1964

Cestoda

Diphyllobothrium lanceolatum, (Krabbe, 1865); King, 1964
Diphyllobothrium cordatum, (Leuckart, 1863); Delyamure, 1955
Diphyllobothrium schistochilus, (Germanos, 1895); Guiart, 1935

Nematoda

Phocascaris phocae, Höst, 1932
Contracaecum osculatum, (Rudolphi, 1802); King, 1964
Porrocaecum decipiens, (Krabbe, 1878); Baylis, 1916
Otostrongylus andreewaae*, King, 1964

Acanthocephala

Corynosoma strumosum, (Rudolphi, 1802); King, 1964

Anoplura

Echinophthirius horridus, (Olfers, 1816); King, 1964

Cystophora cristata (Hooded Seal)

Trematoda

Metrochis albidus, (Braun, 1893); Delyamure, 1955
Opisthorchis tenuicollis, (Rudolphi, 1819); Stiles and Hassall, 1896
Pseudamphistomum truncatum, (Rudolphi, 1809); Delyamure, 1955

Cestoda

Diphyllobothrium latum, (Linnaeus, 1758); King, 1964
Diplogonoporus tetrapterus, (Siebold, 1848); Delyamure, 1955
Pyramicocephalus phocarum, (Fabricius, 1780); Monticelli, 1890

Nematoda

Contracaecum osculatum, (Rudolphi, 1802); Baylis, 1920
Dirofilaria immitis, (Leidy, 1856); King, 1964
Phocasaris ceptophora, Berland, 1963
Phocasaris osculatum, Berland, 1963
Porrocaecum decipiens, (Krabbe, 1878); King, 1964

Acanthocephala

Corynosoma bullosum, (Linstow, 1892); King, 1964
Corynosoma semerme, (Forssell, 1904); King, 1964
Corynosoma strumosum, (Rudolphi, 1802); King, 1964

---

* Same as *Otostrongylus andreewoi,* Skjabin, 1933.

Anoplura

Echinophthirius horridus, (Olfers, 1816); King, 1964

Mirounga angustirostris (Northern Elephant Seal)

Trematoda

Cryptocotyle lingua, (Creplin, 1825); Delyamure, 1955
Zalphotrema hepaticum, (Stunkard and Alvey, 1929); King, 1964

Nematoda

Anisakis similis, (Baird, 1853); Caballero and Peregrina, 1938
Porrocaecum decipiens, (Krabbe, 1878); Baylis, 1916
Contracaecum osculatum, (Rudolphi, 1802); Caballero and Peregrina, 1938

Acanthocephala

Corynosoma sp., King, 1964

Acarina

Halarachne miroungae, Ferris, 1925

Mirounga leonina (Southern Elephant Seal)

Cestoda

Baylisiella tecta, (Linstow, 1892); Markowski, 1952
Diphyllobothrium tectum, (Linstow, 1892); Delyamure, 1955

Nematoda

Anisakis patagonica, (Linstow, 1880); King, 1964
Anisakis similis, (Baird, 1853); Baylis, 1920
Contracaecum radiatum, (Linstow, 1907); King, 1964
Contracaecum osculatum, (Rudolphi, 1802); Baylis, 1920
Contracaecum rectangulum, (Linstow, 1907); King, 1964
Porrocaecum decipiens, (Krabbe, 1878); Baylis, 1916
Uncinaria hamiltoni, Baylis, 1933
Filaria sp., King, 1964

Acanthocephala

Corynosoma bullosum, (Linstow, 1892); Delyamure, 1955

Acarina

Halarachne sp., King, 1964

Anoplura

Lepidophthirius macrophini, King, 1964

Lobodon carcinophagus (Crab-eating Seal)

Trematoda

Ogmogaster antarcticum, Johnston, 1931

Cestoda

Baylisia baylisi, Markowski, 1952

Nematoda

Contracaecum radiatum, (Linstow, 1907); King, 1964
Contracaecum osculatum, (Rudolphi, 1802); Delyamure, 1955
Contracaecum rectangulum, (Linstow, 1907); Delyamure, 1955

Acanthocephala

Corynosoma hamanni, (Linstow, 1892); Railliet and Henry, 1907
Corynosoma bullosum, (Linstow, 1892); Gower, 1939

Anoplura

Antarctophthirius lobodontis, King, 1964

Hydrurga leptonyx (Leopard Seal)

Cestoda

Phyllobothrium delphini, (Bosc, 1802); King, 1964
Diphyllobothrium ventropapillatum, Delyamure, 1955
Diphyllobothrium quadratum, (Linstow, 1892); King, 1964
Diphyllobothrium tectum, (Linstow, 1892); King, 1964
Diphyllobothrium scoticum, Rennie and Reid, 1912
Diphyllobothrium wilsoni, Shipley, 1907

Nematoda

Contracaecum osculatum, (Rudolphi, 1802); Delyamure, 1955
Contracaecum radiatum, (Linstow, 1907); Yamaguti, 1961
Contracaecum rectangulum, (Linston, 1907); Yamaguti, 1961
Contracaecum stenocephalum, (Railliet and Henry, 1907); King, 1964
Contracaecum ogmorhini, Johnston and Mawson, 1941
Porrocaecum decipiens, (Krabbe, 1878); King, 1964
Anisakis similis, (Baird, 1853); King, 1964

Phocascaris hydrurgae, Johnston and Mawson, 1945
Parafilaroides hydrurgae, Mawson, 1953

Acanthocephala

Corynosoma hamanni, (Linstow, 1892); Yamaguti, 1963
Corynosoma australe, Johnston, 1937
Corynosoma clavatum, Johnston and Best, 1942

Anoplura

Antarctophthirus ogmorhini, Enderlein, 1906

Leptonychotes weddelli (Weddell Seal)

Trematoda

Ogmogaster antarcticus, Johnston, 1931

Cestoda

Diphyllobothrium quadratum, (Linstow, 1892); Delyamure, 1955
Diphyllobothrium lashleyi, Leiper and Atkinson, 1914
Diphyllobothrium archeri, Leiper and Atkinson, 1914
Diphyllobothrium perfoliatum, (Railliet and Henry, 1912); King, 1964
Diphyllobothrium tectum, (Linstow, 1892); King, 1964
Diphyllobothrium rufum, Leiper and Atkinson, 1914
Diphyllobothrium wilsoni, (Shipley, 1907); Railliet and Henry, 1912
Phyllobothrium delphini, (Bosc, 1802); King, 1964

Nematoda

Contracaecum osculatum, (Rudolphi, 1802); Baylis, 1920
Contracaecum radiatum, (Linstow, 1907); Baylis, 1920
Contracaecum rectangulum, (Linstow, 1907); Baylis, 1920
Contracaecum stenocephalum, (Railliet and Henry, 1907); King, 1964
Porrocaecum decipiens, (Krabbe, 1878); Baylis, 1916

Acanthocephala

Corynosoma antarcticum, Rennie, 1907
Corynosoma hamanni, (Linstow, 1892); Nickol and Holloway, 1968
Corynosoma sipho, Railliet and Henry, 1907

Acarina

Halarachne sp., King, 1964

Anoplura

Antarctophthirius ogmorhini, (Enderlein, 1906); Murray, *et al.*, 1965

Ommatophoca rossi (Ross Seal)

Cestoda

Diphyllobothrium mobile, (Rennie and Reid, 1912); King, 1964
Diphyllobothrium scotti, Shipley, 1907
Diphyllobothrium wilsoni, Shipley, 1907

Nematoda

Contracaecum radiatum, (Linstow, 1907); Yamaguti, 1931
Porrocaecum decipiens, (Krabbe, 1878); King, 1964

Acanthocephala

Corynosoma hamanni, (Linstow, 1892); Golvan, 1959

Anoplura

Antarctophthirus mawsoni, King, 1964

Monachus monachus (Mediterranean Monk Seal)

Cestoda

Diphyllobothrium elegans, (Krabbe, 1865); King, 1964
Diphyllobothrium hians, (Diesing, 1850); Delyamure, 1955
Diphyllobothrium latum, (Linnaeus, 1758); Delyamure, 1955
Diphyllobothrium lanceolatum, (Krabbe, 1865); Joyeux and Baer, 1936
Diphyllobothrium tetrapterus, (Siebold, 1848); Ariola, 1900
Diphyllobothrium coniceps, (Linstow, 1905); King, 1964
Bothriocephalus sp., King, 1964
Cysticercus cellulosae, King, 1964

Nematoda

Contracaecum osculatum, (Rudolphi, 1802); Delyamure, 1955
Porrocaecum decipiens, (Krabbe, 1878); Delyamure, 1955
Anisakis pegreffii Campana-Rouget and Biocca, 1955

Monachus schauinslandi (Hawaiian Monk Seal)

Cestoda

Diphyllobothrium hians, (Diesing, 1850); Chapin, 1925
Diphyllobothrium cameroni, Rausch, 1969

Nematoda

Contracaecum turgidum, Chapin, 1925

Acanthocephala

Corynosoma rauschi, Golvan, 1959

Monachus tropicalis (Carribbean Monk Seal)

Acarina

Halarachne americana, (Banks, 1899); Newell, 1947

CARNIVORA

Enhydra lutris (Sea Otter)

Trematoda

Microphallus pirum* (Afanas'ev, 1941); Rausch, 1953
Orthosplanchnus fraterculus, (Odhner, 1905); Rausch, 1953
Phocitrema fusiforme, (Goto and Ozaki, 1930); Rausch, 1953
Pricetrema zalophi, (Price, 1932); Rausch, 1953

Cestoda

Diplogonoporus tetrapterus, (Siebold, 1848); Rausch, 1964
Pyramicocephalus phocarum, (Fabricius, 1780); Rausch, 1953

Nematoda

Porrocaecum decipiens, (Krabbe, 1878); Schiller, 1954

Acanthocephala

Corynosoma strumosum, (Rudolphi, 1802); Rausch, 1953
Corynosoma villosum, van Cleave, 1953
Corynosoma enhydris, Afanas'ev, 1941
Corynosoma macrosomum, Neiland, 1962
Corynosoma sp., (Rausch and Locker, 1951); Jellison and Neiland, 1965
Corynosoma sp., (Rausch, 1953); Jellison and Neiland, 1965

Acarina

Halarachne miroungae, Kenyon, *et al.,* 1965

CETACEA

Platanista gangetica (Blind River Dolphin or Susu)

Trematoda

Cyclorchis campula, (Cobbold, 1876); Baylis, 1932
Echinochasumus andersoni, (Cobbold, 1876); new combination

Nematoda

Contracaecum lobulatum, (Schneider, 1866); Linstow, 1907b

---

* Same as *Microphallus enhydrae,* Rausch and Locker, 1951.

Inia geoffrensis (Amazon River Dolphin or Boutu)

Trematoda

Hunterotrema caballeroi, McIntosh, 1960
Unidentified eggs, Layne and Caldwell, 1964

Nematoda

Anisakis insignis, (Diesing, 1851); Delyamure, 1955
Halocercus sp., New Host Record

Pontoporia blainvillei (La Plata Dolphin or Franciscana)

Nematoda

Contracaecum sp., New host record

Acanthocephala

Corynosoma sp., New host record

Steno bredanensis (Rough-toothed Dolphin)

Cestoda

Tetrabothrius forsteri, (Krefft, 1871); Baylis, 1932
Stobilocephalus triangularis, (Diesing, 1850); Delyamure, 1955

Nematoda

Anisakis sp., Kagel, *et al.*, 1967

Sotalia fluviatilis (Amazon River Dolphin or Tookashee)

Trematoda

Amphimerus lancea, (Diesing, 1950); Baylis, 1932

*Sotalia guianensis** (Guiana Dolphin)

Trematoda

Halocercus brasiliensis, Lins de Almeida, 1933

Sousa chinensis (Chinese White Dolphin)

Nematoda

Anisakis alexandri, Hsü and Hoeppli, 1933

* Same as *Sotalia brasiliensis*.

Tursiops truncatus (Bottlenosed Dolphin)

Trematoda

Braunina cordiformis, (Wolf, 1903); Delyamure, 1955
Nasitrema sp., Neiland, *et al.* (1970)
Synthesium tursionis, (Marchi, 1873); Baylis, 1932
Zalophotrema hepaticum, (Stunkard and Alvey, 1929); *Brown, et al.,*
  1960

Cestoda

Diphyllobothrium sp., Delyamure, 1955
Monorygma delphini, (Gervais, 1847); Baylis, 1932
Monorygma grimaldii, (Moniez, 1889); Delyamure, 1955
Phyllobothrium delphini, (Bosc, 1802); Baylis, 1932

Nematoda

*Anisakis simplex,** Delyamure, 1955
Crassicauda crassicauda (Creplin, 1829); Baylis, 1932
Halocercus lagenorhynchus (Baylis and Daubney, 1925); Delyamure,
  1955
Stenurus ovatus (Linstow, 1910); Baylis, 1932

Acanthocephala

Corynoroma cetaceum (Johnston and Best, 1942)—Delyamure, 1955

Tursiops gillii (Pacific Bottlenosed Dolphin)

Trematoda

Nasitrema sp. Neiland *et al.,* 1970

Grampus griseus (Risso Dolphin)

Cestoda

Phyllobothrium delphini, (Rudolphi, 1819); Baylis, 1932

Nematoda

Crassicauda grampicola, Johnston and Mawson, 1941
Stenurus minor, (Kühn, 1829); Tomilin, 1957

---

* Same as *Anisakis tursionis,* Crusz, 1946.

Lagenorhynchus albirostris (White-beaked Dolphin)

Nematoda

Anisakis simplex, (Rudolphi, 1809); Baylis, 1932
Halocercus lagenorhynchi, (Baylis and Daubney, 1925); Baylis, 1932
Phocanema sp., Van Thiel, 1966

Lagenorhynchus acutus (Atlantic White-sided Dolphin)

Cestoda

Monorygma chamissonii, (Linton, 1905); Baylis, 1932
Monorygma grimaldii (Moniez, 1889); Baylis, 1932
Phyllobothrium sp., Linton, 1905; Baylis, 1932
Strobilocephalus triangularis, (Diesing, 1850); Baylis, 1932

Lagenorhynchus obliquidens (Pacific Striped Dolphin)

Cestoda

Phyllobothrium sp., New host record

Trematoda

Nasitrema globicephalae Neiland *et al.*, 1970

Lagenorhynchus obscurus (Dusky Dolphin)

Nematoda

Anisakis simplex, (Rudolphi, 1809); Baylis, 1932

Stenella longirostris (Long Beaked Dolphin)

Trematoda

Campula laevicaecum, (Yamaguti, 1942); Delyamure, 1955
Delphinicola tenuis, (Yamaguti, 1933); Delyamure, 1955
Lecithodesmus nipponicus, (Yamaguti, 1942); Delyamure, 1955

Cestoda

Diphyllobothrium fuhrmanni, (Hsü, 1935); Delyamure, 1955
Phyllobothrium sp. New host record
Monorygma sp. New host record

Nematoda

Anisakis simplex, (Rudolphi, 1809); Delyamure, 1955

Acanthocephala

Corynosoma sp., Delyamure, 1955

Stenella roseiventris (Hawaiian Spinner Dolphin)

Trematoda

Lecithodesmus sp., New host record

Cestoda

Monorygma sp., New host record
Phyllobothrium sp., New host record

Stenella caeruleoalba (Striped Dolphin or Euphrosyne Dolphin)

Cestoda

Phyllobothrium sp., New host record
Monorygma sp., New host record

Nematoda

Anisakis sp., Kagel, *et al.,* 1967

Stenella attenuata (Narrow-snouted Dolphin)

Cestoda

Monorygma sp., New Host Record
Phyllobothrium sp., New Host Record

Stenella graffmani (Eastern Pacific Spotted Dolphin)

Trematoda

Braunina cordiformis, (Wolf, 1903); McIntosh, 1953
Nasitrema stenosomum, Neiland, *et al.* 1970

Cestoda

Monoryma sp., New host record
Phyllobothrium sp., New host record
Strobilocephalus sp., New host record

Nematoda

Anisakis simplex, (Rudolphi, 1809); New host record
Crassicauda sp., New host record

Delphinus delphis (Crisscross or Common Dolphin)

Trematoda

Braunina cordiformis, (Wolf, 1903); Delyamure, 1955
Campula delphini, (Poirier, 1886); Baylis, 1932
Campula palliata, (Looss, 1885); Baylis, 1932
Campula rochebruni, (Poirier, 1886); Baylis, 1932
Galactosomum erinaceum, (Poirier, 1886); Baylis, 1932
Nasitrema delphini, Neiland, *et al.,* 1970

Cestoda

Diphyllobothrium stemmacephalum, (Cobbold, 1858); Baylis, 1932
Monorygma delphini, (Gervais, 1847); Baylis, 1932
Tetrabothrius forsteri, (Krefft, 1871); Baylis, 1932

Nematoda

Anisakis simplex, (Rudolphi, 1809); Baylis, 1932
Halocercus delphini, (Baylis and Daubney, 1925); Baylis, 1932
Halocercus kleinenbergi, (Delyamure, 1951); Delyamure, 1955
Skrjabinalius cryptocephalus, (Delyamure, 1942); Delyamure, 1955

Acanthocephala

Bolbosoma vasculosum, (Rudolphi, 1819); Delyamure, 1955
Corynosoma cetaceum, (Johnston and Best, 1942); Delyamure, 1955
Corynosoma sp., Delyamure, 1955

Delphinus sp.

Cestoda

Monorygma grimaldii, (Moniez, 1889); Delyamure, 1955
Strobilocephalus triangularis, (Diesing, 1850); Baylis, 1932

Nematoda

Anisakis simplex, (Rudolphi, 1809); Baylis, 1932

Lissodelphis borealis (Northern Right Whale Dolphin)

Trematoda

Nasitrema globicephalae Neiland *et al.,* 1970

Cestoda

Phyllobothrium sp., New Host Record

*Peoponocephala electra** (Broad-beaked Dolphin)

Trematoda

Nasitrema sp., New host record

Cestoda

Monorygma sp., New host record

Nematoda

Halocercus sp., New host record, (R. J. Harrison, per com.)

Pseudorca crassidens (False Killer Whale)

Trematoda

Nasitrema attenuata, Neiland, *et al.*, 1970
Nasitrema globicephalae Neiland *et al.*, 1970

Nematoda

Anisakis simplex, (Rudolphi, 1809); Delyamure, 1955

Acanthocephala

Bolbosoma capitatum, (Linstow, 1880); Baylis, 1932

Globicephala melaena (North Atlantic Pilot Whale)

Trematoda

Orthosplanchnus arcticus, (Odhner, 1905); Cowan, 1967

Cestoda

Diphyllobothrium sp., Cowan, 1967
Monorygma grimaldii, (Moniez, 1889); Delyamure, 1955
Phyllobothrium delphini, (Bosc, 1802); Delyamure, 1955
Plicobothrium globicephalae, Rausch and Margolis 1969
Trigonocotyle lintoni, (Guiart, 1935); Delyamure, 1955

---

* Same as *Lagenorhynchus electra* and *Electra electra*.

Nematoda

Anisakis simplex, (Rudolphi, 1809); Baylis, 1932
Pharurus convolutus, (Kühn, 1829); Baylis, 1932
Stenurus globicephalus, (Baylis and Daubney, 1925); Baylis, 1932

Acanthocephala

Bolbosoma capitatum, (Linstow, 1880); Baylis, 1932

*Globicephala macrorhyncha** (Short-finned Pilot Whale)

Trematoda

Campula gondo, Yamaguti, 1942
Lecithodesmus nipponicus, Yamaguti, 1942
Nasitrema gondo, Yamaguti, 1951
Nasitrema lanceolata, Neiland, *et al.*, 1970
Nasitrema globicephalae, Neiland, *et al.*, 1970

Cestoda

Anophryocephala sp., New host record (R. J. Harrison, per com.)
Monorygma sp., New host record
Phyllobothrium sp., New host record

Nematoda

Anisakis sp., Kagel, *et al.*, 1967
Pharurus convolutus, (Kühn, 1829); Dougherty, 1943

Orcinus orca (Killer Whale)

Trematoda

Fasciola skriabini, Delyamure, 1955

Cestoda

Trigonocotyle spasskyi, Gubanov, 1952; Delyamure, 1955
Phyllobothrium sp., New host record

Nematoda

Anisakis simplex, (Rudolphi, 1809); Delyamure, 1955

* Also includes species identified as *Globicephala scammoni*

Orcaella brevirostris (Irrawaddy River Dolphin)

Trematoda

Amphimerus lancea, (Diesing, 1850); Baylis, 1932

Phocoena phocoena (Harbor Porpoise)

Trematoda

Campula oblonga, (Cobbold, 1858); Baylis, 1932
Lecithodesmus nipponicus, Yamaguti, 1951
Opisthorchis tenuicollis, (Rudolphi, 1819); Baylis, 1932
Pholeter gastrophilus, (Kossack, 1910); Baylis, 1932

Cestoda

Diphyllobothrium lanceolatum, (Krabbe, 1865); Delyamure, 1955
Diphyllobothrium latum, (Linnaeus, 1758); Delyamure, 1955
Diphyllobothrium stemmacephalum, (Cobbold, 1858); Baylis, 1932

Nematoda

Anisakis simplex, (Rudolphi, 1809); Baylis, 1932
Halocercus invaginatus, (Quekett, 1841); Delyamure, 1955
Halocercus ponticus, (Delyamure, 1946); Delyamure, 1955
Halocercus taurica, (Delyamure and Skrjabin, 1942); Delyamure, 1955
Pharurus convolutus, (Kühn, 1829); Baylis and Daubney, 1925;
   Delyamure, 1955
Porrocaecum decipiens, (Krabbe, 1878); Delyamure, 1955
Pseudalius inflexus, (Rudolphi, 1809); Baylis, 1932
Stenurus minor, (Kühn, 1829); Baylis, 1932

Acanthocephala

Corynosoma alaskensis, Golvan, 1959
Corynosoma semerme, (Forssell, 1904); Delyamure, 1955
Corynosoma strumosum, (Rudolphi, 1802); Delyamure, 1955

Phocoenoides dalli (Dall Porpoise)

Trematoda

Nasitrema dalli, Yamaguti, 1951

Cestoda

Phyllobothrium sp., New host record (W. J. Houck, per com.)

Nematoda

Anisakis sp., Kagel, *et al.*, 1967
Halocercus kirbyi, (Dougherty, 1944), Delyamure, 1955
Placentonema sp., Ridgway, 1966
Stenurus sp., Norris and Prescott, 1961

Neophocoena phocoenoides (Black Finless Porpoise or Common Chinese Porpoise)

Trematoda

Campula folium, (Ozaki, 1935); Delyamure, 1955
Nasitrema spathulatum, (Ozaki, 1935); Delyamure, 1955
Orthosplanchus elongatus, (Ozaki, 1935); Delyamure, 1955

Cestoda

Diphyllobothrium furhmanni, (Hsü, 1935); Delyamure, 1955

Nematoda

Crassicauda fuelleborni, (Hoeppli and Hsü, in Hoeppli, Hsü, and Wu, 1929); Baylis, 1932
Halocercus pingi, (Wu, 1929); Baylis, 1932
Stenurus auditivus, (Hsü and Hoeppli, 1933); Delyamure, 1955

Monodon monoceros (Narwhal)

Nematoda

Anisakis simplex, (Rudolphi, 1809); Baylis, 1932
Stenurus alatus, (Leuckart, 1848); Baylis, 1932
Porrocaecum decipiens, (Krabbe, 1878); Delyamure, 1955

Delphinapterus leucas (Beluga or White Whale)

Trematoda

Odhneriella seymouri, (Price, 1932); Delyamure, 1955
Leucasiella arctica, Delyamure and Kleinenberg, 1958
Leucasiella mironovi, (Krotov and Delyamure, 1952); Delyamure, 1955
Orthosplanchnus sudarikovi, Treshchev, 1966
Orthosplanchus albamarinus, Treshchev, 1968

Cestoda

Diphyllobothrium lanceolatum, (Krabbe, 1865); Delyamure and Kleinenberg, 1958

Nematoda

Anisakis simplex, (Rudolphi, 1809); Baylis, 1920
Crassicauda giliakiana, (Skrjabin and Andreeva, 1934); Delyamure, 1955
Otophocaenurus oserskoi, (Skrjabin, 1942); Delyamure, 1955
Stenurus arctomarinus, Delyamure and Kleinenberg, 1958
Stenurus minor, (Kuhn, 1829)
Stenurus pallasii, (Van Beneden, 1870); Delyamure, 1955
Porrocaecum decipiens, (Krabbe, 1878); Scott and Fisher, 1958

Acanthocephala

Corynosoma cameroni, van Cleave, 1953
Corynosoma strumosum, (Rudolphi, 1802); Delyamure, 1955

Physeter catodon (Sperm Whale)

Trematoda

Zalophotrema curilensis, (Gubanov, 1952); Delyamure, 1955

Cestoda

Dipogonoporus sp., Delyamure, 1955
Hexagonoporus physeteris, (Gubanov, 1952); Delyamure, 1955
Phyllobothrium delphini, (Bosc, 1802); Baylis, 1932
Priapocephalus grandis, (Nybelin, 1922); Rees, 1953
Tetrabothrius curilensis, (Gubanov, 1952); Delyamure, 1955
Tetrabothrium wilsoni, (Leiper and Atkinson, 1914); Rees, 1953
Trigonocotyle sp., Delyamure, 1955

Nematoda

Anisakis ivanizkii, (Mozgovoi, 1949); Delyamure, 1955
Anisakis physeteris, (Baylis, 1923); Baylis, 1932
Anisakis simplex, (Rudolphi, 1809); Baylis, 1932
Anisakis skrjabini, (Mozgovoi, 1949); Delyamure, 1955
Placentonema gigantissima, (Gubanov, 1951); Delyamure, 1955

Acanthocephala

Bolbosoma brevicolle, (Malm, 1867); Baylis, 1932
Bolbosoma capitatum, (Linstow, 1880); Baylis, 1932
Bolbosoma physeteris, (Gubanov, 1952); Delyamure, 1955
Corynsoma curilensis, (Gubanov, 1952); Delyamure, 1955

Kogia breviceps (Pygmy Sperm Whale)

Cestoda

Phyllobothrium delphini, (Bosc, 1802); Delyamure, 1955
Monorygma grimaldii, (Moniez, 1889); Baylis, 1932

Nematoda

Anisakis simplex, (Rudolphi, 1809); Van Thiel, 1966
Crassicauda magna, (Johnston and Mawson, 1939); Delyamure, 1955
Crassicauda duguyi, Dollfus, 1966
Phocanema sp., Van Thiel, 1966
Psedoterranova kogiae, (Johnston and Mawson, 1939); Delyamure, 1955

Kogia simus (Dwarf Sperm Whale)

Cestoda

Phyllobothrium sp., New host record

Mesoplodon bidens (Sowerby Beaked Whale)

Cestoda

Phyllobothrium delphini, (Bosc, 1802); Delyamure, 1955
Strobilocephalus triangularis, (Diesing, 1850); Delyamure, 1955
Tetrabothrius forsteri, (Krefft, 1871); Baylis, 1932

Nematoda

Anisakis simplex, (Rudolphi, 1809); Baylis, 1932

Acanthocephala

Bolbosoma vasculosum, (Rudolphi, 1819); Delyamure, 1955

Mesoplodon mirus (True's Beaked Whale)

Nematoda

Crassicauda anthonyi, Chabaud, 1962

Ziphius cavirostris (Goose Beaked Whale or Cuvier Beaked Whale)

Cestoda

Phyllobothrium sp., Tomilin, 1957

Nematoda

Crassicauda boopis, (Baylis, 1920); Baylis, 1932
Crassicauda crassicauda, (Creplin, 1829); Delyamure, 1955

Berardius bairdi (Giant Bottlenosed Whale)

Trematoda

Oschmarinella sobolevi, (Skrjabin, 1947); Delyamure, 1955

Cestoda

Diphyllobothrium sp., Delyamure, 1955
Phyllobothrium delphini, (Bosc, 1802); Delyamure, 1955
Trygonocotyle sp., Delyamure, 1955

Nematoda

Anisakis simplex, (Rudolphi, 1809); Margolis and Pike, 1955
Anisakis skrjabini, (Mosgovoy, 1949); Delyamure, 1955
Crassicauda giliakiana, (Skrjabin and Andreeva, 1934); Delyamure, 1955
Delamurella hyperoodoni, (Gubanov, 1952); Delyamure, 1955

Hyperoodon ampullatus (Northern Bottlenosed Whale)

Cestoda

Strobilocephalus triangularis, (Diesing, 1850); Baylis, 1932

Nematoda

Anisakis simplex, (Rudolphi, 1809); Baylis, 1932

Acanthocephala

Bolbosoma turbinella, (Diesing, 1851); Baylis, 1932
Bolbosoma balaenae, (Gmelini, 1790); Delyamure, 1955

Hyperoodon planifrons (Southern Bottlenosed Whale)

Nematoda

Crassicauda bennetti, (Spaul, 1926); Baylis, 1932

Eubalaena glacialis (Black Right Whale, Pacific Right Whale)

Cestoda

Priapocephalus grandis, (Nybelin, 1922); Baylis, 1932

Acanthocephala

Bolbosoma brevicolle, (Malm, 1867); Delyamure, 1955
Bolbosoma turbinella, (Diesing, 1851); Delyamure, 1955

Balaena mysticetus (Greenland Right Whale, Bowhead Whale)

Trematoda

Lecithodesmus goliath, (van Beneden, 1858); Baylis, 1932
Ogmogaster pilcatus, (Creplin, 1829); Tomilin, 1957

Cestoda

Phyllobothrium delphini, (Bosc, 1802); Baylis, 1932

Acanthocephala

Bolbosoma balaenae, (Rudolphi, 1814); Baylis, 1932

Nematoda

Crassicauda crassicauda, (Creplin, 1829); Delyamure, 1955

Eschrichtius gibbosus (Gray Whale)

Trematoda

Ogmogaster antarcticus, New host record
Ogmogaster pentalineatus, Rausch and Fay, 1966

Cestoda

Priapocephalus sp., Rice, 1963*
Pseudophyllidae, Tomilin, 1957

Acanthocephala

Corynosoma sp., New host record (Rice, per com.)

Balaenoptera acutorostrata (Little Piked Whale, Minke Whale)

Trematoda

Fasciola skrjabini, Delyamure, 1955
Lecithodesmus goliath, (van Beneden, 1858); Balyis, 1932
Ogmogaster plicatus, (Creplin, 1829); Baylis, 1932

---

* Same as *Tetrabothius sp.*, Rice per com.

Nematoda

Anisakis simplex, (Rudolphi, 1809); Baylis, 1932
Crassicauda crassicauda, (Creplin, 1829); Delyamure, 1955
Porrocaecum decipiens, (Krabbe, 1878); Delyamure, 1955

Acanthocephala

Bolbosoma balaena, (Gmelin, 1790); Baylis, 1932
Bolbosoma brevicolle, (Malm, 1867); Baylis, 1932
Bolbosoma nipponicum, (Yamaguti, 1939); Delyamure, 1955

Balaenoptera borealis (Sei Whale)

Trematoda

Lecithodesmus goliath, (van Beneden, 1858); Baylis, 1932
Lecithodesmus spinosus, Margolis and Pike, 1955
Ogmogaster plicatus, (Creplin, 1829); Baylis, 1932

Cestoda

Diphyllobothrium sp., Delyamure, 1955
Diplogonoporus balaenopterae, (Lönnberg, 1892); Baylis, 1932
Priapocephalus grandis, (Nybelin, 1928); Baylis, 1932
Tetrabothrius affinis, (Lönnberg, 1891); Baylis, 1932
Tetrobathrius arsenyevi, Delyamure, 1955
Tetrabothrius wilsoni, (Leiper and Atkinson, 1914); Baylis, 1932

Acanthocephala

Bolbosoma balaenae, (Gmelin, 1790); Baylis, 1932
Bolbosoma brevicolle, (Malm, 1867); Baylis, 1932
Bolbosoma nipponicum, (Yamaguti, 1939); Delyamure, 1955
Bolbosoma turbinella, (Diesing, 1851); Baylis, 1932

Nematoda

Crassicauda crassicauda, (Creplin, 1829); Baylis, 1932
Crassicauda delamureana, Skryabin, 1966
Anisakis sp., Rice, 1963

Balaenoptera physalus (Fin Whale)

Trematoda

Lecithodesmus goliath, (van Beneden, 1858); Delyamure, 1955
Ogmogaster antarcticus, (Johnston, 1931); Delyamure, 1955
Ogmogaster plicatus, (Creplin, 1829); Baylis, 1932

Cestoda

Diplogonoporus balaenopterae, (Lönnberg, 1892); Delyamure, 1955
Phyllobothrium delphini, (Bosc, 1802); van Beneden, 1870; Tomilin, 1957
Priapocephalus grandis, (Nybelin, 1928); Delyamure, 1955
Priapocephalus minor, (Nybelin, 1928); Delyamure, 1955
Tetrabothrius affinis, (Lönnberg, 1891); Lönnberg, 1892; Delyamure, 1955
Tetrabothrius ruudi, (Nyblin, 1928); Baylis, 1932

Nematoda

Anisakis simplex, (Rudolphi, 1809); Tomilin, 1957
Contracaecum sp., (Baylis, 1929); Baylis, 1932
Crassicauda boopis, Delyamure, 1955
Crassicauda crassicauda, (Creplin, 1829); Delyamure, 1955
Crassicauda pacifica, Margolis and Pike, 1955

Acanthocephala

Bolbosoma balaenae, (Gmelin, 1790); Delyamure, 1955
Bolbosoma brevicolle, (Malm, 1867); Baylis, 1932
Bolbosoma hamiltoni, (Baylis, 1929); Baylis, 1932
Bolbosoma nipponicum, (Yamaguti, 1939); Delyamure, 1955
Bolbosoma turbinella, (Diesing, 1851); Delyamure, 1955

Balaenoptera musculus (Blue Whale)

Trematoda

Ogmogaster antarcticus, (Johnston, 1931); Delyamure, 1955
Ogmogaster plicatus, (Creplin, 1839); Baylis, 1932

Cestoda

Priapocephalus grandis, (Nybelin, 1922); Baylis, 1932
Tetrabothrius affinis, (Lönnberg, 1891); Baylis, 1932

Nematoda

Anisakis simplex,[*] (Rudolphi, 1809); Baylis, 1932
Crassicauda crassicauda, (Creplin, 1829); Baylis, 1932
Porrocaecum decipiens, (Krabbe, 1878); Delyamure, 1955

Acanthocephala

Bolbosoma balaenae, (Gmelin, 1790); Baylis, 1932
Balbosoma brevicolle, (Malm, 1876); Baylis, 1932

[*] Same as *Ascaris angulivalis.*

Bolbosoma hamiltoni, (Baylis, 1929); Baylis, 1932
Bolbosoma turbinella, (Diesing, 1851); Baylis, 1932

Megaptera novaengliae (Humpback Whale)

Trematoda

Lecithodesmus sp., Rice, 1963

Cestoda

Diplogonoporus balaenopterae, (Lönnberg, 1892); Rice, 1963

Nematoda

Anisakis sp., (Baylis, 1929); Baylis, 1932
Crassicauda boopis, (Baylis, 1920); Baylis, 1932
Crassicauda crassicauda, (Creplin, 1829); Delyamure, 1932

Acanthocephala

Bolbosoma balaenae, (Gmelin, 1790); Baylis, 1932
Bolbosoma turbinella, (Diesing, 1851); Baylis, 1932

Ectoparasites and Epizoites on Cetaceans

A wide variety of organisms are found attached to cetaceans, ranging from diatoms to lampreys and whalesuckers. No summarized host records are given, but the following groups and genera are reported from cetaceans:

Diatoms

Cocconeis ceticola and species of *Gyrosigma, Licmophora, Navicula Plumosigma,* and *Stauroneis*
(Hart, 1935; Nemoto, 1956 and 1958)

Sessile Barnacles

Coronula, Cryptolepas, Tubicinella, and *Xenobalanus*
(Thoracica: Balanidae)
(Dollfus, 1968; Ross and Newman, 1967)

Stalked Barnacles

Conchoderma auritum and *Conchoderma virgatum*
(Thoracica: Lepadidae)
(Clarke, 1966; Perrin, 1969)

Copepod

Balaenophilus, Penella, and *Harpacticus*
(Caligoida: Lernaeoceridae)
(Humes, 1964; Rice, 1963)

Whalelice

Cyamus, Isocyamus, Neocyamus, Platycyamus, and *Syncyamus*
(Amphipoda: Cyamidae)
(Leung, 1965 and 1967)

Lampreys

Lampetra and Petromyzon
(Hyperoartii: Petromyzontidae)
(Nemoto, 1955; Pike, 1951, Utrecht, 1959)

Whalesucker or Remora

Remora australis
(Discocephali: Echineididae)
(Follett and Dempster, 1960; Rice and Caldwell, 1961; Radford and Klawne, 1965)

SIRENIA

*Dugong dugon** (Dugong, Sea Cow)

Trematoda

Indosolenorchis hirudinaceus, Crusz, 1951
Lankatrema mannarense, Crusz and Fernand, 1954
Opisthotrema dujonis, (Leuckart, 1874); Price, 1932
Taprobanella bicaudata, Crusz and Fernand, 1954
Solenorchis trauassosi, Hilmy, 1949
Solenorchis gohari, Hilmy, 1949
Solenorchis naguibmahjouzi, Hilmy, 1949
Solenorchis baeri, Hilmy, 1949
Rhabdiopoeus taylori, Johnston, 1913
Pulmonicola pulmonalis, (Linstow, 1904); Poche, 1925

Nematoda

Heterocheilus tunicatus, Diesing, 1839
Paradujardinia halicoris, Owen, 1833

* Synonyms are *Halicore dugon, Halicore cetacea* and *Halicore australe.*

*Trichechus manatus*** (Caribbean Manatee)

Trematoda

*Chiorchis fabaceus,**** (Diesing, 1838); Fischoeder, 1901

Opisthotrema cochleotrema, (Travassos and Vogelsang, 1931); Price, 1932

Anthropoda

Copepoda

Harpacticus pulex, Humes, 1964

Trichechus senegalensis (West African Manatee)

Trematoda

Chiorchis fabaceus, (Diesing, 1838); Dollfus, 1955

Trichechus inunguis (Amazon Manatee)

Trematoda

Chiorchis fabaceus, (Diesing, 1838); Dollfus, 1955

LIST OF PARASITE GENERA AND LOCALITY IN HOST

Pinnipedia

Trematoda	Locality in Hosts
Family Campulidae	
Zalophotrema	Liver
Orthosplanchnus	Liver (bile duct)
*Hadwenius**	Intestine
Family Opisthorchiidae	
Metorchis	Gall bladder & bile duct
Phocitrema	Intestine
Pseudamphistomum	Liver (bile duct)
Opisthorchis	Liver (bile duct)
Family Microphallidae	
Microphallus	Intestine

** Synonym is *Trichechus latirostris.*

*** Same as *Schizamphistoma manati,* Skoloff and Caballero, 1932.

* Same as *Odhneriella.*

Family Heterophyidae
    Pricetrema   Intestine
    Stictodera   Intestine
    Cryptocotyle   Intestine
    Rossicotrema*   Intestine
Family Echinostomatidae
    Stephanoprora   Intestine
    Echinostoma   Intestine
Family Notocotylidae
    Ogmogaster   Intestine

Cestoda   Locality in Hosts

Family Diphyllobothriidae
    Baylisiella   Intestine
    Diphyllobothrium   Intestine
    Diplogonoporus   Intestine
    Pyramicocephalus   Intestine
    Adenocephalus   Intestine
    Schistocephalus   Intestine
    Plicobothrium   Intestine
    Glandicephalus   Intestine
Family Phyllobothriidae
    Phyllobothrium   Tissue
Family Tetrabothriidae
    Anophryocephalus   Intestine
    Trigonocotyle   Intestine
Family Lecanicephalidae
    Polypocephalus   Tissue (?) not given by King, 1964

Nematoda   Locality in Hosts

Family Ascarididae
    Ascaris   Intestine (?) not given by King, 1964
Family Ancylostomatidae
    Uncinaria   Intestine
Family Psuedaliidae
    Halocercus   Lungs (?) not given by King, 1964
    Parafilaroides   Lungs
Family Heterocheilidae
    Anisakis   Stomach
    Porrocaecum   Stomach

* Same as *Apophallus*.

Pocanema	Stomach
Contracaecum	Stomach
Dujardinia	Stomach
Terranova	Stomach
Phocascaris	Stomach
Family Dirofilariidae	
Dirofilaria	Heart
Family Dioctophymidae	
Eustrongylides	(?) not given by King, 1964
Dioctophyma	Kidney (?) not given by King, 1964
Family Dipetalonematidae	
Skjabinaria	Heart
Dipetalonema	Muscle fascia
	Heart
Family Dictyocaulidae	
Otostrongylus	Lungs, circulatory system
Family Trichinellidae	
Trichinella	Tissue

Acanthocephala   **Locality in Hosts**

Family Polymorphidae	
Corynosoma	Intestine
Bolbosoma	Intestine

Cetacea

Trematoda   **Locality in Hosts**

Family Fasciolidae	
Fasciola	Liver
Family Campulidae	
Campula	Liver
Lecithodesmus	Liver
syn. *Hadwenius*	Intestine
Leveasiella	Intestine
Odhneriella	Liver
Orthosplanchus	Liver
Oschmarinella	Liver
Zalophotrema	Liver
Synthesium	Intestine
Hunterotrema	Lung
Family Ratziidae	
Cychlorchis	Liver

Family Troglotrematidae
   Pholeter   Stomach
Family Opisthorchidae
   Nasitrema   Air sinuses
   Opisthorchis   Bile ducts
   Amphimerus   Not indicated, bile ducts (?)
   Delphinicola   Bile ducts
Family Echinostomatidae
   Echinochasmus   Intestine
Family Herterophyidae
   Galactosomum   Intestine
Family Notocotylidae
   Ogmogaster   Intestine
Family Brauninidae
   Braunina   Stomach and intestine

Cestoda   Locality in Hosts

Family Tetrabothriidae
   Tetrabothrius   Intestine
   Anophryocephalus   Intestine
   Priapocephalus   Intestine
   Strobilocephalus   Intestine (rectum)
   Trigonocotyle   Intestine
Family Diphyllobothriidae
   Diphyllobothrium   Stomach and intestine
   Diplogonoporus   Intestine and liver
   Hexagonoporus   Intestine
Family Phyllobothriidae
   Phyllobothrium   Blubber
   Monorygma   Abdominal cavity

Nematoda   Locality in Hosts

Family Pseudaliidae
   Pseudalius   Lungs, heart
   Delamurella   Lungs (trachea)
   Halocercus   Lungs
   Otophocaenurus   Air sinus
   Pharurus   Lungs, heart, air sinus
   syn. *Torynurus*
   Pseudostenurus   "Accessory nasal cavity"
   Skrijabinacius   Lungs
   Stenurus   Air sinus, lungs, heart

Family Heterocheilidae
  Anisakis   Stomach, intestine
  Contracaecum   Stomach, intestine
  Pseudoterranova   Stomach
  Phocanema   Stomach
  Porrocaecum   Stomach
Family Crassicaudidae
  Crassicauda   Kidneys, muscle, urogenital system

  Placentonemma   Placenta, mammary gland, subdermis

Acanthacephala   **Locality in Hosts**

Family Polymorphidae
  Corynosoma   Intestine, stomach
  Bolbosoma   Intestine

Sirenia

Trematoda   **Locality in Hosts**

Family Paramphistomatidae
  Chiorchis   Large intestine
  Solenorchis   Intestinal cecum
  Indosolenorchis   Intestinal cecum
Family Pronocephalidae
  Taprobanella   Stomach
  Lankatrema   Stomach
  Opisthotrema   Esophagus, stomach, eustachian tubes, and nasal passages
  Pulmonicola   Lungs
Family Rhabdiopoeidae
  Rhabdiopoeus   Intestine

Nematoda   **Locality in Hosts**

Family Heterocheilidae
  Heterocheilus   Stomach
Family Filocapsulariinae
  Paradujardinia   Stomach

REPRESENTATIVES OF COMMON PARASITIC GROUPS FOUND IN MARINE MAMMALS

Figure 9–1. *Braunina cordiformis* in the stomach of *Tursiops truncatus*.

Genus *Braunina* (Trematoda: Brauninidae)

Braunina cordiformis, the stomach fluke, is one of the most common parasites found in the bottlenosed dolphin, *Tursiops truncatus*. The small, heart-shaped trematodes are found in both the fundic and pyloric stomach where they cause a small focus of chronic gastritis at each site of attachment. Schryver, *et al.* (1967), reports as many as "several hundred" of these parasites from a single host.

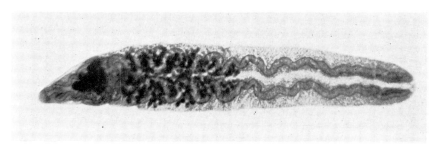

Figure 9–2. Adult *Nasitrema globicephalae* from the air sinus of a pilot whale (*Globicephala macrorhyncha*).

Genus *Nasitrema* (Trematoda: Nasitrematidae)

Nasitrema globicephalae Neiland, *et al.* (1970) is common in the head sinuses of the pilot whale *Globicephala macrorhyncha*. One hundred and sixty-five of these trematodes have been recovered from the sinuses of a single host (Neiland, *et al.* 1970). There are currently nine species recognized in this genus. These range in length from 9 to 12 mm (*Nasitrema stenosomum*) to 28 to 35 mm (*Nasitrema gondo*).

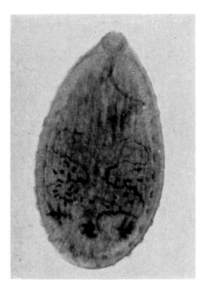

Figure 9–3. Adult *Ogmogaster antarcticus.*

Genus *Ogmogaster* (Trematoda: Notocotylidae)

Ogmogaster antarcticus from the intestine of a gray whale (*Eschrichtius gibbosus*) has been reported from both pinnipeds and cetaceans. It has also been reported from the Antarctic and northern Pacific Ocean. These flukes cause no known damage to the host.

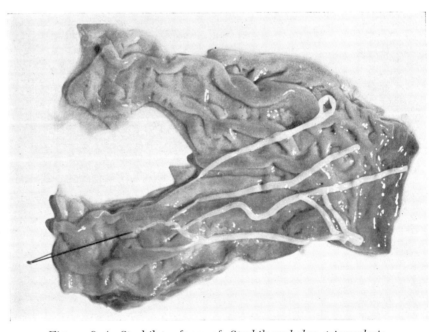

Figure 9–4. Strobilate form of *Strobilocephalus triangularis.*

Genus *Strobilocephalus* (Eucestoda: Tetrabothriidae)

Strobilocephalus triangularis collected from the rectal area of *Stenella graffmani*. This parasite was figured by Baer (1955) from an unidentified host. Note the inflated scolex buried in the rectal wall. Massive infections of these cestodes have been found to completely fill the lumen of the rectum.

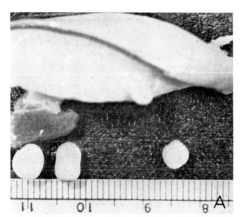 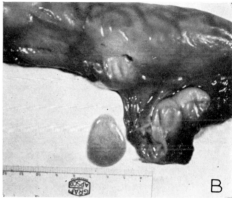

Figure 9–5A, B. Larval stage of *Phyllobothrium delphini* and *Monorygma* sp.

Genera *Phyllobothrium* (A) and *Monorygma* (B) (Eucestoda: Phyllobothriidae)

Other than stomach "worms," the larval phyllobothriid cysts *Phyllobothrium* and *Monorygma* are the most commonly encountered parasites in cetaceans. Because of the confusion in the literature concerning the identification and the locality in the host of these plerocercoids, we have combined the discussion of these two important genera. These larval tapeworm infections occur mainly in odontocetes. There are several records from the baleen whales, and *Phyllobothrium* has been reported from five species of pinnipeds. Dollfus (1964) has reviewed the literature from 1864 to 1955 on these larval cestodes in cetaceans. The most recent discussion since Dollfus is Williams (1968).

Linton (1905) is probably the first to show that two kinds of larval cysts occur in cetaceans. Members of *Phyllobothrium* have scoleces at the end of a short (12 to 15 mm), filament-like invagination, and *Monorygma* has a considerably longer invagination (12 cm to 1 m). *Monorygma* is the larger of these two cysts and is always found internal to the blubber. *Phyllobothrium* in cetaceans is only found in the blubber, usually around the anal orifice. Reports of Baylis (1932), Meggitt (1924), Williams (1968), Ridgway and Johnston (1965), and Cowan (1967) state that *Phyllobothrium* cysts occur in the mesentery of cetaceans. The first three authors misquote Linton (1905), who stated that *Phyllobothrium* came from the blubber and *Taenia chamissonii** were obtained from the body cavity. Ridgway and Johnston (1965) figure a tapeworm cyst *Phyllobothium delphini*, which by its size and length appears to be *Monorygma*. Cowan (1967) reported *Phyllobothrium* plerocercoids from the blubber and adominal cavity without a description of either cyst.

Figure 9–6. Scolex of adult *Diphyllobothrium* sp.

Genus *Diphyllobothrium* (Eucestoda: Diphyllobothriidae)

Diphyllobothrium (Cobbold, 1858) was established for tapeworms taken from a porpoise *Phocoena phocoena*. This genus is one of seven in the family (five parasitic in marine mammals) Diphyllobothriidae which includes 70 to 75 species from cetaceans, pinnipeds, carnivorous land mammals, fish-eating birds, humans, and one snake. Man is the host for the adults of *Dibothriocephalus latus*. Wardle, McLeod, and Steward (1947) have reviewed the species of this genus as adopted by Lühe (1910).

Genus *Uncinaria* (Nematoda: Ancylostomatidae)

Adult hookworms are common in various immature pinnipeds. The large oral opening and two sharp buccal teeth are typical of *Uncinaria*. These parasites are found in the small intestine and feed on blood. Olsen and Lyons (1965) have shown that *Uncinaria lucasi* in the fur seal (*Callorhinus ursinus*) is carried by the milk of the mother to the nursing young. A massive infection can be fatal to pups.

Subgenus *Contracaecum* (Nematoda: Filocapsulariinae)

Members of this subgenus are one of the most common parasites found in the stomachs of pinnipeds. In California sea lions (*Zalophus californi-*

* Same as *Monorygma*.

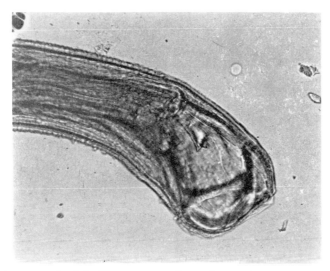

Figure 9–7. Anterior of adult *Uncinaria* sp. from the small intestine of a four month old *Zalophus californianus*.

anus) large parasitic granulomas have been found in association with *Contracaecum osculatum* infections. How detrimental these granulomas are to the host is unknown.

The life history of *Contracaecum osculatum baicalensis* is given by Dely-amure (1955) as worked out by Sudarikov and Ryzhikov (1951) for the Baikal seal (*Pusa sibirica*). The latter workers suggest that the most probable intermediate host is the sand hopper (*Macrohectopus branickii*) with the supplementary or transfer host being the yellow goby (*Cottomephorus grewingki*).

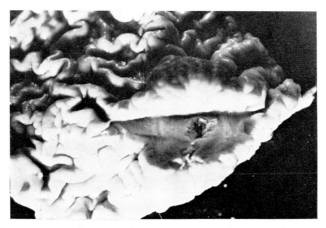

Figure 9–8. Parasitic granuloma in the stomach of *Zalophus californianus* caused by *Contracaecum osculatum*.

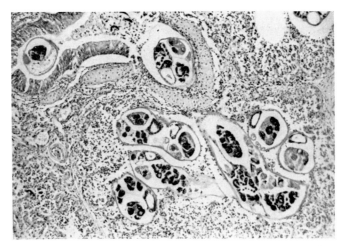

Figure 9–9. Adult *Parafilaroides decorus* in section of *Zalophus californianus* lung.

Genus *Parafilaroides* (Nematoda: Pseudaliidae)

Adult stages of this genus are found in the lungs of various pinnipeds—*Parafilaroides gymmurus* (Dougherty, 1946) from the harbor seal (*Phoca vitulina*); *Parafilaroides decorus* (Dougherty and Herman 1947) from the California sea lion, and three species (*Parafilaroides nanus, Parafilaroides prolificus* and *Parafilaroides sp.*, (Dougherty and Herman, 1947) from the Steller's sea lion (*Eumetopias jubata*). No mixed infections have been reported.

The life cycle of *Parafilaroides decorus* uses the opal eye fish (*Girella nigricans*) as an intermediate host at the San Nicholas Island rookery (Dailey, 1970). Massive numbers of infective third-stage larvae have been found in naturally infected fish. These fish are coprophagous and consume the first-stage larva in sea lion excrement. The fish is then eaten by the foraging sea lion. It is probable that lungworm disease is responsible for much of the mortality seen in both captive and wild California sea lions during their first three years of life.

Genus *Anisakis* (Nematoda: Heterocheilidae)

Adult stages of this nematode are found only in marine mammal stomachs (Van Thiel, 1966). Infective third-stage larvae of this genus are common in herring which, in turn, are a common food species of marine mammals. Larvae first invade the submucosal or mucosal tissue of the stomach where they moult to the fourth stage. These nematodes then leave the tissue and attach to the inner lining of the stomach. After further development another ecdysis takes place, with the adult stage emerging (Kikuchi *et al.*, 1967).

Numerous species have been described due to the widespread occurrence

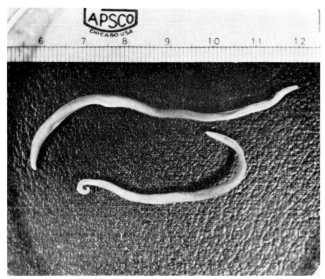

Figure 9–10. Adult male and female *Anisakis simplex* from the stomach of *Tursiops truncatus*.

of this genus in marine mammals. Baylis (1932) placed *Anisakis angulivalvis* in synonomy with *Anisakis simplex*. Dollfus (1948) stated that *Anisakis typica, Anisakis dussumieri* and *Anisakis kukenthali* are all synonymous with *Anisakis simplex* (also see Margolis and Pike (1955) for comments on the taxonomy of various species of this genus). Van Thiel (1966) has suggested that all the various named species belong to a single species and has adopted *marina* for the specific name. The name *simplex* has been retained here because of its long time and universal use. An older generic name *Filocapsularia* was used by Yamaguti (1961) to replace *Anisakis*. *Filocapsularia* should be treated as a *nomen oblitum*.

Yokogawa and Yoshimura (1967) reported larval anisakiasis in the gastrointestinal tract of Japanese people. The infections were probably acquired by eating raw marine fish and squid.

Genera *Corynosoma* (A) and *Bolbosoma* (B) (Acanthocephala: Polymorphidae)

Approximately sixty genera occur in the phylum Acanthocephala. Primarily only two of these *Corynosoma* and *Bolbosoma* occur in marine mammals. The genus *Bolbosoma* is primarily found in cetaceans (only two species, *bobrovi* and *nipponicum* from pinnipeds) while *Corynosoma* occurs mainly in pinnipeds.

These parasites can be identified by bulbous, spiny foretrunks and long hindtrunks. They attach to the intestinal mucosa by a long proboscis covered with recurved hooks. The life cycle of aquatic acanthocephalans usually involves two intermediate hosts—crustaceans and fishes.

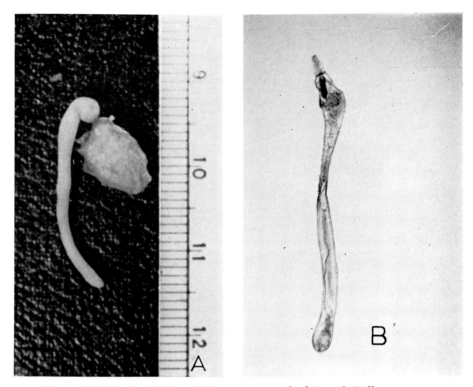

Figure 9–11A, B. Adults of *Corynosoma enhydris* and *Bolbosoma sp.*

Genus *Orthohalarachne* (Arthropoda: Acarina)

Orthohalarachne diminuata (A) is a very common lung mite of the California sea lion. These can be recovered in large numbers from the mucus of the trachea and bronchioles.

Orthohalarachne attenuata (B) has been reported from the nasopharynx of the northern fur seal and Steller's sea lion. The females are found attached anteriorly while the elongated posterior portion of the body extends free into the nasal cavity. The six-legged larval forms are very active and move throughout the infested area. Little is known of the pathogenicity or life history in either of these species.

Genus *Antarctophthirius* (Arthropoda: Anoplura)

Antarctophthirius microchir is a common louse found infesting the skin of both the California and Steller's sea lion. In rookery areas, pups are seen with massive infestations of these parasites, while older animals are very seldom infested. Attempts by various workers to incriminate these arthropods as intermediate hosts for filarid nematodes have been unsuccessful.

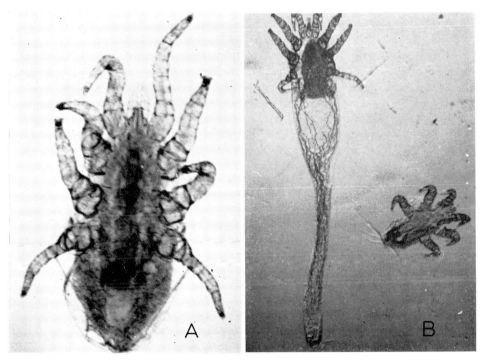

Figure 9-12A, B. Adult mites of the genus *Orthohalarachne* found commonly in sea lions.

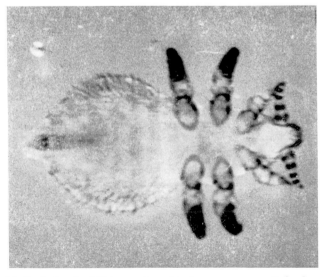

Figure 9–13. Adult *Antarctophthirus microchir* from a young *Zalophus californianus*.

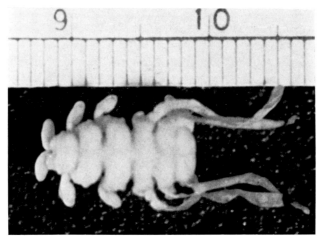

Figure 9–14. Adult *Cyamus ceti* from a California gray whale (*Eschrichtius gibbosus*).

Genus *Cyamus* (Arthropoda: Amphipoda)

Whale-lice of the family Cyamidae infest both whalebone whales (Mystacoceti) and toothed whales (Odontoceti) throughout the world. The family is composed of five recognized genera with seventeen named species (Leung, 1967).

✻   ✻   ✻

The authors would like to express their appreciation to Mrs. Mary Dailey, Miss Barbara Harvey, and Mr. Thomas McIntyre for their help in the preparation of this paper.

REFERENCES

Afanas'ev, V.P.: *Corynosoma enhydris* n. sp. (In Russian text with German summary on the parasite fauna of fur animals of the kormandorskii islands.) Uchenie Zapiski, *Ser. Biol. Nauk.*, 18:115, 1941.

Anderson, R.C.: The taxonomy of *Dipetalonema spirocauda* (Leidy, 1858) n. comb. (*Skrjabinaria spirocauda*) and *Dirofilaria roemeri* (Linstow, 1905) n. comb. (*Dipetalonema roemerii*). *Canad. J. Zool.*, 37:481–493, 1959.

Ariola, V.: Sopra alcuni dibotrii nuovi o poco noti e sulla classificazione del gen. *Bothriocephalus*, *Bull. Mus. Zool.* Genova (52) 2:22 1900.

Baer, J.G.: Contribution à l'étude des cestodes de cétacé. *Rev. Suisse Zool.*, 39:195–228, 1932.

Baer, J.G.: Cestodes d'un dauphin de l'ocean pacifique. *Bull. soc. neuchatel. sci. nat.*, Series 3, 78:33–36, 1955.

Baird, W.: Descriptions of some new species of entozoa from the collection of the British Museum. *Proc. Zool. Soc. London*, Part 21, 18–25, 1853.

Ball, G.H.: *Corynosoma strumosum* from the harbor seal. *Univ. Calif. Publ. Zool.* 33, 1930.

Banks, N.: A new species of the genus Halarachne. *Proc. Ent. Soc. Washington,* 4:212–214, 1899.

Banks, N.: New American mites (Arachnoidea: Acarina). *Proc. Ent. Soc. Washington, 12*:2–12, 1910.

Barabash-Nikiforov, I.I.: The sea otter. (1947). Jerusalem, Israel Program for Scientific Translations, 1962.

Baylis, H.A.: Some Ascarids in the British Museum (Natural History). *Parasitology, 8*(3):360–378, 1916.

Baylis, H.A.: On the classification of the Ascaridae. I. The systematic value of certain characters of the alimentary canal. *Parasitology, 12*(3):253–264, 1920.

Baylis, H.A.: Parasitic Nematoda and Acanthocephala collected in 1925–1927. *Discovery Rep., 1*:541–59, 1929.

Baylis, H.A.: A list of worms parasitic in Cetacea. *Discovery Rep., 6*:393–418, 1932.

Baylis, H.A.: A new species of the nematode genus *Uncinaria* from a sea lion with some observations on related species. *Parasitology, 25*:308–316, 1933.

Baylis, H.A. and Daubney, R.: A further report on parasitic nematodes in the collection of the zoological survey of India. *Rec. Ind. Mus. Calcutta 25:* 551–578, 1923.

Baylis, H.A. and Daubney, R.: A revision of the lung-worms of Cetacea. *Parasitology, 17*:201–215, 1925.

Beneden, P.J. van.: Mémoire sur le vers intestinaux. *Paris, 2*:1 376, 1848.

Beneden, P.J. van.: Les Cétacés, leurs commensaux et leurs parasites. *Bull. Acad. Roy. Sci. Belg., 29*:347–368, 1870.

Berland, B.: *Phocascaris cystophorae* sp. nov. (Nemtoda) from the hooded seal, with an emendation of the genus. *Arbok Univ. Bergen Mat. Naturv. Serie, 17*:1–22, 1963.

Blanchard, R.: Notices sur les parasites de l'homme, 3-me serie, sur le *Krabbea grandis* et remarques sur la classification des Bothriocephalines. *C. R. Soc. Biol.* (*Paris*), *46*:699–702, 1894.

Bosc, L.A.Y.: Historie Naturelle des Vers Contenant Leur Description et Leurs Moeurs. In Costell, K.K. (Ed.): *Buffon, Historie Naturelle,* Paris, 1802, vol. 3.

Braun, M.: Üeber die Distomen in der Leber des Hauskatzen. *Zool. Anz. Leipzig. Bd. 16*:347–355, 1893.

Brown, D.H., McIntyre, R.W., Delli Quardi, C.A., and Schroeder, R.J.: Health problems of captive dolphins and seals. *J. Amer. Vet. Med. Ass., 137*:534–538, 1960.

Bruyn, W.M.: Beitrage zur Kenntnis von *Strongylus circumlitus* Railliet aus dens Lungen des Deehundes: die neue Gattung. *Otostrongylus. Zool. Anz. Leipzig. Bd., 103*:142–153, 1933.

Caballero, Y., Eduardo, C., and Peregrina, D.I.: *Nemátodo de los mamiferos de México. An. Inst. Biol., Univ. Nac. Mexico., 9*:289–306, 1938.

Cameron, T.W.M., Parnell, I.W., and Lyster, L.L.: The Helminth parasites of seldge-dogs in northern Canada and Newfoundland. *Canad. J. Res. 18:* 325–332, 1940.

Campana-Rouget, Yvonne and Biocca, E.: Une nouvelle espéce d' Anisakis chez un phogue Méditerranéen. *Ann. Parasit.*, 30:477–48,0 1955.

Chabaud, A.G.: Description de *Crassicauda anthonyi* n. sp., nematode parasite renal de *Mesoplodon mirus* True. *Bull. Mus. Nat. Hist. Nat.* (*Paris*) 34:397–403, 1963.

Chapin, E.A.: Descriptions of new internal parasites. *Proc. U.S. Nat. Mus.* 68, att. 2:1–4, 1925.

Cholodkovski, N.A.: Cestodes nouveaux ou peu connus. *Troisième Série, Ezhegodnik Zool. Mus. Imp. Nauk.* 20:164–166. 1915.

Ciurea, J.: Les Vers Parasitories de l'Homme, de Mammaiferes et des Oiseaux Provenant des Poissons du Danube et de le Mer Noire. *Arch. Roumaines Path. Exp. Microbiol.* 6:150–171, 1933.

Clarke, R.: The stalked barnacle *Conchoderma*, ectoparasitic on whales. *Norsk Hvalfangst Tid.*, 55:153–168, 1966.

Cobbold, T.S.: Observations on entozoa, etc. *Trans Linnean Soc. London*, 22: 155–172, 1858.

Cobbold, T.S.: Synopsis of the Distomidae. *J. Proc. Linnean Soc. Zool. London*, 49:1–56, 1860.

Cobbold, T.S.: Trematode Parasites from the Dolphins of the Ganges, *Platanista gangetica* and *Orcella brevirostris*. *J. Proc. Linnean Soc. Zool. London*, 65: 35–46, 1876.

Cowan, D.F.: Helminth parasites of the pilot whale *Globicephala melaena* (Traill, 1809). *J. Parasit.* 53:166–167, 1967.

Creplin, F.C.: *Observations de Entozios Gryphiswaldiae*, 1825.

Creplin, F.C.: Filarie et Monostomi Speciem Novam in *Balaena rostrata* Repartam. *Nova Acta Leop. Carol.*, 14:871–882, 1829.

Crusz, H.: Contributions to the helminthology of Ceylon. II. Notes on some parasitic nematodes, with a description of *Anisakis tursiopis* sp. nov. *Ceylon J. Sci.* (B), 23:57–66, 1946.

Crusz, H.: A new amphistome fluke, *Indosolenorchis hirudinaceus*, gen. et sp. nov., from the caecum of a dugong from the Indian Ocean. *Ceylon J. Sci.* (B), 24:135–141, 1951.

Crusz, H. and Fernand, V.S.V.: The trematode parasites of the dugong with descriptions of two new monostomes and histopathological changes in the host, *J. Parasit.*, 40:449–507, 1954.

Dailey, M.D.: *Stictodera ubelakeri* a new species of heterophyid trematode from the California sea lion (*Zalophus californianus*). *Bull. S. Calif. Acad. Sci.*, 68:82–85, 1969.

Dailey, M.D.: The transmission of *Parafilaroides decorus* (Nematoda: Metastrongyloidea) in the California sea lion (*Zalophus californianus*). *Proc. Helm, Soc. Wash.*, 37:215–222, 1970.

Delyamure, S.L.: In Skrjabin, K.I.: The paths of phylogenetic evolution of nematodes of family pseudaliidae parasites of the auditory apparatus, the circulatory system, and respiratory organs of marine mammals. *Doklady Akademii Nauk SSSR*, 37:41–46, 1942.

Delyamure, S.L.: Tri vida legonykh nematod ot del'finov Chernogo i Azovskogo morei (Three species of Pulmonary Nematodes from Black and Azov Sea Dolphins). *Gel'mintologicheskii sbornik, posvyashchennyi akademiku K. I. Skryabinu. Izdatel'stvo Akademii Nauk SSSR*, 104–144, 1946.

Delyamure, S.L.: Navaya psevaliida-parazit legkikh del'fina-belobochki (A new pseudaliid parasite of the lung of the common dolphin). *Trudy Gelmintologicheskoi Laboratorii Akademii Nauk SSSR*, 5:93–97, 1951.

Delyamure, S.L. and Kleinenberg, S.E.: In Kleinenberg, S.E., Yablokov, A.V., Bel'kovich, B.M., and Tarasevich, M.N.: Results of monographic investigation of Beluga (*Delphinapterus leucas*) investigation of the species. Jerusalem, Israel Program for Scientific Translations, 1969.

Delyamure, S.L.: *Helminthofauna of Marine Mammals (Ecology) and Phylogeny)*, Academy of Science USSR, Moscow, 1955. Jerusalem, Israel Program for Scientific Translations, 1968.

Delyamure, S.L. and Alekseev, E.V.. (*Parafilaroides arcticus* n. sp., a parasite of the ringed seal of Chukchi Sea.) In Russian. Parzity, Promezhutochnye Khozyaeva: Perenocchiki. *Nauka Dumka*, Kiev, :11–15, 1966.

Diesing, K.M.: Abbildungen neuer Gattungen brasilianischer Binnenwurmer (Entozoen) (Secretary's abstract). *Ber. Versamml. deutsch. Naturf. und Aerzte in Prag.* Sept. 1837, 1838.

Diesing, K.M.: Neue Gattungen von Binnenwurmern nebst einem Nachtrage zur Monographie der Amphistomen. *Ann. Wien Mus. Naturg.*, 2:219–242, 1839.

Diesing, K.M.: *Systema Helminthum I*. Wien, 1850.

Diesing, K.M.: *Systema Helminthum II*. Wien, 1851.

Doetschman, W.H.: The occurrence of mites in pinnipeds, including a new species from the California sea lion, *Zalophus californianus*. *J. Parasit.*, 27 (6):23, 1941.

Dollfus, R.P.: Nématode à Oesophage Sigmoïde de l'Estomac d'une *Orca orca* (L. 1789) ♀ (Cetacea—Odontocete). Liste des *Anisakis* des Cétacés et des Pinnipèdes. *Ann. Parasit.*, 23(5–6):305–322, 1948.

Dollfus, R.P.: Parasites—Sireniens. *Traité Zool.*, 17:981–983, 1955.

Dollfus, R.P.: A Porpos de la Reccolte, a Banyuls d'un Crystique de Cestode Chez *Tursiops truncatus* (Montagu, 1821). Les Cystiques des Cestodes chez les Cétacés et Pinnipèdes. *Vie Milieu*, 17:177–204, 1964.

Dollfus, R.P.: Helminthofaune de *Kogia breviceps*. *Ann. Soc. Sci. Nat. Charente-Maritime*, 4:3–6, 1966.

Dollfus, R.P.: *Xenobalanus globicipitis* Steenstrup (*Cirripedia thoracica*) récolté sur *Tursiops truncatus* (Montagu) à proximité de la Côte Nord du Maroc. *Bull. l'Inst. Peches Maritimes Maroc.*, 16:55–62, 1968.

Dougherty, E.C.: Notes on the lungworms of porpoises and their occurrence on the California coast. *Proc. Helm. Soc. Washington*, 10:16–22, 1943.

Dougherty, E.C.: The lungworms (Nematoda: Pseudaliidae) of the Odontoceti: Part I. *Parasitol.*, 36:80–94, 1944.

Dougherty, E.C.: The Genus *Aelurostrongylus* Cameron, 1927 (Nematoda: Metastrongylidae) and its Relatives: with descriptions of *Parafilaroides* gen nov. and *Angiostrongylus gubernaculatus* sp. nov. *Proc. Helm. Soc. Washington,* 13:16–26, 1946.

Dougherty, E.C., and Herman, C.M.: New species of the genus *Parafilaroides* Dougherty, 1946 (Nematoda, Metastrongylidae), from seal lions, with a list of the lungworms of the Pinnipedia. *Proc. Helm. Soc. Washington,* 14:77–87, 1947.

Enderlein, G.: Lausestudien 5. Schuppen als sekundare Atmungsorgane, soure uber eine neue antarktische Echinophthiriiden-Gattung. 12. Beitrag zur Kenntris der antarktischen Fauna. *Zool. Anz.,* 29:659–665, 1906.

Fabricius, D.F.: *Fauna Groenlandica, Systematice Sistens Animalia Groendandicae Occidentalis Hactenus Indagata, etc. Haforiae et Lipsiae* (1780).

Faust, E.C.: Mammalian heart worms of the genus *Dirofilaria. Festschrift Bernhard Nocht zum 80, Geburtstag,* pp. 131–139, 1937.

Ferris, G.F.: Anoplura from sea lions of the Pacific Ocean. *Ent. News,* 27:366–370, 1916.

Ferris, G.F.: On two species of the genus *Halarachne* (Acarina, Gamasidae). *Parasitol.,* 17:163–167, 1925.

Finnegan, Susan: On a new species of mite of the family Halarachnidae from the southern sea lion. *Discovery Rep.,* 8:319–327, 1934.

Fischoeder, F.: Die Paramphistomiden der Saugethiere. *Zool. Anz.,* 24:367–375, 1901.

Follett, W.I. and Dempster, L.J.: First records of the echeneidid fish *Remilegia australis* (Bennett) from California, with meristic data. *Proc. Calif. Acad. Sci.,* 31:169–184, 1960.

Forssell, A.: *Echinorhynchus semermis* n. sp. Fauna Flora Fennica, *Med. Soc.* 30:175–179, 1904.

Fujita, T.: On the parasites of Japanese fishes II. *Dobuts Zasshi,* 33:1–8, 1921.

Gedoelst, L.: *Synapsis de Parasitologie de l'Homme et des Animaux Domestiques.* Lierre er Bruxelles, 1911.

Germanos, N.K.: *Bothriocephalus schistochilos* n. sp. Ein neuer Cestode aus dem Darm von *Phoca barbata. Jenaische Ztschr. Naturw.,* 30:1–38, 1895.

Gervais, P.: Sur quelques entozoaires taenioides et hydatides. *Acad. Sci. Montpel., Mem. Sect. Sci.,* 1:85–103, 1847.

Gmelin, J.F.: Caroli à Linné . . . Systema naturae per regna tria naturae, secundum classes ordines, genera, species cum characteribus, differentiis, synonymis, locis, vol. 1. Editio decima tertia, aucta, reformata, cura J. Fred. Gmelin, pt. 6 (vermes) 3021–3910, 1790.

Goeze, J.A.E.: *Versuch einer Naturgeschichte der Eingeweidewürmer thierischer Körper.* Blankenburg, 1782.

Golvan, Y.J.: Acanthocéphales du genre Coryonsoma Lühe, 1904 Parasites de mammifères de'Alaska et de Midway. *Ann. Parasit.,* 34:288–321, 1959.

Goto, S. and Ozaki, Y.: Brief notes on new trematodes. *Jap. J. Zool.,* 3:72–82, 1930.

Gower, W.C.: Host-parasite catalogue of the helminths of ducks. *Amer. Midland Natur.,* 22:580–628, 1939.

Gubanov, N.M.: Gigantskaya nematoda iz platsenty kitoobrazynykh *Placentonema gigantissima* nov. gen. nov. sp. *Doklady Akademiia Nauk SSSR, Novaia seriia*, 77:1123–1125, 1951.

Gubanov, N.M.: Gel'mintofauna promyslovykh zhivotnykh okhotskogo morya i tikhogo okeana. (The helminthofauna of commercial animals of the sea of Okhotsk and Pacific Ocean.) Report & Thesis, 1952.

Guiart, J.: Cestodes Parasites Provenant des Campagnes Scientifiques de S.A.S. le Prince Albert 1-er de Monaco (1886–1913). *Res. Camp. Sci. Monaco*. 91, 1935.

Hart, T.J.: On the diatoms of the skin film of whales, and their possible bearing on problems of whale movements. *Discovery Rep.*, 10:247–282, 1935.

Herman, C.M.: The effect of Higueronia on nematodes and nemathelmintic gastric ulcers of California sea lions. *Rev. Med. Trop. Parasit., Bact., Clin. Lab.*, 8:45–47, 1942.

Hilmy, I.S.: New paramphistomes from the Red Sea dugong, *Halicore halicore*, with description of *Solenorchis* gen n and Solenorchinae subf. n. *Proc. Egypt. Acad. Sci.*, 4:1–14, 1949.

Hoeppli, R., Hsü, H.F., and Wu, H.W.: Helminthologische Britrage aus Fukien and Chekiang. *Arch Schiffs Tropenhyg.*, 33:44, 1929.

Höst, M.G.: *Phocascaris phocae*, n. g., n. sp., line neue Ascaridenart aus *Phoca gronelandica* Fabr. *Zbl. Bakt. Jena. Org. Bd.*, 125:335–340, 1932.

Hsü, H.F.: Contributions a l'Etude de Cestodes de China. *Rev. Suisse Zool*, 42:447–570, 1935.

Hsü, H.F. and Hoeppli, R.: On some parasitic nematodes collected in Amoy. *Peking Nat. Hist. Bull.*, 8:155–168, 1933.

Humes, A.G.: *Harpacticus pulex*, a new species of copepod from the skin of a porpoise and a manatee in Florida. *Bull. Marine Sci. Gulf Caribbean*, 14:517–528, 1964.

Jägerskiöld, L.A.: Uber den Bau des *Ogmogaster plicatus* (Creplin) (*Monostomum plicatum* Creplin). *Kongl. Svenska Vetenskaps-Akad. Handl.*, 24:1–32, 1891.

Jellison, W.L. and Neiland, K.A.: *Parasites of Alaskan vertebrates*. Norman, Okla., University of Oklahoma Research Institute, Proj. 1508 (Processed, 73), 1965.

Johnston, S.J.: On some Queenland trematodes with anatomical observations and descriptions ot new species and genera. *Quart. J. Micr. Sci.*, 59:361–400, 1913.

Johnston, T.H.: New Trematodes from the Subantarctic and Antarctic. *Aust. J. Exp. Biol. Med. Sci.*, 8:91–98, 1931.

Johnston, T.H. and Best, E.W.: Acanthocephala. *Sci. Rep. Australia Antarctic Expedition*, 1911–1914., 10:1–20, 1937.

Johnston, T.H. and Best, E.W.: Australian Acanthocephala No. 3. *Trans. Roy. Soc. S. Aust.*, 66:250–254, 1942.

Johnston, T.H. and Mawson, P.M.: Internal parasites of the pygmy sperm whale. *Rec. S. Aust. Mus.*, 6:263–274, 1939.

Johnston, T.H. and Mawson, P.M.: Nematodes from Australian marine mammals. *Rec. S. Aust., Mus.*, 6:429–434, 1941.

Johnston, T.H. and Mawson, P.M.: Parasitic nematodes. *Rep. B.A.N.Z. Antarctic Research Exped.* 1929–1931., 5:73–159, 1945.

Johnson, M.L., Fiscus, C.H., Ostenson, B.T. and Barbour, M.L.: Marine mammals. In Wilimovsky, N.J. (Ed.): *Environment of the Cape Thompson Region, Alaska*, U.S. Atomic Energy Commission, Washington, 33:877–924, 1966.

Joyeux, C. and Baer, J.G.: Fauna de France. 30. *Cestodes*. Paris, 1936.

Kagel, N., Oshima, T., Kobayashii, A., Kumada, M., Koyama, T. Komiya, Y., and Takemura, A.: Survey of *Anisakis* spp. (Anisakinae, Nematoda) in marine mammals on the coast of Japan. *Jap. J. Parasit.* (In Japanese; English summary, p. 435), 16:427–435, 1967.

Kenny, D.: Personal communication, 1968.

Kenyon, K.W., Yunker, C.E., and Newell, I.M.: Nasal mites (Halarachnidae) in the sea otter. *J. Parasit.*, 51:960, 1965.

Keyes, M.C.: Pathology of the northern fur seal. *J. Amer. Vet. Med. Ass.*, 147: 1090–1095, 1965.

Kikuchi, S., Hayashi, S., and Nakajima, M.: Studies on anisakiasis in dolphins. *Jap. J. Parasit.*, (In Japanese: English summary, p. 166.) 16:156–166, 1967.

King, Judith E.: *Seals of the World*. London, British Museum of Natural History, 1964.

Kossack, W.: Neue Distomen. *Centralbl. Bakt. Parasitenk.*, Abt. I, 56:114–120, 1910.

Krabbe, H.: Helminthologiske Undersogelser i Denmark og pae Island, ned saerligt Hensyn til Blaerormlidelserne paa Island. *Dansk. Videnski. Selsk. Sur., naturvid.-math afd.*, 7:347–408, 1865.

Krabbe, H.: Saelernes og tandhvalernes Spelorme. *Overs. d. Kong. Danks. Vidensk. Selsk. Forhondl.*, 43:51, 1878.

Krefft, G.: On Australian entozoa, with descriptions of new species. *Trans. Ent. Soc. N. S. Wales*, 11:206–232, 1871.

Kreis, H.A.: Beitrage zur Kenntnis Parasitischer Nematoden. 6. Parasitische Nematoden aus dem Zoologischen Garten in Basel. *Centralbl. Bakt., Parasitenkunde Infekt. I Abt., Org. Bd.* 141, Heft. 5/6:279–304, 1938.

Krotov, L.V. and Delyamure, S.L.: Materialy k faune paraz022iticheskikh chervei mlekopitayuschikh i ptits SSSR (Data on the parasitic worm fauna of mammals and birds of the USSR). *Trudy gel'mintologicheskoi laboratorii Akad. Nauk USSR*, 6:278–292, 1952.

Kühn, J.: Description d'une nouvelle espèce de strongle trouvée dans le marsouin. *Bull. Sci. Nat. Geol.*, 17:150–153, 1829.

Layne, J.N. and Caldwell, D.K.: Behavior of the Amazon dolphin, *Inia geoffrensis* (Blainville), in captivity. *Zoologica*, 49:81–108, 1964.

Leidy, J.: Synopsis of Entozoa and some of their ectocongeners observed by the author. *Proc. Acad. Nat. Sci. Phila.*, 8:42–58, 1856.

Leidy, J.: Contributions to helminthology. *Proc. Acad. Nat. Sci.*, 10:110–112, 1858.

Leiper, R.T. and Atkinson, E.L.: Helminths of the British Antarctic Expedition 1910–1913. *Proc. Zool. Soc. London,* 1:222–226, 1914.

Leuckart, K.G.: Beschreibung Zweier Neuen Helminthen. *Arch Naturg., 14:* 26–29, 1848.

Leuckart, K.G.: *Die Menschilchen Parasiten und die von ihnen herruhrenden Krankeisen.* Ein Hand-und Lehrbuch fur Naturferscher und Aerzte. Leipzig, Heidelbert. 1863 vol. 1.

Leuckart, R.: Bericht über die wissenschaftlichen Leistungen in der Naturge-schichte der niederen Thiere während der Jahre 1872–1875. *Arch Naturg., Jahr., 40:*401–505, 1874.

Lent, H. and de Freitas, T.: Uma collecao de nematodeos, parasitos de verte-brados, do Museo de Historia Natural de Montevideo. *Mem. Inst. Osw. Cruz., 46:*1–71, 1948.

Leung, Y.M.: A Collection of whale-lice (Cyamidae: Amphipoda). *Bull. S. Calif. Acad. Sci., 64:*132–143, 1965.

Leung, Y.. An illustrated key to the species of whale-lice (Amphipoda, Cyami dae), ectoparasites of Cetacea, with a guide to the literature. *Crustaceana, 12:*279–291, 1967.

Lincicome, D.R.: Acanthocephala of the genus *Corynosoma* from the California sea lion. *J. Parasit.,* 29:102–106, 1943.

Linnaeus, C.: Systema naturae, 10th ed. Holmiae, 1758.

Lins de Almeida, J.: Nouveau nématode parasite de cétacés du Brásil, *Halo-cercus brasiliensis* n. sp. *Compt. Rend. Soc. Biol., 114:*955–958, 1933.

Linstow, O. von: Helminthologische Untersuchunge. *Arch. Naturg. (Berlin),* 46. *1:*41–54, 1880.

Linstow, O. von: Helminthen von Sud-Georgien Nach der Ausbeute der deutschen station von 1882–1883. *Jahrb. Ham. Wissensch.,* 9:59–77, 1892.

Linstow, O. von: Neue Helminthen. *Centralb Bakt., Parasit Infekt.,* Abt. 1, orig., 37:678–683, 1904.

Linstow, O. von: Helminthen aus Ceylon aund aus arktischen Breiten. *Z. Wiss. Zool., 82:*182–193, 1905.

Linstow, O. von: Nematoden aus dem Koniglichen Zoologischen Museum zu Berlin., *Mitteil. Zool. Mus. Bd.* 3, ss. 251–259, 1907a.

Linstow, O. von: *Ascaris lobulata,* Schneider, ein Parasit des Darms von *Platanista gangetica. J. Proc. Asiatic. Soc.* Bengal., 3:37–38, 1907b.

Linstow, O. von: *Pseudalius ovatus* n. sp. *Centralbl. Bakt. Parasitenk.,* Abt. I, 55:133–135, 1910.

Linton, E.: Notes on cestode cysts, *Taenia chamissonii,* new species, from a porpoise. *Proc. U.S. Nat. Mus.,* 28(1410):819–822, 1905.

Looss, A.: Beitrage zur Kenntnis der Trematoden. *Distomum palliatum* nov. spec. und *Distomum reticulatum* nov. spec. *Z. Wiss. Zool., 41:*390–446, 1885.

Lönnberg, E.: Mitteilungen über einige Helminthen aus dem zool. Museum der Universität zu Kristiania. *Biol. Fören. Forhandl., Verh. Biol. Ver., (Stock-holm),* 3:64–78, 1891.

Lönnberg, E.: Antaomische studien über Skandinavische Cestoden, II. Zwei

Parasiten aus Walfischen und zwei aus *Lamna cornubica. Kongl. Svensk. Vetensk. Akad. Hand.*, 24:1–30, 1892.

Lühe, M.: *Cestoden.* In A. Brauer Die Susswasserfauna Deutschlands. Heft. 18, 1910.

Lühe, M.: *Acanthocephalen.* In A. Brauer Die Susswasserfauna Deutschlands. Heft. 16, 1911.

Lyster, L.L.: Parasites of some Canadian sea mammals. *Canad. J. Res.*, 18:395–409, 1940.

Malm, A.W.: *Monographie Illustrée du Baleinoptere trouve le 29 Octobre 1865 sur la cote occidentale de Suede.* Stockholm, 1867.

Marchi, P.: Sopra una specie nouva di Distomum trovata nelle intestina del *Delphinus tursio. Atti Soc. Ital. Sci. Nat.*, (*Milano*), 15:304, 1873.

Margolis, L.: Parasitic Helminths and Arthropods from Pinnipedia of the Canadian Pacific Coast. *J. Fish. Res. Bd. Canada*, 13:489–505, 1956.

Margolis, L. and Pike, G.C.: Some helminth parasites of Canadian pacific whales. *J. Fish Res. Bd. Canada*, 12:97–120, 1955.

Markowski, S.: The cestodes of pinnipeds in the Arctic and other regions. *J. Helmenth.*, 26:171–214, 1952.

Mawson, P.M.: Parasitic nematoda collected by the Australian National Antarctic Research Expedition: Heard Island and Macquarie Island, 1948–1951. *Parasit.*, 43:291–297, 1953.

McIntosh, A.: New host and distribution records for the Trematoda genus *Braunina*, Heider, 1900. *J. Parasit.*, 39:31, 1953.

McIntosh, A.: A New Campulid trematode, *Hunterotrema caballeroi*, n.g., n. sp. from an Amazon dolphin, *Inia geoffrensis.* In Libro homenaje al Dr. Eduardo Caballero y Caballero, Jubile 1930–1960, Mexico D.F. (Instituto Politechnico Nacionál):207–208, 1960.

Meggitt, F.J.: *The Cestodes of Mammals.* H. Pohle, Jena-London, 1924.

Moniez, R.: Sur la larve du *Taenia grimaldii*, nov. sp., parasite du Dauphin. *Comp. Rend. Acad. Sci.*, 109:825, 1889.

Monticelli, F.S.: Note elminthologiche. *Bull. Soc. Natural. Napoli*, 4:189–208, 1890.

Montrevil, P.L.: *Corynosoma magdaleri* sp. nov. (Acanthocephala). A parasite of the gray seal in Eastern Canada. *Canad. J. Zool.*, 36:205–215, 1958.

Mozgovoi, A.A.: Askaridaty Zhivotnykh (Ascarids of Animals), USSR Thesis, 1949.

Mozgovoi, A.A.: Askaridaty mlekopitayushchikh SSSR (Anisakoidea) (Ascarids of mammals of the USSR) (Anisakoidea) *Trudy Gel'mintologicheskoi Laboratorii Akademii Nauk. SSSR*, 5:14–22, 1951.

Mozgovoi, A.A. and Ryzhikov, K.M.: Vopros o pro skhozhdenii baikal's Kogo tyulenya v suete gel'minthologicheskoi nauki. (The problem of the origin of the Baikal Seal in the light of helminthological science). *Dokiady Akademii Nauk SSSR*, 72:997–999, 1950.

Murray, M.D., Smith, M.S.R., and Soucek, Z.: Studies on the ectoparasites of seals and penguins, II. The ecology of the louse *Antarctophthrius ogmorhini*

Enderlein on the Weddell seal, *Leptonychotes weddelli* Lesson. *Aust. J. Zool.*, 13:761–771, 1965.

Muller, O.F.: *Zoologiae Danicae prodomus seu animalium Daniae et Norvegiae indigenarum characteres.* Nomina. et synonyma imprimis popularum., 1776.

Neiland, K.A.: Suspected role of parasites in non-rookery mortality of fur seals (*Callorhinus ursinus*). *J. Parasit.*, 47:732, 1961.

Neiland, K.A.: Alaskan species of acanthocephalan genus *Corynosoma* Luehe, 1904. *J. Parasit.*, 48:69–75, 1962.

Neiland, K.A., Rice, D.W., and Holden, Barbara L.: Helminths of marine mammals, Part 1. The genus *Nasitrema*, nasal-flukes of delphinid cetacea. *J. Parasit.*, 56:305–316, 1970.

Nemoto, T.: White scars on whales: I. lamprey marks. *Sci. Rep. Whales Res. Inst.*, 10:69–77, 1955.

Nemoto, T.. On the diatoms of the skin film of whales in the northern pacific. *Sci. Rep. Whales Res. Inst.*, 11:99–132, 1956.

Nemoto, T.: *Cocconeis* diatoms infected on whales in the Antarctic. *Sci. Rep. Whales Res. Inst.*, 13:185–191, 1958.

Newell, L.M.: Studies on the morphology and systematics of the family Halorachnidae Oedemans, 1906 (Acari, Parasitoidea). *Bull. Bingham Oceanogr. Coll.*, 10:235–266, 1947.

Nickol, B.B. and Holloway, H.L., Jr.: Morphology of the presoma of *Corynosoma hamanni* (Acanthocephala: Polymorphidae). *J. Morph.*, 124:217–226, 1968.

Norris, K.S. and Prescott, J.H.: Observations on Pacific cetaceans of Californian and Mexican waters. *Univ. Calif. Publ. Zool.*, 63:291–402, 1961.

Nybelin, O.: Anatomisch-systematische studien über Pseudophyllideen. *Kungl. Vetensko Vitterh. Samh. Handl.*, 26:1–228, 1922.

Nybelin, O.: Zwei neve cestoden aus Bartenwalen. *Zool. Anz.*, 78:309–314, 1928.

Nybelin, O.: Saugetiere and Vogelcestoden von Juan Fernandez. The natural history of Juan Fernandez and Easter Island. *Uppsala*, 3–4:493–523, 1931.

Odhner, T.: Die Trematoden des Arktischen Gebietes. (In *Romer and Schaudinn-Fauna Arctica*, 1905, vol. 4, part 2, Jena S. pp. 291–372.

Olfers, I.F.M.: *De vegetativis et animatis corporibus in corporibus animatis reperiundis commentarius.* Berolini, 1816.

Olsen, O.W., and Lyons, E.T.: Life cycle of *Uncinaria lucasi* Stiles, 1901 (Nematoda: Ancylostomatidae) of fur seals, *Callorhinus ursinus* Linn., on the Pribilof Islands, Alaska. *J. Parasit.*, 51:689–700, 1965.

Oudemans, A.C.: Acarologische Aantecheningen. *Ent. Ber.*, 41:311–313, 1916.

Owen, A.: Description of a microscopic entozoon infesting the muscles of the human body. *Trans. Zool. Soc. London*, 1:315–324, 1835.

Ozaki, T.: Trematode parasites of Indian porpoise *Neophocaena phocaenoides* Gray. *J. Sci. Hiroshima Univ. (Zool.)*, 3:115–138, 1935.

Perrin, W.F.: The barnacle, *Conchoderma auritum*, on a porpoise (*Stenella graffmani*). *J. Mammal.*, 50:149–151, 1969.

Perry, Mary Lou: A new species of *Dipetalonema* from the California sea lion and a report of Microfilariae from a Steller sea lion (Nematoda: Filaroidea) *J. Parasit.*, 53:1076–1081, 1967.

Pike, G.C.: Lamprey marks on whales. *J. Fish. Res. B. Canada,* 8:275–280, 1951.

Poche, F.: Das System der Platodaria. *Arch. Naturg. A.* 91(2–3), 1926.

Pourier, J.: Trematodes Nouveaux ou Peu Connus. *Bull. Soc. Philomat.,* 10:20–40, 1886.

Price, E.W.: The trematode parasites of marine mammals. *Proc. U.S. Nat. Mus.,* 81:1–68, 1932.

Quekett, J.: Anatomy of four species of entozoa of the genus *Strongylus* from the common porpoise. *Ann. Mag. Nat. Hist.,* 8:151–152, 1841.

Radford, K.W., and Klawne, W.L.: Biological observations on the whalesucker *Remilegia australis* Echeneiformes: Echeneidae. *Trans. San Diego Soc. Nat. Hist.,* 14:65–72, 1965.

Railliet, A.: Sur queques parasites rencontres a l'autopsie d'une Phoque (*Phoca vitulina* L.) *C. R. Soc. Biol.* (*Paris*), 51:128–130, 1899.

Railliet, A., and Henry, A.C.L.: *Nemathelminthes Parasites.* Expid. Antarctique Francaise (1903–1905), Vers., 1907.

Railliet, A., and Henry, A.: Helminthes Recueillis par l'expedition Antarctique Francaise du Pourquoi-Pass II. Cestodes de Phoques. *Bull. Mus.* (*Paris*), pp. 153–159, 1912.

Ransom, B.: Synopsis of the trematode family Heterophyidae with descriptions of a new genus and five new species. *Proc. U.S. Nat. Mus. Washington,* 57:527–573, 1920.

Rausch, R.: Studies on the helminth fauna of Alaska XIII. Disease in the sea otter, with special reference to helminth parasites. *Ecology,* 34:584–604, 1953.

Rausch, R.L.: Diphyllobothriid cestodes from the Hawaiian monk seal, *Monachus schauinslandi* Matschie, from Midway Atoll. *J. Fish. Res. Bd. Canada,* 26:947–956, 1969.

Rausch, R.L. and Fay, F.H.: Studies on the helminth fauna of Alaska, XLIV. Revision of *Ogmogaster* Jägerskiöld, 1891, with a description of *O. pentalineatus* sp. n. (Trematoda: Notocotylidae). *J. Parasitol.,* 52:26–38, 1966.

Rausch, R. and Locker, B.: Studies of the helminth fauna of Alaska II. On some helminths parasitic in the sea otter, *Enhydra lutris* (L). *Proc. Helm. Soc. Washington,* 18:77–81, 1951.

Rausch, R.L. and Margolis, L.: *Plicobothrium globicephalae* gen. et sp. nov. (Cestoda: Diphyllobothriidae) from the pilot whale, *Globicephaca melaena* Traill, in Newfoundland Waters. *Canad. J. Zool.,* 47:745–750, 1969.

Rees, G.: A record of some parasitic worms from whales in the Ross Sea area. *Parasitology,* 43:27–34, 1953.

Rennie, J.: 'Scotia" collections. On *Echinorhynchus antarcticus* n. sp. and its allies. *Proc. R. Soc. Edinburgh,* 26:437–446, 1907.

Renniee, J. and A. Reid: The Cestoda of the Scottish Antarctic Expedition (Scotia). *Trans. Roy. Soc. Edinburgh,* 48:441–454, 1912.

Rice, D.W.: Progress report on biological studies of the larger cetacea in the waters off California. *Norsk Hvalfangst Tid.,* 52:181–187, 1963.

Rice, D.W. and Caldwell, D.K.: Observations on the habits of the whalesucker (*Remilegia australis*). *Norsk Hvalfangst Tid.,* 50:181–189, 1961.

Rice, D.W. and Scheffer, V.B.: A list of the marine mammals of the world. U.S. Fish and Wildlife Serv., Special Scientific Rept., 579:1–16, 1968.

Ridgway, S.H. and Johnston, D.G.: Two interesting disease cases in the wild cetaceans. *Amer. J. Vet. Res.*, 26:771–775, 1965.

Ridgway, S.H.: Dall porpoise, *Phocoenoides dalli* (True): observations in captivity and at sea. *Norsk Hvalfangst Tid.*, 55:97–110, 1966.

Ross, A. and Newman, W.A.: Eocen balanidae of Florida, including a new genus and species with a unique plan of "turtle-barnacle" organization. *Amer. Mus. Nov.*, 2288:1–21, 1967.

Roth, H. and Madsen, H.: Die Trichinose in Grønland, abschliessender Bericht der Jahre 1948–1953. *Proc. 14th Int. Cong. Zool.*, Sec. X Parasit., 1953, pp. 340–341.

Rudolphi, C.A.: Fortsetzung der Beobachtungen uber die Eingeweidewurmer. *Arch. Zool. Zoot.*, 2:1 67, 1802.

Rudolphi, C.A.: *Entozoorum sive uermium intestinalium historia naturalis.* Amsteaedami 1809, vol. 1.

Rudolphi, C.A.: *Entozoorum synopsis cui accedunt mantissa duplex et indices locupltissimi.* Berolini, 1819.

Shchupakov, I.G.: [Parasitic fauna of the Caspian Seal] (Russian text). *Uchen. Zapiski Leningr. Gasudarstv. Univ. Bubnov* (7) *s. Biol.*, 3:134–143, 1936.

Schiller, E.I.: Studies on the helminth fauna of Alaska, XVII. Notes on the intermediate stages of some helminth parasites of the sea otter. *Biol. Bull.*, 106:107–121, 1954.

Schneider, A.: *Monographie der Nematoden.* Berlin, 1866.

Schryver, H.F., Medway, W., and Williams, J.F.: The stomach fluke *Braunina cordiformis* in the Atlantic bottlenose dolphin. *J. Amer. Vet. Med. Ass.*, 151: 884–886, 1967.

Scott, D.M. and Fisher, H.D.: Incidence of a parasitic ascarid *Porrocaecum decipiens*, in the common porpoise *Phocoena phocoena*, from the lower Bay of Fundy. *J. Fish. Res. Bd. Canada*, 15:1–4, 1958.

Shipley, A.E.: Cestodes (*National Antarctic Expedition 1901–1904*). *Nat. Hist.*, vol. 3, Zool. and Bot., 1907.

Siebold, C. and Stannius: Lehrbuch der vergleichenden Anatomie. Bd. 2, Berlin, 1848.

Skrjabin, K.I.: *Odheriella rossica*, n.g., n. sp. Vosbuditel' pechenochnoglistnoi bolezni morzhei (*Odhneriella rossica* n.g. n. sp., an agent of worm liver diseases in walruses. *Arkhiv veterinarnykh*, 45:1058–1064, 1915.

Skrjabin, K.I.: *Kutassicaulus* n.g., nouveau representant des Nematodes de la sousfamille des Dictyocaulinae Skrjabin, 1933. *Ann. Parasitol.*, 2:359–363, 1933.

Skrjabin, K.I.: The ways of the phylogenetic evolution of nematodes of the family Pseudaliidae, parasitic of the auditory apparatus, circulatory system and respiratory organs of marine mammals. *Dokl. Akad. Nauk. USSR.*, 37: 35–40, 1942.

Skrjabin, K.I.: *Oschmarienella sobolevi* n.g., n. sp.—New trematode from the liver of the whale. *Dokl. Adad Nauk. USSR*, 57:857–859, 1947.

Skrjabin, K.I. and Andreeva, N.K.: Un nouveau Nematode *Crassicauda giliakiana* n. sp. Trouve dan les Reins de *Delphinaptera leucas. Ann. de Parasit.*, 12: 15–28, 1934.

Skryabin, A.S.: (*Crassicauda delamureana* n. sp., a parasite of the Sei Whale.) (In Russian). Kraeuaya Parazitologiya i Prirodnoy. Ochagovast Transmissivnykh Boleznei. "Nauka Dumka" Kiev., 1966.

Sokoloff, D. and Caballero, E.: Una nueva especie de trematodo parasito del intestino del manati. *Ann., Inst. Biol., Universidad Nacional*, Mexico City, 2:163–167, 1932.

Spaul, E.A.: *Crassicauda bennetti*, sp. n., a new nematode parasite from the bottlenosed whale (*Hyperoodon*). *Ann. Mag. Nat. Hist.*, 17:581–584, 1926.

Stiles, C.W.: Uncinariosis (anchylostomiasis) in man and animals in the United States. *Texas Med. News*, 10:523–532, 1901.

Stiles, C.W. and Hassall, A.: Notes on parasites. 42 *Veterin. Mag.*, 3:6–9, 1896.

Stiles, C.W. and Hassall, A.: Internal parasites of the fur seal, *In* Jordan, D. S., *et al.: The Fur Seal and Fur Seal Islands of the North Pacific Ocean, Washington.* 1899, part 3, pp. 99–177.

Stiles, C.W. and Hassall, A.: Index catalogue of medical and veterinary zoology subjects: Cestoda and Cestodaria—U.S. Pub. Health and Mar. Hosp. Sever. *Hyg. Lab. Bull.*, 85:467, 1912.

Stunkard, H.W.: Pseudophyllidian cestodes from Alaskan pinnipedia. *J. Parasit.*, 34:211–228, 1948.

Stunkard, H.W. and Alvey, C.H.: A new liver fluke, *Zalophotrema hepaticum*, from the California sea lion *Zalophus californianus. J. Parasit.*, 16:106–107, 1929.

Sudarikov, V. E. and Ryzhikov, K.M.: [On the biology of *Contracaecum osculatum baicalensis*—Nematode from *Phoca sibirica*] (Russian text). *Trudy Gel'-mint. Lab., Akad. Nauk. USSR.*, 5:59–66, 1951).

Taylor, A.L.R., Brown, D.H., Heyneman, D., and McIntyre, R.W.: Biology of filaroid nematode *Dipetalonema spiracauda* (Leidy, 1858) from the heart of captive harbor seals and sea lions, together with pathology of the hosts. *J. Parasit.*, 47:971–976, 1961.

Tomilin, A.G.: Mammals of the U.S.S.R. and adjacent countries (1957). Jerusalem, Israel Program for Scientific Translations, 9:1–717, 1967.

Travassos, L. and Vogelsang, E.: Novo tipo de Trematodeo Opisthotrematidae. *Bol. Biol.*, Rio de Janeiro, 19:143–147, 1931.

Treshchev, V.V.: (A new trematode *Orthosplanchnus sudarikovi* nov. sp. (Campuldae) from the beluga) (In Russian.) Mat. K. Nauch. Konf. Vsesoyoir. Ob-va Gel'minthol. 3 *Izdat. Akad. Nauk.* USSR, Moscow (1966).

Treshchev, V.V.: (The new campulid *Orthosplanchnus albamarinus* sp. n. (Trematoda, Campulidae)—parasite of the white whale). *Zool. Zhur.*, 47:937–940, (In Russian, English summary), 1968.

Trouessart, E.L. and Neumann, L.G.: Le pou de l'otaire (*Echinophthirius microchir* n. sp.) *Le Naturaliste*, An. 10, S2, 2:80–81, 1888.

Tubb, J.A.: Archnida. In Reports of the McCoy Society, Lady Julia Percy Island. *Proc. Roy Soc. Vict.*, 49:412–419, 1937.

Van Cleave, H.J.: Acanthocephala of North American mammals. *Illinois Biol. Monogr.*, 23:1–179, 1953.

Van Thiel, P.H.: The final hosts of the herringworm *Anisakis marina*. *Trop. Geogr. Med.*, 18:310–328, 1966.

Wardle, R.A., McLeod, J.A., and Stewart, I.E.: Lühe's "Dipyllobothrium" (Cestoda). *J. Parasit.*, 33:319–330, 1947.

Williams, H.H.: The taxonomy, ecology and host specificity of some phyllobothriidae (Cestoda: Tetraphyllidea), a critical revision of *Phyllobothrium*, Beneden, 1849 and comments on some allied genera. *Phil. Trans. Royal Soc. London, Series B, Biol. Sci.*, 253:231–307, 1968.

Wolf, K.: Beitrage zur kenntnis der Gattung *Braunina* Heider. *Sitz. Ber. Akad. Wiss. Wien, Bd.*, 112:603–626, 1903.

Wu, H.W.: On *Halocercus pingi*, n. sp. a lung-worm from the Porpoise, *Neomeris phocoenoides*. *J. Parasit.*, 15:276–279, 1929.

Yamaguti, S.: Studies on the helminth fauna of Japan. Part I, Trematodes of birds, Reptiles and mammals. *Jap. J. Zool.*, 5:1–134, 1933.

Yamaguti, S.: Studies of the helminth fauna of Japan. Part 29. Acanthocephala II. *Jap. J. Zool.*, 8:317–351, 1939.

Yamaguti, S.: Studies on the helminth fauna of Japan Part 40. Three new species of trematodes from the bile ducts of marine mammals. *Trans. Biogeog. Soc. Japan.*, 3:399–407, 1942.

Yamaguti, S.: Studies on the helminth fauna of Japan. Part 45. Trematodes of marine mammals. *Arb. Med. Fak. Okayama*, 7:283–294, 1951.

Yamaguti, S.: Studies on the helminth fauna of Japan. Part 46. Nematodes of marine mammals. *Arb. Med. Fak. Okayama*, 7:295–306, 1951.

Yamaguti, S.: *Systema Helminthum Vol. III*. Part I. Nematodes. Interscience, 1961.

Yamaguti, S.: *Systema Helminthum Vol. V*. Acanthocephala. Interscience, 1963.

Yokogawa, M. and Yoshimura, H.: Clinicopathological studies on larval anisakiasis in Japan. *Amer. J. Trop. Med. Hyg.*, 16:723–728, 1967.

Yurakhno, M.V.: *Microphallus orientalis* n. sp. (Trematoda: Microphallidae), a parasite of the Pacific walrus and bearded seal.) *Zool. Zh.*, 77:630–631, 1968.

Zschokke, F.: Die Arktischen cestoden in Romer und Schaudinn, *Fauna Arctica*, 3:1–32, 1903.

Chapter 10

HOMEOSTASIS IN THE AQUATIC ENVIRONMENT

Sam H. Ridgway

Marine mammals have made many interesting and important physiological adjustments in adapting to aquatic life. Numerous anatomical variations reflect changes that have occurred in mammalian respiratory function, thermoregulation, circulation, renal physiology, and neural mechanisms. There is a striking degree of integration in the physiological modifications that marine mammals have achieved. Different species often have achieved these adjustments in diverse ways, depending upon the specific ecological demands made upon them. All of these specialized aquatic adaptations must be considered by anyone who wishes to work with this group of mammals. Homeostatic mechanisms must have consideration in the clinical management of the various aquatic species. As Robin (1966) points out, "comparative physiology on the one hand and clinical medicine on the other constitute a broad two-way street. Each discipline is capable of making important contributions to the other because there is a basic unity among living forms."

BACKGROUND

Over twenty centuries ago, Aristotle recognized that dolphins were mammals and that they were much better suited for the marine environment than their land-dwelling counterparts. Galileo Galilei (1603), the founder of experimental physics and astronomy, reasoned that whales were not affected by gravity in quite the same way as terrestrial mammals. He theorized that their relative weightlessness in the aquatic environment made them exempt from the law of skeletal scaling which to a great extent limits the size of mammals on land. Little additional progress on the physiology of weightlessness as it applies to marine mammals has been made since Galileo's day! Paul Bert (1870) made the first solid contribution to the diving physiology of the vertebrates. Richet (1899) and

590

Bohr (1897) also concerned themselves with diving mechanisms of vertebrates.

The classical work of Irving and Scholander in the 1930's and 1940's
defined many of the physiological capabilities that enable marine mammals
to dive for prolonged periods. There appears to be a continuum in the
degree of adaptation, beginning with the nondiving mammals, progressing
to semiaquatic divers such as beavers, muskrats, and trained humans, and
culminating with the champions of all, the sperm and bottlenosed whales.

RESPIRATION

Respiratory Rate

Resting respiratory rate among marine mammals varies according to
body size, metabolic rate, and degree of aquatic adaptation. Table 10–1
summarizes some of the available data on respiratory rates in marine mammals. Because they must have considerable three-dimensional freedom in
the aquatic environment, these mammals have evolved an apneustic plateau.
As with almost all aquatic adaptations, this feature is most pronounced in
cetaceans. Porpoises breathe two to three times per minutes or less. Lawrence and Schevill (1956) have shown that *Tursiops truncatus* can blow
(expiration and inspiration) in 0.3 seconds. With a tidal volume of 5 to
10 L, the flow rates through the air passages would range from about 30
to 70 L per second during the breath. Thus, when leisurely swimming on
the surface, the animal exhales and inhales in a fraction of a second and
then holds its breath for the 20 to 30 sec apneustic period. The muscles
that control the blowhole act primarily in contracting to open the orifice;

TABLE 10–1
RESTING RESPIRATORY RATES IN SOME MARINE MAMMALS

Species	No. of Animals	Avg. Wt. (kg)	RR/Min	Reference
Fin whale, *Balaenoptera physalus*	. . .	. . .	1–2	Scholander (1940)
Bottlenosed whale, *Hyperoodon rostratus*	. . .		1–2	Scholander (1940)
Killer whale, *Orcinus orca*	2	2,100	0.8	*
Bottlenosed porpoise, *Tursiops truncatus*	10	150	2.2	*
Bottlenosed porpoise, *Tursiops truncatus*	. . .	. . .	1.0	Irving, *et al.* (1941)
Common dolphin, *Delphinus sp.*	2	68	3.4	*
White-striped dolphin, *Lagenorhynchus obliquidens*	4	85	3.2	*
Harbor porpoise, *Phocoena phocoena*	. . .	. . .	2–4	Scholander (1940)
Dall porpoise, *Phocoenoides dalli*	3	110	3.1	*
Amazon dolphin, *Inia geoffrensis*	2	60	1.0	*
Harbor seal, *Phoca vitulina*	1	39	3.6	*
Elephant seal, *Mirounga angustirostris*	1 (young)	100	3.0	*
California sea lion, *Zalophus californianus*	5 (young)	50	6.0	*
Manatee, *Trichechus manatus*	. . .	. . .	1.0	Scholander (1940)
Man *Homo sapiens*	. . .	. . .	15.0	

* Data gathered by the author at the NUC, Marine Bioscience Facility, Point Mugu, California.

thus the nasal plug and blowhole are in a closed position except when opened by muscular action. The vestibular and tubular sacs that relate directly to the nares also contribute to sealing the respiratory passage between breaths.

Even when hauled out on land, the elephant seal will take several breaths in fairly rapid succession and then hold for three to twenty minutes before repeating the process. As mentioned in Chapter 1, the larger whales usually blow several times while swimming near the surface and then make a longer and usually deeper dive for several minutes. In general, it may be said that marine mammals have developed a style of breathing that allows them the most freedom in their environment, permits them to take more oxygen from the air that they breathe, and enables them to conserve water and body heat that might be lost with a more rapid turnover of lung air (Coulombe *et al.*, 1965). Thus, respiratory rate can be taken as a prime example of the remarkable degree of integration of the physiological adjustments achieved in aquatic adaptation.

Mechanics of Breathing

As mentioned previously, most marine mammals breathe less frequently than their terrestrial counterparts. In order to compensate, they take "deeper" breaths and take more oxygen from the air that they breathe. Irving *et al.* (1940) found 80 percent tidal air in bottlenosed porpoises, and Olsen *et al.* (1969a, b) found up to 88 percent air in the pilot whale. Olsen *et al.* also determined that the whale, like man, inspires actively and expires passively. The elastic recoil of the inflated lungs and the diaphragm facilitate the almost complete emptying of the lungs. The large amount of elastic tissue of the lungs (Chap. 5) is probably a manifestation of this adaptation.

Although their expiration is normally passive, all marine mammals with which I have worked are quite capable of forced exhalation. This is especially apparent in the "snorting" behavior of porpoises and whales. In addition, awake porpoises with an endotracheal tube in place often manifest "tube bucking" in which they may exert 60 mm Hg or more pressure against the respirator.

Between the alveoli and major bronchi of many marine mammals there is a series of sphincters that can segment the lower bronchi into compartments (see Chap. 5). The function of these sphincters is not completely clear. When porpoises die in the water, histological examination often reveals many of these sphincters to be closed. In one case where a healthy *Tursiops truncatus* was caught in a net underwater and drowned, the number of closed sphincters that could be seen in histological sections was particularly impressive. This was also observed after a trained porpoise performing in an oceanarium suffered a severe head injury and died in the water (see Chap. 5, Fig. 5–29).

In the bottlenosed porpoise, the expired breath may contain as little as 1.5 percent oxygen after prolonged breathholds (Ridgway and Kanwisher, 1969). In order to achieve such a low value for the entire breath, even though porpoises have a relatively small dead space, some mixing of lung air must occur during the apneustic plateau. These smooth muscle sphincters may serve to promote circulation of gas in the periphery of the respiratory tree. The smooth muscle may also function in limiting the amount of residual air in the lungs at the end of exhalation.

The early proposal by Feibiger (1916) that the sphincters served to trap air in the alveoli during deep dives has been shown to be incorrect (Ridgway *et al.*, 1969).

During deep dives, these sphincters may function to reduce the passage of nitrogen into the blood. As the animal dives, alveolar collapse probably occurs at a depth of about 100 m as a result of hydrostatic pressure (Figs. 10–1a, b). The sphincters may close during the deeper part of the dive and remain closed during much of the ascent. Thus, the peripheral bronchi would be segmented into a series of small compartments and conversely into a series of small pressure gradients, which together would make a large pressure gradient between the central airways and the alveoli (Goudappel and Slijper, 1958). This would further reduce the amount of nitrogen entering the bloodstream during a dive.

The larger whales that are thought to be very deep divers, such as Baird's beaked whale, lack the bronchial sphincters (Murata, 1951). The sphincters are, however, replaced by extensive and continuous smooth muscle lining of the peripheral bronchioles. In seals, a similar situation exists, and there is a long alveolar duct with an extensive smooth muscle lining.

Diving on Inhalation or Exhalation

My observation has been that elephant and harbor seals always dive after exhalation. Other true seals, such as Weddell seals, also dive after exhalation (Kooyman, 1966). California sea lions usually dive on at least partial inspiration but may vent air on the way down. Bottlenosed porpoises dive with lungs full of air. The simplest explanation for this difference in diving habits is probably specific gravity. Cetaceans have no body hair coat or fur, and bottlenosed porpoises have an average of about 18.5 percent of body weight as fat (an amount very similar to that of the large rorquals and of *Homo sapiens*). On full inspiration, a bottlenosed porpoise has approximately neutral buoyancy. Elephant seals and harbor seals, on

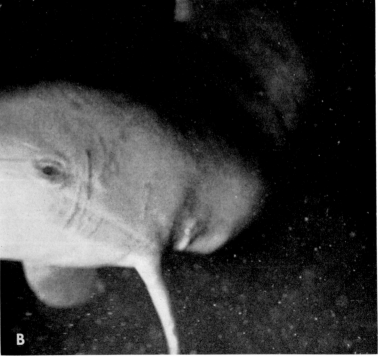

Figure 10–1A. Photograph of Tuffy at 300 m. The picture was taken as the porpoise pushed the plunger of a deep diving test switch located at the end of a cable. B. Side view of Tuffy at 300 m. Thoracic collapse is quite apparent in the area behind the left flipper. The photograph was reproduced with the permission of *Science*. (Official U.S. Navy Photo by Naval Missile Center underwater photographic unit.)

the other hand, must exhale a goodly portion (the amount depends upon how fat the seal is) of their lung air to attain neutral buoyancy. California sea lions appear to fall somewhere in between. Some cetaceans with exceedingly high percentages of body fat, such as the Greenland right whale, may also dive on exhalation, but I have no firsthand knowledge of their diving behavior. Many other factors, including cardiovascular anatomy, pulmonary structure, blood volume, and metabolic rate, may also be involved.

Lung Air and Diving

Scholander (1940) pointed out that the deeper-diving whales have relatively smaller lungs and that marine mammals in general have lungs no larger than other mammals. This would seem to emphasize the minimal role played by lung air in prolonged diving. Lung air is apparently of little importance as an oxygen supply during diving in the elephant seal. A seal in our laboratory was trained to completely submerge on command and then exhale into an inverted underwater collecting funnel at the end of a prescribed period of time (Fig. 10–2). Analysis of respiratory gas

Figure 10–2. The elephant seal holds its breath for a period prescribed by the trainer and then exhales into the inverted funnel. Expired air is collected in the syringe that the trainer is holding in his hand.

(Table 10–2) indicates that the elephant seal uses very little of the oxygen in the lung air after the first minute of submersion. Ferrante (1970) found in another diving mammal, the nutria, that the rate of decline of the partial pressure of oxygen in arterial blood (PaO_2) during the first minute of a dive was much greater than during the remainder of the period of submersion. Elsner *et al.* (1964b) showed that the elephant seal relies at least partially on blood oxygen stored during prolonged dives. The extremely large blood volume of the elephant seal, about 20 percent of body weight (Simpson *et al.*, 1970), and high hematocrit appear to give this seal an extraordinary capability for blood oxygen storage.

TABLE 10–2
EXHALED AIR CONTENT FROM A NORTHERN ELEPHANT SEAL
AFTER SUBMERGED BREATHHOLDS*

	20 sec	*40 sec*	*60 sec*	*180 sec*	*360 sec*	*600 sec+*
O_2	11.8 ± 2.1	9.9 ± 2.5	10.3 ± 1.6	7.4 ± 1.6	6.0 ± 1.2	5.3 ± 0.2
CO_2	5.7 ± 0.7	5.9 ± 0.4	5.6 ± 0.7	5.9 ± 0.7	6.2 ± 0.5	5.5 ± 0.6

* The 600 sec.+ column represents submersion of 10 to 13 minutes. Each column represents values for at least 12 breathholds.

The bottlenosed porpoise has a metabolic rate considerably higher than that of the elephant seal. Pulmonary oxygen is apparently somewhat more important, but even in this case, pulmonary oxygen is not utilized during the deeper part of deep dives. Damant (1934) and Scholander (1940) hypothesized that alveolar collapse would occur at about 100 m depth and that no pulmonary respiratory exchange occurs below that depth. Recent experiments (Ridgway *et al.*, 1969) employing a trained porpoise in the open ocean have substantiated this earlier hypothesis.

Deep-Diving Adjustments

As ambient pressure increases, air within the animal is compressed in accordance with Boyle's law. These four aquatic adaptations, therefore, appear to be of primary importance for deep diving: (a) flexible thoracic structure that allows the thorax to collapse as the hydrostatic pressure increases, (b) large distensible veins, venous sinuses, and *retia mirabilia* that can engorge with blood and fill space as air is compressed, (c) lungs that contain large amounts of elastic tissue (see Chap. 5), allowing them to become atelectic without separating from the chest wall, and (d) a resilient trachea (bottlenosed porpoise, Ridgway, 1968; Weddell seal, Kooyman, 1969) that allows the respiratory passages to collapse beyond the limits of the sea-level dead-space volume. The degree of development of these characteristics varies from species to species, depending upon the ecological need for deep diving. Among the deeper-diving animals, there is also variation in the degree of development of individual characteristics. The beaked whales, for example, appear to have a somewhat more rigid thoracic structure but a greater degree of development of expansible vasculature in the thorax. This is but one example among many of how evolution has solved the same problem in different ways.

CARDIOVASCULAR ADJUSTMENTS

Bradycardia

Bradycardia is the most frequently mentioned and well documented cardiovascular response of diving aquatic animals. Seals manifest the most profound bradycardia. It has a rapid onset during which the heart rate falls to 10 percent of the predive rate (Scholander, 1940). In most cetaceans, the diving bradycardia is not as intense (Table 10–3). Elsner *et al.* (1964a) demonstrated that bradycardia was more pronounced when a sea lion was forced to dive than when it was trained to immerse its head in a pail of water and that cardiac output, as well as heart rate, decreased during immersion. Blood pressure in the central arteries of the seal (*Phoca vitulina*) remained almost constant during the profound bradycardia of an experimental dive (Irving *et al.*, 1942).

Just what triggers the bradycardia in marine mammals is not clear. Immersion in water causes a bradycardia (to about 50 percent of the resting rate) of gradual onset in some human subjects (Craig, 1963). The bradycardia in man is more pronounced when the subject is in water than when he is breathholding in air (Hong *et al.*, 1967). The bradycardia is

TABLE 10–3
BRADYCARDIA OBSERVED IN SOME AQUATIC MAMMALS

1. Beaver	75–90	10	Irving and Orr (1961)
2. Nutria	115–180	10–30	Ferrante (1970)
3. Hippopotamus	100	10–20	Elsner (1966)
4. Seal	100–150	10	Scholander (1940)
(*Halichoerus grypus* and *Cystophora cristata*)			
5. Sea Lion	95	20	*
(*Zalophus californianus*)			
6. Beluga	100	12–20	King *et al.* (1953)
(*Delphinapterus leucas*)			
7. Killer whale	60	30	Spencer *et al.* (1967)
(*Orcinus orca*)			
8. Pacific bottlenosed porpoise	90	12–20	Elsner *et al.* (1966)
(*Tursiops gilli*)			
9. Atlantic bottlenosed porpoise	100	50	Irving *et al.* (1941)
(*Tursiops truncatus*)	90	35	*
10. Dall porpoise	120	15	**
(*Phocoenoides* dalli)			

The first column gives the average values prior to the breathhold and the second column gives the bradycardia rates.
* Author's personal observations.
** Out of water.

just as pronounced when a porpoise is out of the water, provided the animal is not highly excited.

Whayne and Killip (1967) implicated temperature as the primary factor in man and stated that the colder the facial stimulus, the more intense the depression in heart rate. The application of a wet towel to the subject's face caused bradycardia (Brick, 1966; Harding *et al.*, 1965).

Increasing the venous return to the heart will cause bradycardia in man. This can be produced by tilting the head downward, by elevating the feet, by vertical immersion (standing) in water, and by Valsalva's maneuver (Craig, 1963). It has been suggested that bradycardia is reflexly initiated by distention of stretch receptors in the atrial walls (Harding *et al.*, 1965).

Anderson (1966) has identified the ophthalmic branch of the trigeminal nerve as the afferent nerve pathway for initiation of bradycardia in the duck. Harrison and Tomlinson (1963) observed that grasping the seal's muzzle with the hand and clamping the nostrils was sufficient to produce bradycardia and that the efferent portion of the bradycardia reflex is mediated by the vagus nerve. Atropine abolishes the diving bradycardia in the seal (Murdaugh *et al.*, 1961a).

Heart rate and respiration are very intimately associated in marine mammals. The heart rate of bottlenosed porpoises increases just after inspiration to a rate of 70 to 100 per minute whether they are swimming or resting on a mat out of the water. As the apneustic plateau continues, the heart rate falls to 30 to 40 per minute and remains at this rate until the next breath, regardless of whether the breathhold (apneustic plateau) lasts for twenty seconds or four minutes. Thus, when a porpoise is breathing normally at two or three respirations per minute, the heart manifests a normal respiratory arrhythmia. The rate rises on inspiration and slows during the apneustic plateau. I have noted this respiratory arrhythmia in every cetacean species with which I have worked, including *Orcinus orca, Globicephala scammoni, Lagenorhynchus obliquidens, Phocoenoides dalli, Delphinus sp., Inia geoffrensis,* and *Tursiops gilli.* Kanwisher and Sundness (1965) reported this in *Phocoena phocoena.*

During prolonged breathholds, the heart usually slows only to the same basal rate as between normal breaths but beats more rapidly when the animal inspires. In this case, the heart rate remains rapid until the respiratory rate returns to normal.

A free-swimming bottlenosed dolphin with telemetry gear on its harness (Fig. 10–3) had a heart beat of 80 to 90 per minute just after blowing. This slowed in a few seconds to 33 to 45 beats per minute and remained at this rate until the next blow, immediately after which the tachycardia appeared again (Ridgway and Kanwisher, 1969). Longer breathholds did not cause a more profound bradycardia. The heart rate seemed to fall to a

Figure 10–3. Acoustic telemetry gear was attached to the dolphin by a harness. Data could be telemetered from the animal while it was swimming in a tank or in the open ocean.

basal level and remain there until the next blow. The longer the breathhold, however, the more pronounced the tachycardia that followed, and the heart rate stayed higher for a longer period of time. Expired air collected after experimental breathhold dives (Fig. 10–4) showed that the tachycardia persisted until the exhaled carbon dioxide level had returned to normal. Thus, after a long breathhold, the respiratory rate increases to five times the resting rate (or more), and the heart rate increases from the diving bradycardia rate of about 35/min to about 150/min and remains high until the excess carbon dioxide is blown off.

The elephant seal prefers to breathe several times in succession and then hold the breath for several minutes. Again, the heart rate is rapid during breathing and slows rapidly as the long breathhold begins. Resting sea lions have a similar pattern, but their apneustic periods are relatively short and generally more like that of porpoises than of elephant seals.

The normal respiratory cardiac arrhythmia is obliterated whenever a porpoise or sea lion is under anesthesia. In the well-ventilated, anesthetized porpoise or sea lion, the heart rate is extremely regular. If the patient is made apneic, however, a bradycardia of slow onset is manifested. The heart rate gets slower and slower until oxygen is administered and the heart rate recovers. The anesthetized porpoise or sea lion appears to be only slightly more resistant to anoxia than land mammals. This further

Figure 10–4. The porpoise holds his breath underwater for a prescribed period and then blows in the funnel.

suggests that central mechanisms are important in the diving responses of marine mammals.

The bradycardia of the anesthetized, hypoxic marine mammal appears to be analogous to the general responses to anoxia that can be demonstrated in most mammals. Bradycardia of the awake aquatic mammal has its onset before the animal becomes hypoxic. Therefore, the bradycardia observed is more than just a simple response to hypoxia.

Bottlenosed porpoises have large, well-developed eustachian tubes (Fig. 10–5) that lead from the nares into the middle-ear cavity. Often I have noted swallowing-like movement of the larynx and gular musculature just after inspiration. This movement could be related to something like Valsalva's maneuver which might serve to trigger bradycardia. At any rate, it is clear that we still do not understand the control mechanisms for various "diving reflexes" including bradycardia.

Peripheral Vasoconstriction

It has been shown that during a dive the heart rate slows and the cardiac output declines but the mean arterial blood pressure in central vessels appears to remain about the same (Irving *et al.*, 1942). Scholander (1940) noted that the lactic acid concentration in the blood of seals remained constant during a dive but increased rapidly when breathing resumed. Irving (1938) used a hot wire flowmeter in several animals, including the beaver and muskrat, to show that during asphyxia the blood flow to the muscle decreased and the blood flow to the brain increased. Scholander *et al.* (1942) observed that muscle oxygen was depleted faster than oxygen in the circulating blood. Thus, it appears that peripheral vessels and muscle are effectively isolated from the central circulation during a dive. In fact, Scholander (1940) found that incisions made in a seal's muscle during submersion would not bleed but such incisions bled profusely when the seal was breathing.

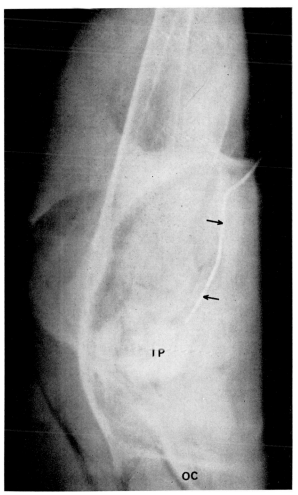

Figure 10–5. Radiograph showing path of the eustachean tube (arrows) from the nares to the tympanoperodic bone (TP). (OC) Occipital condyle.

Irving *et al.* (1942) observed that the blood pressure in the femoral artery of a seal remained constant, but the pressure in a toe artery decreased during submersion. This indicates that the peripheral vasoconstriction is quite widespread and involves vessels much larger than capillaries.

Pronounced peripheral vasoconstriction would seem to be a great advantage not only as an oxygen-conserving mechanism but for thermoregulation during dives. The seawater is generally much colder at depth than near the surface. This marked peripheral vasoconstriction would conserve considerable heat and the peripheral tissues might cool, slightly reducing their oxygen consumption.

Redistribution of Blood Flow

In spite of the profound bradycardia and marked peripheral vasoconstriction, it would appear that continuous perfusion of the brain and heart is essential. R. H. Burne (1909) was probably the first to suggest that diving mammals might be capable of preferentially shunting blood to certain vital organs during submersion and employing vasoconstriction to reduce or completely interrupt the blood supply to tissues less sensitive to temporary oxygen deprivation. Irving (1934, 1938) and Scholander (1940, 1962, 1963) have expanded this hypothesis and furnished a great deal of experimental evidence in its support.

Many early anatomists cited by Harrison (1968) mentioned the bulbous dilatation in the ascending aorta of seals. Elsner *et al.* (1966) noted the presence of this enlargement in several species of cetaceans and pinnipeds. In every marine mammal that I have dissected or necropsied, this enlargement has been present just distal to the left ventricle. Harrison and Kooyman (1968) suggest that this elastic bulb may help to maintain diastolic arterial pressure and would certainly assist in coronary blood flow. The blood vessel walls must be highly elastic in order to pump blood against a tightly constricted arterial network. This "natural aneurysm" should, in effect, act as a passive heart to help insure circulation during the prolonged diastolic period (Strauss, 1969).

The caval sphincter was mentioned in Chapter 4. Most marine mammals have some sort of anatomical arrangement in the vena cava at the level of the diaphragm that is capable of interrupting, to a varying extent, the blood flow through that vessel. The caval sphincter is best developed in Ross seals and elephant seals (Harrison and Tomlinson, 1956). The large posterior vena cava and hepatic sinus form a sizable blood reservoir. The caval sphincter and the large venous sinuses may play a role in preventing fluid overload of the heart during diving. They may also help to displace some of the thoracic volume as the lungs are compressed during a deep dive. Elsner *et al.* (1964a) suggested that blood in the caval reservoir is a major oxygen storage depot during prolonged submersion. These investigators observed that in the elephant seal the oxygen concentration fell more rapidly in the arteries than in the veins, and in the latter part of the dive the blood of the caval reservoir had a higher oxygen concentration than that in the arterial system.

Neurohumoral Control During Submersion

The profound vasoconstriction and selective blood flow redistribution are evidently quite necessary for enabling the animal to remain submerged for prolonged periods. This leaves many questions, however, regarding neurohumoral control. What happens to adrenal function, renal activity, and digestion during a prolonged dive?

It has been demonstrated that the kidneys are effectively isolated from circulation during prolonged submersion (Murdaugh *et al.*, 1961b). There appears to be a definite possibility that the adrenal circulation is also compromised. To compensate, aquatic mammals may have developed a more active central nervous control for implementation during dives. The rich nerve supply to the thoracic rete (Fig. 5–47) may be a manifestation of such an adjustment. The effects of the various diving adjustments on liver function, digestion, and the gastrointestinal tract have not been studied.

OXYGEN STORES

It has long been recognized that the oxygen stores in blood and muscle of marine mammals are not sufficient to maintain a long dive. However, when compared with terrestrial animals, most species have increased oxygen transport and storage capabilities.

Respiratory Properties of the Blood

VOLUME

A relatively larger blood volume was one of the first aquatic adaptations that was noticed. Bert (1870) found that the blood volume was greater in ducks than in hens. Later, Bohr (1897) found the blood volume of the guillemot and the puffin to be greater than that of nondiving birds. Many subsequent investigators have reported high blood volumes in various diving mammals. Some of the results are listed in Table 10–4.

TABLE 10–4

BLOOD VOLUME IN VARIOUS MARINE MAMMALS

	% Blood Volume	Maximum Submersion	Hct	Hb	Technique	Reference
Bottlenose dolphin *Tursiops truncatus*	7–9	6 min	44	14.8	131I dilution	Ridgway and Johnston (1966) Ridgway et al. (1970)
Pacific white-striped dolphin *Lagenorhynchus obliquidens*	10–11	6 min or less	53	18.0	131I dilution	Ridgway and Johnston (1966)
Dall porpoise *Phocoenoides dalli*	14–15	8 min	57	20.0	131I dilution	Ridgway and Johnston (1966)
Harbor seal *Phoca vitulina*	11 18	23 min	54	18.5 16.0	Dye dilution 131I dilution	Harrison and Tomlinson (1956) Wasserman and MacKenzie (1957?)
California sea lion *Zalophus californianus*	12–13	20 min	49		131I dilution	**
Elephant seal (young) *Mirounga angustirostris*	19–20	35 min	64	21.2	131I dilution and Evans blue dye	Simpson et al. (1970)
Elephant seal (adult) *Mirounga angustirostris*	12	45 min +			Bleed out and oxygen capacity	Elsner (1964b)
Elephant seal (adult) *Mirounga leonina*	16				Bleed out	Bryden and Lim (1969)
Hooded seal *Cystophora cristata*	15	20 min			Bleed out and estimate	Scholander (1940)
Killer whale *Orcinus orca*	8–10	15 min	45	16.2	131I dilution	**
Weddell seal *Leptonychotes weddelli*	15	55 min	57	20.8	51Cr tagged cell dilution	Lenfant et al. (1969)

* Compared to observed submersion times, hematocrit, and hemoglobin concentration.
** Unpublished observations made at the Navy Marine Bioscience Facility.

RED BLOOD CELLS AND HEMOGLOBIN

Early investigators reported relatively large sizes for cetacean red blood cells, but more recent studies have revealed smaller cell sizes (Tables 10–5, 10–6). There is still little good hematological data on the very large cetaceans, but information has been developing quite rapidly on those up to the size of the killer whales that are being kept at oceanariums and research laboratories. In our studies at the Marine Bioscience Facility, we have found no real correlation between size of the animal and red blood cell (RBC) diameter. The mean corpuscular volume (MCV) is relatively high, usually over $100\mu^3$. In terrestrial mammals, the MCV is usually less than 100. This suggests that the RBC in marine mammals is slightly different in shape. Whereas the human and canine RBC is disc shaped and somewhat thinner in the center than around the edges, the marine mammalian RBC may be more pronounced in the direction of a fatter periphery, giving it the shape of a doughnut with the thin part of the cell replacing the hole. The erythrocytes of porpoises also appear to be slightly more fragile than those of most other mammals (Ridgway *et al.*, 1970).

TABLE 10–5
RED BLOOD CELL MEASURES IN SOME CETACEANS*

N	Diameter (Microns) Mean ± SD	N	RBC Count ($10^6/mm^3$) Mean ± SD	N	PCV (HCT) (%) Mean ± SD	N	Hemoglobin (Gm/100 ml) Mean ± SD
			Ten ♂ *Tursiops truncatus*				
130	7.1 ± 0.2	134	4.14 ± 0.5	180	45 ± 4	141	15.2 ± 1.5
			Eleven ♀ *Tursiops truncatus*				
150	7.2 ± 0.2	157	3.97 ± 0.4	165	43 ± 4	155	14.4 ± 1.4
			Three ♂ *Lagenorhynchus obliquidens*				
31	6.6 ± 0.1	33	5.31 ± 0.5	46	50 ± 5	40	17.8 ± 1.6
			Two ♀ *Lagenorhynchus obliquidens*				
21	6.7 ± 0.1	31	5.83 ± 0.5	33	54 ± 3	27	19.8 ± 1.9
			One ♂ *Phocoenoides dalli*				
11	6.9 ± 0.2	11	5.50 ± 0.6	11	53 ± 4	11	19.7 ± 1.8
			Two ♂ *Orcinus orca*				
6	6.8 ± 0.1	6	4.00 ± 0.3	6	45 ± 6	6	16.2 ± 0.9
			Two ♂ *Globicephala scammoni*				
9	6.8 ± 0.1	13	3.87 ± 0.4	13	46 ± 4	10	16.5 ± 1.9
			Five ♂ *Inia geoffrensis*				
20	6.9 ± 0.2	20	3.90 ± 0.5	20	42 ± 3	18	14.4 ± 1.4
			Three ♀ *Inia geoffrensis*				
4	6.8 ± 0.1	4	3.80 ± 0.3	4	40 ± 4	4	13.3 ± 0.3

* These values are from animals that were at the Marine Bioscience Facility for at least three months. When trained porpoises were maintained in the open ocean and required to make frequent deep dives, a training effect was observed. This was evidenced by an increased RBC, hemoglobin, PCV, and blood volume, and a decrease in RBC diameter. One of the female *Lagenorhynchus obliquidens* used in our studies was being worked daily in the open sea. Thus the values for the female *Lagenorhynchus obliquidens* are more similar to those we have found in wild animals. The values for the male *Lagenorhynchus obliquidens* and *Phocoenoides dalli* that were maintained in tanks are lower than those we have recorded from the same animals at the time of capture.

TABLE 10–6
RED BLOOD CELL MEASURES IN SOME NORMAL AND SICK PINNIPEDS

N	Diameter* (Microns) Mean ± SD	N	RBC Count (10⁶/mm³) Mean ± SD	N	PCV (HCT) (%) Mean ± SD	N	Hemoglobin (Gm/100 ml) Mean ± SD
			Five *Phoca vitulina* (normal)				
2	6.4 ± 0.3	6	5.45 ± 0.7	7	52 ± 6	5	19.2 ± 1.3
			Phoca vitulina (sick) #1				
1	6.6	1	7.73	1	60.5		
			Phoca vitulina (sick) #2				
1	7.4	1	3.30	2	33 ± 0	1	13.8
			Phoca vitulina (sick) #3				
1	7.5	1	2.06	1	18.5	1	7.3
			Eight *Zalophus californianus* (normal)				
6	7.1 ± 0.2	8	4.38 ± 0.7	8	45 ± 5	8	15.0 ± 2.1
			Zalophus californianus (sick) #1				
1	6.8	1	4.8	1	45.0	1	15.0
			Thirteen *Mirounga angustirostris* (normal)				
2	7.6 ± 0	2	5.55 ± 0.26	13	63.5 ± 4.9	3	25.0 ± 1.0
			Mirounga angustirostris (sick) #1				
4	7.6 ± 0	4	3.77 ± 0.43	4	55.6 ± 2.4	4	24.2 ± 2.6

* N = number of determinations and the values are means ± standard deviation (SD)

As seen in Table 10–4, many of the better divers among marine mammals manifest a high hematocrit and hemoglobin level. These, along with the large blood volume, indicate a greatly increased capacity for oxygen transport and storage by the blood. Contrary to early beliefs, a smaller red cell size would improve the oxygen transport and storage capabilities of the blood. A decrease in erythrocyte size may also be an advantage in resisting the affects of vascular stasis and provide some degree of resistance to decompression sickness.

BLOOD pH

In bottlenosed porpoises, the normal arterial pH of an animal resting on a pad out of the water is about 7.35 and well within the normal range for most mammals. However, during and just after a prolonged submergence, the blood may become quite acid due to the buildup of carbon dixoide and the release of lactic acid from the muscle as the dive is completed. In accordance with the Bohr effect, more oxygen would be dissociated from oxyhemoglobin when the blood is acid, thus allowing for more complete utilization of the blood oxygen during a dive.

The oxygen dissociation curve has been determined for several marine mammal species (Horvath *et al.*, 1968; Lenfant *et al.*, 1969; Lenfant, 1969). Interspecies comparison of diving capability and swimming speed have been correlated with a shift to the left in the dissociation curve (Horvath *et al.*, 1968).

Muscle Myoglobin

The capability of certain tissues, especially muscle, to function anaerobically and remain isolated until the end of a dive is one of the major diving adjustments made by marine mammals. The muscle hemoglobin or myoglobin, however, represents about 50 percent of the total oxygen storage capability in many marine mammals, and this stored oxygen is apparently isolated from the general circulation and preserved for muscle metabolism during the period of submersion.

Scholander (1940) noted that the darkness of the muscle tissue of a diving mammal is indicative of its myoglobin content. He says, "The striking positive correlation between the darkness, i.e. myoglobin content of the muscles and ability for protracted diving, appears to indicate that conditions in the muscles during diving are hardly entirely anaerobic. It is rather to be supposed that they received a very small but steady oxygen supply at probably a low tension."

THERMOREGULATION

Water transports heat away from a submerged mammal's body about twenty-five times as fast as compared with the same body in air. Beckman (1963), who has investigated the thermoregulatory problems of Navy divers, summarizes this effect as follows: "The rate at which heat is conducted away from the immersed body is so rapid that heat loss is limited primarily by the rate at which heat is transferred by the blood from the central core of the body to the skin."

As seen in Chapter 1, marine mammals are widely distributed from the equator to the Arctic and Antarctic. The majority of species and the largest populations of pinnipeds are found on the Arctic and Antarctic ice. Thus, these mammals represent a special case so far as comparative metabolic and thermoregulatory physiology is concerned, and they have developed morphological and physiological adjustments to deal with this stress.

Cetaceans and pinnipeds have the following five primary means of dealing with the thermoregulatory problem: integumentary modifications, restriction in body surface area, circulatory adjustments, metabolism, and respiratory modifications.

Integumentary Modifications

Integumentary modifications have probably received the most attention. Improved insulative properties of the integument have been achieved in several different ways. As mentioned in Chapter 2, the sea otter relies on a thick fur coat that entraps air and provides good insulation. Pinnipeds

have hair or fur which provides some insulation as well as a thick layer
of subcutaneous fat. Cetaceans have glabrous skin without hair follicles
or glands except for a few vestigial whiskers on the head (see Chapter 5).
The integument is, however, highly modified for thermoregulation and
hydrodynamic efficiency (Parry, 1949; Kramer, 1960; Lang, 1966; Sokolov
et al., 1969). The tough hypodermis (blubber layer), containing fibrous
connective tissue interspersed with a large amount of fat, provides good
insulation.

Body Surface Area

Compared with terrestrial mammals of similar size, pinnipeds have a
somewhat smaller limb size. Cetaceans have eliminated the rear limbs
entirely and the forelimbs are considerably reduced. The major muscles
concerned in propulsion are primarily in the main body axis. The reduction
in limb size and the spindle shape of the body has served to reduce the
total surface area to mass ratio and thus restricts the amount of exterior
area with which blood must come in contact. This results in a reduced
radiation of heat.

Table 10–24 gives average body surface areas for 100 kg porpoises of
three different species. Terrestrial mammals of equivalent size have a
considerably greater body surface area.

Circulatory Adjustments

Scholander and Schevill (1955) have described the countercurrent heat-
exchange system found in the flipper, dorsal fin, and flukes of cetaceans.
This is an interesting arrangement (Figs. 4–2, 5–97) whereby the peripheral arteries are surrounded by numerous veins. Pinnipeds also have
veins surrounding many arteries in the limbs. Thus, much of the heat of the
warm blood coming to the periphery is lost not to the surface but to the
venous blood returning to the body core. This arrangement provides a
minimum surface area for heat radiation by the vessels. In porpoises, even
the carotid arteries are surrounded by an extensive network of veins
(Ridgway *et al.*, 1970b).

Cetaceans can become overheated, and when necessary, secondary
venous channels near the surface can carry more blood and help to cool
the animal. Overheating can occur during prolonged fast swimming, in
warm water, and when the animal is out of the water. Under these circumstances, the blood pressure rises and the central artery (Fig. 5–97)
increases in diameter, reducing the capacity of the surrounding veins and
favoring the return flow of blood in the more superficial secondary veins
draining the same area.

The circulatory adjustments that occur during diving also play an important role in heat conservation. Restriction of the peripheral circulation, a major diving adjustment, keeps blood away from the surface and preserves heat. As already mentioned, this takes on added significance because most ocean waters, even in the tropics, are considerably colder at depth than near the surface.

The water cools the more external portion of the integument, and the skin temperatures of most cetaceans and pinnipeds are very close to those of the water. A temperature gradient is thus created from the skin to the deep body tissues (Hart and Irving, 1959; Sokolov, 1959; and Bel'kovich, 1965). Circulation to the more peripheral portions of the integument is probably controlled by the temperature. Thus, in warmer waters or when the animal's core temperature is increased, the peripheral circulation increases, eliminating more heat. In cetaceans, the vessels of the dermal papillae (Chap. 5) appear well suited for such a function.

The larger rete in the thorax, around and in the spinal canal, around the optic nerve and behind the eye, at the base of the cranial vault and around the ear, and in a number of other areas (see Chapter 4, Table 4–1) may play a big role in temperature regulation. Although no direct physiological evidence is available, it appears to me that the mass of blood vessels may serve to maintain temperature in certain local areas. During dives the ears, eyes, cranial nerves, and base of the brain may be kept warm while nearby tissues are allowed to cool somewhat.

Metabolism

Several authors have stated that marine mammals in general have higher metabolic rates than terrestrial mammals of similar size (Scholander, 1940; Irving *et al.*, 1941; Scheffer, 1958; Kanwisher and Sundness, 1965; Pierce, 1970). The high-protein diet alone contributes considerably to a high metabolic rate. Porpoises have relatively large thyroid glands (Harrison, 1969) and an increased output of thyroid hormone (Ridgway and Patton, 1970).

The higher rate of metabolism also contributes to thermoregulation because it provides for increased heat production. In some cetacean species, it appears that flipper size (as an indication of surface area) may give a good indication of relative metabolic rate. Small porpoises that inhabit colder waters have a more restricted body surface area (smaller flippers) and higher metabolic rates than those in tropical waters.

Metabolism and Diving

The best breathholders among aquatic vetebrates appear to be able to function for a period of time with a drastically reduced rate of aerobic metabolism. Scholander *et al.* (1942) demonstrated a reduction in body temperature during diving in seals. They observed that seals shivered during the recovery phase of strenuous dives and considered this to be due to a general depression in the metabolic process during the dive to as much as 50 percent of the resting level. At the end of the dive, peripheral circulation is reestablished, but the peripheral tissue has cooled. Thus, cooled blood is flowing back to the body core as the metabolism is returning to normal. This is thought to result in the shivering which was observed.

Pickwell (1968) showed that Peking ducks undergoing prolonged submersion may experience a reduction in total energy metabolism in excess of 90 percent of stable, presubmersion resting levels. The ability of organ systems within the animal's body to tolerate total or near total reduction in the rate of metabolism for some period of time explains the smallness of the observed oxygen debt payoff following long, quiet dives by experimental ducks (Pickwell, 1968). Scholander (1940) observed that the calculated oxygen debt incurred by seals during experimental dives was not completely paid off after the dive. In experimental dives with trained porpoises and sea lions in the open ocean, we at the Navy Marine Bioscience Facility noted that the major factor in determining when an animal will repeat a dive appears to be the elimination of carbon dioxide rather than the consumption of oxygen. These experiments will be discussed in greater detail later.

Respiratory Modifications in Heat Conservation

In man and other terrestrial mammals, 10 to 30 percent of the body heat produced is lost in pulmonary ventilation. Because marine mammals breathe less frequently, they conserve considerable heat that would normally be lost during the expiratory phase of respiration. In addition, some porpoises, at least, expire air that is not saturated with water vapor (Coulombe *et al.*, 1965). The exhalation of drier air conserves considerable heat that would normally be lost by evaporative cooling.

Thermoregulation and Taking Food Whole

An interesting but as yet unstudied thermoregulatory problem involves the feeding habits of marine mammals. These animals feed on poikilothermic species, and in most cases the food is taken whole. A dolphin may seize a fish of 1 kg or more and swallow it whole. As we have already discussed, the marine mammal's body has five major defenses against the cooling effects of the medium in which it is immersed. However, when a dolphin or seal in very cold waters swallows a 1 kg fish, and especially a number of such fish in rapid succession, he is taking into his body core a considerable thermal representation of his surrounding environment and quite a cold load. An increase in activity and metabolism during feeding might help to ameliorate this problem. Much of the feeding is probably done on prolonged dives, and the additional cooling effect in the body core would seem to be not wholly compatible with the overall diving adjustments.

OSMOREGULATION

Portier (1910) was one of the first to examine the problems of water balance in marine mammals. He raised the problem, but at that time it could not be solved. Laurie (1933) analyzed the urine from a number of blue and fin whales and found the chloride values to be quite variable. The first extensive study on osmoregulation in a marine mammal was made by Irving *et al.* (1935) on *Phoca vitulina*. These investigations showed that seals fed fresh herring derived all the water necessary for urine formation, fecal moisture, and insensible pulmonary loss from the water in the fish plus the metabolic water obtained from the combustion of fat and protein. Smith (1936) also examined the urine of the seal and, like Irving *et al.* (1935), found the concentrations of urea and other constituents to be well within the range produced by other mammalian kidneys.

Krogh (1939) suggested that the conclusions arrived at by Irving *et al.* (1935), i.e. that the water obtained from the food is sufficient for the normal requirements of the animal, can no doubt be extended to include all of the seals and whales feeding on vertebrates. However, for the baleen whales feeding on zooplankton, the walrus feeding on clams, and the many odontocetes and pinnipeds that feed on squid, the case is somewhat more complex.

All of these invertebrate food animals are isosmotic with the seawater and their blood is, practically speaking, isotonic with seawater. Smith (1936) fed a seal on clams and found that the urinary chloride concentration rose to only 510 mM/L, and even after ten hours the seal had not eliminated all of the ingested salts. Krogh (1939), however, gave calculations showing that even when feeding on invertebrates, the marine mammal can stay in water balance with no more than the urinary concentrating capability of the normal mammalian kidney.

Fetcher and Fetcher (1942) carried out the first experiments on water balance in a cetacean. They used two *Tursiops truncatus* (70 and 140 kg) as their experimental subjects. Each animal was given 2 L of 0.5 Molar sodium chloride (approximately isosmotic with seawater). Urine, feces, and saliva* (probably mucous secretion) were collected during a nine-hour

---

* Fetcher and Fetcher (1942) were collecting the copious mucoid excretion from the throat of *Tursiops truncatus*. This is not saliva. To my knowledge, salivary glands have not been demonstrated in this species.

experiment. The "saliva" was slightly hyperosmotic to the blood but not enough to play any significant part in eliminating the excess salt. The fecal material was generally hypotonic to the blood indicating that preferential salt uptake had occurred in the gut. The chloride concentration of the urine rose rapidly to nearly 600 mM/L and remained high, but after nine hours, 84 percent of the water and only 53 percent of the salt had been excreted. A considerable volume of feces was produced which was roughly isosmotic to the blood. At the end of the experiment, the choride concentration of the blood was higher than at the beginning. Fetcher and Fetcher (1942) concluded that there was a net shift of water from the tissues to the blood or that *Tursiops truncatus* possessed some means of extrarenal salt excretion.

Routes of Water Loss

Urine Production

The urinary bladder is relatively small in all cetaceans with which I am familiar. This indicates that little urine is stored. Porpoises fed methylene blue were observed to urinate at intervals of about thirty-five minutes (Prescott, 1965). Nevertheless, cetaceans on a normal diet of fish or squid do produce a large amount of urine. The California sea lion has a larger urinary bladder and a much greater capability for urine storage.

Urine production by porpoises and sea lions under varying conditions are shown in Table 10–7 to 10–19. A fasting 183 kg female *Tursiops*

TABLE 10–7

COMPARISON OF TWENTY-FOUR HOURS' URINE AND FECAL VOLUME AND
ELECTROLYTE VALUES IN FOUR *Zalophus californianus**

Animal	Squid Wt. kg	Urine			Feces			Moisture %
		Vol. ml	Na mEq/L	Cl mEq/L	Wt gm	Na mEq/kg	Cl mEq/kg	
Sea lion B (25kg)	4.3	2270	369	402	360	81	140	71
Sea lion B	4.3	2250	324	419	633	41	126	74
Sea lion B	4.5	2350	260	432	325	58	118	78
Sea lion S (30kg)	4.5	2495	317	442	409	102	184	80
Sea lion P (26kg)	4.5	2280	369	428	430	48	167	72
Sea lion P	4.5	2330	382	501	360	68	101	71
Sea lion P	6.0**	3213	418	606	460	191	129	79
Sea lion P	6.0**	3100	491	760	667	212	130	76
	Smelt wt.							
Sea lion P	4.5	2140	44	87	273	91	70	73
Sea lion P	4.5	2125	45	72	109	182	82	64
Sea lion P	4.5	2525	43	168	221	168	109	68
	HPTR wt.							
Sea lion T	0.9	465	181	307	13	131	108	60

* After being fed squid, squid + salt,** smelt and high-protein test ration (HPTR). All analyses were done on an aliquot of the total volume. The salt was placed in gelatin capsules and 15 gm were fed with squid. The last urine sample (from sea lion T) had an osmolality of 2,403 mOsm per kilogram of water.

truncatus produced 0.23 ml/kg/hr (Table 10–11), while a fasting 39 kg sea lion produced 0.31 ml/kg/hr (Table 10–8). As seen in Table 10–12, a porpoise on a normal diet of 7 kg of fish produces considerable urine in a day. The daily urine production for an animal on a normal diet of fish or squid is four to ten times the fasting urine production.

FECAL WATER

Water is also lost through the feces but in considerably smaller amounts than in the urine. In our tests, fecal moisture content for porpoises and sea lions has ranged from 60 to 85 percent.

TEARS

The tear secretion contains no unusual amounts of sodium or chloride. Cetacean tears are very viscous and it appears that a relatively large amount is secreted for protection and lubrication of the cornea. All analyses that we have done indicate that these tears contain slightly less sodium and cloride than a similar amount of blood. Sea lion tears are less viscous, and the three specimens that we examined contained sodium and chloride in amounts roughly equal to the blood concentration.

WATER LOSS FROM SKIN

For animals immersed in water, evaporation would not appear to be an efficient method of cooling. Cetaceans have no glands in the skin. Pinnipeds do have sweat glands and sebaceous glands but do not appear to sweat. Water loss from this route is assumed to be negligible.

RESPIRATORY WATER LOSS

Krogh (1939) pointed out that the slower respiration and more complete lung oxygen utilization by cetaceans would result in considerable water conservation. Coulombe *et al.* (1965) have shown that a 140 kg *Tursiops truncatus* loses only 30 percent of the water via respiration that would ordinarily be lost by a theoretical terrestrial mammal breathing dry air. This is accomplished by reduced ventilation (including increased oxygen consumption from each breath) and also by expiring air that is not completely saturated with water. The ability to exhale less-than-saturated air was attributed to the special structure and functioning of the nares and nasal sac system.

MILK

The period of lactation is a stressful one for the mother. The marine mammal that must produce milk and remain in water balance presents a problem of considerable physiological interest. The milk of both cetaceans and pinnipeds is very high in fat and relatively low in water content. This appears to offer an advantage from the standpoint of osmoregulation as Krogh (1939) points out. However, the richest milk appears to be from Arctic and Antarctic animals, and the higher water and lower fat content milks are from *Tursiops truncatus* and *Stenella plagiodon*, species that live primarily in tropical waters (Table 10–38). This appears to emphasize the importance of environmental temperature and the need for the young to have a rich food supply early in life while the body surface area to mass ratio is quite small.

Aldosterone and Sodium Loss

Animals living in the ocean would seem to have little need to conserve electrolytes. This brings up questions concerning adrenocortical secretions and the ability of the kidney to conserve sodium. To elucidate this question, distilled water was given by stomach tube to porpoises and sea lions (Tables 10–8, 10–15). Both species exhibited a substantial capability for

TABLE 10–8

URINE PRODUCTION, SODIUM, CHLORIDE, OSMOLALITY, AND UREA FOR A
Zalophus californianus UNDER 3 DIFFERENT CONDITIONS*

Hour	Volume ml	Sodium mEq/L	Chloride mEq/L	Osmolality mOsm	Urea gm
(A) 7	492	16	20	508	13.1
14	465	9	17	304	3.3
17	58	17	24	330	0.7
18	180	11	16	330	3.1
19	49	11	15	347	0.7
22	19	13	19	356	0.2
23	76	16	22	494	1.6
25	105	14	19	520	2.4
TOTAL:	1,444				25.1
FECES:	None				
(B) 9	292	74	96	1916	17.6
FECES:	None				
(C) 9	270	320	398	2260	22.5
12	150	328	368	2298	11.2
15	10	321	383	2303	0.9
17	55	223	310	945	4.9
TOTAL:	485				39.5
FECES:	126Gms, sodium 72.0mEq/kg, chloride 18.0mEq/kg				

* Thirty-nine kilogram male, under these three different conditions (a) 1,500 ml of distilled water given by stomach tube at start of test, (b) the last 25 hours of a 47-hour fast, (c) fed 1kg of high-protein test ration during the 8 hours prior to the start of the test at 0 hour. The sea lion was kept in the collecting cage for 25 hours in each case. Hour designations indicate the number of hours after the animal was placed in the collecting cage when each urine specimen was collected.

secreting urine low in sodium. These animals also had urinary aldosterone excretion within the normal range of values found in man (Table 10–20).

Diuresis

Smith (1936) showed that large amounts of urine were produced after a meal and the rate of urine production decreased to a relatively low value during fasting. Hiatt and Hiatt (1942) found that this increase was due to a rise in glomerular filtration rate (GFR) and renal plasma flow. These investigators suggested that the postprandial diuresis was related to the protein content of the food rather than to the increased amount of water available as a result of the meal. This conclusion was based on the finding that neither water, saline solution, nor protein-free herring extract would produce the diuresis.

Malvin and Rayner (1968) found that the introduction of tap water (2.5 per cent of body weight) by stomach tube did not increase urine flow in a dolphin (*Tursiops gilli*) during a two-hour experiment. These investigators state that "the mechanism by which the dolphin regulates urine flow following a meal is as yet unclear."

Circulatory changes already mentioned apparently have a profound effect on kidney function, and urine flow decreases during simulated dives (Bradley and Bing, 1942; Murdaugh *et al.*, 1961b). The decreased urine flow observed during apnea is not affected by the water and electrolyte load of the body (Todd *et al.*, 1951; Bradley *et al.*, 1950, 1954). Lawrence *et al.* (1956) also noted a decrease in urine flow in the seal both during apnea and during partial anoxia (breathing 10 per cent oxygen in nitrogen). They reported that water and sodium output were decreased due to increased tubular reabsorption of sodium.

Murdaugh *et al.* (1961c) also reported that osmotic diuretics did not increase urine flow in *Phoca vitulina* unless they were administered with food. Plasma volume expanders did produce a diuresis similar to that observed after normal feeding. These investigators also found it possible to cause a diuresis with mercurial diuretics and to abolish it by administering pitressin.

Schmidt-Nielsen *et al.* (1959) reported that in the harbor seal, urea excretion increases after feeding because of an increased plasma urea concentration, GFR, and urine flow. Malvin and Rayner (1968) discount the role of urea in producing a postprandial diuresis in dolphins.

ANTIDIURETIC HORMONE (ADH)

In reporting their experiments on water balance in dolphins, Malvin and Rayner (1968) suggested that ADH does not seem to be involved in the way it is usually pictured and indeed may play no role at all. Malvin *et al.* (1970) have carried out ADH assays on blood plasma and whole fresh pituitary glands of *Tursiops truncatus.* The antidiuretic activity was very low or completely absent. Even when the dolphins were fasted for three days, the plasma ADH levels were negligible.

In my view, the absence of ADH in significant quantities is not an incongruous discovery, particularly when the overall physiology of the aquatic mammal is considered. In his natural environment of seawater, the marine cetacean is suspended in a state very close to neutral buoyancy. Therefore, his body as a whole is in a state of weightlessness. In man, one of the most striking physiological manifestations of immersion is diuresis. Immersion is thought to cause a hydrostatic pressure gradient forcing blood from the veins of the lower extremities into the central circulation. The consequent distention of cardiac atrial stretch receptors by a concurrent increase in intrathoracic blood volume causes an inhibition of the release of ADH with the resulting diuresis. A similar problem of diuresis results from the weightlessness of space flight. ADH depression may be a natural consequence of immersion in water, but porpoises apparently replace ADH with some other mechanism for control of diuresis.

Some Experiments on Water Balance

Neither in Smith's (1936) nor in Fetcher's and Fetcher's (1942) experiments had the animals returned to a state of osmotic equilibrium at the termination of the test, nine or ten hours after the start. For the purpose of elucidating the physiology of water balance in marine mammals, therefore, we have carried out a number of more prolonged experiments (twenty-four hours in most cases) at the Navy Marine Bioscience Facility.

The two primary experimental species have been the California sea lion *Zalophus californianus* and the bottlenosed porpoise *Tursiops truncatus.* For experiments, sea lions were placed in a collecting cage (Fig. 10–6) so that the animals could be observed frequently and feces and urine harvested when the animals provided them. Porpoises were placed in transport sling which had apertures to accommodate the flippers and the genital slit (Fig. 10–7). After a urinary retention catheter and rectal catheter were inserted, the animal (in his sling) was lifted into a transporter carton equipped with a spray system that provided for cooling the upper half of the body. The container was then filled with water to the porpoise's eye level; thus a goodly portion of the animal's weight was supported by the water. Figure 10–8 is a drawing of the experimental setup for urine collection. The animals employed in these tests were accustomed to spending long hours in the transport container.

Figure 10–6. Sea lion in urine- and feces-collecting cage.

TESTS ON SEA LIONS

Our first experiments were aimed at determining the urine and fecal volume and sodium and chloride content for sea lions on an all squid diet. Three yearling *Zalophus californianus* gained weight rapidly and became very fat on a diet of 3 to 5 kg of squid daily. Some twenty-four-hour urine and fecal values for these sea lions are presented in Table 10–7.

Since it was evident that sea lions could easily maintain water balance on a complete squid diet, salt (NaCl) was added to the squid to try to determine the extent of the sea lion's ability to excrete sodium and chloride. The animals often vomited the food containing salt, and diarrhea usually accompanied salt administration. However, some successful tests were made and two of these are shown in Table 10–7. It appears that the sea

Figure 10–7. Porpoise in a transport sling. This type of sling was also used to suspend the animal for water-balance tests.

lion can excrete a urine more concentrated in both sodium and chloride than seawater. When the sea lions were fed fish (smelt), or a special high-protein test ration, the urinary sodium and chloride content was much lower (Table 10–7).

Sometimes newly captured sea lions will refuse food for as long as two

TABLE 10–9

URINE PRODUCTION, SODIUM, CHLORIDE, OSMOLALITY, AND UREA FOR A
*Zalophus californianus**

Hour	Volume Urine ml	Volume Feces gm	Sodium Urine mEq/L	Sodium Feces mEq/kg	Chloride Urine mEq/L	Chloride Feces mEq/kg	Osmolality mOsm	Urea gm
1	190		243		260		679	2.4
2	456		303		299		727	5.1
3	206		339		346		863	2.2
5	428		370		300		1330	10.4
8	420	14.1	332	29	297	36	1863	24.4
11	150	29.7	138	33	134	36	2119	17.8
13	82	21.9	116	90	136	41	2027	9.3
17	115	27.1	74	62	183	67	2171	14.4
19	95		66		162		2119	11.1
23	131	62.3	65	104	175	36	2056	16.6
26	155	90.5	90	124	202	35	2006	15.5
29	192		21		196		1996	19.1
TOTAL	2967	155.1						148.3

* Thirty-nine kilogram male, fed 3.8 kg of smelt containing an additional 45 gm of Instant Ocean in capsules. The smelt was fed during the 30 minutes prior to 0 hour and the sea lion had been fasted for 24 hours prior to the test. The product contains 65.226% sodium chloride, 1.737% potassium chloride, 12.762% magnesium chloride, and 3.251% calcium chloride in addition to other constituents.

TABLE 10–10
URINE PRODUCTION, SODIUM, CHLORIDE, OSMOLALITY, AND UREA FOR A
*Zalophus californianus**

Hour	Volume ml	Sodium mEq/L	Chloride mEq/L	Osmolality mOsm	Urea gm
2	430	300	372	892	6.0
3	628	334	442	879	5.3
4	496	358	514	992	4.9
6	307	395	594	1183	4.0
9	478	438	608	1448	10.6
16	414	442	516	2003	25.7
19	85	353	392	2223	6.4
24	15	310	330	2111	0.9
TOTAL	2853				63.8

* Thirty-nine kilogram male, fed 2.5kg of smelt containing an additional 100 gm of Instant Ocean in capsules. The smelt was fed during 20 minutes just prior to 0 hour and the sea lion had been fasted for 24 hours prior to the test.

weeks. We took advantage of this situation to get some urine specimens from animals that had been fasting for relatively long periods. Some single sample values are presented in Table 10–34 and those for a twenty-four-hour specimen are presented in Table 10–8. The urine uric acid levels of these sea lions are in the same range as those of man. Urine osmolality increases to a level of 2,250 to 2,500 mOsm during the first forty-eight to seventy-two hours and remains at that level while urine output decreases to a base level of 0.20 to 0.35 ml/kg/hr.

We noticed that Instant Ocean[®]* a product manufactured for the purpose of serving as the solute for seawater aquariums that must be supplied with fresh water, was tolerated somewhat better by our sea lions that was ordinary table salt. Two tests were made (Table 10–9 and 10–10) in which 45 gm and then 100 gm were fed to a sea lion. The 100 gm of Instant Ocean in 2.5 kg of smelt yields a total electrolyte load considerably more concentrated than seawater. It appears from Table 10–10 that the sea lion eliminates more water than was contained in the fish and therefore could not maintain water balance on this ration.

The sea lion's kidney can apparently handle electrolyte loads up to about the concentration of seawater. In order to handle higher concentrations, it appears that the animal must sacrifice some of his own body water for increased urine production.

TESTS WITH PORPOISES

Several experiments were carried out in which animals were fed fish, while urine and blood were collected hourly for analysis. Some data on blood and urine constituents after a fish meal are shown in Tables 10–12 to 10–14.

* "Instant Ocean" is a product of Aquarium Systems, Inc. Wickliffe, Ohio.

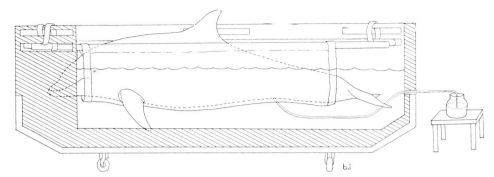

Figure 10–8. An illustration of the setup for water-balance tests with porpoises. The fecal collecting bag is not shown. The animal was immersed to eye level in water and the upper half of the body was sprayed with water.

The characteristic pattern of postprandial diuresis is evident in all of these tests. In general, potassium elimination increased when sodium excretion was lowest. Urinary sodium and chloride levels were relatively low because of the comparatively small amounts of these electrolytes in fish. It was evident that the water available in fish is quite ample for waste product elimination.

Malvin and Rayner (1968) reported that 4 L of tap water introduced into the stomach of a 160 kg *Tursiops gilli* failed to produce a diuresis

TABLE 10–11

URINE PRODUCTION, SODIUM, CHLORIDE, OSMOLALITY, UREA AND BLOOD UREA NITROGEN FOR A *Tursiops truncatus**

Hour	Volume ml	Sodium mEq/L	Chloride mEq/L	Osmolality mOsm	Urea gm	BUN mg/100 ml
1	57	. . .	. . .	. . .	1.5	40
2	64	161	164	1311	3.3	41
3	54	138	159	1334	1.3	42
4	56	131	157	1312	0.9	40
5	41	88	127	912	1.8	38
6	51	79	127	1227	2.2	
7	50	67	107	900	2.4	40
8	48	63	100	798		42
9	52					
10	31	65	99	811	3.1	41
11	45					
12	48	83	114	982	1.8	40
13	40					
14	41	124	171	1242	3.5	44
15	41					
16	34	105	139	1172	3.3	40
17	28					
18	49	113	141	1327	1.8	44
19	53					
20	41	132	183		3.1	42
21	50	167	202	1494	3.5	41
22	20	172	182	1596	1.1	41
TOTAL	994					

* 183kg female, during the last 22 hours of a 40-hour fast.

TABLE 10–12

URINE PRODUCTION, SODIUM, CHLORIDE, POTASSIUM, OSMOLALITY, UREA, AND BLOOD UREA NITROGEN FOR A *Tursiops truncatus**

Hour	Urine Volume ml	Sodium mEq/L	Potassium mEq/L	Chloride mEq/L	Osmolality mOsm	Urea gm	BUN mg/100 ml
1	289	179	80	204	1743	15.6	43
2	408	179	77	218	1838	24.0	
3	334	150	74	194	1832	26.2	45
4	276	126	70	173	1944	18.0	
5	310	151	68	216	2006	16.9	47
6	322	145	65	246	2082	21.8	
7	279	119	53	209	2000	18.5	47
8	313	111	54	190	1991	21.1	
9	311	115	43	178	1954	25.1	50
10	370	116	45	174	1767	26.6	
11	210	77	49	135	1489	10.8	42
12	215	52	61	110	1388	11.4	
13	179	62	71	128	1389	9.2	
14	115	79	90	157	1511	5.1	37
15	95	67	100	152	1549	5.7	
16	85	51	145	149	1562	5.1	
17	78	61	121	173	1671	4.8	
18	78	61	117	165	1664	4.4	35
19	70	81	123	204	1648	3.9	
20	67	97	121	213	1778	4.6	42
21	65	143	101	233	1822	2.9	
22	63	153	103	252	1814	3.3	42
23	55	162	107	259	..	2.9	
24	65	205	89	284	1804	3.1	40
TOTAL	4652					291.0	

Feces: 1450 gm; Sodium 103 mEq/kg; Chloride 56 mEq/kg; Moisture 82%

* One hundred and eighty-seven kilogram female, fed 7 kg of Spanish mackerel during 20 minutes preceeding 0 hour. The animal was fasted overnight prior to the test.

during a two-hour experiment. We decided to repeat these tests with another member of the same genus. Five 24-hour tests were conducted with four different *Tursiops truncatus* females. The results were similar in all cases, with a marked diuresis beginning in the second hour after water administration. Some results of one of these experiments are shown in Table 10–15. These porpoises definitely absorbed water from the gastro-intestinal tract. The feces contained less moisture than it generally does after a fish meal. The amount of urea excreted during these tests was one-half to two-thirds as great as would be expected if the animal had consumed an equal amount of fish and the BUN decreased. The sodium excretion, however, dropped to a very low level in about two hours and remained low. Plasma electrolytes varied only slightly from hour to hour and remained within the normal range during the entire period. Urine osmolality dropped to about one-fourth of pretest levels and then gradually climbed, but at the twenty-fourth hour it was less than two-thirds of the pretest value. The creatinine clearance varied only slightly and was much lower than when the porpoises were fed fish or given seawater (Fig. 10–12).

TABLE 10–13

URINE PRODUCTION, SODIUM, POTASSIUM, CHLORIDE, OSMOLALITY, UREA, AND BLOOD UREA NITROGEN (BUN) FOR A *Tursiops truncatus**

Hour	Volume ml	Sodium mEq/L	Potassium mEq/L	Chloride mEq/L	Osmolality mOsm	Urea gm	BUN mg/100ml
1	96	72	75	107	1500	4.0	42
2	180	89	91	150	1570	8.4	43
3	176	97	86	141	1655	11.9	45
4	185	83	97	131	1527	11.5	45
5	168	84	95	137	1630	13.2	48
6	145	76	95	123	1533	12.1	46
7	171	61	99	133	1589	11.4	46
8	161	53	94	129	1592	13.9	48
9	137	52	69	111	1787	19.8	
10	132	61	71	131	1692	15.6	50
11	206	72	69	125	1534	16.7	
12	163	69	66	118	1524	14.9	52
13	114	64	54	99	1477	9.7	
14	84	72	78	121	1568	6.6	52
15	95	77	30	101	1566	4.9	
16	83	59	84	124	1554	4.7	52
17	54	69	38	79	1596	5.3	
18	51	40	82	121	1570	5.1	58
19	63	49	105	159	1520	3.1	
20	37	75	54	176	1770	4.9	57
21	52	43	95	160	1860	4.6	
22	45	56	104	169	1725	3.0	52
TOTAL	2597					205.3	

* One hundred and seventy-seven kilogram female, after being fed 5 kg of Spanish mackerel.

TABLE 10–14

URINE PRODUCTION, SODIUM, CHLORIDE, OSMOLALITY, UREA AND BLOOD UREA NITROGEN FOR A **Lagenorhynchus obliquidens**

Hour	Volume ml	Sodium mEq/L	Potassium mEq/L	Chloride mEq/L	Osmolality mOsm	Urea gm	BUN mg/100ml
1	105	147	104	121	1334	5.8	40
2	274	145	107	132	1461	19.9	
3	217	164	92	87	1640	18.1	47
4	160	175	83	59	1629	9.9	43
5	138	171	88	104	1683	11.8	50
6	109	142	71	111	1933	8.8	
7	96	130	81	149	1889	8.2	50
8	98	128	79	113	1946	10.6	
9	122	124	88	90	1992	14.5	
10	117	126	87	54	1836	14.1	
11	111	129	89	86	1964	12.7	
12	102	128	95	92	1996	11.4	
13	77	131	128	99	1985	6.9	
14	77	104	135	96	1997	6.8	
15	69	80	133	97	1962	6.8	
16	76	67	99	93	1930	7.6	60
17	65	63	164	98	1945	5.6	
18	78	67	162	91	1931	8.4	
19	80	81	176	101	1928	8.5	
20	67	91	110	102	1939	6.6	
21	73	92	112	97	1964	8.8	
22	90	138	43	93	1988	10.9	
23	83	150	84	109	2001	9.5	
24	83	143	77	112	1986	10.9	65
TOTAL	2567					243.1	

* Eighty-two kilogram female, fed 4.6 kg of Spanish mackerel.

Our results are at variance to those of Malvin and Rayner (1968). Perhaps their tests were too short, but all of our test animals were showing a diuresis by the end of the second hour. Perhaps a species difference could account for these conflicting observations.

We had no *tursiops gilli*. A newly captured 82 kg female *Lagenorhynchus obliquidens* was, however, available for a test. Two liters of distilled water were given by stomach tube. No diuresis was observed during the twenty-four-hour test. Urine production was about 800 ml and close to the amount that would be expected from this animal during a fast; however, the porpoise produced 2600 ml of feces that contained 88 percent moisture. Thus it appeared that the water had remained in the gut and passed through without being absorbed. This porpoise had a much higher than normal respiratory rate during the test and appeared to be quite distressed by the situation. Close observation of this animal during the next few days revealed that she had a severe diarrhea. Whether our test caused the diarrhea or the diarrhea affected our test results is still not clear. We have not as yet had an opportunity to repeat these tests in other species and can only say that fresh water does produce a diuresis in *Tursiops truncatus* and *Zalophus californianus*.

TABLE 10–15

URINE PRODUCTION, SODIUM, CHLORIDE, OSMOLALITY, UREA, AND BLOOD UREA NITROGEN FOR A *Tursiops truncatus**

Hour	Urine Volume ml	Sodium mEq/L	Chloride mEq/L	Osmolality mOsm	Urea gm	BUN mg/100ml
1	95	223	291	1442	4.4	40
2	272	179	226	1443	18.2	
3	298	39	91	878	14.5	40
4	331	17	48	527	12.1	
5	305	17	46	482	6.6	
6	262	16	45	509	9.2	
7	141	13	46	614	6.2	38
8	126	10	49	775	6.6	
9	127	7	45	709	5.5	
10	173	7	45	684	7.7	
11	132	8	50	736	5.7	
12	151	7	55	785	7.9	
13	115	8	55	742	4.8	
14	106	9	54	812	5.1	
15	81	9	51	899	4.0	
16	84	8	54	884	4.4	
17	81	8	52	835	3.7	29
18	93	9	58	937	5.5	
19	95	8	52	918	5.7	
20	128	8	51	906	7.0	
21	57	7	44	953	2.6	
22	100	8	46	880	4.8	
23	79	9	43	862	3.7	
24	76	8	40	873	2.9	35
TOTAL	3507				158.8	

Feces: 510 gm; 62% moisture; 115 mEq Sodium; 31 mEq Chloride.

* One hundred and eighty-seven kilogram female after receiving 4 L of distilled water by stomach tube after fasting overnight.

TABLE 10–16

URINE PRODUCTION, SODIUM, CHLORIDE, OSMOLALITY, UREA, AND
BLOOD UREA NITROGEN IN A *Tursiops truncatus**

Hour	Urine Volume ml	Sodium mEq/L	Chloride mEq/L	Osmolality mOsm	Urea gm	BUN mg/100ml
1	176	290	302	1613	9.5	60
2	367	416	542	1474	13.8	65
3	328	374	500	1252	6.2	60
4	157	330	512	1195	5.1	35
5	136	348	526	1419	4.4	
6	112	369	542	1607	4.2	35
7	90	374	592	1752	4.7	
8	100	370	612	1844	4.0	45
9	52	333	606	1968	5.1	
10	60	399	602	1957	2.7	
11	63	282	534	1953	3.1	
12	62	292	530	1947	3.1	
13	66	296	528	1891	3.1	
14	51	313	544	1913	3.1	
15	50	288	552	1950	2.7	
16	57	285	534	1960	2.4	
17	52	251	528	1944	3.1	
18	42	255	514	1940	2.7	35
19	46	237	550	1960	2.4	
20	52	203	500	1913	2.7	34
21	49	230	446	1928	3.1	
22	38	208	430	1901	2.7	40
23	38	189	388	1893	2.2	
24	34	174	356	1892	2.2	34
TOTAL	2684				98.2	

Feces: 1476 gm; Moisture 85%; Sodium 137 mEq/kg; Chloride 93 mEq/kg.

* One hundred and seventy-seven kilogram female, fed 3 L of seawater by stomach tube. The animal was fasted overnight prior to the test.

We wanted to see how a porpoise responded to seawater ingestion. For our next test, 3 L of seawater was taken from one of our holding tanks and given by stomach tube to a 177 kg female *Tursiops truncatus*. The results are shown in Table 10–16. The characteristic postprandial diuresis followed the seawater administration. Urine electrolyte levels increased, but plasma electrolyte values remained within normal range. Urine urea excretion was about one-half to two-thirds as great as would be expected from the consumption of an equal amount of fish, and the BUN dropped. At the end of the test, the porpoise had excreted all of the water administered plus an amount just about equal to that excreted during a complete fast. The fecal moisture content was high, and though the total fecal sample had sodium and chloride levels slightly lower than those of the blood, the feces at the end of the test appeared to be isotonic with the blood. The salt not excreted in the urine or feces could be easily accounted for by the amount retained in the gut. It appeared that the animal could handle a seawater load without substantial loss of its body water, but it was also clear that the animal derived little or no net water gain from the seawater.

In the next test, a 101 kg female *Tursiops truncatus* was fed 4.7 kg of Spanish mackerel (*Trachurus symmetricus*) and two hours later at the

TABLE 10–17

URINE PRODUCTION, SODIUM, CHLORIDE, POTASSIUM, OSMOLALITY, UREA,
AND BLOOD UREA NITROGEN IN A *Tursiops truncatus**

Hour	Urine Volume ml	Sodium mEq/L	Potassium mEq/L	Chloride mEq/L	Osmolality mOsm	Urea gms	BUN mg/100ml
1	293	182	93	116	1396	15.2	38
2	387	265	52	222	1594	21.6	
3	338	310	60	330	1769	21.8	55
4	270	294	66	368	1902	16.0	
5	225	262	60	362	1990	14.2	53
6	173	214	54	308	1977	12.9	
7	140	168	58	257	1912	10.9	46
8	56	140	105	248	1766	3.8	
9	61	108	129	230	1709	3.8	
10	46	87	148	222	1584	2.7	
11	55	68	169	207	1542	2.0	
12	29	65	174	212	1533	1.6	
13	51	69	179	222	1587	2.6	
14	41	72	176	228	1589	2.0	
15	67	83	169	236	1653	3.8	45
17	95	79	120	188	1548	2.1	
18	10	66	111	178	1659	0.7	45
19	102	64	108	174	1568	6.4	
20	93	65	105	159	1469	5.7	34

TOTAL 2530 153.6

Feces: 679 gm; Sodium 80 mEq/L; Chloride 37 mEq/L; Moisture 76%.

* One hundred and one kilogram female, fed 4.7 kg of Spanish mackerel and 2 hours later near the height of diuresis given 1 L of sea water by stomach tube. Hour one is thus the 3rd hour after Spanish mackerel and the first hour after seawater administration.

height of diuresis she was given 1 L of seawater by stomach tube. The results are shown in Table 10–17. Urine sodium, chloride, and osmolality values increased as did the BUN, but all of these values declined from the seventh hour on as the potassium increased. Fecal moisture was about normal. Fecal sodium and chloride were low. It appeared that the porpoise could easily handle a liter of seawater with a meal of fish.

Wolf *et al.* (1959) have pointed out that a mammal on a high-protein diet commits a certain amount of water for the urine needed to excrete urea. This same urine could also be used for the excretion of electrolytes. To test this hypothesis in porpoises, we used a special high-protein test ration that was undergoing feeding trials to determine the feasibility of its use as a fish substitute for porpoises or sea lions. Two kilograms of this ration and 2 L of sea water were homogenized in a large, high-speed blender. The porpoise was removed from the water and the 4 L of blend given by stomach tube. The animal was then placed back in the water for eight hours, well after the fecal appearance had changed to that normally observed when the animals were on the test ration. The porpoise was again removed from the water, given 4 L of the same blend, and the test started.

The first test (Table 10–18) employed a 140 kg *Tursiops truncatus* female and was carried on for thirty hours with urine and feces being

TABLE 10–18

URINE PRODUCTION, SODIUM, CHLORIDE, OSMOLALITY, UREA, AND
BLOOD UREA NITROGEN FOR A *Tursiops truncatus**

Hour	Volume ml	Sodium mEq/L	Chloride mEq/L	Osmolality mOsm	Urea gm	BUN mg/100ml
9	144	391	455	1681	5.7	35
10	207	422	510	2007	10.3	43
11	230	410	480	2142	14.1	50
12	203	406	486	2259	12.5	
13	184	396	506	2388	12.3	45
14	320	380	521	2291	21.1	
15	265	394	531	2213	16.9	45
16	308	406	534	2155	18.9	
17	207	422	588	2236	12.8	40
18	140					
19	130	442	632	2458	10.3	35
20	125					
21	110	410	595	2300	10.0	35
22	100					
23	66	327	404	267	4.6	35
24	55					
25	45	260	387	2012	3.3	37
26	48					
27	52	292	387	1996	3.2	40
28	58					
29	42	243	342	1857	2.5	40
30	58	220	308	1763		38

TOTAL   3097
FECES: 1226 gm; Sodium 76mEq/kg; Chloride 20mEq/kg; Moisture 69%.

* One hundred and forty kilogram female, after receiving 2 kg of high protein test ration blended in 2 L of seawater at 0 hour and an additional 2 kg of the ration in 1.5 L of seawater at hour 8. Urine, blood, and feces collection began at hour 8.

TABLE 10–19

URINE PRODUCTION, SODIUM, CHLORIDE, OSMOLALITY, UREA, AND
BLOOD UREA NITROGEN FOR A *Tursiops truncatus**

Hour	Volume ml	Sodium mEq/L	Chloride mEq/L	Osmolality mOsm	Urea gm	BUN mg/100ml
10	225	380	494	2072	14.1	40
11	191	370	407	2424	17.6	
12	156	370	416	2592	14.2	45
13	208	400	462	2658	19.2	
14	175	410	491	2554	14.5	40
15	260	428	563	2371	19.8	
16	196	416	503	2084	12.1	40
17	210					
18	205	460	555	2078	12.2	37
19	188	430	513	2042	10.0	
20	162	350	450	1995	8.8	28
21	117	294	398	1784	5.5	
22	102	222	350	1604	4.4	40
23	88	182	347	1747	4.9	40

TOTAL   2483
FECES: 1433 gm; Sodium 54 mEq/kg; Chloride 35 mEq/kg; Moisture 68%.

* One hundred and thirty kilogram male, after receiving 2 kg of high protein test ration blended in 2 L of sea water. The animal had received an additional 2 kg of the ration with 2 L of sea water (4 L of blend) 9 hours before urine and fecal collection started.

collected during the last twenty-two hours. The urine sample collected at hour 19 was hypertonic to seawater and contained about 8 percent urea. In another test a slightly smaller male *Tursiops truncatus* was employed. The results are shown in Table 10–19. This experiment yielded the highest urine osmolality that we have observed from a cetacean—2658 mOsm. Fecal moisture was within the normal range observed when the porpoises were feeding on fish. Fecal sodium and chloride were low in both cases. From the results of both tests, it appeared that the electrolytes contained in the seawater were excreted along with urine containing relatively large amounts of urea.

Creatinine and Creatine

Creatine was present in all urine samples that we have collected from marine mammals and analyzed for this substance. Plasma levels of creatine increase rapidly after a fish meal (Fig. 10–9) and then decrease as the excess creatine is excreted. Small transient increases in plasma creatine were observed in animals fed seawater or fresh water. During a fast, the plasma creatine levels remain fairly constant at around 1.0 mg per 100 ml.

The total twenty-four-hour urinary creatine ranged from 7.0 to 10.7 gm in porpoises fed 5 to 7 kg of fish. The high creatine output after a fish meal is probably a result of the creatine content of whole raw fish. The human body contains roughly 2 gm of creatine per kilogram of body weight. Judging from the excretion of creatine by our porpoises, the whole fish body may have a similar concentration of creatine. When porpoises were given seawater, distilled water, or fasted, the total twenty-four-hour urinary creatine ranged from 1.3 to 1.7 gm. Creatine output in two *Tursiops truncatus* given 2 L dextrose plus 2 L of distilled water was less than 0.5 gm in both cases. Rates of creatine excretion in *Tursiops truncatus* under different conditions are shown in Fig. 10–10.

Creatinine excretion ranged from 2.8 to 4.0 gms daily in three large female *Tursiops truncatus* (177, 183, and 187 kg). The creatinine excretion on a milligram-per-kilogram basis was in the upper half of the normal range for the human female (Best and Taylor, 1967, p. 1306). The creatinine excretion was similar whether the animal was fasted or fed fish, distilled water, or seawater. The creatinine excretion was so constant that we used it as a measure of the adequacy of urine collection. On one occasion when a leak developed in the urine collection line and urine samples were contaminated by the water in which the animal was immersed, the creatinine level reflected the dilution that had occurred.

In a fasting *Tursiops truncatus* female, the creatinine clearance averaged 257 ml/min during a twenty-four-hour test. This is an average of 1.45 ml/kg/min, and on this basis is within the normal human range (Fig. 10–

Mammals of the Sea

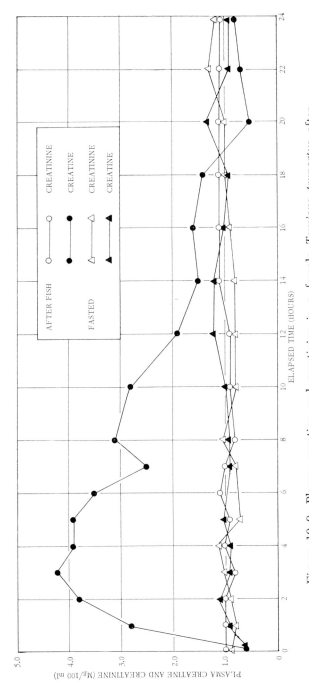

Figure 10–9. Plasma creatine and creatinine in a female *Tursiops truncatus* after
being fed fish and after fasting.

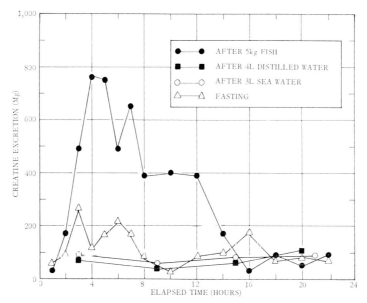

Figure 10–10. Creatine in the urine of female *Tursiops truncatus* after being fed 5 kg of fish, after receiving 4 L of distilled water by stomach tube, after receiving 3 L of seawater by stomach tube, and after fasting for twenty-four hours.

11). After a fish meal, the creatinine clearance increased to a peak of almost 400 ml/min at four hours and then decreased to the normal range by the tenth hour. Urine flow remained elevated after the creatinine clearance had returned to normal (Fig. 10–12) in a porpoise which was fed fish. However, in the animal fed seawater, the creatinine clearance remained high after urine flow subsided. The creatinine clearance for a *Tursiops truncatus* given 4 L of distilled water remained within normal range during the entire twenty-four hours of the test even though there

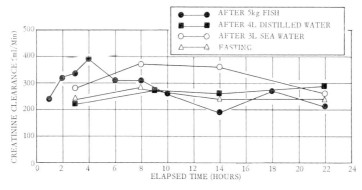

Figure 10–11. Creatinine clearance in female *Tursiops truncatus* (177 to 187 kg) after being fed 5 kg of fish, after receiving 4 L of distilled water by stomach tube, after receiving 3 L seawater by stomach tube, and after fasting for twenty-four hours.

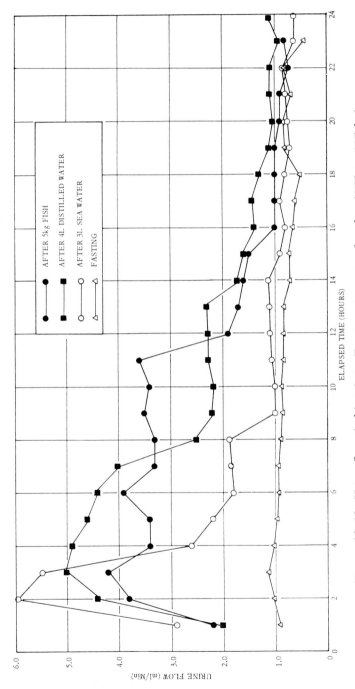

Figure 10–12. Urine flow (ml/min) in *Tursiops truncatus* females (177 to 187 kg) after being fed 5 kg of fish, after receiving 4 L of distilled water by stomach tube, after receiving 3 L of seawater by stomach tube, and after fasting for twenty-four hours.

was a marked diuresis. The diuresis following distilled water administration appears to be regulated at the renal tubular level and is apparently not a response to an increased clearance.

Do They Drink Seawater?

Earlier workers have generally concluded that marine mammals do not drink seawater and therefore rely wholly on their food as a source of water (Irving *et al.*, 1935; Smith, 1936; Krogh, 1939; Fetcher and Fetcher, 1942; Malvin and Rayner, 1969). Irving *et al.* (1935) reported that under ordinary conditions, none of their seals were observed drinking seawater, but four seals shipped to Toronto in a warm express car drank fresh water greedily as soon as a clean supply was available. When our *Zalophus californianus* were being fed high-protein test ration containing about 55 percent moisture, they readily drank fresh water that was provided in buckets (apparently in preference to seawater in their tanks). The sea lions did not ordinarily lap water as a dog or cat does but rather immersed the whole muzzle in the water and drank much as a thirsty horse does. A 35 kg sea lion with a consumption of 2 kg of the test ration regularly drank 800 to 1200 ml of water daily.

We have no direct evidence of seawater drinking in normal pinnipeds on a fish or squid diet. As already mentioned, *Zalophus californianus* can certainly concentrate urine sufficiently to allow it to consume seawater along with fish. No doubt the water in the normal diet of pinnipeds is quite adequate. As Harrison and Kooyman (1968) point out, seawater consumption by pinnipeds is still an open question.

There is some evidence that porpoises take in seawater. We found that when copper sulphate is placed in the pool water, the copper level in the porpoise's forestomach increases. In another experiment (Ridgway, 1968), porpoises were moved back and forth between freshwater and seawater pools and their blood and urine constituents monitored. When *Tursiops truncatus* were placed in fresh water, plasma electrolytes and osmolality remained unchanged but the urine electrolytes and osmolality dropped to values equal to, or lower than, those shown in Table 10–15. When these animals were returned to seawater, the urine electrolytes increased twenty-fold to one hundredfold in three hours and before any fish were given. Calculations based upon the electrolyte dilution of the fish fed to the animals in fresh water indicated that an average of about 1.5 L of water were consumed each day. Porpoises in seawater were also fed mackerel of a known electrolyte content (Table 10–21). Urine samples collected averaged somewhat higher in sodium and chloride content than could be expected from the fish alone. Calculations again based on dilution indi-

TABLE 10–20

ALDOSTERONE IN URINE OF FOUR PORPOISES AND A SEA LION
UNDER DIFFERING CONDITIONS

Hour	Tursiops truncatus *Given* 4 L Distilled H₂O Total μg	% μg/100ml	Tursiops truncatus *Given* 3 L Sea H₂O Total μg	% μg/100ml	Tursiops truncatus *Given* 5 kg Fish + 1 L Sea H₂O Total μg	% μg/100ml
1–6	2.0	0.13	0.9	0.06	4.0	0.24
6–12	1.0	0.12	0.6	0.12	2.0	0.52
12–18	1.0	0.18	0.9	0.27	1.0	0.38
18–24	0.9	0.17	0.5	0.19	0.8	0.41

Hour	Lagenorhynchus obliquidens *Given* 4.7 kg Fish Total μg	% μg/100ml	Zalophus californianus *Given* 3.9 kg Fish + 45 gm Instant Ocean Total μg	% μg/100ml
1–6	2.0	0.20	2.0	0.16
6–12	2.0	0.31	2.0	0.35
12–18	2.0	0.45	1.0	0.34
18–24	2.0	0.42	3.0	0.44

cated that our *Tursiops truncatus* must consume 500 ml to 1500 ml of sea-water daily.

Telfer *et al.* (1970) have recently carried out an experiment with three species of small cetaceans. They treated the tank water with radioactive isotope material and then monitored the levels of radioactivity in the animals blood at regular intervals. In each case, there were increases in the blood levels and the investigators concluded that the animals must have consumed seawater.

The urinary concentrating capability of our porpoises and sea lions appear similar to those of the camel (Schmidt-Nielsen, 1964) or the cat

TABLE 10–21

ANALYSES OF FOODS AND SEAWATER USED IN WATER-BALANCE TESTS*

	Sodium mEq/L	Potassium mEq/L	Chloride mEq/L	Protein % (N × 6.25)	Fat %	Moisture %
Squid (*Loligo sp.*)	355	64	374	14.0	1.4	80.0
Spanish mackerel (*Trachurus symmetricus*)	102	118	80	19.5	4.4	71.9
Pacific mackerel (*Scomber diego*)	99	116	74	20.0	8.0	69.6
Columbia River smelt (*Thaleichthys vetulus*)	33	58	25	16.4	4.0	68.0
High-protein test ration	124	90	196	26.0	8.0	55.0
Sea water	441	9.4	504			

* The whole fish and squid were liquefied by thorough blending in a large laboratory blender. Thus the electrolytes are reported as mEq/L rather than on a weight basis. The whole body analyses of fish and squid were performed on specimens that were received frozen at the Navy Marine Bioscience Facility from commercial sources. It should be noted that the analyses probably reflect any changes that occurred due to capture, freezing, handling and storage. The seawater was taken from a beach well which is the source of pool water at the Marine Bioscience Facility.

(Wolf *et al.*, 1959) but definitely inferior to several rodents including the kangaroo rat (Schmidt-Nielsen, 1964) and Australian hopping mice (Mac-Millen and Lee, 1967). The kidney can readily handle the added load of seawater consumption if the animal is eating teleosts and the mammal gets the advantage of osmotic work already done by the fish. It seems evident, however, that seawater consumption is not essential for water balance. The seawater may be consumed for some other reason such as the nutritional need for trace elements that it contains.

REPRODUCTIVE PHYSIOLOGY

The reproductive cycles of most pinnipeds are fairly well understood because they gather in large breeding congregations at particular times of the year (see Chap. 1 and Harrison, 1969). The cetacean's reproductive habits are not as easily observed. Captive births of *Tursiops truncatus* were mentioned in Chapter 6.

The Female Reproductive Cycle

Although the experimental data currently available allows only specu-lation on the subject, it appears to me that the female *Tursiops truncatus* is a seasonally polyestrous animal that reaches the peak of estrus in spring or autumn (or both). Animals not bred in the spring probably come into estrus again in the autumn. The overall reproductive rate is probably low, with most females calving every two years. The breeding season is prob-ably influenced by day length and perhaps by water temperature.

Species that migrate extensively and those that dwell primarily in waters of high latitudes probably have shorter breeding seasons, and most of these are probably restricted to one breeding season per year (see Chap. 1). This rhythmic breeding activity is probably under photoperiodic control.

THE VAGINAL SMEAR

Sokolov (1961) has reported that the vaginal smear can be employed to differentiate stages of the estrous cycle in *Delphinus delphis*. He ex-amined 114 common dolphins and found that their vaginal smears re-vealed epithelial cells of basically the following three size groups: small cells with a large nucleus and a small amount of cytoplasm, average-size cells, and large, flattened cells with a pyknotic nucleus. In immature fe-males, there was a predominance of epithelial cells of medium size with a well-developed nuclear structure. In mature females ready for fertilization (as indicated by subsequent examination of the ovaries), the smears showed epithelial cells of a medium size, many of which had pyknotic nuclei; and there were also large, flattened cells. Females in early pregnancy showed a predominance of epithelial cells of medium dimensions, a large number of pyknotic nuclei; large, flattened cells, leucocytes, and numerous horny scales. In lactating females, there were small and middle-sized epithelial cells with large nuclei with a clearly visible structure. There were many leucocytes and by the end of lactation, middle-size epithelial cells were the predominate cell type.

I have examined too few porpoises in estrus to add much to Sokolov's description. However, in captive *Tursiops truncatus* that appear to be (behaviorally and from the appearance of the vulva) in estrus, there is a great increase in mucous production and an increase in the number of bacteria that are seen in the vaginal smear. This increase in the number of bacteria may be related to a higher level of bacteria in the tank water and may not be a feature of estrus in wild animals. In the *Tursiops truncatus* that I have observed, the apparent period of estrus was roughly thirty-six hours.

The Male Reproductive Cycle

The breeding season appears to be a very stressful time for mature males of most species of marine mammals. The testes, prostate, and muscles associated with the reproductive organs increase in size. In addition to the stress of fighting to control territory and/or females, food consumption may decrease markedly. This appears to be the time of greatest mortality for such animals, and the breeding season seems to be truly a test of survival of the fittest. The enlargement of the reproductive organs is attended by increased exposure to infection, and severe orchitis is apparently common based on the number of cases that have been found. The orchitis can progress to peritonitis and death. Fights between males, reduced nutrition, parasitism, and other incidental infections also combine to eliminate many individuals.

TABLE 10–22

PLASMA TESTOSTERONE LEVELS IN TWO MALE *TURSIOPS TRUNCATUS**

	Mar	Apr	Jun	Jul	1969 Aug	5 Sep	25 Sep	Oct	Nov	Dec
M	135 ng	500+	140	138	229	1026	1635	1560	707	170
A	39	62	11	7	48		85	167	24	

	Jan	Feb	Mar	1970 Apr						
M	608	548	685	1379						
A	47	44		38						

* Testerone level in the plasma of a young 215 kg male (M—estimated age 10 to 15 years) during his sixth and seventh years in captivity. These values are compared to another young male 135 kg in weight (A—estimated age 7 to 10 years) during his fourth and fifth years in captivity. The testosterone levels are reported in nanograms (ng). Adult human male levels range from 400–1200 ng and prepubertal children have levels lower than 100 ng.

Some characteristics of the male *Lagenorhynchus obliquidens* and *Delphinus sp.* in rut have been discussed by Ridgway and Green (1967). At the Navy Marine Bioscience Facility, we have gathered data correlating testis size, plasma testosterone levels, and month of the year in *Tursiops truncatus* (Harrison and Ridgway, 1970). Animals that had previously been regarded as mature (125 to 150 kg in weight and 2.3 to 2.6 m in length) invariably had plasma testosterone levels comparable to human children. One male that came to Point Mugu in September, 1962 (2.0 m and about 95 kg), still did not exhibit an adult male testosterone level in early 1970 when he was 2.5 m long and weighed 146 kg. Table 10–22 compares the testosterone levels of a 215 kg male that apparently attained maturity during his sixth year at Point Mugu and an immature male at the same facility. These data appear to support the Caldwells' conclusion (see Chap. 6) that *Tursiops truncatus* males mature at about fifteen years of age. The plasma testosterone level for our mature male is between 400 and 700 ngm during most of the year with a sharp rise to 1,200 ngm or more during early spring and early fall.

MISCELLANEOUS PHYSIOLOGICAL CONSIDERATIONS

Training the Animal to Cooperate in Experiments

Most of the reports on the physiology of aquatic mammals have been obtained through the use of uncooperative experimental animals. A seal or porpoise tied to a board or strapped to a sling is immediately under a stressful situation, thus it may be difficult to separate the responses to the distressing situation from the normal responses to be studied. Experiments in which the natural behavior of the animal is an important factor may be altered if conducted under highly unnatural conditions. To overcome these problems, we at the Navy Marine Bioscience Facility have trained marine mammals to work free and untethered in the open sea or in a large lagoon (Fig. 10–13). Six species have been worked in this manner, including *Tursiops truncatus* (Fig. 10–14), *Lagenorhynchus obliquidens* (Fig. 10–15), *Zalophus californianus, Mirounga angustiorstris, Phoca vitulina,* and *Orcinus orca*. Of these, *Tursiops truncatus* and the sea lion have been used most extensively.

The first porpoise to be trained and work free and untethered in the open sea was released for the first time at the Navy Marine Bioscience Facility in the summer of 1964 (Bailey, 1965). During that same summer, a trained porpoise was used for swimming speed tests in the open sea off Hawaii (Norris, 1965). Since that time, ten additional porpoises have

Figure 10–13 (*Top*). View of the Marine Bioscience Facility from the air. Mugu Lagoon is on the left and the Pacific Ocean is on the right.

Figure 10–14 (*Left*). Two trained bottlenosed porpoises leap on command.

Figure 10–15 (*Right*). A trained *Lagenorhynchus obliquidens* leaps by her trainer's boat in the open ocean off the Marine Bioscience Facility. Photograph provided by John Hall and A. B. Irvine.

been trained at the Navy Marine Bioscience Facility and worked free in the open sea.

The most highly publicized achievement took place in 1965 when we trained an Atlantic bottlenosed porpoise, "Tuffy," to act as guide, messenger, rescuer, (Fig. 10–16, 10–17), and errand boy for aquanauts engaged in the Navy SEALAB II experiment off La Jolla, California. This was the first demonstration of the capability of these animals to serve useful functions for man in the scientific investigation of the sea (Wood and Ridgway, 1965; Ridgway, 1966).

Figure 10–16. Tuffy and divers near underwater SEALAB habitat.

Operant conditioning techniques (see Breland and Breland, 1968, for a good review) have been employed in all of our training. Food is the only overt and systematic reward; however, it is always augmented by other factors such as the development of a special rapport and confidence between the animal and the trainer, and by stroking, which cetaceans often appear to enjoy and solicit (Fig. 10–18).

The desired behaviors are reinforced by the delivery of fish (several small fishes or several chunks of cut fish). One trainer says that porpoises and sea lions can count and thus he prefers to present several small bits rather than a larger unit of food. Absence of performance or incorrect behavior is not rewarded. If the animal fails to respond over several trials, it is punished by a time out during which the trainer turns his back or leaves the area. It is important to reward desired behaviors at the instant they occur. To facilitate this instantaneous reward, a bridging stimulus is employed. An ordinary police whistle is most commonly used to signal the correct response.

Figure 10–17. Tuffy demonstrated his capability to carry a rescue line to a lost diver during the SEALAB II experiment in 1965.

In newly acquired naive animals, the bridging stimulus is introduced at feeding time. As the animal turns or swims toward the trainer, the whistle is sounded and a reward is given. After this bridge becomes firmly associated with food reward, it is established as a secondary reinforcement and serves to communicate to the animal the fact that he has performed correctly and food reward will be presented shortly. The animal soon learns the game and tends to repeat behaviors that have brought the whistle and reward.

Animal training takes patience. The long journey to a highly reliable finished product is started with a single small step. The most rapid progress is attained by a long sequence of small individual steps. If the trainer tries to go too fast, the animal may become confused and frightened and the resultant time consumed will be far greater than if slow but systematic progress is made. Each new step should be a variation of a natural behavior or a well-established acquired behavior. The trainer should be careful to keep all of these variations oriented in the direction of the finished task. Behaviors that have already been learned are repeated again and again in order to build the animal's confidence in the training situation.

The animal is required to come to the trainer and take food from his hand, to station himself in front of the trainer, and to permit the touch

Figure 10–18. Porpoises appear to enjoy being stroked.

of the trainer. Coming to and touching an object with the snout is the next requirement. If the animal is to be taught to paddle-press, the task is usually introduced by cautiously touching the animal's snout with the paddle and sounding the bridging stimulus. In successive trials, the paddle is held a few centimeters in front of the snout and the animal is required to press it. Soon the paddle can be placed anywhere in the pool and the animal will swim over and press it. The paddle-pressing behavior can be used in many experimental situations as a yes-no choice or as a switch to indicate the accomplishment of a task.

It is essential for an animal being used for experiments in the open ocean to return to the trainer on command. Thus, the animal is trained to answer a recall signal. We have used sound sources varying from metal "crickets" and battery-powered doorbell buzzers to specially designed underwater "pingers" as recall signals. The animal is required to come to the recall signal and touch it with his snout. This must be the animal's primary behavior and will be repeated again and again. This signal must be answered whenever it is heard under any conditions, and, since the animal will be returned to its pen at the end of each training session, it is next required to answer the recall signal by swimming through gates in the tank. Most animals are initially fearful of this and must be coaxed a little at a time until they have made several passes through the gate and lose their fear of the situation.

When a porpoise's recall response is highly reliable, he is ready for secondary training in the lagoon (Fig. 10–13). Here in the holding pens all prior behaviors are repeated many times and strengthened.

When the trainer judges that the porpoise is reliable enough, he opens the gate and starts using the open lagoon as a training area. The next major task is generally an easy one—to teach the animal to ride the wake of a small boat (Fig. 10–19). This is done by calling the animal to the boat and then rewarding him for swimming beside the boat as it moves away. Porpoises very quickly take up surfing in the boat's stern wake rather than the much more tiresome swimming. In this way the porpoise and trainer can travel several miles in a fairly short time.

After the animal performs all tasks reliably in the lagoon, he is taken to an ocean pen where the behaviors are again repeated. The animal is then released for work in the open ocean as the experimental program requires.

Figure 10–19. Porpoise riding in stern wake of a boat. In this way the porpoise actually surfed to the deep-dive site.

Many of the techniques mentioned for cetaceans are used with pinnipeds. The pinnipeds are, however, amphibious and can be readily trained to enter a cage for transport to the work area. The first task generally taught a new sea lion is to mount a training seat (Fig. 10–20). Such props have been employed in the trained "seal" acts of zoos and circuses for many years. The following are several advantages to having the animal on a seat: (a) It brings his attention to the trainer. (b) The trainer remains in front of the seat and the animal must ordinarily get down from the seat to attack the trainer, thus allowing the trainer time to retreat if a new animal becomes aggressive. (c) It brings the sea lion to height roughly equal to that of the trainer. (d) It provides a convenient platform for applying a harness and otherwise manipulating the animal. All new signals, manipulanda, and many of the new behaviors are introduced to the animal on the training seat. For example, the sea lion is taught to paddlepress on the seat. The paddle is then gradually moved away into the water until the animal is forced to enter the water to press it.

The next step is to accustom the sea lion to a cage. He is first enticed into the cage with fish and then is fed there. He might be required to

Figure 10–20. Sea lion on a training seat. This sea lion is wearing a harness and muzzle which are used with animals that work in the open ocean.

spend the night in the cage. Thus, the cage becomes home base and the recall signal (which may well include a visual as well as an auditory signal) always calls the animal back to his cage. All behaviors for sea lions in the open ocean start and end in the cage.

The desired behaviors are chained together in a tank then transferred to the lagoon. When the sea lion has become quite reliable, he is required to perform in the open ocean. Overall, sea lions have not proved quite as reliable as porpoises in the open ocean. Thus, the animal is trained to return to his cage for reward after each task, and the total period of freedom is reduced.

Irvine (1970) has recently reviewed the techniques employed in training cetaceans and pinnipeds for work in the open sea.

Marine Mammals and the "Bends"

Why don't marine mammals get the bends when they dive? This is a question that I have frequently heard. First of all, they are breathhold divers and thus are not exposed to compressed gas (except for that in the lungs) as are SCUBA and "hard-hat" divers. For a long time, this was thought to be a sufficient explanation, but Paulev (1965) demonstrated that man was susceptible to decompression sickness following repeated breathhold dives.

We still do not know how resistant marine mammals actually are to decompression sickness. Again, the total physiological picture of the animal must be considered, and no one system or capability can be considered as providing the whole answer.

My associates and I have recently conducted tests with an Atlantic bottlenosed porpoise (Ridgway *et al.*, 1969) and a California sea lion, both of which were trained to dive and work in the open sea.

The experiments were carried out with a male *Tursiops truncatus* 225 cm in length and weighing 138 kg, and a castrated male *Zalophus californianus* weighing 65 kg. The porpoise (Tuffy) flown from Gulfport, Mississippi, to Point Mugu in September, 1962, had been in training of one type or another since that time. Since December, 1964, he had been housed almost continuously in ocean pens and was worked free and untethered in the open ocean. This animal has participated in numerous studies, including the Navy SEALAB II experiment (Fig. 10–17). On a number of occasions, he was employed to find and mark underwater equipment containing acoustic beacons. The sea lion has been in captivity for almost two years and was trained specifically for this project.

The animals were trained to perform two tasks. The first required them to dive on acoustic command to a diving test switch located at the end of a cable. The switch was pressed, turning the sound off. Each of the animals returned to the surface and exhaled into an inverted water-filled funnel placed with the large opening about 50 cm below the surface (Fig. 10–21). The porpoise was also taught to breathhold just under the surface, again in response to a sound, and exhale into the funnel on command. Thus, expired air samples could be collected from any depth or duration of dive that the animal was willing to make.

Tuffy had previously been trained to work with divers on the ocean bottom. We took advantage of this training to have him swim rapidly

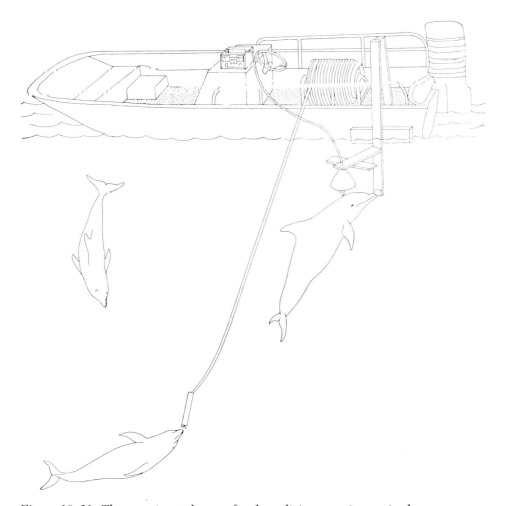

Figure 10–21. The experimental setup for deep-diving experiments in the open ocean. The porpoise (or sea lion) dives down when the go signal is turned on. He pushes the plunger on the end of the diving test switch, turning the signal off, and then returns to exhale into the funnel before surfacing. Reproduced with the permission of *Science*.

back and forth between two divers at 20 m depth in order that an expired air sample could be collected from the animal after he had exercised at that depth. He could also be commanded to come to, and exhale into, the funnel on any given breath after a deep dive or after a surface breathhold. In this way, we collected air samples from breaths varying from the third to the fifteenth after a dive, third to fifteenth after a surface breathhold, and random breaths during normal leisurely swimming on the surface. We also interrupted hyperventilation, which occurred in anticipation of deep dives to collect expired air samples.

For deep-diving experiments, the porpoise was released from his pen to swim beside a small outboard-powered boat to a diving site up to five miles offshore. The porpoise usually took up a position in the boat's stern wave and thus actually rode or surfed for most of the trip (Fig. 10–19).

The sea lion rode on a boat in a cage. When the diving test setup was ready, the animal was released from his cage to make the dive. He normally dove directly from the boat and down to press the plunger on the test switch. Then he returned to the surface to blow in the funnel. After blowing in the funnel, he would climb back on the boat and go into his cage to be rewarded (Fig. 10–22).

The deep-diving device consisted of an acoustic beacon, off switch, temperature sensor, and pressure transducer in a housing at the end of 308 m of five-wire marine cable. A control box in the boat registered depth and temperature and had a switch to activate the dive signal and gauges. A hydrophone permitted monitoring of the acoustic signal from the deep-dive device. In calm seas, with little current, the cable hung straight down from the boat and the pressure-depth reading was almost identical with

Figure 10–22 A. The diving test switch is lowered over the side. B. The sea lion dives down to press it. C. The sea lion returns, climbs back on the boat after blowing in the funnel.

the measured length of cable over the side of the boat. As the surface winds or currents increased, the cable curvature increased as a result of relative water motion. Under these conditions, the pressure-depth reading could be considerably less than the length of cable in the water.

When the porpoise or the sea lion returned to the surface and exhaled, the respiratory gas displaced the water in the funnel (Figs. 10–23, 10–24); a stopcock was then opened and water pressure forced the gas through

Figure 10–23. Tuffy blowing in the funnel after the completion of a deep dive. Photograph reproduced with the permission of *Science*. (Official U.S. Navy Photograph.)

polyethylene tubing into a lubricated 100 ml glass syringe. The first 100 ml was disposed of through a three-way stopcock and the second 100 ml collected for analysis. Duplicate samples were taken on each dive.

Initial analyses were done on a Scholander analyzer. With these for calibration, we felt secure in using a less laborious method. This involved an infrared carbon dioxide analyzer (Godart capnograph) in series with a nitrogen analyzer. The oxygen content was determined by subtracting the sum of carbon dioxide and nitrogen values from 99 percent (100 minus 1 percent inert gas). The instruments were calibrated before and after each day's analyses with four cylinders of gas that had been analyzed on a

Haldane apparatus. Water vapor pressure was accounted for by calibration within the nitrogen values. All of the air samples were assumed to be saturated, since they were exhaled through water. One set of samples was done on a gas chromatograph that was calibrated by frequent comparison with results of Haldane analyses. Other random samples which were analyzed on the Haldane were within a standard deviation of results derived by the other methods.

Figure 10–24. Sea lion blowing in funnel.

For these experiments, the porpoise made over 500 deep dives, more than 120 breathholds at the surface, and 4 dives in which he swam back and forth between two divers on the bottom at 20 m depth. The results of the respiratory gas analyses are presented in Fig. 10–25. The pulmonary oxygen was much higher after dives to depth than after the surface breathholds of identical periods of time. After rapid swimming at 20 m depth, the exhaled oxygen was considerably lower than after a 200 m dive requiring a similar amount of time and at least as much exercise. Carbon dioxide values for dives of 100 to 300 m were almost identical. Values of carbon dioxide for all dives were much lower than for surface breathholds.

Increased depth with its greater pressure should force more of the oxygen into the blood. Yet it was found that less was used. This indicated that some (or all) of the gas in the lungs was isolated from the alveoli. Because we have not obtained a breath sample from the animal at depth, we cannot estimate the rapidly changing tensions in the lungs, as Schaefer *et al.* (1968) have been able to do for man.

Because the porpoise expires explosively (Fig. 10–26), much of the gas is not caught by the funnel. In spite of this, we usually caught at least 3 L. There clearly had been no massive absorption of nitrogen.

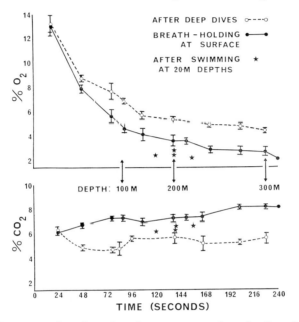

Figure 10–25. Oxygen and carbon dioxide in porpoise breath after deep dives, after breathholding just under the surface, and after swimming at a depth of 20 m. Each point represents seven to twenty dives or surface breathholds. The arrows indicate the average times and points on each graph that represent or correspond to dives of 100, 200, and 300 m.

Our porpoises dive on inspiration. This was obvious from close observation of numerous dives and from the fact that Tuffy returned from depth and exhaled several liters of air into the funnel. Numerous authors have suggested that all marine mammals dive on expiration. This appears to be true for Weddell, elephant, and harbor seals but definitely not for porpoises.

The average rate of descent for the porpoise was around 3.0 m/sec for dives of 200 m and less. The rate of ascent was about the same. The amount of time it took the porpoise to stop, press the switch, and start back toward the surface varied from five to nine seconds. For a 300 m dive, his average rate of descent slowed to 2.67 m/second, and the rate of ascent averaged about 2.88 m/second.

Figure 10–26. The porpoise often blows explosively and much of the air is not caught by the funnel.

In one thirty-four minute session, the porpoise made ten dives to 200 m. Twelve minutes and fifty-two seconds of the thirty-four minutes were spent at depths in excess of 100 m. In another such session twelve dives were made in fifty-eight minutes, and about fifteen minutes were spent below 100 m. In three additional sessions, the porpoise was able to make ten dives to 260 m in sixty minutes. (This animal has made as many as forty-eight dives to depths of 40 to 260 m in a single four-hour session.) Between dives, the porpoise would blow eight to fifteen times in one minute and dive again. Random expired air samples collected showed the oxygen and carbon dioxide levels of the first breath after these 200 to 260 m dives to be as seen in Table 10–23. However, analysis on subsequent breaths after such dives gave oxygen values of 13 percent or more, but the carbon dioxide values were 7.5 to 9 percent for the first few breaths after the dive. By the eighth to tenth breath after the dive, the exhaled air was usually back to the normal range, and the porpoise was willing to dive again. It appeared that the calculated oxygen debt incurred during the dive was not completely paid off after the dive, and the blowoff of carbon dioxide appeared to be the determining factor as to when the porpoise would dive again. This carbon dioxide unloading is compatible with the measurements Scholander (1940) made on restrained porpoises.

TABLE 10–23

PERCENTAGE OF OXYGEN AND CARBON DIOXIDE IN THE PORPOISE'S EXPIRED BREATH AFTER DIVES TO 200m*

	1st Exhalation	*3rd Exhalation*	*6th Exhalation*	*9th Exhalation*
O_2	5.4 ± 0.4	11.9 ± 1.9	13.0 ± 1.2	13.2 ± 1.4
CO_2	5.7 ± 0.5	8.2 ± 0.6	7.5 ± 0.4	6.3 ± 0.7

* Each column represents a figure from a different dive. On one dive, the breath was collected on the first exhalation, on the next the ninth, followed by the third and so on, randomly.

Tuffy's tidal air, measured by having him exhale completely into a large, calibrated canister, ranged from 5 to 6 L. If we assume that tidal air is 80 percent of respiratory volume (RV), then RV is about 7 L. Based on Boyle's law, at 300 m depth, all of the air in Tuffy's lungs must be compressed into a volume of 200 to 260 ml. This volume is smaller than that of the trachea and bronchi, to say nothing of the nares and nasal sacs. When a large *Tursiops truncatus* weighing 200 kg died at our facility, an endotracheal tube was inserted in an attempt to revive the animal. When this failed, we measured the respiratory volume by first inflating the animal to the greatest extent possible and then deflating as much as possible. The measured respiratory volume was 11 L. The body with deflated lungs weighed 10 kg under water. On full inflation, the body was just about neutral or very slightly buoyant. Tests on the fully inflated, freshly excised porpoise lungs in a pressure chamber indicated that the bronchi and trachea collapse at depth, also. The interlocking cartilaginous rings of the trachea are heavy and strong, but they are structured in such a way as to make the trachea flexible and resilient rather than rigid (Ridgway, 1968). The bony nares seem to be the only structure of the respiratory system not collapsible, and their volume is no more than 50 ml. The air sinuses of the head have venous plexuses associated with them that probably expand at depth in the same manner as has been proposed for seals and sea lions (Odend'hal and Poulter, 1966). Man is limited in the depth of his breath-hold dives by his ability to make such pulmonary and circulatory adjustments (Schaefer, *et al.*, 1968).

As the porpoise dives, the thorax starts to collapse. Divers have observed this at only 10 m, and by 60 m, thoracic collapse is quite apparent. This has also been observed with an underwater camera and surface television monitor to a depth of 300 m (Fig. 10–1). The lungs have a great deal of elastic tissue (See Chap. 5) and the flexible bronchi and trachea together with a flexible rib cage with long, thin cartilage connecting with the sternum give the porpoise a resilient thorax that continuously changes shape.

The capability of breathholding is a necessary part of staying beneath the surface for extended periods. It alone does not allow the animal to go deep. This ability comes from adaptations in structure that provide for flexibility, so that air is compressed away from the alveoli during the increasing pressure of a dive. The nitrogen is prevented from going into solution in significant quantities; thus, the animal avoids any problem of the bends.

The deepest dives made by the sea lion were to a depth of 250 m. On the shallower dives (50 m or less), the sea lion exhaled 1 to 3 L of gas into the funnel, but as the dives got deeper, less gas was collected. We were unable to collect a representative air sample from a dive deeper than about

100 m. After the deeper dives, the sea lion would push his muzzle directly into the funnel (Fig. 10–24) as if to exhale. Generally, however, only 25 to 50 ml of air could be collected and that was quite high in oxygen and low in carbon dioxide content. It was clear that the animal simply did not have any air left after these deeper dives. Apparently the sea lion would exhale on the way down, as divers observed on a number of occasions. This exhalation of lung air may be an important diving adjustment for this species.

In summary, there are three primary adjustments and perhaps a number of secondary adjustments that appear to provide protection from decompression sickness. These adjustments vary among the species. The first primary adjustment involves the isolation of lung air from the alveoli during deeper portions of a dive. Apparently this can be accomplished completely by lung collapse, as in porpoises; or by exhalation before the dive, as in seals; or by exhalation on the way down as in the case of our sea lion. The second adjustment involves the flexible thoracic structure (Fig. 10–1), rete, and highly distensible veins in the thorax, all of which probably allow the alveoli to collapse without the danger of thoracic squeeze seen in human divers. The third adjustment involves the respiratory mechanics and an improvement in the efficiency of gas exchange on the surface. After a deep and prolonged dive, the respiratory rate may increase to ten times the resting value. The heart and circulatory rates also speed up to reduce the recovery time. Thus the blood and myoglobin are rapidly reoxygenated, the accumulated carbon dioxide is quickly purged, and any nitrogen that might be accumulated during a dive is rapidly blown off.

Some Interspecies Physiological Comparisons

Ridgway and Johnston (1966) observed an interesting physiological comparison between three species of odontocetes that appeared to vary somewhat in ecology and in swimming and diving habits. The species studied were the bottlenosed porpoise. *Tursiops truncatus* (see Chap. 1, p. 97), the Pacific white-striped porpoise, *Lagenorhynchus obliquidens* (see Chap. 1, p. 89), and the Dall porpoise, *Phocoenoides dalli* (see Chap. 1, p. 115).

The bottlenosed porpoise frequents inshore waters including bays and estuaries. Some individuals or groups appear to take up permanent residence in such areas. The other species, *Lagenorhynchus obliquidens* and *Phocoenoides dalli* are more pelagic, swim much faster, and probably dive deeper than does *Tursiops truncatus*.

In captivity, *Tursiops truncatus* adapts very readily and can be kept for many years. *Lagenorhynchus obliquidens* has been kept successfully at several locations but does not adapt nearly as well as *Tursiops truncatus*.

The Dall porpoise has been very difficult to keep, and only one has been maintained in captivity for over a year.

Table 10–24 compares the three species from the standpoint of heart size, brain weight, thyroid weight, and body surface area. *Lagenorhynchus obliquidens* is intermediate in all cases. *Tursiops truncatus* has the larger brain and surface area, whereas *Phocoenoides dalli* has the larger thyroid and heart. *Phocoenoides dalli* also has a relatively larger body muscle mass and a thinner blubber layer (hypodermis). Other areas of comparison can be seen in Tables 10–4 and 10–5. The highest blood volume, hematocrit and hemoglobin content, and the smallest red-blood-cell diameter are observed in *Phocoenoides dalli*. These factors combine to give *Phocoenoides dalli* at least a threefold increase in oxygen-carrying and storage capabilities.

TABLE 10–24

APPROXIMATE RELATIONSHIP OF HEART, BRAIN, THYROID AND
BODY SURFACE AREA IN THREE ODONTOCETES

	Heart Weight (% of Body Weights)	Brain Weight (% of Body Weight)	Thyroid Weight (mg/kg Body Weight)	Body Surface Area (Average for a 100 kg Animal)
Tursiops truncatus	0.54	1.1–2.3	300–400	1.85m²
Lagenorhynchus obliquidens	0.85	1.0–1.4	500–600	1.70m²
Phocoenoides dalli	1.31	0.7–1.0	750–900	1.50m²

The extremely large heart of the Dall porpoise seems to be an adaptation to the great power required for fast swimming, rather than for prolonged diving or as an adaptation to handle the large blood volume. The elephant seal, which has the largest blood volume known, does not have an unusually large heart. The large heart may help the animal to make frequent deep dives because it can beat at a slower rate during the dive and still maintain blood pressure. It appears that the heart can respond faster and with a greater stroke volume when the animal surfaces, thus allowing for a faster payoff of the oxygen debt incurred during the dive and a quicker blowoff of carbon dioxide accumulated. Since Dall porpoises feed on deep water fishes such as hake (Norris and Prescott, 1961), as well as on squid, they apparently have need to make frequent deep dives.

The Physiology of Hearing in Cetaceans

Although senses were discussed in Chapter 7, some recent experiments have yielded significant information on the physiology of hearing that can appropriately be discussed here.

Since at least as early as the work of Camper in 1777, scientists have speculated about the function of hearing in cetaceans (Purves, 1966).

Based on dissections of dead material, numerous and divergent theories have been advanced to explain the acoustic functions of the cetacean meatus, bulla, ossicular chain, eardrum, and jawbone.

Particularly in recent years, the motivation to obtain a definitive explanation for cetacean hearing has been high. A behavioral study by Johnson (1966) demonstrated a wide frequency range of hearing for a bottlenosed porpoise. The same species is known to have a highly sophisticated underwater sonar system (Busnel, 1967). Also, the cortical and subcortical acoustic centers of the porpoise brain are well developed (Breathnach, 1960). Bullock *et al.* (1968) reported the first neurophysiological experiments on hearing and echolocation in cetaceans.

The cetaceans, in a sense, provide an example of "evolutionary pressures in reverse." The ear of land mammals evolved from an aquatic ear. And with land mammals as ancestors (Romer, 1966), the cetaceans have completed the cycle by returning to the sea.

Under the direction of Wever, a program was initiated in 1966 to elucidate the physiology of hearing in the small cetaceans *Tursiops truncatus* and *Lagenorhynchus obliquidens.* Clearly, a test of hearing in live anesthetized porpoises was necessary. Wever's group decided to assess the role of auditory structures through experiments in which the cochlear potentials of porpoises could be recorded (Wever, 1966). Surgical manipulations of the meatus, eardrum, and middle ear structures were carried out and their affect upon the cochlear potential recorded.

Although, as stated above, it is generally accepted that porpoises evolved from a land mammal with an "air" ear, the results of the work by Wever's group supported the idea that the meatus and eardrum of porpoises no longer functions in the hearing process. Since cochlear potentials resulting from point source vibration of the lateral meatus were not altered by dissection and separation of the meatus pathway, It was concluded that the meatus of the porpoise was no more important for sound conduction than the surrounding tissue of the head. The fact that relatively high pressure applications at the eardrum failed to damp the cochlear potential argued strongly for the disinvolvement of the eardrum with the hearing process. Bisection of the tympanic ligament did not affect the cochlear potential. This disinvolvement of the eardrum was also confirmed by a fine anatomical study of the middle ear which revealed that the eardrum was not directly connected to the malleus.

Since no direct coupling between the degenerated aerial system of the porpoise and the middle ear ossicular chain was found, further cochlear potential studies were directed at analyzing the system in terms of direct vibration modes of stimulation such as bone conduction and tissue conduction. A point source bone stimulator driven at a constant frequency of 20 kHz was systematically moved over the body surface of the porpoise while the varying amplitude of the cohlear potential was monitored. Thus, the whole body was mapped for acoustic transmission characteristics. This study revealed that the skull was acoustically isolated from the ear; however, the lateral aspect of the lower jaw was apparently the most sensitive area of the body so far as sound transmission is concerned.

The fact that the axis of the stapes of the porpoise was noted to project on an imaginary line through the aspect of the lower jaw which was found to be the most sensitive reception area in the body mapping study suggested the operation of Barany's translational bone conduction phenomena for porpoises (Barany, 1938).

An 18 dB drop in cochlear potential observed with the damping of the porpoise ossicular chain during high frequency bone stimulation supported the assumption that the ossicular chain was operational in accord with the idea that porpoises hear by translational bone conduction.

The major findings of Wever's group concerning the auditory system of porpoises will be published in forthcoming papers dealing with the surgical approach (Ridgway *et al.*, 1970b) and the anatomy and physiology of the ear. To date, the following reports of the porpoise auditory study have been made: McCormick (1968a), McCormick (1968b), and McCormick *et al.* (1969 and 1970).

HEMATOLOGY AND BLOOD CHEMISTRY

The White Blood Cells

In my experience, marine mammals usually, but not always, manifest a strong neutrophilic response to infections. Animals with bacterial pneumonias, erysipelas, gastrointestinal infections, abscesses, and urinary tract infections have manifested white blood cells (WBC) as high as 45,000 per cubic millimeter. One porpoise with chronic dental alveolitis had a WBC count of 27,000 to 44,000 per cubic millimeter for a period of four months. An abscess then developed on the lower jaw and two affected teeth were removed, after which the WBC rapidly fell to within the normal range (Table 10–25).

A strong neutrophilic response is, of course, a good clinical sign when an animal has an infection. In my experience, animals that have been in captivity for a long period of time will usually show a strong neutrophilic response. However, newly captured animals that have not yet adapted rarely do.

The high percentage of eosinophils in the differential analysis (Table 10–25) of white blood cells has been reported previously (Laurie, 1933;

TABLE 10–25

AVERAGE VALUES (± STANDARD DEVIATION) FOR TOTAL WHITE CELL
COUNTS AND DIFFERENTIAL ANALYSIS ON BLOOD FROM SMALL ODON-
TOCETES MAINTAINED AT THE MARINE BIOSCIENCE FACILITY

| | | | | Differential Count | | | |
N	Total WBC's (10³/mm³) Mean ± SD	N	Neutrophils (%) Mean ± SD	Stabs (%) Mean ± SD	Lymphocytes (%) Mean ± SD	Monocytes (%) Mean ± SD	Eosinophils (%) Mean ± SD
			Ten ♂ *Tursiops truncatus*				
154	10,675 ± 4,864	155	61 ± 13	1 ± 2	22 ± 10	3 ± 3	13 ± 9
			Eleven ♀ *Tursiops truncatus*				
167	9,780 ± 3,087	163	61 ± 13	1 ± 2	20 ± 11	2 ± 2	15 ± 9
			Three ♂ *Lagenorhynchus obliquidens*				
41	7,922 ± 2,295	42	43 ± 15	1 ± 1	29 ± 14	5 ± 3	21 ± 11
			Two ♀ *Lagenorhynchus obliquidens*				
31	6,668 ± 1,295	30	41 ± 11	1 ± 1	28 ± 9	5 ± 3	24 ± 10
			One ♂ *Phocoenoides dalli*				
12	5,513 ± 1,941		48 ± 19	1 ± 1	43 ± 17	4 ± 2	5 ± 3
			Two ♂ *Orcinus orca*				
6	10,380 ± 3,804	6	78 ± 12	3 ± 2	15 ± 10	3 ± 2	2 ± 1
			Two ♂ *Globicephala scammoni*				
13	11,450 ± 1,553	10	66 ± 10	6 ± 6	19 ± 6	3 ± 2	7 ± 7
			Five ♂ *Inia geoffrensis*				
9	14,586 ± 3,135	9	66 ± 16	4 ± 2	21 ± 7	4 ± 3	5 ± 4
			Three ♀ *Inia geoffrensis*				
4	12,200 ± 2,100	4	67 ± 14	3 ± 1	20 ± 8	3 ± 3	4 ± 3

TABLE 10–26

WHITE BLOOD CELLS OF PINNIPEDS*

| | | | | Differential Count | | | |
N	Total WBC's (10³/mm³) Mean ± SD	N	Neutrophils (%) Mean ± SD	Stabs (%) Mean ± SD	Lymphocytes (%) Mean ± SD	Monocytes (%) Mean ± SD	Eosinophils (%) Mean ± SD
			Five *Phoca vitulina* (Normal)				
6	8,016 ± 1,000	6	59 ± 20	1 ± 1	33 ± 22	4 ± 2	1 ± 1
			Phoca vitulina (Sick) #1				
1	30,800	1	46	51	2	1 ±	0
			Phoca vitulina (Sick) #2				
2	11,025 ± 3,147	2	64 ± 14	6 ± 2	24 ± 4	5 ± 5	1 ± 1
			Phoca vitulina (Sick) #3				
1	23,900	1	54	1	36	5	3
			Eight *Zalophus californianus* (Normal)				
8	9,232 ± 1,533	9	58 ± 7	6 ± 6	28 ± 10	4 ± 2	4 ± 4
			Zalophus californianus (Sick) #1				
1	34,100	1	63	2	23	2	10
			Three *Mirounga angustirostris* (Normal)				
3	9,526 ± 1,856	2	55 ± 11	0	38 ± 14	3 ± 1	4 ± 1
			Mirounga angustirostris (Sick) #1				
4	24,437 ± 3,051	4	72 ± 7	10 ± 8	12 ± 8	4 ± 3	3 ± 3

* Average values (± standard deviation) for total white cell counts and differential analysis on blood from some normal and sick pinnipeds maintained at the Marine Bioscience Facility.

Miller and Ridgway, 1963; Medway and Geraci, 1964; Anderson, 1966; and Ridgway, 1965, and 1968). When first captured, the Pacific white-striped dolphins often manifest a very high (50 to 80%) lymphocyte value in the differential court, but after a few months in captivity, these values decrease (Table 10–25). Otherwise, the differential can be interpreted much as in other mammals. Our pinniped data are limited, but WBC values from some normal and sick animals are shown in Table 10–26.

Blood Clotting

All cetaceans tested (*Tursiops truncatus, Lagenorhynchus obliquidens, Orcinus orca, Delphinus sp., Globicephala scammoni,* and *Phocoenoides dalli*) have had prolonged blood clotting times. Lee and White clotting times for bottlenosed porpoises have averaged about forty-five minutes (Ridgway, 1968). Clot retraction is also slow, and it has been demonstrated that several species, at least, lack blood clotting factor 12 or Hageman factor (Lewis, 1969; Robinson *et al.*, 1969). This does not mean that these cetaceans are "bleeders." The deficiency does not affect clotting of blood in normal wounds, venipuncture, or other tissue damage. It does affect *in vitro* clotting, and perhaps it might influence intravascular clotting. Decreased propensity for intravascular clotting might be an advantage for a diving mammal, since disseminated intravascular coagulation has been shown to be a major factor in severe cases of decompression sickness (Holland, 1969). In man, disseminated intravascular coagulation also occurs in shock, and it is a transient coagulation that may obstruct the microcirculation. It is thought to involve the transformation of fibrinogen to fibrin, agglutination of red blood cells, and sticking of platelets.

Circulatory changes that occur in diving marine mammals have already been mentioned. During prolonged dives, circulation is restricted, carbon dioxide levels increase, and the blood becomes more acid. In man, slow-flowing acid blood is hypercoagulable. It seems reasonable to assume that diving mammals would have to evolve blood factors that would resist this situation.

The anticoagulant activity for whale heparin has been shown to be quite high (Hashimoto *et al.*, 1963; Yoshizawa, 1964; Abe *et al.*, 1965). Whale heparin has been employed as an anticoagulant in human clinical cases (Abe *et al.*, 1968) and satisfactory results were reported. These workers suggested that whale heparin had an influence on the activation of the fibrinolysis system.

It appears, therefore, that cetacean hematology is a fruitful field for research that might have direct human clinical application in the treatment of decompression sickness, shock, and other disorders that involve blood clotting.

Blood Groups

Two blood group alleles (Ju 1 and Ju 2) have been demonstrated in fin whales and sperm whales (Fujino, 1954; Cushing *et al.*, 1963). A study of bottlenosed porpoise blood has shown the presence of "naturally occurring" saline agglutinins in the serum, which demonstrate the likelihood of several blood groups (Myhre *et al.*, 1969). These blood groups influence the survival of transfused cells and thus have clinical significance. Before transfusion, donor bloods must be crossmatched with the recipient, even when the recipient has had no prior transfusions.

Plasma Enzymes

Values of serum glutamic oxalacetic transaminase (SGOT) or lactic dehydrogenase (LDH) activity (Tables 10–27 to 10–29) have not always been of significant diagnostic benefit, but probably with continued accumulation and evaluation of these data, they will prove more useful. Extensive damage to skeletal muscle will definitely produce an increased LDH and SGOT. In one porpoise that died of an extensive myositis and peritonitis, the SGOT and LDH were both elevated over 2000 units, while the serum glutamic pyruvic transaminase activity (SGPT) remained within the normal range (Table 10–30). A beached *Delphinus sp.* had extensive icterus that was evident from observing the plasma. The bilirubin was elevated, the SGOT was 2280 units, the SGPT was 680, and the ornathine carbamyl transferase (OCT) was 801.* Subsequent postmortem examination revealed a severely damaged liver with a fluke infestation. The LDH isoenzymes that are thought to be associated with skeletal muscle are

TABLE 10–27

SERUM GLUTAMIC OXALACETIC TRANSAMINASE AND
ALKALINE PHOSPHATASE*

= *Species*	*Sex*	*No. Studied*	*N*	*SGOT (Henry Units) Mean ± SD*	*N*	*Alk. Phos. (King-Armstrong-Units) Mean ± SD*
Tursiops truncatus	M	10	73	225 ± 109	22	42 ± 27
Tursiops truncatus	F	11	99	188 ± 89	49	30 ± 14
Lagenorhynchus obliquidens	M	3	19	255 ± 115	2	23 ± 4
Lagenorhynchus obliquidens	F	2	15	193 ± 63	4	42 ± 8
Phocoenoides dalli	M	1	11	406 ± 181	. .	. . . .
Orcinus orca	M	2	4	61 ± 11	4	38 ± 17
Globicephala scammoni	M	2	5	199 ± 52	5	42 ± 29
Inia geoffrensis	M	5	9	175 ± 101	7	15 ± 8
Inia geoffrensis	F	3	3	150 ± 62	3	21 ± 6

* Average values (± standard deviation) for serum glutamic oxaloacetic transaminase (SGOT) and alkaline phosphatase from small odontocetes maintained at the Marine Bioscience Facility.

* Our normal *Tursiops truncatus* have OCT values less than 10 nanomoles of carbon dioxide.

TABLE 10-28

LACTIC ACID DEHYDROGENASE AND ISOENZYMES*

Specimens	Total LDH (Units)		I.E. 1 (Cardiac) %		I.E. 2 (Cardiac) %		I.E. 3 (Muscle)** %		I.E. 4 (Muscle)** %		I.E. 5 (Hepatic) %	
	N	Mean ± SD	N	Mean ± SD	N	Mean ± SD	N	Mean ± SD	N	Mean ± SD	N	Mean ± SD
10 ♂ *Tursiops truncatus*	80	271 ± 181	8	7.8 ± 3.7	8	27.8 ± 6.8	8	38.3 ± 2.0	8	19.6 ± 3.7	8	6.0 ± 4.1
11 ♀ *Tursiops truncatus*	100	234 ± 133	15	11.13 ± 6.2	15	32.47 ± 4.24	15	36.60 ± 6.2	14	14.86 ± 6.8	14	4.71 ± 2.2
3 ♂ *Lagenorhynchus obliquidens*	18	507 ± 193	2	11.5	2	30.5	2	36.5	2	14.5	2	5.5
2 ♀ *Lagenorhynchus obliquidens*	11	372 ± 262	2	14.0	2	27.5	2	32.5	2	19.0	2	7.0
2 ♂|♀ *Orcinus orca*	5	263 ± 178	5	16.4 ± 4.5	5	34.2 ± 7.2	5	31.6 ± 6.0	5	11.0 ± 5.1	5	6.8 ± 1.6
2 ♂|♂ *Globicephala scammoni*	7	347 ± 100	5	9.8 ± 4.2	5	25.4 ± 4.0	5	36.2 ± 2.6	5	18.8 ± 4.4	5	9.8 ± 2.4
7 ♀ & ♂ *Inia geoffrensis*	9	378 ± 196	8	18.9 ± 7.0	8	35.9 ± 3.7	8	25.5 ± 7.7	8	12.8 ± 4.1	8	7.0 ± 3.4

* Average values (± standard deviation) for LDH and the isoenzymes in some odontocetes maintained at the Marine Bioscience Facility.
** The 3rd and 4th isoenzymes are thought to come primarily from skeletal muscle but may originate in many other tissues.

TABLE 10–29
PLASMA ENZYMES IN PINNIPEDS*

	SGPT (Units)		SGOT (Units)		LDH (Units)		Alk. Phos. (Units)
N	Mean ± SD	N	Mean ± SD	N	Mean ± SD	N	Mean ± SD
			Five *Zalophus californianus* (Normal)				
3	49 ± 6	6	64 ± 17	4	337 ± 178	5	11.2 ± 6.7
			One *Mirounga angustirostris* (Normal)				
		5	102 ± 27	4	310 ± 162		

* The SGOT and SGPT are reported in Henry units, the LDH in Wracker units, and the alkaline phosphatase in King-Armstrong units.

always increased in porpoises as compared with man (Table 10–28). The SGOT, LDH, and SGPT activity values are normally highest in porpoises with higher metabolic rates (Table 10–27, 10–28, 10–30). The SGPT activity values appear to be diagnostically useful. Values of over 100 units in bottlenosed porpoises have been recorded only from sick animals (Table 10–30). Although data on plasma OCT activity is scant, it appears to be elevated in cases with liver damage.

TABLE 10–30
SERUM GLUTAMIC PYRUVIC TRANSAMINASE*

		N	Normal Mean ± SD	N	Sick Mean ± SD
Lagenorhynchus obliquidens	Males	8	99 ± 33	5	340 ± 100
Lagenorhynchus obliquidens	Females	6	88 ± 22	1	660
Tursiops truncatus	Males	45	40 ± 24	2	330
Tursiops truncatus	Females	43	38 ± 18	5	125 ± 55
Globicephala scammoni	Males	6	27 ± 17		
Orcinus orca	Males	2	12.5		
Inia geoffrensis	Both	5	21 ± 8	2	86

* SGPT values from cetaceans at Point Mugu. The sick animals were observed to be ill by other signs such as loss of appetite, loss of weight, or a high WBC. N = the number of animals, and SD = standard deviation from the mean.

Plasma Electrolytes and Osmolality

The mean plasma osmolality in marine porpoises shown in Table 10–31, was between 330 and 340 mOsm, values about 40 to 50 mOsm higher than those found in horses, cattle, and man but only slightly higher than values reported for pigs and sheep. The mean plasma sodium concentration in porpoises (Table 10–31) was about 153 mEq/L and the mean value for chlorides was a little less than 110 mEq/L; thus these ions occur in the plasma of porpoises at concentrations roughly 10 mEq/L higher than in man but in the same general range as pigs, sheep, and dogs. *Inia geoffrensis*, a freshwater species, had lower sodium, chloride, and osmolality values. The serum potassium values (Table 10–31) were slightly lower than those reported for man. This is interesting in view of the fact that fish, on which porpoises subsist, contain large amounts of potassium (Thurston, 1958).

TABLE 10–31

ELECTROLYTES AND OSMOLALITY (mOsm/kg OF WATER) IN THE PLASMA
OF SEVERAL SPECIES OF SMALL ODONTOCETES MAINTAINED AT THE
MARINE BIOSCIENCE FACILITY

N	Sodium (mEq/L) Mean ± SD	N	Chloride (mEq/L) Mean ± SD	N	Potassium (mEq/L) Mean ± SD	N	Osmolality (mOsm) Mean ± SD
			Ten ♂ *Tursiops truncatus*				
99	153 ± 7	98	106 ± 9	94	3.7 ± 0.4	89	331 ± 12
			Eleven ♀ *Tursiops truncatus*				
117	155 ± 7	120	110 ± 8	116	4.0 ± 0.7	107	336 ± 14
			Three ♂ *Lagenorhynchus obliquidens*				
19	153 ± 9	24	107 ± 9		3.6 ± 0.4	11	332 ± 9
			Two ♀ *Lagenorhynchus obliquidens*				
16	153 ± 7	19	108 ± 8		3.5 ± 0.5	8	335 ± 13
			One ♂ *Phocoenoides dalli*				
5	155 ± 9	5	107 ± 6	5	4.4 ± 0.8		
			Two ♂ *Orcinus orca*				
5	155 ± 8	5	112 ± 7	5	3.8 ± 0.2	5	337 ± 17
			Two ♂ *Globicephala scammoni*				
8	149 ± 4	8	109 ± 9	7	3.6 ± 0.6	8	333 ± 15
			Five ♂ *Inia geoffrensis*				
9	144 ± 5	9	102 ± 11	9	3.6 ± 0.7		315 ± 12
			Three ♀ *Inia geoffrensis*				
4	142 ± 6	4	98 ± 6	4	3.9 ± 0.7	4	315 ± 15

Plasma Cholesterol

Cholesterol content has varied between the species studied at the Navy Marine Bioscience Facility (Ridgway *et al.*, 1970). In white-striped porpoises and Dall porpoises, the concentration was well under 200 mg per 100 ml, whereas other species had greater amounts than this. There seems to be a correlation with metabolic rate and body size. In man, plasma cholesterol is only partially influenced by dietary intake, and it must be assumed that this is also the case in cetaceans. Biosynthesis of cholesterol appears to be the major factor in determining the amount of blood cholesterol. Of particular interest is the finding that, while human beings and bottlenosed porpoises have similar blood cholesterol concentrations, the former subsist on a diet relatively high in saturated fat, whereas porpoises live on a fish diet that is high in unsaturated fats. Both the killer whale, whose values are shown in Table 10–32, and the elephant seal (Table 10–33) are immature. Accordingly, the high plasma cholesterol content of these young animals seems quite remarkable. Cholesterol levels are commonly high in the Weddell seal, and Prathap *et al.* (1966) were unable to find any correlation between cholesterol and arterial lesions in this species. During periods of fasting by *Zalophus californianus*, the plasma

TABLE 10–32

AVERAGE VALUES (± STANDARD DEVIATION) FOR VARIOUS THYROID MEAS-
URES AND CHOLESTEROL IN THE PLASMA OF SMALL ODONTOCETES

N	T_4 ($\mu g/100\ ml$)	Total I ($\mu g/100/ml$)	f T_4 ($m\mu g/100\ ml$)	N	PBI ($\mu g/100\ ml$)	N	Cholesterol ($Mg/100\ ml$)
		Fifteen ♂ *Tursiops truncatus* (70–205 kg)					
15	8.18 ± 1.46	15.65 ± 4.80	3.48 ± 0.85	135	14.54 ± 4.43	120	219 ± 32
		Sixteen ♀ *Tursiops truncatus* (61–189 kg)					
71	7.38 ± 1.72	15.34 ± 5.42	3.58 ± 0.99	196	11.79 ± 5.70	181	223 ± 27
		Two ♂ *Lagenorhynchus obliquidens* (70–75 kg)					
4	2.58 ± 1.06	5.10 ± 1.47	1.73 ± 0.45	19	4.03 ± 1.25	43	152 ± 43
		Five ♀ *Lagenorhynchus obliquidens* (55–94 kg)					
6	3.72 ± 0.95	5.32 ± 1.08	2.30 ± 0.51	21	4.67 ± 0.71	49	155 ± 31
		Two ♂ *Globicephala scammoni* (390–520 kg)					
8	4.26 ± 1.57	8.96 ± 1.88	3.99 ± 1.58	8	6.67 ± 1.98	12	281 ± 63
		Two ♂ *Orcinus orca* (1,730–2,240 kg)					
6	6.05 ± 1.70	17.47 ± 4.55	2.78 ± 0.71	6	13.28 ± 4.00	6	335 ± 61
		One ♂ *Phocoenoides dalli* (120 kg)					
				9	12.0 ± 4.6		131 ± 23
		Seven *Inia geoffrensis* ♂ + ♀					
8	1.5 ± 0.6					8	203 ± 95
		Ranges for *Homo sapiens*					
	$2.9–6.4$		$1.0–2.1$		$4.0–8.0^5$		$150–250$

cholesterol level remains fairly constant while the unesterified fatty acids (UFA) and triglycerides usually decrease and the phospholipids more frequently show a slight increase (Table 10–34). Puppione (1969) has recently characterized the serum lipoproteins of several species of marine mammals.

TABLE 10–33

BLOOD CHEMISTRY*

N	Sugar ($mg/100\ ml$) Mean ± SD	N	BUN ($mg/100\ ml$) Mean ± SD	N	Bilirubin ($mg/100\ ml$) Mean ± SD	N	Cholesterol ($mg/100\ ml$) Mean ± SD
			Two *Phoca vitulina* (Normal)				
2	150 ± 2	2	46 ± 13				
			Seven *Zalophus californianus* (Normal)				
8	129 ± 37	7	29 ± 11	5	$0.2 \pm .16$	5	229 ± 77
			One *Mirounga angustirostris* (Normal)				
6	118 ± 26	5	27 ± 2			6	297 ± 118

Plasma Iron

The total iron-binding capacity (Table 10–35) has been shown to be quite high in all odontocetes that I have studied. In the killer whale and the freshwater porpoises shown in Table 10–35, the degree of saturation was found to be relatively low. In man, the saturation of iron-binding protein is normally 20 to 50 percent. Iron metabolism in captive cetaceans should be investigated more thoroughly. Supplementation of the diet with this mineral may be advisable, especially in newly captured cetaceans. Intramuscular injections of liver extract and injectable iron have been effective in increasing the plasma iron concentration and hematocrit.

TABLE 10–34
SOME BLOOD AND URINE VALUES FOR 6 ADULT FEMALE
Zalophus californianus AFTER A PROLONGED FAST

Animal No.	310	311	312*	313	314	315
Days fasted	7	6	6	5	5	6
Weight (kg)	50	47	48	46	70	77
Hematocrit (PCV)	50	47	48	47	43	55
Plasma sodium (mEq/L)	156	153	152	149	155	155
Plasma chloride (mEq/L)	115	125	114	112	115	113
Plasma osmolality (mOsm)	333	335	330	325	330	340
Blood urea nitrogen (mg/100ml)	21	30	23	22	. . . .	25
Plasma uric acid (mg/100ml)	0.4	0.9	0.4	0.7	. . . .	0.4
Triglycerides (mg/100ml)	11	38	79	10	6	9
Chlosterol (mg/100ml)	223	434	357	348	. . . .	497
Unesterifled fatty acids (mEq/L)	0.37	0.36	0.40	0.91	0.32	0.29
Phospholipids (mg/100ml)	236	500	325	358	407	474
Glucose (mg/100ml)	139	130	147	125	123	120
Total protein (gm/100ml)	8.4	8.7	7.7	8.2	8.1	9.0
Albumin (gm/100ml)	3.8	2.4	2.5	2.9	3.5	3.4
Urine osmolality (mOsm)	. . . .	. . . .	825	2250	2264	2391
Urine uric acid (mg/L)	. . . .	. . . .	. . . .	. . . .	260	460
Urine urea nitrogen (gm/L)	. . . .	. . . .	. . . .	. . . .	20	16

* Animal No. 312 struggled considerably during the blood sampling procedure. This probably influenced the blood glucose and urine osmolality values.

Thyroid Hormones

Porpoises have relatively large thyroid glands. The bottlenosed porpoise has about 300 to 400 mg of thyroid per kilogram. An average-sized Dall porpoise of 80 kg had a thyroid of 70 gm while the average thyroid size for human beings in North America is 15 to 25 gm (Williams, 1962).

The strong possibility of thyroid abnormalities and dysfunction in some cetaceans has recently been mentioned by Harrison (1969). Thyroid function may be especially important in the clinical evaluation and maintenance of white-striped porpoises and Dall porpoises. Values for some plasma metabolic measures in various species are given in Table 10–32. Although plasma cholesterol seems to correlate fairly well with other comparative indicators of metabolic rate, the measures of thyroid activity appear to correlate well only in the bottlenosed porpoises, river porpoises, and possibly the killer whales.

The metabolic rate, based primarily on oxygen consumption data, was

662   *Mammals of the Sea*

TABLE 10 35

AVERAGE VALUES (± STANDARD DEVIATION) FOR PLASMA IRON
MEASURES AND CALCIUM AND PHOSPHORUS IN SOME ODONTOCETES

Calcium (mEq/L)		Phosphorus (mg/100 ml)		Iron (µg/100 ml)		T.I.B.C. (µg/100 ml)		% Saturation	
N	Mean ± SD	N	Mean ± SD	N	Mean ± SD	N	Mean ± SD	N	Mean ± SD
Ten ♂ *Tursiops truncatus*									
76	5.0 ± 0.8	41	5.7 ± 1.1	14	253 ± 118	14	486 ± 144	14	49.5 ± 20.8
Eleven ♀ *Tursiops truncatus*									
90	4.9 ± 1.1	61	5.6 ± 1.0	21	173 ± 72	19	454 ± 140	19	37.0 ± 14.0
Three ♂ *Lagenorhynchus obliquidens*									
19	5.0 ± 0.8	4	5.0 ± 0.6	3	116 ± 28	3	590 ± 84	3	19.7 ± 3.8
Two ♀ *Lagenorhynchus obliquidens*									
10	5.2 ± 0.8	3	4.1 ± 0.3	4	144 ± 56	4	528 ± 201	4	28.5 ± 12.4
One ♂ *Phocoenoides dalli*									
11	4.8 ± 1.4	1	5.5 ± —	—	—	—	—	—	—
Two ♂ *Orcinus orca*									
4	5.4 ± 1.5	4	6.9 ± 1.3	4	72 ± 44	4	672 ± 34	4	9.5 ± 2.1
Two ♂ *Globicephala scammoni*									
4	4.9 ± 0.3	6	4.9 ± 1.0	7	210 ± 133	7	490 ± 95	7	45.8 ± 34.7
Five ♂ *Inia geoffrensis*									
8	4.5 ± 0.4	8	5.7 ± 0.9	4	57 ± 41	4	356 ± 58	4	18.2 ± 5.6
Three ♀ *Inia geoffrensis*									
4	4.6 ± 0.5	4	6.0 ± 1.4	2	51 ± —	2	378 ± —		13.5 ± —

138 kcal/m^2/hr for a bottlenosed porpoise. This is considerably higher than the resting metabolic rate of terrestrial mammals of comparable size and appears to be reflected by a high thyroxine (T_4), protein-bound iodine (PBI), and total iodine. The lower values for the white-striped porpoises, even though the metabolic rate is higher, may be a reflection of a more rapid thyroid hormone turnover rate. In addition, triiodothreonine (T_3), which we were not able to measure, may be more important in this species as it is in the rat (Sterling, 1970). Triiodothreonine is about eight times more potent in increasing the metabolic rate than is thyroxine (T_4).

Plasma Proteins

Other investigators have recently studied the plasma proteins of several species of cetaceans (Medway and Geraci, 1966; Medway and Moldovan, 1966; Gallien *et al.*, 1967; DeMonte and Pilleri, 1969). Table 10–36 gives plasma protein data from five species of small cetaceans maintained at the Navy Marine Bioscience Facility. As expected, the globulins increase and the albumin often decreases during severe infections.

Plasma Uric Acid, Bilirubin, and Blood Urea Nitrogen

The Amazon River porpoise was found to have high concentrations of plasma uric acid (Table 10–37). What this means in relation to purine metabolism or metabolic end products is not certain, but the finding was

TABLE 10-36

PLASMA PROTEINS IN SOME ODONTOCETES

Specimens	N	Total Protein (gm/100 ml) Mean ± SD	N	Albumin Mean ± SD	Alpha Globulin 1 Mean ± SD	Alpha Globulin 2 Mean ± SD	Beta Globulin Mean ± SD	Gamma Globulin Mean ± SD
10 ♂ *Tursiops truncatus*	58	8.0 ± 0.7	45	3.3 ± 1.1	0.50 ± 0.21	0.55 ± 0.22	0.56 ± 0.24	1.09 ± 0.45
11 ♀ *Tursiops truncatus*	75	8.0 ± 0.8	64	3.5 ± 1.5	0.47 ± 0.18	0.62 ± 0.31	0.59 ± 0.35	1.29 ± 0.70
3 ♂ *Lagenorhynchus obliquidens*	6	9.0 ± 0.7	6	3.6 ± 1.5	0.33 ± 0.10	0.86 ± 0.41	1.0 ± 0.31	1.88 ± 0.92
2 ♀ *Lagenorhynchus obliquidens*	4	8.9 ± 0.4	4	4.3 ± 1.9	0.25 ± 0.16	1.05 ± 0.60	0.68 ± 0.27	2.03 ± 1.02
2 ♂/♀ *Orcinus orca*	4	8.3 ± 0.8	4	4.0 ± 0.1	1.00 ± 0.21	0.72 ± 0.37	1.10 ± 0.55	1.6 ± 0.19
2 ♂/♂ *Globicephala scammoni*	6	7.0 ± 0.4	6	3.5 ± 0.4	0.86 ± 0.27	0.61 ± 0.34	0.61 ± 0.34	1.3 ± 0.40
4 ♂ *Inia geoffrensis*	5	8.9 ± 1.2	5	2.7 ± 0.6	0.41 ± 0.10	1.20 ± 0.70	0.70 ± 0.35	3.8 ± 2.10
3 ♀ *Inia geoffrensis*	4	8.6 ± 1.6	4	2.8 ± 0.8	0.36 ± 0.13	1.30 ± 0.60	0.71 ± 0.69	3.0 ± 1.40

consistent in all animals of this species and might be an interesting area for investigation both from the standpoint of evolutionary comparisons of the various supposedly primitive river species and from the standpoint of physiological comparisons of freshwater adaptation in cetaceans.

Considered from the standpoint of water and electrolyte metabolism, the high uric acid level presents a paradox. Urea contains two hydrogen atoms per nitrogen atom, while the amount of hydrogen in uric acid is only one per nitrogen atom. Therefore, the yield of water from oxidation of protein is greater (0.396 gm/gm of protein if urea is formed versus 0.499 gm/gm of protein if uric acid is formed) when uric acid is the end product of protein metabolism. Thus, if the high plasma uric acid level can be interpreted to mean that uric acid is a major end product, it would appear that *Inia geoffrensis*, a species that lives in fresh water, may have a slight advantage in metabolic water production over the marine species.

The plasma bilirubin level appears to be consistent with findings in other mammals. The BUN, however, is always high as compared with terrestrial mammals. In my experience, the BUN in cetaceans is slightly higher than that of pinnipeds. The high BUN may be a reflection of the elevated metabolic rate and high-protein diet. The high BUN is probably a major factor in the relatively high plasma osmolality and represents an osmotic advantage for the kidney when excretion of a concentrated urine is necessary. The high BUN may also be a factor in the prolonged blood clotting time already mentioned.

Plasma Glucose and the Glucose Tolerance Test

Fasting blood sugar levels in marine mammals that we have observed generally range well above 100 mg/100 ml (Table 10–33 and 10–37). The values are comparatively high but the findings have been consistent. An adrenalin response that results from catching and restraining the animal for venipuncture can produce elevations in the blood glucose level. Animals that become highly excited when caught or struggle a great deal usually have blood sugar levels 10 to 30 percent higher than more docile animals.

Bottlenosed porpoises given a glucose load (1.0 to 175 gm/kg) by oral, intraperitoneal or intravenous injection respond with an increase in plasma glucose that does not return to normal for six to fourteen hours (Figs. 10–27 and 10–30). These glucose tolerance tests can be compared with a twenty-four-hour fast and a 6 kg fish meal (Tables 10–31, 10–32).

Carbohydrate Metabolism

There are several interesting aspects to the problem of carbohydrate metabolism in marine mammals. The following are some preliminary observations that I have made:

TABLE 10–37
AVERAGE VALUES (± STANDARD DEVIATION) FOR PLASMA
CHEMISTRY VALUES FOR SOME ODONTOCETES

Uric Acid (mg/100 ml)		Sugar (mg/100 ml)		BUN (mg/100 ml)		Bilirubin (mg/100 ml)	
N	Mean ± SD	N	Mean ± SD	N	Mean ± SD	N	Mean ± SD
			Ten ♂ *Tursiops truncatus*				
43	1.1 ± 0.7	110	131 ± 36	111	53 ± 12	44	0.5 ± 0.5
			Eleven ♀ *Tursiops truncatus*				
64	1.1 ± 0.7	121	127 ± 27	121	50 ± 13	65	0.3 ± 0.2
			Three ♂ *Lagenorhynchus obliquidens*				
5	1.1 ± 0.9	28	123 ± 23	34	36 ± 8	6	0.6 ± 0.6
			Two ♀ *Lagenorhynchus obliquidens*				
4	0.9 ± 0.5	24	110 ± 27	28	39 ± 9	4	0.2 ± 0.1
			One ♂ *Phocoenoides dalli*				
1	0.8 + —	15	138 ± 39	11	40 ± 12	—	—
			Two ♂ *Orcinus orca*				
4	0.8 ± 0.4	5	203 ± 61	3	33 ± 8	4	0.2 ± 0.1
			Two ♂ *Globicephala scammoni*				
6	0.5 ± 0.3	6	145 ± 28	6	52 ± 11	—	—
			Five ♂ *Inia geoffrensis*				
9	11.4 ± 5.1	9	127 ± 44	9	38 ± 11	1	0.1
			Three ♀ *Inia geoffrensis*				
4	10.0 ± 3	4	116 ± 16	4	44 ± 10	1	0.3

1. The milk is either relatively low in lactose or there is none at all (Table 10–38).

2. Disaccharidase in the intestine is low or absent in the species that have been investigated (Ketchmer and Sunshine, 1967).

3. Porpoises, at least, have no salivary glands and thus no salivary amylase. The numerous glands opening into the pharynx are mucous glands. The serum amylase levels of *Tursiops truncatus* and *Globicephala scammoni* are negligible (Allen, 1970).

4. There are only minute amounts of carbohydrate in the natural diet of most marine mammals, squid being a minor exception, containing about 1.5 per cent carbohydrate.* This may help to explain why sea lions, who lack intestinal disaccharidase, always have a loose stool when they are on a squid diet. Some keepers and trainers like to use squid as a laxative.

5. Bottlenosed porpoises fasted for seventy-two hours showed no increase in plasma acetone and acetoacetic acid levels and no ketones in the urine (Fig. 10–34). The dietary protein yields amino acids whose metabolic effect is primarily glucogenic rather than keto-

---

* The diet of the walrus is another exception. It feeds on clams (see Chapter 1) which contain larger amounts of carbohydrate.

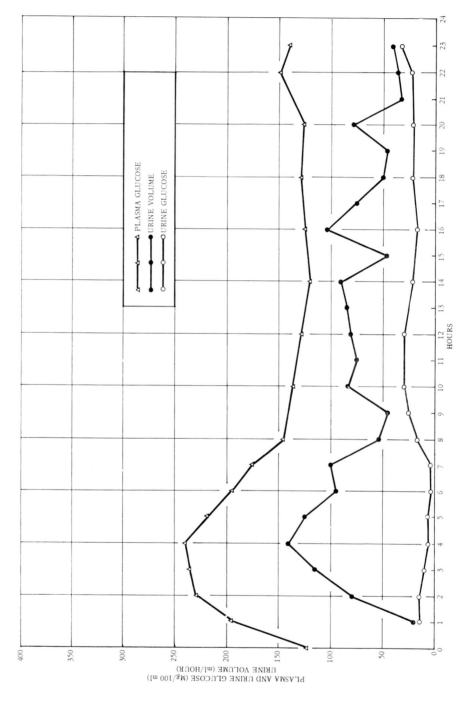

Figure 10-27. Response of 183 kg female *Tursiops truncatus* (wave) after receiving 2 L of 10% dextrose by stomach tube.

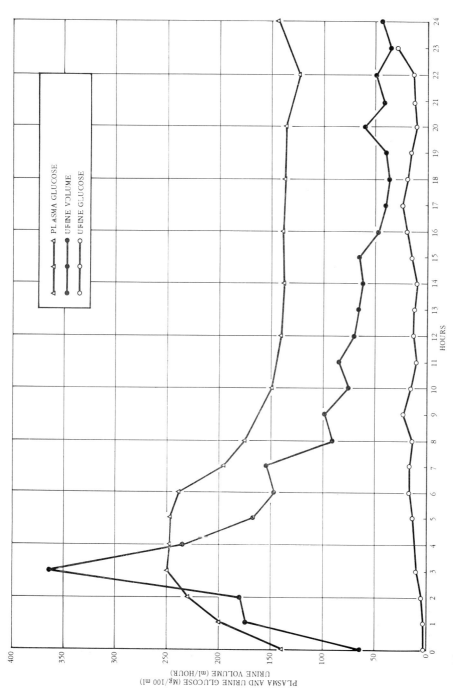

Figure 10–28. Response of a 187 kg female *Tursiops truncatus* (Cynthia) after receiving 2 L of 10% dextrose by stomach tube.

genic. The same is apparently true for fasting porpoises, and glucose is produced as body protein is metabolized.

6. In animals (dolphins and elephant seals) fed 1.75 gm/kg of glucose,
   the respiratory quotient (RQ) remains at about 0.70, actually lower
   than when they are fed fish or fasted for short periods. When most
   other mammals are fed glucose, the RQ approaches 1.0.

7. In bottlenosed porpoises, immunologically measurable insulin is
   very low even after a glucose load (Fig. 10–29), and beta cells of
   the pancreas that normally secrete insulin appear to be sparse.

8. The fasting urine urea-nitrogen levels are relatively high, indicating
   that much of the glucose may be obtained through gluconeogenesis.

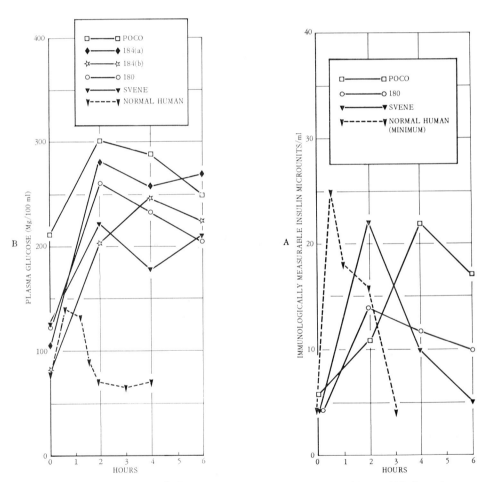

Figure 10–29A. Response of five young *Tursiops truncatus* 61 to 109 kg after receiving 15 ml/kg of 10% dextrose intraperitoneally. The response is compared to the
normal human glucose tolerance curve. B. Insulin response of three of these five
animals as compared to the human minimum response.

It appears that fasting *Tursiops truncatus* and *Lagenorhynchus obliquidens* lose muscle almost as fast as they lose body fat. The glucose requirement is apparently met by conversion of protein to glucose. DuBois *et al.* (1948) found dolphin muscle to be high in glycogen (0.98 volume percent). This glycogen is thought to be a readily available substrate for glycolysis during fast swimming and diving when muscular activity is great.

9. If we assume bottlenosed dolphins are similar to other mammals and have a glucose space of about 33 percent (Forsham, 1966), we can roughly estimate the glucose consumption of a resting animal after a glucose load (Fig. 10–28). About 4.1 kilocalories are produced for each gm of glucose consumed and the total amount

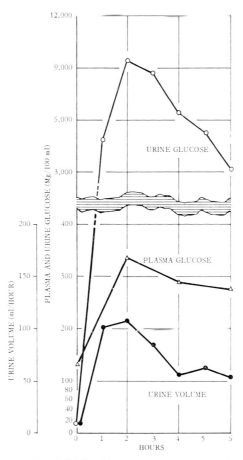

Figure 10–30. Response of a 107 kg *Tursiops truncatus* male (No. 179) after administration of 1.5 L of 10% dextrose I.P. Urine volume and urine glucose were measured hourly, while blood glucose was measured every two hours.

consumed by the animal represented in Fig. 10–28 would equal the number of kilocalories calculated to be necessary for brain and CNS metabolism during the fourteen hours that the glucose level was elevated. If we assume that the brain consumes 20 to 25 percent of the oxygen used by the dolphin and that the nervous tissue is consuming glucose with an RQ of 1.00, then the dolphin's RQ would be 0.75 to 0.78, which is very similar to the RQ found by Pierce (1970) in *Tursiops truncatus*.

10. When enough dextrose is given (1.5 liters 10% dextrose to a 108 kg *Tursiops truncatus*) to raise the plasma glucose to about 300 mg/100 ml, glucose starts to spill over into the urine in large amounts (Fig. 10–30). In fact, the young *Tursiops truncatus* involved in the experiment illustrated in Fig. 10–30 was excreting a 9% glucose

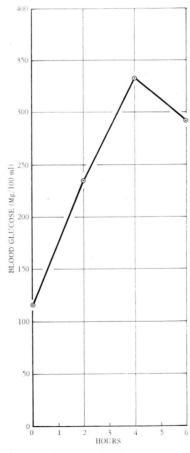

Figure 10–31. Response of a 105 kg female elephant seal (*Mirounga angustirostris*) fed 1.75 gm/kg of dextrose in about 1 kg of fish.

solution for a time. When 2 L of 10% dextrose plus 2 L of distilled water was given to a 187 kg *Tursiops truncatus* (Fig. 10–28), the glucose clearance was not increased to the point where it exceeded tubular reabsorption. Both urea and creatine were reduced in the urine of animals fed glucose as compared to those given sea water or distilled water. In the experiment illustrated in Fig. 10–28, the BUN also decreased from a pretest value of 35 mg/100 ml to 20 mg/100 ml at hour 24. This was probably a result of decreased gluconeogenesis. It appears that the glucose administered spares body protein that would ordinarily be consumed for glucose production. This is also suggested by the low creatine excretion, since muscle catabolism ordinarily results in increased creatine excretion.

11. There are many similarities in the glucose measures of clinically normal bottlenosed dolphins that closely resemble the physiological picture that has been described for hyperthyroid diabetics (Best and Taylor, 1966, p. 1338). This may have some significance in diving physiology. Considerable lactate is produced during a dive. Lactate is well used by the diabetic heart, whereas its glucose utilization is extremely low. When insulin is supplied, the heart increases its utilization of glucose but not of lactate; whereas, brain metabolism of glucose is little affected by insulin (Best and Taylor, 1966, p. 1339). Increased lactate consumption by the heart might be an advantage to an animal making frequent dives. Scholander (1949) showed that the blood glucose level closely followed the lactate level and increased slightly after a dive.

12. From our experiments with a diving porpoise in the open ocean, we concluded that an almost complete anaerobicity exists throughout the animal during the latter part of a prolonged dive (Ridgway *et al.*, 1969). The data indicated that the brain must also operate with at least partial reduction in oxygen consumption during this period. It is known that brain tissue can function anaerobically for a time if sufficient glucose is available as a substrate for anaerobic metabolism.[*] Thus it is understandable that all of the healthy diving mammals that we have sampled have a relatively high blood glucose level (Tables 10–33, 10–34, 10–37). During the latter part of a dive, the circulation is probably functioning only poorly as an oxygen transport mechanism while brain circulation is thought to be maintained or increased. Glucose transport is probably quite efficient.

---

[*] Reduction in oxygen consumption could also be brought about by other means such as a lowering of cortical temperature.

Mammals of the Sea

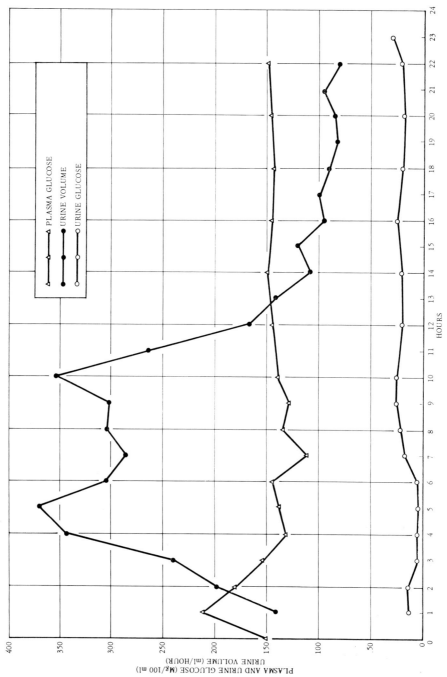

Figure 10-32. Response of a 183 kg female *Tursiops truncatus* (wave) fed 6 kg of Spanish mackerel.

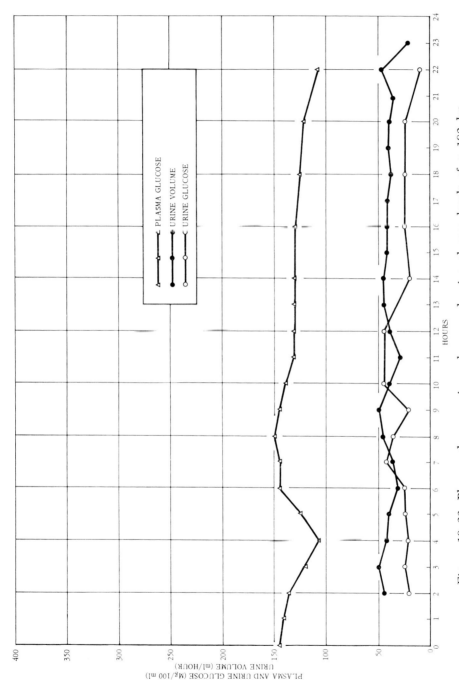

Figure 10–33. Plasma glucose, urine volume, and urine glucose levels of a 183 kg *Tursiops truncatus* (wave) female during a twenty-four-hour fast.

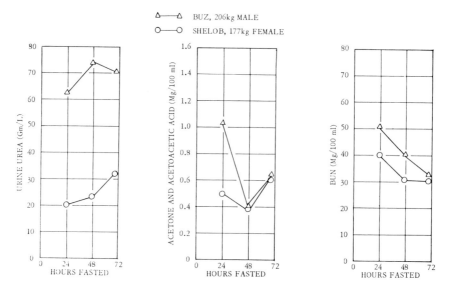

Figure 10–34A. Some blood and urine values for an adult male (Buz) and an adult female (Shelob) *Tursiops truncatus* during a seventy-two-hour fast. Urine urea, plasma acetone, and acetoacetic acid, and BUN.

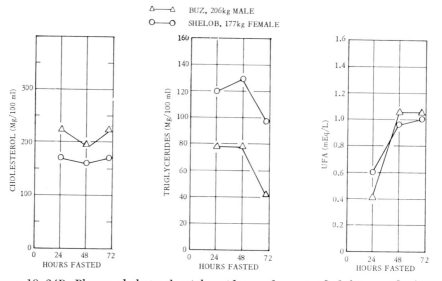

Figure 10–34B. Plasma cholesterol, triglycerides, and unesterified fatty acids (UFA).

INSULIN

Pinniped insulin has not, to my knowledge, been chemically analyzed. The only cetacean insulin that has been investigated is that of the sperm whale (Harris *et al.*, 1956). The structures of sperm whale insulin and porcine insulin are the same. Human insulin differs from porcine insulin only in the substitution of threonine for alanine at amino acid 30 on the carbonyl end of beta chain. Because of this similarity, porcine insulin has been used in the treatment of diabetic or resistant diabetic human patients. It can be less antigenic and is generally more effective than bovine insulin. Because of the probable similarity in structure, the porcine extract is probably the best for use in porpoises.

Husbandry Problems

As with most wild animals brought into captivity, chances of mortality of the marine mammal are far greater during the initial adaptation to the captive environment than at any other time. Examination by the veterinarian on arrival or very soon after is essential. Laboratory tests and physical examination at the outset will facilitate later diagnosis. Disease conditions should be attended as soon as possible. The animal must be vaccinated and wormed during the first few days if he is in acceptable physical condition. Some animals may require three months or more to adapt to captivity. Others never adapt and these should not be kept. Occasional animals have to be rejected for behavioral or health reasons. Wise selection at the outset may save months or even a year of unsuccessful training effort.

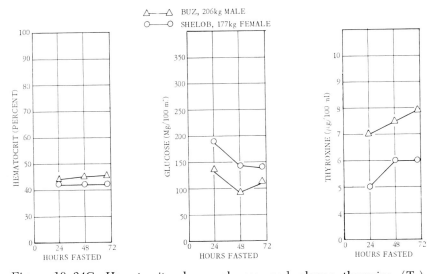

Figure 10–34C. Hematocrit, plasma glucose, and plasma thyroxine (T_4).

New arrivals should ordinarily remain separated from resident animals for at least a month. During that period, they should be slowly accustomed to human contact. Medical problems should be treated, and the animals' diets adjusted.

As any traveler knows, it takes humans some time to get adjusted to the food and water of a foreign land. How much more traumatic it must be for a dolphin or seal experiencing captivity for the first time! If the animal could, he might warn newcomers: Don't drink the water and be very careful of the food!

Porpoises which survive the initial three months in captivity are likely to adapt well and live for many years if given proper treatment. Very young animals are not nearly as likely to survive and adapt to captivity as are larger, older animals. We prefer not to acquire *Tursiops truncatus* less than about 2 m (6½ ft) in length because of the high mortality of the younger animals. Pinnipeds may be acquired just after weaning, though older animals usually adapt quite readily.

According to Keyes' (1968) survey, about fifteen species of pinnipeds are being kept in captivity. The California sea lion and *Phoca vitulina* are the most frequently encountered of the pinnipeds. Among cetaceans, *Tursiops truncatus* is by far the one most commonly seen in captivity. These animals, usually referred to as bottlenosed porpoises, are hardier and adapt much more readily to captivity than any other species of cetacean with which I am familiar. This might be explained in part by the fact that this species frequents bays and estuaries and even on occasion swims into freshwater rivers where it may come in contact with many of the microorganisms of the terrestrial environment. Pelagic cetaceans which remain farther at sea would not be nearly as likely to come in contact, for example, with terrestrial animal pathogens. No doubt physiological differences are an important factor as well.

The killer whale has also proved to be a hardy species. In Japan and some other areas, *Grampus griseus* has been quite popular as a display animal. The beluga has been displayed at several locations, and recently *Neophocoena phocoenoides* has been performing in Japanese oceanariums. In Hawaii, *Pseudorca crassidens*, various *Stenella*, and the local *Tursiops* have been prominent attractions. In California, *Lagenorhynchus obliquidens* is commonly seen and some have been exported to other parts of the world. Pilot whales are kept at many locations, but their mortality is higher than that of *Orcinus orca* or *Grampus griseus*. *Delphinus sp.* have also been relatively difficult to maintain in general. Among the freshwater species, *Inia geoffrensis* has been the most popular. The blind river dolphin, *Plantanista gangetica*, has recently been brought into captivity (Herald *et al.*, 1969; Nishiwaki, 1970).

Whereas the more pelagic cetaceans are captured in deep water with "hoop nets" (Fig. 10–35) or "tail grabbers," *Tursiops truncatus* is usually captured in shallow water. A group of animals is encircled with a fishing net. Generally the entrapped porpoises become entangled in the net and are removed individually into a small boat and then transported to a larger craft. Sometimes beach sets are used. In this case, the entrapped porpoises are drawn right up to the shore. In a technique pioneered by Griffin and Goldsberry (1968), killer whales are surrounded in relatively shallow water with a large purse seine (Fig. 10–36). The whales are then carefully separated and caught individually with a net. The driving of large groups of *Stenella* into bays was described in Chapter 1.

The newly caught porpoise is laid on a mattress or suspended in a hammock-like sling, which is covered with a wet sheet and kept moist. Minor wounds are often incurred, for example lacerations induced by the capture net line and other handling procedures. Early treatment of these wounds is mandatory.

Occasionally, a new cetacean will have difficulty orienting itself and swimming when placed back into the water. This is more likely if the newly captured animal spends a long time out of water during transport to holding pens. Sometimes human assistance is needed to keep the porpoise from running into the walls of the tank and to start it swimming on its own. Since they are air breathers, porpoises need not be "walked" as sharks sometimes do. They simply should be given strong pushes and made to swim on their own. Attendants should position themselves around the edge of the tank. If it appears that an animal is going to strike the wall, the attendants should turn it, hold it with its blowhole out of the water until it takes one breath and then should push it across the pool rather than walk it or hold it in the water. Since porpoises have been known to assist each other, the presence of an already adapted animal in the pool might be beneficial to the new animal. It may later be necessary to separate the newcomers if the already adapted animal(s) interferes with attempts to feed.

One of the first problems encountered in the animal's adaptation to its new environment is its introduction to food. The animal is enticed with dead fish which are thrown into the water in front of the animal's rostrum. Some animals will eat almost immediately after being captured, but it is more common to have them go two to five days before commencing to feed on dead fish. Usually the animal will evidence interest by nudging the fish with its snout. Then it will take a fish in its mouth, shake it a little, and throw it out. Finally it will take a fish, and in the customary manner swallow the whole fish, head first.

Some individuals will refuse food for a week or more. In some cases,

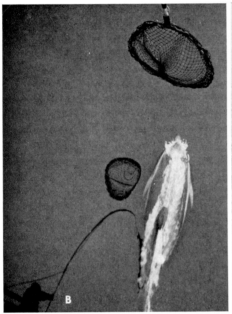

Figure 10–35A. In deep water porpoises are often captured one at a time with a hoop net. The operator works from a pulpit secured to the bow of the boat. A second net is on the deck and ready for use (arrow). B. When a porpoise rides the bow of the boat, and blows in the proper position just in front of the boat, the hoop net is plunged down, just in front of the animal. C. The porpoise is thus caught in a bag-like net which envelopes the forward portion of the body. A buoy attached to the hoop net line is thrown overboard and retrieved when the porpoise surfaces. A swimmer usually goes in and attends the animal as it is towed to the boat. D. The porpoise is secured in a lifting sling and hoisted aboard the capture boat.

Figure 10–36 (*Top*). A group of killer whales surrounded by a net. Several from this herd were selected for research or display and the remainder were released. (*Bottom*) One of two killer whales brought to the Marine Bioscience Facility undergoes preliminary training.

feeding can be started by introducing live fish into the pool. When the animal starts to feed on live fish, dead fish are thrown into the water. The animal may start to eat the dead fish as well.

Rarely will an animal refuse food for such a long period that it is in danger of starvation. In this case, it can be fed via stomach tube. One part fish, one part Ringer's solution (or water), vitamin-mineral capsules, and an essential fatty acid supplement may be mixed in a blender and administered via stomach tube in these cases.

A similar blend containing some added medication was employed to feed an adult female *Tursiops truncatus* twice daily for six weeks while she had numerous severe ulcers of the forestomach and refused fish. She progressed well on the 8 L of "gruel" that were pumped in each day. After the second day of treatment, she would swim over to the side of the pool and allow the stomach tube to be inserted without restraint. During the sixth week of treatment, she refused the tube and started taking whole fish. Subsequent endoscopic examination revealed that the ulcers were healed.

Because pinnipeds are comparatively smaller in size, they can be maintained out of water without the close attention required to keep cetaceans comfortably suspended and properly cooled. Therefore, the pinnipeds with which we have worked are considerably easier to capture and transport than the cetaceans.

There are two main methods of capturing California sea lions and other pinnipeds, one method based on land, the other in a boat working offshore near the rookeries or haul-out areas. In the first, several personnel work themselves into a position between the animals and the water, if possible without being seen, and on signal begin to move toward the desired group. If this is done cautiously, so that the herd does not alarm and begin a frenzied rush to the water, the animals are relatively easy to herd away from the beach to where the cages and nets have been left. Sticks, jackets, bags, and even umbrellas can be used to herd the animals in a group. Once the group of animals is away from the beach and sufficiently calmed, the large and smaller animals and all others not wanted are allowed to return to the water. The desired ones are retained. When this is accomplished, the remaining individuals can be removed and placed in the cages by a variety of methods. Smaller animals (less than 35 to 40 kg) can be grabbed by the hind flippers and lifted into the cage. Others may either be herded directly into the cages or, if this does not work, hoop netted or entangled in a piece of netting held on both ends by attendants and then placed into cages. Since the animals that adapt most readily to captivity are usually nine months to three years old (in the case of *Zalophus californianus*), they are small and relatively easier to handle. The problems in capture mutiply rapidly with increased size.

During the herding, care must be taken not to drive the animals too fast or to head them toward cliffs or other obstacles which they may climb in their fright and exhaust themselves. The capture should be accomplished as soon as possible and the remaining animals allowed to return to the water at their own pace. Care must be exercised in handling sea lions, especially in warm weather. Since they do not sweat, they can rapidly become over-heated and die.

In the second method, the animals are driven into the water and allowed to entangle in a set net. The captured animals are collected one at a time by a crew working from a small boat. They are removed from the net and placed in a cage for transport.

The Water Supply

Probably the most important single factor in keeping marine mammals healthy in captivity is the environmental water. For all the animals, but particularly for the cetaceans which spend their entire lives in the water, it is essential that the water be kept clean and as free of contamination as possible. The professional aquarist must be concerned with a broad area of biological and water management problems. Only a few of the major considerations concerning the water supply for marine mammals are presented here.

The main contaminants which can pose a threat to captive marine mammals are as follows: (a) animal excrement, (b) bacteria, (c) parasites, (d) foreign bodies, (e) insecticides, and (f) toxic chemicals. Any adequate system of filtration, water exchange, treatment, and management must deal with these problems.

Bacteria represent a substantial threat to captive marine mammals (per-haps fungi and viruses should also be included). There are some bacteria present in all surface waters, and in a porpoise holding tank those are supplemented both by those introduced by handlers, trainers, and visitors to the tanks and by those from the porpoises' flora (normal or abnormal) which are continuously shed into the water. Further, in a porpoise tank where a 136 kg (300 lb) animal on 6.6 kg (15 lbs) of fish a day can pass over a gallon (4 L) of urine and about 1.4 kg (3 lbs) of feces a day, these bacteria have an excellent medium for growth if the water is not kept clean. Therefore, an adequate means must be available to remove the bacteria and to prevent the buildup of those organisms pathogenic to the aquatic animals which are being maintained.

The life cycles of most marine mammal parasites are not clearly under-stood. However, it is reasonable to assume that there are parasites that might infect the animal directly from the water either by skin penetration or ingestion.

Ingestion of the fourth type of contaminants, foreign bodies, is summarized in another portion of this chapter. It is essential that the area around the pools be kept clear of all items which might fall or be blown into them. Some of the most valuable porpoises and pinnipeds at various oceanariums have been lost because they swallowed foreign objects. All toys and props should be large enough to prevent this possibility.

The fifth potential contaminant in a captive environment is insecticides. Since porpoises possess little, if any, of the enzyme plasma cholinesterase, organophosphate insecticides should not be used in the vicinity of their tanks. If spraying becomes essential, other insecticides should be employed.

Contamination of the water by chemicals must also be avoided. Chlorine or copper, while useful additives, may cause permanent damage to animals if used in excess. Any chemical that is to be placed in the pool water must be thoroughly investigated first.

Water supplies for marine mammals can be provided in several ways. One of the simplest involves the construction of a pen or netted enclosure in a bay or inlet in order to keep the animals in their natural ocean environment. Sometimes this is not a practical approach, and land-based tanks or pools must be utilized. In these cases, most facilities employ filtration in some form or another to keep water supplies clean and clear.

Some seaside oceanariums and aquaria pump water directly from the ocean through the pool and then out again. Others have collection cisterns or pervious pipe buried in beach sand or the ocean bottom. Others use seawater wells drilled on the beach at depths up to 100 m. These systems have the advantage of natural filtration as the ocean water seeps through the beach or bottom sand; therefore, the water is consistently clear and free of most marine organisms, some of which can foul pipes and water systems.

In most oceanaria, pool water is recirculated through filters while 5 to 10 per cent "makeup" water is pumped in from the main source to compensate for that lost due to evaporation and/or discharge through overflow systems, etc. The water is generally filtered through conventional sand and gravel filters, sand pressure filters and/or diatomaceous earth filters. Some aquaria use two types of filters in conjunction. Dirty water from the pool passes through a sand or sand and gravel filter and then is "polished" by a diatomaceous earth filter. If sufficient flow is maintained, this type of system can yield beautiful, crystal-clear water.

When fish or invertebrates and marine mammals are maintained together, a biological filter may be the most practical, since chlorine, copper, and other water additives are not generally tolerated by fishes and invertebrates. The biological filter is constructed of rock, gravel, and sand. Water flows through the top of the filter by gravity and is pumped from the bottom and recirculated through the animal pool. A rich growth of microorganisms and invertebrates up to the size of large worms which gradually establishes itself in the filter is, to a large measure, responsible for the filtration. In order to be efficient, a filter of this type must be relatively large—about one-half the volume of the pool being filtered.

An adequate rate of water turnover must be maintained, regardless of whether water is pumped directly through tanks and out or circulated through a filter. The rate of water turnover is based upon the water capacity of the tank and the number of animals that are being maintained. The following formula provides a good minimum turnover rate for maintaining porpoise pools:

$$(4 \times \frac{TC}{1000}) + (0.5 \times \frac{TC}{1000} \times \frac{AW}{100}) = GPM$$

Where:

TC = tank capacity in gallons
AW = animal weight in kg
GPM = gallons per minute (one GPM = almost 4 liters per minute)

Adherence to this formula will generally produce a water turnover rate of about two hours. The rate will be faster for crowded tanks and somewhat slower for sparsely populated tanks.

Even though the filter system may be otherwise adequate, chemical additives are sometimes advisable. Chlorine, added in sufficient quantities to maintain a concentration of from 0.1 to 0.4 ppm in the water, is sufficient to kill harmful bacteria and control the growth of various other microorganisms. Since some organisms and parasite larvae are resistant to chlorine, the addition of sufficient quantities of copper to maintain 0.3 to 0.4 ppm, may also be required. Though the pH of ocean water is just slightly over 8.0, the pH in artificial sea water pools is best maintained at 7.6 to 7.9.

When porpoises are maintained at inland aquaria, fresh water with sufficient quantities of salt (NaCl) to make a solution of at least 20 parts per thousand (ppt) or 2% sodium chloride must be added. This concentration of 20 ppt appears to be about the minimum salinity at which bottle-nosed porpoises can be maintained for long periods of time. Seawater generally has a salinity of 27 to 35 ppt.

Seals and sea lions are maintained with apparent success in areas where they have access only to fresh water for long periods of time. One zookeeper who maintains his pinnipeds in freshwater pools to which he adds a large amount of salt only once each month feels that this practice has been highly beneficial to the pinnipeds in his exhibit. Though the corneal opacities frequently seen in captive pinnipeds are sometimes blamed on fresh water, other factors such as parasites, trauma, malnutrition, chemical contamination, and infections must also be considered in these cases. However, it does seem reasonable that pinnipeds which have access only to fresh water should have their salt and trace element requirements provided for in some way, particularly if the diet consists solely of fish. Marine lice which often infest sea lions and some seals can frequently be eliminated by putting lousy animals in a freshwater environment for about two weeks.

The cells of the epithelial layers of porpoise skin reproduce rapidly. Thus the external layers are constantly being shed. For animals in training, a frequent rubdown is quite desirable. When this is not practical, large brushes may be placed in the tank. The porpoises will usually rub on these, thus preventing the buildup of dead skin.

Nutrition

The food and feeding behavior of each species was mentioned in Chapter 1. This discussion will therefore be confined primarily to those species that are maintained in captivity. We know far too little about the food requirements of marine mammals and the nutrient value of the foods that are provided for them. Table 10–21 gives the gross moisture, electrolyte, fat, and protein composition of some marine mammal foods as they were received from commercial sources. The food can vary considerably depending upon when and how it is caught, how it is processed, and how long it has been in storage.

Food Handling

Food fish or squid for marine mammals is normally acquired from commercial seafood dealers. It is usually stored frozen. Fish does deteriorate even at freezer temperatures. It appears that $-7.0°$ ($+20°F$) is about the maximum temperature at which food fish should be stored. At this temperature, fish should be stored no more than a few weeks. Storage life can be prolonged by lowering the temperature. Most fish can be kept for about six months at $-18°C$ ($0°F$). At $-29°C$ ($-20°F$) fish can probably be kept fairly well for over a year; but in general it is preferable not to use fish that have been stored longer even at these very low temperatures. Careful handling of fish, from the time they are acquired until the animal eats them, will minimize the chances of food-acquired diseases (nutritional, parasitic, infectious) in the marine mammals being maintained. Freezer stock should be rotated so that no food is kept in storage too long. The food must be thawed before it is fed. It is usually taken from the freezer and allowed to partially thaw in air. Running water (clean seawater is probably best) is used to complete the thawing. After the fish is thawed, it should not be left in the thaw water, but should be placed in clean containers and used as soon as possible. Unused thawed fish should be kept in a refrigerator. A bucket of thawed fish used during a training session should be covered and kept as cool as possible. As the temperature of thawed fish increases, a number of changes occur, and they are all bad. Bacteria multiply and the toxic chemical histamine builds rapidly in some fish (Geraci and Gertsmann, 1966). Fish on the bottom of a bucket of warm water are an excellent anaerobic medium for the multiplication of clostridial organisms. If fish is kept in a bucket of cool water during a training session, the water should be changed frequently. Thawed fish should not be stored overnight for use in feeding the next day.

The food preparation area, the food containers, personnel, and any items that come in contact with the food should be kept clean. There are several advantages to wearing rubber gloves when handling fish. It promotes good santitation, it may prevent transmission of disease from the trainer or keeper to the animals, and it will likely prevent cases of erysipeloid (fish-handler's disease, blubber finger, etc). This disease (and its variations that may be caused by other bacteria) is common among people who handle fish and who work with marine mammals. It usually begins as a reddened swelling of a finger or hand and can be quite painful. The condition warrants immediate medical attention.

FEEDING RATES

Sergeant (1969) summarizes the feeding rates of several species of odontocetes. The food requirements for young and growing animals are greater than for adults. Adult odontocetes from the size of *Tursiops truncatus* up to the size of the killer whale have an average daily food consumption of 4 to 6 percent of body weight. Smaller odontocetes require more food on a ratio to body weight basis. *Phocoenoides dalli* may consume fish equal to 10 to 12 percent of body weight and *Phocoena phocoena* has food requirements almost as high.

Other delphinids such as *Delphinus sp.* and *Lagenorhynchus obliquidens* require food equal 7 to 8 percent of body weight. In my experience, small sea lions usually require food equal to about 10 percent of body weight, but as the animal approaches adulthood this amount is reduced toward 5 percent. The comparatively large food requirement of the sea otter was mentioned in Chapter 2.

DIETETICS

Keyes (1968) succinctly summarized what is known about nutrition in both wild and captive pinnipeds. The information on captive animals was obtained from questionnaires answered by thirty-four different institutions which maintain a total of fifteen different pinniped species. Of the captive species mentioned, all were fed on various fish (mackerel, smelt, bonito, etc.) or squid, except for the walrus which was fed clams.

Wood *et al.* (1966) reported that *Tursiops truncatus* maintained at Marineland of Florida were kept in good health on butterfish (*Poronotus*) and blue runner (*Carnax crysos*) without the addition of food supplements. Under conditions existing at that oceanarium, these two species of fish apparently provided all the necessary dietary requirements to maintain the animals in good health. Herbivorous fishes apparently do not store sufficient vitamins, and thus porpoises subsisted on mullet developed avitaminosis (Wood *et al.*, 1966).

Porpoises (*Tursiops truncatus* and *Lagenorhynchus obliquidens*) fed only mackerel (*Scomber diego*) developed mouth lesions like those seen in scurvy. The lesions regressed after the administration of high levels of ascorbic acid (Miller and Ridgway, 1963). These porpoises were maintained in water of 10° to 21°C. It is possible that animals maintained in tropical waters might have lower vitamin C requirements. Thiamine deficiencies in cetaceans and pinnipeds have been encountered on a number of occasions (Rigdon and Drager, 1955; Hubbard, 1968; White, 1970).

As already mentioned, factors involved in handling, processing, and storage of the fish may affect its nutritional quality, and thus there may be variations in food value between different lots of fish of the same species. Some species of fish may be nutritionally adequate while others apparently are not. Therefore, it is desirable to feed two or three different kinds of fish and/squid. The varied diet is considered desirable not only from a nutritional standpoint, but also because animals (especially porpoises) sustained on one type of fish may develop exclusive preference for that food and refuse other types. Thus, difficulty may arise if that particular type of food happens to come into short supply.

The results of Keyes survey (1968) revealed that most of the institutions (28) supplemented the animals' diets with vitamins, usually multivitamin capsules, and that one institution gave cod liver oil. To my knowledge no comprehensive work has yet been done to establish the requirements of any of the vitamins or minerals in any marine mammal. At the Navy Marine Bioscience Facility, we normally include multivitamin capsules and ascorbic acid in the daily diet.

FEEDING YOUNG ANIMALS

Often young or orphaned marine mammals, especially seals and sea lions, are brought to the oceanarium or laboratory for rearing. Hubbard

(1968) and Keyes (1968) have discussed their experiences in rearing young sea lions and fur seals. A number of formulae have been devised for feeding such animals (Brown, 1962; Hubbard, 1968; Keyes, 1968). In general, it is probably desirable to use a food that provides the same nutrients as the mother's milk. Analyses of milks from various marine mammals are shown in Table 10–38.

TABLE 10–38

GROSS COMPOSITION OF MILK FROM SOME MARINE MAMMALS*

CETACEANS	Water	Total Solids	Fat	Protein	Lactose	Ash	Reference
Bottlenosed dolphin (*Tursiops truncatus*)	71.4	28.6	16.7	9.6	0.77	——	Eichelberger et al. (1940)
Spotted dolphin (*Stenella plagidon*)	70.0	30.0	18.0	9.4	0.63	——	Eichelberger et al. (1940)
Harbor porpoise (*Phocoena phoccena*)	41.1	58.9	45.8	11.2	1.33	0.57	Grimmer (1925)
Fin whale (*Balaenoptera physalus*)	57.9	42.1	28.6	11.1	2.58	1.59	Lauer and Baker (1969)
Beluga (*Delphinapterus leucas*)	59.0	41.0	26.9	10.6	0.74	0.83	Lauer and Baker (1969)
Blue whale (*Balaenoptera musculus*)	43.6	56.4	42.0	11.7	1.24	——	Gregory et al. (1955)
	47.2	52.8	38.1	12.8	——	1.43	Ben Shaul (1962)
PINNIPEDS							
California sea lion (*Zalophus californianus*)	47.3	52.7	36.5	13.8	0.00	0.64	Pilson and Kelly (1962)
Northern fur seal (*Callorhinus ursinus*)	36.4	63.6	51.1	11.3	0.10	0.49	Ashworth (1966)
Hooded seal (*Cystophora cristata*)	49.8	50.2	40.4	6.7	——	0.86	Sivertsen (1941)
Harp seal (*Pagophilus groenlandicus*)	45.1	54.9	46.9	6.8	0.77	0.39	Cook and Baker (1969)
Gray seal (*Halichoerus grypus*)	32.3	67.7	53.2	11.2	2.60	0.70	Amoroso and Matthews (1952)
OTHERS							
Polar bear (*Thalarctos maritimus*)	55.9	44.1	31.1	10.2	0.49	1.17	Baker et al. (1963)
Cow (*Bos taurus*)	87.5	12.5	4.0	3.6	4.65	0.70	

* A very recent analysis, that of Pilson and Waller (1970), was not received in time to be included in the table. In 8 *Stenella graffmani* they found 25.3% fat, 1.9% lactose and 8.28% protein. In one *Stenella microps* they found 26.2% fat, 1.03% lactose and 7.09% protein.

The period of nursing should be considered by anyone attempting to rear orphaned marine mammals. Nursing periods range from several months to over a year with the exception of most phocids which can be weaned after about eight weeks. A young *Tursiops truncatus* may nurse for a year to eighteen months. Walrus calves require a similarly long period. The otariids require six to nine months' nursing.

Just after birth, the young should be fed about six times daily. The number of feedings can be decreased as the animal grows. We have reared one *Zalophus californianus* and several *Phoca vitulina* on a simple formula that consists of five parts whole fish, three and one-half parts of water, one-half part cod liver oil, and one part essential fatty acid supplement homogenized in a large blender. The mixture is fed by stomach tube (Fig. 10–37). As the animals come to accept the tube quite readily, it is less time consuming than teaching the animal to nurse.

Lactose should be omitted from the diet of most young marine mammals, since all milks analyzed show low levels or no milk sugar at all. Sea lions lack intestinal disaccharidase, and the inclusion of lactose in their diet is detrimental (Ketchmer and Sunshine, 1967). The walrus, whose diet is primarily clams (comparatively high in carbohydrates), has been successfully reared on a rich diet composed mainly of whipping cream and clams (Brown, 1962).

Figure 10–37. An orphaned harbor seal is fed formula by stomach tube.

SYNTHETIC RATIONS

Recently we have maintained several (two to five years old) sea lions and one elephant seal on various versions of a fish-based prepared ration. The high-protein test ration mentioned previously (Table 10–21) was one of these synthetic food products. Further studies are being conducted to develop a highly nutritious, parasite-free, shelf-stable prepared ration for marine mammals which will significantly reduce diseases communicated by food and may facilitate storage and handling. Some results of this work are reported by Patachnik (1970) and by Simpson and Leatherwood (1970).

Catching and Handling Marine Mammals

PORPOISES

In the water, porpoises are all power and grace. When out of the water they are almost helpless and may be easily injured if they are not handled gently. It is necessary to capture animals whenever they must be examined out of the water, when they are to be transported to another location, or when their tanks must be drained and cleaned. We have found the following procedures of catching and handling animals to be efficient and relatively safe.

When the tank is equipped with the proper water system, it may be most practical to drain the water down and carefully strand the animals. However, it is often more desirable to separate and catch each animal with a net. The net should be slightly larger than the distance across the pool. The animal's trainer or a designated crew leader supervises the operation. Only this individual gives instructions while the animal is being caught.

The net is pulled across the end of the pool separating the animal (or animals) that are to be caught. The net forms a sort of bag that goes along each wall and the bottom so that an animal cannot swim around or under it. Swimmers are evenly spaced along the net to guard it and to be available in case a porpoise becomes entangled in the net. The net is closed slowly, forcing the porpoises into a gradually decreasing area. No attempt is made to grab an animal until it is forced into a very restricted area and is almost immobile. Diving to grab a moving animal or racing to try to catch it will only serve to frighten the porpoise and frustrate the capture crew. If an animal swims into the net, the swimmers withdraw or push the porpoise out. Should the porpoise become entangled, the swimmers rapidly grab the animal in the net and hold its head above water so it can breathe.

Normally the porpoise will "give up" and remain fairly still when surrounded (or crowded against a wall) by the net. Two men then take hold of the animal. One secures a "bear hug" with a wristlock just before or just aft of the flippers. The other man holds the animal just behind the dorsal fin. Grabbing the porpoise by the flukes must be avoided. If an animal seems likely to fight, leave a small portion of the net over his head until he is in the sling. The porpoise may be restrained by the base of the flippers but should not be grabbed by the ends of the flippers. This could cause a dislocation or a break.

When the animal is caught, the net is pulled away and the porpoise removed as gently as possible into a sling or stretcher. Three swimmers are generally required for the safe execution of this procedure. The procedure should not be attempted with fewer people. The porpoise is fitted into the sling carefully so that the flukes just clear the rear of the sling. The flippers are folded back along the body and the eyes protected from exposure to straps, buckles, netting or anything that might injure them. As soon as the netting operation is complete the net is removed from the pool. A net should never be left in a pool unattended. A porpoise could become entangled in it and drown.

A porpoise out of the water is suspended in a sling and placed on a padded table or on a foam rubber mattress. For examination, the animal is generally placed on its side with the flipper on the underside in correct position alongside the body.

The animal is kept moist when out of the water. If it is to be out of the water for more than five or ten minutes, the animal is covered by a wet sheet or cloth which is kept wet. The eyes should be protected from direct exposure to sunlight; therefore a cupped hand, moist gauze pad or part of the cover sheet can be used to shade them. Precautions are taken to see that nothing obstructs the blowhole.

No animal is left unattended while out of the water. If the veterinarian is making an examination, at least two people are on hand at all times to help in restraining the animal. They also are responsible for keeping the porpoise wet.

When it is time to carry the porpoise back to the tank, the supervisor must be sure that there are enough men to lift the animal easily. Usually it takes two men on each end of the sling or stretcher. The animal is lowered into the water. Two swimmers remove it from the sling, pull the porpoise clear and after it takes one breath, push it away toward the center of the tank. The porpoise is never released in the direction of a near wall or corner, or under an obstruction.

WHALES

Catching and moving a whale is, of course a major undertaking but procedures for handling animals such as *Globicephala scammoni* and *Orcinus orca* are similar to those outlined above except that heavy equipment rather than human muscle is required for all lifting (Fig. 10–38). A soft, bag-like net can be placed over the animal's head, and large pieces of cloth such as bed sheets may be placed under the whale for use as handles in guiding the animal into the lifting sling.

SEALS AND SEA LIONS

Seals and sea lions are amphibious and can remain out of the water for long periods of time. They are much more dangerous to handle than are

Figure 10–38A. Killer whale in a transporter. B. killer whale being lowered into a pool.

porpoises because they have very flexible bodies and a decided willingness to bite.

The animal to be handled should first be isolated and put into a cage by itself. If it is small (25 kg or under), it may be restrained by two men. One, wearing elbow-length protective gloves, holds the animal behind the head and presses it down against a flat surface such as a table top or floor. The second man holds the rear flippers, pressing down and pulling, stretching the animal out. Larger sea lions should be handled by use of a specially designed sea lion squeeze cage (Fig. 10–39).

Transportation

Porpoises were first transported in water-filled boxes (Townsend, 1914). That method of transport was also used by Lilly (1962). The disadvantages of this system (such as the considerable weight of the container, the danger that the animal might crash against the side of the box, the sloshing of water when the transport vehicle accelerates or stops, and the possible difficulties in respiration due to water slosh and movement of the animal) appear to outweigh the advantages.

In a more recent evolution of animal transport techniques, animals were placed on their sides in shallow boxes lined with some kind of padding material (see Chapter 7, Fig. 7–3). Though this technique, like the first, has been used rather extensively, there is considerable overheating on the underside of the animals. In addition, if the attendants were not careful, by the end of the transport the animals were lying in and perhaps breathing their own urine and feces.

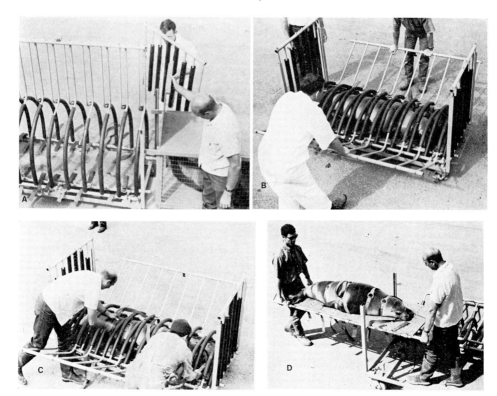

Figure 10–39A. Sea lion is driven from transport cage to restraining cage. B. Sea lion completely restrained by the cage bars. C. In this position, the sea lion is strapped down. D. The cage bottom containing the securely restrained animal is picked up and carried to surgery or examination. The slots in the cage bottom allow this same bottom to be used with animals of various sizes. Reproduced with the permission of the *AVMA Journal.*

Today, the most frequently used method of transport consists of suspending the animal in a hammock-like sling designed to evenly distribute his weight and allow for the maximum possible amount of evaporative cooling. These porpoise carriers are equipped with pectoral holes, to allow the flippers to hang at a normal angle, with genital and anal slits to allow the drainage of urine and feces, and with tail pockets to support the tail flukes. The box is lined to hold water and to collect wastes.

Terrycloth covers for the body, dorsal fin, and pectoral flippers and water sprayed, poured, or sponged over the animal's body assist in keeping the animal cooled. One oceanarium, Marineland of the Pacific, adds packed ice around the tail flukes or the entire body to further reduce overheating, particularly when transporting killer whales (Prescott, 1969).

During the past few years, extensive experiments have been conducted at the Navy Marine Bioscience Facility to find a method of transporting odontocetes which is least traumatic to the animals with minimum logistical difficulty (Irvine, 1969). Those experiments have resulted in a method acceptable for long-term transport of some porpoises (*Tursiops truncatus* and *Lagenorhynchus obliquidens*) and intermediate-sized odontocetes (*Globicephala scammoni* and *Orcinus orca*). This method is illustrated in Figs. 10–7 and 10–40.

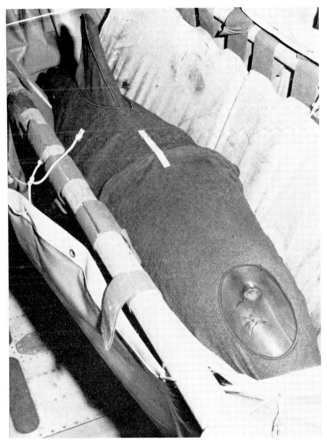

Figure 10–40 A porpoise in a transporter sling covered by a terrycloth jacket, taken in by Velcro® tabs between the dorsal fin and blowhole to prevent the cloth from sliding over the blowhole. A spray system that attaches to the transporter keeps the animal moist.

Even this most recent method, however, is not without its problems. The animal may still overheat along the ventrum, and heat sores may develop if the animal is unevenly distributed in the sling. If the animal is not properly fitted to the sling, sores may develop from abrasion, especially in the axillary region. Additional abrasions have occurred along the chin and the tail stock, where these parts hang over the sling. Such injuries may later cause discomfort to the animal, adversely affect his behavior, and provide access for infection.

Whatever method is employed, it must take into account the extensive adaptations of marine mammals to life in the water. Thermoregulation is of primary importance. The animal must be kept cool and moist to prevent overheating or airburn. The highly flexible thorax is also a matter of special concern because the animal's lungs are forced to expand against much of the weight of its body when being carried out of the water. Because of this stress on the lungs and the increased exposure to various contaminants, respiratory infections are more likely to occur just after transport than at any other time.

Gastrointestinal Foreign Bodies

ODONTOCETES

As reported in Chapter 1, a sperm whale discovered with a glove in its stomach was rumored to have swallowed the owner of that glove. Though it is highly unlikely that this actually did occur, sperm whales and other odontocetes are known to ingest many other kinds of exotic foreign objects. Sperm whales are frequently found with the first stomach one-third filled with sand. Others have swallowed pieces of rocks and wood, and a relatively large number of those captured have coconuts in their stomachs. It is not uncommon to find sand and small stones in the forestomach of newly captured or beached porpoises. It is known, therefore, that at least some wild odontocetes ingest foreign objects. Though it is not known why this occurs and though it may be accidental in some cases, Slijper (1958) proposed that the stones might be beneficial to these animals in the digestion of their food, which is generally swallowed whole.

It is not too surprising in the light of these findings in wild animals, therefore, that captive odontocetes also frequently ingest some strange foreign bodies. Brown *et al.* (1960), Amemiya (1962), Ridgway (1965), and Nakajima *et al.* (1965) have reported such varied items as soft drink bottles, plastic toys, coins, flash bulbs, balls, net floats, tin cans, and other assorted paraphernalia retrieved from stomach contents. Nakajima *et al.* (1965) reported that eighteen of ninety-two dolphins that died at Enoshima Aquarium in Japan between 1958 and 1965 had foreign bodies in their stomachs. The authors attributed the high incidence of foreign objects to "some morbid condition of the animals on the one hand and excitement in training, showing, or playing on the other." The largest item recovered by this group was a $35 \times 20 \times 20$ cm object which weighed 5 kg. In one case which we encountered at the Marine Bioscience Facility, an animal had swallowed three nails, a steel wool cleaning pad, and two washers. In another, an animal swallowed a silicone rubber eye cup which fell from the eye of its tank mate. The suction cup remained in the fore-stomach for over a year and was ultimately removed after the animal accidentally became entangled in a net and drowned. Postmortem also yielded two large plastic bags, a gauze pad, and a considerable amount of marsh grass. In another incident at Sea Life Park in Hawaii, an im-mature porpoise swallowed a 7 cm long by 4 cm in diameter plastic net float. The float was removed by reaching into the forestomach and with-drawing the object.

Though the reasons for these incidents are not absolutely clear, several plausible suggestions have been offered. Since captive animals are taught to eat dead fish, they may consider any object thrown in the pool as edible. The excitement of training and performing may be a contributory factor.

The swallowing of foreign bodies might also be attributable to the diminished gustatory sense of odontocetes (Slijper, 1962). Nutritional problems may contribute to foreign body ingestion. Vitamin and mineral deficiencies have been implicated in foreign body ingestion by cattle. Still another explanation, which receives support from parallels known in other animals, is that the animals are attempting to cope with gastrointestinal upsets such as parasites, enteritis, or ulcers. Parasites such as *Anisakis* in cetaceans and *Contracaecum* in pinnipeds often burrow into the gastroin-testinal tract walls and cause ulcers which no doubt result in considerable pain.

PINNIPEDIA

In describing the pinnipeds, Linnaeus remarked that they "swallow stones to prevent hunger, by distending the stomach" (Turton, 1806). Though it is true that a wide variety of pinnipeds, like cetaceans, are known to ingest foreign bodies, both in the wild and in captivity, there is far from agreement concerning the reasons for this behavior. There is certainly not the matter-of-factness Linnaeus suggested. Some of the in-gestions must surely be accidental as animals play with objects or chase fish or other food, but as Keyes points out (1968), the fact that rocks are found so frequently in the stomachs of collected animals does not permit easy rejection of the theories that they are associated with some physio-logical function. *Arctocephalus pusillus* pups take wood chips and stones along with their first food as they begin to learn to fend for themselves. Yearlings, which may still be nursing, take an even larger number of stones, suggesting that they may be attempting to allay hunger while the mother is away at sea (King, 1964). *Mirounga leonina* appear to take a larger number of stones just prior to the breeding season. King (1964) goes on to summarize briefly the most prevalent theories on why pinnipeds swallow stones. These are as follows: (a) accidental swallowing, (b) to aid in grinding up parasitic worms which may irritate the gastrointestinal tract, (c) to aid in grinding up food items, (d) to provide mass to assist in ejecting undigested fish bones, (e) to ballast and stabilize themselves while they are in the water, and (f) to provide bulk to allay hunger during periods of fast. Harrison and Kooyman (1968) briefly review these theories, rejecting the ballasting and stabilizing theory because there is no evidence that the animals can ingest and regurgitate stones easily as they need them and because the small quantity normally swallowed can hardly be expected to significantly influence drag, bouyancy, etc. Whatever the reason or reasons for it, however, stone swallowing is a widespread behavior and is believed to be relatively noninjurious to the animals (Hubbard, 1968). Recovery of stones has been reported from wild animals of the following species: *Zalophus californianus* (Scheffer and Neft, 1948), *Eumetopias jubata* (Mathisen *et al.* 1962; King, 1964; Nesterov, 1964; Spaulding, 1964; Fiscus and Baines, 1966; Panina, 1966), *Calorhinus ursinus* (Kajimura, 1968), *Arctocephalus doriferus* (Lewis, 1929); and *Otaria byronia, Mirounga leonina,* and *Neophoca hookeri* (King, 1964). In addition, Harrison and Kooyman (1968) reported seeing a *Mirounga angustirostris* playing with and presumably swallowing stones.

Stones and other foreign objects have also been recovered from captive animals. Schneider retrieved 69 lb (31.5 kg) of stones from a *Zalophus californianus* in a zoo (Mohr, 1952). Another California sea lion from Japanese Deer Park in Buena Park, California, swallowed a small rubber ball about 6 cm in diameter (Fig. 10–41). Hammond (1969) mentioned that a Weddell seal died after consuming considerable foam rubber that was used to line its transport carton. A two-year-old female *Mirounga angustirostris* which died of accidental drowning at the Marine Bioscience Facility had stones and tiles from the side of the pool in her stomach, and *Phoca vitulina sp., Zalophus californianus, Mirounga sp.,* and *Arctocephalus pusillus* at the Antwerp Zoo reportedly ate considerable amounts of sand and pebbles (Keyes, 1968). The results of Keyes (1968) survey indicated that eight institutions observed without concern the ingestion of rocks and sand by their pinnipeds and three organizations even provided stones especially for this purpose.

Management of the Foreign Body Problem

There is probably no single explanation which will cover all instances of foreign body ingestion in all species. I prefer the explanation of Naka-

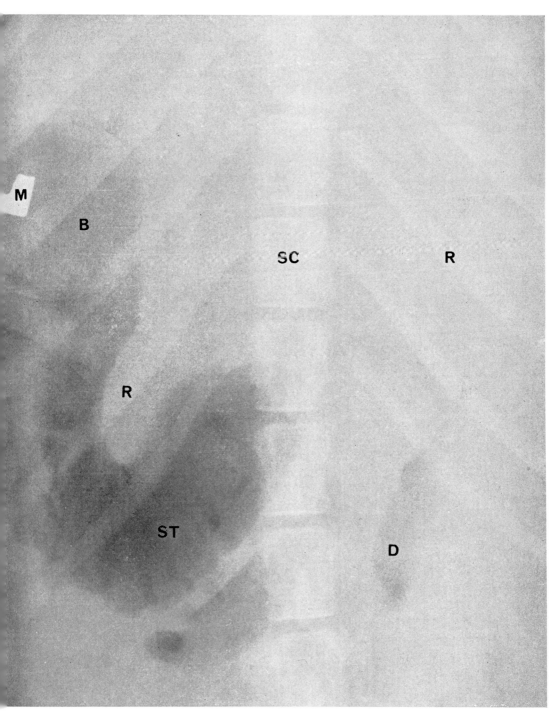

Figure 10–41. Radiograph of the midsection of a California sea lion showing a foreign body, (B), a ball in the stomach. (SC) spinal column, (R) rib, (M) lead marker, (ST) stomach, (D) duodenum.

jima, *et al.* (1965) and suggest that during times of excitement, marine
mammals are most likely to ingest a foreign object. Pryor (1965) described
an incident which illustrates this point. A highly trained Pacific bottlenosed porpoise was performing in a show. Concurrently an experiment
was being done to see if the animal would work for rewards other than
food. Thus the porpoise was being rewarded with small plastic floats
about 7 cm long and 4 cm in diameter. The animal was taught to deposit
these in a container to be later traded for fish at the end of the act. On this
occasion, the porpoise was given the reward and was carrying it across the
pool when another animal gave chase and the float was swallowed.

In addition, gastrointestinal pain is no doubt a factor in many cases
of foreign body ingestion. This pain can result from hunger, parasites,
ulcers, enteritis, and perhaps other causes. Dietary factors must also be
considered.

Small stones and sand are not likely to cause problems, but I can think
of no real benefit that could be derived from such objects. Sharp objects
can cause injury. Rubber balls and pieces of cloth can degenerate and
cause blockage of the intestine at some later date. The best treatment is,
of course, prevention. The animals should not be allowed access to objects
that are small enough to be swallowed. Control of parasites and an adequate diet will no doubt help to eliminate some foreign body ingestion.
Medical treatment of this problem will be discussed later.

Monitoring Animal Health

Maintaining healthy marine mammals is the responsibility of everyone
who feeds or trains the animals or who works with their environmental
water system. The basic and most important factor is genuine concern.
Keen observation by those feeding and training marine mammals is very
important. Early detection of abnormal situations will often prevent the
development of more serious problems. Some signs that may indicate
illness are as follows:

1. Poor appetite. Loss in appetite or complete refusal of food is, unfortunately, the first sign of illness that we usually recognize. It does
   not always mean that the animal is ill. However, animals that refuse
   food or exhibit a diminished appetite should be examined for possible
   illness.
2. Evident weight loss. Porpoises will display weight loss by a hollow-
   ing or caving in on either side of the dorsal fin or on the tail stock.
   In very thin animals it is possible to distinguish a constriction behind the head, and the animal's neck is much more evident. If
   possible, animals should be weighed about once a month.

3. Vomiting or diarrhea. Diarrhea is particularly difficult to observe when the animal is in the water, but if it is suspected, porpoises can be placed in shallow, clear water where the frequency and character of their defecation can be observed. Pinnipeds can be isolated from the water and observed closely for a few hours.
4. Unusual fluid discharges. There is normally a viscous tear secretion. Fluid coming from the nose (blowhole), mouth, or urethra may be a sign of disease and is sufficient cause for an examination.
5. Skin damage. Skin sores, swellings, tattoos, or cuts and scratches.
6. Lameness. This is manifested in cetaceans by failure to use the flipper or flukes.
7. Very foul-smelling breath. The marine mammal's breath is not normally pleasant and usually smells a little fishy. A particularly foul or rancid breath may be present in respiratory infections or sinusitis.
8. Unusual behavior. (Also see Chapter 6.)
   a. The animal is breathing faster than normal (Table 10–1). Difficulty in breathing is evidenced by hoarse or rasping breathing.
   b. The animal is swimming in a stereotyped pattern, failing to take notice of people, other animals, or things in the water.
   c. The animal is trembling.
   d. The animal evidences a continued lack of movement.

Some frequently manifested behaviors of cetaceans that are not usually associated with illness are as follows:

1. Lob tailing is a behavior characterized by lifting the flukes out of the water and bringing them down with a slap to the water surface. This action seems to be a warning gesture and appears to be analogous to the pawing of the ground by a bull (bovine). This behavior may be seen when the animal is irritated for any reason, and it may be used as a bluffing gesture during play.
2. Underwater exhalation is characterized by the release of large quantities of air under water. This usually creates a large bubble which wells up to the surface. In our porpoises, this is often seen at feeding time and is probably a means of getting attention.
3. Jaw snapping is usually a warning and indicates that the animal is angry. The jaws are opened and snapped together forcefully. This may be accompanied by rigid, jerking up-and-down movements of the head. In those rare cases where people have been bitten by porpoises the bite has usually been preceded by jaw-snapping behavior.
4. Aroused surfacing is characterized by the animal swimming around the tank with the upper portion of the head and eyes out of the water. The snout may be slightly above the surface, with the rest

of the head parallel to the surface. The animal may do this in order to get a better view of people and activities around the tank.

5. Snorting is another behavior that may indicate displeasure. It is characterized by the animal expelling air in such a way as to create a snorting sound. It may be seen in conjunction with aroused surfacing or lob tailing. Snorting must be differentiated from sneezing which may occur during respiratory conditions.

MEDICATION

Promiscuous drug usage is wasteful of money and likely to be harmful to the animal. It may also make any illness more difficult to treat when actually diagnosed. No medicine at all is usually better than the wrong medicine.

Medication given by mouth is usually placed in the food. Tablets or capsules may be placed into the gills or mouth of the fish. Liquids can be injected into the body cavity of the fish with a syringe. The medication should get into the first fish fed to the animal. If appetite is poor, at least the medication is taken. If the animal is in the same pool or enclosure with others, these may have to be distracted by someone else so that the sick animal alone gets the medicated fish. It is especially important to give medication at the prescribed times during the day. The effect of the drug is usually dependent upon maintaining a certain blood level. If too long a time elapses between medications, the beneficial effects may be lost. The higher metabolic rate of many marine mammals may speed the degradation and excretion of some drugs; thus, proper timing of medication is essential.

DISEASES
A TABULATION OF KNOWN MARINE MAMMAL DISEASE

I. CETACEA
  A. Cardiovascular system
    1. Myocardial conditions   Truex *et al.* (1961)
                                         Cowan (1966)
                                         Simpson and Ridgway (1970)
        a. Focal Inflammation
        b. Sarcocystis
        c. Basophilic degeneration of myocardial fibers
        d. Focal fibrosis
        e. Infarction
    2. Atherosclerosis and Arteriosclerosis   Truex *et al.* (1961)
                                           Roberts *et al.* (1965)
                                           Cowan (1966)
                                         Hashimoto *et al.* (1967)
    3. Parasites   Truex *et al.* (1961)
        a. Vasculitis
  B. Digestive system
    1. Gastric ulcers   Schroeder and Wegeforth (1935)
                                           Brown and Norris (1956)
                                           Geraci and Gerstmann (1966)
                                           Ridgway and Johnston (1965)
                                           Simpson and Ridgway (1970)

2. Ulcers of forestomach and esophagus   Ridgway and Johnston (1965)
3. Enteritis   Stolk (1953a)
    Ridgway (1966)
4. Foreign bodies   Brown *et al.* (1960)
    Amemiya (1962)
    Nakajima *et al.* (1965)
    Ridgway (1965 and 1968)
5. Colitis   Stolk (1953)
6. Gastrointestinal parasitism   See Chapter 9
    Margolis (1954)
    Delyamure (1955)
    Cockrill (1960)
    Ridgway (1965)
    Ridgway and Johnston (1965)
    Woodard *et al.* (1969)
7. Hepatic cirrhosis and other hepatic pathology   Stolk (1953)
    Stolk (1954)
    Brown *et al.* (1960)
    Cockrill (1960)
    Tomilin (1968)
    Woodard *et al.* (1969)
    Simpson and Ridgway (1970)

      a. Purulent necrotic nodules
      b. Flukes
      c. Fatty degeneration and other toxic changes
8. Pancreatic fibrosis   Ridgway (1968)
    Woodard, *et al.* (1969)
    Simpson and Ridgway (1970)
9. Clostridial enterotoxemia   Klontz (1969)
C. Integumentary system and somatic musculature
    1. Erysipelas   Seibold and Neal (1956)
    Simpson *et al.* (1958)
    Geraci *et al.* (1966)
    Wood *et al.* (1966)
    2. Parasitic cysts   Delyamure (1955)
    Norris (1961)
    Ridgway and Johnston (1965)
    (See Chapter 9)
    3. Dermatoses   Nemoto (1955)
    Hoshina and Siguira (1965)
    Miller and Ridgway (1963)
    Simpson and Ridgway (1970)

      a. Mycotic dermatitis (*Trichophyton*)
      b. Cutaneous abscesses
      c. Urticaria
      d. Nonspecific dermatoses
    4. Clostridial Infections   Heller (1920)
    Slijper (1936)
    Case (1948)
    Simpson and Ridgway (1970)

      a. Myositis (equivalent to blackleg)
      b. Gas gangrene
    5. Ectoparasites   (See Chapter 9)
    6. Husks (encapsulated abscesses)   Stolk (1953 and 1954a)
    7. Trichinosis   Cockrill (1960)
    8. Sarcosporidiosis   Owen (1968)
D. Eye, ear, nose, and throat
    1. Corneal edema and ulceration   Simpson and Ridgway (1970)
    2. Conjunctivitis   Simpson and Ridgway (1970)
    3. Parasitic infestation   See Chapter 9
    Ridgway (1966)

      a. Nasal sinuses
      b. Eustach an tube
      c. Middle ear
    4. Erosion and ulceration of mouth and throat   Miller and Ridgway (1963)
    5. Whalebone disease (gingivitis and loss of baleen plates)   Rice (1961)
    Tomilin (1968)
    6. Tonsilitis   Stolk (1953a)
    Cockrill (1960a)

E. Respiratory system
    1. Pulmonary aspirgillosis   Carrol, *et al.* (1968)
    2. Pulmonary nocardiosis   Cowan (1968)
                                                             Pier *et al.* (1970)
    3. Pneumonia   Brown *et al.* (1960)
                                                             Slijper (1962)
                                                             Miller and Ridgway (1963)
                                                             Ridgway (1965 and 1968)
                                                             Cowan (1966 and 1968)
                                                             Testi and Pilleri (1969)
                                                             Woodard *et al.* (1969)

        a. Bacterial
        b. Parasitic
        c. Unknown etiology
    4. Pleuritis   Stolk (1954a)
                                                             Ridgway (1966)

F. Urogenital system
    1. Mastitis   Cockrill (1960)
    2. Orchitis, testicular necrosis   Cockrill (1960b)
                                                             Uys and Best (1966)
                                                             Tomilin (1968)
                                                             Simpson and Ridgway (1970)
    3. Ovarian cyst   Tomilin (1968)
    4. Purulent nephritis   Miller and Ridgway (1963)
    5. Urinary calculi   Legendre (1925)
                                                             Simpson and Ridgway (1970)
    6. Abortions and stillbirths   Essapian (1963)
                                                             Ridgway (1966)

G. Neoplasms
    1. Benign tumors of the uterus and ovaries   Rewell and Willis (1949)
    2. Benign melanotic tumor of the lip   Uys and Best (1966)
    3. Dermal fibroma   Stolk (1952)
    4. Ganglinoneuroma-anterior mediastinum   Rewell and Willis (1950)
    5. Hepatic adenoma   Stolk (1952)
    6. Hepatic hemangioma   Stolk (1953c)
    7. Hodgkins disease   Stolk (1962)
    8. Lingual fibroma   Stolk (1952)
    9. Lingual papilloma   Rewell and Willis (1950)
    10. Lipoma   Cockrill (1960a)
    11. Brain lipoma   Pilleri (1966)
    12. Ovarian carcinoma   Stolk (1950)

H. Miscellaneous
    1. Dental caries in *Inia* geoffrensis   Ness (1966)
    2. Other dental disease   Tomes (1873)
                                                             Colyer (1938)
                                                             Cockrill (1960b)
                                                             Simpson and Ridgway (1970)

        a. Alveolitis
        b. Pulp abscesses
        c. Pulp infections
    3. Vitamin C deficiency   Miller and Ridgway (1963)
                                                             Ridgway (1965)
    4. Vitamin B$_1$ deficiency   White (1970)
    5. Peritonitis   Cockrill (1960b)
                                                             Simpson and Ridgway (1970)
    6. Fetal defects and neonatal disease   Cockrill (1960b)
                                                             Simpson and Ridgway (1970)
    7. Jaundice   Medway *et al.* (1966)
                                                             Simpson and Ridgway (1970)
    8. Thyroid pathology   Cowan (1966)
                                                             Harrison (1969)
    9. Bone pathology   Slijper (1936 and 1962)
                                                             Cowan (1966)

        a. Spinal osteoarthritis
        b. Spondylitis deformans
        c. Deformed lower jaw (sperm whale)
    10. Septicemias (primarily erysipelas)   Heller (1920)
                                                             Seibold and Neal (1956)
                                                             Geraci *et al.* (1966)
                                                             Simpson and Ridgway (1970)

11. Salmonellosis   Brown *et al.* (1960)
12. Injury by sting ray spine   Allen (1970)

II. PINNIPEDIA

A. Cardiovascular system
   1. Heartworm   Taylor *et al.* (1961)
            MacDonald and Gilchrist (1969)
            (See Chapter 9)
   2. General vascular and cardiac disease   Fox (1921 and 1923)
            Kelly and Jensen (1960)
            Prathap *et al.* (1966)
            Stout (1969)
     a. Atherosclerosis
     b. Aortitis
B. Digestive system
   1. Enteritis   Fox (1923)
            Wolinski and Landowski (1962)
            Keyes (1965)
            Hubbard (1968)
            Simpson and Ridgway (1970)
   2. Gastrointestinal parasites   Hubbard (1960)
            Keyes (1965)
            Simpson and Ridgway (1970)
            (See Chapter 9)
   3. Gastric and intestinal ulceration   Schroeder and Wegeforth (1935)
            Herman (1941)
            Hubbard (1968)
            Simpson and Ridgway (1970)
   4. Hepatitis   Simpson and Ridgway (1970)
   5. Pancreatitis   Murray (1915)
            Simpson and Ridgway (1970)
   6. Gastrointestinal foreign bodies   Appelby (1962)
            Harrison (1968)
            Simpson and Ridgway (1970)
C. Integument and somatic musculature
   1. Seal Pox   Wilson (1969)
   2. Dermatoses   Mohr (1952)
            Scheffer (1958)
            Hubbard (1968)
            Simpson and Ridgway (1970)
     a. Ulcers
     b. Papules
     c. Granulomas
     d. Nonspecific lesions
   3. Ectoparasites   See Chapter 9
D. Eye, ear, nose and throat
   1. Ocular pathology   Hamerton (1933)
            Kelly (1950)
            Hubbard (1968)
            Simpson and Ridgway (1970)
     a. Corneal edema
     b. Corneal ulceration
     c. Cataracts
     d. Conjunctivitis
   2. Ulceration and erosions of mouth and throat   Simpson and Ridgway (1970)
E. Respiratory system
   1. Pneumonia   Mohr (1952)
            Brown *et al.* (1960)
            Hubbard (1968)
            MacDonald and Gilchrist (1969)
            Simpson and Ridgway (1970)
            (See Chapter 9)
     a. Bacterial
     b. Parasitic
     c. Mycotic
   2. Empyema   Simpson and Ridgway (1970)
   3. Bronchitis   Blessing (1969)
   4. Obstructive emphysema   Saunders and Hubbard (1966)
F. Urogenital system
   1. Chronic interstitial nephritis   Fox (1923)
            MacDonald and Gilchrist (1969)

2. Abortion   Simpson and Ridgway (1970)
G. Neoplasms
  1. Adrenal hypernephroma   Fox (1923)
  2. Adenocarcinoma and myosarcoma of   Fox (1921)
    mammary gland
  3. Fibroma of the neck   Simpson and Ridgway (1970)
  4. Adenocarcinoma of eccrine glandular tissue   Simpson and Ridgway (1970)
                                               See Chapter 5
  5. Lymphosarcoma   Griner (1970)
  6. Granulosa cell tumor   Griner (1970)
  7. Adrenocortical carcinoma   Griner (1970)
H. Miscellaneous
  1. Dental disease   Stirling (1969)
  2. Erysipelas   Simpson and Ridgway (1970)
  3. Pasteurellosis   Keyes (1968)
  4. Blastomycosis   Williamson *et al.* (1959)
  5. Tuberculosis   Blair (1912)
  6. Peritonitis   Plimmer (1915)
  7. Otariid ataxia   Rigdon and Drager (1955)
                                               Hubbard (1968)
                                               Simpson and Ridgway (1970)

    a. Thiamine deficiency
    b. Clostridial enterotoxemia
  8. Hypoglycemia   Hubbard (1968)
  9. Salmon disease (rickettsial)   Farrell (1969)
                                               Keyes (1969)
  10. Trichinosis   Roth (1949)
  11. Osteomalacia   Todd (1913)
  12. Botryomycosis   Fox (1923)
  13. Salmonellosis   Griner (1970)
  14. Septicemia   Hill (1951)
  15. Jaundice   Hill (1951)
                                               Simpson and Ridgway (1970)

DIAGNOSIS AND THERAPY

Although most of those subjects already discussed must be considered when attempting to make a diagnosis on a marine mammal, this discussion deals more specifically with some basic clinical techniques employed in diagnosis and therapy. The major emphasis is on those aspects that vary from techniques used and responses found in other animals.

Some Clinical Techniques Used in Diagnosis

Body Temperature Measurements

Cetaceans with pneumonia, urinary tract infections, enteritis, erysipelas, and myositis have manifested fevers ranging from 38° to 39°C (102.2°F). We have recorded fevers as high as 41°C (105.8°F) in an elephant seal with severe pneumonia. Pinnipeds usually remain out of the water when they are very ill. Immersion of the animal in water may, in effect, place a limit on the fever.

Normal body temperatures for several species are listed in Table 10–39. We employ an electronic thermometer with a flexible thermistor probe for measuring body temperature. Glass thermometers should be avoided because they are generally too short to obtain a reliable reading in most

TABLE 10–39
RECTAL TEMPERATURES OF SOME MARINE MAMMALS
FOUND IN CAPTIVITY

Pinnipeds	Rectal Temperature (C°)	Reference
Odobenus rosmarus	36.6	Ray and Fay, 1968
Leptonychotes weddelli	37.0	Ray and Smith, 1968
Callorhinus ursinus	37.0	Bartholomew and Wilkie, 1966
Mirounga angustirostris	36.9	Bartholomew, 1954
Pagophilus groenlandicus	36.0	Irving and Hart, 1957
Zalophus californianus	37.5	Ridgway, 1965
Phoca vitulina	36.9	*
Cetaceans		
Lagenorhynchus obliquidens	37.2	Ridgway, 1965
Globicephala scammoni	36.5	*
Orcinus orca	36.4	*
Tursiops truncatus (normal)	36.9	Ridgway, 1965
Tursiops truncatus (with severe infection)	38.1	*
Tursiops truncatus (Out of water and dried out)	38.5	*

* Data collected by the author at the Navy Marine Bioscience Facility.

marine mammals. If the animal struggles, the glass thermometer can be broken, causing injury.

In *Tursiops truncatus*, the thermistor probe is inserted 25 cm into the rectum, where the normal temperature is usually just under 37°C (98.6°F). At lesser depths, the temperature is more variable and averages progressively lower toward the anus. In seals and sea lions, this standard depth is also desirable although not essential in the smaller animals. In larger odontocetes such as *Globicephala scammoni* and *Orcinus orca,* the probe is inserted to a depth of 40 cm.

If an animal checked out of the water has a slightly increased temperature, say 38°C (100.4°F), the temperature should probably be taken again after the porpoise is placed back in the water to ensure that the increased temperature was not due to the animal being out of the water and insufficiently cooled. Pinnipeds that struggle a great deal and become excited can have very large elevations in body temperature, especially on warm days.

MacKay (1964) and Reid (1966) used a small ingested radio transmitter to telemeter body temperature from a *Tursiops truncatus* swimming in a small pool. McGinnis (1968) employed such telemetry in pinnipeds. In the future, such endoradiosons may offer a practical means of observing body temperature for clinical purposes.

BLOOD COLLECTION

In cetaceans, the best site for venipuncture is in most cases the ventral aspect of the tail flukes, but occasionally the dorsum of the flukes or the

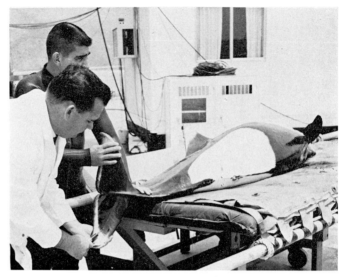

Figure 10–42. Blood samples for porpoises are usually collected from the central veins on the ventral aspect of the tail fluke. For bleeding, the animal is placed on a soft mat and kept wet. The *Phocoenoides dalli* shown here was the only member of that species to survive in captivity for more than sixty days. It lived at the Marine Bioscience Facility for about twenty months.

veins of a flipper are used (Medway and Geraci, 1964). The vessels employed are the central veins which form part of the countercurrent vascular system found in the extremities of cetaceans (Figs. 4–2, 5–97). A 1½ in, 18- or 20-gauge needle is normally used for venipuncture in cetaceans.

Cetacean red blood cells are more fragile than those of dog or man as measured by the saline osmotic fragility test and the Fragilograph.* To minimize hemolysis in blood collection and handling, we have used disposable plastic syringes and test tubes. When glass syringes or test tubes are required, they are treated with a silicone solution. In addition, the blood is centrifuged in a 25 cm centrifuge at low speeds (1,000 to 1,500 RPM) to separate serum or plasma from the cells.

Since values for serum enzyme activity and electrolyte content are subject to change if the serum is allowed to stand on the cells, the blood is centrifuged within one hour after it has been collected, whether or not a clot has formed. A fibrin clot that later forms in the serum is removed. A small amount of EDTA** is added to hemogram specimens, but for most other samples requiring an anticoagulant, sodium heparin or lipo-heparin is employed.

In preparation for taking samples, cetaceans are usually removed from the tank or enclosure in slings and placed on a padded table (Fig. 10–42).

* Fragilograph, Model D-12, Elron Electronic Industry, Ltd., Haifa, Israel.
** Sequestersol®, Cambridge Chemical Products, Inc., Detroit, Michigan.

Larger animals such as *Globicephala scammoni* and *Orcinus orca* may be held in slings or stranded on the tank bottom. Water is sprayed over the animal to keep it moist and to maintain normal body temperature. Blood specimens are usually collected before the animal is fed and thus after a fast of twelve to twenty-four hours.

In Phocidae such as *Phoca vitulina* and *Mirounga angustirostris* blood specimens are usually collected from one of the extradural veins that lie above and just lateral to the spinal column (Fig. 10–43). In Otariidae, a vessel inside the spinal canal is entered by inserting the needle into an intervertebral space in the lumbar region. Small blood samples from the Phocidae and Otariidae may be taken from the interdigital vessels of the flippers. Pinniped blood generally clots much faster than that of cetaceans; thus slightly more anticoagulant is used.

URINE COLLECTION AND ANALYSIS

In porpoises, urine is collected by catheterization. In female porpoises of the species which I have studied, the urethral orifice lies just below the

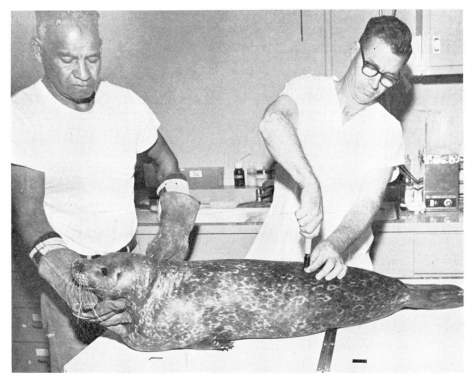

Figure 10–43. The Harrison method for bleeding the harbor seal demonstrated by Dr. Richard Hubbard of Stanford Research Institute. The sample is drawn from the intravertebral extradural vein.

relatively large clitoris and is of adequate diameter so that a No. 8 to 14 French catheter is easily passed. Since the penis of the male contains a sigmoid flexure, a 40 to 50 cm 6 or 8 French male canine catheter seems to work best. I prefer to collect urine from pinnipeds by placing them in a collecting cage (Fig. 10–6).

Urine electrolytes, osmolality, and other characteristics involved in osmoregulation have already been discussed. The urine specific gravity ranges between 1.020 and 1.055 for animals on a fish diet and up to 1.075 for animals on a squid diet or fasting. Tests for albumin and sugar are normally negative and the pH is acid. The urine color is normally clear to yellow and may be deep amber in fasting animals.

We have observed an interesting phenomenon regarding urine color in the Dall porpoise (Ridgway, 1965). In every member of that species that we catheterized, the urine was voided pale green but rapidly turned to a straw color when exposed to sunlight. Thus there was probably some green pigment in the urine that was changed in sunlight. We can only speculate as to the nature of this pigment; and whether or not it is a normal condition in *Phocoenoides dalli*, we still do not know. The colorless bile pigment urobilinogen is normally present in mammalian urine. Upon oxidation it is converted to the greenish fluorescent pigment urobilin. Perhaps the Dall porpoise excretes an unstable urobilin that is reduced when exposed to sunlight (or air).

The Dall porpoise as well as several other pelagic species of cetaceans have bright green feces when they are first captured at sea. This indicates to me an absence of bile-reducing intestinal microflora. Since the intestinal microflora of other mammals is involved in the reduction of bile pigments, such a condition could possibly be responsible for the green urine observed. Ray (quoted in Wood *et al.*, 1966) mentioned that the *Delphinapterus leucas* which he maintained in the New York Aquarium had a sterile gut and green feces. He did not mention the urine color, however.

FECAL COLLECTION AND ANALYSIS

Fecal samples from pinnipeds can be collected by isolating the animal from the water or putting it in a collecting cage. The fecal sample can then be picked up when it is produced. Small fecal samples can be collected from porpoises when they are being examined out of the water. For large specimens, or twenty-four hour specimens, a small endotracheal tube is employed as a rectal catheter and inserted into the rectum. In this way, the feces can be collected over a long period of time. The catheter should not fit too tightly or be forced into the rectum. In one such case, necrosis was produced in the lower rectum and severe peritonitis followed.

Geraci (1969) fed charcoal to seals in order to observe the gastrointestinal clearance rate. Charcoal appeared in the feces one and one-half to three and one-half hours after feeding. I have noted that the majority of the feces is passed in the first six hours after feeding in *Tursiops truncatus*.

Fecal examination for parasites is accomplished by standard techniques. Sea lion stools should be carefully examined for lung worm larvae, and at least three fecal specimens in one week from each new animal should be checked.

The color and consistency of the feces of four species of marine mammals that we have observed is shown in Table 10–40. Ray (quoted in Wood *et al.*, 1966) noted that his *Delphinapterus leucas* at the New York Aquarium had smoky gray feces after feeding, which gradually turned to

TABLE 10–40
CHARACTERISTICS OF FECES OF PORPOISES AND SEA LIONS

	Tursiops truncatus	*Lagenorhynchus obliquidens*	*Phocoenoides dalli*	*Zalophus californianus*
Color	Tan to light green*	Grey to bright green	Gray to bright green	Tan to brown
Consistency	Thick liquid	Thick liquid	Thick liquid	Firm on fish diet, liquid on squid diet

* Bright or dark green feces in *T. truncatus* is usually a sign of ill health or possibly heavy antibiotic medication. Observed at the Navy Marine Bioscience Facility.

green. Thus the animal had green feces in the morning before feeding and gray feces in the afternoon after feeding. This appears comparable to the situation that I observed in *Lagenorhynchus obliquidens* and *Phocoenoides dalli*. In *Tursiops truncatus*, green feces has been a sign of ill health (Wood *et al.*, 1966). In addition, heavy antibiotic therapy may produce a green feces in this species. Some disease conditions, as well as antibiotic therapy, produce a change in intestinal microflora to such an extent that the bile-reducing bacteria are eliminated with the resultant green feces. The color difference between the feces of *Tursiops truncatus* and that of the other species mentioned may partially explain why *Tursiops truncatus* adjusts more readily to captivity and is hardier. Because it goes into estuarine areas, perhaps *Tursiops truncatus* is exposed to more terrestrial bacteria and can better adjust to the microfloral changes in captivity.

THE ELECTROCARDIOGRAM (EKG)

In *Tursiops truncatus* and all other cetaceans that I have observed, there is a normal cardiac arrhythmia whether the animal is swimming or resting out of the water. Within about one second after inspiration, the heart rate of *Tursiops truncatus* increases to around 100 or 120 beats per minute and then slows to 30 to 60 beats per minute as the period of apnea increases. Therefore, the heart rate slows and speeds up in a cyclic fashion with respiration. Irving *et al.* (1941) first reported this in *Tursiops truncatus,* and Kanwisher and Sundness (1966b) observed it in *Phocaena phocaena.* The arrhythmia is not manifested if the animal is very excited, such as just after capture. Several drugs that depress the CNS and many illnesses also eliminate the normal respiratory arrhythmia.

For cetaceans we have standardized lead placement (Ridgway, 1968). The left arm lead is placed at the left axilla with the right arm lead at the right axilla and the chest lead at the center of the dorsum of the thorax, since the animal is usually resting on its underside. If the animal is resting on its back, the chest lead is placed on the ventral midline of the thorax. For recording the EKG, silver-silver chloride electrodes imbedded in a silicone suction cup are employed (Fig. 10–45). These electrodes work equally as well underwater or in air.

Senft and Kanwisher (1960) made cardiographic observations on a beached fin whale. Spencer *et al.* (1960) reported on the killer whale. King *et al.* (1955) reported on the EKG of the beluga. Murdaugh *et al.* (1961a) recorded the electrocardiogram of a diving *Phoca vitulina.* Hamlin *et al.* (1970) have characterized the EKG of *Tursiops truncatus* and have described its vectors as similar to those of Equidae (horses, mules, and zebra) and swine. The ventricular activation process of the dolphin seems similar to that of animals classed in group B of mammals based on complete penetration of Purkinje's fibers to the epicardium of the ventricular free walls. Hamlin *et al.* (1970) state that "the electrocardiogram in the dolphin will be of limited value for the detection of diseases which would produce characteristic changes in the electrocardiogram if these diseases occurred in primates, carnivores, and Felidae."

RADIOGRAPHY

Radiographs can be valuable aids to diagnosis and have wide areas of application in experimental procedures with marine mammals. Bron *et al.* (1966) used x-ray to demonstrate the arterial constrictor response in a seal and Nagel *et al.* (1968) illustrated the cerebral circulation in *Tursiops truncatus* with radiography.

Foreign bodies are often observed with x-ray. Soft foreign bodies (Fig. 10–41) and other gastrointestinal problems can often be observed with a barium series. For a barium series in a 125 to 200 kg *Tursiops truncatus,* 0.5 kg of barium sulphate are blended with equal parts of fish and water and homogenized in a large blender. This mixture is given by stomach tube and reaches the anus in one to three hours. Radiographs should be taken at brief intervals. The normal blend of barium and water can be employed, but it is vomited somewhat more readily than the barium-fish-water mixture.

ESOPHAGEAL PALPATION

Porpoises have relatively large mouths and throats. The esophagus of most *Tursiops truncatus* over about 100 kg can accommodate the average human hand and arm. A technique has been described for removing foreign bodies from the forestomach of small delphinids (Ridgway, 1965) that consists of simply reaching in, grasping the object with the hand, and pulling it out. This has been the simplest and most successful method of treating the foreign-body problem.

Cornell (1969) has adapted this technique for manual palpation of the lungs, heart, pleura, and liver in addition to the forestomach.

ENDOSCOPIC EXAMINATION

The forestomach of cetaceans and stomach of pinnipeds can be examined by means of a gastroscope or endoscope. At the Navy Marine Bioscience Facility we have a 1.8 m (6 ft) fiberoptic gastroscope that has been quite useful. A stomach tube is usually passed along with the endoscope so that air can be injected for improved visibility of the gastrointestinal tract walls and contents.

Esophageal erosions, ulcers of the forestomach, and foreign bodies have been diagnosed with the gastroscope. Alternate closing and opening of the cardiac sphincter between the forestomach and mainstomach (Fig. 4–12) and the spillover of gastric juice from the mainstomach to the forestomach have been observed with this tool.

Therapeutic Techniques

INJECTIONS

In cetaceans, intramuscular (IM) injections may be made in the abdominal muscles or in the dorsal musculature on either side of the dorsal fin. It is essential that the needle used for the injection penetrate the blubber layer and go into the muscle. A needle at least 3.3 cm (1½ in) must be used in *Tursiops truncatus* unless the animal is large and fat, in which case a 4.4 cm (2 in) needle must be employed. In pilot whales and killer whales, needles 8.8 to 13.2 cm (4 to 6 in) should be used for IM

injections. In small pinnipeds, a 3.3 cm needle is sufficient, but in larger
animals longer needles must be used.

The technique for intravenous injection is the same as mentioned earlier
for venipuncture (Fig. 10–42, 10–43). Intraperitoneal injections are also
acceptable for administration of fluids. Blood levels of glucose are increased within ten minutes after the IP injection of 10% dextrose solution.
In pinnipeds, the subcutaneous route is often used when indicated. The
subcutaneous injection of hydrating fluids (50 ml per site) has been well
tolerated and effective.

ORAL MEDICATION

If the animal is eating, medication may be placed in food fish or squid.
When the patient is off food, a stomach tube is passed for administration
of oral-type medication, for hydration, or for feeding.

VACCINATION

We immunize all newly aquired animals against erysipelas. This is repeated at six-month intervals. For some time, attenuated live erysipelas
vaccine was employed, but during 1968 there were several incidents of
multiple animal deaths occurring at three different oceanariums or laboratories that were using the attenuated product. Currently, most organizations
employ the bacterin. Some facilities give enterotoxemia bacterin. Immuniza-
tion against other Clostridia (probably blackleg) many prove desirable.

One virus disease of sea lions (seal pox) has recently been reported
(Wilson *et al.*, 1969). Virus hepatitis has been suspected in porpoises but
not proven. The "tattoos" that sometimes occur on porpoises may also be
of viral origin, but in general, the virus diseases of marine mammals have
not been investigated. Thus there are no vaccines.

TOPICAL MEDICATION

A clean water supply is the best medication for most wounds, cuts, and
scratches. Wounds acquired during capture or transport are scrubbed with
surgical soap and cleaned with alcohol or ether. If the water is clean, no
further treatment is generally required.

Pinnipeds can be held away from the water during treatment. They can
also be allowed periodic access to a small medicated bath. Cetaceans
cannot be treated so easily, however. Most medication will wash off in
the water, but dyes such as gentian violet and pyoktanol will adhere for
a day or so. Silicone rubber suction cups have been used to hold medication over a small wound or an eye of porpoises for up to a few hours.

Wounds on the flukes, flippers, and tip of the snout are particularly difficult to manage, since these areas are more exposed to trauma in the animal's daily activities. These body parts are especially susceptible to injury when the porpoise has to be caught for any reason. Such lesions often bleed slowly or leak plasma, causing the animal to be anemic in the first case. In the second case, they may be unthrifty and difficult to keep in good flesh. Since the snout is often used for rooting, pushing, bumping, and all sorts of things, even the healthiest porpoises usually have roughened, sore, or scarred areas on the tip of the snout (Fig. 10–46).

Airburn or sunburn is sometimes seen in newly captured cetaceans or animals that are ill. These individuals rest on the surface with the blowhole and sometimes the dorsal fin out of the water for long periods of time. In light-colored animals, the affected area becomes dark in color. The skin cracks, peels, and becomes roughened. In severe cases, the cracks may bleed. The condition is just as severe in animals kept inside buildings as it is in those exposed to sunlight. Therefore, in my judgment, the condition results from drying of the skin and is not an effect of sunlight. To prevent these conditions, zinc oxide ointment can be applied to the exposed areas, but a frequent spraying with water is more effective.

PARASITE CONTROL

It can be assumed that every marine mammal brought in from the wild is parasitized to some extent. At the Marine Bioscience Facility, a complete fecal examination is made at the outset and thiabendazole* is given in some of the first food fish. This compound appears to be quite effective against some of the most ubiquitous and damaging of the marine mammal parasites including genera such as *Anisakis* and *Contracaecum*. This medication (45 mg/kg) is repeated in about three months and is then routinely given every six months. In very severe cases, the initial dose may be increased to 70 mg/kg followed by a 45 mg/kg dose in one to three weeks. When tapeworms are diagnosed, the animal is treated with diphenthane 70.**

Each year, numerous obviously ill young *Zalophus californianus* come onto southern California beaches. They are usually thin; the breathing is rapid; sometimes there is a nasal exudate, and they cough. Although there is often a secondary respiratory infection, the primary problem in a severe lung worm infestation that has been mentioned in Chapters 5 and 9.

* Thibenzole®, a product of Merck and Co., Inc., Rahway, N.J.
** Teniatol®, a product of Pitman-Moore, Co., Indianapolis, Ind.

These animals invariably die within two or three days after coming to the beach.

In one instance, lung worm larvae were found in stool specimens of two young *Zalophus californianus*. Both had lost weight. One frequently coughed and had shown some respiratory distress after exertion. The animals were treated with diethylcarbamazine citrate† (3 mg/kg daily in the food fish) for about three months. No further larvae have been seen, and there have been no other symptoms of lung worm disease in these animals in the two years since.

Some *Zalophus californianus* recover spontaneously from lung worm infestation. Others no doubt live for long periods with light to moderate lung worm infestation. Thus it is not possible to be certain about the efficacy of the diethylcarbamazine citrate treatment.

In southern California, heart worms have frequently been found in *Phoca vitulina* and occasionally in *Zalophus californianus* (see Chapter 9). The microfilaria can be observed in a blood smear. The life cycle is not yet known and to my knowledge there are no reports on modes of therapy.

SLEEP AND ANESTHESIA IN CETACEANS

Some questions about natural sleep in cetaceans are particularly germane to a consideration of anesthetic procedures; viz, Is respiration strictly voluntary and controlled at higher levels of the CNS or does it involve reflex acts still not fully understood? Do cetaceans lose consciousness during sleep, and if so, do they awake for each breath?

Several observers have reported on the behavior of porpoises during what was apparently natural sleep. Gray (1927) was the first to record observations of sleeping whales (Greenland right whales and a narwhale) in the scientific literature. McBride and Hebb (1948) and McCormick 1967) describe a passive surface sleep during which the porpoise hangs near the surface, both eyes closed, with the head and trunk nearly parallel to the water surface and the tail dangling somewhat. In the absence of water current, the animal rests almost motionless except for about twice each minute when the tail strokes, slowly lifting the animal to the surface to breathe. Tomilin (1948) who also mentions this type of sleep, attributes the porpoise's surface sleep respiration to a reflex mechanism involving the stroking of the tail flukes and exposure of the blowhole to air (emergence reflex).

McCormick (1967) also describes another type of sleep referred to as bottom sleep, during which the animal rests on or near the bottom, coming

† Caricide®, a product of American Cyanamid Co., Princeton, N.J.

up periodically to breathe. The *Tursiops truncatus* that McCormick (1967) observed would catnap in this manner for as long as four minutes before they surfaced to breathe. After ten to twenty quick breaths, they may or may not resume the nap. McBride and Hebb did not mention bottom sleep, but they did observe that in a tank with particularly strong current, the porpoises would make a few rapid swimming strokes and then coast around the tank as the eyes drooped.

Lilly (1964) maintains that the sleep behavior of porpoises is considerably different. The animals he observed closed only one eye at a time and thus Lilly (1964) proposes that only one-half of the brain sleeps at any one time. This allows the porpoise to actively surface under conscious volition for each breath taken during periods of sleep. He further proposes that inhibition of respiration takes place at a thalamocortical level.

I have observed *Tursiops truncatus, Tursiops gilli, Lagenorhynchus obliquidens, Globicephala scammoni* and *Orcinus* orca that appeared to be asleep. The most common type of sleep that I have observed is the surface sleep which has previously been seen by McBride and Hebb (1948), Tomilin (1948), McCormick (1967), and Spencer *et al.* (1967). However, at the Marine Bioscience Facility, there seem to be some individual variations in the behavior exhibited during apparent sleep.

In our main holding tank (16 × 2.5 m), a 215 kg mature male *Tursiops truncatus* and five females of the same species have been the primary residents for the past year. At night when the facility is quiet, I have noted characteristic behaviors on a number of occasions by quietly approaching the tank in rubber shoes. The large male is always stationed next to the boards of the weir over which water flows from the tank into Mugu Lagoon. Both of his eyes are closed, and the tail fluke droops about 1 m below the water. He breathes at intervals of thirty-five to seventy-five seconds. The dorsum of his head and the blowhole remain out of the water. The largest female, an animal that currently weighs 224 kg, sleeps immediately on his left in the characteristic surface sleep posture, i.e. tail drooped down, both eyes closed, resting just below the surface and stroking the flukes just slightly to rise for breaths at thirty to fifty second intervals. A 180 kg spayed female usually sleeps to the left of the largest female but has on occasion been on the right of the male. Another large female occupies the second or third position to the left of the male. In the far side and center of the tank, a large female (183 kg) and an immature female (115 kg) swim in a slow, counterclockwise circle about 8 m in diameter. They surface to breathe at intervals of about thirty seconds (about once each time around the tank). The smaller animal swims just to the rear of the larger and keeps her left pectoral flipper extended slightly so that it remains in contact with the large female's right side as they swim. Although

I cannot be absolutely certain, it appears that both animals have both eyes closed.

The only periods of bottom sleep that I have observed in a cetacean occurred when a young male *Tursiops truncatus* was placed in a tank of fresh water for some studies of renal physiology. While in fresh water, this animal was often observed catnapping on the bottom as described by McCormick (1967). The Aquarama where McCormick made most of his long-term observations is an inland oceanarium. A 1% salt solution is used as an environmental water supply. Thus it appears that bottom sleep may occur more frequently in water of lower specific gravity, although surface sleep was also observed under both conditions.

Considerable neurophysiological investigation will be required before we understand the complicated central nervous system control of respiration and the physiology of sleep in cetaceans. Control of the large specialized larynx and the muscles of the blowhole are probably very important factors in CNS respiratory control. Neuromuscular control of respiration could possibly involve the stroking of the tail flukes and exposure of the blowhole to air as Tomilin (1948) has suggested.

The first attempts to anesthetize porpoises were not successful. Langworthy (1932) made the first known attempt. He used ether given by a cone held over the blowhole of a *Tursiops truncatus*. The porpoise did not survive. In 1955, a group of researchers used intraperitoneal sodium pentobarbital in attempts to anesthetize several *Tursiops truncatus* for electrophysiological studies of the brain. All of these porpoises died from the anesthesia (Lilly, 1962).

In 1965, Dr. Forrest Bird of the Bird Corporation, Palm Springs, California, developed an apneustic plateau control unit compatible with the Bird Mark 9 large animal respirator. This unit effectively imitates the natural respiration of the porpoise by inflating the lungs rapidly, holding an apneustic plateau for a variable period and then deflating and rapidly filling the lungs again. Nagel *et al.* (1964) employed the Bird equipment in an attempt to produce barbiturate anesthesia in a *Tursiops truncatus*. Methohexital (5 mg/kg) and thiopental sodium (13 mg/kg) were given intraperitoneally and an anesthetic death resulted. In the same report, a technique of employing 50 to 70 percent nitrous oxide (NO_2) for anesthesia was outlined. In 1965 Nagel *et al.*, reported on the use of NO_2 supplemented with succinyldicholine as an anesthetic preparation for major surgery in porpoises.

After consulting Nagel's group, my associates and I attempted to anesthetize several porpoises (*Lagenorhynchus* and *Tursiops truncatus*) with NO_2 (Ridgway 1965; Ridgway and McCormick, 1967). We decided not to employ succinyldicholine because it has no anesthetic or analgesic properties and paralyzes the skeletal muscle to such an extent that muscular reflexes cannot be used to assist in judging the depth of anesthesia. In addition, porpoises have very low levels of or a complete lack of plasma cholinesterase and thus the action of succinyldicholine is prolonged (Nagel *et al.*, 1965). From these experiments, we concluded that NO_2 was quite inadequate for major surgery in porpoises (Ridgway and McCormick, 1967 and 1970).

Since we were not satisfied with NO_2 as an anesthetic for use in major surgery in porpoises, we decided to test a more potent agent. We chose halothane* for the following reasons: (a) it is a potent agent, (b) it

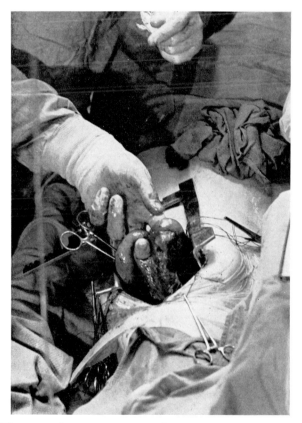

Figure 10–44. The ovariohysterectomy on this porpoise was an essential lifesaving measure because of a chronic endometritis. A sterile form-fitting clear plastic drape covers the entire abdominal area. The horns of the bicornuate uterus have been drawn up through the ventral midline incision in the abdomen. This animal, a 150 kg *Tursiops truncatus* recovered rapidly and has had no apparent health problems in the 4 years since the operation. She now weighs over 200 kg and is a well trained experimental animal.

* Fluothane®, a product of Ayerst Laboratories, Inc. New York, N.Y.

provides rapid induction and rapid recovery, (c) halothane is not spasmo-
genic to the larynx and bronchi, (d) it is not irritating to mucous membrane, (e) it fortifies nitrous oxide and can readily be used with that
agent, and (f) it is nonflammable and chemically stable.

Probably the most important single consideration so far as porpoises are
concerned is rapid recovery with no aftereffects. Porpoises are slightly
negatively buoyant, but their overall buoyancy is near neutral. Because
cetaceans are approximately weightless in their aquatic environment, being
out of the water subjects the animal to several stresses including the
necessity to breathe and maintain circulation against the weight of its own
body. Thus it is important to get the animal back into the water as soon as
possible after a surgical procedure (Fig. 10–44). For long-term surgery,
we employ a special tank so that much of the body is submerged (Fig.
10–45).

The several disadvantages of halothane were also considered. It is
expensive, and difficulty in monitoring makes it more complicated to use
in a closed system. Fortunately, our laboratory was equipped with a gas
chromatograph on which inspired and expired halothane, as well as blood
levels, could be measured during our initial experiments. We chose to use

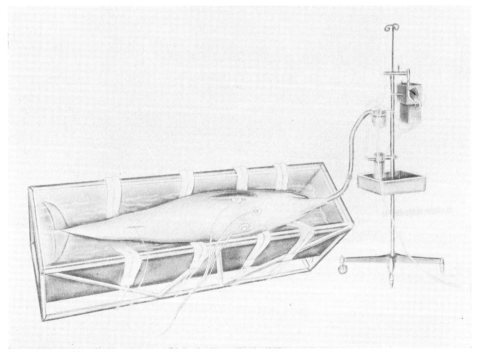

Figure 10–45. Porpoise in surgery tank. Suction cup electrodes are used for monitoring
the electrocardiogram, and a thermistor probe is placed into the rectum for monitoring
body temperature.

a controlled open system because of the added safety factor. Halothane also may depress circulation and cardiac action, especially if administered together with succinyldicholine. However, this factor became less important to us, since we felt that succinyldicholine was contraindicated in porpoises due to low levels or absence of plasma cholinesterase. Because it precluded using most muscular reflexes as indications of the depth of anesthesia, we did not plan to use it.

Our earlier experiments with halothane and barbiturates and the development of our present technique have recently been reviewed (Ridgway and McCormick, 1970). Therefore, only our present technique which has been employed successfully on numerous occasions will be discussed here.

The only preanesthetic medication is atropine. In our initial experiments, the porpoises were intubated awake and halothane was used for induction. However, in subsequent investigations we found that thiopental sodium or thiamyl sodium* (10 mgkg) injected in a fluke vein safely and rapidly relaxed and calmed the animal, greatly facilitating intubation.

Barbiturates have several disadvantages that possibly contributed to the 100 percent mortality observed by earlier investigators who gave these drugs IP (Lilly, 1962; Nagel *et al.*, 1964). Some of those factors that should be considered when giving barbiturates to marine mammals are as follows:

1. Due largely to their high-protein diet, marine mammals excrete an acid urine. Barbiturate excretion is slowed when the pH is lower. If the plasma pH is increased and the urine made alkaline, barbiturate excretion may triple.
2. In some species, injections of glucose (or its intermediary metabolites) can increase the cerebral depression of barbiturate, probably by increasing the rate at which the drug enters brain cells (Lamson *et al.*, 1951). Since porpoises normally have a high blood glucose level (and lactate), the effect of barbiturates may possibly be enhanced.
3. The sensitivity of medullary centers to pH and CO_2 is reduced by barbiturates. Since marine mammals already have such a diminished sensitivity (Irving, 1939), this barbiturate effect may be more profound in this group of animals.
4. If the barbiturate is injected outside the vein or into an artery, considerable inflammation may develop and tissue necrosis result. For this reason we use solutions of 1 to 2.5% to minimize the damage caused should the animal struggle and some barbiturate be injected outside the vein.

* Surital®, a product of Parke-Davis, Detroit, Michigan.

5. Laryngospasm is one of the primary complications of barbiturate anesthesia in other mammals. Porpoises have a large and complex larynx. Postanesthetic laryngospasm for an animal swimming in the water would be especially dangerous.

6. Body temperature depression is more pronounced when barbiturates are used than when halothane is employed alone. Thus, temperature is carefully monitored and if the rectal (25 cm depth) temperature drops below about 36.2°C, warm water is applied until the temperature approaches normal.

A dosage of 15 to 25 mg/kg of thiopental sodium produced periods of surgical anesthesia ranging from ten to twenty-five minutes. Recovery of respiration, however, required one to two and one-half hours. In our experience, the *Lagnorhynchus obliquidens* require a slightly larger dosage to achieve the same effect than does *Tursiops truncatus*. In each of six cases, the animals recovered completely from thiopental sodium anesthesia and the surgical or clinical procedure that accompanied it. These preliminary observations indicate that barbiturate anesthesia can be safely employed in porpoises, but the animal must spend four to ten minutes on positive pressure ventilation for every minute of surgical anesthesia.

After the inductive dose of thiopental sodium or thiamyl sodium (10 mg/kg) is given intravenously, the animal will relax quite rapidly and the mouth may be opened easily. For endotracheal intubation, 24 to 30 mm Rusch modified equine endotracheal tubes with inflatable cuff are employed. The hand is inserted into the pharynx. The larynx (Fig. 4–1) is grasped and pulled from its intranarial position (Lawrence and Schevill, 1965). Two fingers are inserted into the glottis and the tube is guided in through the palm of the hand.*

When the tube is in place, the cuff is inflated with 25 to 50 ml of air and positive pressure respiration is started. Halothane administration is begun at 1.5 to 2.0% and adjusted in response to heart rate, clinical signs, and reflexes.

Swimming movements of the free tail flukes were found to be a reliable indication of depth of anesthesia. When these movements disappeared, the subject was sufficiently anesthetized for surgery to begin. During induction, the swimming movements disappeared just after the loss of strong corneal and eyelid reflexes. The proper degree of anesthesia was maintained with the lowest concentration of halothane necessary to inhibit movement of the tail fluke. The heart rate also appeared to be a reliable indicator as were the lid and corneal reflexes.

---

* Some very small delphinds are difficult to intubate in this manner. Rieu and Gautheron (1968) have employed a method of introducing the tube through the blowhole in *Delphinus delphis* and *Stenella styx*.

During anesthesia, the mean arterial blood pressure (MABP) in *Tursiops truncatus* averaged about 115 mm Hg. Before anesthesia, MABP usually ranged from 120 to 130 mm Hg in the *Tursiops truncatus*, although in one animal it was 140 mm Hg. The *Lagenorhynchus obliquidens* averaged 145 mm Hg MABP prior to surgery and 130 mm Hg during anesthesia. In pelagic odontocetes such as *Lagenorhynchus obliquidens* and *Phocoenoides dalli*, MABP is normally higher than in *Tursiops truncatus*. This is probably due in part to the higher hematocrit and higher total blood volume (Ridgway and Johnston, 1966).

Arterial pH averages about 7.35, while pO_2 is usually maintained at 100 to 120 mm Hg and pCO_2 is 30 to 50 mm Hg. Rectal temperature (25 cm from the anal opening) is maintained between 36.7 and 37.2°C. The heart rate is generally 100 to 120 per minute in smaller *Tursiops truncatus* and 85 to 110 in large individuals.

Animals are allowed to recover on 60 percent ambient air and 40 percent oxygen. After two to four hours of anesthesia, all reflexes except the blowhole reflex (evidenced by movement of the blowhole in response to a touch, a pinprick or insertion of a finger) usually return in about fifteen minutes. Spontaneous movement of the jaw and flipper are often evidenced. The animal's eyes may follow a finger moved near them. Depending on the duration of anesthesia, movements of the blowhole are noticed approximately fifteen to forty-five minutes after the start of the recovery period. At this time, extubation can usually be performed safely.

The removal of the endotracheal tube is a most critical period in a porpoise anesthesia procedure. The tube must not be removed or positive pressure ventilation terminated until the animal is completely capable of breathing on its own. This will be manifested by movements of the animal's blowhole, movements of the thorax, struggling during inspiratory and expiratory cycles, and "tube bucking" or applying back pressure against the respirator. When these signs have become clearly evident, the endotracheal tube is removed and the larynx replaced into its normal intranarial position. If the animal does not blow within two to three minutes, or if the heart rate falls below about 60 beats per minute, the tube is reinserted and positive pressure ventilation resumed for a few more minutes. However, reintubation has been necessary only five times in over fifty procedures.

SLEEP AND ANESTHESIA IN PINNIPEDS

Although captive pinnipeds do most of their sleeping out of the water, elephant seals and harbor seals will frequently nap underwater on the tank bottom. Sea lions will nap both on the surface and on the tank bottom (see Nishiwaki's discussion in Chapter 1 on how fur seals sleep on the sea surface). A young elephant seal in our laboratory has been observed to remain on the bottom of her tank for as long as twenty-three minutes, apparently napping. Young harbor seals have been observed to remain underwater for over ten minutes with both eyes closed and apparently asleep.

Unlike cetaceans, pinnipeds can be anesthetized without the use of a respirator. The anesthetized sea lion breathes ten to fifteen times per minute, while the same animal breathes about six times per minute when awake and only three or four times per minute during natural naps (Table 10–41). As in cetaceans, the anesthetized sea lion's pulse is very regular

TABLE 10–41

AVERAGE RESPIRATORY RATES OF *Tursiops truncatus* AND *Zalophus californianus* UNDER DIFFERING CONDITIONS

	T. truncatus RR/min	Z. californianus RR/min
Actively swimming	3.0	8.0
Very leisurely swimming or resting	2.2	6.0
Dozing or resting out of water	2.0	3.0
Nonassisted breathing during anesthesia	———	12.0
Awake breathing 5% CO_2 20% O_2 in closed chamber	5.0	10.0
After a 4 min dive (1st min)	12.0	20.0

and the rate is around 80 to 120 per minute depending somewhat upon the animal's size. This regular heart rate varies from the respiratory arrhythmia of the awake animal and is observed whether or not atropine[*] is given.

A method for anesthesia and restraint of the California sea lion (Fig. 10–39) has recently been reported by Ridgway and Simpson (1969). The same technique has also been used with *Mirounga angustirostris* and *Phoca vitulina*.

Inhalant anesthesia employing halothane and methoxyfurane has been practiced effectively. In addition, intravenous thiamyl sodium and thiopental sodium have been used quite successfully. The intraperitoneal and intramuscular use of barbiturates has not been satisfactory and should be avoided.

The animal should not be allowed access to the water until it is thoroughly recovered from any effects of the anesthesia. The effect of the anesthetic agent on peripheral circulation and body temperature is the primary concern. If barbiturate anesthesia is employed, body temperature may have to be controlled for the duration of its effect.

SOME PHARMACOLOGIC CONSIDERATIONS

Several factors involving the adaptation of cetaceans and pinnipeds to the aquatic environment must be taken into consideration when adminis-

[*] Atropine, 2.0 mg/100 kg, is usually given as a preanesthetic medication.

tering drugs. The fact that the animal must swim, and that with empty or only partly filled lungs it sinks, is of primary importance. The marine mammal lives in a relatively cold environment. Heat would diffuse rapidly away from the body without the special thermoregulatory mechanisms already discussed. Clinicians who administer any agent that will produce peripheral vasodilatation, ganglionic blockage, or a marked depression of the hypothalamus must be prepared to control body temperature for the duration of their effect.

The effects of one phenothiazine-derived tranquilizer were observed in a wild pilot whale. Thirty minutes after injection of the drug with a projectile syringe,* the dorsal fin was noticed to be quivering. During the next fifteen minutes, the quivering became more pronounced. The animal started swimming in circles and tended to exhale just before reaching the surface for each blow. A line was looped over the whale's head and he was guided into an inflatable raft. The animal periodically vomited squid. The heart rate was very rapid and the rectal temperature was 32°C. The animal died about two hours after the injection.

In order to better understand what was observed, a test was carried out on a captive 78 kg female *Lagenorhynchus obliquidens*. The porpoise was caught in her tank and given an IM dose of 20 mg of acepromazine maleate.† About twenty minutes, later the dorsal fin started to quiver slightly. By thirty minutes after the injection, the quivering of the dorsal fin was more pronounced. The animal was making some premature exhalations as she came up to blow, and was swimming in a tighter circle near the center of the tank. At thirty-five minutes, it appeared that the animal's blowhole was also quivering and that she was taking on water. The porpoise was quickly removed from the water. After an endotracheal tube was inserted, she was put on positive pressure ventilation. The rectal temperature was 27.8°C (82°F) and the heart rate was 180 beats per minute. The porpoise was wrapped in moist warm towels. Warm water was poured over her. After three hours of this treatment, her rectal temperature returned to a normal 37.2°C (99°F). The blowhole started to move and the animal appeared quite alert. When the endotracheal tube was removed, the porpoise started to breathe on its own. She was returned to the water. At the outset, she swam quite normally. However, in about thirty minutes, the quivering of the dorsal fin was observed again and the whole initial episode was repeated. She was removed from the water and reintubated. This time the rectal temperature was 33°C (91.4°F) and the warming procedure was repeated. The body temperature returned to normal in less than two hours. When the endotracheal tube

---

* Cap-chur Syringe®, Palmer Chemical and Equipment Co., Douglasville, Ga.
† Acepromazine®, a product of Ayerst Laboratories, New York, N.Y.

was removed, the porpoise started to breathe without aid. This time she was held out of the water for an additional two hours and returned to the pool without a recurrence. Similar but less pronounced effects have been observed with other phenothiazine derived tranquilizers, trifluromeprazine HCl,† and hydroxyzine HCl§). The observations appear to emphasize the importance of the circulatory mechanisms described by Scholander and Schevill (1951) and Bel'kovich (1965) in temperature regulation.

Some newer tranquilizers, chlordiazepoxide HCl¶ and diazepam,** do not appear to cause the problems encountered with the phenothiazine-derived drugs. We have used chlordiazepoxide HCl in a number of cases involving *Zalophus californianus, Tursiops truncatus* and *Globicephala scammoni*. The drug appears quite effective in calming excitable animals.

McBride and Kritzler (1951) reported that paraldehyde was administered in fish to excited male porpoises in the large tank at Marineland of Florida during a period when females in the same tank were giving birth. The paraldehyde was reportedly effective in calming aroused males.

In my experience, morphine and apomorphine tend to be excitatory to *Tursiops truncatus, Lagenorhynchus obliquidens* and *Zalophus californianus*. Meperidine* and pentazocine† deserve consideration when an analgesic agent is required. However, neither has had sufficient pharmacologic evaluation in these species.

A number of different antibiotics have been employed for treatment of infections in marine mammals. Intramuscular, intravenous, and oral routes of administration have been used. Those antibiotics that can produce ototoxicity should be used with special caution. Because of the higher metabolic rate, dosages should be increased over those ordinarily given to land mammals of comparable size, and dosages should be well spaced to maintain an adequate blood level. Absorption, blood levels, metabolic fate, and excretion in relation to various antibiotics have not been studied in marine mammals.

Nitrofurantin§ (oral and IV) has been employed in the treatment of urinary tract infections. Various sulfonimides have also been used but are recommended only if the animal is eating and is well hydrated.

Several steroid compounds have been used. Dexamethasone has probably been employed more extensively than any other. To date, we have

---

* Nortran®, a product of Norden Laboratories, Lincoln, Nebraska.
† Trilafon®, a product of Schering Corporation, Bloomfield, N.J.
§ Atarax®, a product of Charles Pfizer Company, New York, N.Y.
¶ Librium®, a product of Roche Laboratories, Nutley, N.J.
** Valium®, a product of Roche Laboratories, Nutley, N.J.
* Demerol®, a product of Winthrop Laboratories, New York, N.Y.
† Talwin®, a product of Winthrop Laboratories, New York, N.Y.
§ Furadantin®, a product of Eaton Laboratories, Norwich, N.Y.

noted no reactions or results that have not been encountered in other mammals.

Enteritis and diarrhea can cause a cetacean or pinniped to lose water very rapidly. Kaolin and pectin products, along with antibiotics, have been used quite effectively in these cases. Constipation has not been a common finding in cetaceans or pinnipeds. In most odontocetes, the large intestine is quite short and apparently does not function like the lower bowel of most mammals (also see Chapter 5). However, I have encountered cases in *Globicephala scammoni* and *Orcinus orca* where the clinical signs pointed to a constipation. Mineral oil was given by stomach tube (12 liters to a 2,100 kg killer whale and 4 liters to a 500 kg pilot whale). Fecal output increased markedly within one hour, and normal appetite returned the next day.

Peterson (1965) discussed his use of several drugs for handling fur seals. Ling and Nicholls (1963) used succinylcholine chloride in immobilizing elephant seals. They found the elephant seals more tolerant of the drug than sea lions. We have noted that *Zalophus californianus* have low levels of plasma cholinesterase, while *Tursiops truncatus* have none at all. (At least the five blood samples we tested showed no activity.) This was first reported by Nagel *et al.* (1965).

Flyger (1964) proposes the use of succinylcholine chloride for killing or capturing whales. This has serious drawbacks, since most cetaceans[*] sink when they are paralyzed. Schevill *et al.* (1967) warned against the use of drugs in swimming marine mammals. Research is needed on the pharmacodynamics of various drugs in marine mammals. Perhaps some day we will be able to effectively and humanely catch whales with an injection. However, the experiments needed to achieve this goal should employ captive animals under controlled conditions rather than animals in the wild (Schevill *et al.*, 1967).

SURGERY AND POSTSURGICAL CARE

Local anesthetics are quite effective and have been employed for many minor surgical procedures and biopsies. Lidocaine HCl[**] (2% solution) has been used extensively in local infiltration.

In most cetaceans, the skin and blubber are contiguous and together form a tough, fibrous integument. Therefore, heavy needles such as those used in bovine surgery are employed for external suturing. After abdominal surgery, the thick ventral musculature must be well sutured, since the

---

[*] I have heard that sperm whales and belugas usually float when killed, but I have no first hand knowledge of this.

[**] Xylocaine® HCl, a product of Astra Pharmaceutical Products, Inc. Worcester, Mass.

animal must use these muscles for swimming very soon after the operation. For the same reason, care should be taken to stay in the midline when making initial abdominal incisions.

The vascular anatomy of cetaceans and pinnipeds was discussed in Chapters 4 and 5. If one could ascribe a motto to the construction of marine mammal vascular anatomy it would be "divide and conquer." Physiologically this appears to be quite a sound structural approach. However, it usually makes surgery more difficult. The extensive vascular networks (especially in cetaceans) around the ear, behind the eye, at the base of the cranial vault, in the dorsum of the thorax, in the spinal canal, and around the genitalia complicate surgical procedures in these areas.

Pneumonias involving gram negative organisms such as *Pseudomonas aeruginosa* have not been uncommon in marine mammals. Many of these organisms are primary contaminants of surface waters. Thus, after a procedure requiring general anesthesia, I give penicillin and colymycin for three days.

Clean seawater is a good medium for wound healing. Therefore, exposure of the freshly closed surgical incision is not detrimental. In tanks where an animal is recovering from surgery, we are especially careful to see that the chlorine level of about 0.2 ppm is maintained.

THE FUTURE

Prediction of the future carries with it an element of danger. One is likely to come up with many apparently foolish ideas when engaging in such activity. My efforts are probably no different; however, I feel it necessary to mention something about the potential future of man's use of and relationship with aquatic mammals.

Behavioral Engineering

It has already been demonstrated that some marine mammals can be trained to work under human control in the open sea. Training aquatic animals to perform useful tasks for man may become common in the future. Marine mammals are likely to play "sheep dog" and "sea horse" roles.

Small cetaceans may be trained to assist men underwater in numerous ways. They might herd or locate schools of fish, and some such as the killer whale might be used in the roundup of larger baleen whales (Fig. 10–47).

The California sea lion *Zalophus californianus* has been worked free and untethered in the open sea for the performance of a number of research

Figure 10–46. The adult female *Tursiops truncatus* seen here with her calf has an erosion at the tip of the lower jaw and her snout tip is generally scarred. Since porpoises use the snout for rooting, pushing, probing, and all sorts of things, even the healthiest of animals as those shown here, usually have a roughened snout. Photograph by J. W. Latourrette provided courtesy of Mr. Burton Clark of Wometco Miami Seaquarium.

tasks. Life guards on dangerous beaches such as those in Australia, in South Africa or in Hawaii might be well advised to have trained sea lions that could plunge rapidly through even the most dangerous undertow or rip tide to locate a person in danger and help tow him to shore. Sea lions

Figure 10–47. Whales and fish in a feed lot of the future.

might also assist in rescue operations at sea and should be especially helpful during stormy weather and at night.

Mariculture

Wild stocks of pelagic animals on which whaling and fishing industries depend will be depleted. A number of species are already extinct or in danger of extinction as result of human exploitation. The challenge of harvesting the sea lies not in how well we can catch fish or whales but in how well we can hatch or breed, cultivate, grow, and market them.

Advanced technology of the future may make it possible for man to more extensively utilize marine resources for food production. Certain baleen whales may be fattened in large aquatic feedlots (Fig. 10–48), much as beef and pork are produced today. Some pinnipeds such as the crabeater seal may be prospects for commercial production. Pinchot (1966) proposed that large lagoons in the South Pacific be employed in whale culture. The consumption of zooplankton would be more feasible economically. However, cultural eating habits will probably be more important than nutritional needs in dictating the diet of the peoples of various countries around the world.

Figure 10–48. Killer whales might be used as "sheep dogs" to herd the larger baleen whales.

The growth of population on the land mass will greatly increase the need for electrical power and nuclear generating stations will develop along our coasts. The resulting thermal pollution of the ocean and the need to process waste products from the cities might produce situations favorable for the culturing of krill or other organisms for feeding large whales and fish. The basic products and byproducts of the whales and fish would in turn contribute to the food supply. Many things now regarded as waste and discarded to pollute the earth and its atmosphere will be regarded as valuable resources and recycled. Production of controlled food chains terminating in fish, mollusks, crustaceans, turtles, seals, or whales could provide satisfactory solutions to the problem of recycling some organic waste.

Conservation

Informed people are becoming more concerned about the conservation of marine wildlife. It is likely that more international biological control programs such as the one involving the northern fur seal will be established. There will be a continual need for more information on the biology and diseases of marine animals in order to promote their conservation.

Laboratory Animals

Marine mammals as research laboratory animals will help man in numerous ways as he probes the marine environment and learns the secrets of the adaptations of marine animals. What better way for man himself to learn to adapt to the marine environment than to study other mammals who have taken eons to make the necessary adjustments?

In order to maintain marine animals for research, studies will be required on disease control, husbandry and maintenance, reproduction, ecology, etc. Biomedical research involving the marine environment and aquatic animals will make outstanding contributions. The increased use of aquatic animals in the laboratory will provide vital knowledge and capabilities in (a) medical research and student training, (b) diseases of fish and other aquatic animals used as food, (c) ecology and conservation, (d) pollution effects and biological control pollution, (e) nutrition and new food species development, (f) development of new drugs from the sea, (g) controlling dangerous marine animals such as sharks, rays, and poisonous fishes, (h) bionic research in diving, hydrodynamics, underwater acoustics, circulation, biocybernetics, and neural control mechanisms, (i) behavioral research, and (j) public education and recreation.

❋   ❋   ❋

I am indebted to F. G. Wood, Dr. Clinton Maag, Dr. A. L. Hall, E. Q. Smith, D. F. Sullivan, Adm. K. C. Childers and the Naval Missile Center Foundation Research Board for supporting my earlier work. The more recent research has been supported by the Naval Undersea Research and Development Center and its sponsors. I am particularly grateful to Dr. C. Scott Johnson, George Anderson, Dr. Don Wilson, Dr. W. B. McLean, Captain C. B. Bishop, Allen Jewett, Commander Tor Richter, John Ropek, Stanley Marcus, Dr. Sam Rothman, Dr. J. J. Collins and H. B. Stone.

I thank James S. Leatherwood and Mr. Dan Pearson for assistance in editing and Maria Ridge for typing the manuscript. Dr. James McCormick summarized our experiments on audition; Dr. John Simpson reviewed much of the literature for the disease list. Dr. C. Scott Johnson, Dr. John Kanwisher, Dr. Richard Malvin, Mr. F. G. Wood, Dr. Joel Mattsson and Dr. Don Van Dyke reviewed the manuscript. Their comments were very much appreciated.

I am especially grateful to the staff of the Marine Bioscience Facility for their continual support. Many individuals deserve a special word of gratitude. I particularly appreciate the contributions of W. G. Gilmartin, M. F. Wintermantel, S. P. O'Brien, B. L. Scronce, A. F. Langguth, A. B. Irvine, Wallace Ross, Roland Raffler, Frank Harvey, John Hall, Ralph Penner, Martin Conboy, William Chamberlain, Dr. D. G. Johnston, Frank Braun and Gloria Patton.

REFERENCES

Abe, T., Kazama, M., and Matsuda, M.: Anticoagulant activity of whale heparin and it characteristics. *Israel J. Med. Sci., 1*:862, 1965.

Abe, T., Kazama, M., Matsula, M., Ikemori R., and Shibate, T.: Anticoagulant activity of whale intestine heparin and its clinical application. *Bibl. Haemat., 29*(4):1141, 1968.

Allen, J.: Personal communication. Naval Undersea Research and Development Center, Kaneohe M.C.A.S., Oahu, Hawaii, 1970.

Amemiya, I.: The dolphin that swallowed a football. *Intern. Zoo Yearbook, 4*:34, 1962.

Amoroso, E.C. and Matthews, L.H.: Reproduction and lactation in the seals. Copenhagen, Denmark, *Rep. 2d Int. Congr. Physiol. and Path. of Animal Reproduction and of Artificial Insemination,* 1952.

Andersen, H.T.: The reflex nature of the physiological adjustments to diving and their afferent pathway. *Acta Physiol. Scand., 18.*109, 1964.

Andersen, H.T.: Physiological adaptations in diving vertebrates. *Physiol. Rev., 46*:212, 1966.

Andersen, H.T.: Cardiovascular adaptations in diving mammals, *Amer Heart J., 74*:295, 1967.

Andersen, S.: The physiological range of formed elements in the blood of the harbor porpoise, *Phocaena phocaena. Nord. Vet. Med., 18*:51, 1966.

Andersen, S.: Electrocardiography of the harbor porpoise, *Phocoena phocoena* (L.). In Pilleri, G.: *Investigations on Cetacea.* Waldau, Berne, Switzerland, G. Pilleri, 1969, vol. 1, p. 199.

Anonymous: 16th Ann. Rep. Washington Park Zoo, Milwaukee, 1926.

Appelby, E.C.: A case of gastric perforation by a foreign body in an elephant seal (M*irounga leonina*). *Nord. Vet. Med., 14*:164, 1962.

Ashworth, V.S., Ramaiah, G.D., and Keyes, M.C.: Species difference in the composition of milk with special reference to the northern fur seal. *J. Dairy Sci., 49*:126, 1966.

Bailey, R.E.: Training and open ocean release of an Atlantic bottlenose porpoise, *Tursiops truncatus* (Montagu), China Lake, California, Naval Ordnance Test Station Tech. Paper 3838:1, 1965.

Baker, B.E., Harington, C.R., and Symes, A.L.: Polar bear milk I: gross composition and fat constitution, *Canad. J. Zool., 41*:1035, 1963.

Barany, E.A.: Contribution to the physiology of bone conduction, *Acta oto-laryng., 26*:223, 1938.

Bartholomew, G.A.: Body temperature and respiratory and heart rates in the northern elephant seal. *J. Mammal., 35*:211, 1954.

Bartholomew, G.A. and Wilkie, F.: Body temperature in the northern fur seal, *Callorhinus ursinus. J. Mammal., 37*:327, 1956.

Baylis, H.A.: A list of worms parasitic in Cetacea. *Discovery Rep., 6*:393, 1932.

Beckman, E.L.: Thermal protection during immersion in cold water. *Proc. 2nd Symp. Underwater Physiol., 2*:247, 1963.

Bel'Kovich, V.M.: Particular features of thermoregulation in an aquatic environment (From the example of mammals) *Bionika* (*Bionics*) *Moscow*, 215, 1965.

Ben Shaul, D.M.: The composition of the milk of wild animals, *Intern. Zoo Yearbook*, pp. 337, 1962.

Bert, P.: *Lecons sur la Physiologie Comparee de la Respiration*. Paris, Bailliere, 1870.

Best, C.H. and Taylor, N.B.: *The Physiological Basis of Medical Practice*. 8th ed. Baltimore, Williams and Wilkins, 1967.

Blair, W.R.: Report of the veterinarian. *17th Annual Report*, N.Y. Zoological Society, 1912.

Blessing, M.H.: Morphology of bronchitis in the seal *Phoca vitulina* L. *Deutsch Tieraerztl. Wschr.*, 76:457, 1969.

Bohr, C.: Bidrog til Svommefuglernes Fysiologi. *K. danske Vidensk. Forh.*, 2:207, 1897.

Bradley, S.E., Mudge, G.H., and Blake, W.D.,: Water and electrolyte excretion by the harbor seal (*Phoca vitulina*). *Fed. Proc.*, 9:16, 1950.

Bradley, S.E., Mudge, G.H., and Blake, W.D.: The renal excretion of sodium potassium, and water by the harbor seal (*Phoca vitulina*): Effect of apnoea, sodium, potassium and water loading; pitressin and mercurial diuresis. *J. Cell. Comp. Physiol.*, 43:1, 1954.

Breathnach, A.S.: The cetacean central nervous system. *Biol. Rev.*, 35:187, 1960.

Breland, K. and Breland, M.: *Animal Behavior*. New York, Macmillan, 1968.

Brick, I.: Circulatory responses to immersing the face in water. *J. Appl. Physiol.*, 21:33, 1966.

Bron, K.M., Murdaugh, H.V., Jr., Miller, J.E., Lenthall, R., Raskin, P. and Robin, E.D.: Arterial constrictor response in a diving mammal. *Science*, 152:540, 1966.

Brown, D.H. and Norris, K.S.: Observations of captive and wild cetaceans, *Mammalia*, 37:3, 1956.

Brown, D.H., McIntyre, R.W., Delli Quardri, C.A., and Schroeder, R.J.: Health problems of captive dolphins and seals. *J. Amer. Vet. Med. Ass.*, 137(9):534, 1960.

Brown, D.H.: The health problems of walrus calves, and remarks on their general progress in captivity. *Intern. Zoo Yearbook*, 4:13, 1962.

Bullock, T.H., Grinnell, A.D., Ikezono, E., Kameda, K., Katsuki, Y., Nomoto, M., Sato, O., Suga, N., and Yanagisawa, K.: Electrophysiological studies of central auditory mechanisms in cetaceans. *Verg. Physiol.*, 59:117, 1968.

Burgess, K.: The behavior and training of a killer whale at San Diego Sea World. *Intern. Zoo Yearbook*, 8:202, 1968.

Burne, R.H.: Notes on the viscera of a walrus (*Odobenus rosmarus*). *Proc. Zool. Soc. London*, pp. 732, 1909.

Busnel, R.G. (Ed.):*Les systémes sonars animaux biologie et bionique*. France, Jouy-en-Josas, Laboratoire Acoustique de Physiologie, 1967, Vols. I and II.

Bryden, M.M. and Lim, G.M.K.: Blood parameters of the southern elephant seal (*Mirounga leonina*, Linn.). In relation to diving. *Comp. Biochem., Physiol.*, 28:139, 1969.

Bryden, M.M.: Insulating capacity of the subcutaneous fat of the southern elephant seal, *Nature (London)*, 203:1299, 1964.

Carroll, J.M., Jasmin, A.M., and Baucom, J.N.: Pulmonary aspergillosis of the bottlenose dolphin (*Tursiops truncatus*), *Amer. J. Vet. Clin. Path.*, 2:139, 1968.

Case, R.A.M.: A study of the incidence of disease in a whaling expedition to the Antarctic pelagic whaling ground, 1946–7. *Brit. J. Soc. Med.*, 2:1, 1948.

Cockrill, W.R.: Pathology of the Cetacea, Part I. *Brit. Vet. J.*, 116:133, 1960a.

Cockrill, W.R.: Pathology of the Cetacea, Part II. *Brit. Vet. J.*, 116:175, 1960b.

Colyer, J.F.: Dento-Alveolar Abscess in a Grampus (*Orca gladiator*, Bonn.) *Scott. Naturalist*, 230:1, 1938.

Cook, H.W. and Baker, B.E.: Seal milk I, harp seal (*Pagophilus groenlandicus*) milk: composition and pesticide residue content. *Macdonald College J. Series*, P.Q. Canada, 1969.

Cornell, L.A.: Personal communication, Marineland of the Pacific, Palos Verdes Estates, California, 1969.

Coulombe, H.N., Ridgway, S.H., and Evans, W.E.: Respiratory water exchange in two species of porpoise. *Science*, 149:86, 1965.

Cowan, D.F.: Pathology of the pilot whale. *Arch. Path.*, 82:178, 1966.

Cowan, D.F.: Lung diseases in whales and dolphins. *Proc. 2nd Conference on Disease of Aquatic Mammals*, Boca Raton, Fla., 1968.

Craig, A.B., Jr.: Heart rate responses to apneic underwater diving and to breath holding in man. *J. Appl. Physiol.*, 18:854, 1963.

Cushing, J.E., Fujino, K., and Calaprice, N.: The JU blood-typing system of the sperm whale and specific soluble substances. *Sci. Rep. Whales Res. Inst.*, 17:67, 1963.

Damant, G.C.C.: Physiology of deep diving in the whale. *Nature (London)*, 133:874, 1934.

Delyamure, S.L.: *Helminthofauna of Marine Mammals*. Academy of Science USSR, Moscow, 1955, (translated from Russian), U.S. Dept. of the Interior and Nat. Sci. Found., Washington, D.C., 1968.

DeMonte, T. and Pilleri, G.: Haemoglobin of *Delphinus delphis* and plasma-protein fractions in some species of the family Delphinidae, determined by microelectrophoresis on cellulose acetate gel. *Blut.*, 17:25, 1968.

DuBois, K.P., Geiling, E.M.K., McBride, A.F., and Thompson, J.F.: Studies on intermediary carbohydrate metabolism of aquatic animals I. The distribution of acid-soluble phosphrous and certain enzymes in dolphin tissues. *J. Biol. Chem.*, 347:359, 1948.

Dudok van Heel, W.H. and Tiebor, J.: Observations in flight reactions of *Tursiops truncatus* (Mont.) with some suggestions for flight planning. *Sunderdruck aus Z.F. Saugetierkunde*, 31:370, 1966.

Eichelberger, L., Fetcher, E.S., Geiling, E.M.K., and Vos, B.J.: The distribution of water and electrolytes in the blood of dolphins. *J. Biol. Chem.*, 133:145, 1940a.

Eichelberger, L., Fetcher, E.S., Geiling, E.M.K., and Vos, B.J.: The composition of dolphin milk. *J. Biol Chem.*, 134:171, 1940b.

Eichelberger, L., Geiling, E.M.K., and Vos, B.J.: The distribution of water and electrolytes in skeletal muscle of the dolphin (*Tursiops truncatus*). *J. Biol. Chem., 133*:661, 1940c.

Elsner, R.W., Franklin, D.L., and Van Citters, R.L.: Cardiac output during diving in an unrestrained sea lion. *Nature (London) 202*:809, 1964a.

Elsner, R.W., Scholander, P.F., Craig, A.B., Diamond, E.G., Irving, L., Pilson, M., Johansen, K., and Bradstreet, E.: Venous oxygen reservoir in the diving elephant seal. *Physiologist, 7*:124, 1964b.

Elsner, R.W., Kenney, D.W., and Burgess, K.: Diving bradycardia in a trained dolphin. *Nature (London), 212*:407, 1966.

Elsner, R.W.: Diving bradycardia in the unrestrained hippopotamus. *Nature (London), 212*:408, 1966.

Elsner, R.W.: Cardiovascular adjustments to diving. In Andersen, H.T. (Ed.): *The Biology of Marine Mammals.* New York, Academic Press, 1969, vol. 1, p. 117.

Essapian, F.S.: Observations on abnormalities of parturition in captive bottlenosed dolphins *Tursiops truncatus* and concurrent behavior of other porpoises. *J. Mammal., 44*:405, 1963.

Evans, W.E. and Harmon, S.R.: Experimenting with trained pinnipeds in the open sea. In Harrison, R.J., Hubbard, R.C., Rice, C.E., and Schusterman, R.J. (Eds.): *The Behavior and Physiology of Pinnipeds.* New York, Appleton-Century-Crofts, 1968, vol. 1, p. 196.

Farrel, R.K.: Personal communication, Agricultural Research Service, Pullman, Washington, 1969.

Fay, F.H. and Ray, C.: Influence of climate on the distribution of walruses, *Odobenus rosmarus* (Linnaeus). I. Evidence from thermoregulatory behavior. *Zoologica, 53*:1, 1968.

Ferrante, F.L.: Oxygen conservation during submergence apnea in a diving mammal, the nutria. *Amer. J. Physiol., 218*:363, 1970.

Fetcher, E.S. and Fetcher, G.W.: Experiments on the osmotic regulation of dolphins (*Tursiops truncatus*). *J. Cell. Comp. Physiol., 19*:123, 1942.

Fiscus, C.H. and Baines, G.A.: Food and feeding behavior of Steller and California sea lions. *J. Mammal, 47*:195, 1966.

Flyger, V.: Succinylcholine chloride for killing or capturing whales. *Norsk Hvalfangst Tid., 4*:88, 1964.

Forsham, P.H.: Insulin and the pancreas. In Hall, V.E. (Ed.) *Annual Review of Physiology.* Palo Alto, Annuals Reviews, 1966, p. 28.

Fox, H.: Comparative pathology of the heart as seen in captive animals at the Philadelphia Zoological Gardens. *Trans. Coll. Phys.,* 3d Series, *43*:130, 1921.

Fox, H.: *Disease in Captive Wild Mammals and Birds.* Philadelphia, Lippincott, 1923.

Fox, H: Report of the Penrose Research Lab, 1941.

Fujino, K.: On the serological constitution of the sperm and Baird beaked whales (I) Blood groups of the sperm and Baird beaked whales, *Sci. Rep. Whales Res. Inst., 9*:105, 1954.

Galileo, G.: *Dialogues Concerning Two New Sciences* (1603). Translated by Henry Crew and Alfonso de Salvio, New York, McGraw-Hill, 1963.

Gallien, M.C., LeFoulgoc, M.T.C., and Fine, M.J.: The Serum Proteins of *Delphinus delphis* (Linn.), *C. R. Acad. Sci.*, (*Paris*), *264*:1359, 1967.

Geiling, E.M.K., Vos, Jr., B.J., and Oldham, J.K.: The pharmacology and anatomy of the hypophysis of the porpoise. *Endocrinology*, *27*:309, 1940.

Geraci, J.R., Saver, R.M., and Medway, W.: Erysipelas in dolphins. *Amer. J. Vet. Res.*, *27*:597, 1966.

Geraci, J.R. and Gerstmann, K.E.: Relationship of dietary histamine to gastric ulcers in the dolphin. *J. Amer. Vet. Med. Ass.*, *149*:884, 1966.

Geraci, J.R.: Personal communication. Dept. of Zoology, University of Guelph, Ontario, Canada, 1969.

Geraci, J.R.: *The Effects of Thiaminase Ingestion on the Harp Seal.* Doctoral thesis, Montreal, McGill University, 1970.

Goudappel, J.R. and Slijper, E.J.: Microscopic structure of the lungs of the bottlenose whale. *Nature* (*London*), *182*:479, 1958.

Gray, R.W.: The sleep of whales. *Nature* (*London*), *119*:636, 1927.

Gregory, M.E., Kon, S.K., Rowlands, S.J. and Thompson, S.Y.: The composition of the milk of the blue whales. *J. Dairy Res.*, *22*:108, 1955.

Griffin, T. and Goldsberry, D.: Personal communication. Seattle Marine Aquarium, Seattle, Washington, 1968.

Grimmer, W.: *Tabulae Biol.*, Beil., *2*:536, 1925.

Griner, L.: Personal communication. Pathology Department, San Diego Zoo, San Diego, California, 1970.

Halloran, P.O.: Disease of wild mammals and birds, *Amer. J. Vet. Res.*, *16*:216, 1955.

Hammond, T.: Personal communication. Scripps Institution of Oceanography, La Jolla, California, 1969.

Hamerton, A.E.: Reports of deaths occurring in the Societies gardens during the year 1932. *Proc. Zool. Soc. London*, pp. 451, 1933.

Hamlin, R.L., Jackson, R.F., Himes, J.A., Pipers, F., and Townsend, A.C.: Electrocardiogram of bottle-nosed dolphin (*Tursiops truncatus*). *Amer. J. Vet. Res.*, *31*:501, 1970.

Harding, F.E., Roman, C., and Whelan, R.F.: Diving bradycardia in man, *J. Physiol.*, *181*:401, 1965.

Harkness, D.R. and Grayson, V.: Erythrocyte metabolism in the bottle-nosed dolphin, *Tursiops truncatus. Comp. Biochem. Physiol.*, *28*:1289, 1969.

Harris, J.I., Sanger, F., and Naughton, M.A.: Species differences in insulin. *Arch. Biochem. Biophys.*, *65*:427, 1956.

Harrison, R.J.: Experiments with diving seals, *Nature* (*London*), *188*:1068, 1960.

Harrison, R.J. and Tomlinson, J.D.W.: Observations on the venous system in certain pinnipedia and cetacea. *Proc. Zool. Soc. London*, *126*:205, 1956.

Harrison, R.J. and Tomlinson, J.D.W.: Normal and experimental diving in the common seal (*Phoca vitulina*). *Mammalia*, *24*:386, 1960.

Harrison, R.J. and Tomlinson, J.D.W.: Anatomical and physiological adaptations in diving mammals. In Carthy, J.D. and Duddington, C.L. (Eds.): *Viewpoints in Biology,* London, Butterworths, vol. 2, p. 115.

Harrison, R.J. and Tomlinson, J.D.W.: Observations on diving seals and certain other mammals. *Symp. Zool. Soc. Lond.,* 13:59, 1964.

Harrison, R.J. and King, J.E.: *Marine Mammals.* London, Hutchinson, 1965.

Harrison, R.J., Johnson, F.R., and Tedder, R.S.: Underwater feeding, the stomach and intestine of some delphinids. *J. Anat.,* pp. 101–186, 1967.

Harrison, R.J. and Kooyman, G.L.: General physiology of the pinnipedia. In Harrison, R.J., Hubbard, R.C., Peterson, R.S., Rice, C.E., and Schusterman, R.J. (Eds.): *The Behavior and Physiology of Pinnipeds.* New York, Appleton-Century-Crofts, 1968, vol. 1, p. 212.

Harrison, R.J.: Endocrine organs: hypophysis, thyroid and adrenal. In Andersen, H.T.: *The Biology of Marine Mammals,* New York Academic Press, 1969, vol. 1, p. 349.

Harrison, R.J. and Ridgway, S.H.: Anatomical and biochemical observations on the reproductive status of male dolphins. Unpublished data, 1970.

Hart, J.S. and Irving, L. The energetics of harbor seals in air and in water with special consideration of seasonal changes. *Canad. J. Zool.,* 37:447, 1959.

Hart, J.S. and Fisher, H.D.: The question of adaptations of polar environments in marine mammals. *Fed Proc.,* 23:1207, 1964.

Hashimoto, K., Matsumo, M., Yoshizawa, Z., and Shibata, T.: A dextro-rotatory polysaccharide of very high anticoagulant activity newly isolated from whale's lung and intestine. *Tohoku J. Exp. Med.,* 81:93, 1963.

Hashimoto, S., Dayton, S., and Roberts, J.C.: Aliphatic wax alcohols and other lipids in atheromata and arterial tissues of cetaceans. *Comp. Biochem. Physiol.,* 20:975, 1967.

Heller, H.H.: Etiology of acute gangrenous infections of animals: a discussion of blackleg, braxy, malignant edema and whale septicemia. *J. Infect. Diseases,* 27:385, 1920.

Herald, E.S., Brownell, R.L., Frye, F.L., Morris, E.J., Evans, W.E., and Scott, A.B.: Blind river dolphin: first side-swimming cetacean. *Science,* 166:1408, 1969.

Herman, C.M.: The effect of Higueronia on the nemathelminthic gastric ulcers of California sea lions. *Science,* 94:129, 1941.

Hiatt, E.P. and Hiatt, R.B.: The effect of food on the glomerular filtration rate and renal blood flow in the harbor seal (*Phoca vitulina* L.). *J. Cell. Comp. Physiol.,* 19:221, 1942.

Hill, W.C.O.: Report of the society's prosector. *Proc. Zool. Soc. London,* 121:650, 1951.

Holland, J.A.: Discussion of disseminated intravascular coagulation in decompression sickness. *U.S. Naval Submarine Medical Center,* Report No. 585, Groton, Conn., 1969.

Hong, S.K., Song, S.H., Kim, P.K., and Suh, C.S.: Seasonal observations on the cardiac rhythm during diving in the Korean ama. *J. Appl. Physiol.,* 23:18, 1967.

Horvath, S.M., Chiodi, H., Ridgway, S.H., and Azar, S.: Respiratory and electrophoretic characteristics of hemoglobin of porpoises and sea lion. *Comp. Biochem. Physiol.*, *24*:1027, 1968.

Hoshina, T. and Sigiura, Y.: On a skin disease and a nematode parasite of a dolphin, *Tursiops truncatus* (Montagu 1821). *Sci. Rep. Whales Res. Inst.*, 1956.

Hubbard, R.C.: Husbandry and laboratory care of pinnipeds. In Harrison, R.J., Hubbard, R.C., Peterson, R.S., Rice, C.C. and Schusterman, R.J. (Eds.): *Behavior and Physiology of Pinnipeds.* New York, Appleton-Century-Crofts, 1968, vol. 1, pp. 299.

Hubbard, R.C.: Chemotherapy in captive marine mammals. *Bull. Wildlife Dis. Ass.*, *5*:218, 1969.

Irvine, A.B.: Transporation of small cetaceans. *Naval Undersea Research and Development Center Technical Paper*, in press, 1970.

Irvine, A.B.: Conditioning marine mammals to work in the sea *Mar. Tech. Soc. J.*, *4*:47, 1970.

Irving, L.: On the ability of warm-blooded animals to survive without breathing. *Sci. Monthly*, *38*:422, 1934.

Irving, L.: The protection of whales from the danger of caisson disease. *Science*, *81*:560, 1935.

Irving, L.: Changes in the blood flow through the brain and muscles during the arrest of breathing. *Amer. J. Physiol.*, *122*:207, 1938.

Irving, L.: Respiration in diving mammals, *Physiol. Rev.*, *19*:112, 1939.

Irving, L., Fisher, K.C. and McIntosh, F.C.: The water balance of a marine mammal, the seal. *J. Cell. Comp. Physiol.*, *6*:387, 1935.

Irving, L., Scholander, P.F., and Grinnell, S.W.: Significance of the heart rate to the diving ability of seals. *J. Cell. Comp. Physiol.*, *18*:283, 1941a.

Irving, L., Scholander, P.F., and Grinnell, S.W.: The respiration of the porpoise, *Tursiops truncatus. J. Cell. Comp. Physiol.*, *17*:145, 1941b.

Irving, L., Scholander, P.F., and Grinnell, S.W.: The regulation of the arterial blood pressure in the seal during diving. *Amer. J. Physiol.*, *135*:557, 1942.

Irving, L. and Orr, M.D.: The diving habits of the beaver. *Science*, *82*:569, 1961.

Irving, L.: Temperature regulation in marine mammals. In Andersen, H.T. (Ed.): *Marine Mammals.* New York, Academic Press, 1969, vol. 1, p. 147.

Johnston, D.G. and Ridgway, S.H.: Parasitism in some marine mammals. *J. Amer. Vet. Med. Ass.*, *155*:1064, 1969.

Kajimura, H.: Pup feeding before leaving Pribilof Islands in 1966. In *Fur Seal Investigations* (1967), Manuscript report, 74, Marine Mammal Biol. Lab., Seattle, Bur. Comm. Fish., 1968.

Kanwisher, J. and Sundnes, G.: Thermal regulation in cetaceans. In Norris *Whales, Dolphins and Porpoises.* Berkeley, University of California, *1*:397 (1966a).

Kanwisher, J. and Sundnes, G.: Physiology of a small cetacean. *Hvaldrad. Skr.*, *48*:45, 1966b.

Kelly, A.L.: Report of the hospital and research committee (conjunctivitis). *Zoo Nooz*, San Diego Zoo, San Diego, Calif., 1950.

Kelly, A.L. and Jensen, D.: Chronic aortitis in the California sea lion, *Zalophus californianus. Nature* (*London*), pp 731, 1960.

Ketchmer, N. and Sunshine, P.: Intestinal disaccharidase deficiency in the sea lion. *Gastroenterology, 53*:123, 1967.

Keyes, M.C.: Pathology of the northern fur seal. *J. Amer. Vet. Med. Ass., 147:* 1090, 1965.

Keyes, Mark C.: The nutrition of pinnipeds. In Harrison, R.J., Hubbard, R.C., Peterson, R.S., Rice, C.C., and Schusterman, R.J. (Eds.): *The Behavior and Physiology of Pinnipeds.* New York, Appleton-Century-Crofts, 1968, vol. 1, p. 359.

Keyes, M.C., Crews, F.W., and Ross, A.J.: *Pasteurella multocida isolated* from a California sea lion (*Zalophus californianus*). *J. Amer. Vet. Med. Ass., 153:* 803, 1968.

King, J.E.: *Seals of the World.* London, Trustees of the British Museum of Natural History, London, 1964, p. 154.

King, R.L., Jenks, J.L., and White, P.D.: The electrocardiogram of the Beluga whale. *Circulation, 8*:337, 1953.

Kleinenberg, S.E., Yablokov, A.V., Bel'Kovich, V.M., and Tarasevich, M.N.: *The White Whale.* Moskova, Izdatelstvo Nauka, 1964.

Knoll, W.: Unlersuchungen uber die Morphologie des Saugetierblutes. *Folia haemat., 47*:201, 1932.

Kooyman, G.L.: Maximum diving capacities of the Weddell seal (*Leptonychotes weddelli*). *Science, 151*:1553, 1966.

Kooyman, G.L. and Drabek, C.M.: Observations on milk, blood and urine constituents of the Weddell seal. *Physiol. Zool., 41*:187, 1968.

Kooyman, G.L.: The Weddell seal. *Sci. Amer., 221*:100, 1969.

Kramer, M.O.: The dolphins' secret. *New Scientist, 7*:1118, 1960.

Krogh, A.: Physiology of the blue whale. *Nature* (*London*), *133*:635, 1934.

Krogh, A.: *Osmotic Regulation in Aquatic Animals.* Cambridge, Cambridge University Press, 1939.

Lamson, P.D., Greig, M.E., and Hobdy, C.J.: Modification of barbiturate anesthesia by glucose, intermediary metabolites and certain other substances. *J. Pharmacol. Exper. Therap., 103*:460, 1951.

Ladd, M., Raisz, L.G., Crowder, G.H., Jr., and Page, L.B.: Filtration rate and water diuresis in the seal, *Phoca vitulina. J. Cell Comp. Physiol.. 38*:157, 1951.

Lang, T.G.: Hydrodynamic analysis of cetacean performance. In Norris, K.S. (Ed.): *Whales, Dolphins and Porpoises.* Berkeley, University of California Press, 1966, vol. 1, p. 410.

Langworthy, O.R.: A description of the central nervous system of the porpoise (*Tursiops truncatus*). *J. Comp. Neurol., 54*:437, 1932.

Larsen, S.: A survey of the post mortem findings in Pinnipedia autopsied during a ten-year period 1952–1961. *Nord. Vet. Med., 14*:150, 1962.

Lauer, B.H. and Baker, B.E.: Whale milk I. Fin whale (*Balaenoptera physalus*) and beluga whale (*Delphinapterus leucas*) milk: Gross composition and fatty acid constitution. *Canad. J. Zool., 47*:95, 1968.

Laurie, A.H.: Some aspects of respiration in blue and fin whales. *Discovery Rept.,* 7:363, 1933.

Lawrence, B. and Schevill, W.E.: *Tursiops* as an experimental subject. *J. Mammal.,* 35:225, 1954.

Lawrence, B. and Schevill, W.E.: The functional anatomy of the delphinid nose. *Bull. Mus. Comp. Zool.,* 114:103, 1956.

Lawrence, B. and Schevill, W.E.: Gular musculature in delphinids. *Bull. Mus. Comp. Zool.,* 133:5, 1965.

Legendre, R.: Calcul de l'uretere chez un dauphin. *Comp. Rend. Soc. Biol.,* 92, 1925.

Lenfant, C., Elsner, R., Kooyman, G.L., and Drabek, C.M.: Respiratory function of the blood of the adult and fetus Weddell seal, *Leptonychotes weddelli. Amer. J. Physiol.,* 216:1595, 1969.

Lenfant, C.: Physiological properties of blood of marine mammals. In Anderson, H.T. (Ed.): *The Biology of Marine Mammals.* New York Academic Press, 1969, vol. 1, p 95.

Lewis, F.: Report of the chief inspector of fisheries and game on an investigation into the feeding habits, etc. of seals in Victorial waters. *Rep. to Parliament, Melbourne, Victoria Government Printer,* 23:1, 1929.

Lewis, J.H., Bayer, W.L., and Szeto, I.L.F.: Coagulation factor 12 deficiency in the porpoise, *Tursiops truncatus. Comp. Biochem. Physiol.,* 31:667, 1969.

Lilly, J.C.: *Man and Dolphin.* London, Gallancz, 1962.

Lilly, J.C.: Animals in aquatic environments: Adaptation of mammals to the ocean. In *Handbook of Physiology: Environment.* Washington, American Physiology Society, vol. 1, p. 741.

Ling. J.K.: Functional significance of sweat glands and sebaceous glands in seals. *Nature (London),* 208:560, 1965.

Ling, J.K. and Nicholls, D.G.: Immobilization of elephant seals using succinylcholine chloride. *Nature (London),* 200:1021, 1963.

Lowrance, P.B., Nickel, J.F., Smythe, C.M., and Bradley, S.E.: Comparison of the effect of anoxic anoxia and apnea on renal function in the harbor seal (*Phoca vitulina* L.), *J. Cell. Comp. Physiol.,* 48:35, 1956.

Lucas, F.A.: The swallowing of stones by seals. *Science,* 20:537, 1904.

MacDonald, D.W. and Gilchrist, E.W.: *Dipetolonema spirocaulu* and *Pseudomonas aeruginosa* infection in a harbor seal (*Phoca vitulina*). *Canad. Vet. J.,* 10(8):220, 1969.

MacKay, R.S.: Deep body temperature of untethered dolphin recorded by ingested radio transmitter. *Science,* 144:864, 1964.

MacMillen, R.E. and Lee, A.K.: Australian desert mice: independence of exogenous water. *Science,* 158:383, 1967.

Malvin, R.L. and Rayner, M.: Renal function and blood chemistry in Cetacea. *Amer. J. Physiol.,* 214:187, 1968.

Malvin, R.L., Bonjour, Jean-Philippe, and Ridgway, Sam H.: Antidiuretic hormone in porpoises. In preparation, 1970.

Margolis, L.: List of parasites recorded from sea mammals caught off the west coast of North America. *J. Fish. Res. Bd. Canada, 11:*267, 1954.

Mathisen, O.A., Baade, R.T., and Lopp, R.J.: Breeding habits, growth, and stomach contents of the Steller sea lion in Alaska. *J. Mammal, 43:*469, 1962.

McBride, A.F. and Hebb, D.O.: Behavior of the captive bottlenose dolphin, *Tursiops truncatus. J. Comp. Physiol. Psychol., 41:*111, 1948.

McBride, A.F. and Kritzler, H.: Observations on pregnancy, parturition, and postnatal behavior in the bottlenosed dolphin. *J. Mammal, 32:*251, 1951.

McCormick, J.G.: *Theory of Hearing for Delphinids.* Doctoral dissertation. Department of Psychology, Princeton, New Jersey, Princeton University, May 1968a.

McCormick, J.G.: Cochlear potential studies of the porpoise (*Tursiops truncatus*): Implications for theories of cetacean hearing. 16mm, 30 min. color film. Presented at the *Eastern Psychological Association Annual Meeting,* April 1968b.

McCormick, J.G.: Relationship of sleep, respiration and anesthesia in the porpoise; a preliminary report. *Proc. Nat. Acad. Sci. U.S.A., 62:*697, 1969.

McCormick, J.G., Wever, E.G., Ridgway, S.H., and Palin, J.: Physiology of hearing in odontocetes as indicated by their cochlear potentials. *Proc. Acoustical Soc, Amer., 47:*68, 1969.

McCormick, J.G., Wever, E.G., Ridgway, S.H., and Palin, J.: Sound conduction in the dolphin ear. *J. Acoustical Soc. of Amer.,* in press, 1970.

McGinnis, S.M.: Biotelemetry of pinnipeds. In Harrison, R.J., Hubbard, R.C., Peterson, R.S., Rice, C.C., and Schusterman, R.J. (Eds.): *The Behavior and Physiology of Pinnipeds.* New York, Appleton-Century-Crofts, 1968, vol. 1, p. 54.

Medway, W. and Geraci, J.R.: Hematology of the bottlenose dolphin *Tursiops truncatus. Amer. J. Physiol., 207:*1367, 1964.

Medway, W. and Geraci, J.R.: Blood chemistry of the bottlenose dolphin, *Tursiops truncatus. Amer. J. Physiol., 209:*169, 1965.

Medway, W., Schryver, H.F., and Bell, B.: Clinical jaundice in a dolphin. *J. Amer. Vet. Med. Ass., 149:*891, 1966.

Medway, W. and Moldovan, F.: Blood studies in the north Atlantic pilot whale, *Globicephala melaena. Physiol. Zool., 39:*110, 1966.

Medway, W., Geraci, J.R., and Klein, L.: Hematologic response to administration of a corticosteroid in the bottle-nosed dolphin (*Tursiops truncatus*). *J. Amer. Vet. Med. Ass., 157:*563, 1970.

Medway, W., McCormick, J.G., Ridgway, S.H., and Crump, J.F.: Effects of prolonged halothane anesthesia on some cetaceans. *J. Amer. Vet. Med. Ass., 157:*576, 1970.

Miller, R.M. and Ridgway, S.H.: Clinical experience with dolphins and whales. *Small Animal Clinician, 3:*189, 1963.

Mohr, E.: *Die Robben der europoischen Gewasser.* Frankfurt Am Main, Paul Schops, Monographien der Wildsaugetiere, Band 12, 283, 1952.

Morimoto, Y., Takata, M., and Sudzuki, M.: Untersuchungen uber Cetacea. *Tohuko J. Exp. Med.*, 2, 1921.

Murdaugh, H.V., Jr., Seabury, J.C., and Mitchell, L.: Electrocardiogram of the diving seal. *Circ. Res.*, 9:358, 1961a.

Murdaugh, H.V., Jr., Schmidt-Nielsen, B., Wood, J.W., and Mitchell, W.L.: Cessation of renal function during diving in the trained seal *Phoca vitulina*. *J. Cell. Comp. Physiol.*, 58:261, 1961b.

Murdaugh, H.V., Jr., Mitchell, W.L., and Seabury, J.C.: Volume receptors and post prandial diuresis in the seal (*Phoca vitulina* L.). *Proc. Soc. Exp. Biol. Med.*, 108:16, 1961c.

Murdaugh, H.V., Jr., Brennan, J.K., Pyron, W.W., and Wood, J.W.: Function of the inferior vena cava valve of the harbor seal. *Nature (London)*, 194:700, 1962.

Murray, J.A.: Report of deaths of animals in the gardens in 1914. *Proc. Zool. Soc. London, 13*, 1915.

Myhre, B.A., Simpson, J.G., and Ridgway, S.H.: Blood groups in the Atlantic bottlenose porpoise. *Fed. Proc., 28*, 1969.

Nagel, E.L., Morgane, P.J., and McFarland, W.L.: Anesthesia for the bottlenosed dolphin. *Science, 146*:1591, 1964.

Nagel, E.L., Morgane, P.J., and McFarland, W.L.: Anesthesia for the bottlenose dolphin and author's addendum. *Vet. Med.—Small Animal Clinic., 61*:933, 1965.

Nagel, E.L., Morgane, P.J., McFarland, W.L., and Galliano, A.E.: Rete mirabile of dolphin: Its pressure-damping effect on cerebral circulation. *Science, 161*: 898, 1968.

Nakajima, M., Sawaura, K., Fujimoto, A., and Oda, T.: Foreign bodies in the stomachs of the captive dolphins. *Enoshima Marineland Reports, 2*:27, 1965.

Nemoto, T: White scars on whales. *Sci. Rep. Whales Res. Inst., 10*:69, 1955.

Ness, A.R.: Dental caries in the platanistid whale, *Inia geoffrensis. J. Comp. Path., 76*:271, 1966.

Nesterov, G.A.: Information on the biology and population size of the sea lions (*Eumetopias stelleri*) of the Commander Islands. *Izvestiya TINRO, 54*:173, 1964.

Nishiwaki, M.: Personal communication. Ocean Research Institute University of Tokyo, Tokyo, Japan 1970.

Norris, K.S., and Prescott, J.H.: Observations on Pacific cetaceans of California and Mexican waters. *University of California Publications in Zoology (Berkeley), 63*:291, 1961.

Norris, K.S.: Trained porpoise released in the open sea. *Science, 147*:1048, 1965.

Olsen, C.R., Hale, F.C., and Elsner, R.: Mechanics of ventilation in the pilot whale. *Resp. Physiol., 7*:137, 1969.

Olsen, C.R., Elsner, R., Hale, F.C., and Kenney, D.W.: "Blow" of the pilot whale. *Science, 163*:953, 1969.

Owen, C.G. and Kakulas, B.A.: Sarcosporidiosis in the sperm whale. *Aust. J. Sci., 31*:46, 1968.

Panina, G.K.: Food of Steller sea lion and seals on Kuril Islands. *Izvestiya TINRO*, 58:235, 1966.

Parry, D.A.: The structure of whale blubber and a discussion of its properties. *Quart. J. Micr. Sci.*, 90:1, 1949.

Patashnik, M. and Kangas, P.: Tek-Food—A pasteurized whole fish ration for captive marine mammals. Seattle, Technological Labs, Bur. Comm. Fisheries, U.S. Dept. of Interior, 1970.

Paulev, P.: Decompression sickness following repeated breathhold dives. *J. Appl. Physiol.*, 20:1028, 1965.

Peterson, R.S.: Drugs for handling fur seals. *J. Wildlife Management*, 29:688, 1965.

Pickwell, G.V.: Energy metabolism in ducks during submergence asphyxia: Assessment by a direct method. *Comp. Biochem. Physiol.*, 27:455, 1968.

Pier, A.C., Takayama, A.K., and Miyahara, A.Y.: Cetacean nocardiosis. *J. Wildlife Dis.*, 6:112, 1970.

Pierce, R.W.: *The Design and Operation of a Metabolic Chamber for Marine Mammals.* Doctoral Thesis, Berkeley, University of California, 1970.

Pilleri, G.: Brain lipoma in the humpback whale, *Megaptera novaengliae. Path. Vet.* (*Basel*), 3:341, 1966.

Pilson, M.E.Q. and Kelly, A.L.: Composition of the milk from *Zalophus californianus*, the California sea lion. *Science*, 135:104, 1962.

Pilson, M.E.Q. and Waller, D.W.: The composition of milk from spotted and spinner porpoises, *J. Mammal*, 51:74, 1970.

Pinchot, C.B.: Whale culture—A Proposal, *Perspect. Biol. Med.*, 10:33, 1966.

Plimmer, H.G.: Reports of the deaths which occurred in the zoological gardens during 1914. *Proc. Zool. Soc. London*, 11:123, 1915.

Portier, P.: Pression Osmotique des liquides des oiseaux et mammiferes marins. *J. Physiol. Path. Gen.*, 12:202, 1910.

Prathap, K., Ardlie, N.G., Paterson, J.C., and Swartz, C.J.: Spontaneous arterial lesions in Antarctic seal. *Arch. Path.*, 82:287, 1966.

Prescott, J.H.: Personal communication. Marineland of the Pacific, Palos Verdes Estates, California, 1969.

Puppione, D.L.: *Physical and Chemical Characterization of the Serum Lipoproteins of Marine Mammals*, Doctoral Thesis, Berkeley, University of California, 1969.

Purves, P.E.: Anatomy and physiology of the outer and middle ear in cetaceans. In Norris, K.S. (Ed.): *Whales, Dolphins, and Porpoises*, Berkeley, University of California Press, 1966.

Ray, C. and Fay, F.H.: Influence of climate on the distribution of walruses, *Odobenus rosmarus* (Linnaeus). I. Evidence from physiological characteristics. *Zoologica*, 53:19, 1968.

Ray, C. and Smith, M.S.R.: Thermoregulation of the pup and adult Weddell seal, *Leptonychotes weddelli* (Lesson), in Antarctica. *Zoologica*, 53:33, 1968.

Reid, M.H.: *A Mathematical Contribution to System Identification with Appli-*

cation to Dolphin Temperature Regulation and Intraocular Pressure Control,* Doctoral Thesis, Berkeley, University of California 1966.

Rewell, R.C. and Willis, R.A.: Some tumors found in whales. *J. Path. Bact.,* 1:454, 1949.

Rewell, R.E. and Willis, R.A.: Some tumors of wild animals. *J. Path. Bact., 26:* 450, 1950.

Pryor, T.A.: Personal communication. The Oceanic Institute, Waimanalo, Oahu, Hawaii, 1955.

Rice, D.W.: Sei whale with rudimentary baleen. *Norsk Hvalfangst. Tid.,* 5:1, 1961.

Richet, C.: De la resistance des canards a l'asphyxie. *J. Physiol. Path. Gen., 1:* 641, 1899.

Ridgway, S.H. and Johnston, D.G.: Two interesting disease cases in wild ceta- ceans. *Amer. J. Vet. Res., 26:*771, 1965.

Ridgway, S.H.: Medical care of marine mammals. *J. Amer. Vet. Med. Ass., 147:* 1077, 1965.

Ridgway, S.H.: Experiments on diving depth and duration in *Tursiops truncatus. Proc. 3rd Conf. of Bio-Sonar and Diving Mammals,* Stanford Research Insti- tute, Palo Alto, Calif., 3:151, 1966a.

Ridgway, S.H.: Dall porpoise, *Phocoenoides dalli* (True): Observations in captivity and at sea. *Norske Hvalfangst. Tid.,* 5:97, 1966b.

Ridgway, S.H. and Johnston, D.G.: Blood oxygen and ecology of porpoises of three genera. *Science, 151:*456, 1966.

Ridgway, S.H. and McCormick, J.G.: Anesthesia for surgery in porpoises. 16mm 20 min. color sound film. Presented at the April 1967, *Eastern Psychological Association Annual Meeting,* and 1968 *American Psychological Association Meeting.* Available through N.I.H. film library.

Ridgway, S.H. and Green, R.: Evidence for a sexual rhythm in male porpoises, *Norsk Hvalfangst. Tid.,* 1:1, 1967.

Ridgway, S.H. and McCormick, J.G.: Anesthesia for major surgery in porpoises. *Science, 158:*510, 1967.

Ridgway, S.H.: The bottlenose dolphin in biomedical experimentation. In Gay, W.I. (Ed.): *Methods of Animal Experimentation,* New York, Academic Press, 1968, vol. III, p. 387.

Ridgway, S.H. and Simpson, J.G.: Anesthesia and restraint for the California sea lion. *J. Amer. Vet. Med. Ass., 155:*1059, 1969.

Ridgway, S.H., Scronce, B.L., and Kanwisher, J.: Respiratory function and deep diving in a bottlenose porpoise. *Science, 166:*1651, 1969.

Ridgway, S.H. and Simpson, J.G., Gilmartin, W.G., and Patton, G.S. Hematologic findings in some small cetaceans. *J. Amer. Vet. Med. Ass., 157:*566, 1970a.

Ridgway, S.H. and Patton, G.S.: Dolphin thyroid: Some anatomical and phy- siological findings. *Verg. Physiol.,* in press, 1970.

Ridgway, S.H. and McCormick, J.G.: Anesthetization of porpoises. In Soma, L.R. (Ed.): *Introduction to Veterinary Anesthesia.* Baltimore, Williams and Wilkins, in press, 1970.

Ridgway, S.H. and Kanwisher, J.: Carbon dioxide unloading and heart rate in a free swimming porpoise. Unpublished data collected at the Navy Marine Bioscience Facility, 1970.

Ridgway, S.H., McCormick, J.G., and Wever, E.G.: Surgical approach to the ear in porpoises, in preparation, 1970.

Rieu, M. and Gautheron, B.: Preliminary observations concerning a method for introduction of a tube for anesthesia in small delphinids. *Laboratoire D'Acoustique Animale,* 78:1, 1968.

Rigdon, R.H. and Drager, G.A.: Thiamine deficiency in sea lions (*Otaria californianus*) fed only frozen fish. *J. Amer. Vet. Med. Ass., 127*:453, 1955.

Roberts, J.C., Boice, R.C., Brownell, R.L., and Brown, D.H.: Spontaneous atherosclerosis in Pacific toothed and baleen whales. In Roberts, J.C. and Straus, R. (Eds.): *Atherosclerosis.* New York, Harper and Row, 1965, p. 151.

Robin, E.D.: of seals and mitochondria. *New Eng. J. Med., 275*:646, 1966.

Robinson, A.J., Kropatkin, M., and Aggeler, P.M.: Hageman factor (Factor 12) deficiency in marine mammals. *Science, 166*:1420, 1969.

Romer, A.S.: *Vertebrate Paleontology,* 3rd ed. Chicago, University of Chicago Press, 1966.

Roth, H.: Trichinosis in Arctic animals. *Nature (London), 163*:805, 1949.

Saunders, A.M. and Hubbard, R.C.: Studies on pinnipeds #1: Obstructive emphysema in an elephant seal (*Mirounga angustirostris*). *Lab Animal Care, 16*:217, 1966.

Schaefer, K.E., Allison, R.D., Dougherty, J.H., Jr., Carey, C.H., Walker, R., Yost, F., and Parker, D.: Pulmonary and circulatory adjustments determining the limits of depths in breathhold diving. *Science, 162*:1020, 1970.

Scheffer, V.B.: *Seals, Sea Lions and Walruses.* Stanford, Stanford University Press, 1958.

Scheffer, V.B. and Neff, J.A.: Food of California sea lions. *J. Mammal, 29*:67, 1948.

Schevill, W.E., Ray, C., Kenyon, K.W., Orr, R.T., and Van Gelder, R.G.: Immobilizing drugs lethal to swimming mammals. *Science, 157*:630, 1967.

Schmidt-Nielsen, B., Murdaugh, H.V., Jr., O'Dell, R., and Bacsanyi, J.: Urea excretion and diving in the seal (*Phoca vitulina* L.). *J. Cell. Comp. Physiol., 53*:393, 1959.

Scholander, P.F.: Experimental investigations on the respiratory function in diving mammals and birds. *Hvalrad. Skr., 22*:1, 1940.

Scholander, P.F. and Irving, L.: Experimental investigations on the respiration and diving of the Florida manatee. *J. Cell. Comp. Physiol., 17*:169, 1941.

Scholander, P.F., Irving, L., and Grinnell, S.W.: Aerobic and anaerobic changes in the seal muscles during diving. *J. Biol. Chem., 142*:432, 1942a.

Scholander, P.F., Irving, L., and Grinnell, S.W.: On the temperature and metabolism of the seal during diving. *J. Cell and Comp. Physiol., 19*:67, 1942b.

Scholander, P.F. and Schevill, W.E.: Counter current heat exchange in the fins of whales. *J. Appl. Physiol., 8*:279, 1955.

Scholander, P.F., Hammel, H.T., LeMessurier, H., Hemmingsen, E., and Garey,

W.: Circulatory adjustments in pearl divers. *J. Appl. Physiol., 17*:184, 1962.

Scholander, P.F.: The master switch of life. *Sci. Amer., 209*:92, 1963.

Schroeder, C.R. and Wegeforth, H.M.: The occurrence of gastric ulcers in sea mammals of the California coast, their etiology and pathology. *J. Amer. Vet. Med. Ass., 87*:333, 1935.

Seibold, H. and Neal, J.E.: Erysipelas septicemia in the porpoise. *J. Amer. Vet. Med. Ass., 128*:537, 1956.

Senft, A.W. and Kanwisher, J.: Cardiographic observations on a fin-back whale. *Circulation Res., 8*:961, 1960.

Sergeant, D.E.: Feeding rates of cetacea. *Tisk Dir. Skr. Der. Hav. Unders, 15*: 246, 1969.

Simpson, C.F., Wood, F.G., and Young, G.: Cutaneous lesions on a porpoise with erysipelas. *J. Amer. Vet. Med. Ass., 133*:558, 1958.

Simpson, J.G., Gilmartin, W.G., and Ridgway, S.H.: Blood volume and other hematologic parameters in young elephant seals *Mirounga angustirostris. Amer. J. Vet. Res., 31*:1449, 1970.

Simpson, J.G. and Ridgway, S.H.: Unpublished diagnostic data from the Marine Bioscience Facility, Point Mugu, California, 1965–1970.

Simpson, J.G. and Leatherwood, J.S.: Development and testing of prepared ration for porpoises, seals and sea lions. NUC Technical Report (in preparation).

Sivertsen, E.: On the biology of the harp seal, *Phoca groenlandica. Hvalrad Skr., 26*:1, 1941.

Slijper, E.J.: Die Cetaceen. *Cap. Zool., 7*:1, 1936.

Slijper, E.J.: Organ weights and symmetry problems in porpoises and seals. *Arch. Neerl. Zool., 13*:97, 1958.

Slijper, E.J.: *Whales.* New York Basic Books, 1962.

Smith, H.W.: The composition of urine in the seal. *J. Cell. Comp. Physiol., 7*: 465, 1936.

Sokolov, A.S.: Particular features in the size and distribution of certain blood vessels in aquatic (seals) and terrestrial (dog) mammals. *Arch. Anat., Hostol. Embryol., 38*:12, 1959.

Sokolov, V. Ye: Determining the phase of the reproductive cycle in female *Delphinus delphis* L. by vaginal smears. *Proceedings of Meetings of the Ichthyological Commission of the Academy of Sciences, USSR, 12*:68, 1961.

Sokolov, V., Bulina, I., and Rodionov, V.: Interaction of dolphin epidermis with flow boundary layer. *Nature (London), 222*:267, 1969.

Spaulding, D.J.: Comparative feeding habits of the fur seal, sea lion, and harbour seal on the British Columbia Coast. *J. Fish. Res. Bd. Canada, 146*:1, 1964.

Spencer, M.P., Gornall, T.A., and Poulter, T.C.: Respiratory and cardiac activity of killer whales. *J. Appl. Physiol., 22*:974, 1967.

Sterling, K.: Personal communication. Bronx Veterans Administration Hospital, New York, 1970.

Stirling, I.: Tooth wear as a mortality factor in the Weddell seal, *Leptonychotes weddelli. J. Mammal, 50*:559, 1969.

Stolk, A.: Tumors in whales. *Amsterdam Natural.,* 1:28, 1950.

Stolk, A.: Some tumors in whales. *Amsterdam Natural.* 55:275, 1952.

Stolk, A.: Some inflammation in whales. *Proc. Kon. Nederl. Akad. Wet.* (*Biol. Med.*) 56(1):364, 1953a.

Stolk, A.: Hepatic cirrhosis in the blue whale, (*Balaenoptera musculus*). *Proc. Kon. Nederl. Akad. Wet.* (*Biol. Med.*), 56(8):375, 1953b.

Stolk, A.: Some tumors in whales II, *Proc. Kon. Nederl. Akad. Wet.,* (*Biol. Med.*), 56(3):360, 1953c.

Stolk, A.: Some inflammation in whales II, *Proc. Kon. Nederl. Akad. Wet.,* (*Biol. Med.*), 57(3):254, 1954a.

Stolk, A.: A new case of hepatic cirrhosis in the blue whale, (*Balaenoptera musculus*). *Proc. Kon. Nederl. Akad. Wet.* (*Biol. Med.*), 57(3):258, 1954b.

Stolk, A.: Tumors in whales III. *Proc. Kon. Nederl. Akad. Wet.* (*Biol. Med.*), 65: 250, 1962.

Stout, C.: Atherosclerosis in exotic carnivora and pinnipedia. *Amer. J. Path.,* 57:673, 1969.

Strauss, M.B.: Mammalian adaptations to diving. *U.S. Naval Submarine Medical Center,* Groton, Conn., 562:1, 1969.

Taylor, A.E.R., Brown, D.H., Heyneman, D., and McIntyre, R.W.: Biology of filaroid nematode (*Dipetalonema spirocauda*) from the heart of captive harbor seals and sea lions, together with pathology of the hosts. *J. Parasitol.,* 47:971, 1961.

Telfer, N., Cornell, L.H., and Prescott, J.H.: Do dolphins drink water? *J. Amer. Vet. Med. Ass.,* 157:555, 1970.

Testi, F. and Pilleri, G.: Verminous pulmonitis induced by nematoda (*Halocoercus, Pseudaliidae*) in the dolphin (*Delphinus delphis* L.). In Pilleri, G. (Ed.): *Investigations on Cetacea.* Switzerland, Waldau Berne, G. Pilleri, 1969.

Thurston, C.E.: Sodium and potassium content of 34 species of fish, *J. Amer. Diet. Ass.,* 34(4):396, 1958.

Todd, T.W.: Report of deaths of animals in the Gardens during 1912. *Proc. Zool. Soc. London,* 855, 1913.

Tomes, C.S.: On a case of abscess of the pulp in a Grampus (*Orca gladiator*). *Trans. Odont. Soc.* (*Great Britain*), 5:1, 1873.

Tomilin, A.G.: On the biology and physiology of black sea dolphins. *Zool. Zhurn.,* 27:1, 1948.

Tomilin, A.G.: Cetacea. In *Mammals of the USSR and Adjacent Countries, vol. 9. Jerusalem,* Israel Program for Scientific Translation, 1967.

Tomilin, A.G. and Smyshlyayev, M.I.: Some factors affecting whale mortality, *Byulleten Moskovskogo Obschestva Ispitateley Priorody,* Otdel Biologicheskiy, 3:1, 1968.

Townsend, C.H.: The porpoise in captivity. *Zoologica,* 16:289, 1914.

Truex, R.C., Nolan, R.G., Truex, R.C., Jr., Schneider, H.P., and Perlmutter, H.I.: Anatomy and pathology of the whale heart with special reference to the coronary circulation. *Anat. Rec.,* 141(4):325, 1961.

Turton, W.: *A General System of nature through the three grand kingdoms.* By Sir Charles Linne', London, Lockington Allen and Co., 7 cols. 1806.

Tyler, J.C.: Erythrocytes and hemaglobin in the crabeater seal. *J. Mammal., 41:* 527, 1960.

Uys, C.J. and Best, P.B.: Pathology of lesions observed in whales flensed at Saldahna Bay, South Africa, *J. Comp. Path., 76:*407, 1966.

Wasserman, K. and Mackenzie, A.: Studies on the seal during the dive reflex. *Bull. Tulane Fac. Med., 16:*105, 1957.

Wever, E.G.: Electrical potentials of the cochlea. *Physiol. Rev., 46:*102, 1966.

Whayne, T.F. and Killip, T.: Simulated diving in man: Comparison of facial stimuli and response in arrhythmia. *J. Appl. Physiol., 22:*800, 1967.

White, J.R.: Thiamine deficiency in an Atlantic bottle-nosed dolphin (*Tursiops truncatus*) on a diet of raw fish. *J. Amer. Vet. Med. Ass., 157:*559, 1970.

White, P.D. and Kerr, W.J.: The heart of the sperm whale with especial reference to the A-V conduction system. *Heart, 6:*207, 1917.

Williams, R.H.: *Textbook of Endocrinology,* 3rd ed. Philadelphia, W.B. Saunders, 1962, p. 101.

Williamson, W.M., Lombard, L.S., and Getty, R.E.: North American blastomycosis in a Northern sea lion. *J. Amer. Vet. Med. Ass., 135:*513, 1959.

Wilson, T.M., Cheville, N.F., and Karstad, L.: Seal pox. *Bull. Wildlife Disease Ass., 5:*412, 1969.

Wislocki, G.B. and Belanger, L.: The lungs of larger cetacea compared to those of smaller species. *Biol. Bull., 78:*289, 1940.

Wolf, A.V., Prentiss, G., Douglas, L.G., and Swett, R.S.: Potability of sea water with special reference to the cat. *Amer. J. Physiol., 196:*663, 1959.

Wolf, S.: The bradycardia of the dive reflex—a possible mechanism of sudden death. *Trans. Amer. Clin. Cliamatol. Ass., 76:*192, 1964.

Wolinski, Z. and Landowski, J.: Uber die Krankheits-und Todesfalle der Seelowen in den Polnischen Zoologischen Garten, *Nord. Vet. Med., 14:*125, 1962.

Wood, F.G. and Ridgway, S.H.: Project SEALAB Report; SEALAB II Project Group. Edited by D.C. Pauli and G.P. Calapper, Office of Naval Research, Washington, D.C. (1967).

Wood, F.G., Norris, K.S., Dudok van Heel, W.H., and Ray, C.: Round table: practical problems. In Norris, K.S. (Ed.): *Whales, Dolphins and Porpoises,* Berkeley, University of California Press, 1966, vol. 1, p. 640.

Woodard, J.C., Zam, S.G., Caldwell, D.K., and Caldwell, M.C.: Some parasitic diseases of dolphins. *Path. Vet., 6:*257, 1969.

Yoshizawa, Z.: A new type of heparin, "W-heparin" isolated from whale organs. *Biochem. Biophys. Res. Commun., 16:*336, 1964.

NAME INDEX

749

SUBJECT INDEX

A

Abashiri Aquarium, *Eumetopias jubata* specimens, 140

Abscesses, 653

Abundance of
Arctocephalus australis, 149
Arctocephalus forsteri, 154
Arctocephalus gazella, 155
Arctocephalus philippii, 153
Arctocephalus pusillus, 151
Balaenoptera acutorostrata, 27–28
Balaenoptera edeni, 25
Balaenoptera musculus, 20
Balaenoptera physalus, 22
Berardius bairdi, 46
Callorhinus ursinus, 158–159
Cystophora cristata, 189
Delphinapterus leucas, 66
Delphinus capensis, 79
Delphinus delphis, 77–78
Dugong dugon, 195–196
Erignathus barbatus barbatus, 168
Erignathus barbatus nauticus, 169
Eschrichtius gibbosus, 17
Eumetopias jubata, 139
Halichoerus grypus, 169
Histriophoca fasciata, 178
Hydrurga leptonyx, 187
Hyperoodon ampullatus, 49
Kogia breviceps, 43
Lagenorhynchus acutus, 93
Lagenorhynchus obliquidens, 90
Leptonychotes weddelli, 184
Lissodelphis borealis, 74
Lobodon carcinophagus, 188
Megaptera novaeangliae, 32–33
Mirounga angustirostris, 191–192
Monachus schauinslandi, 181
Monachus tropicalis, 182
Monodon monoceros, 67–68
Neophoca cinerea, 146
Odobenus rosmarus, 163

Ommatophoca rossi, 185
Orcinus orca, 131
Otaria byronia, 144
Pagophilus groenlandicus, 179
Phoca vitulina, 173
Phocoena phocoena, 119
Phocoenoides dalli dalli, 116
Physeter catodon, 37
Pusa hispida botnica, 176
Pusa hispida krascheninikova, 176
Pusa hispida ladogensis, 176
Pusa hispida ochotensis, 175–176
Stenella caeruleoalba, 81
Trichechus manatus, 198
Zalophus californianus, 142
Zalophus californianus japonicus, 142
Zalophus californianus wollebaeki, 143
Ziphius cavirostris, 52
see also *Distribution, and Migrations*

Acanthocephala, 529–560 *passim*
families, 564, 566
locality in hosts, 564, 566

Acarina, 529–544 *passim*

Acoustic system of
Cetacea, 466–470
pinnipeds, 486–489
sea otters, 486–489

Activity cycles of
cetaceans, 435–436
pinnipeds, 450–452

Adenocarcinoma, 405

Adenocephalus pacificus, 529, 531

Adenocephalus septentrionacis, 533

ADH, water balance studies, 615–616

Adjustments to aquatic life, 590

Adoption of pups, 449

Adrenal gland, microscopic anatomy, 386–392

Adrenocortical secretions, 614

Affectional behavior of
cetaceans, 423–428
odontocetes, 424

African manatee, characteristics, 200
see also *Trichechus senegalensis*

M